SEX, POWER, AND SLAVERY

from post to pediment
the architecture of knowing
surpasses the outline.

subvention by
Figure Foundation

SEX, POWER AND SLAVERY

Edited by

Gwyn Campbell

and Elizabeth Elbourne

OHIO UNIVERSITY PRESS

ATHENS

Ohio University Press, Athens, Ohio 45701
ohioswallow.com

Printed in the United States of America
Ohio University Press books are printed on acid-free paper ∞ ™

25 24 23 22 21 20 19 18 17 16 5 4 3 2 1

Library of Congress Cataloging-in-Publication Data

Sex, power, and slavery / edited by Gwyn Campbell and Elizabeth Elbourne.
pages cm
Includes bibliographical references and index.
ISBN 978-0-8214-2096-6 (hc : alk. paper) — ISBN 978-0-8214-2097-3 (pb : alk. paper) — ISBN 978-0-8214-4490-0 (pdf)
1. Slavery—History. 2. Sex crimes—History. 3. Women slaves—Social conditions. 4. Slaves—Social conditions. I. Campbell, Gwyn, 1952– editor of compilation. II. Elbourne, Elizabeth, editor of compilation.
HT861.S33 2014
306.3'6209—dc23

2014036293

CONTENTS

Art, Sexuality, and Slavery

Queering the Study of Slavery

Legacies: Discourse, Dishonor, and Labor

ACKNOWLEDGMENTS

The editors acknowledge with gratitude the support of the Social Sciences and Humanities Research Council of Canada. They are also very grateful to Rachel Sandwell, Renée Saucier, and Marie-Luise Ermisch for expert assistance; to Joan Sherman for sharp copyediting; and to Gillian Berchowitz, Nancy Basmajian, and Beth Pratt of Ohio University Press for guiding this project to the end with skill and insight.

INTRODUCTION

Key Themes and Perspectives

ELIZABETH ELBOURNE

This collection looks at the intersections between the history of sexuality and the history of slavery in broad comparative perspective. The obligation to provide sexual labor was a critical feature of enslavement for women (and to a more limited extent and in certain circumstances for men) in almost every society in which slavery existed. Control of the bodies of the enslaved was central to slavery, no matter the theological or legal underpinnings of particular societies. Ideas about honor and debasement, furthermore, affected how the sexuality of the enslaved was understood and harnessed in a range of different contexts. The obligation of the enslaved to provide sex had implications at every level, whether at the micro scale of individual personal experience or the macro scale of the economics of long-distance slave trades. At the same time, the entangled histories of sexuality and slavery cannot be limited to the sexual interaction between master and slave, nor, indeed, can they be reduced to a history of rape—even if rape was a constant feature of the experience of enslaved women.

A growing body of work in many areas of the world attests to the value of a fuller understanding of the sexual dimensions of slavery, as well as to the importance of reinscribing the history of slavery and colonialism into the history of sexuality. Yet, as the studies in this volume suggest, scholars do not agree about what *kind* of a difference it makes to our understanding of slavery to take account of the history of sexuality more fully, nor do they share a uniform approach to studying sexuality and slavery. Here, we seek to showcase a range of ways in which sexuality mattered, to look at a number of possible approaches to studying sexuality and slavery together, and to provide the opportunity for contrast and comparison among different societies. The essays in this collection are drawn from many regions, and this in itself invites comparison between various scholarly traditions.

The study of sexuality and slavery is well under way in different regions of the world, even if there are still many areas in which the history of sexuality needs to be more thoroughly understood and many archival silences that may never be filled. The very diversity of this project provides a significant opportunity to bring together scholars whose works might not otherwise be read against one another. Particularly fruitful space for collaboration might exist, for example, between feminist scholars interested in gender and sexuality and others who define themselves as primarily scholars of slavery and the slave trade (despite the important overlap between these categories). Similar opportunities for comparison and collaboration are opened up by bringing work on the Atlantic world into dialogue with work on other regions, including the Indian Ocean world.

Points of Departure

There are thus numerous entry points to the study of sexuality and slavery. It would be foolhardy to seek to provide an overview of the many large and diverse scholarly literatures on which histories of sexuality and slavery in very different places have drawn or might potentially draw in the future. Nonetheless, it may be useful to gesture at some critical questions and methodological approaches that have provided points of departure for at least some of the essays in this collection, before exploring certain overarching themes that the essays seem, despite their considerable diversity, to raise.

In recent years, the impetus to examine the history of slavery and sexuality has come from several directions, perhaps leading to some rather distinct scholarly languages. A great deal of pioneering work, particularly in the Americas, derived from the desire to understand more clearly the experience of enslaved women.[1] Much of this work puts sexual violence at the heart of the experience of such women.[2] In line with ongoing trends in the field, feminist historians in particular have more generally built on the study of women's experience to analyze the wider dynamics of sexuality, race, and class through the lens of gender, including the dynamics of masculinity. How did ideas about gender and sexuality, broadly conceived, maintain power relationships?[3] The linked fields of women's history and gender history, informed by feminist perspectives, have thus been major points of departure for at least some of the work in this volume. Conversely, sexual violence—the "everyday wound," in Edward Baptist's evocative phrase—also framed men's experience of slavery, whether as enslaved men unable to prevent masters from sleeping with enslaved women, as masters whose views of enslaved women were shaped by the expectation of sexual dominance, or as male slaves who were themselves sexually abused.[4]

Another key point of departure, overlapping with work on women and gender, has been scholarship on the slave family, informed by, among other things, an interest in the family as a locus both of resistance and solidarity, on the one hand, and of gendered power struggles between men and women, on the other hand.[5] Work on the family opens, in turn, the question of "interracial" sexuality and the formation of what Catherine Clinton, in an American context, terms "shadow families."[6]

However, as a number of essays here make clear, families and the roles of the enslaved within them looked quite different in many regions outside the Atlantic world, characterized as the latter was by the putatively monogamous patriarchal nuclear family and a sharp distinction (in theory if not in practice) between "free" and "unfree." Gwyn Campbell and others have argued that the structure of slavery was very different in the Indian Ocean world and that one key difference was that societies in that region were largely characterized by webs of dependence, rather than by a free/unfree binary.[7] In this context, the enslaved woman often, in some sense, joined the acknowledged kinship networks of the patriarch, at times openly bearing his children and at times becoming a recognized concubine or even wife. Although kinship and "family" relationships and accompanying ways of thinking about the family are central vectors in analyzing sexuality in slave societies, sexuality and slavery were woven together differently in societies with different kinship structures.

Another point of departure for some historians in the anglophone world is found in work on gender and empire.[8] A growing number of historians, often but not necessarily also working within an explicitly feminist tradition, have become interested in colonialism and sexuality, with attention to, among other things, sexual relationships between colonizers and the colonized as well as the regulation of sexuality by the colonial state.[9] Although this work tends to start from an interest in colonialism rather than slavery, it raises the issue of how the supposedly "private" realm of sexuality was both a target of an often obsessive interest by colonial states and a critical way in which colonial power was upheld. In other words, this work breaks down the barriers between private and public, and it makes a case for the importance of the control of sexuality to state power.[10] As Gabeba Baderoon points out in her chapter, feminist historians interested in colonialism and sexuality further raise the issue of how ideas about sexuality and ideas about "race" were linked; thus, Baderoon cites Philippa Levine's argument that ideas about the supposedly perverse sexuality of the colonized were used to justify colonial rule, just as similar ideas were used to justify slavery.[11] But even as the history of colonialism has increasingly focused on ways in which colonized peoples also worked within colonial structures, studies on sexuality and colonialism have raised the central issue of how (and whether) enslaved and colonized women alike were able to turn oppressive structures to their own advantage. In addition, these studies have considered whether talking about agency in this context is simply securing the "fetters of subjection" while "proclaiming the power and influence of those shackled and tethered," in the words of Saidiya Hartman.[12]

In general terms, as the burgeoning historiography of sexuality and colonialism suggests, the history of sexuality is, of course, an increasingly significant field in its own right. The study of queer history is an important part of the rapidly growing field of the history of sexuality, even if queer history has not yet engaged as much as it might with the history of slavery and of colonialism. In this volume, Ronaldo Vainfas provides a striking example of the effort to mine well-known archival sources (in his case, in colonial Brazil) with new questions in mind, including the life experiences of homosexual people and the legal regulation of sexuality defined as transgressive. Brian Lewis reexamines the life of Roger Casement, queer antislavery activist and Irish nationalist, with attention to his sexual encounters in colonial contexts. Queer history, with its interest in why certain practices (not necessarily only gay sex) are considered outside some wider social "norm," also poses questions of why and how certain kinds of sexuality, such as sex between slave and free, might come to be seen as transgressive in the first place.

It might be somewhat artificial to separate various fields of study in approaching the history of sexuality and slavery. Nonetheless, despite substantial areas of overlap between the approaches discussed here, it is also important to underscore that much significant work on women, sexuality, and slavery asks macroeconomic questions or tries to come to some larger conclusions about the structures of enslavement and the slave trade.[13] In what ways did the sexual work of slaves matter economically, for example? Can this help explain why women outnumbered men among slaves within Africa and throughout the Indian Ocean world? Here, there is perhaps an intriguing confluence of interest between certain feminist theorists and economic historians, both interested in sex as a form of labor.

This type of work is part of a long-standing rethinking of the role of women in slavery among historians of slavery and the slave trade. Not least among the macro-level insights offered by this radical rethinking of slavery through attention to gender has been recognition of the fact that the male-dominated plantation slavery systems of the Americas were actually relatively anomalous. In Africa itself, as also within Indian Ocean slave-trading systems and in household slavery in many parts of the world outside the Americas, women were preferred by the purchasers of slaves, and in general, more women than men were both trafficked and used as slaves.[14] Why this was so remains a subject for debate. There is disagreement among specialists over themes such as the relative importance of women's productive labor (especially in regions of the world, such as Africa, where women carried out the bulk of agricultural labor) versus the importance of women's reproductive roles. In the current collection, Martin Klein revisits his own debates with the classic work of Claude Meillassoux regarding the relative significance of reproductive and productive labor by women. Other studies point to the economic importance of a slave trade in young women as items of luxury consumption required to perform sexual labor, as well as to the need for women in order to staff the harems of powerful men in many areas of the non-Christian world, including the Middle East, North Africa, and much of Asia.[15] In an African context, Joseph Miller has made a trenchant case that what mattered most about female enslavement over the long term, or *longue durée*, was that women could be brought in from outside communities and assimilated, allowing households to replenish themselves.[16] In terms of the dynamics of the slave trade, it is also clearly important that women and children could be captured and transported with greater ease, especially in open warfare (when men were often killed and women and children kidnapped). This was a particularly vital supply dynamic in often chaotic and violent frontier zones on the fringes of empires or in congenitally war-torn regions.[17] This, in turn, often led to captive women providing sex and reproduction. At the same time, however, women and children could be sold more readily by their families than could adult men, as debt bondage came to replace direct violence as a key motor in the replenishment of the slave trade in Africa in the eighteenth century.[18] Much of the work in this volume starts from the standpoint of slavery studies and draws on these and similar questions about economics and material power.

Another critical question arising both from more macro-level work and from textured local studies is that of routes to manumission: how often and in what ways were enslaved women able to use sexuality, especially the fact of bearing the master's children, as a route to emancipation for themselves and their offspring? And did this—to return to the issue of women's experience with which we began—mean that men and women experienced slavery in radically different ways?

In this extensive and sometimes contested work of revision across many fields, the question of the intersections between sexuality and slavery has obviously been a crucial issue. It has not, however, always been foregrounded on its own terms. This volume attempt to do precisely that. To that end, it brings together scholarship on a wide variety of places and time periods, although with a particular focus on the period from the late eighteenth to late nineteenth centuries. The collection also seeks to place male and female sexuality in a common frame and thereby escape the popular (if not academic) equation of "gender" with "women"—an equation feminist historians have complained about since the 1990s.[19] The study of masculinity is decidedly a central aspect of the history of slavery, and male and female sexual experience in slave societies cannot be disentangled.[20] In sum, this collection, though certainly not comprehensive, tries to represent regional, temporal, and gender diversity while also pointing to some larger trends; furthermore, it is relatively interdisciplinary within the confines of historical studies, as the authors approach the topic of sexuality from many perspectives. The work covers a wide gamut of societies and slave systems, whether the Atlantic slave system and chattel slavery in the Americas, slavery in a variety of forms in Africa, the Indian Ocean slaving system (with its greater orientation to procuring slaves for household labor), the trafficking of prostitutes in the British imperial world, the sale of wives in Qing China, or concubinage within the harem.

The history of sexuality and enslavement should not, of course, be limited to the history of sexual intercourse between female slaves and male masters, even if this is easiest to document from available records (albeit still quite hard to authenticate). A number of chapters in this volume struggle with the question of what it might be possible to know about same-sex sexuality in slave societies, for instance, or sexual relationships between slaves. Broadening the focus helps illuminate complex interactions across societies between slave and free, even among those who were not involved in sexual relationships with one another. To take just one example in this collection, Ann McDougall's contribution argues that in twentieth-century Mauritania, the fertility of slave women enabled and, indeed, underpinned the diminished fertility of "fattened" free wives.[21] Furthermore, we must consider what "counts" as sexuality? Is it possible that the enslaved might not have seen a difference between intercourse and the daily invasion of their bodies in other ways informed by the erotics of power relationships? More generally, a focus on sexuality also allows us to raise questions about gendered systems of power in slave societies and how ideologies and material power relationships undergirded one another.[22]

Finally, it must be underscored that slavery is not over (even if it is not always easy to label and identify) and that it remains intimately linked to sexual exploitation. Global sex trafficking provides one modern instance, at least for some historians, as does the covert continuation of household slavery in a number of contexts. The 1956 United Nations Supplementary

Convention on the Abolition of Slavery, the Slave Trade, and Institutions and Practices Similar to Slavery placed bonded labor, serfdom, servile marriage, and the transfer of children to the end of exploitation on the same legal footing as chattel slavery, while scholars and international lawyers continue to debate and expand definitions of enslavement.[23] The capture and sexual exploitation of children and young women by militias in conflict zones such as Uganda or the Democratic Republic of the Congo is a further example of the confluence between sexual exploitation and enslavement in a modern context.[24]

Methodological Concerns

Before turning to some of the themes raised by essays in this collection, I would like to acknowledge certain ethical and methodological issues, even if they might not admit of easy resolution. Any project of comparison across time and space necessarily raises methodological concerns, but perhaps this is doubly true with reference to a topic such as sexuality and slavery. The broad topic of sexual relations between enslaved and enslaver touches on particularly difficult issues and needs to be approached with sensitivity. At what point is the researcher's or reader's gaze prurient in itself?[25] And how does one amass and discuss information on what has sometimes been termed "difficult knowledge"?[26] This task may not be so different from research on knowledge more broadly; perhaps, in a sense, all knowledge is difficult. Nonetheless, there are distinct challenges in discussing material that may seem to be both particularly repugnant and particularly personal (just as there are challenges in displaying so-called difficult knowledge in a museum context).[27] On a more purely technical level, the broad topic of sexual relations, including the varying meanings individuals and societies ascribe to sex, is often simply quite difficult to research, given a frequent paucity of source material; sparse material is interspersed, furthermore, with telling stories from records such as legal archives that are often shocking but may not be representative. Silences mark the history of sexuality, reflecting both lacunae in historical records and the hush surrounding certain sexual practices in many times and places.[28] Silences can be read, but to do so often requires resort to unconventional types of source material as well as recognition of the fact that not all silences (such as the frequent silences of enslaved women) can be filled with confidence.

Comparison also raises its own issues. Is it, in fact, helpful to compare sexual dynamics across different "systems" of slavery? This current collection has a particularly large number of studies drawn from the worlds of two key trading systems. On one hand are those trading networks that helped knit together an Indian Ocean world where a majority of the enslaved were probably women living in households. On the other hand are those that drew together an Atlantic world where more slaves worked on plantations and on farms than within households and where the majority of human beings imported as slaves were male. Slavery worked very differently in these diverse environments. The current project confronts the inherent risk, familiar in other contexts, of essentializing different systems. Comparison in itself entails the danger of creating reified models and thus of oversimplifying. It also runs the risk of appearing to make value judgments in a field in which orientalism is already prevalent, as many scholars from Edward Said onward have taught us, and in which much crucial evidence amassed by observers was itself premised on what we might call orientalist assumptions.[29] On a more general level, again familiar in other contexts, it is hard to compare across very dissimilar linguistic systems, in which common terms such as *slave* (or even *freedom*) have markedly different meanings.

Yet, despite real pitfalls, comparison of the interaction between sexuality and slavery in widely variant contexts does provide useful insights and questions. Not least is the universal frequency of sex between (in particular) enslaved women and free men: we will suggest, in the pages that follow, that the obligation to provide sex might be seen as a central characteristic of enslavement, whatever the putative taboos against sexual relations between slave and free and whatever the legal frameworks. Comparison also points to the significance of cultural conceptions of gender and sexuality, for example. More generally, comparison is useful as a tool to think with, even if its conclusions can never be taken as definitive. It destabilizes and thus exposes more distinctly the assumptions particular societies take, or have taken, for granted. The diverse case studies here are thus also useful for pointing to local particularity and breaking down the very idea of universal systems.

Given that these are, to some extent, intractable issues, it is not surprising that the authors in this collection approach them differently. With due attention to particularity and diversity, what are some of the recurring themes, whether local or transnational, that their essays identify?

Blurring the Lines

The definition of slavery has long been a topic for debate among scholars. The study of slavery in comparative perspective, of course, raises the issue with particular force, but it also perhaps points to the futility of seeking a clear definition of *slavery* and *freedom* in all contexts.[30] One might, in fact, suggest that a distinct binary was the product of Western commercialized society, with its need for juridical clarity in the marketplace, in contrast to other societies where fluidity of status was more useful. Be that as it may, if a slave in the Atlantic slave system was defined by being alienable and therefore plainly set off in law (if not in reality) from the "free," even in this context it makes sense to see a spectrum of free and unfree labor rather than a rigid dichotomy—as suggested, for instance, by the history of masters and servants legislation or the history of convict transportation.[31] In many other parts of the world, the line between slave and free was even less clear. Thus, across Asia and the Middle East, as several chapters in this collection illustrate, the sale of laborers who were not hereditary slaves was common, and this included the permanent or temporary sale of family members by their own kin. But slaves were not always sold as commodities.[32] In all societies, the model of the free person was the male.[33] In the current collection, Joost Coté uses the example of the Dutch East Indies to argue that the colonial discourse of what did or did not constitute slavery served colonial ends, since colonial reformers defined certain coercive labor relationships as slavery and other, more favored relationships as freedom, "thus legitimating the more general condition of 'unfreedom' that was colonialism."[34]

To focus on sexual relations further muddies the juridical line between slave and free in several interesting ways. In many societies, supposedly free women were less free than men in terms of controlling their own sexuality. In many contexts, women in particular status groups had no choice but to provide coerced sexual labor, even if they were not considered slaves. At the same time, even in more overt conditions of bondage, sexual relationships often moved across what were allegedly impermeable boundaries. In some societies, such relationships were not supposed to happen, especially given the ascription of debased status to enslaved people, even if they were widely and tacitly accepted in reality. Caribbean plantation societies provided compelling examples, combining as they did widespread and often open sexual relations between slaves and masters with a theoretical theological opposition to extramarital sexual relations, including relationships between slave and master.[35] In this collection, Sandra Evers offers a fascinating analysis of peasant society in Madagascar, where those ascribed slave status slept with males who described themselves as masters by the river at night, despite the existence of very strong taboos against such contact and concern over the ritual impurity it was held to impart.[36] In societies with relatively rigid category distinctions (particularly legal distinctions) between slave and free, sexual relationships provided a reality that was messier than the theory and compelled slave societies to come to terms, at least in some minimal way, with the children who were the products of such relationships.[37]

In many other societies, especially those in which monogamy was not a religiously prescribed norm, sexual relationships between slaves and masters were acknowledged and offspring ascribed particular legal statuses, depending on circumstances. A number of essays in this volume point to the codification of the status of slave concubines in Islamic and Confucian law, for instance, including chapters by Abdul Sheriff, Ann McDougall, and Johanna Ransmeier. In these societies, it could be argued, female slaves had more rights and clearer potential benefits arising from sexual contact with masters, as Abdul Sheriff suggests in his contribution, "*Suria:* Concubine or Secondary Slave Wife? The Case of Zanzibar in the Nineteenth Century."[38] Yet it could conversely be argued that nonslave women tended to have more legal restrictions on their actions; authors seem to disagree on this issue and on whether the codification of rights for slave concubines was or was not a sign of a more humane system. It is also significant that there were many factors in addition to legal custom that determined the status of slave women in particular local hierarchies. In this collection, George Michael La Rue, in his chapter "The Fatal Sorbet: An Account of Slavery, Jealousy, Pregnancy, and Murder in a Harem in Alexandria, Egypt, ca. 1850," outlines the tragic case of a young Sudanese slave woman in a nineteenth-century Egyptian harem who had a sexual relationship (under unclear circumstances) with her owner. The wife of the master abused the slave woman and had her severely beaten, eventually even murdering her child; the slave, in turn, murdered the wife and was then executed. However embellished the story (recounted by Charles Didier) may have been, it points to the underlying reality of the frequent powerlessness in social practice of enslaved women at the bottom of racial hierarchies.

Several areas of experience explored in a number of chapters illustrate the blurring of lines between slavery and freedom and its significance with particular force. In the remainder of this introduction, I will first focus on three specific areas, namely, marriage and concubinage, prostitution and sex trafficking, and motherhood and the politics of reproduction. Since slavery was a juridical relationship as well as one determined by social practice, I will in each case consider both legal issues and some of the arguments that the authors make about the much messier nature of lived social realities.

I will then discuss the more scattered evidence provided by chapters in this collection on same-sex sexuality and sexual relationships between slaves themselves. Finally, I will return to the wider themes of what might be termed the "emotional geographies of enslavement" and the systems of honor and shaming around sexual relationships that, I argue, were integral to slavery in a wide variety of settings. In this context, I will also consider observers' representations of enslaved women and their sexuality, a theme raised by a number of essays in this collection.

Marriage, Concubinage, and Slavery

Across many societies, the experience of enslaved women and the sexual demands placed on them were intimately related to wider views of marriage and the relative degree of freedom wives (and, where pertinent, concubines) knew. Thus, slave women had different kinds of status in societies where wives, concubines, and slaves lived together in separate spaces than in those where slaves were largely separated as a group, allowing living space to be governed dominantly by slave status and race rather than dominantly by gender. The harem has been said by some scholars to have provided a separate woman's space, for example.[39] Enslaved wives, concubines, and casual sexual partners also had different statuses in societies that sanctioned polygamy as opposed to those that paid lip service to monogamy. In the former environment, one might argue, the sexual labor of unfree women was more openly acknowledged.

It might further be argued that a sharp distinction between slave and free, or freedom and unfreedom, was a binary juridical model that was being developed in Europe and the Americas in the eighteenth century in part through the experience of struggles over emancipation and debate over the meaning of a free labor economy. That binary did not necessarily apply to European imperial worlds, whether before or after emancipation. An enormous amount of scholarship has been devoted to the reality of the coercive elements of free labor regimes, including the legal coercion of taxation policy in colonial contexts, the imperial use of masters and servants legislation, and the lack of freedom of the indentured laborer. Nonetheless, the discursive binary between slave and free still had an intellectual, political, and legal impact, not least in framing discourses of emancipation. It helped build discursive walls between slave and free communities that otherwise lived very closely together. Is it possible this was particularly true of Protestant societies with strong proscriptions against extramarital sexuality and a heavy stress on the purity of the core community?

Nevertheless, there was certainly an enormous disjuncture between theory and practice when it came to sexual relationships in the Americas. In theory, in eighteenth- and nineteenth-century Christian slave societies and in a strictly juridical sense only, wives had the obligation to provide sexual labor to their husbands. There was no legal concept of marital rape. Indeed, in the Scottish Presbyterian Church, women could be rebuked in front of the congregation for refusing sex to their husbands.[40] Conversely, in theory, men could not demand sex from women other than their wives, including slave women: such women had no legal or religious obligation to provide sex.

The reality was, of course, quite different. An enormous amount of scholarship has documented the widespread sexual abuse of enslaved women, as well as the opportunities that such sexual relationships opened up for a few women and their children. In his chapter on "Slavery, Sex, and Dehumanization," David Brion Davis convincingly documents the extent of sexual relationships between slaves and masters in the American Atlantic world, including some horrific examples of abuse. Arguably, the existence of the free wife with strong claims to monogamy and the expectation of inheriting most of her husband's property made the treatment of enslaved sexual partners worse than it might otherwise have been because such relationships were frequently unregulated and covert. Yet, as some chapters in this volume contend, if a slave woman was extremely lucky, she might broker sexual relationships and, above all, motherhood into manumission, particularly on the death of the master.

The contributions in this collection suggest that the manumission of slave mistresses was more common and more socially accepted in certain slave societies than in others, whether because of greater cultural tolerance of extramarital relationships or because of the reality of gender-skewed colonial societies. In "Strategies for Social Mobility: Liaisons between Foreign Men and Slave Women in Benguela, ca. 1770–1850," Mariana Candido argues that in the slave-trading entrepôt of Benguela in what is now Angola, men preferred female slaves over males because they could exploit them sexually. Ironically, this sexual exploitation sometimes opened possibilities for enslaved women to use sex with slave owners, usually foreign men posted to Benguela to work in the slave trade, as a strategy to "enhance their lifestyle and status" and perhaps to win manumission. More generally, sexual relationships with colonial men involved in the slave trade enabled some enslaved women in slave-trading coastal regions in Africa to access power, and a number of these women became involved in the slave trade in turn.[41] The example of Angola (and other societies, such as colonial Brazil) contrasts with more tightly policed plantation societies in the anglophone West Indies, where the white family provided a stronger putative model, however little the exemplar was followed in practice.

Other legal regimes openly recognized sexual relationships beyond the marital. A number of essays in this collection look at Islamic law and the regulation of sexuality in North Africa, the Middle East, and the Sudan. Again, authors are often concerned with the gap between legal theory and reality, but the gap seems to have been less wide in these settings. Islamic law permitted slavery, which was a fact of everyday life at the time of the Prophet, although it also placed significant restrictions on who could be enslaved and under what circumstances (in theory, only war captives and those born into slavery). Slave masters were permitted to sleep with slave women if they made them concubines. Concubinage was, in theory, a legal status, and a man was permitted to have slave concubines in addition to up to four free wives. If a slave concubine bore a child to her master (the authors in this collection disagree about whether the child had to be male), she became *umm al-walad* (mother of the child; the variant *umm walad* is also used in English-language scholarship) and could no longer be sold. She was, in other words, a permanent household member. Upon her master's death, according to some traditions she was to be freed. A man might also marry his slave concubine, and in theory, the children of the union would be free. In this sense, slave women who slept with their masters had some legal advantages, even if they did not have the legal option of refusing to provide sexual services to those masters. Indeed, many women were bought and sold with the open expectation that they would provide sexual and reproductive labor, particularly in the Indian Ocean world. In the Atlantic slave system, by contrast, the dominant expectation was that the women would primarily provide nonsexual labor, whether in the household, on the farm, or on the plantation (albeit with the significant caveat that some women were clearly bought for sexual exploitation in the Americas as well).[42] There appears to be a division in the scholarship, recognizable in the diverse approaches taken by the authors of the essays in this collection, over whether and how often women were purchased primarily for sexual and reproductive purposes rather than primarily to provide manual labor.

Under Confucian law in China, concubinage was also a legally recognized status, which opened the door to the recognition of some rights for slave concubines. However, the Chinese slave concubine may have been less protected than her peers under Islamic law because she could be sold and resold with impunity: the provision of children did not confer immunity from sale. Essays by Griet Vankeerberghen and Johanna Ransmeier in the current collection provide perspectives on sexuality and slavery in China, as well as illustrating the diversity of possible sources. Drawing on classical texts together with more fragmented bureaucratic sources, Griet Vankeerberghen makes an important argument that the status of free wives was consolidated and hedged about with more protection in the Han period, during which slave concubinage and polygamy were more common than has been hitherto recognized. Johanna Ransmeier looks instead at the local complications of the sale of family members in the late Qing period, drawing on Qing local legal records (rather than central law codes). Ransmeier's work seems to suggest that a woman who had proven fertile was a more salable commodity during the Qing period. There was a market in fertile women to provide children to men whose wives had not had offspring; indeed, Ransmeier argues that wives themselves were sometimes involved in the purchase of concubines to give the family children—above all, it was hoped, male children who would be able to tend the shrines of the ancestors.

Legal theory was not always an accurate guide to the reality of intimate relationships. Much of Ransmeier's work, for instance, explores the many ways in which the putative legal system was subverted. Thus, Ransmeier tells the story of a Miss Men in the late Qing period who was returned to her natal family by a dissatisfied husband and whose aunt then sold her as a concubine; en route to service as a concubine, Miss Men was kidnapped by another man who planned to sell her in his turn, probably as a prostitute. The author shows how the magistrate adjudicating this case weighed the options of where to send Miss Men, which included allowing her to stay with her abductor, before ultimately returning the young woman to her own family. This case does not, however, show women entirely without agency, if only of a very limited kind. The girl was sold by her own matchmaking aunt, and she herself consented to the sale, on at least some level, because her body-price would pay for medical care for her ailing mother. This raises the issue of the network of obligations and personal ties in which women were bound up, again complicating a free/unfree binary and showing how illusory was the clarity putatively provided by elite legal codes. Despite efforts at legal reform in the Republican period, the gray zones between various forms of marriage, concubinage, and enslavement continued to make legal clarity difficult.[43]

In the chapter "'To Marry One's Slave Is as Easy as Eating a Meal': The Dynamics of Carnal Relations within Saharan Slavery," Ann McDougall argues that there were many possibilities open in Mauritania to those who wanted to follow legal custom. "Ask a question about marriage or slavery or just about anything, and a Mauritanian (like most Muslims) will first refer to 'what Islam says.' By that, they mean some part or combination of the Qur'an, the 'law' that interprets it (*fiqh*), and/or the stories told of the Prophet Mohamed that are meant to lead by example (*hadith*). What actually happens is usually a combination of these understandings and local realities and/or customs (*'ada*), which of course, change over time."

In her work, McDougall tries to unpack ambiguity and slippage between the status categories of "slave," "wife," and "concubine." Ambiguity was such that it was even possible for a woman whose purchase had been shared to be considered the slave of one man and the freed wife of another at the same time, depending on her relationship with each man. Thus, McDougall cites the example of the enslaved woman Miriam mint Matellah, whose master's friend purchased a share in her for sexual purposes. Her children by the second master were considered free, implying that the mother herself had become *umm al-walad* and thus eligible to be freed on her master's death; at the same time, however, her other children remained enslaved and stayed within the family of the first master, suggesting that they were the children of a slave father. McDougall asserts it is significant that through such legal sleights of hand, as well as through marriages between enslaved women and the dependent clients of their owners' families, women could bring children into more than one family grouping, particularly in an era in which the slave trade itself had (in theory) been abolished. Many of these actions were strategies to boost the overall fertility of the family group, especially given the reduced fertility of fattened noble women, and they need to be seen as part of wider family strategies.

These examples suggest that for women in many societies, there was a continuum of degrees of self-ownership and corresponding obligations to provide sexual services, rather than a clear-cut distinction between "slave" and "free." How much control a woman had over with whom she had sex, and under what circumstances, reflected her status, but very few women (including wives) had complete freedom to choose or refuse sex. The individual's degree of obligation to provide sexual labor was a marker both of freedom and of status, in ways that overlapped. In societies with very strong distinctions between slave and free, this was arguably more likely to be a private rather than a publicly recognized obligation; in societies that openly recognized a more subtle gradation of statuses and degrees of duty to one another among members of the household, there may have been more of a sliding scale for the degrees of obligation. That being said, however, marriage certainly constituted a moment of transition from slavery to nominally free status for many slave women. It appears that it was much easier for an enslaved woman to marry a free man in a society that did not, in fact, have a deeply entrenched binary distinction between free and unfree members or a high degree of legal freedoms for women.

It is important to note that the variation in degrees of self-ownership and sexual obligations created status ambiguities that could be exploited from many directions. Several chapters in this book provide striking examples of colonial states refusing to recognize the inconvenient unfreedom of women in the wake of the supposed abolition of slavery. For instance, Marie Rodet shows how in colonial Mali, French officials tacitly accepted the marriages of masters with former slaves in a manner that enshrined the slave status of the wives. At the same time, women in Rodet's study used status ambiguity themselves to try to increase their freedom, often by moving from one area to another and sometimes by denouncing husbands to colonial officials. Status ambiguities might be particularly pronounced when legal regimes overlapped,[44] but women often fought hard to exploit the ambiguities and loopholes in the law, whatever legal constraints were placed on them.

Finally, it is also crucial that enslavement had a profound impact on the way men experienced marriage. In the Americas, men were often sold away from their families, for example, and were emasculated by their inability to limit sexual access to their own wives (as I will discuss further). In this collection, Matthew Hopper sensitively shows how important it was for enslaved pearl divers in the Arabian Peninsula to have access to the wives who had been provided by their masters: issues of access were a significant source of tension between slave and master. More generally, control over the marriages of enslaved male members of the household bolstered the power of the male patriarch across the Indian Ocean world, providing yet another example of the differences between slave systems.

Prostitution and Sex Trafficking

Sex work is another area in which a focus on sexuality and the obligation to provide sex blurs the line between freedom and unfreedom, although, again, there is obviously room for debate over the meaning of slavery, just as the discussions on the meaning of human trafficking suggest. In the nineteenth century, increasingly far-ranging and dense networks of sex trafficking accompanied globalization. Transnational trafficking networks frequently took women from areas where they were sold (or where they sold themselves), often to provide money to highly impoverished families, to areas with skewed sex ratios and a high demand for prostitutes. Such women were not clearly slaves, and sometimes they had the theoretical possibility of buying back their freedom. Yet they were often compelled to remain in brothels and were often deliberately enmeshed in debt in order to immobilize them. Francesca Mitchell describes sex trafficking in Thailand and Cambodia as a modern form of slavery, although she also points to the difficulty of drawing a firm line between free and coerced labor in sex work. Roseline Uyanga and Marie-Louise Ermisch see sex slavery as a global phenomenon assisted by but not coincidental with human trafficking. They similarly explore the role of coercion in the modern trafficking of young Nigerian women into European locations, citing the use of juju charms, the theft of the women's passports, and the creation of unrepayable debts as mechanisms employed to keep women in prostitution—even as they also acknowledge that some women enter the trade voluntarily, if only, in many cases, to be coerced later.[45] James Warren investigates the trafficking of young women from rural Japan in the late nineteenth and early twentieth centuries to the imperial enclave of Singapore, with its dominantly male workforce of Chinese migrants. Poor rural Japanese and Chinese women were also sent to areas as diverse as tin-mining regions of Malaya, Sumatran tobacco plantations, and even pearling settlements in Australia. This suggests that there was a tight link between prostitution networks and the provision of migrant labor by men across the workfaces of empires. Here, too, the line between choice and coercion blurred.

As status relationships within households were transformed into long-distance commodity relationships, one might see parallels with the transformation in Africa of local forms of slavery, including coerced household labor, via the creation of salable "chattel" individuals who could then be inserted into long-distance capital markets. There are limits to the parallel: the frequently covert nature of markets in sex workers made them less open to the public ascription of a financial "value" that would be recognized by capital markets than was the case with chattel slaves, for example. In the slave-era American south, in contrast, commodification was so advanced that slaves might be mortgaged and used as a source of credit.[46] At the same time, there were hugely complicated markets in debt, as well as complex uses of household members as pawns to provide security for debt, in many areas of the world that provided people for long-distance markets both as chattel slaves and as sex workers. Be that as it may, it is also noteworthy that in areas where women and children were frequently sold to become prostitutes, sales between households in which the provision of sexual services was only part of a wider gamut of obligations were transformed into direct long-distance sales of women to carry out sexual labor alone. At the same time, the brothel mimicked the household in some contexts. James Warren shows how women in Japanese brothels in Singapore used kinship terminology: prostitutes were "daughters" and madams "mothers," and kinship obligations were transferred onto these relationships.

Overall, trafficking shows the commodification of sexual services that allows us to see sex work as a form of migrant labor, in some contexts, as well as a form of labor that had financial consequences far back in the supply chain. The process stretched notions of household bondage in a way that went well beyond existing legal notions, and yet it also worked within local understandings (such as in the cases discussed here of Japan and China) of the fundamental alienability of surplus women. At the same time, the paradigm of slavery does not entirely fit trafficked prostitutes; some had the ability to become madams or to marry out of the trade, for example. Here, too, different authors accord different weights to the elusive issue of the sex worker's agency and degree of choice.

In this collection, Shigeru Sato looks at a less equivocal example of coerced sexual labor by trafficked women, namely, the work of the *ianfu*, or comfort women, who were compelled to provide sex to Japanese soldiers during World War II. As Sato demonstrates, there is considerable debate today, in the context of lawsuits for compensation, about many features of the system, including the number of women involved (with a lowest estimate of 21,000 and a highest estimate of 410,000); the number who were professional prostitutes before the war; and what percentage were from Korean and other non-Japanese backgrounds. At the same time, authorities agree that Japanese women were better paid, were more likely to have worked in brothels before the war, and had higher-status work.[47] It is clear, though, that there were many overlaps between how women were produced for the international sex trade and how they were procured as prostitutes for the Japanese army. In both cases, for instance, families sold girls at times of great poverty, and these girls might have ended up as long-distance sex workers; other women were lured to carry out different jobs only to find themselves coerced into prostitution. The example of comfort women is a reminder of a pivotal area of female experience not fully covered in this collection—the coercion of women in wartime to provide sexual service to men. The kidnapping of girls by the Lord's Resistance Army (LRA) in Uganda to be both child soldiers and sexual partners is a compelling (and complicated) illustration of sexual servitude that does not fully fit the paradigms we have discussed so far.

Reproduction

From the perspective of slave owners, much of the "value" of female slaves was tied up in the fact that they reproduced and thus potentially replenished the group of people under the control of masters and mistresses, whether in households or on plantations. This was, of course, a critical difference between male and female enslavement. Again, generalizations across very diverse slave systems and societies are hugely difficult: there was, for instance, a great difference in the ways in which children of enslaved women fit into kinship networks in much of the Indian Ocean world as compared to the Atlantic world. Yet despite central points of contrast, some key issues arguably recurred in a wide variety of contexts.

For masters, then, the reproductive labor of the enslaved woman was a critical source of value. In some times and places, it could be monetized with a remarkable degree of precision. David Brion Davis cites the example of discussions over the price of a young and potentially fertile slave.[48] Reproduction could thus be turned into a commodity itself, unhinged from familial relationships. It was also an important measure of the exchange value of women in African societies that affixed less precise monetary values to reproductive potential but still saw the ability to reproduce as a critical—and possibly *the* critical—source of value for enslaved women.

The children of enslaved women might be perceived as particularly malleable and therefore available to be shaped as new members of a particular society. Indeed, women and children were generally more prone to be adopted into societies, rather than seen as perpetual outsiders. In this sense also, having children may have improved the status of enslaved women.

It is difficult, however, to generalize about the benefits accruing from children (as debate about the prevalence of abortion and infanticide in American plantation societies suggests). For enslaved women, children were a potential route to a better life, especially if the fathers were free men, but also a source of profound vulnerability. A child might be a means to manumission, but women conversely faced the far more likely, heart-wrenching possibility of losing their children, whom others "owned," through sale; further, there was the pain of seeing children grow up in slavery. The offspring of enslaved women and free men met widely divergent fates not only in different societies but also as a function of the willingness of men to acknowledge their children. In societies in the Americas with a sharp legal dividing line between slave and free, such children quite frequently went unacknowledged and remained enslaved. Yet in some cases, men would manumit both their mistresses and their children outright, particularly in their wills. In his essay in this collection, David Brion Davis discusses the wide range of legal and cultural possibilities even within the nominally Christian slaveholding communities in the Americas in the eighteenth and nineteenth centuries—including laws put in place to curtail individual manumissions, limit interracial sexuality (at least at a publicly recognized level), and forbid the recognition of interracial children.

In the polygamous households of the Indian Ocean world, there were (at least in theory) stronger obligations owed to the child of a female slave on the part of a master who was also the father, as well as to the mother. As I discussed earlier, for a woman to bear her master's child in Islamic societies imposed obligations on the father; he would certainly be forbidden under Islamic law from selling her away from the household, and he might be obliged to manumit her upon his death. Of course, this was not necessarily manumission into complete freedom; in many places, the families of former slaves would often remain as dependents of their deceased masters' families. In all the societies under discussion in this collection, having children potentially raised the status of an enslaved mother—but this was frequently a high-risk strategy (if it could even be called a strategy in some cases), and the emotional issues were doubtless profoundly difficult.

Throughout this discussion, it is important to recognize that the children of slave women were often not treated as children. Charmaine Nelson argues that black children stood apart from another emerging Western binary, namely, that between childhood and adulthood. They were called on to labor from an early age and were treated as commodities. In this sense, the labor of the black child helped undergird the far more extended childhood of the white child, just as the labor of black women in the household enabled the ideals of genteel feminine domesticity enacted by white women. As Tara Inniss demonstrates, many children were also subjected to sexual exploitation themselves. Although it was, in theory, possible to pursue lawsuits against men who violated enslaved children in the West Indies, such children were surely among the most vulnerable members of plantation societies, as of other slaveholding societies. It is particularly hard to speak of the "agency" of the targets of sexual advances in this context.

Same-Sex Sexuality

There is a great deal that is not known—and probably cannot be known—about sexuality in slave societies. Same-sex sexuality is perhaps especially difficult to uncover, given severe legal prohibitions against sodomy in most societies. Same-sex sexuality, particularly between master and slave, was further over the boundary of the acceptable than male-female sex between master and slave, and it apparently was less likely to have been accepted tacitly or seen as part of a wider honor system. Not least of all, same-sex sexuality left no children and was therefore intrinsically more private. At the same time, the very fact that sodomy was often punished harshly when it was discovered has left a trail of legal records that historians are only beginning to exploit. Most of these historians are finding that more can be known than was once thought possible, as is, of course, the case for scholars of queer history more generally.

In this collection, Ronaldo Vainfas attempts to uncover evidence about same-sex sexuality in a small town in the slave colony of Brazil, largely through using Inquisition records. He finds that it is difficult to locate a gay subculture in small colonial towns, in contrast to the major urban centers on the Iberian Peninsula of the eighteenth and nineteenth centuries. Same-sex activity did, however, clearly exist, and there were limits to how far the Inquisition was willing or able to police it. Vainfas's study includes sex between slaves and masters that he sees for the most part as exploitative because it was based in unequal power relationships; indeed, same-sex relationships between master and slave arguably had fewer potential advantages for the slave, in the absence of children.

In other contexts, same-sex sexuality was more readily accepted and more woven into the fabric of slavery. Eunuchs were often traded across the Indian Ocean world. Salah Trabelsi shows that they provided sexual services to men and women, but for obvious reasons, they were uncoupled from reproduction. The trade in male eunuchs as items of sexual consumption for certain elite households should also be placed alongside the trade in young women. There was, to be sure, far more to the employment of eunuchs than occasional sexual labor. Although eunuchs could be perceived as agents of sexual aggression, they were also, among other functions, trusted to run harems. They thus acted as crucial intermediaries between women's worlds and men's worlds in elite environments in the Middle East. They could also help maintain internal hierarchies within harems, as La Rue's example of a wife using eunuchs to beat the enslaved mistress of her husband implies.

Brian Lewis details the extensive same-sex sexual activities of Roger Casement, a passionate antislavery activist who was deeply involved in the campaign against Belgian atrocities in the Congo in the late nineteenth century. Casement kept a series of diaries, the so-called black diaries, in parallel with his more routine journals. These diaries show that he frequently paid for sex with young men of many different background across the world, including African men. Lewis hypothesizes that this contact contributed to empathy, but it has been read as well as a form of exploitation. This study, in turn, raises the issue of how exploitative, or even how consequential, such sexual exchanges were. They were obviously dangerous: Casement's black diaries were used by the British government to help ensure a death sentence against him and eliminate international support after Casement was found guilty of seeking German backing for an uprising in Ireland during World War I.

Sex among Slaves and the Emotional Geographies of Enslavement

Much less scholarly work has been carried out on sexual relationships between slaves than on relationships between slaves and slave owners. Relationships between slaves are far harder to document than sexual relationships between masters and enslaved persons. Here again, the question of silence and perhaps the need to respect the limits of knowledge remain important. Nonetheless, some generalizations are possible. In the current collection, Ulrike Schmieder sensitively explores a range of information about the sexual worlds of the enslaved in colonial Cuba. She shows, for example, competition between enslaved men over access to women, sometimes ritualistically expressed in dance competitions or song. Her chapter addresses the "victimization both of slave women through the sexual assaults of their owners and that of all slaves by the intervention of masters in their private lives and the various obstacles placed to forming couples and families," while also exploring the "everyday struggle" of slaves to defend their personal lives and family ties.

Competition between men (including between slaves and masters) over sexual access to enslaved women was a key feature of many slave societies. In the Americas in particular, the formation of families was blocked by the sale of slaves. Enslaved men had to see white men sleeping with their own sexual partners and consistently not only elbowing them aside but also denying the validity of slave families and men's ownership of their own offspring. Variants of such experiences are explored in a number of essays in this collection. In the very different context of serfdom in Russia, Richard Hellie shows complex power struggles over sexuality as serfdom degenerated into de facto slavery, including the sexual abuse of serfs by landlords.

This type of evidence places emasculation at the heart of the slave experience and the complex emotional geographies that maintained and justified slavery. It is surely not surprising that a critical concern for previously enslaved men in the aftermath of abolition was the control of women and their sexuality: this was, in itself, a marker of freedom.[49] The quest for sexual self-ownership was a vital aspect of ideologies of freedom, whether to choose and control sexual partners or to care for the children that resulted. In the meantime, enslaved females often formed communities of women, drawing on complex female networks that provided a different model of sociability and support than the nuclear family preferred by Western abolitionists.

Honor, Slavery, and Sexual Self-Ownership

Sexuality and the control of sexuality were critical elements of what might be termed the "emotional geography" of slavery in many other ways. Slavery was accompanied by ideas of honor and dishonor. Many of the chapters in this collection, taken together, seem to suggest that across a multitude of slave societies, there were links between slavery, the control of sexuality (including a slave's lack of self-ownership and corresponding obligation to provide sexual labor), and perceptions of honor and dishonor. In China, for instance, as Johanna Ransmeier argues, only those women who were "debased" could be sold, such as a wife who had committed adultery. In reality, there was tremendous slippage, and those who were enslaved or sold came to be defined as debased, rather than vice versa. So-called debased women, in turn, were no longer able to refuse sexual services and could be sold as concubines. In the empires of the western Sudan, as Martin Klein shows, the stigma of slave status persisted long after the formal abolition of slavery, and slave women were described as vulgar, dishonorable, and sexually voracious; Klein ties the persistence of status distinctions to regionally persistent honor codes.[50] Similar things could be said about a multitude of different societies.

This association seems to have held even in situations without formal enslavement. In late twentieth-century Madagascar, well after the supposed abolition of slavery, as Sandra Evers agues, the "andevo" were assumed both to owe labor and to be sexually promiscuous, and those higher-status men who slept with andevo women needed to remove ritual impurity after sexual contact. Subho Basu's essay, "Wages of Womanhood," looks at the working conditions of free women mill workers in early twentieth-century Bengal, again in the absence of actual slavery. He argues that these women workers, whose range of choices was severely limited by economic circumstances and entrapment through debt even if they were legally free agents, were described as prostitutes by mill owners, who refused to provide social services and workplace benefits to them on that basis. The chapter underscores the strength of the link between sexual dishonor and the presumed obligation to provide labor.

In the Americas, many racial stereotypes turned (and continue to turn) around sexuality, honor, and the capacity for self-control. The honorable man had control of his own sexuality, yet African-origin men and women were often portrayed as highly sexed and unable to control their own sexuality, as several authors in these volumes argue, including David Brion Davis, Ana Lucia Araujo, and Charmaine Nelson. Such stereotypes arguably validated the sexual abuse of women. They also permitted a vision of the hypermasculinity of enslaved men that paradoxically functioned as a form of emasculation: slave masculinity was supposedly out of control and thus could be portrayed as dishonorable and dangerous.

These kinds of views of the wrong sort of masculinity were arguably also at work in emancipationist stereotypes of the debased and dangerous West Indian planter who exploited the bodies of his slaves, both sexually and through outrageous violence. Here, too, one sees a critical nexus between ideas of sexual self-ownership, honor, and freedom. Western feminists in the early nineteenth century who opposed slavery told of the sexual abuse of slave women by male slave owners. In some ways, this was also an affirmation of their own status, as Brion Davis asserts here, and a broader attack on male sexual predation, reflecting as well many of the later concerns of wider social purity movements in Britain, the United States, and Canada.[51] Would this critique have proved so powerful had the freedom from an obligation to sexual labor not been so central a component of definitions of freedom and dignity for women?

At the same time, slave women were also often portrayed by European observers as lascivious and as the willing sexual partners of white men. In this collection, Ana Lucia Araujo's analysis of paintings of colonial Brazil shows that painters often portrayed enslaved women as beautiful and available; given the collaborative nature of the production of prints and the widespread dissemination of images, she suggests that this was a widespread view. Such stereotypes are also evident in Charmaine Nelson's analysis of early Canadian artwork and in Ulrike Schmieder's discussion of colonial Cuba. The view of the enslaved woman as eagerly sexual was arguably the flip side of the abolitionist view of the enslaved woman as entirely chaste: in some sense, both views reflected the desires and needs of the European observer. With an emphasis on resistance, in contrast, Gabeba Baderoon analyzes South African art and fiction that recovers the "traumatic history of slavery and sexual subjection hidden within the picturesque colonial landscape," and she crafts images of the "resilience and interiority of enslaved people." Here, art has an emancipatory potential through demystifying the fantasies that undergirded subjection.

Concluding Reflections

Running through much of the preceding discussion, as through many of the essays in this collection, is the issue of the agency (to use a vexed, problematic, and much-debated term) of the enslaved. Take, for example, the central issue of enslaved women who had sex with their masters. Was this an opportunity, however precarious and limited, for self-advancement and the possible advancement of a woman's children? Or was this a central feature of the exploitation of enslaved women? The two options are not mutually exclusive. Nonetheless, even the authors in this particular collection differ in terms of tone and emphasis on victimization or agency. Mariana Candido, though arguing that women in Benguala sought to exploit sexual relationships to gain freedom, is also unequivocal that "white men viewed all non-white females, whether free or servile, as available to service their sexual needs, and systematically asserted their sexual dominance, especially over enslaved women who were in control neither of their bodies, nor of their sexuality. Indeed, sexual abuse was recognized as one of the mechanisms through which white male power, dominance and control was exercised over the slave population."[52] Other works in this collection, including the chapters by Salah Trabelsi and Abdul Sheriff, emphasize the considerable advantages that could be won by enslaved people, including slave concubines and eunuchs, who were able to negotiate through hierarchies of power. This was all the more true at particular times and places, among them, as Trabelsi points out, the Abbasid Caliphate centered on Baghdad, when enslaved outsiders were structurally able to seize power at the court, even if only a few slaves had such opportunities. Some would suggest that the greater ability of slaves to advance was actually a key feature of Indian Ocean slavery. At a different social level and in a very different environment, Matthew Hopper describes the capacity of enslaved pearl divers in the twentieth-century

Arabian Gulf to negotiate with owners over family relationships, albeit, as he argues, in very limited and constrained ways.

However, a critical issue at stake in the more particular discussion of sexual relationships between owners and the enslaved is that enslaved women and in certain contexts enslaved men (including eunuchs) almost never had a choice about rejecting the advances of their masters: the ownership of the body by another was a fundamental defining feature of slavery. Even further down the hierarchies of a slave society, others besides the master (such as fellow slaves in positions of power or European visitors to the household) could control the sexuality of the enslaved. In this broad context but with particular attention to the American slave South, Saidiya Hartman claims that the discourse of the "seduction" of powerful masters by slave women who thereby gained the weapons of the weak was, in fact, a fantasy of domination: "The presumed mutuality of feelings in maintaining domination enchanted the most brutal and direct violence of master-slave relations."[53]

As this brief discussion suggests, a focus on sexuality shows starkly both how central the control of the body was to slavery and to wider concepts of freedom and how embedded slavery was in a wider discourse about gender and power. The enslaved might struggle adroitly to exploit structures of victimization. These very struggles, however, reinforced the structures and beliefs that maintained slavery. For example, if some enslaved women gained pecuniary advantages from long-term relationships with free men, this does not suggest that other women did not suffer profoundly from the system that made these relationships possible or that the enslaved partners themselves did not experience the relationship as abusive.

Sexuality was, in sum, a controversial, difficult, and multifaceted element of enslavement, even as sexuality itself is clearly complex and multifaceted, and the limits to the subject are hard to define. Taken together, the essays in this collection suggest, nonetheless, that sexuality was actually at the heart of how slavery worked in many different societies. Although controversies will continue and although scholars differ widely in their views of how and why sexuality mattered, we hope that this collection demonstrates the centrality of the history of sexuality to the history of slavery and the mutual entanglement of slavery and sexuality.

The chapters in this volume are grouped by theme and should ideally be read as a composite whole. The collection begins with three overview essays about sexuality and enslavement in particular regions, by David Brion Davis on the Americas, Martin Klein on the vast northern regions of West Africa known as the western Sudan, and the late Richard Hellie on Russia and the Russian Empire. These essays lay out some paradigmatic arguments. Brion Davis links the control of the bodies of the enslaved to the dehumanization contingent on slavery. Klein gives a magisterial overview of diverse interactions between sexuality and slavery in the western Sudan. Hellie similarly looks at sexuality and both serfdom and slavery in Russia; his analysis suggests that female slaves and serfs were objects of sexual predation, individuals without rights who were categorized as shameful, and that related attitudes persisted even after the formal abolition of serfdom.

The next section examines concubinage, law, and family in polygamous societies. Griet Vankeerberghen's essay in this section addresses concubinage, marriage, and slavery in China during the Han period. The remaining essays all explore Islamic societies in diverse contexts. Abdul Sheriff and George Michael La Rue dissect relationships within elite harems, in Zanzibar in the case of Sheriff and in nineteenth-century Egypt in the case of La Rue (a theme that is later picked up by Salah Trabelsi in his chapter on eunuchs in the Abbasid Caliphate). E. Ann McDougall examines the dynamics of carnal relations within slaveholding families in Mauritania, with attention to the status ambiguity between "wife" and "concubine" and to the ways in which enslaved concubines and the children they produced fit into wider economic and familial structures. Matthew Hopper looks at the family relationships of enslaved pearl divers, most of African origin, in the Arabian Gulf between the late nineteenth and early twentieth centuries. Finally, Marie Rodet echoes Hopper's emphasis on the strategies of the enslaved, focusing on the "sexual and migratory strategies" of slave women in French Sudan in the region of Kayes at the time of emancipation. Rodet continues the theme of ambiguities in the overlapping and fluid status of concubines, wives, and female slaves, showing how both slaves and slave owners tried to exploit these status ambiguities at the moment of the putative abolition of slavery. Like several other essays, Rodet's work also demonstrates that the legal end of slavery often did not mean the actual end of enslavement, especially when European imperial masters were primarily interested in brokering arrangements with local slaveholding elites. Women were particularly vulnerable; looking at concubinage and sex makes it clearer how readily women might slip from being slave concubines to enslaved "wives."

The next section looks at sexuality, slavery, and the family in the Atlantic trading system. The chapters in this section all investigate societies in which, at a minimum, local imperial masters were Christian and in which there was some expectation that households (or at least those headed by Europeans) would be monogamous. Ulrike Schmieder provides an ambitious overview of sexual relations not only between slaves and nonslaves but also between the enslaved themselves in nineteenth-century Cuba; she explores in particular how the enslaved struggled in brutal environments to protect their personal lives and family relationships. Tara Inniss seeks to overcome the silences in both the historical record and subsequent scholarship around the sexual exploitation of enslaved children to examine the abuse of children in Barbados (and, by extension, in the British Caribbean more broadly) in the final half century of slavery in the British Empire. Mariana Candido examines sexual liaisons between foreign men and enslaved women in the slave-trading center of Benguela, in what was then the Portuguese colony of Angola. Sexual relationships between white men and enslaved women were extremely prevalent (given the mostly all-male composition of the European workforce). She argues that sexual exploitation was thus central to slavery and the slave trade; within these difficult parameters, however, women tried to use sexual relationships to improve their situations and, in some cases, to obtain manumission.

The volume then homes in on some key themes. One cluster of essays addresses sex trafficking and prostitution. James Warren describes the trafficking of Japanese girls and women to colonial Singapore and the daily life of Singaporean brothels between 1870 and 1940. These women were only ambiguously free, and they were often unable to escape the brothels. If Warren focuses on the lives of trafficked prostitutes at their destination, Johanna Ransmeier looks at the mechanisms that saw Chinese women trafficked in the first place, in her analysis of the sale of women at the end of the Qing dynasty from the late nineteenth to early twentieth centuries.

Roseline Uyanga and Marie-Luise Ermisch explore the current trafficking of Nigerian women and compare this to enslavement. Although some women willingly go overseas as prostitutes, they are often constrained by financial and familial obligations, and once in the trade, they are trapped and unable to leave. In addition, many women and children are, in fact, trafficked and prostituted involuntarily. Francesca Mitchell makes similar observations about the rise of sex trafficking in Thailand and Cambodia from the 1960s forward. Shigeru Sato provides a sobering comparison with the trafficking and exploitation of comfort women by the Japanese army in World War II.

The next section turns to art and the light that it can shed on the relationship between sexuality and slavery. Gabeba Baderoon analyzes contemporary South African art and fiction that seeks to recapture the traumatic but often hidden history of slavery in the Cape Colony. Charmaine Nelson examines how black girls were portrayed in Canadian art from the time of slavery. She uses this study as a springboard to argue that the childhood of white children, in an era in which childhood was being reinvented as an idyllic and protected space, actually depended on the denial of the childhood of exploited slave children. Finally, Ana Lucia Araujo analyzes the representations of slaves and slavery in colonial Brazil by European artists and the ways in which they perpetuated particular stereotypes about the enslaved, including their sexuality. Like all the authors of essays in this section, Araujo engages with the ways slavery has been remembered and the continuing power of visual images.

We then turn to three chapters that "queer" the study of slavery. The covert sexual life of Roger Casement, eminent antislavery activist and voracious purchaser of sex with young men, has proved almost as controversial in scholarship as it was in his lifetime, when his secret diaries were produced in evidence at his sedition trial for his activities in support of Irish independence. Brian Lewis reexamines the sexual life of Casement in the context of his antislavery activities. Ronaldo Vainfas combs through sources to uncover information about sex between men in Minas Gerais in eighteenth-century Brazil (and shows, among other things, that sexual exploitation was not limited to the exploitation of enslaved women). Salah Trabelsi writes about eunuchs in the early Islamic world, mining Arabic-language chronicles and travelers' accounts from the period to gain glimpses of the lives of the enslaved (including women) and the nature of relationships in elite households.

The final section of the book brings together three essays that discuss aspects of the ideological structures that accompanied slavery but in environments without formal juridical enslavement. Joost Coté studies abolitionist rhetoric in the Dutch East Indies, as well as ways in which coerced labor continued after the formal abolition of slavery (echoing, as I suggested earlier, a number of other essays in the collection). In contemporary Madagascar, Sandra Evers argues, peasants in the community she studied continued to believe that some people were the slaves of others and owed them labor because they did not have ancestral tombs or land rights; those perceived as enslaved were considered to be sexually dishonorable, even if they were also sought out as covert sexual partners, and young women defined as enslaved struggled to use these sexual relationships to their advantage. The final essay in the collection, by Subho Basu, looks at the labor of women mill workers in twentieth-century Bengal. It is hard to define this labor as coerced, but women were often forced into it by debt bondage and other more nebulously coercive economic circumstances. The low-caste status of these women and their limited bargaining power conspired to make it easy for mill owners to define them as sexually promiscuous and therefore undeserving of rights.

The collection is structured to highlight comparisons across time and space, while also bringing out some common themes and clustering studies on particular regions. Despite the differences between these essays, which range across markedly different worlds, we hope that the comparisons, contrasts, and similarities prove fruitful in inspiring future work.

Notes

I am very grateful for comments on this chapter and other assistance to Pierre Boulle, Gwyn Campbell, Marie-Luise Ermisch, Joseph Miller, Jason Opal, Laila Parsons, Johanna Ransmeier, Rachel Sandwell, Renee Saucier, Jon Soske, and Daviken Studnicki-Gizbert, as well as to Carrie Rentschler and other participants for a very helpful seminar at the Institute for Gender, Sexuality, and Feminist Studies, McGill University, at which I presented some of these ideas. All errors are of course my own.

1. Some foundational works in the 1980s and 1990s that focused on the experiences of enslaved women (including sexual experiences) are Deborah Gray

White, *Ar'n't I a Woman? Female Slaves in the Plantation South* (1985; New York: W. W. Norton, 1999); Elizabeth Fox-Genovese, *Within the Plantation Household: Black and White Women of the Old South* (Chapel Hill: University of North Carolina Press, 1998); A. McLaurin, *Celia: A Slave* (Athens: University of Georgia Press, 1991); Barbara Bush, *Slave Women in Caribbean Society, 1650–1838* (Bloomington: Indiana University Press, 1990); and Marcia Wright, *Strategies of Slaves and Women: Life Stories from East/Central Africa* (London: James Currey, 1993).

2. Saidiya V. Hartman, *Scenes of Subjection: Terror, Slavery and Self-Making in Nineteenth-Century America* (Oxford: Oxford University Press, 2007).

3. Among many possibilities in English-language literature, see Catherine Clinton and Michele Gillespie, eds., *The Devil's Lane: Sex and Race in the Slave South* (New York: Oxford University Press, 1997); Kathleen Brown, *Good Wives, Nasty Wenches and Anxious Patriarchs: Gender, Race and Power in Colonial Virginia* (Chapel Hill: University of North Carolina Press, 1996); Dorothy L. Hodgson and Sheryl McCurdy, eds., *"Wicked" Women and the Reconfiguration of Gender in Africa* (Oxford: James Currey, 2001); Jennifer Morgan, *Laboring Women: Reproduction and Gender in New World Slavery* (Philadelphia: University of Pennsylvania Press, 2004); and Pamela Scully and Diana Paton, eds., *Gender and Slave Emancipation in the Atlantic World* (Durham, N.C.: Duke University Press, 2005).

4. Edward E. Baptist, "'Cuffy,' 'Fancy Maids' and 'One-Eyed Men': Rape, Commodification and the Domestic Slave Trade in the United States," *American Historical Review* 106, no. 5 (December 2001): 1619–30. For enslaved men's experience of sexual abuse, see, for example, Thomas A. Foster, "The Sexual Abuse of Black Men under American Slavery," *Journal of the History of Sexuality* 20, no. 3 (September 2011): 445–64.

5. For example, see Brenda E. Stevenson, *Life in Black and White: Family and Community in the Early South* (New York: Oxford University Press, 1997); Pamela Scully, *Liberating the Family? Gender and British Slave Emancipation in the Rural Western Cape, South Africa, 1823–1853* (Portsmouth, N.H.: Heinemann, 1997); or the seminal work of Eugene Genovese, *Roll, Jordan, Roll: The World the Slaves Made* (New York: Pantheon Books, 1974).

6. Catherine Clinton, "Breaking the Silence: Sexual Hypocrisies from Thomas Jefferson to Strom Thurmond," in *Beyond Slavery: Overcoming Its Religious and Sexual Legacies*, ed. Bernadette J. Brooten, with the assistance of Jacqueline Hazelton (New York: Palgrave Macmillan, 2010), 213.

7. Gwyn Campbell, "Introduction: Slavery and Other Forms of Unfree Labour in the Indian Ocean World," in *The Structure of Slavery in Indian Africa and Asia*, ed. Gwyn Campbell (Abingdon, UK: Frank Cass, 2006), vii–xxxii.

8. For an overview of the field of gender and empire from a British perspective, see Philippa Levine, ed., *Gender and Empire* (Oxford: Oxford University Press, 2004).

9. Ann Stoler, *Carnal Knowledge and Imperial Power: Race and the Intimate in Imperial Rule* (Berkeley: University of California Press, 2002); Ann Stoler, *Haunted by Empire: Geographies of the Intimate in North American History*, 2nd ed. (Berkeley: University of California Press, 2006); Philippa Levine, *Prostitution, Race and Disease: Policing Venereal Disease in the British Empire* (New York: Routledge, 2003); Durbha Ghosh, *Sex and the Family in Colonial India: The Making of Empire* (Cambridge: Cambridge University Press, 2006); and Timothy Mitchell, *Colonizing Egypt* (Berkeley: University of California Press, 1988).

10. A number of scholars in this tradition have been influenced by Michel Foucault's pioneering work on the history of sexuality. See Foucault, *Histoire de la sexualité*, 3 vols. (Paris: Gallimard, 1976–1991); Ann Stoler, *Race and the Education of Desire*, with author's preface (1995; repr., Los Angeles: University of California Press, 2010).

11. Levine, *Prostitution, Race and Disease*, 325.

12. Hartman, *Scenes of Subjection*, 89. For an early version of this debate in a British imperial context, compare Ronald Hyam, *Empire and Sexuality: The British Experience*, and Mark Berger, "Imperialism and Sexual Exploitation: A Response to Ronald Hyam's *Empire and Sexuality*," *Journal of Imperial and Commonwealth History* 17, no. 1 (1988): 83–89.

13. For example, see David Eltis and Stanley L. Engerman, "Fluctuations in Sex and Age Ratios in the Transatlantic Slave Trade, 1664–1864," *Journal of Economic History* 46, no. 2 (1993): 308–23. Also see several of the essays in Paul E. Lovejoy, *Slavery, Commerce and Production in the Sokoto Caliphate of West Africa* (Trenton, N.J.: Africa World Press, 2005), for arguments about the relationship between the sexual labor of concubinage and wider economic implications.

14. Claire Robertson and Martin Klein, eds., *Women and Slavery in Africa* (Madison: University of Wisconsin Press, 1983); Gwyn Campbell, Suzanne Miers, and Joseph C. Miller, "Strategies of Women and Constraints of Enslavement in the Modern Americas," in *Women and Slavery*, vol. 2, *The Modern Atlantic*, ed. Campbell, Miers, and Miller (Athens: Ohio University Press, 2008), 1–24.

15. Claude Meillassoux, "Female Slavery," in *Women and Slavery in Africa*, ed. Claire Robertson and Martin Klein (Madison: University of Wisconsin Press, 1983), 49–66; see Martin Klein's reevaluation of his debate with Meillassoux in chapter 2 of the current collection. Joseph E. Inikori, "Export versus Domestic Demand: The Determinants of Sex Ratios in the Transatlantic Slave Trade," *Research in Economic History* 14 (1992): 117–66.

16. Joseph C. Miller, "Domiciled and Dominated: Slaving as a History of Women," in *Women and Slavery*, vol. 2, *The Modern Atlantic*, ed. Campbell, Miers, and Miller, 284–312.

17. In a southern African context, a covert slave trade (unacknowledged by pertinent governments) mainly involved captured women and children, for example, as demonstrated in several essays in Elizabeth Eldredge and Fred

Morton, eds., *Slavery in Southern Africa: Captive Labour on the Dutch Frontier* (Boulder, Colo.: Westview Press, 1994). In Australia in the early nineteenth century, Aboriginal women were (covertly) traded along the coast of New South Wales, and sealers in Tasmania captured or purchased women to provide sexual and economic services such as catching mutton birds for food, oil, and feathers during the mutton birding season: G. A. Robinson, speech to (Australian) Aborigines Protection Society, October 19, 1838, *Colonist*, October 31, 1838, reproduced at www.law.mq.edu.au/scnsw/Correspondence/vdlspeech.htm; N. J. B. Plomley, ed., *Friendly Mission: The Tasmanian Journals and Papers of George Augustus Robinson, 1829–1834*, rev. ed. (Hobart, Australia: Quintus Publishing, 2008); Elizabeth Elbourne, "Between Van Diemen's Land and the Cape Colony," in *Reading Robinson: Companion Essays to Friendly Mission*, ed. Anna Johnston and Mitchell Rolls (Hobart, Australia: Quintus Publishing, 2008). On other aspects of supply dynamics, see Paul Lovejoy, "Internal Markets or an Atlantic-Sahara Divide," in *Women and Slavery*, vol. 1, *Africa, the Indian Ocean World, and the Medieval North Atlantic*, ed. Gwyn Campbell, Suzanne Miers, and Joseph C. Miller (Athens: Ohio University Press, 2007), 259–79; here, Lovejoy suggests that ethical considerations constrained slave traders in Muslim West Africa from selling slaves to Christian Europeans and kept a disproportionate number of women in the West African internal market.

18. Campbell, Miers, and Miller, "Strategies of Women," 3–4.

19. Joan Wallach Scott, "Preface to the Revised Edition" and "Some More Reflections on Gender and Politics," in Scott, *Gender and the Politics of History*, rev. ed. (New York: Columbia University Press, 1999), ix–xiii and 199–222.

20. This point is made forcefully, for example, in Scully, *Liberating the Family*.

21. See chapter 6.

22. Brooke N. Newman, "Gender, Sexuality and the Formation of Racial Identities in the Eighteenth-Century Anglo-Caribbean World," *Gender and History* 22, no. 3 (November 2010): 585–602.

23. United Nations Human Rights, Office of the High Commissioner for Human Rights, www.ohchr.org/EN/Professionalinterest/Pages/SupplementaryConventionAbolitionofSlavery.aspx (accessed June 15, 2014).

24. Annie Bunting argues, for example, that "forced marriage" in African conflict situations is best understood as a form of enslavement, in which sexual services overlap with other forms of coerced labor. Annie Bunting, "'Forced Marriage' in Conflict Situations: Researching and Prosecuting Old Harms and New Crimes," *Canadian Journal of Human Rights* 1, no. 1 (2012): 165–85. On aspects of the continuation of slavery, see *inter alia* Benedetta Rossi, ed., *Reconfiguring Slavery: West African Trajectories* (Liverpool: Liverpool University Press, 2009); Joel Quirk, "Ending Slavery in All Its Forms: Legal Abolition and Effective Emancipation in Historical Perspective," *International Journal of Human Rights* 13, no. 4 (2009): 529–54; Joel Quirk, *The Anti-Slavery Project:*

From the Slave Trade to Human Trafficking (Philadelphia: University of Pennsylvania Press, 2011).

25. On the scholarly reception of the display and postmortem dissection of Sarah Baartman, the "Hottentot Venus," in Europe in the 1810s, compare, for example, Zine Magubane, "Which Bodies Matter? Feminism, Poststructuralism, Race, and the Curious Theoretical Odyssey of the 'Hottentot Venus,'" *Gender and Society* 15, no. 6 (December 2001): 816–34; Yvette Abrahams, "Images of Sara Bartman: Sexuality, Race and Gender in Early Nineteenth-Century Britain," in *Nation, Empire, Colony: Historicizing Gender and Race*, ed. Ruth Roach Pierson and Nupur Chaudhuri (Bloomington: Indiana University Press, 1998), 220–36.

26. Museum curators, for instance, have begun to discuss the particular challenges involved in curating "difficult knowledge."

27. An interesting example is provided in Shelley Ruth Butler, *Contested Representations: Revisiting "Into the Heart of Africa"* (1999; repr., Peterborough, Ontario, Canada: Broadview Press, 2008), which examines reactions to a highly controversial exhibit on British colonialism in Africa at the Royal Ontario Museum in Toronto, Canada.

28. J. D. Wrathall, "Provenance as Text: Reading the Silences around Sexuality in Manuscript Collections," *Journal of American History* 79, no. 1 (1992): 165–78.

29. Edward Said, *Orientalism* (1978; New York: Vintage Books, 2003). Debates over the nature of the harem and Western perceptions of the harem illustrate some of these themes with particular force. Fatima Mernissi, *Etes-vous vacciné contre le harem?* (Casablanca: Éditions le Fennec, 1998); Leila Ahmed, "Western Ethnocentrism and Perceptions of the Harem," *Feminist Studies* 8, no. 3 (Autumn 1982): 521–34.

30. Gwyn Campbell, "Introduction: Slavery and Other Forms of Unfree Labour in the Indian Ocean World," and Susanne Miers, "Slavery: A Question of Definition," in *The Structure of Slavery in Indian Ocean Africa and Asia*, ed. Gwyn Campbell (London: Frank Cass, 2004): vii–xxxi, 1–16.

31. E.g., Douglas Hay and Paul Craven, eds., *Masters, Servants and Magistrates in Britain and the Empire, 1562–1955* (Chapel Hill: University of North Carolina Press, 2004); Paul Lovejoy and Nicholas Rogers, "Introduction," in *Unfree Labour in the Development of the Atlantic World*, ed. Lovejoy and Rogers (Ilford, UK: Frank Cass, 1994); and Bruce Kercher, *An Unruly Child: A History of Law in Australia* (Sydney: Allen & Unwin, 1995).

32. See chapters 13 and 14.

33. Carole Pateman makes this argument with reference to John Locke's theory of the social contract (which assumes a prior "sexual contract" in which the patriarch controls the family), but her arguments are clearly applicable in many other contexts. Pateman, *The Sexual Contract* (Stanford, Calif.: Stanford University Press, 1988).

34. See chapter 24.

35. On eighteenth-century Jamaica, for example, see Newman, "Gender, Sexuality and the Formation of Racial Identities," and Trevor Burnard, *Mastery, Tyranny and Desire: Thomas Thistlewood and His Slaves in the Anglo-Jamaican World* (Chapel Hill: University of North Carolina Press, 2004).

36. See chapter 25.

37. On the broad theme of the children of sexual relationships across colonial lines, compare Stoler, *Carnal Knowledge and Imperial Power.*

38. See chapter 4.

39. Martin Klein, "Sex, Power, and Family Life in the Harem: A Comparative Study," in *Women and Slavery*, vol. 1, *Africa, the Indian Ocean World, and the Medieval North Atlantic*, ed. Gwyn Campbell, Suzanne Miers, and Joseph A. Miller (Athens: Ohio University Press, 2008), 63–82.

40. In a South African context, compare Karel Schoeman, "*A Thorn Bush That Grows in the Path*": *The Missionary Career of Ann Hamilton, 1815–1823* (Cape Town: South African Library, 1995); as Schoeman discusses, in the early 1820s, the Scottish missionary Robert Moffat forced Ann Hamilton, the wife of a fellow missionary, to confess to the congregation at Kuruman that she was refusing sex to her husband and to promise publicly to sleep with him in the future as a condition of receiving communion. For a canonical Victorian argument that the obligation to provide sex to husbands was a hallmark of the "slavery" of wives, see John Stuart Mill, *On the Subjection of Women* (London: Longmans, Green, Reader, and Dyer, 1869).

41. Contrast Pernille Ipsen, "Koko's Daughters: Danish Men Marrying Ga Women in an Atlantic Slave Trading Port in the Eighteenth Century" (Ph.D. diss., Copenhagen University, 2008).

42. On trading for sexual purposes in the American South, see Baptist, "'Cuffy,' 'Fancy Maids' and 'One-Eyed Men,'" as well as chapter 1 in this book and Walter Johnson, *Soul by Soul: Life inside the Antebellum Slave Market* (Cambridge, Mass.: Harvard University Press, 1999).

43. On legal reform in the Republican period, compare Lisa Tran, "The Concubine in Republican China: Social Perception and Legal Construction," *Études chinoises* 28 (2009): 119–50.

44. For example, Fiona Vernal shows one woman's struggles in the interstices of Roman-Dutch and British law at the Cape: Vernal, "'No Such Thing as a Mulatto Slave': Legal Pluralism, Racial Descent and the Nuances of Slave Women's Sexual Vulnerability in the Legal Odyssey of Steyntje van de Kaap, c. 1815–1822," *Slavery and Abolition* 29, no. 1 (2008): 23–47.

45. There was a long history to such trafficking, which had, in turn, been influenced by colonialism and the legacies of slavery, even though colonial officials long refused to recognize it; compare Saheed Aderinto, "'The Problem of Nigeria Is Slavery, Not White Slave Trade': Globalization and the Politics

of Prostitution in Southern Nigeria, 1921–1955," *Canadian Journal of African Studies* 46, no. 2 (2012): 1–22.

46. Bonnie Martin, "Slavery's Invisible Engine: Mortgaging Human Property," *Journal of Southern History* 76, no. 4 (November 2010): 817–66.

47. See chapter 17.

48. See chapter 1.

49. E.g., Scully, *Liberating the Family*.

50. Compare John Iliffe, *Honour in African History* (Cambridge: Cambridge University Press, 2004).

51. E.g., Clare Midgley, *Women against Slavery: The British Campaigns, 1780–1870* (London: Routledge, 1995).

52. See chapter 12.

53. Hartman, *Scenes of Subjection*, 88.

PARADIGMS AND OVERVIEWS

Points of Departure and Return

1

SLAVERY, SEX, AND DEHUMANIZATION

DAVID BRION DAVIS

Let me begin with the neglected but seemingly obvious point that sexual intercourse can exemplify the closest possible moment of love, merging two humans in an equal sharing of joy with an equal sharing of genes that magically give rise to a new human life. Yet the same physical movements can exemplify the most dehumanizing, degrading, and exploitative act of conquest or warfare, including the infliction of the conquerors' genes on an enemy group. Here, one thinks, for example, of the modern Sudanese Janjaweed, who have used repeated gang raping for the ethnic cleansing of blacks in Darfur and eastern Chad. Though usually far less organized, such military gang raping is nothing new; the Russians applied it against the Germans late in World War II.[1]

There is clearly a very wide spectrum of sexual experiences between these two extraordinary extremes. Sexual intercourse can be casual, commonplace, random, habitual, or even purchased. But despite this variation and diversity, the relationship between a slave and a free person, especially a master, could never reach the ideal level of the first model I described, since the slave, as chattel property, could never achieve even temporary equality. A classic example would be the relationship between Sally Hemings and Thomas Jefferson.

As the historian Mia Bay points out, since the 1998 DNA testing that confirmed the high probability of some of the oral traditions of the descendants of Hemings's and Jefferson's sexual alliance, certain historians have tended to romanticize the relationship and overplay Hemings's ability to consent and negotiate the terms of their union.[2] Moreover, though there is hardly any documentary evidence, we know that Hemings was the half sister of Jefferson's deceased wife and was described by contemporaries as "mighty near white." Yet whatever affections Jefferson may have felt for his enslaved chambermaid and her four surviving children, he never failed to include her and the children in his plantation inventory, along with their market value. As Bay concludes, sexual associations between masters and slaves fall "outside the categories we use to describe relationships in which neither party is classed as chattel property."[3] And she reminds us of a famous passage Jefferson wrote, after his affair with Hemings is believed to have begun, concerning the impact of slavery upon the slaveholder: "The whole commerce between master and slave is a perpetual exercise of the most boisterous passions, and the most unremitting despotism on the one part, and degrading submission on the other. Our children see this and learn to imitate it; for man is an imitative animal. . . . The man must be a prodigy who can retain his manners and morals undepraved by such circumstances."[4]

As we find even as early as the Hebrew Bible, free women could also exploit the sexual vulnerability of male slaves. In what was by no means a unique incident in a slave society, Joseph, the highly favored son of the Israelite leader Jacob, was sold by his jealous brothers to some Ishmaelite slave traders, whose caravan moved on to Egypt. Then, Potiphar, the pharaoh's chief steward, purchased Joseph, who, like many privileged slaves throughout history, became his master's personal attendant; he was put in charge of Potiphar's entire household. Since we are told that Joseph, still in his twenties, was "well built and handsome," it is not surprising that Potiphar's unnamed wife began to cast her eyes upon him. "Lie with me," she demanded. For many days, Joseph resisted her efforts, what he termed "the most wicked thing, a sin before God." He also knew that being found in such a relationship could lead to his death. But then, after she caught hold of him and ripped off a garment as evidence, the wife informed Potiphar that the Hebrew slave whom he had brought into their house had tried to rape her but had fled when she screamed at the top of her voice. Potiphar was, of course, furious. It was only because of God's intervention that Joseph spent just two years in prison, and then, thanks to his remarkable interpretation of dreams, he became the de facto ruler of Egypt, second only to the pharaoh himself.[5]

The traditions and fables regarding male slaves and lascivious free women were sometimes subjects of ribald humor. The famous *Life of Aesop*, a fictional slave biography from Roman Egypt in the first century CE, portrayed one wife of a slave master as a "sex-crazed slut" on the lookout for a "young, handsome, athletic, good-looking blond slave." As the historian Keith Hopkins puts it, "The baths, cleanliness, heat and lust were a heady mixture; and the close association between powerful female mistresses and their male slave attendants in public and in private stimulated the anxieties of husbands . . . and of later Christian moralizers." Aesop himself, a slave who began by severely rebuking his new mistress for her immorality, ended up seducing her, in revenge for his master's ingratitude. If such tales exemplified the primacy of sex in human nature, they also conveyed the dehumanizing aspects of human bondage and the most extreme forms of human inequality.[6]

Turning to colonial North America, such relationships between male slaves and free women were not uncommon but became increasingly subject to punishment. In Latin America and the Caribbean, a dramatic shortage of white women encouraged a much greater acceptance of racial intermixture between female slaves and white men, though a popular Brazilian adage proclaimed, "White women are for marriage, mulattoes for fornication, and Negresses for work."[7] Partly for cultural reasons, colonial Virginia and Maryland were less open to interracial concubinage, to the manumitting of at least some mulatto children of slaves, or to the belief that each step toward greater generational whiteness was a way to blend inevitable intermixture with social progress. Yet the presence of thousands of white female indentured servants in the seventeenth-century Chesapeake meant that "approximately one-quarter to one-third of the illegitimate children born to white women had fathers of African descent."[8]

According to the ancient Roman rule of *partus sequitur ventrem*, which was observed throughout the New World—the rule that the offspring of slaves must follow the condition of the mother—the *white* servants' mulatto children were free. In both Virginia and Maryland, the legislators became increasingly alarmed by this sexual intermixture and passed laws against racial intermarriage; they also established legal punishments for white women who gave birth to mulatto children—"that abominable mixture and spurious issue," as the Virginia Assembly put it.[9]

In Maryland, the legislators were so upset by the belief that women servants of English origin enjoyed connections with black slaves, "always to the satisfaction of their lascivious and lustful desires," that they reversed the old Roman rule in 1664 and decreed that such mulatto children should inherit the status of slavery from their fathers; their white mothers were required to serve the fathers' owners for the rest of their lives.[10] This measure caused considerable confusion and conflict with Virginia, to which many mixed couples fled. In 1681, Maryland repealed the law and returned to the rule of *partus sequitur ventrem.* But in response to the same problem, Virginia in 1691 imposed thirty-one years of servitude on the children of such white mothers and even on the *grandchildren* of the original offenders.[11] If the white mothers of these children could not pay a large fine, they were condemned in the Chesapeake to a five- or seven-year term of servitude. Even so, unions continued to take place, and in Maryland in 1681, when a white indentured servant called Irish Nell married a black slave named Negro Charles, a few white neighbors actually attended the wedding and wished the couple well.[12] Of course, no laws applied to the white fathers who had raped or won some kind of sexual consent from slave women, including those who appeared nearly white.

As matters developed, there were many earlier precedents for Thomas Jefferson's notorious lines, in his *Notes on the State of Virginia,* about blacks themselves preferring whites, "as uniformly as is the preference of the Oran-ootan [*sic*] for the black women over those of his own species."[13] One must always balance this appalling claim that black women had sexual relations with orang-outangs (really meaning chimpanzees) with Jefferson's contradictory reassurance that blacks were equal to whites in their innate "moral sense," even if they were inferior to whites "in the endowments both of body and mind" and were more crudely "ardent after their female." (Of course, we now know that he himself was almost certainly "ardent" after one African American female.)[14] Jefferson did not go as far as the earlier famous Jamaican historian Edward Long, who declared, "I do not think that an oran-outang husband would be any dishonour to an Hottentot female"; he also observed that the orang-outang "has in form a much nearer resemblance to the Negroe race, than the latter bear to White men."[15]

Stereotypes of the black Africans' superior and uninhibited sexuality can be found in the writings of medieval Arabs and even in Greco-Roman antiquity, in part, no doubt, because of the Africans' relative absence of protective clothing. Though some early European explorers and travelers commented on the West Africans' agility, gracefulness, and amazing custom of taking daily baths, it was their near nakedness that took front stage. Nor was the trader Richard Jobson alone when, in 1621, he took note of "the enormous Size of the virile Member" among male Negroes, which he saw as "infallible Proof" that they were descended from the biblical Canaan, who had been cursed for uncovering his father Noah's nakedness (an egregious sin actually committed in the Bible by Canaan's father, Ham). For blacks of both genders, it was commonly said, the sexual act was as "libidinous and shameless" as it was for monkeys and baboons. African women, throughout these English, French, and Dutch travel accounts, were said to be "incredibly hot and lascivious" and willing to "prostitute themselves for a trifling quantity of European goods"—even though whites were also surprised by the harsh punishments Africans inflicted on adulterous wives.[16]

Many of these sexual myths were clearly used to justify the Europeans' own sexual exploitation of black slaves, from the shoreline markets in Africa on to the slave ships and New World plantations. In North America, we find the pervasive image of the slave woman as Jezebel, whose powerful libido is unrestrained by piety, modesty, or reason. Though some Southern white wives used cruel treatment as a threat to potential Jezebels, others could even find a bit of comfort by believing that their weak husbands had been seduced or led astray by a Jezebel—the polar opposite of the Victorian ideal of sexless womanhood. Some Southern writers and lecturers even argued that the Jezebels were beneficial to the South, especially when compared with the Northern reliance on prostitutes. But in time, Jezebel became paired with and negated by the counterimage of the fat black Mammy, long portrayed on the Aunt Jemima Pancakes box—the asexual, maternal, deeply religious, and above all unthreatening household servant.[17]

American abolitionists focused attention on the way slavery allowed Southern white men to cast off all restraints and exploit the highly vulnerable slave women—though it is clear that the slave Harriet Jacobs was not alone in finding ways to resist. A few abolitionists also stressed that slavery could encourage black men to strike back by raping white women. Only emancipation, they claimed, could free planters' wives and daughters from this danger and bring on a peaceful and truly monogamous social order.[18] Oddly enough, in the antebellum era, a surprising number of male slaves were acquitted of the charge of raping white women or were not executed even when they were convicted—an indication, perhaps, of the high value of slave property. But in the postwar decades, after emancipation, such limited toleration of interracial relationships became unthinkable. The Ku Klux Klan and other terrorist groups resorted to whipping, torture, castration, and lynching as a way, they said, of protecting white womanhood from the lustful eyes of black males.[19]

The obsession with black male sexuality had a long history and could seldom be deeply repressed. It was the Haitian Revolution, from 1791 to 1804, that reinforced the conviction of male slaveholders, in particular, that slave emancipation in any form would lead to economic disaster as well as to the rape and massacre of whites.[20] The waves of fear traveled even faster than the thousands of Dominguan refugees who streamed westward to Cuba and Jamaica and northward to Spanish Louisiana and the port cities and towns of the United States. Throughout the Americas, planters and government officials learned to live in a state of alert in the 1790s. The very words *Santo Domingo,* which English-speakers used to refer to the doomed French colony Saint Domingue, once the wealthiest colony in the New World, evoked at least a moment of alarm and terror in the minds of slaveholders throughout the hemisphere.

Beginning in 1793, two years after the first massive slave uprising in northern Saint Domingue, Toussaint-Louverture's armies defeated the Spanish, the French royalists, the English, and a large mulatto army and then checked the invasion by Napoleon's huge force of veteran troops—before Napoleon's brother-in-law captured Toussaint by a ruse and shipped him off to die in a dungeon in France. Then, after the French withdrew in humiliation in 1803, Jean-Jacques Dessalines, Toussaint's sadistic successor, declared Haiti's independence and slaughtered most of the remaining whites, many of whom Toussaint had persuaded to return to Saint Domingue in order to build a productive plantation regime based on wage labor. Although the blacks' military feats were often wrongly minimized by emphasizing the tropical diseases that decimated the British and French armies, it was widely believed that the slaves would never have rebelled if they had not been inspired by the subversive ideology of the French abolitionists, whose principles won increasing support by the fifth year of the French Revolution. Few arguments were more damaging to the antislavery cause, especially after three major slave uprisings in the British Caribbean were attributed to abolitionist agitation in the early 1800s. Abolitionists, in both Britain and the United States, vacillated between a policy of ignoring the explosive subject of Haiti and warning that insurrections and racial war would be inevitable unless the slaves were *peacefully* emancipated and converted into grateful free peasants.

But whether the Haitian Revolution hastened or delayed the numerous emancipations from the 1830s to the American Civil War, imagery of the great upheaval hovered over the antislavery debates like a bloodstained ghost. No Internet was required to distribute the unforgettable descriptions of the famous British West Indian Bryan Edwards, who had witnessed firsthand an early stage of the Haitian Revolution. His best-selling book pictured a white infant impaled on a stake and then reported that even though "a general massacre of the whites took place in every quarter, on some few estates indeed the lives of the women were spared, but they were reserved only to gratify the brutal appetites of the ruffians; and it is shocking to relate, that many of them suffered violation on the dead bodies of their husbands and fathers!" Nothing, however, could match the fate of Madame Sejourné: "This unfortunate woman (my hand trembles while I write) was far advanced in her pregnancy. The monsters, whose prisoner she was, having first murdered her husband in her presence, ripped her up alive, and threw the infant to the hogs.—They then (how shall I relate it) sewed up the head of her murdered husband in——!!!——Such are thy triumphs, Philanthropy!"[21]

Similar imagery moved back and forth between the printed page and oral traditions. And both French and English publications made repeated use of animal imagery: when once aroused, it was said, blacks were savage, tigerlike men or ferocious beasts gorged with blood. Yet there were no reports in 1831 of women being raped when Nat Turner and his fifty to sixty followers killed all the whites in one farmhouse after another in Southampton County, Virginia, even though most of the nearly sixty victims were women and children.[22] Nevertheless, the Southerners' underlying assumptions linking rape with slave insurrections were reinforced by some of the slave confessions following the alleged Denmark Vesey conspiracy. They are vividly revealed in a record kept by a rich Mississippi planter, Lemuel P. Conner, of slave testimony given to a secret examination committee at an isolated racetrack in Adams County, Mississippi, in September and October 1861, five to six months after the Civil War began. Other evidence confirms the fact that these Mississippi slaves had planned a major insurrection. The interrogation of the slaves, apparently conducted with severe torture, led to the execution of over forty blacks, including several privileged drivers of family carriages.[23]

Despite the planters' belief that, as a result of their paternalism and goodwill, most slaves were happy, loyal, and content with their lot, many of the blacks at the racetrack were clearly filled with rage and resentment. Moreover, the examinations gave them a chance for self-assertion—for shocking some of the whites they had planned to murder. Knowing that they would soon be hauled to the gallows, they had little to lose. It is therefore difficult to judge the frequent report in Conner's record that specific slaves said they intended to "take," "ravish," and "ride" specific white women, often the wives or daughters of their owners.[24] For the slaves, it seems, nothing could exemplify the meaning of freedom better than inverting the slave/master relationship: kill the master, possess and rape the white mistress or daughter, and seize the land. In recent times, the systematic rape of women in Bosnia, Liberia, Darfur, and other locations has added new meaning to the view of rape as a means of revenge, a weapon of war and dishonor.

Yet another possibility arises when one considers that white women in the antebellum and Civil War South expressed little fear of black males, despite the long American tradition of white males imagining and fantasizing that black slaves were oversexed, licentious, and secretly eager to rape the best-looking white women.[25] In view of these traditional white male preconceptions, why should we not expect the examiners to have asked the captured slaves: "What did you intend to do with the ladies?" "Who was Simon, or Albert, or Peter going to ravish?" "After you killed master and Mrs. Mosby, did you plan to ride Miss Anna?" And if the slaves were being savagely flogged or tortured in other ways, why would they not have told the inquisitors what the inquisitors wanted to hear? There is really no way of knowing the answers to such questions.

From the very start, abolitionists centered much attention on the sexual exploitation of slave women, beginning with the transatlantic slave ships, on which the women were always separated from the men. According to Alexander Falconbridge, a former slave ship surgeon, "On board some ships, the common sailors are allowed to have intercourse with such of the black women whose consent they can procure . . . [and] the officers are permitted to indulge their passions among them at pleasure; and are sometimes guilty of such brutal excesses as disgrace human nature."[26]

On April 2, 1792, as the British House of Commons debated the abolition of the British trade, William Wilberforce horrified members of Parliament by describing how John Kimber, the captain of the slave ship *Recovery*, owned by Bristol merchants, had assaulted and killed a fifteen-year-old African girl who had refused to dance naked for him on the deck. This accusation evoked an immediate public outcry, especially in Bristol, as newspapers highlighted the story and as copies of Wilberforce's speech soon sold out at bookstores. Kimber, who denied the charge and claimed that the girl had died of disease, was then arrested and taken to London for trial. But despite the publicity and assumptions of guilt, there was not sufficient evidence to convince the jury, which acquitted Kimber without even retiring to deliberate. This outcome was at least a temporary disaster for Wilberforce and the abolitionists. That said, the testimony of many slave trade participants such as Falconbridge made it clear that young African women were regularly raped even before they entered New World slave societies.[27]

For American abolitionists, a central question with respect to Southern slavery and sex was the practice of "breeding"—in the most simplistic conception, the alleged effort to increase the slave population and thus the value of investment in human property by requiring black male "studs" to systematically impregnate large numbers of young slave women. Records indicate that the Romans used similar techniques to acquire more slaves in a period of relative peace, when wars and expansion no longer brought streams of captives from nearly all directions. In the American Upper South, the slave population had been rapidly increasing by natural means from as early as the 1720s, in sharp contrast to the slave populations in the Caribbean and Brazil.[28] This fact was troubling to abolitionists, since Southerners could claim that the natural increase, which soon spread to all the slave states, proved that their form of bondage was far more humane and benign than that in other parts of the hemisphere.

But in 1839, the great abolitionist Theodore Dwight Weld opened the way for a totally different answer in his landmark work, *American Slavery as It Is: Testimony of a Thousand Witnesses.* In this long collection of testimonies from travelers, Southern newspapers, and Southern clergy and political leaders, Weld not only documented the appalling cruelty and dehumanization of Southern slavery but also "attributed the high rate of natural increase to the deliberate practice of 'slave breeding,' by which he meant the application of practices employed in animal husbandry in order to obtain the greatest number of slaves for sale on the market."[29] Weld made no mention of male studs or of assembly-like reproduction. But he did document the violent coercion used to force slave girls to have "criminal intercourse," as well as the common Southern talk of slaves as "brood mares," "breeding wenches," and "the best stock." Furthermore, he argued that in the Upper South, where the tobacco economy had faltered, "the only profit their masters derive from [slaves] is, repulsive as the idea may justly seem, in breeding them like other livestock for the more southern states."[30]

Robert William Fogel, a Nobel Prize–winning economist, has shown that breeding had no effect on slave population growth; on the contrary, he has noted, any planter intervention in the private lives of slaves had a negative impact on population growth.[31] Nevertheless, slaveholders were acutely aware of the reproductive value of slave women as the markets for slaves expanded toward Louisiana and Texas. Far too often, slavery in the American South has been pictured as a fixed and static institution, almost frozen in time. In reality, an immense domestic or internal slave trade transported close to 1 million blacks from the Chesapeake and other Atlantic coastal regions to the "Old Southwest," centering on the lower

Mississippi valley. Weld was correct in stressing that Virginia's economy was becoming dependent on the production and sale of slaves to markets in the Old Southwest and that the impact of this trade on African American families was disastrous. Again and again, he described the breakup of marriages and the separate sale of children and even babies who were taken from their mothers. Moreover, a recent study shows that first-time buyers, such as Jefferson McKinney in New Orleans, chose young female slaves instead of males because of their lower price and promise of reproduction. As McKinney put it, "She is sixteen years old in May [1856] and is verry wel grone. If she should breed she will be cheap in a few years and if she does not she wil always be a deer Negro."[32] It should be added that during slave auctions, women's bodies were routinely exposed and examined to determine their capacity for childbearing. And the sight of naked or nearly naked slave women was clearly arousing for white males, especially in an era when white women could be provocative just by lifting a skirt slightly above an ankle.

In New Orleans especially, traders openly discussed their sexual exploitation of attractive, light-skinned enslaved women. Known as "fancy maids," these near-white victims could sell for arbitrarily high prices, ranging from $2,000 to $5,233, values that reflected their sexual allure to white buyers. As the historian Walter Johnson points out, these prices measured not only the slaveholder's sexual desire but also his reputation and dominance and his courage in pushing the boundaries of socially accepted behavior. This so-called fancy trade was not limited to New Orleans but could also be found in Richmond, Virginia; St. Louis, Missouri; and Charleston and Columbia, South Carolina. As it happened, these developments gave abolitionists the opportunity to portray Southern society as a place where man's lowest instincts and desires, his "animal nature," could run wild. Hence, abolishing slavery could be part of a *much* larger struggle for civilization and self-control.[33]

Ironically, although Southerners had traditionally accused the abolitionists of promoting miscegenation by demanding racial equality, which would lead to intermarriage, the increasing reports of Southern mulatto slave mistresses allowed the abolitionists to turn the tables. One Southern white women, Mary Chesnut, observed that "every lady tells you who is the father of all the mulatto children in everybody's household but those in her own she seems to think drop from the clouds or pretends so to think." Chesnut added: "Who thinks any worse of a negro or mulatto woman for being a thing we can't name?" If any white woman behaved like either white men or black women, she wrote, they would be "sent out of any decent house elsewhere."[34]

Catherine Hammond clearly shared similar feelings of outrage when she left her highly distinguished husband, James Henry Hammond, after discovering that he had had a long relationship and had sired children with both a household slave seamstress, Sally Johnson, and her daughter Louisa. Hammond, one of the South's most brilliant defenders of slavery, had served as a US congressman and as the governor of South Carolina before becoming a prominent senator from 1857 to 1860. He felt some compassion for his slave lovers and refused to sell them, as his wife demanded. He also knew that his legitimate white son, Harry, had been involved with at least one of the Johnson women. In 1856, after Catherine had returned, Hammond wrote a letter to Harry stating that according to his last will, Harry would inherit both Sally and Louisa and "all the children of both":

> Sally says Henderson is my child. It is possible, but I do not believe it. Yet act on her's rather than my opinion. Louisa's first child *may* be mine. I think not. Her second I believe is mine. Take care of her & her children who are both of *your* blood if not of mine. . . . I cannot free these people & send them North. It would be cruelty to them. Nor would I like that any but my own blood should own as slaves my own blood or Louisa. I leave them to your charge, believing that you will best appreciate & most independently carry out my wishes in regard to them. Do not let Louisa or any of my children or possible children be the Slaves of Strangers. Slavery *in the family* will be their happiest earthly condition.[35]

In contrast to Latin America society, Southern planter society officially condemned interracial sexual unions and tended to blame lower-class white males for fathering mulatto children. Yet there is abundant evidence that many slave owners, sons of slave owners, and overseers took black mistresses, in effect raping the wives and daughters of slave families. This abuse of power may not have been quite as universal as Northern abolitionists claimed. But the ubiquity of such sexual exploitation was sufficient to deeply scar and humiliate black women, to instill rage in black men, and to arouse both shame and bitterness in white women. When a young slave named Celia finally struck and killed her owner and predator, a prosperous Missouri farmer named Robert Newsom, her action led to a major trial that opened a rare window on the nature of this forbidden subject.[36]

As the historian Melton A. McLaurin has put it, "Celia's trial, its causes and consequences, confront us with the hard daily realities of slavery rather than with the abstract theories about the workings of that institution." And McLaurin vividly shows that these daily realities involved personal decisions by both blacks and whites "of a fundamental moral nature."[37]

In 1850, Robert Newsom was a highly respected family man who lived with his two grown daughters and three grandchildren. His four male slaves helped him profit from growing livestock as well as wheat, rye, and corn.[38] But at age sixty, Newsom had been a widower for nearly a year, and he longed for a sexual partner. Instead of courting one of the available white women in his own Callaway County, he slipped over to Audrain County and purchased Celia, who was approximately fourteen, and raped her as he took her home. While Celia was purportedly a housekeeper for his daughters, Newsom built her a brick cabin of her own and used it as the site for his sexual exploits. During the next five years, Celia gave birth to two infants: as a concubine, she exemplified one of the less publicized uses of enslavement.[39]

But by 1855, Celia had become romantically attached to Newsom's slave George, who demanded that she cease all sexual contact with their master. Celia first appealed without success to Newsom's grown daughters, who clearly felt no bond of sisterhood with her. Then, after Newsom himself refused to listen to her pleas, Celia killed him and then burned and buried his remains. George, fearful for his own safety, soon betrayed her and cooperated with those investigating the crime. After being repeatedly threatened by whites, Celia confessed. Most remarkable, perhaps, was the nature of the trial that followed, in which she was given a defense team of three court-appointed lawyers, one of them a respected three-term US congressman. Even after her conviction, Celia was somehow helped to break out of jail in order to avoid execution before the Missouri Supreme Court could consider an appeal. Still, on December 21, 1855, Celia went to the gallows, her death representing the culmination of a series of decisions that underscored the ultimate powerlessness of slaves.[40] This story, with all its complexities, highlights the central and basic contradiction of slavery: namely, the tortured and sometimes creative ways in which slaves expressed their humanity when confronted by an institution dedicated to their ultimate dehumanization.

No outsiders were better able to expose this cruel contradiction than the Northern women abolitionists who eventually came to see that their empathy for slaves, especially slave women, sprang from their own subservience in a patriarchal culture, a subservience they had long taken for granted.

In what is often labeled the Anglo-American Victorian culture, middle-class women supposedly possessed a moral superiority over males, a superiority that enabled them to purify the world through motherhood and participation in church activities and voluntary societies for promoting temperance, observing the Sabbath, disseminating tracts and Bibles, and furthering other such nonthreatening causes. Increasingly, female reformers sought ways to suppress humanity's so-called animal nature and to uplift the downtrodden. But in order to avoid contamination and preserve their purity, these activists could not enter the brutal world of politics or publicly reveal any awareness of the nature of sexual relations. Nonetheless, when male abolitionists began to reveal that the unlimited power of slaveholders had a shocking sexual dimension, women such as Lydia Maria Child zeroed in on the sexual exploitation of their black sisters in the South.

"The facts are so important," Child declared, "that it is a matter of conscience not to be fastidious." Child, who published *An Appeal in Favor of That Class of Americans Called Africans* in 1833, acknowledged that restrictive standards of decency kept her from unveiling the subject "so completely as it ought to be." Yet a slave woman and her daughters, Child assured her audience, were "allowed to have no conscientious scruples, no sense of shame . . . [but] must be entirely subservient to the will of their owner." "Those who know human nature," she shrewdly stated, "should be able to conjecture the unavoidable result, even if it were not betrayed by the amount of [racially] mixed population."[41] When addressing the Boston Female Anti-Slavery Society, Child asked: "Where women are brutalized, scourged, and sold, shall we not inquire the reason? My sisters, you have not only the right, but it is your solemn *duty*."[42] The famous Grimké sisters, who became refugees from the South and then abolitionists after growing up on a South Carolina plantation, confirmed these accusations, and Angelina Grimké broke new ground by lecturing to what were termed promiscuous audiences, that is, audiences that included both men and women.

After many male abolitionists cautioned and criticized these women reformers, some fearing that any violation of the boundaries of gender would provoke a backlash and bring a fatal setback to the antislavery movement, radicals such as Abby Kelly replied, "In striving to strike [the slave's] irons off, we found most surely that we were manacled ourselves."[43]

Thus, identification with the female slave increasingly revealed a more universal "lust for domination" on the part of all white men, a domination that deprived *all* women of the right to vote, to own property, to enter the professions, to receive a genuine education, or even to reject a husband's demand for sex without facing his chastisement.[44]

Despite the defeats suffered by female abolitionists and advocates of women's rights at the 1840 meetings of the American Anti-Slavery Society and the London Anti-Slavery Convention, women abolitionists prepared the way for new feminist movements on both sides of the Atlantic. For a time, following the landmark 1848 convention at Seneca Falls, New York, the movement for female equality became closely linked to the movement for the emancipation of slaves. Recognition of the strong and yet subtle ways in which slavery inevitably strove to dehumanize the slave ultimately revealed how a patriarchal culture used the concept of *love* to denigrate one-half of the so-called free population.

Notes

1. Norman M. Naimark, *The Russians in Germany: A History of the Soviet Zone of Occupation, 1945–1949* (Cambridge, Mass.: Harvard University Press, 1995), 69–140.

2. Mia Bay, "In Search of Sally Hemings in the Post-DNA Era," *Reviews in American History* 34, no. 4 (2006): 407–26.

3. Ibid., 416–17, 422–23.

4. Thomas Jefferson, *Notes on the State of Virginia*, ed. William Peden (Chapel Hill: University of North Carolina Press, 1955), 162. Although Jefferson freed no other members of a slave family, his will manumitted Sally's two youngest children, Madison and Eston, who then lived as whites and were joined by their mother after Jefferson's daughter, Martha Jefferson Randolph, allowed her to leave Monticello without being formally freed from slavery. In 1822, four years before his death, Jefferson seems to have permitted Sally's older son and daughter, Beverly and Harriet, to flee Monticello and disappear into white society. For the definitive account of the Jefferson-Hemings relationship, see Annette Gordon-Reed, *The Hemingses of Monticello: An American Family* (New York: W. W. Norton, 2008).

5. Genesis 38–41.

6. Keith Hopkins, "Novel Evidence for Roman Slavery," *Past and Present* 138 (February 1993): 17–18.

7. David Brion Davis, *The Problem of Slavery in Western Culture* (Oxford: Oxford University Press, 1966), 274.

8. Ira Berlin, *Many Thousands Gone: The First Two Centuries of Slavery in North America* (Cambridge, Mass.: Harvard University Press, 1998), 45.

9. Edmund S. Morgan, *American Slavery, American Freedom: The Ordeal of Colonial Virginia* (New York: W. W. Norton, 1975), 335.

10. Davis, *Problem of Slavery*, 277.

11. Berlin, *Many Thousands Gone*, 124.

12. Martha Hodes, *White Women, Black Men: Illicit Sex in the Nineteenth-Century South* (New Haven, Conn.: Yale University Press, 1998), 19–20.

13. Jefferson, *Notes on the State of Virginia*, 138.

14. Ibid., 143, 139.

15. Winthrop D. Jordan, *White over Black: American Attitudes toward the Negro, 1550–1812* (Chapel Hill: University of North Carolina Press, 1968), 492–93. For a comparison of the views on black slavery expressed by Jefferson and by two Caribbean "men of the Enlightenment," Bryan Edwards and Moreau de Saint-Méry, see David Brion Davis, *The Problem of Slavery in the Age of Revolution, 1775–1823* (Ithaca, N.Y.: Cornell University Press, 1975), 184–95.

16. Davis, *Problem of Slavery in Western Culture*, 452, 462–63, 469.

17. Deborah Gray White, *Ar'n't I a Woman? Female Slaves in the Plantation South* (New York: W. W. Norton, 1985), 27–61.

18. Ronald G. Walters, *The Antislavery Appeal: American Abolitionism after 1830* (New York: W. W. Norton, 1984), 73.

19. Hodes, *White Women, Black Men*, 59–66, 176–78.

20. The most recent history of the Haitian Revolution is Laurent Dubois, *Avengers of the New World: The Story of the Haitian Revolution* (Cambridge, Mass.: Harvard University Press, 2004).

21. Bryan Edwards, *The History, Civil and Commercial, of the British Colonies in the West Indies*, 3 vols. (London: Printed for John Stockdale, 1807), 3:94, 99. See also Olwyn M. Blouet, "Bryan Edwards and the Haitian Revolution," in *The Impact of the Haitian Revolution*, ed. David P. Geggus (Columbia: University of South Carolina Press, 2001), 44–56.

22. David Brion Davis, *Inhuman Bondage: The Rise and Fall of Slavery in the New World* (Oxford: Oxford University Press, 2006), 208.

23. Winthrop D. Jordan, *Tumult and Silence at Second Creek: An Inquiry into a Civil War Slave Conspiracy* (Baton Rouge: Louisiana State University Press, 1996).

24. Ibid., 149–80.

25. Jordan, *White over Black*, 32–35, 38–40, 150–54, 398, 458–60. Despite this long tradition, which even ties in with medieval Arab stereotypes of black sexuality, Jordan notes in *Tumult and Silence* that white women in the South never seemed to share this phobia, at least in the pre–Civil War period (p. 159). And they seldom if ever alluded to black rapists in their letters and diaries. This point receives additional support from Martha Hodes, who makes the following observation about Southern white women during the Civil War: "Although white Southerners lived in fear of slave uprisings during the war, white women were not necessarily engulfed by sexual alarm when white men went off to war and left them alone with slave men." Hodes even quotes a white Virginia woman who as late as 1864 made no explicit mention of rape when describing hundreds of Negroes moving through the countryside, robbing and looting every house and committing "every crime that can be imagined"; see Hodes, *White Women, Black Men*, 140.

26. Alexander Falconbridge, *An Account of the Slave Trade on the Coast of Africa* (London: James Phillips, 1788), 24.

27. Peter Marshall, "The Anti-Slave Trade Movement in Bristol," in *Bristol in the Eighteenth Century*, ed. Patrick McGrath (Newton Abbot, UK: David and Charles, 1972), 206–11; Madge Dresser, *Slavery Obscured: The Social History of the Slave Trade in an English Provincial Port* (London: Continuum, 2001), 163.

28. Davis, *Inhuman Bondage*, 80, 104, 125.

29. Robert William Fogel, *Without Consent or Contract: The Rise and Fall of American Slavery* (New York: W. W. Norton, 1989), 119–20.

30. Theodore Dwight Weld, *American Slavery as It Is: Testimony of a Thousand Witnesses*, reprint ed. (New York: Arno Press, 1968), 15, 39, 110, 175, 167, 183.

31. Fogel, *Without Consent or Contract*, 151–53.

32. Walter Johnson, *Soul by Soul: Life inside the Antebellum Slave Market* (Cambridge, Mass.: Harvard University Press, 1999), 82.

33. Ibid., 113–14; Edward E. Baptist, "'Cuffy,' 'Fancy Maids' and 'One-Eyed Men': Rape, Commodification, and the Domestic Slave Trade in the United States," *American Historical Review* 106 (December 2001): 1619–50; Walters, *Antislavery Appeal*, 78.

34. C. Vann Woodward, *Mary Chesnut's Civil War* (New Haven, Conn.: Yale University Press, 1981), 29.

35. Drew Gilpin Faust, *James Henry Hammond and the Old South: A Design for Mastery* (Baton Rouge: Louisiana State University Press, 1985), 86–87, 314–15. It should be stressed that even though Catherine continued to live with her husband, they never fully reconciled.

36. Melton A. McLaurin, *Celia, a Slave: A True Story of Violence and Retribution in Antebellum Missouri* (Athens: University of Georgia Press, 1991).

37. Ibid., ix–xi.

38. Newsom also owned a five-year-old slave boy; see ibid., 17–18.

39. Ibid., 1–24.

40. Ibid., 24–114.

41. Ruth Bogin and Jean Fagan Yellin, "Introduction," in *The Abolitionist Sisterhood: Women's Political Culture in Antebellum America,* ed. Yellin and John C. Van Horne (Ithaca, N.Y.: Cornell University Press, 1994), 5–6, 8.

42. Ibid., 8.

43. Bonnie S. Anderson, *Joyous Greetings: The First International Women's Movement, 1830–1860* (Oxford: Oxford University Press, 2000), 122.

44. For an eloquent list of such "absolute tyranny" over married women, see Elizabeth Cady Stanton and Lucretia Mott, "Declaration of Sentiments, 1848," in *History of Woman Suffrage,* vol. 1, *1848–1861,* ed. Elizabeth Cady Stanton, Susan B. Anthony, and Matilda Joselyn Gage (Rochester, N.Y.: Fowler and Wells, 1889), 70–71.

2

SEXUALITY AND SLAVERY IN THE WESTERN SUDAN

MARTIN A. KLEIN

In 1983, Claire Robertson and I published *Women and Slavery in Africa.*[1] For the book, we invited the late Claude Meillassoux to write a theoretical chapter. We gave him all the articles, and he produced a typically lucid, Meillassoux-type piece that argued female slaves were desired not for reproduction but for labor.[2] He treated two other factors, sexuality and ease of integration, as marginal. The data collected in the volume posed a central question: Why was it that almost everywhere in Africa, the price of women was higher than the price of men? Furthermore, female slaves were almost everywhere more numerous than males, and in the interior the price of females was always higher than the price of males. This was true in spite of the fact that Europeans were buying twice as many men as women and paying higher prices for men at the coast. Meillassoux's argument derived from a simple observation: many of the articles in the book indicated that slaves did not reproduce themselves. He believed that if offspring were the major concern, masters would have made arrangements to increase the rate of reproduction. He argued that men married free women to have children and bought slaves for their value as workers. For both Robertson and myself, the first reaction was, Why didn't I think of that? But then, as I thought over my data, I found his explanation inadequate. His arguments were interesting and suggestive, but there was a problem with the data.

My article dealt with the western Sudan, the area where both Meillassoux and I had done research.[3] In this area, slaves went through a series of stages, which Meillassoux has described elsewhere. The newly acquired slaves worked full-time for their masters. Meillassoux calls them *esclaves de peine* (drudge slaves).[4] As the slaves became integrated, they worked part of the week for their masters and part for themselves. Meillassoux called them *esclaves mansés* (allotment slaves).[5] This situation was, in fact, one of the limitations on slave reproduction, for the slave household had a limited amount of labor time available to meet its own needs and could not afford too many dependent persons.[6] This was true in the third stage as well, in which the slaves became *esclaves casés* (settled slaves); at this stage, the slave household worked for itself and paid a fixed sum to the master.[7] What was interesting was that the male slave paid a sum equivalent to what an adult male needed to feed himself for a year, but the female slave paid half that amount. And that observation takes us back to the original question. If the female ended up paying half what the male slave paid, why was the price of the female slave always higher? I will try to answer that question in this chapter.

Sexuality

Let me start by laying out some simple assumptions. The first is that during most of their lives, the vast majority of human beings feel a strong sexual desire for other persons, in most cases persons of the opposite sex. This may seem like belaboring the obvious, but there is a good bit of sociological and historical writing that talks about sex as if it were merely a desire to have offspring. Meillassoux is critical of this approach. In his writing, he describes sexual exploitation, but he treats it as a result of the slave's status rather than as a crucial element in it.[8] The second assumption is that much of culture is concerned with controlling and channeling human sexuality. The rules about who may do what with whom and when vary from society to society, but all societies draw some kind of lines and set some kind of limits. These limits are necessary for the orderly operation of society. The three Abrahamic religions have tried, with varying degrees of success, to channel sexuality. All three are sexually repressive, not necessarily because they regard sex as wrong or immoral but because they accept the carnal nature of human beings and seek to channel it within marriage. Therefore, sex within marriage is usually seen as a good thing because it produces offspring. Only in extreme versions of Abrahamic morality or in fictional dystopias is sexual pleasure seen as an undesirable by-product of the way we reproduce ourselves.[9] The problem is that no matter how strict the sexual morality, the drive to violate it tempts many human beings. All three Abrahamic religions are also patriarchal and are concerned with paternal rights to the fruits of the married woman's body. Of course, when marriage becomes an alliance between families or a way to maximize power, people find an added incentive to develop outlets for their sexuality outside of marriage and in direct violation of the teachings of the Abrahamic religions.

If the omnipresence of sexual desire is obvious, so, too, is the reason why slaves were sexually exploited. Slaves were owned. Although there were some limitations on what could be done to a slave, particularly within Islam, there were few limitations on a man having sexual relations with his female slaves. Christian churches forbade sexual exploitation of slaves as either adultery or fornication, but that does not seem to have strongly inhibited the practice. Masters have usually regarded the sexual enjoyment of their slaves as a right. In Islam, this right was channeled with laws on concubinage, the right to take a concubine being conditioned only by the obligation to support the concubine and to recognize any offspring of that sexual relationship. In slave societies, some female owners may have used male slaves sexually, but there were strong restrictions on this practice, due to the fear of pregnancy from an illicit relationship and the control that husbands and fathers had over their women.[10]

The diary of the Jamaican plantation manager and slave owner Thomas Thistlewood indicates what can happen when men have absolute control over women. He kept a record of sexual encounters, which suggests that he had the power to demand sexual favors whenever and wherever he wished.[11] Furthermore, when a male guest spent the night, a female slave was often provided for his pleasure. Many of my black female students have raged at the rape of their foremothers, but it is not clear that society saw this exercise of male authority as rape; certainly, the men involved did not. For slave women there was often no alternative to submission. Acquiescence or seeking a protector were frequently the only long-term strategies open to them, but there were usually few potential protectors available.[12]

Thistlewood was often not the owner, but even as a plantation manager, he had an authority over the slaves that was rooted in the property relationship. The West Indies and in particular Jamaica were unusual in that there were few European women in the region and the planters themselves were far away. In fact, most of the planters were absentee owners living with their families in England. The men who went out to Jamaica were therefore not seriously restrained by female opinion or by the authority of others. The American South, at the other end of the spectrum, was a monogamous area, where Christian churches were strong. This did not prevent sexual exploitation, but it meant that that the exploitation was more discreet and thus harder to document.

Of course, the use of slave women to provide pleasure for male visitors was not unique to the West Indies. In the western Sudan, when the French sent Eugène Mage to Amadu of Segou in 1866, the expedition was detained for almost two years. During that period, Amadu provided the two officers commanding the expedition with slave women, both of whom were pregnant when the expedition finally left. Similarly, explorers Richard Lander, Gustave Binger, and Gustav Nachtigal were given slave women during their West African travels.[13] When the French explorer Paul Soleillet went to Segou, he was asked to inquire about the children of Mage and his sidekick, Quintin; he was instructed that if Mage's child was a boy, he should bring him out.[14] In the case of Muslim pilgrims and itinerant scholars, slave women were often given to them and became their concubines. Mage wrote that he and Quintin offered to free their concubines and take them to Senegal, but the offer was refused by both women. Soleillet reported that any slave master had not only the droit du seigneur over his slave women but also often provided one of those women to a visitor, in which case she was responsible for both sexual and domestic services.[15]

The place where the sexual vulnerability of slave women was most cruelly underlined was in trade. This was true in the Americas, on the Middle Passage, and on caravans within Africa. During the period between enslavement and incorporation in some social unit, the slave had no social identity. She was a commodity being moved for trade. And her body was there to be used. There was no reason for the men moving the slaves not to have sex with them, and many obviously did. Thus, when one trader claimed that a slave woman in his caravan was his wife, she told the French administrator interrogating her, "You know that any Juula [trader] can take for himself any slave in his troop."[16] There is also an account written in 1959 by a Malian apprentice administrator about an old female slave who remained with his family after the collapse of slavery. He interviewed her for the memoir he had to write for the French École Coloniale. She said that on the trail, she was nightly taken into a hut and subjected to repeated sexual intercourse.[17]

The Preference for Female Slaves

I agreed with Meillassoux about the importance of the female slave's labor obligations. In fact, women throughout African society have always done much more labor than men. They do domestic labor, and they engage in productive labor. And if that is true of free women, it was even more true of slave women. Yet, unlike Meillassoux, I did not think that explained the higher price paid for women, particularly since the only measure I had of the comparative value of male and female labor—the dues paid by slave sharecroppers—suggested that male slaves produced more wealth. I therefore rewrote my article to take issue with Meillassoux's argument. I felt that two things explained the higher price of slave women. The first was that they were easier to incorporate into the society, particularly if they were part of the household and had children.[18] Their sexuality was one of the things that integrated them. The second was that their sexuality was in some sense the cement of the society. Women were a considerable majority of those enslaved and of those being traded at any time. This was, however, useful to the stability of Sudanic societies. Let us look at the ways in which female slaves were used.

First, many of the female slaves went into the harems of the powerful. Rulers and major political leaders often had large harems.[19] When Sikasso fell to the French, the harem was estimated at over 800 women. Similarly, Paul Lovejoy speaks of a high official in Bauchi who was reputed to have over 100 concubines.[20] Though we do not always know a great deal about what went on inside the African harem, what we know suggests that they were not unlike other harems elsewhere. In any large harem, the majority of women were servants. The Kano harem had three categories of women. The wives—Islam allowed a man to have up to four—were free women chosen from elite families. There was a larger group of concubines, usually over 150, chosen from among the daughters of royal slaves, prisoners of war, and women given to the emir. They were secluded but held some major administrative positions involving the collection and storage of grain, the administration of the palace, the operation of its kitchens, and the summoning of the concubines chosen for the emir's companionship. There were also hundreds of slave women, who did manual work within the palace and could be sent out of the palace on errands. These women might be promoted into the ranks of concubines, but most were married off to male slaves or given away after a period of service.[21]

Almost everyone writing about harems makes the argument that they were not about sex. It would be more accurate to say that they were about *more* than sex. Many people studying this subject have reacted against the Western image of the harem as the site of incomparable sexual delights.[22] After reading my paper on the harem, Beverly Mack wrote me: "I have lived long enough in the Kano harem to know that it is all about sons, sons, sons, not sex, sex, sex. One needs a big offspring pool from which king-makers choose if the kingship is to be kept in the family."[23] Fatima Mernissi is even more vigorous in arguing that the harem was the site of family life and that it included a range of dependent women of various ages and different relations to the ruler.[24] Some of the Muslim reformers, however, were troubled by the hedonism and materialism that were the inevitable results of military success. For instance, the victories in the Sokoto jihad made large numbers of women of various social classes available to the victors. Abdullahi, the brother of Uthman dan Fodio, was particularly troubled by the acquisition of concubines during the war and quit the jihad after the fall of Kano. Uthman himself had only one concubine and strongly criticized those who did not recognize a prior commitment to their wives.[25] Masters were supposed to devote their nocturnal attention to their wives, but there is no evidence indicating how many did so or how many faithfully followed the Muslim obligation to divide their time equally between their wives. At the same time, however, there is also no reason to think that many other Muslim statesmen eschewed the pleasures of concubines.

Second, those men with the money to buy slaves did so. West African societies were polygamous. Both the differential in ages of marriage and the surplus of slave women on the market facilitated polygamy. A slave concubine had an advantage over a wife in that she had no family and was totally dependent. Merchants, successful artisans, and wealthy farmers bought slave women. Merchants often had significant harems, though a frugal merchant was likely to put most of the slaves he acquired to work producing something. A successful farmer or artisan might only buy one slave: it was often cheaper than a second marriage.

During the years of the Atlantic slave trade, societies farther in the interior provided a higher percentage of men to this trade. Some have suggested that this occurred because women were shipped north across the Sahara, but I do not think that explains the disparity.[26] During its peak years, the Atlantic slave trade involved ten times the number of individuals shipped across the Sahara. At least half of those enslaved, however, were kept within Africa. And they were almost all women. If we look at the way the trade operated, with a slave often moving toward the coast in multiple stages, it becomes obvious that at every stage, slaves were sold.[27] The trader did not care to whom he sold his slaves as long as he made his profit. Many slaves were moved into agricultural estates (as I will discuss further). Many others, however, were acquired as part of the dynamics of family life. Some writers suggest that men wanted slave concubines to help their wives with domestic work. But there was another dynamic in play. When a woman bore a child, there was a long period of sexual avoidance, both during pregnancy and throughout lactation. A woman usually nursed a child for about two years, and during that time, her husband was not supposed to have sexual relations with her. For the husband, then, having a number of women in his household meant that he had a sexual partner when his first wife was temporarily unavailable to him.[28]

Third, female slaves were acquired by the slave soldiers who proliferated in African states and played a major role up to the colonial conquest and sometimes after. Servile warriors such as the *ceddo* of Senegal or the *tonjon* of the Bambara lived by warfare and raiding. Their culture was hedonistic and involved much display. They were contemptuous of sustained labor in the fields or elsewhere. They were serious drinkers, and they liked to wear brightly colored clothes. The question I asked when I first reflected on the ceddo was how they fed themselves. They were too numerous to be fed by the rulers, but they did not take enough slaves to buy the food they needed.[29] It became clear that they were fed by their slave "wives" and that, in fact, one of the reasons warriors wanted women was so they did not have to cultivate. But women also served them in another way. When Sudanic armies went into the field, they were generally accompanied by a "battalion of women." The women carried some of the soldiers' equipment, and when the march was done, the men relaxed as the women prepared the evening meal. Nominally, this would seem to reinforce Meillassoux's argument about labor, but we can ask why all this labor was done by women. To be sure, the preparation of meals was considered women's work, but beyond that, one major advantage of having women was that when the day's work was done, either in the fields or in the camps, they also became sexual partners.

Female slaves were important to ordinary male slaves as well. The documents on slavery produced by colonial administrators generally ignored the fact that most slaves were women. The questionnaires filled out by all French West African administrators in 1904, for example, generally talk about slaves as if they were men. Thus, we are constantly told masters had to provide every slave with a wife. They never speak of providing husbands for slaves, though, in effect, most female slaves ended under the control of men. Many of the questionnaires speak of male slaves buying a second wife. I was skeptical of this claim, but when I interviewed in Senegal, my informants insisted that many slave ménages acquired a second woman.[30] Richard Roberts was also told in his research among the Maraka that slaves often preferred to buy other slaves rather than buying their freedom.[31] I eventually worked out that marrying a second wife or acquiring a slave of one's own was a way for those slaves who could afford the expense to secure assistance in their old age. There was little advantage to freeing oneself. A freed slave had no family and remained dependent on the former master. Furthermore, he usually lacked the capital to free his wife and children.

The logic of the second wife, like that of the slave of the slave, was rooted in the economics of the slave ménage. A normal peasant family had to produce a surplus capable of feeding unproductive members of the family—the young, the ill, and the elderly. In a sense, the labor that fed the young was a form of insurance because when the parents aged, their children would take care of them. The problem for the slave householders was that the masters had the right to take their children from them. That the masters did not always do so gave them little assurance. Masters also died and changed. Members of the slave ménage were thus under pressure to limit the number of children they had because their surplus was limited. How they did it I do not know, but slave communities tended to have fewer children than free ones. There are other possible explanations for the disparity. There is no evidence that slave women of the western Sudan killed their children as they did in other slave societies, though that is one possibility. It is also possible that slave infants had a high mortality rate. However, I think that the probable method used to control family size was avoidance of sexual relations. Meillassoux was undoubtedly right that if the masters were primarily concerned with reproduction, they would have found a way to encourage it. They also would not have tied up so many women in unproductive harems.[32] The arrangement in which the slave ménage bore the cost of nurturing the child through infancy and up to the years when he or she could become productive worked out quite well for the master, who could then take advantage of the slave's services as a worker; as a servant; or, if the child became an attractive girl, as a concubine. In spite of the constraints on the slave ménage, the possibility of family life was a crucial factor in getting the slave to accept his or her servitude.

Meillassoux, though he did not see sexuality as crucial to the value of the female slave, goes further than other writers in discussing control over the body of the female, as in his description of Gumbu, a desertside town with a very authoritarian form of slavery:

> Even if given a companion, the male slave is not under law "married." This woman is the property of a master . . . to whom she owes labour and whom she obeys. The master or his dependents can have sexual relations with her. The young *hoore* [noble], who is confided to a *komo xoore* [emancipated slave] or a *woroso* [second-generation slave] to learn to work, at the same time, has his sexual apprenticeship with the daughters or the

> wives of his host, who if he inadvertently catches him in the act, has only the right to give him a symbolic blow.[33]

We cannot generalize from Gumbu in the absence of other data, but the attitude suggested is compatible with a belief that the slave woman's body belonged to her master. In effect, the only limitation would be the master's concern that his slaves accept their status. The master who had a sexual relationship with his male slave's partner was humiliating him. Even Thistlewood, who insisted on his right to have sexual relations with any woman under his control, restricted the access of other employees to slave women. He understood that imposing sexual relations on a slave woman could arouse the jealousy or anger of her slave lovers.[34]

Sexuality and the Female Slave

In all of this, two key questions arise. What is sexuality? And how does sexuality fit into the relations that men and women have with each other? In my study of the harem, what was interesting was that most rulers had favorites. Furthermore, their relations with favorites were sometimes lifelong affairs. Suleiman the Magnificent, who expanded the Ottoman Empire to its greatest extent, renounced the Ottoman tradition of ceasing sexual relations with a concubine as soon as she bore a child. He fell in love with Hurrem (known to Europeans as Roxelana), freed her, married her, and got rid of most of the rest of his harem. Mongkut, the great nineteenth-century Thai king, had eighty-two children with thirty-five women, but ten were with the same woman. Even after she aged, he cared for her.[35] Fatima Mernissi argues against conventional notions of what is erotic.[36] The sex act, she suggests, is most satisfying when it is set in an elaborate interaction, and she contends that happened even in a harem where one man owned many women. For Mernissi, sexuality is as much an intellectual exercise as a physical one, and the mind is as important as the body. Certainly, the sexual tastes and values of both men and women vary greatly. What is clear is that many men who had the choice found satisfaction in long-term relationships in which master and partner developed a rich knowledge of each other. In all this, beauty is a much overrated variable. Some women passed through concubinage and as they aged were either given to less powerful men (usually clients or slaves of their masters) or had their sexual role increasingly replaced by a labor role. Others remained in intimate relations, either because they produced sons or because they established affectionate and ongoing relationships with their masters.

What does this have to do with those relations I have already described? Sexual relations are generally embedded in a series of commitments people have to each other. West African men often talk about marriage in terms of having someone to cook for them. For most of those I am writing about, a sexual relationship was part of a complex of obligations between partners. Meillassoux argues that slaves do not marry. That is true in the sense that the members of the ménage, spouses as well as children, do not have the rights in each other that normally are involved in marriage. Richard Roberts's research on court cases suggests that many former slave women used the French courts to escape domestic relations either with masters or with what may have been assigned partners.[37] However, many spouses fled together or sought to reunite after being separated, and they often tried to reconstruct their lives together. The ability to form a ménage integrated the slave couple into slave life. It provided participants with a sexual partner, a partner in the struggle to survive, and a place to call home. Just as marriage was often the beginning of adult life for a free male, so cohabitation gave the slave, both male and female, a measure of autonomy.

It should be emphasized that slave women, whether concubines of the rich or partners of the poor, were rarely where they wanted to be. Slave women had little control over who their partners were or where they lived. Within the harem, some willingly and perhaps eagerly competed for the affections of the master. Others resisted or merely accepted their lot. Those who resisted did so in different ways. Mark Duffill has published a Hausa poem about a concubine named Abinda who deliberately made herself unattractive. She was filthy, did not sweep the house, and was not a good cook.[38] There were also cases of more violent resistence. Lovejoy cites Hugh Clapperton regarding one merchant who slept with loaded pistols under his pillow for fear of his concubines and another who was strangled in his sleep.[39] Female slaves also fled. They were a majority among those who sought their freedom in Saint-Louis du Sénégal.[40] They were also a majority in the liberty villages, where runaway slaves were housed and put to work.[41] Marie Rodet's thesis documents the unhappiness of slave masters who sent slave women to work as cooks, for often, these women never returned. She also describes a case in which a slave woman sent to sell milk to the railroad crews became the mistress of several French officers and finally married an African servant.[42] Rodet discusses the question of the strategies of slave women: "Female slaves could develop different strategies to ameliorate the conditions of their life. They would try to find a new 'husband' with a more interesting social situation, whether free or not. They could flee their masters to attach themselves to a more powerful master. . . . Female slaves could also become concubines of their master, if he was a man, or a member of his lineage. . . . But it seems difficult to speak of strategy. Slavery for women meant in reality that their bodies were the property of their masters."[43] Rodet is skeptical that even bearing a child for the master would always free the slave.[44]

Humphrey Fisher cites cases going back to the Middle Ages of Arab and African Muslim men writing poetically and sensually of the physical beauty of slave women. The Andalusian geographer Al Bakri describes the slave girls of Awdaghast, in what is perhaps an overgeneralization, as "pretty girls with white complexions, good figures, firm breasts, slim waists, fat buttocks, wide shoulders and sexual organs so narrow that one of them may be enjoyed as though she were a virgin indefinitely."[45] Fisher also gives examples of adoring and affectionate relationships. Yet it is clear that the attraction of slave concubines was that they were cheaper to obtain, cheaper to maintain, easier to discard, and thus often more anxious to please.[46] Travelers such as Ibn Batuta bought slave girls to service their needs on the trail. Other men chose to buy a slave girl instead of paying the bride-price for a wife. One of his servants explained to Gustave Nachtigal that if a slave woman was unfaithful, she could easily be sold.[47]

Sexuality and the Colonial Army

Most colonial armies operated in Africa on the cheap and incorporated some of the methods of traditional African armies. The French army was not in Africa to serve the French state but rather to serve its own ends. Stated simply, the officers of the colonial army were recruited from the marine infantry, a branch that had low prestige, and they wanted military action, promotions, and glory.[48] I am convinced that many also sought the sexual freedom that a slave society gave them. Their friends in the Chamber of Deputies were able to win them a certain freedom of action, but they were not able to get the funding or the troops they needed. In fact, French troops were not of much use in the western Sudan because of the climate and the disease environment. The wars of conquest were fought with African soldiers aided by African allies. These soldiers were almost all slaves, essentially the ceddo of the French.[49] Many of them were purchased. They received an enlistment bonus, which was about the price of a male slave and was often paid directly to the master. Others were runaways who found their way to liberty villages and could be reclaimed for three months—but only one month if they volunteered for military service. Officers were frequently given the liberty to find soldiers in any way they could. And slave warriors in defeated armies often served with the visitors in hopes of preserving the privileges of their way of life.

They were generally not disappointed. Booty was essential to the morale of the French army. One young officer who asked that his soldiers be paid before leaving on a campaign was told "that *captifs* [male captives] should not be paid since they were going to war and would surely take *captives* [female captives] which would be their reward."[50] After a victory or a breach in the wall that protected an African stronghold, both French troops and those of their allies took prisoners. Capt. G. Imbert de la Tour, a French officer, has described the capture of Sikasso, the most powerful fortress in West Africa. After the walls were breached, "a cloud of human vultures, bands of two-legged jackals emerged from one knew not where, pillaged, burned and killed throughout the night."[51] Then, everyone joined the pillaging. Children were particularly vulnerable and were often sold to slave dealers before the night was out. The captain reported that before nightfall, "a convoy of several hundred women, they say 800, entirely nude, arrived at the camp . . . the seraglio of Ba Bemba . . . examples of the most beautiful races of the Senegal and Niger." In all, about 2,000 people were gathered from the fortress. At noon of the next day, the distribution took place. Prisoners of both sexes were turned over to relatives. "Europeans were free to take whoever most pleased them, at least among those who remained. Those with copper or almost white skin were quickly taken."[52]

Imbert was horrified by the spectacle. He gave a boy he collected after the fray to the Catholic mission in Segou. Most French officers enjoyed the pleasures of slave society, as did those who served them. They were generous to their agents, who were often sources of intelligence, but also to their servants. One missionary reported a conversation with a gardener who assessed commandants according to their generosity in giving away women. One gave him two, another five.[53] Many of these women were sold, but others moved into the soldiers' households or became part of the "battalion of women." Large households were common among both the French and those who served them.

Most of the French officers were young, male, and interested in an active sex life. Whereas civil administrators often had mistresses and lived in what were considered temporary marriages, the soldiers lived a promiscuous life. In the beginning, they focused on slave women, though in some cases, they commandeered any woman who could be seized. Thus, the mission at Segu received regular complaints about a fifty-two-year-old sergeant who had an African family, probably with slave women, but sent his interpreter and a political agent out every day to get him two attractive young women. When the mission authorities complained, the local commandant was sympathetic but told them that he was not likely to get much help from a regional commander who kept six women, five of them between ten and fifteen years of age.[54] Another sergeant expelled his entourage of women when he was dying of dysentery and wanted to reconcile himself with his god.[55] The missionaries were very disturbed by the dissolute conduct of the officers and tried unsuccessfully to keep their converts from taking jobs as servants with them. After all, the leading source of death in the French military was not combat wounds or any African disease but venereal disease.[56] It is clear that slave women were valued by the African soldiers of the French both for their labor and as sexual partners, but for the French officers, they were primarily sexual servants.

Sexuality and Honor

The sexuality of female slaves became their defining characteristic. Sexual activity was not necessarily something they asked for, though for a few, using sexual attraction was the way they achieved a better life. When I came to study the process of emancipation, one of the problems I encountered involved explaining why slave status persisted after any real economic exploitation had disappeared. Indeed, social status remained important long after economic status. I became convinced that codes of honor were at the heart of this persistence.[57] The only way persons of slave origins could become free of the stigma of their background was to move either to the city or to another cultural area where they were unknown. Most of the peoples of the western Sudan had codes of honor. The one most developed and most studied is the *pulaaku* of the Fulbe, but similar codes existed elsewhere. According to such codes, the noble male was courageous, generous, and disciplined,[58] whereas the slave was crude, vulgar, and dependent. It was, however, members of the elite class who prided themselves on their sexual restraint but imposed themselves on slave women. I have already described how slave women were used on the trade routes, in their slave villages, and within the household. In the nineteenth century, these women were often asked to do sensual dances while singing obscene songs. They were also often available to the very men who prided themselves on their sexual restraint. Olivier de Sardan argues that the availability of the slave woman is "why immodesty and crudity are part of the slave ethnotype, particularly for the female."[59] The slave's discourse, male and female, was marked by "bluntness of speech, obscenity, absence of shame."[60]

In contemporary society, concerns often arise around dancing and music. As stricter Muslim moral codes spread, music in general and dancing in particular were frequently targeted by the moral reformers. The dances done across the Sudan are certainly not obscene to anyone used to Western disco dancing, but they are to many of the reformers. In some villages, all dancing is banned. In many, however, it is banned only for nobles. Members of artisan castes and descendants of slaves have the license to dance. This musical license is one of several ways that the nobles maintain boundaries. Interaction between the descendants of masters and slaves is often structured on these stereotypes. Thus, begging can be profitable for descendants of slaves, as can the crude behavior that the stereotype sanctions. Paul Riesman talks about Fulbe men who like to visit their ex-slave clients and enjoy the crudity, which affirms their nobility. Many descendants of slaves refuse to play the game, but the stereotype of the slave persists and remains important in Sudanese societies where slave origins still carry a stigma. In this process, what is most interesting is that the master class clings most intensely to the status distinctions, even as control of labor declines and then disappears. It is quite possible, in fact, that status distinctions have actually became more important.[61]

Conclusion

Human sexuality is complex, and relationships vary. A slave woman could be many things: a lover, the mother of sons, a field hand, a powerful official, an entertainer, or a servant. Discussions of sexuality have to be read with caution. Descriptions of the sex life of the Other are often highly imaginative, and yet, it is clear that one of the variables that shaped the value of women was that they were property and thus outside all of the inhibitions of Abrahamic moral codes. Women were highly valued for their labor. Those who did not make it to the harem (and some who did) were producing food. In many African harems, most members kept gardens. If they got too old to work the fields and too wizened to be sexually attractive, they took care of children and spun thread. I would also not deny Beverly Mack's pithy observation about sex in the harem. Offspring were desired. The problem is that inside the harem, the reproductive potential of women was not fully exploited, and outside the harem, slaves had good reason to restrict pregnancy because they could not be sure that they would benefit from the children they raised. It is clear, too, that though some men were afraid of their concubines, women were easier to integrate, particularly if they gave birth to children. In spite of all this, the sexuality of women was crucial to the nature of female slavery.

The inequality present in the relationships between men and their slaves probably also shaped gender relationships. These were societies in which men with wealth or power could accumulate large numbers of women over whom they had absolute control, women who never had the possibility of saying no. We will never be able to state with precision how the long-distance slave trade shaped gender relations, but it is evident that the impact was great not only for slave women but also for free women.

Notes

1. Claire C. Robertson and Martin Klein, eds., *Women and Slavery in Africa* (Madison: University of Wisconsin Press, 1983).

2. Claude Meillassoux, "Female Slavery," in Robertson and Klein, *Women and Slavery in Africa*, 49–66. On the notion that women were desired for reproduction, for example, Suzanne Miers and Igor Kopytoff speak of "a marked preference for the more pliable children and for women as reproducers of children rather than for men." See Miers and Kopytoff, eds., *Slavery in Africa* (Madison: University of Wisconsin Press, 1975), 162.

3. Martin Klein, "Women and Slavery in the Western Sudan," in Robertson and Klein, *Women and Slavery in Africa*, 67–92.

4. Claude Meillassoux, *Anthropologies de l'esclavage: Le ventre de fer et d'argent* (Paris: Presses Universitaires de la France, 1986), translated into English by Alide Desnois as *The Anthropology of Slavery: The Womb of Iron and Gold* (Chicago: University of Chicago Press, 1991), 116–17.

5. Meillassoux, *Anthropology*, 117.

6. The notion that a peasant household goes through cycles determined by the number of productive hands and the number of unproductive dependents is attributable to the Russian agricultural economist Alexander Chayanov. See Chayanov, *The Theory of Peasant Economy*, trans. Christel Lane and R. E. F. Smith (Madison: University of Wisconsin Press, 1986).

7. Meillassoux. *Anthropology*, 117–18.

8. Claude Meillassoux, "État et conditions des esclaves à Gumbu (Mali) au XIXe siècle," in *L'esclavage en Afrique précoloniale*, ed. Meillassoux (Paris: Maspero, 1975), 288.

9. A fictional demonstration of this attitude is in Margaret Atwood, *The Handmaid's Tale* (Toronto: McClelland and Stewart, 1985). There are also religious communities such as the Shakers that doom themselves by trying to escape their carnal nature.

10. Martha Hodes, *White Women, Black Men: Illicit Sex in the 19th-Century South*. (New Haven, Conn.: Yale University Press, 1997), deals with interracial sex but not, in general, with planters' wives.

11. Trevor Burnard, *Mastery, Tyranny and Desire: Thomas Thistlewood and His Slaves in the Anglo-Jamaican World* (Chapel Hill: University of North Carolina Press, 2004), esp. 156–64. If Thistlewood actually noted every sexual encounter, he was not unusually active, probably having relations only two or three times a week. What is striking is that his encounters were with a large number of women and at all times of day. Though most of his sexual acts were with a slave mistress, he had sex with almost every woman under his control except the very young and the very old. Many of these sexual encounters were pure biological acts without any emotional context, though presumably he had some feeling for the woman he lived with for most of his adult life. The best evidence for this is that he did not displace her as she aged.

12. Marcia Wright, *Strategies of Slaves and Women* (New York: Lilian Barber, 1993), describes the strategies of enslaved women in the highly anarchic world

of the East African slave trade. Wherever they were, females usually had limited options both in the trade and as slaves.

13. Humphrey Fisher, *Slavery in the History of Muslim Black Africa* (London: Hurst, 2001), 188.

14. Paul Soleillet, *Voyage à Ségou, redigé après les notes et journaux par Gabriel Gravier* (Paris: Challamel, 1887), 463. See also Klein, "Women and Slavery," 88.

15. Soleillet, *Voyage*, 141 and 285.

16. "Affaires-Captifs," Cmdt. Du Cercle Ernest Noirot to Director of Political Affairs, Archives National du Sénégal, K 13, 1893.

17. Cheikna Keita, "Le survivance de l'esclavage et du servage en Afrique noire," Unpublished Memoire, École Nationale de la France d'Outre-Mer, Paris. For a long time, I wondered if this account was written to entertain Keita's French teachers because the exploitation was more blatant and discussed more frankly than in other accounts, but I have since collected so much more information that it seems likely it was largely true or at least that it was recounted as told.

18. Some earlier writers suggested this. See Mamadou Saliou Baldé, "L'esclavage et la guerre sainte au Fuuta-Jalon," in Meillasoux, *L'esclavage*, 183–220. See also Miers and Kopytoff, *Slavery in Africa*, 162. Meillassoux acknowledged it in *L'esclavage*, 56–57.

19. For a discussion of harems, see my "Sex, Power, and Family Life in the Harem: A Comparative Study," in *Women and Slavery: Essays in Honour of Suzanne Miers*, ed. Gwyn Campbell, Joseph C. Miller, and Suzanne Miers (Athens: Ohio University Press, 2007), 63–82.

20. Paul Lovejoy, "Concubinage in the Sokoto Caliphate (1804–1903)," *Slavery and Abolition* 11, no. 2 (1990): 168.

21. Heidi Nast, "Engendering 'Space': State Formation and the Restructuring of the Kano Palace Following the Islamic Holy War in Northern Nigeria, 1807–1903," *Historical Geography* 23 (1993): 62–75. The roles of these powerful concubines were eroded in the late nineteenth century, as they were increasingly secluded and male slaves took over many of their administrative functions. According to Nast, "The Impact of British Imperialism on the Landscape of Female Slavery in the Kano Palace, Northern Nigeria," *Africa* 64, no. 1 (1994): 34–73, there were twelve hundred people living in the palace in 1988, about fifty of them concubines. Many of them were essentially persons who remained voluntarily in slavery. See also Nast's "Islam, Gender and Slavery in West Africa circa 1500: A Spatial Archeology of the Kano Palace, Northern Nigeria," *Annals of the Association of American Geographers* 86, no. 1 (1996): 44–77, and Beverly Mack, "Royal Women in Kano," in *Hausa Women in the Twentieth Century*, ed. Catherine Coles and Beverly Mack (Madison: University of Wisconsin Press, 1991), 109–29.

22. I have discussed this more fully in Klein, "Sex, Power, and Family Life."

23. Beverley Mack, personal communication with the author; Klein, "Sex, Power, and Family Life."

24. Fatima Mernissi, *Scheherezade Goes West: Different Cultures, Different Harems* (New York: Washington Square Press, 2001), 18, and Mernissi, *Êtes-vous vacciné contre le harem?* (Casablanca, Morocco: Editions le Fennec, 1998).

25. Lovejoy, "Concubinage," 168. Lovejoy's data come from Abdullahi Mahadi, "The State and the Economy: The Sarauta System and Its Roles in Shaping the Society and Economy of Kano with Particular Reference to the Eighteenth and Nineteenth Centuries" (Ph.D. diss., Ahmadu Bello University, 1982). On Abdullahi's contempt for those who used the jihad to accumulate concubines and fine clothes, see Fisher, *Slavery in the History of Muslim Black Africa*, 18 and 23. Abdullahi was also angry at the enslavement of free men and, presumably, free women. Shehu Ahmadu, the leader of the Masina jihad, was also reputed to have had "only one concubine, a devout woman who could recite the Quran by heart and had studied the religious law"; see Fisher, *Slavery in the History of Muslim Black Africa*, 199.

26. This is suggested by both Patrick Manning and Paul Lovejoy. See Martin Klein, "La traite transatlantique des esclaves et le développement de l'eslavage en Afrique Occidentale," in *Les dépendances serviles: Approches comparées*, ed. Myriam Cottias, Allessandro Stella, and Bernard Vincent (Paris: Harmattan, 2006), 35–54.

27. This is striking in the few accounts we have of the trade. See Olaudah Equiano, *Equiano's Travels* (1789; repr., Portsmouth, N.H.: Heinemann,1996), chap. 1; Mahommah Baquaqua, *An Interesting Narrative* (1854; repr., Princeton, N.J.: Markus Wiener, 2007); and various chapters of Philip Curtin, *Africa Remembered* (Madison: University of Wisconsin Press, 1968).

28. My understanding of this dynamic came from conversations with Robert and Pauline Lagace. Robert was doing anthropological research in a Wolof village while I was doing research for my thesis in 1963 and 1964. Pauline used to sit with the women when a homosexual Gambian hairdresser visited the village to do their hair. The women treated the hairdresser as if he had no sex and thus talked freely in front of him. He translated for Pauline. The conversation frequently dealt with the tensions involved with nursing and weaning. Women recognized that infant mortality was highest after weaning, when the children were on the ground and eating solid food that was not as sanitary as mother's milk. They were, however, constantly worried about their men having affairs, taking new wives, or becoming enamored of existing rival wives. Ironically, there was an American woman studying weaning at this time who was having problems because women did not want to talk about what was frequently a tense time and a very difficult dilemma. Pauline, by contrast, was a mother and living in the village. On sexual tensions within the Wolof family, see *Xala*, the

brilliant film by Ousmane Sembene, or the novel on which it was based, by the same writer. Ousmane Sembene, *Xala* (Chicago: Chicago Review Press, 1976).

29. On occasion, I have tried to figure out how many slave warriors there were in the western Sudan. The only basis for these calculations was the number of slave warriors in kingdoms I studied. I have, therefore, never tried to publish these amateurish reflections, but it is worth noting that whatever assumptions I built into my calculations, the number of warriors was clearly much higher than the number of people enslaved in any given year. This exercise convinced me that even though the warriors served other functions in the state, many of them were probably more interested in strutting than fighting. Warfare did not keep most of them fed.

30. This analysis is more fully developed in Martin Klein, *Slavery and Colonial Rule in French West Africa* (Cambridge: Cambridge University Press, 1998), chap. 1. The 1904 slave questionnaires are available in Archives Nationales du Sénégal, K 18 to K 20.

31. Richard Roberts, "Ideology, Slavery and Social Formation: The Evolution of Maraka Slavery in the Middle Niger Valley," in *The Ideology of Slavery in Africa*, ed. Paul Lovejoy (Beverly Hills, Calif.: Sage, 1981), 171–200.

32. In a harem, the master has many offspring, but few women have more than one, and many have none at all. If reproduction is the goal, the harem does not contribute to that goal.

33. Meillassoux, "État et conditions," 228. Meillassoux goes on to underline that the male slave has "no right of paternity over the children of his companion," who belong to her master.

34. Thistlewood realized this and restricted sexual predation by his nephew and other employees, but he was unable to restrict his own wandering eye. For an American case in which a slave girl bought for sexual pleasure and her lover killed her master, see Melton McLaurin, *Celia, a Slave* (New York: Avon, 1993). For a planter, the problem was not only fear of violence but also the morale of a servile workforce.

35. Abbot Low Moffat, *Mongkut, King of Siam* (Ithaca, N.Y.: Cornell University Press, 1961), app. 4; Lysa Hong, "Of Consorts and Harlots in Thai Popular History," *Journal of Asian Studies* 57, no. 2 (1998): 333–53.

36. Mernissi, *Sheherazade Goes West* and *Êtes-vous vacciné contre le harem?*

37. Richard Roberts, *Litigants and Households: African Disputes and Colonial Courts in the French Soudan, 1895–1912* (Portsmouth, N.H.: Heinemann, 2005), chaps. 4 and 5. See also his "Women, Household Instability, and the End of Slavery in Banamba and Gumbu, French Soudan, 1905–1912," in Campbell, Miller, and Miers, *Women and Slavery*.

38. Mark Duffill, "Hausa Poems as Sources for Social and Economic History," *History in Africa* 13 (1996): 61–62. See also Lovejoy, "Concubinage," 187n74.

39. Lovejoy, "Concubinage," 187n73. See also Fisher, *Slavery in the History of Muslim Black Africa*, 154–55, for several examples of masters who were murdered by their concubines.

40. Klein, *Slavery and Colonial Rule*, 71–74.

41. Marie Rodet, "Les migrations maliennes à l'époque coloniale, seulement une histoire d'hommes? Les migrantes ignorées du Haut-Sénégal, 1900–1946" (Ph.D. diss., University of Vienna, 2006), 47–48. A published version of this thesis is now available: Marie Rodet, *Les migrantes ignorées du Haut-Sénégal, 1900–1946* (Paris: Karthala, 2009). See also Klein, *Slavery and Colonial Rule*, 87.

42. Rodet, "Migrations," 52.

43. Ibid., 277.

44. Ibid. Many of those writing on this subject are not clear about Muslim law, which only provides that the concubine who has borne her master a child cannot be sold. She is only freed on his death. Roberts, however, was told by some of his informants that a master could deny paternity and thus keep both mother and child in slavery.

45. Cited in Fisher, *Slavery in the History of Muslim Black Africa*, 181.

46. Ibid., 177–202.

47. Ibid., 183.

48. A. S. Kanya-Forstner, *The Conquest of the Western Sudan* (Cambridge: Cambridge University Press, 1969).

49. Myron Echenberg, *Colonial Conscripts: The* Tirailleurs Sénégalais *in French West Africa, 1857–1960* (Portsmouth, N.H.: Heinemann, 1991). See also Klein, *Slavery and Colonial Rule*, chaps. 4–7.

50. Charles Monteil, "Journal d'un jeune administrateur stagiaire 1896-1897-1898," manuscript, 1896–98, 138.

51. G. Imbert de la Tour, "Une épopée française au Soudan de 1894 à 1899," typescript, Institut des sciences humaines, Bamako, Mali, 279.

52. Ibid., 294.

53. *Diaires*, Segu, April 1896, Archives of the White Fathers, Rome.

54. Ibid.

55. *Diaires*, Segu, July 24 and 25.

56. Commandant Louis Baron, personal communication with the author.

57. This argument is explored more fully in Martin Klein, "The Concept of Honour and the Persistence of Servitude in the Western Soudan," *Cahiers d'études africaines* 45 (2005): 831–52.

58. On *pulaaku*, see Paul Riesman, *First Find Your Child a Good Mother: The Construction of Self in Two African Communities* (New Brunswick, N.J.: Rutgers University Press, 2002), 202–3.

59. Jean-Pierre Olivier de Sardan, "The Songhay-Zarma Female Slave: Relations of Production and Ideological Status," in Robertson and Klein, *Women and Slavery in Africa*, 139.

60. This was not dissimilar from the "happy talk" with which African Americans, during slavery and after, dealt with white society.

61. Martin Klein, "Slave Descent and Social Status in Sahara and Sudan," in *Reconfiguring Slavery: West African Trajectories*, ed. Benedetta Rossi (Liverpool, UK: Liverpool University Press, 2009), 26–44. Other contributions to this book also deal with the persistence of forms of slavery.

3

SEX AND POWER IN THE RUSSIAN INSTITUTIONS OF SLAVERY AND SERFDOM

Richard Hellie (†)

The Russian institutions of slavery and serfdom provide interesting comparative data on slavery and its related practices from the beginning of written Russian history at the end of the first millennium CE.[1] This chapter draws on both historical research and literature to investigate what is conventionally viewed as a transition from slavery to serfdom in Russian history and to analyze for that period the relationship between power and sex.

The Transition from Slavery to Serfdom

Slavery was known from the dawn of Russian history and blossomed during the medieval Viking era (750–1050) when Vikings on the famous "route from the Varangians [Scandinavia] to the Greeks [Byzantium]" were massively engaged in the slave trade, providing slaves to the Black Sea and beyond and into the Baltic and beyond. Simultaneously, the Turkic steppe peoples on the East Slavic southern frontier made a living by slave raiding, and, in turn, some of their own were enslaved by the Slavs. Moreover, slaves were a major outcome of the incessant warfare in Kievan

Rus' (the first Russian state, with Kiev as the capital, which Russian tradition considers to have been founded in 862 CE and which lasted to the mid-twelfth century); this warfare raged among the East Slavic tribes, who comprised the majority of the population of Kievan Rus', and between these tribes and their non-Slavic neighbors.

The Turkic steppe peoples continued to engage heavily in slave raiding. Even after 1783, when Catherine the Great (or Catherine II, r. 1762–96) liquidated the Crimean Khanate (founded in 1441 in the Crimean Peninsula), other Turkic peoples kidnapped Russians and sold them into slavery in Central Asia and beyond. Internal East Slavic warfare persisted until the first half of the sixteenth century when Moscow liquidated independent principalities in the north, but warfare among Great Russians, Ukrainians, and Belorussians persisted for decades. Enslavement was the inevitable outcome for those captives who were not killed.

Slaves were also a major concern of legislators. Throughout medieval Rus', individuals who were unable to pay a fine could be legally enslaved. It was also possible for East Slavs to sell themselves into slavery in the absence of either better life alternatives or welfare. In the Kievan period, slaves who sold themselves were deemed "full slaves," just like military captives or enslaved debtors.

Serfdom took up where slavery left off. Serfdom commenced in the 1450s with a measure forbidding selected monastery peasant debtors to move at any time of year other than around St. George's Day (November 26). In 1497, this rule was applied to all peasants. During his Oprichnina (1565–72)—a domestic policy characterized by the extensive use of political police, mass repression, public executions, and confiscation of aristocrats' land—Ivan IV (Ivan the Terrible, r. 1547–84) issued revised "obedience charters" (*poslushnye gramoty*) that made peasants more answerable or responsible to the landlords, who, in turn, rendered the czar invaluable military service. Among other things, this allowed landholders to raise tenfold the rents of their peasants-becoming-serfs. In a decree issued in 1581, Ivan also suspended the right of serfs to transfer, once a year, from one estate to another. This marked the start of the "forbidden years," a long period during which the service obligations of serfs in Russia were progressively tightened. Serfdom became universal in 1592, when all peasants were permanently bound to the land by a statute of limitations that was introduced on the recovery of fugitive serfs. Although this statute was abolished by the Law Code (Sobornoe Ulozhenie) of 1649, the geographic mobility of serfs remained largely restricted until 1906.

As slaves but not serfs were exempted from paying taxes, slavery became an increasingly attractive option for impoverished serfs. By the second half of the sixteenth century, the Muscovites had created the institution of limited-service contract slavery for those who sold themselves into slavery, somewhat like the Parthian institution of antichresis a millennium earlier. In theory, a person borrowed a sum for a year and for that period became a limited-service contract slave, working for the creditor to pay off the interest. In practice, however, the borrower was rarely able to fully pay the interest within the stipulated period, and upon default, this individual became a full slave. However, by the 1590s, the resulting loss of tax revenue pushed the government into decreeing that on the death of their owners (creditors/purchasers), all limited-service contract slaves were to be freed and thus become taxpayers. In response, almost all such freedmen resold themselves again, often to the heirs of their deceased owners. They were perfect manifestations of what is currently called a dependent personality disorder, for when "threatened by self-reliance," they took "shelter in submission."[2]

Self-sale into slavery persisted until the abolition of agricultural slavery (in 1679) and household slavery (by the imposition of the soul tax in 1721) finally transformed all slaves into taxpayers and, to some extent, subjects of the law. Nevertheless, from the 1649 Ulozhenie, a coercive code of law issued by Czar Alexei Mikhailovich Romanov (r. 1645–76) marking what is conventionally viewed as the height of Muscovite autocracy, all peasants were bound irrevocably to the land on which they were registered. Moreover, landlords continued to treat serfs as de facto slaves. For example, during the reign of Catherine the Great, although serfs paid taxes and in some senses were subjects of the law, they were chattel for all practical purposes: their landlord-owners could move them around, have them sent to Siberia for infractions (in the process satisfying the owners' obligation to provide military recruits from among their serfs), discipline them (even kill them, albeit "illegally"), and control their family lives.[3] The personal abasement of the serfs was spelled out in 1790 by

Aleksandr Nikolayevich Radishchev (1749–1802), an aristocratic radical whose picaresque propaganda "novel" *Journey from St. Petersburg to Moscow* depicted the harsh realities of Catherine the Great's socioeconomic policies and earned him exile to Siberia;[4] the similarities between the condition of Russian serfs and that of African slaves in the American South have been nicely laid out by Peter Kolchin.[5]

The conventional belief is that the Russian seignorial serfs were emancipated in 1861, when the slave abasement accretions that had occurred between 1565 and 1796 were abolished and the serf was freed from the landowner. Certainly, the status of the serf as legal chattel ended then. However, the peasant remained enserfed (bound to the land) until 1906. Instead of being tied to a lord, he was bound to his commune, to which he was compelled to pay redemption dues (moneys freedmen had to pay both for the land they acquired in 1861 and in compensation to the lords for the loss of their chattel). Moreover, until 1906, the serf was forbidden to move anywhere without a release from the commune, which was responsible for maintaining order in the countryside.

Sex and Bondage in Russia

The foregoing description of the transition from slavery to serfdom provides a necessary background for a discussion of the complex issue of sex and bondage in Russia. In a juridical sense, Muscovite law of the sixteenth century upheld the formula *po kholopu raba, po rabe kholop*,[6] which translates as "When a free woman marries a slave man, she becomes a slave; when a free man marries a slave woman, he becomes a slave." However, I know of no document that indicates this judicial norm was ever effected in real life. It *may* have been the practice for the lower classes: thus, when a free townsperson or peasant married a slave, he or she may have become a slave himself or herself. Nevertheless, I am aware of no documents showing this. Indeed, if an owner decided to marry a slave, the owner would have manumitted the slave before the wedding so that he or she was not marrying a slave.

It is important to note that the racial/color poignancy of black-white liaisons seems to have been absent in Russia. There were countless cases of interracial miscegenation, such as when white-skinned East Slavs married yellow-skinned Turkic peoples. An offspring from such a union was called a *boldyr'* (half-breed), but there was much of this type of miscegenation on the East European Plain, even at the very top of society, and I am unaware of any stigma being attached to it.[7] We know, too, that names of foreign provenance were completely acceptable: in 1979, Nikolai Aleksandrovich Baskakov (1905–95), the Russian Turkologist, linguist, and ethnologist, published a dictionary of three hundred Russian surnames of Turkic origin.[8] And it is considered that Grand Prince Andrei Bogoliubskii (1111–74) was mainly Turkish because his male ancestors regularly married Turkish women.

Whether a marriage was interracial/international seems to have made no difference either in law or in practice. However, at least some interfaith marriages were forbidden. Borrowing from Byzantium (which forbade Christian-Jewish marriages), Russia imposed a ban on Christian-Muslim marriages, following which a Muslim who married a Christian converted to Christianity—at least in cases where the unions were voluntary; whenever the Muslim "bride" was kidnapped or captured as a military trophy, it was probably just assumed that she converted to Christianity.

By contrast, a slave-cum-free marriage or serf-cum-free liaison seems to have been stigmatized. This is evident as early as the end of the tenth century, when Vladimir Sviatoslavich (980–1015), who Christianized Rus' in 988, was mocked because, as the offspring of Maliusha Liubechanka, one of the concubines of his father, Sviatoslav, he was "a slave's son." Sviatoslavich possessed a large harem, and two of his offspring from the harem were the subsequent martyrs Boris and Gleb, children of a Bulgarian woman who was probably captured by Vladimir in the 990s.[9] That they were the offspring of a slave did not affect the standing of Boris and Gleb in Russian society.

The great scholar of ancient slavery Moses I. Finley claimed that an owner's right of free sexual access to his slaves is "a fundamental condition of all slavery."[10] This, like a number of other generalizations about slavery, did not always hold in eastern Europe. For example, in the twelfth century, owner access to female slaves was limited by a treaty between the Germans and Novgorod, which dictated that the master who raped his slave had to pay a fine and had to manumit her if she became pregnant.[11] However, there is no evidence to indicate if these penalties were ever applied—or could be applied—in an environment where most of the population was illiterate.

The treaty clauses could only have had an impact if the woman victim knew about the law and managed to complain to the appropriate official.

In the 1590s, the government required that all slaves be reregistered and that proof of their slave status be provided[12]—a transparent attempt to clear the slave rolls of as many tax avoiders as possible. Proof of slave status included slave genealogies going back for a century and more. Sometimes, the names of fathers are missing for slaves in these genealogies, but there is no evidence that such slaves were sired by their owners. Flight by both slaves and serfs was common, so one of the missing fathers simply may have run off at some point after he had impregnated his mate.

The slave sex ratio in Muscovy (or the czardom of Russia—the Russian state from 1547 to 1721) was two males for every one female.[13] Only where the ratios were reversed does one suspect that sexual exploitation was the primary purpose of human bondage. In Russia, one wonders what to make of a case in which a buyer purchased a number of young females but no males. He may have been running a harem or brothel, or he may have been buying them to mate with males who were unrecorded.[14] Another piece of evidence that women were purchased primarily for purposes other than sexual exploitation seems to be inherent in the price data: the highest prices were paid for women "past their prime," rather than for female teenagers.[15]

In the seventeenth century, perhaps the heyday of slavery in Muscovy, a slave woman who had conceived and borne a child as a result of sexual assault had the legal possibility of presenting the child to the czar as proof of that assault. The czar was supposed to remand the case to the patriarch. Provisions going back to the Byzantine origins of Muscovite church law prescribed that the woman be manumitted or sold to another owner, but the Russian church statute book (*Kormchaia kniga*) prescribed only that the woman had to be sold to someone else.[16] Also, whereas ordinarily slaves and peasants/serfs found guilty of killing their owners/masters were executed, there were—in cases of proven sexual abuse—rare exceptions. Thus, when on June 24, 1628, two slaves and a peasant killed their lord because he had raped their wives and daughters, the rape was considered a mitigating circumstance: the killers and their wives were exiled to Siberia, and their children were given to the widow and children of the murdered man.[17]

Sexual Abuse of Serfs

In the eighteenth century, the collapse of the moral influence of the Orthodox Church combined with the extraordinary abasement of the serfs into near slaves account for both the widespread sexual abuse of serfs by their landlord-masters and the rise of the serf harem. There is considerable evidence of the continued sexual exploitation of dependents from the start of Russia's Imperial period in 1721, after serfdom had degenerated into de facto slavery. Much of this evidence is reflected in the literature of the time. A celebrated example is Nikolai Mikhailovich Karamzin's sentimentalist story "Poor Liza" (1792). Ivan, Liza's father, was an industrious, rather wealthy farmer (*poselianin*) who by 1792 was almost certainly a serf—a status the very conservative Karamzin avoids discussing. The father dies when Liza is fifteen years old, and she and her sixty-year-old mother (demographically questionable, I should think) are plunged into poverty. Liza is extraordinarily able, hardworking, and attractive. When she is seventeen, she meets Erast, a bored gentry playboy who has money to throw around—in some respects, the forebear of Russian literature's infamous superfluous man (*lishnii chelovek*). They fall madly in love, but she cannot marry him, she claims, because she is a peasant (serf?). This is important for our story because of the implication that peasant/serf-gentry liaisons were taboo. Erast pretends to be insulted, deflowers her, and continues to lead her through a romantic dream world until, finally, he leaves for the army; gambles away his assets; arranges to wed an elderly, rich widow to restore his fortune; and jilts Liza. She faints and then drowns herself, and Erast considers himself her murderer.[18] The crucial line for our story is that, "in public," it was socially unthinkable that a peasant/serf girl could have a romantic affair with a member of the gentry. This notion is reflected in Nikolai Gogol's *Dead Souls* (1842), in which Derebin's aunt disinherits her son for marrying a serf girl.[19]

Arguably the most famous example of such exploitation in Russian artistic literature is found in *Fathers and Sons*, written in 1862 by Ivan Turgenev (1818–1883). The story allegedly takes place in 1859, just before the so-called Emancipation, while the personal-bondage/slavery aspect of serfdom was still in effect. The radical hero of the book, Bazarov, visits the estate of his friend and disciple-follower Arkadii Kirsanov. (Bazarov and Arkadii are the two major "sons" of the novel.) Arkadii's father,

Nikolai Petrovich, is the owner of the estate and a widower. Nikolai owns a number of serfs. He has an intimate liaison with one of them, and a child is born. The mother and babe-in-arms hide when Bazarov comes around because the liaison is considered shameful. Bazarov demonstrates his radical and populist credentials by telling them that they need not hide, for there is nothing shameful about the affair.

For us, the important point is that most people certainly believed such affairs, at least in public, were shameful. Historian Gregory L. Freeze notes that the church tried to require the registration of marriages between lords and serfs but that "the squires—presumably for reasons of status—chose not to have the marriages recorded in parish registers."[20] Again, the toothlessness of the church should be noted. Freeze underscores how powerless the government was in the Russian countryside, where the serf owner was not only the petty tyrant/czar but also the employer of the priest.[21]

In "Poor Liza," Erast uses no compulsion on Liza, who is his very willing victim, but in reality, most liaisons between unfree individuals and members of the gentry were involuntary on the part of the serfs. Freeze, the Brandeis University historian of the Russian clergy, unearthed a number of archival records comprising complaints from Orthodox clergymen to their superiors about masters' abuse of their serfs. In 1820, the archbishop of Iaroslavl' noted a complaint from male serfs that a lord was raping their daughters and wives. A Vladimir diocese priest in 1827 reported to his bishop the case of a master who was raping serf girls aged twelve years and younger, as well as adult serf women. Again, in 1848, a priest of Velikii Ustiug informed his bishop about a lord who was "forcibly depriving serf girls on his estate of their virginity." The church had no authority in such cases and could only pass them on to civil authorities.[22]

Such incidents were so common that they reverberated in the literature of the time. For example, in 1848, Aleksandr Herzen (1812–1870) penned an important fictional piece, "The Thieving Magpie" ("Soroka-vorovka"), about Aneta, a passionate serf actress who rebels against her brutal, lecherous owner. Herzen intended the piece to be a damning indictment of the dehumanizing reality of Russian serfdom.[23] Another of Herzen's works, his famous novel *Who Is to Blame?* (sometimes *Who Is Guilty?* [*Kto vinovat?*]) also deals with the master-serf/mother theme. In this work, the father of Bel'tov, the hero, married Bel'tov's mother, but the father of

Liubochka Krutsiferskaia, the heroine, did not marry her mother.[24] A similar theme is found in F. M. Dostoevskii's *The Adolescent* (sometimes A *Raw Youth* [*Podrostok*], 1875), in which Versilov fathers a child with his serf, who becomes the mother of the hero, Arkadii Dolgorukii. And L. N. Tolstoi—who himself had an affair with a serf, Aksinia Bazykina—describes in *War and Peace* how Prince Bolkonskii had a serf concubine, Alexandra, who as a result of the liaison annually gave birth to a child; further, "Uncle" had a serf who lived with him "like his wife." Later on in his life, Tolstoi condemned such affairs as "immoral," but in the 1860s, he apparently assumed that they were part of everyday life. The persistence of this theme in Russian literature reflects the complex power relations between master and serf that frequently resulted in sexual exploitation.

The Serf Harem

The late eighteenth-century and early nineteenth-century tradition of the large slave harem can be traced to Vladimir Sviatoslavich. In the Primary Chronicle, a history of Kievan Rus' ca. 850–1110, accredited to the monk Nestor and compiled in Kiev in ca. 1113, Sviatoslavich is noted as possessing five wives and eight hundred concubines—nearly all of whom, we may assume, were slaves. Under Russian Orthodoxy, which prescribed monogamy, his five wives were illegal, yet the existence of a law declaring that offspring of nonmonogamous unions should be freed appears to have recognized the existence and even legitimacy of slave concubines. This, together with the reputed size of the harems maintained by members of the Russian elite such as Vladimir, suggests that the harem had existed from at least as early as the sixteenth century, albeit on a considerably smaller scale. Under this rubric, the fate of the offspring of a slave owner and his concubine is of interest. Article 98 of the Russkaia Pravda, a concordance of mainly Russian princely law dating from the eleventh century, prescribed that such a child was to be set free on the father's death. This law was used throughout the sixteenth century in West Russian (Lithuanian) judicial practice. No evidence of its use in later Muscovy has been found, but a similar statute exists in Muscovite church law, which may have had jurisdiction over such cases.[25]

Little research has been done into slave harems of the Imperial period, but an examination of both historical records and the literature of the time reveals sufficient information to highlight specific case studies and draw some broad conclusions about the prevalence and impact of the institution. A major source of information about the serf harem is Priscilla Roosevelt's magnificent *Life on the Russian Country Estate.*[26] A number of the wealthiest landlords owned hundreds or even thousands of serfs and possessed gigantic estates with many buildings. Asking herself what people did with so much space, Roosevelt reasons that they kept harems in them. She reviews for us nearly a dozen such individuals, including Alexander Borisovich Kurakin (1752–1818), a statesman and diplomat; Count Nikolai Petrovich Sheremetev (1771–ca. 1829);[27] and Gen. Lev Dmitrievich Izmailov (1763–1836), a despotic estate owner in the Tula region some 200 kilometers south of Moscow, who was accused of keeping thirty young serf girls for his own and his guests' amusement but was never tried for the offense.[28]

It is difficult to pinpoint precisely when the serf harem as an institution peaked, but in the nineteenth century, certain key developments started to undermine it. The first was the spread of Russian radical thought after the Decembrist uprising of 1825. Another important milestone was the publication of Turgenev's *Sportsman's Sketches* (*Zapiski okhotnika*, 1852), which played the same role for the serfs in Russia as did Harriet Beecher Stowe's novel *Uncle Tom's Cabin* in humanizing the African slave in the United States. This led to the phenomenon of the "repentant noblemen," whereby gentry serf owners outside the Black Soil region of Russia (the richest agricultural area, located some 400 kilometers southwest of Moscow) came to believe that serf ownership was immoral. In turn, this phenomenon greatly facilitated the third major development, the 1861 emancipation of the serfs. In the climate of public opinion that ensued, possession of a serf harem might have been well nigh impossible. Again, this change is reflected in the literature of the time. Relations between serfs and free people would have been limited to the apparently consensual type portrayed, for instance, in *Fathers and Sons*. Lina Steiner has pointed out to me that Tolstoi's late work *Resurrection* (1899) "sums up the nineteenth-century obsession with the female serf as an erotic object and the terrible guilt this passion incurred."[29] This is reflected in the character Katiusha Maslova, a former serf, and her former owner, Prince Dmitrii Nekhliudov, as well as in the dependence of Katiusha on the Nekhliudov family.

Nevertheless, the heritage of master-serf abuse continued to reverberate. Thus, the sexual exploitation of female inferiors is mentioned by the great symbolist poet Aleksandr Aleksandrovich Blok (1880–1921) in his famous 1918 essay "The Intelligentsia and the Revolution": "Why defile the gentry's beloved estates? Because peasant girls were raped and flogged there; if not at this squire's, then at his neighbors."[30] One may conclude that, in reality, female slaves typically and with rare exception were rightless objects of sexual predation from the earliest days of East Slavic slavery through the close of the serf era, laying the basis for the continuation of such practices to the end of Gulag.[31]

Notes

(†) Editors' Note: Unfortunately, Dr. Hellie passed away shortly after completing this article. Because we were unable to consult with him during the editing process, some references in this chapter may be incomplete.

1. I thank Jane Dailey for comments that compelled me to rethink parts of this essay.

2. Harvard Medical School, "Dependent Personality Disorder," *Harvard Mental Health Letter* 23, no. 10 (2007): 1–4.

3. Richard Hellie, "The Great Paradox of the Seventeenth Century: The Stratification of Muscovite Society and the 'Individualization' of Its High Culture, Especially Literature," in *O Rus! Studia litteraria slavica in honorem Hugh McLean*, ed. Simon Karlinsky, James L. Rice, and Barry P. Scherr (Berkeley, Calif.: Berkeley Slavic Specialties, 1995), 116–28.

4. Aleksandr Nikolayevich Radishchev, *Journey from St. Petersburg to Moscow* (Cambridge, Mass.: Harvard University Press, 1958).

5. Peter Kolchin, *Unfree Labor: American Slavery and Russian Serfdom* (Cambridge, Mass.: Harvard University Press, 1987).

6. The major significance of this phrase is that it shows the word *kholop* means "slave." No one questions that *raba* (the feminine form of the masculine *rab*) means "slave," but various people have, from time to time, questioned whether *kholop* actually has the same meaning; for example, some erroneously allege it means "servant."

7. It would never be possible to write a book about Russia along the lines of Martha Hodes's *White Women, Black Men: Illicit Sex in the Nineteenth-Century South* (New Haven, Conn.: Yale University Press, 1997).

8. N. A. Baskakov, *Russkie familii tiurkskogo proiskhozhdeniia* (Moscow: Nauka, 1979).

9. *Pravoslavnaia entsiklopediia*, vol. 6 (Moscow: Pravoslavnaia Entsiklopediia, 2003), 46. The boys were murdered in 1015 by their older half brother, Sviatopolk, in a struggle for the throne after the death of their father, Vladimir.

10. Moses I. Finley, "The Idea of Slavery," in *Slavery in the New World: A Reader in Comparative History*, ed. Laura Foner and Eugene D. Genovese (Englewood Cliffs, N.J.: Prentice-Hall, 1969), 260.

11. V. I. Sergeevich, *Drevnosti russkogo prava*, 3 vols. (St. Petersburg, Russia: Tip. M. M. Stasiulevich, 1908–11), 1:123; A. A. Zimin, *Pamiatniki russkogo prava*, vol. 2, *Feodal'no-razdroblennoi Rusi XII–XV vv.*, ed. L. V. Cherepnin and S. V. Iushkov, 8 vols. (Moscow: Gosudarstvennoe Izdatel'stvo Iuridicheskoi Literatury, 1959), 126 art. 14.

12. On Muscovite slavery, see Richard Hellie, *Slavery in Russia, 1450–1725* (Chicago: University of Chicago Press, 1982).

13. Ibid.

14. A. I. Iakovlev, ed., *Novgorodskie zapisnye kabal'nye knigi 100–104 i 111 godov (1591–1596 i 1602–1603)* (Moscow-Leningrad: Akademiia Nauk SSSR, 1938), 1:246–49.

15. See table 2, "Amount Paid for Single Slave Women by Age," in Richard Hellie, "Women and Slavery in Muscovy," *Russian History* 10, no. 2 (1983): 219.

16. *Akty istoricheskie*, vol. 1., *1334–1598* (St. Petersburg: 1841), xx; Sergeevich, *Drevnosti russkogo prava*, 1:140; E. I. Kolycheva, *Kholopstvo i krepostnichestvo (konets XV–XVI v.)* (Moscow: Nauka, 1971), 236.

17. Nil Aleksandrovich Popov and Dimitrii Akovlevich Samokvasov, eds., *Akty Moskovskogo Gosudarstva [Akty Moskovskogo gosudarstva izdannye imperatorskoiu Akademieiu nauk]* [Acts of the Moscow State Issued by the Imperial Academy of Sciences], vol. 1, *Rozriadnyi prikaz: Moskovskii stol, 1571–1634* (Saint Petersburg: Tip. Imperatorskoi Akademii Nauk, 1890), no. 259, 275–89.

18. The story can be found in English in Harold B. Segel, *The Literature of Eighteenth-Century Russia*, 2 vols. (New York: Dutton, 1967), 2:76–93. The most recent Russian edition, *"Bednaia Liza" Karamzina: Opyt prochteniia* (Moscow: Russkii Mir, 2006), was edited by Vladimir Nikolayevich Toporov, who was awarded the 1998 Aleksandr Solzhenitsyn literary prize. I thank Lina Steiner for many of the literary references in this section of the chapter.

19. Nikolai Gogol, *Dead Souls* (New York: Modern Library, 1965), 260.

20. Gregory Freeze, "The Orthodox Church and Serfdom in Prereform Russia," *Slavic Review* 3 (Fall 1989): 381.

21. Ibid., 382.

22. Ibid., 375.

23. Lina Steiner, "Realism and the Woman: Herzen on Femininity, Domesticity, and Personal Maturity," paper presented at the Thirty-Sixth National Convention of the American Association for the Advancement of Slavic Studies, December 5, 2004.

24. This theme was especially poignant for Herzen, who was also illegitimate: his father, A. Iakovlev, a wealthy Russian landowner, and his mother, Luisa

Haag, who was from Stuttgart, Germany, never married. Moreover, Herzen's name comes from Herz, "from the heart."

25. Kolycheva, *Kholopstvo i krepostnichestvo*, 235–36.

26. Priscilla Roosevelt, *Life on the Russian Country Estate: A Social and Cultural History* (New Haven, Conn.: Yale University Press, 1995). I am indebted to Dan Waugh for refreshing my memory about this work.

27. Sheremetev married one of his serfs, who was a famous actress in his serf theater, Praskov'ia Kovaleva-Zhemchugova; Lina Steiner, e-mail to the author, January 4, 2008.

28. *Russkii biograficheskii slovar'* (Moscow: Tip. Glav. Upravleniia Udelov, 1897), 8:67–68; *Russkii biograficheskii slovar'* (Moscow: Terra, 1999), 7:394–35.

29. Lina Steiner, personal communication with the author. Professor Steiner, a specialist in nineteenth-century Russian and European literature, culture, and intellectual history, is in the Department of Slavic Languages and Literatures at the University of Chicago.

30. The essay is in *Russian Intellectual History: An Anthology*, ed. Marc Raeff (New York: Harcourt, Brace, 1966), 368.

31. On GULag rape, see Anne Applebaum, *Gulag: A History* (New York: Doubleday, 2003), 171–72; Oleg Khlevniuk, *The History of the GULag: From Collectivization to the Great Terror* (New Haven, Conn.: Yale University Press, 2004), 16, 101–3; Varlam Tikhonovich Shalamov, *Kolyma Tales* (New York: W. W. Norton, 1981); and Semen Sanuilovich Vilenskii, ed., *Till My Tale Is Told: Women's Memoirs of the GULag* (Bloomington: Indiana University Press, 1999). I thank Golfo Alexopolous for some of these references. Also, according to Golfo, affairs between former prisoners and members of the Komsomol could get one expelled from the Komsomol, extending the stigma of slave/serf-free relations well into the twentieth century; Alexopolous, e-mail to the author, February 15, 2007.

CONCUBINAGE, LAW, AND THE FAMILY

4

SURIA: CONCUBINE OR SECONDARY SLAVE WIFE?

The Case of Zanzibar in the Nineteenth Century

Abdul Sheriff

A concubine is commonly understood as a "woman cohabiting with a man not legally married," that is, there is no legal recognition of the status of such a woman or of her offspring, who becomes a bastard.[1] This definition, in the words of the *Concise Oxford Dictionary*, is clearly based on the Christian concept of marriage, which eventually recognized unions only between a free woman and a free man. However, in slave societies, men have invariably cohabited with slave women. Christian morality as it had evolved by the sixteenth century was unable to take full cognizance of this reality and acknowledge the rights of women and their children in such situations.

Islam did not invent slavery, nor did it try to abolish it outright. What it tried to do was to humanize the institution through regulations and exhortations on the treatment of slaves. A slave was not merely chattel but also a human being with certain religious and legal rights and social status.[2] Islam recognized the social reality of cohabitation with slave women and went on to explicitly acknowledge the status and rights of those women and of their offspring. It was a society governed by paternity. It permitted unions with slave girls, who became *sarari* (secondary wives, sing. *suria*) when they bore their owners' children. Thereafter, the *umm al-walad* (mother of the child) could not be sold or pawned but was freed on the death of her master (although she did not inherit from him as his free wives did). Moreover, the offspring of such unions were free children of their free fathers, with full rights like those possessed by free mothers. In one of the traditions, the Prophet of Islam stated, "He who, having a female slave, educates and cares for her, and afterwards frees and marries her, shall have a double reward."[3] These were some of the many ways for a slave to move out of servility. Manumission was thus built into the system of slavery in Islam, and it provided its own mechanisms for the assimilation of slaves into the wider fabric of the Muslim community. It offered opportunities for upward social mobility, what Ali Mazrui called "ascending miscegenation," in contrast to the American system, for example, in which white slave owners could not acknowledge the paternity of their children born to slave women, childen who remained slaves like their mothers.[4]

That these were not merely theoretical legal formulations but represented a social reality becomes clear when we examine the history of the ruling dynasty in Zanzibar during the nineteenth century. The patriarch of the Al-Busaid dynasty, Seyyid Said b. Sultan, had three free wives. The first was an Arab, Azza bint Seif of the royal house, and according to R. F. Burton, she had a male child who died at a young age. In 1827, Said married a daughter of the governor of Fars and granddaughter of Fath Ali Shah of the Qajar dynasty of Iran, but after six years of a monotonous life in Muscat, she asked for a divorce. Then, in 1849, he married Sheherezade, another Iranian of "entrancing beauty," according to Said's daughter Salme, who chronicled the royal family's life. Sheherezade went to Zanzibar accompanied by an architect who built her a beautiful *hammam* (steam bath), which is still standing at Kidichi. She liked riding and hunting in broad daylight and was otherwise too wayward and extravagant for her austere and mercantile Ibadhi husband, who divorced her after a short while.[5] However, the sultan was not blessed with surviving children by any of his free wives.

Nonetheless, according to Salme—who eloped with a German trader in 1866 and wrote the first autobiography by a Zanzibari, male or female—he actually left thirty-six children on his death, apart from those who had predeceased him. All of them were by his slave wives. These children inherited substantial property from him according to Islamic law, in plantations, houses, and cash, and many of the sons also acceded to the thrones of Zanzibar as well as Oman. Arab writers generally avoid going into the *haram* (the domestic life of a household), but Salme's autobiography is a firsthand, eyewitness account full of intimate details about life in the royal household—details that are generally missing from diplomatic correspondence, which is often the main source for the history of Zanzibar in the nineteenth century.[6] Salme's autobiography is supplemented by the small but highly informative book on Seyyid Said by Sh. Abdalla Saleh Farsi, a teacher, Muslim scholar, and later chief *qadhi* (Islamic chief justice) of Kenya, Farsi compiled a lot of information about people and events during the lifetime of Said the ruler.[7] Farsi acknowledges that he derived a good deal of information from Salme's book, but he also collected much oral information from many elders in the early 1940s. Unfortunately, some mistakes and discrepancies crept into his book and from there into the footnotes of G. S. P. Freeman-Grenville's and E. van Donzel's editions of Salme's autobiography.[8]

Secondary Slave Wives in Zanzibar

In a maritime and mercantile society with a rapidly growing, floating, and immigrant population, as Zanzibar was in the nineteenth century, one would expect a marked gender disproportion among the immigrants, since women did not cross the sea to the same degree as men. It was not surprising, then, that the British consul in Zanzibar reported in 1844 that there were only four hundred Arab women compared to eight hundred men.[9] Moreover, in a burgeoning slave society with a growing plantation economy, it was to be expected that the deficit in females would be made up by slave women to a considerable extent, although Salme says that a free wife could stipulate in her marriage contract that the husband would not get a suria.[10] According to Burton when he visited Zanzibar in 1857, the easy availability of slave secondary wives affected even the oldest profession. As he observed, "Public prostitutes are here few, and the profession ranks low where the classes upon which it depends can easily afford to gratify their propensities in the slave market."[11]

This was true not only for Muslims, for whom there was a legally recognized procedure to obtain secondary slave wives, but also for Indians, some of whom were Hindus. And the victims were often Indians as well. Burton reported that servile cohabitation by the Bhattia Hindu merchants had caused a scandal some years previously when they were fined 20,000 Maria Theresa thalers by their high priest. Earlier, in 1844, Atkins Hamerton had recorded the case of an Indian slave girl from Hyderabad named Jaffran who, through many transactions, had stayed with Sh. Ahmed Hakim Hindee of Zanzibar for two years. A couple of years later, Mariam, another Indian slave woman, was taken, after a similar series of transactions, to Kilwa by a Khoja Amir Mukhi, with whom she stayed for four years before being sold to an Arab. She was originally a Rajput Hindu from Bombay whose parents had died, but she had converted to Islam. She was manumitted and repatriated to Bombay, but she said she did not want to go back to Baroda in India; instead, she wanted either to return to Zanzibar or to stay in Bombay if she was going to be provided for. In his diary, the British consul, Christopher Rigby, recorded that in 1859, an Indian had purchased a Galla slave girl for $159. Rigby sent her to the qadhi to be manumitted and then imprisoned her master.[12]

Nor were Christian Europeans in Zanzibar innocent of such deeds. Rigby said in 1859 that French residents openly purchased female slaves. Specifically, he charged the French consul for having purchased an Ethiopian slave girl for a considerable sum, and he sent her to the qadhi to be registered as redeemed. In an unpublished marginal note in her autobiography, Salme adds that the concubine—in the correct sense of the word in this case—"had presented him [the French consul] with a pitch-black daughter, who later found shelter in the French mission." Although Rigby, not unexpectedly, had zeroed in on the traditional French rivals, Burton had remarked that "most white residents keep Abyssinian or Galla concubines." In this, he is supported by Salme, who says, "There was great exasperation among the Muslim population of Zanzibar when it was learnt that an Englishman, whose government with grandiloquent morality forbade slavery, had not only bought a female slave himself, but, instead of setting her free, had resold her on his return, and even to an Arab official."[13]

What enraged Salme was the fact that the European Christians, not bound by the ethics of Islamic slaveholding, did the unspeakable—in the case of the French consul by refusing to recognize the paternity of his daughter and in the case of the Englishman by selling the concubine. As Salme makes clear, the sarari were "free as soon as they have children," in the sense that they could no longer be sold, pawned, and so on, although they remained bound to the master until his death. On his death, the sarari became entirely free. Salme adds that if a brother or any other relative of the deceased master wanted to marry the suria, she became a legitimate wife as a free woman. Salme cites the case of one of Seyyid Said's sarari, the Circassian Fatma, who remarried Sultan Majid's minister Sulaiman b. Ali al-Deremky.[14]

Even if the suria's child happened to die, the suria herself was supposed to be free. Salme admits that occasionally a suria was sold after the child's death, but she says this happened only rarely and with petty men "from necessity or boredom."[15] Of course, it was not only the Europeans or petty men who contravened these regulations. A master could refuse to recognize the paternity of the child born of his slave, and in a slave society in the days before DNA identification, there was no way for the slave woman to prove it. Thus, both mother and child could lose the protection of the law. It is widely believed that the only wife of Sultan Barghash of Zanzibar (r. 1870–88) had made a compact with her husband that he could enjoy as many sarari as he wished but that none of their offspring would be recognized as legitimate. And it is true that all his children issued from his only free wife, although he is known to have had dozens of sarari. According to one of them, a pregnant suria was thrown out of the palace as soon as she conceived, which was illegal according to Islamic law.[16]

Salme says that "only a wealthy man can purchase *sarari*." Yet the puritanical first American consul, Richard Waters, recorded in his journal in 1837 that he lectured Zanzibaris that "they commit adultery and fornication by keeping three to four, and sometimes six and eight concubines," and Seyyid Said told the British consul, "Arabs won't work; they must have slaves and concubines."[17] With such low prices charged for local slaves in Zanzibar, sometimes as little as $10 to $20, the practice of buying sarari was probably more widespread. The previously mentioned Indian slave woman Jaffran, for instance, was ultimately sold to Juma Dhobi, a washerman who may have been an Indian.[18] The result of this practice naturally was widespread miscegenation. In one place, according to Burton, to have children by slave girls was "a degradation in the eyes of free-born Arabs," but elsewhere, he noted in his characteristically racist phraseology: "As the Omani chiefs . . . did not disdain servile concubines, many of their issue are negroids: of these hybrids, some are exceedingly fair, showing African pollution only by tufty and wiry hair, whilst others, 'falling upon their mothers,' as the native phrase is, have been refused inheritance at Maskat, and have narrowly escaped the slave market."[19]

What Salme probably had in mind were the more expensive Ethiopian, Circassian, and Indian slave women. Wilson reported from the Persian Gulf in 1831 that Ethiopian slaves sold for 50 to 150 German crowns, "the females being higher," and that a "superior Abyssinian female may sell at 300 Crowns." By 1847, Arnold Kemball had raised the average figure to between $50 and $150 or more for males and $60 to $200 for "Habshi females."[20] These slaves were mostly imported from Hejaz, with the price for boys ranging from $50 to $100 and for girls from $60 to $150. Burton noted the Ethiopians were "exceedingly addicted to intrigue," but they were favorites with men "and, it is said, with Arab women."[21] Rigby reported in 1859 that an Indian had purchased a Galla slave woman for $159 in Zanzibar, and in 1871, a young Iranian had offered $250 for a Pathan (Indian) slave woman named Fatima or Mariam.[22]

Even more expensive were Circassians, from the Turkish Cherkess. Burton said Circassians and white slave girls were exceedingly rare and expensive and were confined to the harems of the rulers. They were imported from Iran and were extravagant in their tastes: "A '*Jariyeh bayza*' [white slave woman] soon renders the house of [a] moderately rich man unendurable."[23] These women came from the Caucasus Mountains, the home of a bewildering variety of ethnic groups speaking many languages. The area was considered a source of the purest Caucasian stock, producing the most striking women, with very pale ivory complexions, blond hair, and blue eyes, as in the case of one of Seyyid Said's sarari; others had extremely long dark hair going down to the knees, as in the case of Salme's mother. There was sometimes confusion in Zanzibar as to their precise origin. Salme uses Circassian as a general name for all these slaves from southeastern Europe, but Farsi often specifies Georgians, and Bulgarians are also mentioned in oral accounts.[24] (See map 4.1.)

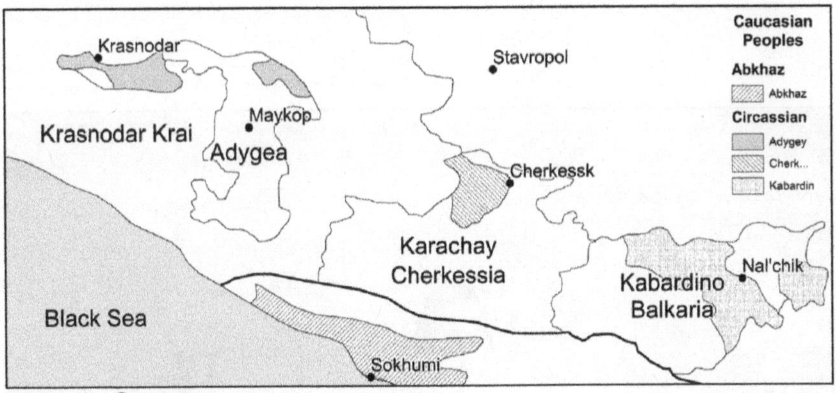

MAP 4.1 Circassia.

The Circassians' culture was strongly dominated by a warrior ethic, and women formerly fought alongside their husbands. Although these people were no longer matriarchal, women were given a high place of respect and dignity. They were Christianized by the Byzantines from the sixth century, but after the capture of Constantinople by the Ottomans, Islam spread in the lowlands of their region; Christian and pagan customs survived in the mountains. Lying across the migration paths of Eurasia, the Circassians were unable to fend for themselves against the Mongols, Huns, and others. Many were enslaved to enter the harems of the rich or the slave armies of Middle Eastern states, some eventually founding slave dynasties such as the Mamlukes of Egypt. Located in the border region between the Ottoman and Russian Empires, they were raided from both directions. The most calamitous invasion was the final conquest by czarist Russia, which led to "the wholesale emigration" of hundreds of thousands of Circassians, described as the biggest genocide of the nineteenth century. It is said that 90 percent of the Circassians were killed or forced to migrate to Turkey, where they now constitute a diaspora of more than 3 million people. In 1856, an American daily reported that as a consequence of the Russian conquest, there was an excess of beautiful Circassian women on the Istanbul slave market, which was causing prices to plummet.[25] (See figures 4.1 and 4.2.)

The Palace Sarari and Their Offspring

Salme says that her father probably had about seventy-five sarari at the time of his death and that they had been purchased gradually over his

FIGURE 4.1 Circassian suria, in Zanzibar. (*Source: Zanzibar National Archives,* AV54:18)

FIGURE 4.2. Circassian suria, in Zanzibar. (*Source:* O. *Baumann*, Afrikanische Skizzen *[Berlin: D. Reimer, 1900]*)

long reign, spanning nearly half a century. She admits that she did not know how many brothers and sisters she had in all, partly because a great number had died young and because some may have been born in Oman, which Salme never visited. She nevertheless hazards a guess that they numbered about a hundred, which may be an exaggeration, but only thirty-six had survived by the time of the sultan's death in 1856. Burton noted that Seyyid Said "always avoided those [slave wives] that bore him children." But if that was true, then he was obviously not very successful. As mentioned earlier, all of his children were by slave girls; "consequently we were all equal and had no need to carry out investigations about the colour of our blood," Salme cheekily adds. The sly remark would suggest that despite Islamic law regarding the rights of children by free and slave mothers, there may have been a difference in the social status of these children. This is confirmed by Burton's remark that children by slave girls were "a degradation in the eyes of free-born Arabs."[26] (See Figure 4.3.)

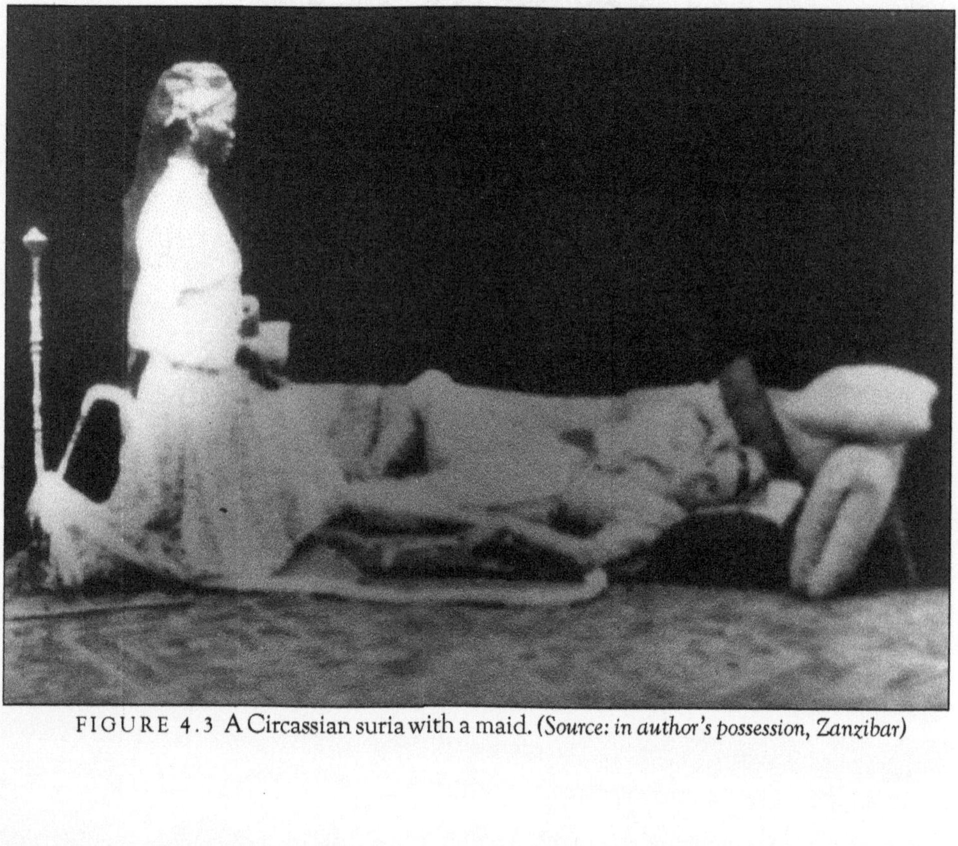

FIGURE 4.3 A Circassian suria with a maid. *(Source: in author's possession, Zanzibar)*

In the incomplete list of forty-one children of Seyyid Said compiled by Farsi, checked against Salme wherever possible, the ethnic origins of fifteen of their mothers are not specified. (See table 4.1.)

TABLE 4.1 THE CHILDREN OF SEYYID SAID

Ethiopian (14)	*Circassian/Georgian (9)*	*Assyrian (3)*	*Unknown (15)*
SONS	SONS	SON	SONS
1. Thuweyny (O 1856–66)	15. Khalid (Georgian)	24. Hilal	27. Abdulaziz 28. Abdullah
2. Muhammad	16. Majid (Z 1856–70)	DAUGHTERS 25. Asha	29. Hamed 30. Talib
3. Turky (O 1870–88)	17. Abdulwahab (Georgian)	26. Khole	31. Abbas 32. Nasor
4. Barghash (Z 1870–88)	18. Jamshid (Georgian)		33. Bedran
5. Ali	19. Hamdan		DAUGHTERS
6. Ghalib	DAUGHTERS		34. Zuweyna
7. Khalifa (Z 1888–90)	20. Khadduji 21. Sharife		35. Reyye 36. Sheykha
8. Ali (Menin) (Z 1890–93)	22. Nunu (Georgian) 23. Salme		37. Sweduu 38. Ghaluje
9. Abd al-Rab			39. Shambua
DAUGHTERS			40. Meyra
10. Meyye			41. Farshuu
11. Shawana			
12. Zeyana			
13. Zamzam			
14. Methle			

O= RULED IN OMAN Z= RULED IN ZANZIBAR

Compiled from: Farsi, *Seyyid Said*; Salme/Ruete, ed. Donzel, *Arabian Princess*; Said-Ruete, ed. Freeman-Grenville, *Memoirs of an Arabian Princess*.

In this table, O stands for rulers in Oman and Z for rulers in Zanzibar; these designations are followed by regnal years. Of the remaining children, fourteen had Ethiopian mothers. Among them were two sons who became sultans in Oman, Thuweyny (r. 1856–66) and Turky (r. 1870–88). Thuweyny was born in Muscat and lived all his life in Oman. He spent most of his time fighting wars to hold on to his father's threatened dominions there while Seyyid Said was in Zanzibar, "to the sorrow of his legitimate wife Ralie [Ghalia] our first cousin who gave him several children," according to Salme.[27] As the eldest surviving son, Thuweyny should have inherited the whole kingdom, but Seyyid Said had realized that it was going to be difficult to hold the far-flung empire together. Although he did not have the right to do so according to the Omani constitutional practice, he wanted to divide his kingdom between two sons. Accordingly, as early as 1844, he secretly approached the British to obtain their support in this effort, but the latter refused to get involved in succession disputes at that time. In any case, the kingdom was divided in 1862 with the sanction of the British authorities in India. Thuweyny was assassinated by his son Salim in 1866, and, following an interregnum, was succeeded in 1870 by his brother Turky, who established a branch of the dynasty that still rules in Oman. Three other brothers by Ethiopian mothers succeeded to the sultanate in Zanzibar. There, after failing to challenge succession by his brother Majid on their father's death in 1856, Barghash (r. 1870–88) succeeded to the throne in 1870, and he presided over a very eventful reign. It ended, however, with the partition of his commercial empire in the late 1880s. He was followed by two fairly weak brothers who ruled for short periods, Khalifa (1888–90) and Ali (1890–93).

Five of the children by Ethiopian mothers were females. Shawana, according to Salme, was very rich and possessed "the most handsome and selected slaves, and loaded them with the most costly weapons and jewels. . . . Even in dying she took care of her town slaves and the upper country slaves. She not only set them free, but also bequeathed to them all their costly arms and jewels, besides one whole estate for their maintenance."[28] Another was Methle, whom Salme describes as being "of so fair a complexion that one would not think of her descent by looking at her." She married a cousin who lived in Zanzibar town and had charming twin boys. The third daughter was Zamzam, who, according to Salme, "was extraordinarily practical, averse to exaggerated luxury, . . . everything prospered under her hands, something which rarely happens in an Arab house"; Salme adds, tongue in cheek, that she "came nearest to the German ideal of a housewife." In proof of this, late in life Zamzam married a distant cousin, Humud b. Ahmed of Bububu, one of the richest men in Zanzibar, who was also "exceedingly stingy." He was the very person who had earlier asked for the hand of another sister and been turned down by Khalid, who was acting as the governor during his father's absence in Oman. As Salme explains, it was a custom among the royals to marry inside the family as much as possible, "so that the blue blood is maintained."[29]

Nine of Seyyid Said's children for whom we have information had Circassian mothers according to Salme, who was very intimate with them (as well as their mothers); Farsi, however, identifies four of them specifically as Georgians. Salme mentions two new Circassian women who had arrived from Egypt and were only a few years older than the children in the house, but they were "rather haughty and indifferent to us," she says, and thus had to be taught a lesson. One day, one of them was sitting on a flimsy Swahili bed, merrily singing her "national song at the top of her voice," and the children decided to play a prank on her to bring her down a peg. They lifted the bed she was sitting on and then suddenly dropped it, thoroughly frightening her. Salme also mentions another Circassian, Medine, who died childless. There were apparently many such women, and Seyyid Said directed in his last will that his childless women should be taken care of for life.[30]

Among his children born of Circassian mothers was Khalid, who was nicknamed "Banyan" because of his mercantile preoccupations. He built the Hadith Mosque adjoining the town palace as well as a house and also a lodge at Sebleni. He had a superb plantation at Machui, which he named Marseille because of his "predilection for France and for everything French." He acted as governor in Zanzibar during Seyyid Said's infrequent visits to Oman and would have succeeded him had he not predeceased his father. His mother was Khurshid, a Circassian or a Georgian according to Salme and Farsi, respectively; Freeman-Grenville speculated that she may have been an Orthodox Christian. According to Salme, Khurshid was very tall and had quite an exceptional appearance; she also "possessed an uncommon strength of will combined with natural, great common sense. . . . In important matters she always proved to have a kind of Solomonic wisdom." It was said that during Seyyid Said's absence from Zanzibar, it was she who actually governed the country.[31] However, Khalid died during Seyyid Said's last visit to Oman in 1854, and when Said himself died on his return voyage, Majid took over as the sultan (r. 1856–70) with the support of the British consul. Majid's mother was a Circassian, Sarah, who was also the mother of his full sister Khadduji, who died at Medina after 1870. According to Salme, Khadduji was domineering and stern by nature, and she blames her for the breakdown of Majid's marriage with his wife Aashe. Khadduji disliked foreign things and was reluctant to meet European women. In other respects, she was very considerate, and according to the same Salme, she sewed and embroidered dresses for the small children of her married slaves "as assiduously as she used to work on the fine shorts of her brother."[32]

In addition to Khadduji, the sultan had three other female children with Circassian mothers. Among them was Sharife, who was, in the words of Salme, "a dazzling beauty with the complexion of a German blonde." She possessed a sharp intellect and was a faithful adviser to their father, but she nevertheless married a cousin who did not seem to possess the qualities of character that her father desired in the husband of his darling daughter. However, Said was reconciled to her choice, and it proved to be a happy one: she remained her husband's only wife, which supported a number of points Salme makes regarding the position of women in a Muslim society.[33] Another daughter was the beautiful but blind Nunu, whose mother was called "*Tadj* (crown) on account of her radiant beauty." Tadj was thus a favorite of Seyyid Said, provoking the envy and jealousy of her fellow wives. After the death of her mother, Nunu was cared for by "an utterly trustworthy Abyssinian slave woman [who] solemnly vowed to the dying Tadj to look conscientiously after Nunu."[34]

The most famous of the group was, of course, Salme herself, who, as mentioned, eloped with the German merchant in 1866. Her mother was Jilfidan, a Circassian by birth who was captured as a child and came into Seyyid Said's possession at the age of seven or eight. Jilfidan was not very pretty, but she was tall and strongly built, with black eyes and hair down to her knees. She was another favorite of Seyyid Said, who, according to Salme, used to rise when she went to visit him. She was also clever with needlework. In addition to Salme, Jilfidan had a second daughter, but she died quite young. When Salme and her mother moved to the town after Seyyid Said's death, Jilfidan attached herself to an experienced Ethiopian woman named Nuren, who taught her some Ethiopian. She also had a Nubian female slave, Zafrane, who had learned the culinary art from her former Iranian mistress in Oman, exemplifying the complex composition and interaction of slaves in the royal household. Jilfidan died in 1859 when a devastating cholera epidemic spread over the town and the whole island of Zanzibar, snatching away human lives almost daily, even in the palace.[35]

Finally, three of Seyyid Said's children had a single mother described by Salme as being from Mesopotamia and by Farsi, more specifically, as Assyrian, whereas Freeman-Grenville speculated that she may have been of Christian origin. These children included Seyyid Said's eldest son, Hilal, who was disinherited because of his addiction to alcohol (seduced by the French consul, according to Salme). The other two were girls. Asha was small and of dark complexion, disfigured by pockmarks that were probably caused by smallpox, which occasionally ravaged Zanzibar. (Her half brother Majid was similarly pockmarked.) She was served by a single Ethiopian slave woman, who was her hairdresser and chambermaid. She was devoted to her brother Hilal, and after his death, she took motherly care of his eldest son, Suud. She was reserved and even cold, but intellectually, she was superior to her younger sister, Khole. The latter was called *nidjm il subh* (Morning Star), according to Salme. Khole was proverbially beautiful, and Salme recounts the story of an Arab chieftain who, while gazing upon her, was so dazzled by her beauty that he did not even notice he was piercing his foot with his lance, a story straight out of *The Arabian Nights*. Khole was her father's favorite and received in her inheritance one of the most beautiful plantations. "The much-loved, much-envied and much-hated" Khole died in 1875.[36]

With such a heterogeneous family, the commentary of a perceptive member is very revealing. In a beautiful paragraph, Salme gives an engaging thumbnail sketch of domestic life in the palace:

> In our gallery at Bet il Sahel a painter would have found many subjects for his brush. . . . At least eight to ten shades of colour could be found in the faces of the multitude fluctuating up and down, and an artist had to paint in the most vivid colours to be able to present a faithful image of the many-tinted garments. . . . For us children the babel of languages in this society was particularly diverting. In fact only Arabic should have been spoken and in my father's presence this order was strictly followed. But no sooner had he turned his back, than a kind

> of *babel*-like confusion of tongues prevailed. Persian, Turkish, Circassian, Swahili, Nubian and Abyssinian were heard promiscuously next to Arabic, not to mention the various dialects of these languages.
>
> As for the kitchen . . . meals were cooked in the Arabic as well as in the Persian and Turkish fashion. In both houses [Mtoni and the town palaces] the various races were indeed living together and the most fascinating beauties as well as their opposites were abundantly represented. But among us only the Arabic fashion was permitted, and among the negroes the Swahili one. When a Circassian woman arrived in her clothes of ample shirts, or an Abyssinian woman in her fantastic attire, within three days she had to lay aside everything and to wear the Arabic clothes assigned to her. . . . Immediately after she had been purchased, a newly arrived *surie* also received the necessary jewels as a present; at the same time the chief eunuch assigned her servants to her.[37]

This was not, of course, one big, happy family. There was a sharp distinction between the free wives, who in Arab society often came from families of equal social status (*kifaya*). Burton noted that men of pure family would not give their daughters to any but fellow clansmen, but in most families, there was rarely more than one free wife. However, men also took slave girls, and in such a situation, the free wife "[ruled] the concubines with a rod of iron."[38] This is amply corroborated by Salme's description of the only free Arab wife, Azza bt. Seif, who was "extremely imperious, haughty and pretentious" toward the other wives and their children. When Salme and her mother went to say good-bye to her "august stepmother," the woman was "pleased to dismiss us standing, an honour with her since she always remained seated when receiving or dismissing people. My mother as well as myself were permitted to bring her delicate hand to our lips before turning our back upon her forever." No suria was permitted to take meals with Seyyid Said, "no matter how favoured." He only ate with his free Arab wife and his sister Aashe. Salme does not mention the fate of the two Iranian free wives, but presumably, he ate with them as well when visiting them in their own separate palaces at Kidichi or Bayt al-Thani in the town. She adds that "this custom is so deep-rooted, that nobody considers such a separation as a personal affront."[39]

Among the sarari, who were of different nationalities, there was superficial amiability but not complete harmony. They talked, laughed, and jested in such high spirits that a stranger would not have believed they were all wives of one and the same man, often jealous about their own relations with the sultan and about the position of their children in the dynasty. According to Salme, there was also an ethnic division among them:

> Even the *sarari* introduced a classification among themselves. The beautiful and expensive Circassians, well aware of their particular value, did not want to take their meals with the coffee-coloured Abyssinians. . . . At Bet il Sahel [the town palace] there was much more luxury and grand style than at Bet il Mtoni [the country palace 5 kilometers north of the town]. The handsome and graceful Circassian women were much more numerous than at Bet il Mtoni, where my mother and her lady friend Medine were the only members of this race. Here [Bet il Sahel] the majority of the women were Circassian, who without any doubt are much more distinguished in appearance than the Abyssinians, though among the latter also quite unusual beauties are to be found. This natural superiority was the cause of a good deal of ill-will and envy. One Circassian woman, favoured with an aristocratic appearance, was avoided and even hated by the chocolate-coloured Abyssinian women through no fault of hers, but simply because she looked majestic.[40]

At one point in her autobiography, Salme protests that "separation based on the colour of the skin did not apply to children," but a couple of pages later, she states:

> Under these circumstances it was bound to happen that occasionally a kind of ridiculous "racism" broke out among my brothers and sisters. In spite of many good qualities, the Abyssinian often is of a fiery and hot-tempered character. Her passion once roused, seldom knows restraint, let alone decency.

> We, the children of the Circassian women, were usually called "cats" . . . because some of us had the misfortune of possessing: blue eyes. Derisively, they called us "Highness," a proof of how annoyed they were about us having been born with lighter skin. My father was of course never forgiven the fact that he had chosen his favourite children Sharife and Chole [Khole]—both by Circassian mothers, Sharife even being blue-eyed—from the hateful race of "cats."[41]

Shawana, daughter of an Ethiopian woman, used to call Salme "You white ape," and Salme's brother Jamshid suffered even more, for he had inherited from his blond mother not only her hair but also her blue eyes.[42]

There was also a division between the princes and princesses born and bred in more luxuriant Zanzibar and those from the more austere Oman. Salme says that the Zanzibari ones did not care much about going to Oman: "The proud Omani ladies treat those of Zanzibar as uncivilised creatures. This arrogance even prevailed among our brothers and sisters; a member of our family born in Oman felt and imagined herself particularly aristocratic vis-a-vis us 'Africans.' They are of the opinion that we, who grew up among the negroes, must also have something from them. Our greatest uncouthness, they think, is that we, (how awful!), speak another language besides Arabic."[43]

The Zanzibari princes and princesses had even taken to chewing betel nuts, which Salme says was a Swahili habit. "We, who had seen the light of the world on the East coast of Africa and had grown up with negroes and mulattoes, readily took over this habit, notwithstanding the scorn of our Arabic brothers, sisters and relatives; only we should not be caught at it by our father."[44]

However, these divisions and natural rivalries should not be overstated. In Islamic law, such distinctions between wives (and their offspring) were not recognized. When the patriarch died, all the wives of the deceased, free as well as slave, had to submit to a special religious mourning, *iddah*, which, according to Salme, lasted four months. (In fact, according to Islamic law, it lasts four months and ten days in the case of free wives and two months and five days in the case of slave wives.)[45] The wives had to mourn their husband or master in a dark room.

At the end of the period, the widows had to go through many other ceremonies, one of which required that they all wash themselves at the same time. Because of the large number of widows left by Said, this ceremony could not take place in the baths and instead had to occur on the beach. Since sarari were not entitled to inherit from their husband, all those who had children received a small amount from their deceased husband, according to Salme, because her father assumed that they would be taken care of by their children from their own inheritance, but that made these women completely dependent on their offspring. For those of his slave women who did not have any children and therefore were not strictly sarari, Said directed that they should be taken care of for life and left some plantations for that purpose.[46]

One critical test came on the death of the patriarch in 1856 and showed that the ethnic and other divisions in the family did not run deep. As mentioned earlier, when the de facto division of the kingdom between Oman and Zanzibar began to surface on the death of Seyyid Said, there was, quite naturally, strong opposition from the eldest surviving son, Thuweyny, who was in Oman. Thuweyny believed he was the rightful successor to the whole kingdom, and he was initially supported in this by Barghash in Zanzibar. Both of their mothers were Ethiopian, whereas the mother of the second-eldest son, Majid, who had been governor of Zanzibar, was Circassian. But the division was not ethnic. The strongest supporter of Barghash, who mounted a palace revolution in 1859, was Khole, whose mother was Assyrian, and she was strongly supported by Salme, whose mother was Circassian, despite the close relationship she shared with Majid. Moreover, they were supported by three brothers, Abd al-Wahab, Jamshid, and Hamdan, whose mothers were all also Circassian.[47]

Although this chapter deals primarily with secondary slave wives in the royal household in Zanzibar, the institution of the sarari was more widespread in Zanzibari society during the nineteenth century. Among the upper echelons of the landowning class, Circassian and Ethiopian sarari were more common, but poorer men also had secondary slave wives, taken from among the other tribes of slaves passing through Zanzibar. Their offspring were assimilated into the general population as free children of their free fathers, resulting in widespread miscegenation. This contrasted sharply with the situation in the American slave-owning class, in which men maintained their racial purity while the children they produced with slave women remained enslaved. Islamic law ameliorated the condition of the sarari after they entered the household, but this could not erase the trauma of capture and sale, nor did it legally provide for their upkeep through inheritance after the death of their husbands. As Princess Salme explains, this made them dependent on their children, who did inherit from their fathers. In practice, husbands, as in the case of Seyyid Said, often did leave them with some property from a third of their property, which they could dispose of as they wished, while the remaining two-thirds had to be distributed according to Islamic law among the legitimate heirs. Ultimately, though, the fate of the sarari lay in the hands of their owners, who could refuse to recognize the paternity of the children they had by their slave wives, as happened with Seyyid Barghash. It should be noted, however, that Princess Salme suggests this was a rare occurrence and considered despicable in the Islamic society.

Notes

1. *Concise Oxford Dictionary*, 7th ed. (Oxford: Clarendon Press, 1982), 195. See "Concubinage," in *Encyclopaedia Britannica*, 11th ed. (New York: Encyclopaedia Britannica, 1910–11), 6:841, for a review of the complex history of concubinage in Europe.

2. J. O. Hunwick, "Black Slaves in the Mediterranean World," in *The Human Commodity*, ed. E. Savage (London: Cass, 1992), 8.

3. W. Arafat, "The Attitude of Islam to Slavery," *Islamic Quarterly* 10 (1966): 12–18. Qur'an 2.178, 221; 4.25, 36, 92; 5.89; 9.60; 23.6; 24.33; 32.50; 47.4; 58.3; 70.30; 90.13.

4. B. Lewis, *Race and Slavery in the Middle East* (Oxford: Oxford University Press, 1990), 6–10; H. A. R. Gibb and J. H. Kramers, eds., *Shorter Encyclopaedia of Islam* (Leiden: Brill, 1961), 1–2; A. A. Mazrui, "Comparative Slavery in Islam, Africa and the West," paper presented at the Conference on Islamic Thought, Istanbul, Turkey, 1997, p. 9.

5. R. F. Burton, *Zanzibar, City, Island & Coast*, vol. 1 (London: Tinsley, 1872), 300–302, 309; Sayyida Salme/Emily Ruete, *An Arabian Princess between Two Worlds*, ed. E. van Donzel (Leiden: Brill, 1993), 154, 186.

6. The best complete translation, with a good introduction and hitherto unpublished "Letters Home," is Salme/Ruete, *Arabian Princess*, 244.

7. Sheikh Abdalla Saleh Farsi, *Seyyid Said Bin Sultan, the Joint Ruler of Oman and Zanzibar*, trans. Shaaban Saleh Farsi (New Delhi: Lancers, 1986).

8. Emily Said-Ruete, *Memoirs of an Arabian Princess*, ed. G. S. P. Freeman-Grenville (London: East-West Publication, 1994).

9. Hamerton to Foreign Office, 2.1.1844, FO 84/540, National Archives, Kew Gardens, London, UK (hereafter cited as NA).

10. Salme/Ruete, *Arabian Princess*, 271.

11. Burton, *Zanzibar*, 380.

12. Hamerton to Bombay, 29.9.1844, 1844–88/1621, 239–40, Maharashtra State Archives Political Department (hereafter cited as MSA-PD), Mumbai, India; Hamerton to Bombay, 23.4.1846, 13.6.1846—Foreign Correspondence—vol. 138, National Archives of India—Foreign Department (hereafter cited as NAI-FD), New Delhi, India; Mrs. Charles E. B. Russell, ed., *General Rigby, Zanzibar and the Slave Trade* (London: George Allen and Unwin, 1935), 80.

13. Rigby to Bombay, 1.4.1859, NAI-FD: Foreign Correspondence—vol. 20; Salme/Ruete, *Arabian Princess*, 329, 330n; Burton, *Zanzibar*, 330, 380.

14. Salme/Ruete, *Arabian Princess*, 272, 365–66, 337; Farsi, *Seyyid Said Bin Sultan*, 19, names her as the Georgian Asha, mother of Jamshid, but Salme was close to Jamshid and his mother and is probably more reliable.

15. Salme/Ruete, *Arabian Princess*, 272.

16. Oral information from Mithu, a tour guide in his eighties who said he remembered a woman selling beans who claimed to be one of the victims.

17. Salme/Ruete, *Arabian Princess*, 272; Waters' Journal I 24.5.1837, Richard P. Waters Papers, Peabody Essex Museum, Salem, Massachusetts; Hamerton to Bombay, 3.1.1842, FO 54/5, p. 269, NA.

18. A. Sheriff, *Slaves, Spices & Ivory in Zanzibar* (London: Currey, 1987), xix, 67–69. The common currency at Zanzibar at that time was the Maria Theresa thaler, also called the German or black dollar, which was roughly equivalent to the US dollar though it varied in local exchange rates. Statement of "Jafran," 6.11.1844, 1844–88/1621, pp. 239–40, MSA-PD.

19. Burton, *Zanzibar*, 309, 374–75.

20. Wilson to Norris, Bushire, 28.1.1831, 1830–2/1/385, 18–21, MAPD; Kemball's Report, 12.11.1847, FO 84/692, p.15, NA. As at Zanzibar (see note 18), the prevalent currency in the Persian Gulf was the Maria Theresa thaler.

21. Burton, *Zanzibar*, 467–68.

22. Rigby's Diary, 6.5.1859, cited in Russell, *General Rigby*, 80; Kirk to Bombay, 8.4.1871, FO 84/1344, NA.

23. Burton, *Zanzibar*, 467; Abbert to Foreign Office, 25.7.1844, FO 85/540, NA.

24. Said-Ruete, *Memoirs of an Arabian Princess*, 203; Salme/Ruete, *Arabian Princess*, 153, 250; Farsi, *Seyyid Said Bin Sultan*.

25. "Caucasia," *Encyclopaedia Britannica*, 11th ed. (New York: Encyclopaedia Britannica, 1910–11), 5:548–50; Stephen D. Shenfield, "The Circassians: A

Forgotten Genocide?" *Circassian World*, http://www.circassianworld.com; Antero Leitzinger, "The Circassian Genocide," http://www.circassianworld.com/new/war-and-genocide/1121-circassian-genocide-leitzinger.html, and http://www.circassianworld.com/new/circassians/1125-history-of-circassians.html.

26. Salme/Ruete, *Arabian Princess*, 154, 244; Burton, *Zanzibar*, 309.

27. Salme/Ruete, *Arabian Princess*, 263.

28. Ibid., 251–52.

29. Farsi, *Seyyid Said Bin Sultan*, 25; Salme/Ruete, *Arabian Princess*, 252–55. Zamzam is the proper English spelling, but in the German edition, it is spelled as Semsem.

30. Salme/Ruete, *Arabian Princess*, 179–80, 242.

31. Ibid., 177, 258–59.

32. Ibid., 167, 249–50.

33. Ibid., 244–45.

34. Ibid., 256.

35. Ibid., 152–53, 160, 166, 247, 334.

36. Ibid., 171, 245–49, 260–61; Farsi, *Seyyid Said Bin Sultan*, 23–24. Farsi seems to be wrongly attributing the mother's name as Najmus-Sabah, instead of being a praise-name of her daughter. Said-Ruete, *Memoirs of an Arabian Princess*, 204n6.25.

37. Salme/Ruete, *Arabian Princess*, 175, 156–57.

38. Burton, *Zanzibar*, 394–95.

39. Salme/Ruete, *Arabian Princess*, 154, 162, 174, 230.

40. Ibid., 174, 176.

41. Ibid., 176.

42. Ibid., 250.

43. Ibid., 230.

44. Ibid., 193.

45. Gibb and Kramers, *Shorter Encyclopedia of Islam*, 157.

46. Salme/Ruete, *Arabian Princess*, 238, 240, 242.

47. Ibid., 340, 343, 366.

5

A SEXUAL ORDER IN THE MAKING

Wives and Slaves in Early Imperial China

Griet Vankeerberghen

Under the Han dynasty (206 BCE–220 CE), a free man was expected to have sexual relations with his wife. There might also be other women in his household, including slaves,[1] whom he could use as sexual partners. Whereas we learn little about how men were to treat their women, starting in late Western Han (206 BCE–8 CE), an elaborate discourse arose that focused on the duties and demeanor of wives. Part of this discourse dealt with sexuality, from the perspective of the wife. It defined the extent of the sexual claims she might make on her husband and sought to guide her in regulating her feelings toward the other women in her household. The underlying argument of this chapter is that through this emerging discourse on wives and sexuality, a new sexual and social order was defined. This sexual order was tailored to a group of newly emerging elite families that asserted themselves on the social and political scene during the latter half of the Han dynasty (the Eastern Han dynasty, 25–220 CE).[2] That the new order was promoted as congruous with the historical practices of the ancients and the prescriptions of the classics was integral to its success. Indeed, this new sexual order so profoundly influenced family structures during subsequent imperial history that it has often been anachronistically or teleologically read into earlier periods of Han history.

Central to my analysis are three texts that deal most directly with the problem of wifely sexuality: some selected biographies from Liu Xiang's 劉向 (79–8 BCE) *Traditions on Outstanding Women* (*Lienü zhuan* 列女傳); the first eight poems of the *Odes* (*Shi* 詩) as they were read and interpreted by Han men of letters (particularly Zheng Xuan 鄭玄 [127–200]); and one chapter of Ban Zhao's 班昭 (45–114 CE) *Lessons for Women* (*Nüjie* 女誡). These texts, steeped in references to the classics, all sought to increase the dignity of the wife's position by hardening the line between her and the other women present in a man's household. In doing so, they inserted themselves as a new element into a social tapestry that was complex, one in which traditional boundaries between primary wives, various sorts of secondary wives, and slaves tended to be fluid and ill defined. In order to situate the genesis of the discourse on wifely virtue, I will first provide a sketch of how, during the Han dynasty, hierarchies of women functioned within households at various levels of the social and political hierarchy, even if doing so entails coming to terms with sources that are inherently limited, scattered, and derived from various modes of discourse.[3]

The Imperial Harem

From the establishment of the empire under Qin (221–209 BCE), China experienced major internal changes that had profound implications for women attached to the ruling court. For one, Qin unification caused a historical shift from the multicentered world of the "warring states" to a world dominated, at least in theory, by one ruler. Henceforth, the imperial palace, situated in the capital, became the main focal point for families who sought to boost their social capital by placing a daughter in the harem.[4] The histories that deal with the Han dynasty almost all contain biographies of empresses and consorts, and in them, we read not only of the social background of the women who became empresses but also of the immense struggles for access to the ruler that took place within the confines of the palace. From the very beginning, attempts were made to manage the women in the imperial palace by placing them into strict hierarchical frameworks. The histories indicate how the number of women in the imperial harem and their titles tended to proliferate with time.[5]

The initial nomenclature, however, was taken over from Qin: "Once the Han was established, it relied on the nomenclature of Qin. The Emperor's mother had the title Dowager, his grandmother that of Grand Dowager, and his main wife that of Empress. The secondary wives all had the title of Spouse. Other designations used were Beautiful Lady, Virtuous Lady, Eighth ranked, Seventh ranked, Senior Attendant, and Junior Attendant. 漢興，因秦之稱號，帝母稱皇太后，祖母稱太皇太后，適稱皇后，妾皆稱夫人。又有美人、良人、八子、七子、長使、少使之號焉。"[6] It was an explicitly polygamous system. The primary wife of the emperor, due to her position at the apex of a hierarchical system in the imperial harem, enjoyed a special title—*di* 適 or 嫡, "empress"—and some special privileges. However, these distinctions separated her little from the secondary wives (*qie* 妾), who were also designated as "spouses" (*furen* 夫人). Indeed, although ritual rules theoretically prohibited inverting the hierarchy of wives, historical evidence shows that, if called upon, a secondary wife could replace the incumbent empress. Best documented is the case of Empress Lü 呂 (d. 180 BCE), who, despite having stood with her husband in the long struggles to establish the Han dynasty, had to resort to extraordinary cruelty in order to withstand challenges to her position from other palace ladies.[7] Zhao Feiyan 趙飛燕, a slave girl who became Emperor Cheng's 成 (r. 33–7 BCE) empress, is often referred to as an example of a woman who used her sexual powers to rise to the highest rank, in the process crushing many of her rivals.[8]

The *Han shu* passage quoted in the preceding paragraph uses "secondary wife" (*qie*) to designate women in the harem who were spouses (*furen*) but not the main wife (*di*) or empress (*huanghou*). It is noteworthy that the usage of the term *qie* in the *Han shu* is very far removed from its usage in later imperial times, when it is commonly translated as "concubine." In later imperial China, a concubine was a woman who was purchased explicitly to provide sexual services to a man and had a kinship status sharply distinguished from that of a wife (*qi* 妻).[9] This is enshrined in the Tang dynasty (617–907) legal code, where the commentary (*shu* 疏) draws a clear line between wives, who stood on a par with their husbands, and concubines, who were acquired via commercial transactions: "The wife is an equal [of her husband] just as the [preimperial] states of Qin and Jin were equals. Concubines are bought or sold and hence have a status very different from that of the wife 妻者，齊也，秦晉┌匹。妾通賣買，等數相懸。"[10] The Tang code banned the taking of more than one wife, thereby explicitly defining marriage as monogamous and establishing a firm legal barrier between the one wife and the concubines beneath her, with the apparent aim of safeguarding the position of the wife.[11] Perhaps the difference between the arrangements prevailing within the emperor's household in early imperial times and the way in which the Tang code sought to regulate the relative positions of women in households under the jurisdiction of the Tang state can best be characterized as one of hierarchical polygamy versus polygynous monogamy.

This chapter postulates that the new discourse on wives that gained prominence in Eastern Han had a role in preparing the ground for this semantic shift in the word *qie*, as well as the accompanying hardening of the legal divide between the primary wife and other women in an elite household. Starting in late Western Han (206 BCE–8 CE), elite men and women developed a classicizing discourse on wifely behavior that, over time, lowered the status of the wife's household competitors into that of persons acquired through "buying and selling." This view presupposes that during the Han dynasty, the divide between primary and secondary wives, even though articulated, was not as wide as hitherto assumed, and it challenges the conventional view that households were monogamous from the start of the imperial period.[12]

Rulers and Ruled

The hierarchical polygamy of the imperial palace extended, through a layered distribution of sumptuary privileges, to other members of the ruling group, especially to kings (*wang* 王) and nobles (*liehou* 列侯). Kings and nobles were at the apex of a state-orchestrated social ranking system, and they were the only ones to receive land in addition to their noble titles, on a hereditary basis.[13] The bamboo strips with legal texts recovered from Zhangjiashan Tomb 247 (hereafter referred to as *ZJS*), dated to early Western Han, stipulate what ranks of females the kings and nobles were allowed to maintain in their harems:[14] "The kings (*zhuhouwang*) are allowed to establish secondary wives[15] at the following ranks: Eighth ranked ladies, Dear Lady, Virtuous Lady. 諸侯王得置姬八子、孺子、良人。Nobles are allowed to establish Dear ladies and Virtuous ladies. 徹侯得

置孺子、良人。" The histories provide ample confirmation of the existence of such harems, including accounts of disputes and intrigues involving queens (*hou* 后 or *wanghou* 王后) and their rivals that mirrored those taking place within the imperial household.[16] Apparently, there was even a measure of rivalry between the emperor's harem and those of his kings. Whereas women from the imperial harem were allowed to remarry, they were explicitly forbidden from marrying into a royal household.[17] The concern that sexual partners not be transferred between agnates—indeed, after 195 BCE, the kings (with only one exception) were members of the Liu imperial patriline—seems to have prevailed widely.[18]

Also below the rank of kings and marquises, people found their places in a carefully graded hierarchy, with different levels of privilege and obligation. The lowest layer of the population was made up of commoners (*shuren* 庶人), slaves, and convicts. Above them came a large group of households whose male heads were ranked within twenty orders of merit, ranks that brought various hereditary privileges, including grants of land and dwellings, as well as the right to commute sentences for crimes.[19] The *ZJS* strips demonstrate that men who held such hereditary ranks were legally permitted to maintain multiple wives. Indeed, the strips indicate that whereas sons of first wives generally inherited their fathers' rank, should the first wife not produce a male heir, the sons of "lower wives" (*xia qi* 下妻) or "side-wives" (*pianqi* 偏妻) could inherit their fathers' titles.[20]

We are poorly informed as to the precise meaning of the terms *lower wives* and *side-wives* and how these categories are distinguished from those of *lesser wives* (*xiao qi* 小妻) and *dependent wives* (*bangqi* 傍妻)—terms that occur with some frequency in the histories of the Han period.[21] Brett Hinsch takes the existence of such terms as pejorative and hence indicative of the monogamous sentiments reigning in the Han dynasty.[22] I argue exactly the opposite: the fact that the term *qi* (wife) was used at all indicates that the women so designated were spouses too and could, potentially, challenge the status of the main wife, who was only a *prima inter pares*. The fact that lesser wives could come from privileged social and economic backgrounds confirms that, from the perspective of the main wife, the secondary wives were indeed forces to be reckoned with, not concubines relegated to an inferior social status.[23]

That the *ZJS* strips make provisions for secondary wives does not prove the ubiquity of households with multiple wives, a phenomenon that was most likely confined to the highest social and economic tiers. Indeed, estimates that the average Han household comprised five individuals indicate that polygamy was limited. Population and land records that archaeologists have discovered at various sites confirm this.[24]

Sex and Slaves

Households in the early imperial period also counted slave women (*bi* 婢) among their adult female members. These servile domestics, such as "the low-ranking female slave Quan from Household XX. Measures 6 feet. XX戶下婢泉長六尺," or "the low-ranking female slave X from the Zheng household. Age 27. 鄭戶下婢X年廿七,"[25] both listed in the Zoumalou records, served the households under which they were registered by performing a wide range of menial tasks.[26] However, male heads of households could, if they so wished, demand sexual services from their slaves. This is made clear in several of the *ZJS* legal strips. *ZJS* 188 tells us that when a master fornicates with his slave, any children that result from such relations will belong to him even if the slave is the wife of a slave from another household. This shows the sexual power of heads of households over their female slaves and over male slaves (*nu* 奴) as well. Male slaves did not enjoy the protection free men enjoyed against the sexual predation on their women by other men.[27]

Moreover, strip *ZJS* 195 indicates that a female slave who has children with her master will be manumitted and made a commoner after her master's death, a rule that would have encouraged female slaves to seek the sexual attention of their masters. With gender roles reversed, the legal rules are very different. *ZJS* 190 forbids, on the pain of death, a male slave fornicating with or taking as his wife either his (female) master or the mother, wife, or daughter of his (male) master.[28] This legal rule seems designed to prevent the male slave in either a female- or male-headed household from attempting to use sexual relations to promote his status. Strip *ZJS* 190 is particularly interesting because it distinguishes little between the "fornication" (*jian* 姦) of a male slave with his owner's relatives or his mistress, on the one hand, and his "taking her as wife" (*yi wei qi* 以為妻)," on the other. Indeed, the rule rather laconically enumerates both possibilities and stipulates the same punishment for them. This begs the question of whether the law, since it entitles female slaves to have sex with their male masters, would consider those who did so as also entering into the qualitative equivalent of a marriage arrangement. If so, this would further underline the fragile position of the main wife.

In Han times, there was also mention of "pleasure slaves" (*yubi* 御婢), female slaves whose main task was to provide entertainment and sexual gratification to their masters. The histories only mention them in passing, when they discuss the cases of kings or marquises convicted and punished for sleeping with their fathers' pleasure slaves.[29] The *ZJS* legal strips, however, indicate clearly that by the early imperial period, ownership of pleasure slaves had expanded outside royal circles and that these slaves had become a common feature of elite households. *ZJS* 195 outlines severe punishments for men who "requit" (*fu* 復) the wives or pleasure slaves of a close male agnate: a brother, paternal uncle, nephew, or cousin.[30] (Interestingly, this list does not include fathers.) What is striking about the legal prescriptions of the time, certainly as compared to later legislation, is that the punishment for sleeping with the agnate's wife or his pleasure slave is the same: what seems to count is the agnate's exclusive claim on her. By contrast, the Tang legal code punished a man two degrees less severely for sexual intercourse with a maid/slave who was sexually favored by his father or paternal grandfather (*jian fuzu suo xing bi* 姦父祖所幸婢) than for sleeping with an agnate's concubine (*qie* 妾) or legal wife, indicating that the status of women in a man's household was far more regulated by that time.[31] *ZJS* 195 again confirms that the existence of sexual relations between a man and a woman in his household influenced that woman's status even if she was a slave, as it made her part of the group of women sexually unavailable to male agnates. That wives and pleasure slaves belonged, from the perspective of this rule, to the same group and that sexual transgressions by or against wives and pleasure slaves were punished with the same degree of severity reflects the lack of sharp lines of division between the various women in a household.

The sexual relationship between a master and his slaves did not necessarily end at the time of the male head of household's death. In some cases, as scattered textual and archaeological evidence for the Han period and beyond attests, slaves were buried with their masters, with the express purpose of providing the latter with sexual pleasure into the afterlife.[32]

Arguing through the *Odes*: The Views of Liu Xiang and Zheng Xuan on the Ideal Consort

A clear wind of change arose around the end of the Western Han period, as the classics increasingly were invoked in political life and as wealthy families accumulated more and more of the land.[33] This shift, interestingly, coincided with the appearance in the written records of an ever more elaborate discourse on wifely virtue. With elite intermarriage on the rise, this discourse should be seen as part of a concerted effort on their behalf to draw a more sharply defined line between a male head of household's first wife and the other women in his household.[34] The classical texts (especially the *Odes* and the *Rites*) and historical precedents from the preimperial era, both of which were central to elite education, played a pivotal role in delineating the responsibilities—including sexual ones—of the new wife.[35]

This discourse on wives, dating as it does to the late Western Han and Eastern Han periods, can be analyzed from a variety of perspectives.[36] Here, I focus on those features of the virtuous wife that are central to her relationship with the other women in her household who are entitled to a sexual relationship with her husband and hence are potential mothers to his children. One key requirement the texts articulate in this regard has to do with jealousy: not only should the wife be above jealousy herself, she should also manage the other women in such a way that jealousies among them remain contained.

Liu Xiang, renowned as an imperial bibliographer but a driven author and memorial writer in his own right, wrote his *Traditions on Outstanding Women* with the explicit purpose of admonishing the emperor for having overstepped the ritual rules (*li zhi* 禮制) by promoting women of an unsuitably low background within the harem.[37] To instruct the emperor on how to make more judicious decisions regarding his harem, Liu Xiang paraded throughout his text exemplary women of the past and present. Thus, Fan Ji 樊姬, wife of King Zhuang of Chu 楚莊王 (r. 613–591), who actively scouted for beauties to serve her husband, earned Liu Xiang's praise for her lack of jealousy (*mi you jidu* 靡有嫉妒).[38] Another example he chose was Zhao Ji 趙姬, a daughter of Lord Wen 文公 (r. 636–628) of Jin 晉, who became the wife of her father's good friend Zhao Shuai 趙衰. Before her father became Lord Wen, he and Zhao Shuai had been exiled from Jin and taken wives among the non-Chinese Di 狄; Zhao Shuai had fathered a son with his non-Chinese wife. Years later, Zhao Ji took the extraordinary step of inviting her husband's "barbarian" wife and son to join her household and insisting on the son's right of primogeniture over her own three sons, thus effectively reducing her own status to that of secondary wife (*pianfang* 偏房). Zhao Ji wins much praise from Liu Xiang for yielding to the birthright of her husband's eldest son and for doing so without the slightest trace of jealousy (*bu du* 不妒).[39] Similarly, Youshen 有莘, consort (*fei* 妃) of Tang 湯, the legendary first ruler of the Shang 商 dynasty, is praised for her lack of jealousy and for her ability "to harmonize the many secondary wives (*hehao zhong qie* 和好眾妾)" in her husband's harem. Liu Xiang links Youshen's story with "Fishhawk" (*Guanju* 關雎), the first poem in the *Odes* (*Shi* 詩), by stating that one of the poem's lines—"Gentle maiden, pure and fair, fit pair for a prince 窈窕淑女。君子好逑"—is applicable to her situation, thus establishing, perhaps for the first time, an association between "Fishhawk" and the consort's skillful management of jealousy.

This association became prominent in the so-called Mao 毛 reading and interpretation of the *Odes*, where a similar reading was extended to the first eight poems of the *Odes* collection. We find this reading in the *Prefaces* (*Xu* 序) and *Commentaries* (*Zhuan* 傳) appended to the Mao version of the *Odes*, as well as in the *Notes* (*Jian* 箋) added to the Mao interpretative apparatus by the classical master Zheng Xuan (127–200).[40] In a general way, the *Prefaces*, *Commentaries*, and *Notes* use the natural and other images invoked in the eight poems—solitary ospreys, thick-growing plantains, trees with drooping boughs, grasshoppers indiscriminate in their mating behavior, nights made sleepless by sexual longing—to paint an image of the aspirations, behavior, and achievements of the ideal consort.

The Mao-Zheng exegesis of "Fishhawk" adds specifics to Liu Xiang's prescription that the virtuous consort should "harmonize" her husband's "multiple secondary wives." First, in order to make conjugal relations harmonious ("no dissonant" *wu bu hexie* 無不和諧), the consort needed to observe proper distinctions between husband and wife (*fufu you bie* 夫

婦有別) and refrain from displaying her sexual charms in his presence (*bu yin qi se* 不淫其色). Second, she needed to be actively engaged in the search for "talented maidens" (*xian nü* 賢女) to join her husband's harem, to the point that she should be consumed by an overwhelming desire to find suitable candidates. Tremendous pleasure was bound to arrive (樂必作) once she had recruited these women and they worked together to, for example, gather the plantain needed for ancestral sacrifices; she and they would become attuned to one another like lutes and zithers (*qi qingyi nai yu qinse zhi zhi tong* 其情意乃與琴瑟之志同). Under the consort's able guidance, the exegetes add, the various female assistants would, instead of harboring jealousies (*jidu* 嫉妒), rejoice in what the consort delighted in (*le houfei zhi le* 樂后妃之樂). In sum, according to the Mao-Zheng exegetes, "Fishhawk" asks the consort not only to voluntarily renounce an openly intimate and sexual relation with her husband but also to serve as the moral and ritual leader of the females of the household.[41]

The exegesis of *Ode* #4, "Tree with Drooping Boughs" (*jiumu* 樛木), returns to the consort's duty to attract other women to her husband's household and manage them so that no jealousies arise, in order to create the greatest possible pleasure and happiness for the lord (其君子) they are all serving. These other women are designated in the preface of "Drooping Boughs" as "those below" (*xia* 下).[42] The exegesis of *Ode* #8, "Plantain" (*fuyi* 芣苢), stresses how once household peace and harmony reign, the wives (*furen* 婦人) will delight in bearing sons to ensure that their lord has appropriate heirs.[43] The exegesis to *Ode* #5, "Locusts" (*zhongshi* 螽斯), also stresses that the consort should allow her husband to father children with his other wives. According to a telling note composed by Zheng Xuan, the locust, alone among sentient living beings, does not experience jealousy, so that "all can receive [the reproductive] *qi* and produce offspring (*ge de shou qi er sheng zi* 各得受氣而生子)." It would be appropriate for the consort, he adds, to do like the locust.[44]

Zheng Xuan's note on the locust clearly indicates an awareness that he and other exegetes required the consort to counter her natural inclinations, as she frees herself of jealousies, tones down her own sexuality, and actively finds and manages other women for her husband. Such behavior was of obvious benefit to her husband, but the consort was offered much in return: recognition, sanctioned by the classics, of her virtue and, perhaps, an admission that such exceptional, almost counternatural virtue would set her off from "those below" as a leader.

It is highly significant that the opposition voiced to this interpretation of the first eight *Odes* came from two women. The first was a fourth-century wife featured in Yu Tongzhi 虞通志's *On Jealousy* (*Duji* 妬記), a text, now only preserved in fragments, that dates to the fifth century. When Xie An 謝安 (320–385), a famous lover of women, desired "to establish female entertainers and secondary wives *li ji qie* 立妓妾," his cousins tried to help him persuade his wife, Lady Liu 劉, that this was an appropriate move: "Fishhawk" and "Locusts," they claimed, were all about the importance of conquering jealousy. After inducing the cousins to state the obvious, that is, that the Duke of Zhou, the presumed author of the *Odes*, was a man, Lady Liu retorted that had the wife of the Duke of Zhou written the *Odes*, "they would not have contained such words (*wu ci yu* 無此語)."[45] This story shows the success of the Mao-Zheng exegesis—indeed, instead of proposing an alternative explanation, Lady Liu read the interpretation in the words of the *Odes* themselves and subsequently had no choice but to attack the *Odes* as such as insensitive to women; it also shows that individual women sometimes resisted the demands placed upon them by society and did so in explicitly gendered terms.

The other voice of resistance is that of Ban Zhao who, unlike Lady Liu, did not reject the *Odes* altogether but preferred an alternative explanation of the poems. Citing *Ode* #4, "Tree with Drooping Boughs," in a comment to her brother's work, she proposed that the poem provides a generalized image of peace and joy (*an le zhi xiang* 安樂之象).[46] The fact that she failed to mention the Mao-Zheng exegesis's understanding that these lines described the efforts of the virtuous lady in attracting subordinate wives for her husband amounted to a rejection of that tradition's elevation of absence of jealousy as the essence of wifely virtue.

Ban Zhao's *Lessons for Women*

In one scholar's words, Ban Zhao's *Lessons for Women* "defines familial roles for men as well as for women in domestic spaces conceived as courts writ small."[47] In the *Lessons*, Ban Zhao outlined those virtues and behaviors she thought would be most conducive to a family's reputation and hence its success in the world; sometimes, she packed controversial messages, such as a strong plea for female education, within passages that ostensibly deliver an entirely conventional message—that husbands should control their wives and wives should serve their husbands.[48]

The *Lessons* provides other candid advice on how to handle various potentially troublesome relationships within the extended family, including those with one's parents-in-law and with the wives of one's husband's siblings. Strikingly, the *Lessons* does not overtly discuss the wife's relation to her husband's other women. Moreover, in a striking contrast with later tracts written in emulation of Ban Zhao's text, it never mentions the absence of jealousy as a female virtue.[49] This silence might well be a studied one, designed, like her reading of the "Tree with Drooping Boughs," to show Ban Zhao's discomfort with the way male colleagues touted this allegedly unnatural virtue.

However, the reader is forced to ask how, in a text ostensibly addressed to daughters of the elite, Ban Zhao can fail to mention the other women with whom they will almost inevitably share their domestic space. According to my reading, Ban Zhao does mention them in the third section of the *Lessons*, "Respect and Caution (*Jingshen* 敬慎)," but she does this so discreetly that her discourse is merely audible. Indeed, the standard translation of the *Lessons* fails to capture her whispered words.

"Respect and Caution" is an intricately composed whole, in which an introductory paragraph is followed by two intertwined chain reasonings (*sorites*)—henceforth, A and B—brought together in a concluding paragraph. For the sake of clarity, I provide a full translation of the chapter here, with A underlined and B italicized:

> Yin and yang are different by nature, men and woman different in their behavior. Yang derives its power from what is hard, whereas yin uses what is soft; men take pride in strength, whereas women find beauty in what is weak. Therefore a common saying states: "Even if a newborn boy is like a wolf, one still fears that he will grow up to be a weakling; even if a newborn girl is like a mouse, one still fears that she will grow up to be a tiger."
>
> <u>Hence, in terms of self-cultivation, respect is what is most important;</u> *to avoid being associated with strength, conformity is crucial.* <u>Now respect comes down to maintaining one's position</u>

> for long, *whereas conformity equals tolerance.* Maintaining one's position for long means knowing where to stop; *as to tolerance, nothing is more important than to respect those below.*
>
> If husband and wife are attracted to one another, they never leave each other's side. What should be confined to the bedroom spreads all around, and excessive intimacy arises. When there is excessive intimacy, exaggerated speech follows. Exaggerated speech, without fail, leads to unrestrained behavior. Unrestrained behavior, in turn, will lead to the wife's contempt for her husband. This all results from not knowing where to stop.
>
> *Now all affairs and all words are both right and wrong. If one cannot avoid fighting for what one believes is right, and one cannot resist reprimanding what one considers to be wrongdoing, anger will result. This all results from not respecting those below.*
>
> However, if she is unable to suppress her contempt for her husband, accusations will fly; *and if she is unable to regulate her anger, there will be beatings.*
>
> When it comes to husband and wife, their duty lies in bringing harmony to the family, and their kindness should bring unity. *When there are beatings, how can this duty be fulfilled?* When accusations fly, how can there be kindness? With kindness and duty destroyed, husband and wife will be divided.

The rhetorical key to the chapter lies in the statement "Even if a newborn boy is like a wolf, one still fears that he will grow up to be a weakling; even if a newborn girl is like a mouse, one still fears that she will grow up to be a tiger." In other words, Ban Zhao raises the possibility that the traditional roles of males and females may be reversed. She then goes on to show, in the remainder of the chapter, that this gender reversal may be caused by the wife's lack of restraint toward her husband and the other women in the household, and she concludes that in such a case, the harmony and unity that a good wife ought to bring to the household will be irretrievably lost.

Chain A describes the process by which a wife can turn her husband into a weakling, whereas chain B describes how she can turn herself into a tiger. As to the first, if she promotes too much intimacy between herself and her husband, her husband will, both in word and deed, become a slave to his passions and come across to the world as weak and unmanly. A crucial injunction is that a wife should "maintain her position for long." Indeed, if she bases her powers over her husband on sexual attraction, her position is bound to be challenged soon by other women; also, she will fall prey to a variety of feelings—including, presumably, jealousy—that will make it impossible for her to maintain her respect for her husband, and she will blame him for her unhappy feelings.

How does a wife turn herself into a tiger? In chain B, the crucial phrase is the need to respect "those below" (*xia* 下), which, curiously, Nancy Swann leaves untranslated but which I believe refers to the other household women, that is, female slaves and secondary wives. Here, the danger is that the wife might become violent toward the women ranked beneath her and thus assume for herself a strength that is properly that of men.[50] Such violence arises where a wife fails to show an appropriate measure of moral tolerance and endlessly faults the other women of the household regardless of what they say or do. (Chain B can be taken to refer to both the household tasks for which the wife is ultimately responsible and the various love affairs between the husband and women of the household.) In other words, she needs to act as the moral leader and be conciliatory rather than vengeful.

Ban Zhao's "Respect and Caution" effectively transposes the values the *Odes* exegetes attributed to the virtuous consorts of China's golden age to the domestic setting of an Eastern Han elite household. However, whatever the similarities in content, Ban Zhao's choice of vocabulary is strikingly different from that of the male authors we encountered. Rather than reveling in descriptions of the joys of the polygynous household and promoting nonjealousy as a female virtue, she talks about jealousy without bringing up the term, and she brings her message of nonviolence toward the secondary women in the household by referring to them obliquely as "those below." Hers seems to be a message that, though also preaching sexual and emotional aloofness in the face of domestic competition, is deliberately more muted in tone.

We know little about the sexual order that prevailed in most households of the early imperial period that were wealthy enough to boast secondary wives and/or slaves. There was a clear term to legally designate a man's primary wife (*di*), but this title might not have meant much more than that her son was first in line to inherit his father's title. The scattered evidence available to us suggests that the hierarchical distinctions between primary wives, secondary wives, and slaves were legally less defined and perhaps also less meaningful in the actual lives of families than during later periods. The ties between couples were also less firm, with divorces, including those initiated by the wife, being common occurrences.

The *Odes* exegetes and Ban Zhao, in contrast, draw a sharp line between the primary wife and those beneath her, and they posit unbreakable ties between a wife and her affines. The distinction they envision between a primary wife and those beneath her is couched in moral terms: the wife is one who excels in the wifely virtues. However, as possession of the wifely virtues was intimately tied to a classical education, a privilege of elite families, it also became a marker of social status. In the absence of a strong legal framework to support a distinction between primary and secondary wives, placing the primary wife on a moral pedestal would, indeed, have been an effective way for elite families to assure that the marriage ties they developed with one another were not threatened by the arrival, in the households of their sons and daughters, of women with superior sexual allure but unsuitable social background.

Did this then lead to the polygynous monogamy encapsulated in the Tang legal code? Much legal, social, and ethnic history, including that of the centuries of division separating Han and Tang, would need to be surveyed in order to substantiate and nuance that claim. However, that the Tang code, in contrast to the Han legal strips uncovered so far, explicitly sought to wed its regulations to the text of the classics may indicate that the new discourse on elite wives, which drew inspiration from those same classics, was of considerable importance for setting the stage for the changes at the heart of the family in the centuries to follow.

Notes

1. I am not using the word *slave* in an analytically rigorous way. The Chinese terms are *bi* 婢 (for females) and *nu* 奴 (for males), and they are often—especially for later periods—translated as "maid" or "servant." On slavery in early China, see C. Martin Wilbur, *Slavery in China during the Former Han Dynasty, 206 B.C.–A.D. 25* (Chicago: Field Museum of Natural History, 1943), and

Robin D. S. Yates, "Slavery in Early China: A Socio-cultural Approach," *Journal of East Asian Archaeology* 3, no. 1–2 (2001): 283–331.

2. Patricia B. Ebrey, "The Economic and Social History of Later Han," in *Cambridge History of China*, vol. 1, *The Ch'in and Han Empires, 221 B.C.–A.D. 220*, ed. Denis Twitchett and Michael Loewe (Cambridge: Cambridge University Press, 1986), 608–48; Han-huang Mao, "The Evolution and Nature of the sMedieval Genteel Families," in *State and Society in Early Medieval China*, ed. Albert Dien (Stanford, Calif.: Stanford University Press, 1990), 73–109; Xudong Hou, "Rethinking Kinship in the Han and the Six Dynasties: A Preliminary Observation," *Asia Major Third Series* 23, no.1 (2010): 29–63.

3. For a general overview on family and kinship in the Han period, see Michael Nylan, "Administration of the Family," in *China's Early Empires: A Re-appraisal*, ed. Michael Nylan and Michael Loewe (Cambridge: Cambridge University Press, 2010), 266–95; Mark E. Lewis, *The Construction of Space in Early China* (Albany: State University of New York Press, 2006), 73–133.

4. Anne B. Kinney, *Representations of Childhood and Youth in Early China* (Stanford, Calif.: Stanford University Press, 2004), 119–31.

5. Hans Bielenstein, *The Bureaucracy of Han Times* (Cambridge: Cambridge University Press, 1980), 73–74.

6. *Han shu* 漢書 (Beijing: Zhonghua, 1962), 97A.3935.

7. Michael Nylan, "Golden Spindles and Axes: Elite Women in the Achaemenid and Han Empires," in *Early China/Ancient Greece: Thinking through Comparisons*, ed. Steven Shankman and Stephen W. Durrant (Albany: State University of New York Press, 2002), 251–81; Hans van Ess, "Praise and Slander: The Evocation of Empress Lü in the *Shiji* and the *Hanshu*," *Nan nü* 8, no. 2 (2006): 221–54.

8. Michael Loewe, *A Biographical Dictionary of the Qin, Former Han and Xin Periods (221 BC–AD 24)* (Leiden, the Netherlands: Brill, 2000), 704.

9. Patricia B. Ebrey, "Concubines in Song China," *Journal of Family History* 11, no. 1 (1986): 1–24.

10. *Tang lü shuyi* 唐律疏議 (Beijing: Zhonghua, 1993), 256–57 (art. 178); Wallace S. Johnson, trans., *The T'ang Code: Specific Articles* (Princeton, N.J.: Princeton University Press, 1997), 155–56.

11. *Tang lü shuyi*, 255 (art. 177); Johnson, *T'ang Code*, 154–55.

12. Thatcher contrasts the Spring and Autumn period (771–481 BCE) to the imperial period generally; see Melvin Thatcher, "Marriages of the Ruling Elite in the Spring and Autumn Period," in *Marriage and Inequality in Chinese Society*, ed. Rubie S. Watson and Patricial Buckley Ebrey (Berkeley: University of California Press, 1991), 29; Brett Hinsch, *Women in Early Imperial China* (Lanham, Md.: Rowman and Littlefield, 2002), 38–39; T'ung-tsu Ch'ü, *Han Social Structure* (Seattle: University of Washington Press, 1972), 46 (but less affirmative on p. 44).

13. Michael Loewe, "Social Distinctions, Groups and Privileges," in *China's Early Empires: A Re-appraisal*, ed. Michael Nylan and Loewe (Cambridge: Cambridge University Press, 2010), 296–307.

14. *ZJS* 221–222, in *Zhangjiashan Hanmu zhujian (ershiqi hao mu)* 張家山漢墓竹簡（二四七號墓）(Beijing: Wenwu, 2001), 163.

15. The term used here is *ji* 姬, not *qie*, but I consider them to be equivalent.

16. For a good example, see the biography of the king of Hengshan, *Shi ji* 史記 (Beijing: Zhonghua, 1959), 18.3095–96; also see *Han shu* 44.2153–55.

17. *Hou Han shu* 後漢書 (Beijing: Zhonghua, 1965), 50.1672.

18. In contrast, there was no taboo on sisters and cousins forming part of the same man's set of wives. See Thatcher, "Marriages of the Ruling Elite," 29–35, and Marcel Granet, *La polygynie sororale et le sororat dans la Chine féodale* (Paris: E. Leroux, 1920).

19. For the view that these ranks "were held on a much wider basis than had been realized," see Loewe, "Social Distinctions," 298.

20. *ZJS* 367–68, in *Zhangjiashan Han mu zhujian*, 182–83; often, the rank was diminished in the transfer from father to son.

21. Wang Zijin 王子今, "'Pianqi' 'xiaqi' kao: Zhangjiashan Han jian ernian lüling yandu zhaji "偏妻" "下妻"考: 張家山漢簡《二年律令》研讀札記," in *Huaxue* 華學 6 (2003): 147–54.

22. Hinsch, *Women in Early Imperial China*, 39. Many translations, including those in Ch'ü, *Han Social Structure*, render all these terms as "concubines," thus obfuscating meaningful historical difference.

23. Ch'ü, *Han Social Structure*, 45–46, cites two cases of daughters of good family becoming "lesser wives"; *Hanshu* 93.3731, *Hou Hanshu* 23.795.

24. Loewe gives 5.2 people as the average family size in Donghai commandery ca. 10 BCE; see Michael Loewe, *The Government of the Qin and Han Empires, 221 BCE–220 CE* (Indianapolis, Ind.: Hackett, 2006), 143. According to Yu Zhenbo 于振波, who studied the Zoumalou population records, household size varied from 1 to 21 members, with the vast majority of households surveyed containing between 3 and 5 members; see Zhenbo Yu, *Zoumalou Wujian chutan* 走馬樓吳簡初探 (Taipei: Wenjin, 2004), 143–48; for the Juyan materials, see Ch'ü, *Han Social Structure*, 44.

25. Note that these female slaves have personal names, just as the wives do.

26. Zoumalou strips 4148 and 5307, in *Zoumalou sanguo wujian: Jiahe limintianjia bie* 走馬樓三國吳簡．嘉禾吏民田家莂, http://rhorse.lib.cuhk.edu.hk/basisbwdocs/rhorse/rhr_intro.html.

27. *ZJS* 188, in *Zhangjiashan Han mu zhujian*, 158.

28. *ZJS* 190, in ibid.

29. For examples, see *Shi ji* 18.884, 95.2666–67, 118.3097; *Han shu* 16.533 and 44.2156;see also Ch'ü, *Han Social Structure*, 274–75n114.

30. *ZJS* 195, in *Zhangjiashan Han mu zhujian*, 159.

31. *Tang lü shuyi* 494–95 (art. 413), Johnson, *Tang Code*, 475–76; Ch'ü, *Han Social Structure*, 274–75n11.

32. For examples, see Stephen R. Bokenkamp, *Ancestors and Anxiety: Daoism and the Birth of Rebirth in China* (Berkeley: University of California Press, 2007), 79, and *Li ji zhuzi suoyin* 禮記逐字索引 *(A Concordance to the Li ji)*, ICS Ancient Chinese Texts Series (Hong Kong: Shangwu, 1992), 4.38/26/23–24. A Han royal tomb at Shizishan 獅子山 near Xuzhou contained the remains of one twenty-eight-year-old woman in a side chamber of the king's tomb complex. For a general treatise on human sacrifice in China, see Zhanyue Huang 黃展岳, *Gudai rensheng renxun tonglun* 古代人牲人殉通論 (Beijing: Wenwu, 2004).

33. On the so-called classical turn in late Western Han, see Michael Nylan, "Classics without Canonization, Reflections on Classical Learning and Authority in Qin (221–210 BC) and Han (206 BC–AD 220)," in *Early Chinese Religion*, pt. 1, *Shang through Han (1250 BC–AD 220)*, ed. John Lagerwey and Marc Kalinowski (Leiden, the Netherlands: Brill, 2008), 721–77.

34. See Nylan, "Administration of the Family," figs. 10.3a–b.

35. Michael Nylan, "The Art of Persuasion from 100 BCE to 100 CE," in *China's Early Empires: A Re-appraisal*, ed. Michael Nylan and Michael Loewe (Cambridge: Cambridge University Press, 2010), 501–3.

36. Lisa Raphals, *Sharing the Light: Representations of Women and Virtue in Early China* (Albany: State University of New York Press, 1998).

37. *Han shu* 36.1957–8; the women explicitly named include the aforementioned Zhao Feiyan.

38. Jing Zhang 張敬, *Lienü zhuan jin zhu jin yi* 列女傳今注今譯 (Taipei: Zhonghua, 1994), 59–61.

39. Ibid., 67–68.

40. Steven Van Zoeren, *Poetry and Personality: Reading, Exegesis, and Hermeneutics in Traditional China* (Stanford, Calif.: Stanford University Press, 1991), 80–115; Mark L. Asselin, "The Lu-School Reading of 'Guanju' as Preserved in an Eastern Han *Fu*," *Journal of the American Oriental Society* 117, no. 3 (1997): 427–43.

41. *Shisanjing zhushu fujiao kanji* 十三經注疏附校勘記 (Beijing: Zhonghua, 1996), 273–74.

42. Ibid., 278c–279a.

43. Ibid., 281b–c. Fuyi is a plant long recognized for its benefits in facilitating pregnancy and birth; see Robin D. S. Yates, "Medicine for Women in Early China: A Preliminary Survey," *Nan nü* 7, no. 2 (2005): 127–81.

44. *Shisanjing zhushu fujiao kanji*, 279a–b.

45. *Taiping yulan* 太平御覽, in *Wenyuange siku quanshu dianzi ban* 文淵閣四庫全書電子版, 521.9b; Wilt Idema and Beata Grant, *The Red Brush: Writing Women of Imperial China* (Cambridge, Mass.: Harvard University Center, Harvard University Press, 2004), 140.

46. Xianqian Wang 王先謙, *Shi sanjia yi jishu* 詩三家義集疏 (Beijing: Zhonghua, 1987), 32.

47. Nylan, "Art of Persuasion," 501.

48. Ibid., 501–3; for the text of the *Lessons*, see *Hou Hanshu* 84.2786–92; for the standard translation, see Nancy Lee Swann, *Pan Chao: Foremost Woman Scholar of China*, Michigan Classics in Chinese Studies 5 (1932; repr., Ann Arbor: Center for Chinese Studies of the University of Michigan, 2001), 82–90.

49. Chia-lien Pao Tao, "Women and Jealousy in Traditional China," in *Zhongguo jinshi shehui wenhua shilun wenji* (Taipei: Institute of History and Philology, Academia Sinica, 1992).

50. A commentary to *Hou Hanshu* preserves a letter by Feng Yan 馮衍 to his brother-in-law in which Feng Yan justifies his decision to send his wife back home. The letter cites the wife's jealousy of and violence toward the family's maid/slave as the most important reason for the divorce. Elements in the letter suggest that Feng Yan had a sexual relationship with the maid; *Hou Hanshu* 28B.1003–4.

6

"TO MARRY ONE'S SLAVE IS AS EASY AS EATING A MEAL"

The Dynamics of Carnal Relations within Saharan Slavery

E. ANN MCDOUGALL

"To marry one's slave is as easy as eating a meal." The elderly informant who shared this thought with me in Atar, Mauritania, some twenty-five years ago contextualized it further: "Yes," he said, "[masters] marrying female slaves happens frequently. Islam only permits four wives. But to marry one's slave is easy; it is like eating a meal. On this, the Qur'an is clear."[1] On first reading, this would seem a strong statement of a Muslim master's power vis-à-vis his female slave, as well as an implicit reference to a special kind of marriage—one that did not make the slave into a proper wife or at least not one who would count among the four accorded by Islamic law (sharia). In this case, it would appear that the status of the woman—free or slave—was what determined the nature of the "marriage" and that this was simply understood in local culture. Outsiders, though, might better understand the special relationship with the slave as concubinage. The ambiguity between marriage and concubinage in Saharan society is, for the most part, in the "ear of the listener"; as we will see, social and religious custom is clear on what should and could be done in any given circumstance—clear to those who live the situation. However, this ambiguity pervades most of the oral testimonies relevant to the subject that I have collected since the early 1980s. It contributes to a kind of silence around the more intimate aspects of sexuality and reproduction that are pertinent in understanding the power dynamics of carnal relationships. Rebecca Popenoe has articulated the problem in her recent study among Saharan Moors in Niger: "Like the veil shrouding women's sexually charged bodies, silence or at least indirectness shrouds the subject of sex in daily conversation, especially in mixed company."[2] The silences and veils are no less problematic when the subject of sex involves master-slave relations among those who would also see themselves as good Muslims.

The Sahara of the Saharan slavery referred to here is the one lived in by the various informants I have interviewed in central Mauritania, especially the Adrar region, but also embraces to some extent northwest Niger (among the Azawagh "Arabs"), where Popenoe carried out interview-based research. This Sahara, therefore, has an experiential rather than geographic delineation. The people who spend their lives in this desert and/or neighboring Sahelian regions are regarded in the dichotomized demographics of the Saharan world as Moors (Arabs), distinct from the rather better-known Tuareg (Berbers—the famous "blue men of the desert"). Certainly, the cultural lines between them blur, just as the postcolonial borders between them are ignored in daily life (and Moors are a small minority among the Tuareg of Niger). They share adherence to Islam and a historical dependence on herding and caravan trade; both have also been slaveholding cultures. But as Popenoe points out, there are some critical differences in how the two societies construct maleness, femaleness, and gender relations that affect their respective cultural situating of "fattening"—another shared practice between them and the subject of her research.[3] As I hope to show that this particular expression of culture also has significance for my questions around marriage and concubinage, I am careful in my use of Tuareg-based research in this chapter, and I have deliberately avoided moving too deeply into the anthropological literature in spite of its richness.

However, there is one significant difference between my analysis and Popenoe's that leads me to incorporate a central Tuareg study: my definition of "Saharan/Moorish society" *incorporates* the functioning of Saharan slavery, rather than relegating it to a related but separate discussion. I have long been very influenced by the early 1980s work of a team of demographers in the Niger delta whose study of nutrition and fertility cut across not only regions but also classes. At that time, "noble" pastoralists still lived in seminomadic fashion with their domestic slaves (*iklan*) and their settled freed slaves (*bella*); fertility and pregnancy could be examined in comparative fashion within neighboring communities. Surprisingly, given assumptions current at the time about the inability of slaves to reproduce because of their treatment (diet, workload, and environment were frequently cited factors), as well as their unwillingness to do so,[4] it was determined that the key variable affecting differences in fertility between free and slave in this region was marriage patterns. This study revealed that iklan were actively encouraged by their masters to produce children outside of marriage.[5] In Muslim societies, children of slave women belonged to their masters (no matter who the father might be); consequently, such illegitimate reproduction automatically enlarged the masters' households. Though out-of-wedlock births were statistically negligible among the nobles, iklan in this particular community had a 35 percent illegitimacy rate.[6] Hence, the authors of the study argued that "the apparently high marital fertility of the delta Tamasheq is probably due to there being some fertility outside marriage, largely amongst the Bella."[7]

These observations were possible because of the study's underlying premise that earlier work had treated pastoralists and sedentary societies as separate entities, instead of looking at how they intersected in order to reproduce. The authors isolated fertility and infant mortality as two critical foci, noting the central role of cultural norms such as marriage patterns.[8] One pair of researchers pushed the "intersection of normally discrete research categories" even further:

> Our thesis is that nobles and *Iklan*, despite their many real and perceived differences, are part of a composite social and economic system and, in description and study of either the nobles or the *Iklan*, reference must be made to the other for a fuller understanding to emerge. . . . It thus follows that demographic analysis must not just analyze data separately for the social classes but should consider their joint dynamics. In discussing household formation, we have implicitly drawn a distinction between a household's

> reproductive and other functions. . . . For nobles we have seen that because of the *Iklan*, households are of limited necessity. . . . [The *Iklan* households are] . . . shaped in two ways by a reproductive function, both of which are dictated by the nobles: one inciting high fertility thus increasing the nobles' slave resources, the other constraining against continued marriage because the owner loses his adult female labour for the duration of the marriage. All this is partly mediated by a high level of *Iklan* illegitimacy and noble manipulation of *Iklan* marriage.[9]

There appears to have been no follow-up to this research that raised so many questions around the social and cultural practices used to manage reproduction and sexual relations in this particular Saharan-Sahelian region.[10] The subjects of the investigation were Tuareg, not Moors, but as noted previously, the two groups share slaveholding and religious traditions. They also share the practice of fattening noble women. Although this practice was not explored directly in the delta demographic project, the authors commented that "of equal interest [to cross-group comparisons] are the within-group differences which generally indicate better weight-for-height indices amongst the dependent groups (*bella* in the case of the Tamasheq) than amongst their former masters." These former "masters" (that is, mistresses) drank three times as much milk as women among the dependent groups.[11] Moreover, it was also noted that iklan and bella children had significantly lower rates of infant mortality, just as their mothers had better weight-for-height ratios.[12] In the following pages, I want to probe further some of the ambiguities arising from our current understanding of reproduction, specifically within the context of Saharan slavery, bringing to bear insights suggested, first, by this (now dated but still valuable) study; second, by Popenoe's fascinating and recent work on fattening; and third but not least important, by the stories told to me by Saharans themselves over the course of my many years of fieldwork.[13]

"Or Those Possessed by Your Right Hand": Marriage, Concubines, and Reproduction

Earlier, I referred to the statement of the Atar elder al-Hadrami, in terms of "first reading," implying that there was more here than immediately met the eye.[14] I went on to discuss the fact that although he used the term *marry* to refer both to wives and to slaves, he clearly understood something different about the latter relationship in the context of Islamic law. What remains unclear, however, is when and why a Saharan master would chose to marry a slave, as in "take a concubine," and when and why he would chose to free her first, then marry her in traditional, legal fashion. When my informants spoke of a master marrying a slave woman, to which situation were they referring? Slave marriage to other slaves and/or to freed slaves, however, occurred frequently in the colonial Adrar region and is more visible. It followed Islamic law. The difference was in the bride-price (*mahr*): for slaves it was much less than for nobles and was largely symbolic.[15] The elder underscored that "the Qur'an was clear" on the question of marrying slaves. But, in fact, as far as interpretive literature is concerned, including the hadiths accepted by many Muslims, that clarity is elusive.

Ask a question about marriage or slavery and Mauritanians (like most Muslims) will first refer to "what Islam says." By that, they mean some part or combination of the Qur'an, the law that interprets it (*fiqh*), and/or the stories told of the Prophet Mohamed that are meant to lead by example (the hadiths). What actually happens is usually a combination of these understandings and local realities and/or customs (*'ada*), which, of course, change over time.[16] It is said in the Qur'an that slaves may marry "both slave and free," but actual examples of free men marrying slave women—in the legal sense of marriage—are hard, if not impossible, to find even in the hadiths that repeatedly question the issue with respect to the Prophet Mohamed himself.[17] Contemporary literature says, "Yes, this is permissible (and presumably happens)"[18] but also "No, a master cannot own, marry and have sexual relations with the same woman."[19] In this respect, perhaps the most helpful guideline is the reported action of Prophet Mohamed himself: upon taking the concubine of a vanquished chief for his own "wife" and being asked what he had paid for mahr, he replied, we are told, "Her self was her *Mahr*"—he had manumitted and then married her.[20] In other words, the precedent was set: manumission fulfilled the first requirement of the marriage process.

Among those I interviewed, it seemed that many different understandings coexisted around this question—on the one hand, about whether in a given situation marriage had, in fact, taken place and, on the other, about what marriage entailed. Al-Hadrami, for example, used the term *marriage* to refer both to free and slave "wives" but only a few minutes later noted that there was a special name given to a slave who was married (to her master) and then freed (either after giving birth or at some later time): "*jari*" (*jariya, jawari* pl.).[21] All his subsequent comments about the status of children born to "married slaves" referred to this category, suggesting that this was actually the norm, at least locally. He noted that it "was understood" that children of jawari were especially valuable, that *metissage* (mixing, of both status and race) was honorable, and that the young man sitting next to us was the son of a jariya —his father was well respected, and he claimed the same inheritance and shared the same respect as his siblings born of a noble mother. That said, there were clearly many instances where concubinage occurred but women were not freed, at least not immediately. Here, the mother's legal status as *umm al-walad*, literally meaning "mother of the child," was the deciding factor. And the key to triggering this status was the master's acknowledgment that the child was his. Once that was acknowledged, the concubine was recognized as such in terms of her treatment. In principle, she could no longer be sold, and she could expect to be freed upon her master's death (if not sooner).[22] Stories of these situations often portray a scenario in terms of "the child was born and the slave mother freed, but she stayed with her master until his death," which was understood as a responsibility on her part.[23] Either way, the child, whether boy or girl,[24] was supposed to be recognized and treated as free by the master's family, thereby remaining a child of that family.[25]

The problem here, for the historian, is being able to see legal marriage (which presumes manumission) as distinct from concubinage, when both short-term and longer-term consequences appear so similar. This problem is compounded when informants do not refer to the nature of the master-slave relationship and simply note that, for instance, "my father was married with one of his slaves and their children are in Nouakchott; my wife's mother was also a slave,"[26] or "the *servantes* in front of you were brought from the north . . . [one of them] was bought by the Ahel so-and-so; she has children; so does [the other one] bought by the Ahel so-and-so."[27] In both of these cases, the interviewees were men and were "noble." In some other cases (such as the interview with al-Hadrami, cited earlier), there is reference to the mother at some point being freed, but usually there is not.[28] What is intriguing is that this apparently does not make a difference to the people recounting their histories. I seemed to be the only one concerned about distinguishing the legal status of wife and concubine. This, in turn, raises a key question: why?[29] I will explore this further, in part by referencing a particular case—that of Hamody of Atar.

Hamody of Atar: The Story Continues

Some aspects of Hamody's story have been told elsewhere,[30] yet many remain to be explored, not least of which are the stories of his extended family, which includes the descendants of hundreds of slaves and *haratin* (freed slaves;[31] *hartani* sing., *hartaniyya* f.). My interviews with family and extended family members in 2004–5 both clarified and muddied this earlier understanding of Hamody's relationship with his Malian slave, Medeym.[32] In my 1988 chapter for a collection edited by Suzanne Miers and Richard Roberts, I wrote that Hamody, *son of a slave* himself, had first purchased his slave from Mali,[33] and then later in his life, he *married her* and had two children. It would now seem that both statements—his being the son of a slave and his having married a slave—need qualification or, at least, explanation. Everyone refers to Hamody's mother, Fatma, as a slave of Malian origin. However, though it is true that she, her sister, and her cousin were initially captured in Mali (the French Sudan at the time), they had first been taken across the Sahara to Goulimine in southern Morocco, where they lived with their masters.[34] The term *marriage* has been used to describe these relationships,[35] but one of Hamody's sons, Mohamed Mahmoud, confirmed that the relations were actually concubinage.[36] At this point, the young girls were legally slaves but in special relationships with their masters. Fatma was then inherited by her master's son, and she gave birth to a child, Hammoud; he was recognized by his father, making Fatma umm al-walad.[37] When I asked if this was the moment Fatma was freed, Mohamed Mahmoud's brother, who was also present, said, "No [understood: there was no need] her son was her paper."[38] In a subsequent interview, a descendant of Fatma's cousin explained that both women were freed upon giving birth to their masters' children, but he added that "there was no ceremony, it was automatic"; moreover, both remained with their masters until these men died. Only then did they enter into legal marriages with "husbands."[39] Fatma married a hartani from the Guebla (southwestern) region, then another of the Awlad Bou Sba clan, with whom she had two children.[40] At some later point, she is said to have married again, this time to a "Sherif" of Tafilelt (northern Saharan) origin. This man was Hamody's father.[41] So in fact, even though there is still ambiguity about exactly when Fatma was freed (or, perhaps more precisely, when Hammoud was born), it would seem there is none about her relationship with the Awlad Bou Sba master who inherited her—she was his concubine. Nor was there any ambiguity about her subsequent marriages, including to Hamody's father: she was a freed wife, a hartaniyya, and no longer a slave.

Hamody's relationship with Medeym is somewhat more difficult to understand, but ultimately, the problem centers on the same issues of ambiguity around the term *marriage.* As I recounted in "A Topsy-Turvy World," Hamody acquired Medeym as his slave in 1947, when she would have been about nine years old; a few years later, in 1952 and 1954, she produced two sons. When I first interviewed Hamody's daughter Swaifya in 1983–84, she said that he had married Medeym.[42] Swaifya's brother Mohamed Said confirmed this in an interview in 2000.[43] But in my 2004–5 interviews, everyone (including a much older and, regrettably, somewhat ill Swaifya) denied that any marriage, in the legal sense, had occurred at all. The relationship was said to have "taken place in the street," another manner of saying the same thing. Moreover, what had not been broached twenty years earlier was now clarified: at the time, the children were assumed by the family to have been the product of Medeym's "marriage" to one of Hamody's freed slaves.[44] Hamody did not acknowledge them until after his death, when the relationship was made public through a posthumous statement.[45] At this time, the eldest was taken into Hamody's household to be raised first by his widow and later by his son; the youngest, Isselmou, stayed with his mother and grandmother.[46] When Medeym "married" again (and had two children), she left Isselmou to be raised by his grandmother, who was also one of Hamody's slaves. It is now clear that the so-called marriage Swaifya and Mohamed Said had long ago spoken of was the same kind of marriage al-Hadrami was referring to, namely, a "marriage-with-a-slave," which produced a "slave wife." In other words, it was concubinage. Both Swaifya and Isselmou affirmed that this was a sexual relationship only.[47] In theory, it is possible that Hamody secretly freed and married Medeym,[48] but Isselmou's statement that "his mother received nothing after Hamody's death because a concubine was not entitled to anything" would seem to confirm that her slave status had been changed only as a consequence of her having given birth, not because she had been manumitted.[49]

It is interesting, however, that the same linguistic ambiguity continued in the interview texts around Medeym's relations with other men. Isselmou spoke of her having married a hartani while she was (presumably) Hamody's concubine,[50] and the former wife of one of Hamody's sons concurred (hence the assumption that her children were the product of that union);[51] he then remarked upon the second marriage after Hamody's death that took Medeym away from his childhood household. Swaifya, by contrast, categorically denied that Medeym was ever married and asserted she had only three sexual relations, two of which produced children. There is one further potential wrench in this works: Isselmou said his mother was freed upon the birth of his brother, Mohamed. This clearly did not happen in the traditional sense because Hamody did not, at the time, recognize Mohamed as his own (nor did he recognize Isselmou, for that matter). But once the posthumous announcement had been made, Medeym would, indeed, have been recognized as freed; consequently, her second marriage to a hartani, the one for whom she left the home of her mother and Isselmou, could well have been a legal marriage if mahr was paid. She was then a hartaniyya with rights to her own children (or rights to them within the boundaries of legal marriage), which meant they belonged to her and her husband—and, most important, no longer to Hamody's family.

Apart from the questions surrounding ambiguities of meaning, which vary both within the insider family perspective and among outsider interpretations,[52] the Hamody-Medeym story reinforces the importance of a point often dropped to a footnote in academic and religious discussions of "those possessed by your right hand"—the acknowledgment of paternity by the master. Hamody provided Medeym's family with land and the means to build a house;[53] he also provided her sons with "free" names at the time they were to be registered for school (his own, Mahmoud, for the eldest and Ahmed Salem, "Isselmou," for the younger), rather than the usual slave names. But still, Mahmoud and Isselmou were nine and seven, respectively, at the time of Hamody's death. And it was only then that they realized their free parentage and their mother's umm al-walad status.[54] It is difficult to know how common this kind of situation may have been.

In my interviews with Hamody's extended family, I encountered one other story in which parentage and its acknowledgment left the slave mother in a form of social limbo.[55] This was the story of Mariem mint Matallah, who had been born and brought up among the Ahmed Salem ould Beyruk, a wealthy and respected family based in Goulimine that established itself in the Adrar during the colonial era. Her master's cousin (another Goulimine merchant) asked her master if he could buy her "to give pleasure." Her master agreed ("she was not asked"[56]). She spent her life between the two families and was considered the property of both; neither wished to relinquish its right to her, even in old age. That said, she lived principally in a house provided to her by ould Beyruk. However, she had had several children, the last two of whom had been freed by her Beyruk master, apparently "at birth."[57] Although my assistant further commented that "he did not know why,"[58] it is understood that this usually means the child was born of a free man—in other words, that in this case, Mariem had been umm al-walad to her Beyruk master.[59] The other children were the progeny of "marriages" with haratin, presumably within the context of the cousin's family.[60] In this instance, that fact that slave women were property that could be shared and inherited meant that a woman could be at one and the same time both slave (to one master) and freed (to another, as the mother of a child or children)—perhaps the most difficult to grasp aspect of this ambiguity we have been exploring. But it apparently was normal in its social context, perhaps, in part, a legacy of colonial negotiations regarding the inheritance and use of female slaves. In 1929, the French had formally recognized the right of masters to include slaves in "customary" inheritance settlements. A few years later, local administrators had been bothered by the fact that what this meant in practice was allocating fractions of slaves—mostly women—to various claimants. When one such administrator suggested that the policy should be modified so that a slave went with only one inheritor, masters objected. "To receive even one-quarter of a female slave gives a possible profit of one or several children tomorrow," they said.[61] And that brings us full circle back to the perplexing question of why.

History, Haratin, and the Evolution of Reproduction

The stories that emerge from the Mauritanian Adrar, especially the towns of Shinqit and Atar (which were and remain home to most of the informants I have drawn upon thus far), certainly suggest that their society is a nuanced and complex one—in many ways, it is silent and invisible to the outsider. Yet the stories also reveal an integration between the free noble and the nonfree slave that is intense and gender specific.[62] This integration seems to hinge on roles played by slave women in various (sometimes ambiguous) capacities as so-called wives. In this respect, slavery cannot be separated from freedom among these Moors any more than it could be in the demographic study looking at fertility and iklan-nobility relations among the Tuareg in the Niger delta (cited earlier). That said, our evidence suggests yet another layer of complexity in focusing attention not just on female slaves but also on *freed* female slaves, hartaniyya. Hartaniyya included slave women who were simply manumitted (for whatever reason), women who were manumitted as part of the marriage process, and concubines who bore children for their masters and were freed at some point following said masters' acknowledgment of those births or upon their death (jawari).

In that rather timeless fashion typical of interviews not focused on specific people, Mohamed Lemine ould Habbot explained that female slaves were rarely freed because their fertility was too valuable: "Their children augmented your slaves if you were her master and if your female slave was married to someone else's male slave, the children also belonged to you."[63] As noted previously, in the early 1930s, local notables responded strongly to the suggestion by authorities that they should cease to divide female slaves as inheritable property, pointing to the potential that even a fraction of a slave held out for producing more children. I have cited this elsewhere to underscore the gender specificity of slavery under colonial rule,[64] but it is only now that its ambiguity fully strikes me. One's first response is to think in terms of master-slave concubinage, with the "profit" being free children who would expand the master's family. But in this instance, the concubine would sooner or later become free, possibly creating the complicated situation of Mariem mint Matallah (described earlier), who seemed at one point in her life to be simultaneously both half freed and half slave. At a time when slave trading had been all but eradicated, this was not a desirable outcome. But it is also possible that these nobles were referring to the profit of coupling (or marrying) the quarter-slave with another slave or hartani, thereby gaining *slave children* who would equally expand the family, albeit in a different way.[65] In effect, this is what the Niger delta study, discussed earlier in this paper, was seeing: masters encouraging iklan to have children illegitimately in order to maximize profit—which, in this situation, encompassed both children belonging to masters and masters' continued rights to their slaves' labor and sexuality. Interestingly, Popenoe observed that the reputation of slaves among the Moors she studied was one of being more sexually active and "wanton." Though she did not attempt to see any connection between their behavior and the nobles with whom she spent her time, she did note that perceived differences in sexuality were central to the female slaves' reputation: "Those [qualities] associated . . . with blacks include lack of willpower, lack of self-restraint, untrustworthiness, uncontrollable sexuality. Sexuality is perceived as a prime arena of physical and moral difference [between slave and noble women]."[66]

Although Mohamed Lemine noted that masters rarely freed female slaves, he also went on to say that if a male slave married a hartaniyya a master would be best off freeing him to be a hartani, for in that way, the master would acquire a "tributary" family. Neither my oral nor my archival evidence suggests that this "marrying down" of a freed female slave happened very often. But his connection of the hartani status and the tributary family is an important one that became increasingly common during the colonial era, especially from the 1930s onward. This was a period of forced agricultural expansion, when masters were being strongly urged to free male laborers to satisfy colonial labor needs. These haratin were literally seen as the new working class.[67] New *adabayes* (haratin-populated cultivation centers in the relatively fertile south) were established, even as older communities of this type saw population growth; female slaves found themselves being given as wives to their masters' haratin.[68]

In the Adrar, such policies were no less influential, as the tale of Hamody himself shows so clearly.[69] During the 1930s and 1940s, he emerged as one of the largest property owners in Atar and began to purchase slaves to cultivate his date-palm groves and fields, as well as to herd his animals. At the time of his death in 1961, he is said to have had over two hundred slaves and haratin. The many stories of this extended family reflect clearly the policies for which Hamody has become famous: buying only "slaves of quality" so that they might be capable of being freed (in keeping with the Islamic precept that one should not free a slave into conditions worse than those he or she has enjoyed in servitude) and rarely freeing female slaves (until his death).[70] That said, there were occasions when circumstances favored manumission, such as when he freed Medeym's mother so that her testimony could be heard in court and she could recover a donkey that had been stolen from her.[71] And then there is the story of Harra mint Mahmoud's mother, whose daughter had been physically abused (some suggest sexually). Hamody had purchased the daughter away from the abusive household. The mother, in turn, sought to be owned by Hamody, who eventually also purchased her two other daughters (presumably including Harra). Hamody immediately freed the mother and Harra (who had a physical deformity) but not the other two sisters.[72] Interestingly, however, contrary to the assertion by the elderly hartani cited earlier—namely, that haratin did not like to marry slave women—Hamody frequently arranged such marriages among his haratin and slaves. In this instance, it would seem that for haratin, the issue of control over offspring was less significant than the benefits to be gained by retaining a close association with a wealthy merchant and property owner.[73] It is this situation in particular that recalls the findings of the Niger delta study, in which nobles were noted to be dictating the reproductive functions of their slaves' households. The authors of the study underscored that "it thus follows that demographic analysis must consider the joint dynamics of these [different] social classes."[74]

Culture and Medicine: The Impact of Fattening on Slavery

That study also raised one further issue that is important to our understanding of Saharan slavery and reproduction—the question of differential fertility (and associated consequences) between noble and slave classes. Although the Niger delta study focused on the somewhat surprisingly higher fertility, better weight-to-height ratio, and lower infant mortality of iklan and bella, I would like to draw attention to the flip side of that database: the fertility, weight, and infant mortality of the noble women. These factors were not examined in the prior study, other than noting the less than favorable weight-to-height ratio of noble women, who also (as mentioned in one substudy) drank three times more milk than dependent women. But medical research that has been carried out since the early 1980s can help us explore the importance of these observations for our own questions about why slave women might have become so central to Saharan society.

Noble Saharan women were (and still are in some regions where resources permit) subject to fattening (*gavage*, in French literature) from as early as age seven or eight through to the arrival of puberty. The process was indicative of class and status—those who could afford to feed their women so well that they had difficulty moving could subsequently afford the loss of these women's labor; as we have seen, the process cut across the Moor-Tuareg cultural frontier.[75] But as Popenoe explained, fattening was about more than class and status. Although reaching a weight that brought on almost total immobility was, indeed, a reflection of the wealth of a woman's family (and hence the status of its patriarchs), it was also the way in which the fruits of men's labor as managers of herds of milk-producing camels were transformed into reproductive value, into cultural capital. It was the way in which "being Moor" was best and most effectively articulated among the Azawagh Arabs Popenoe studied in Niger: "Their beauty ideals also reflect and express social ideals . . . and are predicated on an economic system in which the fruits of men's active labor are 'invested' in passive female bodies."[76] But being of massive weight also left women vulnerable to various health issues that affected their fertility, their ability to bring a pregnancy to term, and their success in delivering healthy babies, as the Niger delta study revealed so long ago.

Popenoe addressed the issue of fertility in her consideration of the meaning of "being fat." She acknowledged that at many times and in many parts of the world, fat was equated with fertility, but she noted, "Fattening has no explicit or implicit association with fertility for Azawagh Arabs. . . . That is, while rich men are likely to have fat wives *and fat wives are, it is hoped, fertile*, feminine corpulence is decidedly not read by Azawagh Arabs, explicitly or implicitly, as a direct indicator of either of these traits."[77] Her exploration of Azawagh Arabs' association of fatness with their Islamic culture is intriguing and makes for a powerful argument; as she put it: "Since women's most noble purpose is to bear sons and Muslims to populate God's earth, it is logical that they should reach the age of childbearing and marriage as soon as possible, a process they believe fattening accelerates. For a girl to fatten, then, is for her to embrace and abet her God-given destiny and purpose."[78] However, it is surprising that such an important corollary—"*fat wives are, it is hoped, fertile*"—was left unquestioned among the silences Popenoe heard in her fieldwork. The current medical understanding of the relationship between obesity and fertility is unequivocal in its conclusion that obesity (a polite, Western term that falls short of appreciating the process and consequences of being forcibly fattened,[79] as these young Saharan women were[80]), negatively affects fertility: "Not only can obesity put a woman and her baby at risk for some serious health complications, but it can actually interfere with fertility. This is because fat stores change the levels of sex hormones that a body produces, making it increasingly difficult to become pregnant."[81]

In addition to compromising fertility, fattening and the obesity it intentionally produces also deleteriously affect the health of the pregnant mother and, potentially, of her child. Obese women are likely to suffer from preeclampsia, which causes high blood pressure, fluid retention, and swelling that can restrict blood flow to the fetus. They may also develop gestational diabetes, which can put the fetus at risk of gaining too much weight, necessitating a slow, prolonged labor and the possibility of a cesarean section that increases the likelihood of postpartum infections.[82] If successfully delivered, the babies are at high risk for neural tube defects, including spina bifida and anencephaly. Although these conditions can be detected through ultrasound imaging when and where this is available, obese women's results are often of poor quality; such defects are not always detected.[83] Moreover, in the historical and geographic context we are dealing with here, such sophisticated options have rarely been provided.

Popenoe noted that people still believe the most important way for a girl to take up her role in society is to become a woman and that fattening brings on womanhood earlier than would otherwise occur: "Moors are remarkable . . . in that fattening begins so young, goes on for so long, and is in fact the central preoccupation of women's lives alongside childbearing, childrearing, and being good Muslims."[84] She spoke in cultural terms of "belief." In fact, her informants were correct:

fattening does bring on early maturity, or menarche. What medical science has noticed recently—that simple weight gain among young girls brings on an early puberty—Saharan society has deliberately exploited for centuries. What is less obvious is that menstruating and being, in principle, ready to bear children is not the equivalent of biological maturity. The growth of reproductive organs—ovaries, uterus, fallopian tubes, and vagina—requires the time involved in a normal adolescence: "These changes are only partly completed at the time of menarche; the mature adult size of the reproductive system is attained only when a girl's growth in height and weight is completed." The pelvis, so essential to successful delivery, "finishes growing even later, not reaching its full size until age 20 or 21."[85] So culture in the form of fattening could force only the *early part* of biological maturity; fattened mothers, in addition to all their own health problems, were the equivalent in many ways of today's obese teenage mothers "[who] give birth to babies who are underweight and have development problems because the mothers have not completed their own growth."[86] As anthropologist Edmund Bernus observed among the Tuareg, when this illusion of womanhood has led to premature marriages and attempted pregnancies, it has often resulted in the deaths of both mothers and babies.[87]

Much of this research is relatively recent, and for the most part (Bernus excepted), it appears not to have been applied to situations in which young girls are *made* obese for express cultural and societal reasons. One might well ask, therefore, if there is any indication in our historical sources that the fattening of noble women might have explained something about the role of slave women in reproduction—any reason we should have brought ourselves to look at research in this particular context earlier. And the answer is yes.[88]

The infamous Dahomean political exile Louis Hunkanrin, who spent ten years in political exile in Mauritania's Adrar-Tagant between 1922 and 1933, wrote a pamphlet about the sexual abuses of slave women by French administrators in these regions, published in 1934.[89] In an unpublished response to these accusations, prepared by local administrators, it was noted that Hunkanrin did not really understand the complex situation in which the women he was concerned about lived. "Black *servantes*" were actually the "base" of the Moorish family, the response noted, and contributed in large part to its reproduction, for "women of the Moorish race" were often sterile and were in any case "insufficient in number."[90] In 1931–32, the commandant of the Cercle of Assaba and the governor-general of the colony each observed that slave women were more fertile and produced more children than their white, noble Mauritanian mistresses.[91] Further east in the Niger bend, colonial authorities took the observation one step further, suggesting that the apparent lack of fecundity of the "white race" (here meaning the Tuareg) threatened its very existence.[92] Perhaps even more telling than French commentary was the concern expressed by a local Tuareg leader, Muhammed 'Ali ag Attaher. He first raised the issue to French authorities in the early 1930s, identifying obesity as a serious obstacle to Tuareg development. This idea was articulated in an impressive and impassioned "modernization manifesto" in 1939: "We have a problem which hinders reproduction even more [than high dowries, which were seen as delaying marriages]. We force our female children to become fat at a young age and as they grow up they become enormously obese. *Too much fat prevents reproduction.*"[93]

Almost a decade later, the intrepid French traveler Odette du Puigaudeau wrote about "the evolution of the black slave in Mauritania." Her unpublished remarks suggest that earlier observations to the effect that female slaves were important to Mauritanian reproduction and that the white race was threatened by obesity had some basis in reality: "Maures are monogamous and their women are not very fertile, much less [fertile] than the *negresses* among the slaves. The acceptable usage of black concubines chosen from among the slaves—happy to find themselves thusly liberated—assured [in the past] a minimal level of birthing, at the same time bringing 'more vigorous [black] blood' to a white people weakened by undernourishment and the Saharan climate. One hardly sees anymore around the tents the groups of happy children—maures, *métis* and black—who were the strength and the future of the tribe."[94]

Managing Carnality

To return to the issue of sexual relations and power, the changes wrought through the implementation of French policy had both class and gender implications. It is totally unclear what these implications were for Saharan mistresses (so-called free wives), as this particular articulation of power has seldom been explored.[95] In the colonial Sahara, it would seem that a noble wife's household authority over slave women may have increasingly been transformed into a kind of charitable noblesse oblige vis-à-vis the hartani community as a whole, but this would need more considered analysis and research before being presented as a hypothesis. What is clear, however, is that through a growing, albeit evolving, hartani class, male masters relinquished considerable personal power to command sexual services as they "freed" women in order to protect slavery (and, by extension, their own wealth and status) in the longer term. In a sense, they became managers, rather than masters, of carnality.

What I have attempted to explore here by drawing on earlier demographic research, ongoing medical research, Popenoe's insightful understandings of the practice of fattening among Nigerian Moors, and the always engaging if not always transparent conversations I have had with Mauritanians during my field interviews is *the way in which local management of societal reproduction situated carnal relations with female slaves at its center*. And because of that centrality, I have investigated how Saharan slavery in general was forced to adapt to the changing colonial (and postcolonial) realities in such a way as to ensure this integral dynamic was protected. To return to the premise of the conference—that, somehow, there was something special about the nature of power as exercised through sexual relations within the institution of slavery—this chapter suggests that such an emphasis obscures a critical dynamic that is not about power per se but rather about reproduction and assuring its success in a culture and society that evolved in particular historical and environmental circumstances. If fattening symbolized the cultural center of society (as Popenoe would argue), slavery assured that both culture and society could survive and would adapt—albeit still to a very large extent "shrouding its silences" when it comes to questions of sexuality and sexual relations.

Notes

My thanks go to the Killam Postdoctoral Fellowship program, the Social Sciences and Humanities Research Council of Canada, and the University of Alberta: their grants made fieldwork possible in 1983–84, 1993–96, 2000, and 2004–5 and also supported conference presentations on this material. In addition, I thank Mohamed Lahbib Nouhi and Zein ould Ahmed Salem for their assistance with interviewing and translations and Louise Rolingher for providing supplementary literature research. Abdel Wedoud ould Cheikh helped me to understand what I was hearing; as always, I am grateful for his support. William Clarence Smith responded to my request to comment upon the manuscript with generosity; thanks are due to him and to Elizabeth Elbourne, coeditor of this volume, for their critical questions and comments.

1. Al-Hadrami, interview by the author, Atar, August 7, 1983.

2. Rebecca Popenoe, *Feeding Desire: Fatness, Beauty and Sexuality among a Saharan People* (London: Routledge, 2004), 81.

3. Ibid., 39.

4. These aspects were assumed to be central and were therefore looked at in these studies. See especially Martie Wagenaar-Brouwer, "Preliminary Findings on the Diet and Nutritional Status of Some Tamasheq and Fulani Groups in the Niger Delta of Central Mali," in *Population, Health and Nutrition in the Sahel*, ed. Allan G. Hill (London: Routledge and Kegan Paul, 1985), 226–53. The belief in slaves' lack of reproduction also became entrenched in the literature at that time with the publication of Claude Meillassoux's influential *Anthropologie de l'esclavage: Le ventre de fer et de l'argent* (Paris: Presses Universitaires de France, 1986; Chicago: University of Chicago Press, 1991); see especially chap. 3, on sterility.

5. No explanation was provided for what *encouraged* might have meant.

6. Sara Randall and Michael Winter, "The Reluctant Spouse and the Illegitimate Slave: Marriage, Household Formation and Demographic Behavior amongst Malian Tamesheq from the Niger Delta and the Gourma," in Hill, *Population, Health and Nutrition*, 182.

7. Allan G. Hill, "The Recent Demographic Surveys in Mali and Their Main Findings Looking at Three Main Groups: Bambara (Sedentary), Fulani and Tamasheq," in Hill, *Population, Health and Nutrition*, 56. There are real differences between iklan and bella, but the fact that the findings concerning their fertility and infant mortality are so similar is what is of interest here. I draw upon Hill, Randall, and Winter collectively for my analysis here.

8. Allan G. Hill and Sara Randall, "Introduction," in Hill, *Population, Health and Nutrition*, 1–19.

9. Randall and Winter, "Reluctant Spouse," 176.

10. Subsequent work by Randall considers some of the same issues but in a different context; see *Fertility of Malian Tamasheq Repatriated Refugees: The Impact of Forced Migration* (Washington, D.C.: Committee on Population National Research Council, National Academies Press, 2004). Also see A. Giuffrida, *Mariage, fécondité et ménage chez les Kel Tamasheq du Mali: Bouleversements socio-économiques et continuité démographique en familles au Nord, familles au Sud, Louvain-la-Neuve* (Paris: L'Harmattan, 2005). Recent studies on pregnancy and birth have the potential to contribute significantly to developing our understanding of the subject; see, for example, Mohamed Ag Erless, *La grossesse et le suivi*

de l'accouchement chez les Touaregs Kel-Adagh (Kidal, Mali) (Paris: L'Harmattan, 2010), which includes a very useful bibliography.

11. Wagenaar-Brouwer, "Preliminary Findings," 245; see also observations on 232–33.

12. Katherine Hilderbrand, Allan G. Hill, Sara Randall, and Marie-Louise van den Eerenbeent, "Child Mortality and Care of Children in Rural Mali," in Hill, *Population, Health and Nutrition*, 186.

13. This point is elaborated on in E. Ann McDougall, "'Si un homme travaille il doit être libre . . . ': Les serviteurs *hrâtîn* et le discours colonial sur le travail en Mauritanie," in *Colonisations et héritages actuels au Sahara et au Sahel: Problèmes conceptuels, état des lieux et nouvelles perspectives de recherche (XVIIIe–XXe siècle)* (Paris: L'Harmattan, 2007), 229–64. See also McDougall, "Topsy-Turvy World: Slaves and Freed Slaves in the Mauritanian Adrar, 1910–1950," in *The End of Slavery in Africa*, ed. R. Roberts and S. Miers (Madison: University of Wisconsin Press, 1988), 366–69.

14. The subheading for this section derives from Qu'ran: *sura* 23 ["The Believers"]: 5–6 "guard their private parts [abstain from sex] . . . except from their wives, or those whom their right hand possess [captives], for indeed they will not be blamed," http://tanzil.net/#23:5/6. (This sura and these verses have been variously translated; the slight differences one finds between them do not change the essential meaning.)

15. Al-Hadrami interview.

16. The term *'ada* is found in several early Saharan *nawazil*, or "learned interpretations," of how to be a good Muslim when engaging with non-Muslims (e.g., peoples of the Sudan). It is not clear whether this term is appropriate for the "local circumstances" of the Mauritanian Sahara, a region that has considered itself Islamic since the eleventh century. Put another way, any perceived differences in appropriate behavior or potential ambiguities between "recognized sharia" and locally understood "Islamic culture" have long since disappeared from discourse.

17. For example, vol. 7, bk. 62, no. 2: [On the Prophet's marriage to Saffiyya]: "The Muslims wondered, 'Is she (Saffiyya) considered as his wife or his slave girl?' Then they said, 'If he orders her to veil herself, she will be one of the mothers of the Believers; but if he does not order her to veil herself, she will be a slave girl.'" What is important for us here is not whether she was or she was not but rather the ambiguity that surrounded the event and the localized understanding of what would indicate one decision or the other. https://www.usc.edu/org/cmje/religious-texts/hadith/bukhari/062-sbt.php.

18. The quotation is from Kecia Ali, "Islam and Slavery," http://www.brandeis.edu/projects/fse/Pages/islamandslavery.html. On this topic more generally, see Murray Gordon, *Slavery in the Arab World* (New York: New Amsterdam Books [English], 1989), 48–104; Mohammed Ennaji, *Soldats, domestiques*

et concubines: L'esclavage au Maroc au XIXème siècle (Casablanca, Morocco: Editions EDDIF, 1994), 61–76.

19. Ali, "Islam and Slavery."

20. Sahih al-Bukhari, "*Volume 1, Book 8, Number 367,*" http://www.truthnet.org/islam/Hadith/Bukhari/8/. .

21. 'Jari' or "concubine"; from Arabic *jâriyya* (or *jariya*), *jawari* pl.: "female slave/s." (My thanks go to Abdel Wedoud ould Cheikh for this confirmation.)

22. Some ambiguity arises around this term *freed* as well—see the discussion of Hamody's mother, Fatma, that follows.

23. "Responsibility" in this case might just as well refer to her relation to her child (or children) as to her master.

24. Other work in this volume suggests that the notion of *umm al-walad* and its implied importance for social status applied only to male children. I have questioned this on several occasions in Mauritania and have always received the same reply: the gender of the child is irrelevant. However, it must be remembered that the requirement of recognition by the master gives a certain license that might well allow for such discrimination in practice.

25. See the larger discussion of differing interpretations and realities in E. Ann McDougall, "A Sense of Self: The Life of Fatma Barka," *Canadian Journal of African Studies* 32, no. 2 (1998): 290–92.

26. Mohamoud ould Mal Lemine d'Eleyé, interview by the author, Shinqit, August 21, 1984.

27. Mohamed Lemine ould Habbott, interview by the author, Shinqit, August 22, 1984.

28. However, as we will see in later discussion of Hamody, some would say the child was literally proof of the mother's freedom.

29. It needs to be kept in mind that it was rare for a man to have more than one wife; serial marriage, rather than polygamy, was the norm during the colonial period; see, for example, Odette du Puigaudeau, *La grande foire des dattes* (1937; repr., Paris: Ibis Press, 2007), 89. This remains true today, the legality of having four wives under Islam notwithstanding. Perhaps this situation lessened the significance of differentiating between the statuses, as it was highly unlikely that a man was in danger of being seen to disregard this religious requirement. (Later, I will suggest a more complex explanation.)

30. McDougall, "Topsy-Turvy World," 362–88, and "Living the Legacy of Slavery: Between Discourse and Reality," *Cahiers d'études africaines*, special double issue titled "Esclavage modern ou modernité d'esclavage?" 179–80, no. 3–4 (December 2005): 957–86.

31. Generally speaking haratin are freed slaves or their descendants but not everyone "seen to be" hartani/hartaniyya acknowledges those origins. Some differentiate between social status and apply different terms to haratin who have done well. In the Adrar (the region of this case study), some families

straddle the southern Morocco border: in southern Morocco the same term means someone very different. Some "warrior" groups also have different relations with so-called haratin. The people referenced here do not question their slave origins.

32. McDougall, "Living the Legacy." I give my sincere thanks to Mohamed Said ould Hamody, who arranged for these extended-family interviews; to Zekeria ould Ahmed Salem Denne, who arranged for an assistant; and to Zein ould Ahmed Salem Denne, for helping me explore his family history. I am indebted to each of them and to their families.

33. McDougall, "Topsy-Turvy World." Medeym went unnamed in my first account of this story, for which I am truly sorry.

34. Fatma's sister remained in Goulimine and had several children with her master. Fatma and her cousin eventually arrived with their masters in Shinqit. All three masters were of the Awlad Bou Sba clan. I hope to develop more of this story in a larger work devoted to Hamody and his extended family.

35. Swaifya mint Hamody used an ambiguous *hassaniya* term that means "led to" or "taken" but can also be understood as "married" to describe how the young girls arrived in Goulimine. *Hassaniya* is the local language, a combination of Arabic and Berber.

36. Mohamed Mahmoud ould Hamody, interview by the author, Nouakchott, December 23, 2004.

37. He died in a battle in Wadan in 1910. The story is well known and frequently retold among the family, perhaps because of its significance vis-à-vis Fatma's status. Swaifya mint Hamody and Mohamed Mahmoud ould Hamody, interviews by the author, Nouakchott, December 22 and 23 (respectively), 2004; Ahmed Salem ould Denne, interview by the author, Atar, December 26, 2004.

38. Mohamed Said ould Hamody, present in Mohamed Mahmoud ould Hamody interview.

39. Ahmed Salem ould Denne, interview by the author, Atar, December 26, 2004.

40. It is not clear what happened with the first marriage, except that no children seem to have issued from it and that it ended, leaving Fatma free to remarry.

41. She married Mahoud ould Ahmed Maloud, sent by his father to study Qur'an with the famed clerical family of Moulay Aly, in Shinqit. She also had a daughter by him. Swaifya mint Hamody and Mohamed Mahmoud ould Hamody, interviews by the author, Nouakchott, December 22 and 23 (respectively), 2004.

42. Swaifya mint Hamody, interview by the author, Atar, summer 1984. To be precise, the French translation by my assistant at the time was "marriage."

43. Mohamed Said ould Hamody, interview by the author, Washington, D.C., November 2000. The interview was conducted in French, and *marriage* was the term used.

44. Swaifya mint Hamody, interview by the author, Nouakchott, December 22, 2004.

45. This statement was delivered publicly by a trusted Muslim friend.

46. There is a lack of consensus on this point, with Swaifya asserting that both boys initially were taken in by Hamody's widow, Selka, and (presumably) only at the time of her death moving into these arrangements; interview, 2004. Isselmou makes no reference to spending this time with Selka; Isselmou ould Hamody, interview by the author, Atar, December 27, 2004.

47. I am not aware of any reason why the term *marriage* would be conveyed in my earlier interviews and not in the later ones. There is no shame involved with respect to the family in either presentation of the relationship. I believe, again, that it is I who have been seeking a distinction and according it an importance that is not locally felt. Nevertheless, I have tried here to dissect the question in response to an anonymous reviewer's query.

48. The term for this is *tasarrâhâ*; (Thanks to Abdel Wedoud ould Cheikh for this explanation.).

49. He and his brother inherited, proof that her concubine status had been recognized.

50. This is somewhat complicated: a Muslim cannot take the wife of another as a concubine; only a slave can be a legal concubine. However, a slave who is married (without manumission) to another slave or hartani remains a slave.

51. Selka mint Ismail, interview by the author, Atar, December 29, 2004. She was the former wife of Mohamed Mahmoud, the son who took Medeym's oldest son and raised him.

52. "Insider-outsider" dichotomies need to be nuanced. I have worked with a Moroccan "outsider" assistant who had, in fact, lived and taught in Mauritania for four years and was himself from the Saharan edge of Morocco. I also have worked with a much younger "insider" assistant from Atar, himself part of this extended family. But his knowledge of his family's past was actually less than my own—I had known his town and family as a researcher before he was even born and had interviewed the last emir of the region and one of the most well-known notables of his town, both of whom were long deceased. He was learning about his own past through our interviews.

53. Medeym's family consisted of her mother (also Hamody's slave); her brother (Hamody's hartani); her sons; and it would seem at one point her "husband," Bilal, also a former slave and now hartani of Hamody.

54. And even at this point, the supposed norm was challenged in that Isselmou remained with Medeym, whereas Mahmoud moved into the main house.

55. It must be said that even the interview left an important issue ambiguous; see discussion, below.

56. Bleil ould Moussa, interview by the author, Atar, January 2, 2005. Ould Moussa (of the Beyruk family) recounted the story of his mother and grandmother.

57. This is where the lack of clarity lies: at the point where the informant Bleil ould Moussa recounted that Beyruk had freed the two children at some later date, his wife, also present during the interview, interjected something not captured fully on tape. She clearly disagreed with her husband, who simply repeated they had been "freed." My assistant translated her correction: they were freed *at birth.*

58. And he was reluctant to pursue the point given the disagreement between ould Moussa and his wife.

59. There are a number of questions here, however. It seems unlikely that she would be taken concubine after having several children with various slave/haratin "husbands" (four in total) unless there was an emotional attachment that was not immediately apparent. Also, if she had been freed upon the birth of the first child, even if she remained with her master as was often the case, it is unclear why the second child, a daughter, would need to be freed. Technically, she would have been born of a freed mother. Yet the dynamic of the interview with Bleil and his wife suggested clearly that it was precisely this issue of umm al-walad that was at play.

60. Bleil ould Moussa interview. The interview never makes clear how her marriages are related to her split ownership. If she was the concubine of her Beyruk master, it would have been improper for her to have had slave marriages while living in his household; therefore, I assume these marriages took place while she was officially living with her other master—remembering that *shared* meant moving back and forth for varying periods of time.

61. This is discussed in McDougall, "Topsy-Turvy World," 376, and later in this chapter. In the article, I further argue that this situation may have been aggravated by French policies that demanded male labor for colonial agriculture and closed down most major slave-trading activities. In other words, masters increasingly saw access to female slave reproduction as their assurance that domestic slavery would survive.

62. I will return to the male-specific aspects of this integration in my concluding paragraphs.

63. Mohamed Lemine ould Habbott interview.

64. McDougall, "Topsy-Turvy World," 376.

65. Remember that children born to slave women belonged to their masters, whether the husband was another slave or a hartani. Ibid., 364–66.

66. Popenoe, *Feeding Desire*, 141.

67. See the development of this point in McDougall, "'Si un homme travaille.'"

68. Meskerem B'hrane, "Narratives of the Past, Politics of the Present" (Ph.D. diss., University of Chicago, 1997). Several of the male life histories

recounted here speak of maternal ancestors and local resistance to female hartaniyya seeking support against *bidan* [Moor] masters in adabayes. See especially chap. 3, "When a Camel Talks: Reclaiming the Past through Oral Narratives of Family History," and chap. 4, "My Master Is My Cousin and Other Ambiguities of Subservience," 163–211.

69. McDougall, "Topsy-Turvy World," 379–82.

70. Bilal ould Mbarak, interview by the author, Atar, December 26, 2004. Isselmou, Hamody's son, married one of his father's former slaves, although it is not known when she was freed.

71. This occasion simultaneously underscores the point: Hamody freed Medeym's brother shortly after purchasing him, but he kept both Medeym and her mother as slaves, until the testimony incident in the mother's case and until his death in Medeym's.

72. Harra mint Mahmoud, interview by the author, Atar, December 29, 2004. The remaining two sisters are believed to have been freed following the national decree declaring slavery illegal in 1980–81; apparently, not all of Hamody's female slaves were freed upon his death.

73. Hamody's gain was both a growing labor force and real local power: at one point in his career, he was appointed *chef de fraction* ('Head' of his Awlad Bou Sba clan in Atar) by the French, and equally as important, he was regarded as a generous patron by all who knew him.

74. Randall and Winter, "Reluctant Spouse," 176.

75. Popenoe, *Feeding Desire*, 39.

76. Ibid., 2.

77. Ibid., 130 (emphasis added).

78. Ibid. Moreover, Popenoe observed, "the sensuous, sexual connotations of fattened female bodies have their roots in Islamic Ideology" (69–70).

79. Although the process was completely accepted culturally, it was (and still is) at times a very uncomfortable one that young girls have often resisted. See the photo of a tool used to "assist" young Tuareg women fatten in Edmond Bernus, "Gavage chez les Touaregs Iwellemeden Kel-Denneg," *Encyclopédie berbère*, vol. 11 (Aix-en-Provence, France: Edisud., 1998), 2996–99.

80. Ibid. The authorship of this piece is credited to J. Akkari Weriemmi, but he appears to have written only the last page. Bernus's article draws from earlier publications, in the 1980s and early 1990s.

81. "Obesity during Pregnancy," http://www.pregnancy-info.net/obesity_pregnancy.html. The literature on obesity and pregnancy frequently cites such cautionary information; see, e.g., Salynn Boyles, "Obesity Increases Risks in Pregnancy: Moms and Babies Have More Problems," http://www.webmd.com/diet/news/20060203/obesity-increases-risks-in-pregnancy and "Obesity" (2013), https://mywiserhealth.com/pregnancy/obesity/learn/.

Weight loss, by contrast, has been shown to restore fertility; see Rose E. Frisch, *Female Fertility and the Body Fat Connection* (Chicago: University of Chicago Press, 2002), 18–19.

82. "Obesity during Pregnancy"; Boyles, "Obesity Increases Risks."

83. Ibid.

84. Popenoe, *Feeding Desire*, 6.

85. Frisch, *Female Fertility*, 66.

86. Ibid.

87. Bernus, "Gavage," 2998.

88. Only very recently have we looked at the connection between being fat and having difficulties with puberty, fertility, birthing, and infant feeding/care, not to mention the additional diseases and other problems mentioned earlier. On this, see Frisch, *Female Fertility*, introduction.

89. Hunkanrin does not, however, emerge unscathed himself in terms of accusations of pimping and abusing female domestics; see E. Ann McDougall, "Setting the Story Straight: Louis Hunkanrin and 'Un forfait colonial,'" *History in Africa: A Journal of Method* 16 (1989): 285–310.

90. Reply to *Un forfait colonial: L'esclavage en Mauritanie*, communication by Louis O Hunkanrin, February 1, 1933, Esclavage, EI 18, April 15, 1933, Archives nationales de la République Islamique de Mauritanie, Nouakchott (hereafter ANRIM).

91. ANRIM, Commandant du Cercle de l'Assaba 1931; Governeur General de la Mauritanie, 1932. I first commented upon these observations in "Topsy-Turvy World," 383, note 45, suggesting that the role of slave women and children was clearly important to the very reproduction of Mauritanian society.

92. Cited in Bruce Hall, *A History of Race in Muslim West Africa, 1600–1960* (Cambridge: Cambridge University Press, 2011), 283. The report he references is from the Cercle of Goundam, 1933.

93. Ibid., 282 (emphasis added). Muhammed 'Ali ag Attaher, chief of Tuareg Kel Entesar, in the 1930s, was concerned with modernization of his people and Niger bend in general and had actually traveled to France, returning in 1931. In 1939, he launched a "modernization manifesto," a program geared to improving the Turareg economy and society. It also was concerned with the problem of a perceived population decline that had to be addressed for fear the people would disappear in future. One issue involved excessively high dowry demands that were preventing too many young and poor from marrying. The other was obesity and reproduction, which also hindered modernization in general—obese women could not and did not work (pp. 282–83). See Hall's full discussion of this modernization program in chap. 8, especially pp. 276–98. My thanks to Bruce for bringing this information to my attention and for discussing it further with me.

94. Odette du Puigaudeau, "L'évolution d'esclave noir en Mauritanie," n.d. (but said to be twelve years after her first visit to the Adrar in 1936), E2-233, ANRIM. To my knowledge, no attempts have yet been made to probe those observations or to consider what they might tell us about the historical functioning of slavery in the Sahara.

95. A notable exception is Elizabeth Genovese Fox's very useful comparative study, *Within the Plantation Household: Black and White Women of the Old South* (Chapel Hill: University of North Carolina Press, 1988).

7

SLAVERY, FAMILY LIFE, AND THE AFRICAN DIASPORA IN THE ARABIAN GULF, 1880–1940

Matthew S. Hopper

In May 1907, Faraj bin Sa'id, an enslaved African pearl diver, entered the British political agency offices in Bahrain seeking manumission from his master. Unlike many other enslaved divers who sought British assistance in that era, Faraj did not appeal for manumission on the grounds of physical abuse. He explained that he had been kidnapped from his home in Ethiopia in 1894 when he was twelve years old and taken to Mecca, where he was purchased and then moved to the Najd region of eastern Arabia. After working three years there, four years at Basra, and two years at Kuwait for three different masters, he was, in 1905, bestowed as a gift upon Bazza bint Sultan, the wife of his most recent master. Bazza sent Faraj pearl diving each season and took all of his earnings, but what made his condition unbearable was that Bazza failed to provide him a wife. When Faraj ran away to the British political agency to seek manumission, Bazza quickly followed to beg his return. In describing the occasion, the agent wrote that he expected Faraj would "probably return to his mistress who has been kissing and stroking his cheeks and promising him a wife."[1]

Although Faraj's case is unique, his experiences are representative of the lives of many enslaved Africans in Arabia in his day. Many pearl divers in the Gulf in the early twentieth century had been kidnapped from Africa as boys and labored in various occupations until, in their teens, they were enlisted as divers. In the early twentieth century, the Gulf pearl industry was at its peak, producing roughly half of the world's supply of pearls—a commodity that had grown increasingly fashionable from the last decades of the nineteenth century. Enslaved pearl divers who provided consistent profits to their masters could expect those masters to arrange a marriage for them, conventionally around the age of twenty-five. As a twenty-five-year-old diver in Bahrain, the center of the Gulf pearl industry, Faraj was near the top of his career and would have had grounds to expect his master to arrange a marriage for him. Bazza's failure to fulfill this obligation justified Faraj's desertion. This chapter examines marriage and family life among enslaved Africans such as Faraj in the Arabian Gulf during the late nineteenth and early twentieth centuries.

Background

Most of the Middle East, including eastern Arabia, was drawn into the expanding global economy in the nineteenth century. Incorporation generated economic growth in some sectors and created wealth in some circles, just as it increased Gulf dependence on global markets and subjected the region to the whims of international consumer tastes, supply, and demand. In the second half of the nineteenth century and the first quarter of the twentieth century, the Gulf experienced a boom in date exports, fueled in part by increased demand from India and new international markets in North America and Europe. Likewise, the pearl industry expanded dramatically in the second half of the nineteenth century due to a revival in demand in Europe and North America, where the fashion for pearls spread beyond royal and aristocratic groups. Growing demand for labor in the date-farming and pearl-diving sectors of the Gulf economy kept the trade in enslaved men and women profitable into the twentieth century and drove many traders to participate in the slave trade from parts of East Africa, Baluchistan, Persia, India, and some regions of Arabia. Demand for African labor fell when the date and pearl industries collapsed in the 1930s, but the decades of importation of Africans created a significant legacy in the demography of the Gulf.

Africans did not account for the Gulf's entire slave population—others from Baluchistan and Persian Mekran, particularly after World War I, comprised a significant portion of the region's enslaved community—but the substantial African population stood out to numerous contemporary observers. As early as 1876, the resident government surgeon in Muscat estimated that a quarter of Muscat and Mutrah's forty thousand residents were "Negroes" and half of the remaining population was of "mixed race" consisting of "different degrees of admixture between the Arab and the Negro, and the Arab and the Abyssinian."[2] In 1905, J. G. Lorimer estimated that the percentage of Africans in the population of the region was significant, ranging from 11 percent in Kuwait, 11 percent in Bahrain, 22 percent in Qatar, 25 percent in Muscat, and 25 percent in Mutrah to 28 percent in the Trucial Coast; Africans also comprised roughly 17 percent of the total population of coastal eastern Arabia between Hormuz and Kuwait. (By contrast, African Americans made up 10 to 12 percent of the US population in 1900 and 1910.)[3]

Many enslaved Africans in the Gulf were well treated, yet slave life in the region presented unique challenges, and physical abuse was common, particularly in the regions surrounding the Gulf pearl banks. Punishment for uncooperative slaves most often took the form of beatings with sticks and imprisonment in shackles.[4] The story of one enslaved African pearl diver is revealing. Mubarak bin Nār was five years old when he was kidnapped from Zanzibar around 1895, taken to Sur, and sold at Dubai, where he became an enslaved pearl diver. Many years later, at the start of the 1930 season, Mubarak was too ill to dive. His master had become heavily indebted to some of Dubai's Arab and Persian merchants due to decreased earnings, and he became desperate. He beat Mubarak for refusing to dive even when he was lying in his sickbed. When Mubarak told his story at the Muscat consulate, officials noted marks of abuse on his back.[5]

Women also experienced abuse. Stories from the Trucial Coast and Qatar reveal that jealous wives of masters could be especially harsh toward enslaved women. A woman named Khadia bint Mabrūk, who as a young girl had been kidnapped from East Africa in the 1890s along with her parents, served in the house of a man in Qatar named Abdul Azīz

Al-Ma'na; she was married to one of his male slaves when she was about twenty years old. After her husband died at the pearl banks around 1926, her master's wife began treating her cruelly. Khadia reported that "as my master's wife treated me with harshness and often beat me with sticks, and as her big daughter hit me on the head with a stone and struck me in the eye, I managed to escape."[6] Another woman complained that when her work slacked a little while she was ill, her masters beat her severely.[7]

In spite of the ever-present threat of beatings, kidnapping, and general abuse, many of the enslaved Africans in the Gulf demanded to be treated with dignity and acted assertively, even if they were punished for their behavior. A frequently asserted grievance was the lack of proper food and clothing. In general in the Gulf, tradition demanded that slave owners provide their slaves with enough food for their subsistence and at least one new item of clothing annually. As the Gulf date and pearl industries floundered after the late 1920s, masters pressed for more work from their slaves, yet at the same time, they failed to meet their obligations to those slaves. In consequence and despite the threats against them, many slaves asserted themselves, demanding that their masters meet their obligations.

The most frequent form of resistance to slavery in the Gulf was flight. Although official British policy generally tended to tolerate the institution of slavery in eastern Arabia, the Gulf administration took exception to cases of physical abuse and blatant neglect within its jurisdiction.[8] It thus maintained a policy, which became systematic from 1921 to 1941, of granting official manumission certificates at British consular offices to runaway slaves who could show evidence of abuse. Embossed with an official government seal, rendered in both English and Arabic, and modeled on Islamic manumission documents, such government manumission certificates were highly valued by their holders and were one means to secure a degree of freedom and respectability in Gulf society—although there was no guarantee against reenslavement by either the slave's original master or another party.

The testimonies that runaway slaves provided when seeking manumission from British officials at Gulf consulates and agencies at Bahrain, Sharjah, and Muscat provide some of the best sources of information about the lives of enslaved Africans in the Gulf. These testimonies give us a window into the family lives of these Africans in the late nineteenth and early twentieth centuries, and they allow us to draw some general conclusions about the treatment of slaves, their labor experiences, and various aspects of their personal lives, including marriage, divorce, concubinage, and childbirth.

Marriage and Divorce

Enslaved men, but not women, sometimes arranged their own nuptials, though rarely the first wedding. Take the case of Sa'id bin Sanqur, born into his master's household in Sharjah around 1913. When Sa'id turned fifteen, his master sent him out for diving and took his earnings, although Sa'id was allowed to retain some of his diving advances. The master also married him to one of his female slaves, named Kaniyah, whom Sa'id divorced after two years. Sa'id then arranged his own marriage to Lattuf, a female slave of another master, with whom he had two daughters. When Sa'id was twenty-three, he divorced Lattuf and after a few months expressed a desire to marry Salluah, the female slave of another master. However, as he lacked the money to do so, he borrowed from his master's wife some gold ornaments that he mortgaged to a Hyderabadi merchant in Sharjah for about one hundred rupees—and that enabled him to marry the woman.[9] Such were the options of some muwalid slave men.

Nevertheless, such cases were rare. Marriage contracts of enslaved men and women in the Gulf were usually arranged by their owners or by other masters.[10] Arranged marriages served the dual purpose of placating valued male slaves and producing offspring who could potentially labor for the master or be sold for profit. Male slaves were traditionally first married when they reached the age of twenty-five, female slaves around age fifteen. Not all arrangements were agreeable to everyone involved, however. One unfortunate man named Mubarak bin Salmīn was sold around 1920 to Hamad bin Saif Al-Suwaidi of Dubai; Hamad then married him to one of his female slaves, Zuhru, who, according to Mubarak, preferred his master.[11] Indeed, as such contracts were arranged without consultation with the slaves involved, many slave marriages were unhappy, and divorce was common throughout the first half of the twentieth century. Divorces initiated by enslaved males were frequent, those initiated by female slaves less common.[12]

A slave's marriage was no guarantee against sale, and enslaved men and women were frequently sold away from their families by their masters.

This was the case with Sadullah bin Sālim. Born a slave in Yemen, he was kidnapped by men from 'Asīr and taken to Qatar via Hasa in the late nineteenth century; he wound up as the slave of Sheikh Qāsim bin Muhammad Al-Thānī, the ruler of Qatar. When Sadullah reached maturity, he was married to Mabruka, one of the sheikh's female slaves. The couple had three sons and two daughters, but only the daughters survived childhood. At the time of Sadullah's manumission, one of the girls was married to the slave of another member of the royal family and the other was fifteen and unmarried. When Sheikh Qāsim died in 1913, Sadullah and his family passed to 'Abd al-'Azīz bin Qāsim, but 'Abd al-'Azīz subsequently sold Sadullah away from his family to a man in Sharjah, who sent him diving.[13] In some cases, masters of male slaves paid dowries to the owners of female slaves in order to contract slave marriages, although the slave couples often continued to work for their respective masters.[14]

A slave could marry a free person, and most arrangements of this kind were between enslaved men and free women. For example, Sulaiman bin 'Abdullah, who had been born in Sudan, kidnapped around 1903 when he was about five years old, and sold via Jedda and Hasa to Qatar and later Darīn, was married to a free woman of Yemeni ancestry when he was twenty-five.[15] Another enslaved diver, named Mabrūk bin 'Ali, born to free parents in Ethiopia and kidnapped at the age of seven around 1905, was similarly married to a freeborn woman of Yemeni ancestry when he was about twenty-five.[16] However, these mixed marriages were subject to special pressures, as the story of Zahra bint Mubarak indicates. Zahra, a muwalid slave born of Swahili slave parents at Sharjah around 1900, was manumitted by her elderly female master. She subsequently married Habush, an enslaved pearling crewman from Batinah. One day, the two got into an argument over a debt Habush had accrued. The disagreement turned into a fistfight, during which Habush fell to the ground, and ten days later, he died from his injuries. Zahra ran away when she perceived local jurists contemplated enslaving her and selling her as repayment for her late husband's debts.[17]

Although polygyny was common in the Gulf, available evidence suggests that male slaves rarely, if ever, had more than one wife, and it is clear from manumission testimonies that enslaved men frequently remarried shortly after divorcing a previous assigned wife. For women, however, being divorced by an enslaved husband could mean the potential of being sold. One thirty-five-year-old enslaved woman named Salhuh bint Ahmad had been married by her master in Umm al-Quwain to a male slave named Mabrūk. When Mabrūk divorced her in 1937, her master prepared to sell her, and she ran away to Sharjah.[18]

Childbirth

Infant mortality among enslaved Africans in eastern Arabia was high in the late nineteenth and early twentieth centuries. Many married couples who were enslaved never had children, few appear to have had more than five children, and rarely did all of a couple's children survive to adulthood. Walaid, who had been kidnapped in East Africa when he was five or six years old, taken to Sur, and sold as a slave to Qatar around 1885, was married when he was about thirty to a female slave of one his master's relatives. Of the couple's two daughters and four sons, all died except a son named Sālim, who became the slave of Walaid's wife's master's son. The marriage may not have been particularly happy: when Walaid's master died around 1923, Walaid passed to his wife's master, who manumitted his wife but kept him as a slave. Seizing her freedom, Walaid's wife left him.[19]

In general, masters controlled the bodies and reproductive lives of their slaves. When a female slave born in his house came of age, a master was entitled to take her as his concubine or marry her to one of his male slaves or the slave of someone else. In some cases, masters availed themselves of all these options. Hilaweh bint Rashid, who was born in her master's house on Za'ab Island around 1907, was married to Nubi, one of her master's male slaves, when she was fifteen years old. She gave birth to a son and a daughter, but in 1938 when her daughter was a year old, her husband died. Her master then took her as his concubine for two years before marrying her to a man from Batinah.[20] Masters could sell away a slave's spouse as easily as marrying slaves to one another. Faraj bin Sulaiman, born on the Mrima coast of East Africa around 1905, was kidnapped as a child by a man who took him to Sur and after a year sold him to 'Isā bin 'Ali on Za'ab Island. 'Isā worked Faraj as a diver for four years before marrying him to a slave woman named Latīfah. Three years later, despite the fact that Latīfah had given birth to a child, 'Isā sold her to Bedouins.[21]

Illicit Sexuality

In the second half of the nineteenth century, slave traders imported so many young boys from East Africa to work in the growing pearl industry that, by the 1870s, the ratio of male to female slaves among captured slave ships on the Arabian coast reversed previous trends, shifting overwhelmingly in favor of males. In 1872, HMS *Vulture* captured a large slave dhow off the coast of Ras al-Hadd at the entrance to the Gulf of Oman. The dhow was carrying 169 slaves from Pemba to Sur and Batinah. Of the slaves found aboard, 124 were males and 45 were females. The majority were children.[22] HMS *Philomel* captured a 63-ton dhow near Ras al-Hadd on October 13, 1884, that was found to have 128 male and 26 female slaves aboard (77 men, 14 women, 51 boys, and 12 girls). The dhow was bound for Batinah from Dar es Salaam, having collected the slaves by canoe between Ras Ndege and Kunduchi.[23] In November 1885, HMS *Osprey* captured a 42-ton dhow around Ras Madraka in Oman bound from Ngao in East Africa to Sur with 49 male and 24 female slaves (8 men, 12 women, 41 boys, and 12 girls).[24] In fact, in the last quarter of the nineteenth century, the evidence from dhows captured by British cruisers off the Arab coast overwhelmingly demonstrated that, by then, the traffic from East Africa comprised mostly male slaves.

In such an environment, not all male slaves were permitted to have socially accepted sexual relations within legally sanctioned marriages. It is perhaps through this lens that we should view evidence of homosexuality and pederasty among some male descendants of enslaved Africans in the Gulf—although the extent to which either was practiced is extremely difficult to gauge from the written record, especially as both were officially prohibited and severely punished when proven by jurists.

Given the unique conditions created by the lopsided ratio of males to females, homosexual relationships may have been common among unmarried men, as suggested by Unni Wikan for the region of Batinah in Oman,[25] particularly on a short-term basis. One record notes that in August 1936, Yūsuf bin Khamīs, "a negro from Basra" (probably an ex-slave or descendant of a slave) working as a teacher of boys in Dubai, was convicted of pederasty and punished accordingly. Yūssuf "was seen from adjacent houses to commit an unnatural offense on a young boy in his room with a friend," and people from the area "rushed on them and caught Yūssuf and his friend." Yūssuf's friend, who tried to escape, "jumped over the wall to the ground with the result that his buttock was fractured." As for Yūsuf, "he was caught by Said bin Bati and was taken to the sheikh. The sheikh sent him to the *qadhi* (judge). When the offense was proved, he was given a very severe beating which caused a wound on his head." The sheikh resolved to send Yūsuf back to Basra as soon as his wound healed, though his friend received no further punishment. After some investigation, it became known that Yūsuf had formerly been sent away from Bahrain, Qatar, and Sharjah for "making mischief."[26]

Concubinage and Questions of Paternity

In the early twentieth century, Arab men in the Gulf frequently took secondary wives or concubines. These women held a lower legal status than a legitimate wife and were generally taken for short periods of time, ranging from a week to a few years. In theory, under Islamic law, children of female concubines had a legally recognized status as free descendants of their fathers. In practice, however, this was often not the case. Masters regularly exchanged female concubines, often for periods as brief as seven to ten days. In a number of cases, when the woman was discovered to be pregnant, she was given in marriage to a male slave and her child treated as the child of slaves. In other cases, the pregnant concubine was sold far away, where the child would not interfere with the father's personal life.

In one case, Sa'id bin Hazim of Dubai purchased Maryami bint Mubrark, a Sudanese woman, and made her a concubine. When he found Maryami to be pregnant (ca. 1903), he married her to Johar, his African slave, and her son took the name Khamīs bin Johar rather than Khamīs bin Sa'id. When Khamīs was twelve years old, Sa'id manumitted the boy along with his mother. But in 1924, Sa'id and Khamīs's parents were all killed when plague hit Dubai. The following year, Sa'id's daughter and her husband decided to reenslave Khamīs, either to sell him or to send him to work for profit. Fearing an unknown fate, he ran away to Sharjah to seek manumission.[27]

Around the turn of the century, Sa'id bin Bilal Al-Gharāhal of Ras al-Khaimah purchased an East African woman named Saluhah and married her to his Swahili male slave. Saluhah and her husband had a daughter named Maryami, and when Maryami was seventeen, Sa'id made her his concubine. Maryami became pregnant and gave birth to a son, named Juma', who legally should have been considered the free son of Sa'id. However, when Juma' was seven years old, Sa'id died and his relatives divided his estate. Sa'id's son 'Ali inherited Maryami and attempted to sell Juma' as a slave, in spite of the fact he was his half brother. In May 1931, Maryami took her son and fled.[28]

Zainab bint Mubarak, another young woman of African ancestry, was born in Yemen, orphaned when she was seven years old (around 1904), and subsequently raised by her uncle. One day while grazing sheep, she was kidnapped and taken first to Jedda and then to Mecca, where she was purchased by a hajj pilgrim named Muhammad bin 'Ali bin Kamil, who took her back by steamer to his hometown of Sharjah. She recalled in 1927 that Muhammad "had sexual intercourse with me for some time and then he married me to a slave named Selim." It is unclear from her account whether she was pregnant at the time she was married to Selim. Zainab subsequently gave birth to five children, three of whom survived infancy. It is possible that her master was the father of her firstborn, if that child died—although Zainab asserted that Selim was the father of the three surviving children. One of the three surviving children was kidnapped, and the other two remained in the service of her master through at least the late 1920s.[29]

Such cases were not limited to enslaved Africans. A Baluchi woman who was kidnapped from Makran was sold to a man from Khan, a dependency of Sharjah near Dubai. Her master, Rashid bin 'Ali, took her as his concubine until she became pregnant. He then married her to a Baluchi slave named Marzūq, and she gave birth to a daughter who took the name Rafia'h bint Marzūq Baluchi. When Rafia'h was six years old, Rashid sold her mother to a man in another town and gave Rafia'h as a present to his brother Abdullah bin 'Ali in Jumairah. Abdullah raised Rafia'h until she was fifteen and then married her to one of his Baluchi slaves, named Sorūr. Rafia'h and Sorūr continued serving Abdullah for ten years. Then, Rashid got into a fight with his brother, went to Jumairah, and took Rafia'h from Abdullah's house by force. Rafia'h subsequently escaped and fled to the British agency in Sharjah to seek a manumission certificate.[30] Surprisingly, although paternal lineage was a vital part of identity in the Gulf, it was uncontested in many ambiguous cases. In the late 1890s, 'Abd al-Rahman bin Khalfan al Mutawwa' of Dubai took as a concubine a muwalid African woman, the daughter of one of his slaves. In about 1899, she gave birth to a son, who took the name Khamīs bin 'Abd al-Rahman and was treated, according to his own account, as 'Abd al-Rahman's legal son. Sometime later, 'Abd al-Rahman turned Khamīs's mother out of his house, but he kept Khamīs with him. Around 1925 (possibly during the Dubai plague of 1924–25), 'Abd al-Rahman died, leaving in the household Khamīs, his three sisters, and three of his father's slaves. Around 1930, Shamsah, one of Khamīs's sisters, began to treat him as if he were a slave, insisting that he go diving with a *nākhuda* (captain) she had selected. Khamīs protested and even asked the British-appointed residency agent at Sharjah to help him, without success. He eventually became so despondent that, fearing enslavement, he traveled to Muscat to request a government manumission certificate.[31]

When the British Political Resident asked the Sharjah agent about Khamīs's case, he replied that after some investigation he had concluded that Khamīs was not 'Abd al-Rahman's son but actually the son of a slave. The details were fuzzy, but the agent alleged that Khamīs's mother had been married thrice before 'Abd al-Rahman took her as his concubine and was pregnant from her last marriage before he had intercourse with her. Although he slept with her several times before Khamīs was born, Khamīs was not his child. Rather, the father was his mother's former husband. 'Abd al-Rahman's slaves called Khamīs his son, according to the agent, but 'Abd al-Rahman "reprimanded the slaves for saying so and so they stopped so doing." Khamīs was thus not 'Abd al-Rahman's son but his slave. Furthermore, the agent reported, 'Abd al-Rahman's daughter had, after her father's death, manumitted Khamīs, who had not only gone diving of his own accord but had also acquired a considerable amount of debt. His flight to Muscat was thus an attempt to escape his debts rather than an effort to regain his paternal rights of freedom.[32] In such cases, paternity was difficult to prove, and in this case specifically, we unfortunately do not know the outcome. Some muwalid slaves never knew their real fathers because their mothers had been concubines who were sold away once they became pregnant. Zamzam bint Awadh, a woman from Dhofar who was probably of African ancestry, was kidnapped as a child from her home by Bedouins, who sold her to Muhammad bin Sa'id of the

Bani Bu 'Ali tribe from Sur. Muhammad kept Zamzam as his concubine for ten years. When she then became pregnant, he sold her to Mohanna bin Sa'id of Wudam, who after a month took her to Abu Dhabi and sold her to a man named Khalaf bin Ataibah. In Khalaf's house, she gave birth to a girl named Safi and married a Kuwaiti man named 'Abd al-Rahman bin Mohanna. Safi's paternal name is not recorded, but it is highly unlikely that she took the name of her biological father or ever met him.[33]

Limits and Negotiations of Sexual Freedom

For most enslaved Africans in the Gulf in the late nineteenth and early twentieth centuries, matters of sexuality, marriage, and reproduction were controlled by others. Still, many enslaved men and women succeeded in dictating some of the terms of their family life. Successful pearl divers such as Faraj bin Sa'id, whose story opened this chapter, negotiated certain aspects of their enslavement from a strong position. However, with the collapse of the Gulf date and pearl industries in the 1920s, even the most accomplished divers faced an uncertain future.[34]

One final story perhaps best illustrates both the limitations and the possibilities for negotiating degrees of sexual freedom in the Gulf in this period. Letters intercepted en route to Bahrain from Doha attest to the sale of some women in Qatar in April 1935. 'Abd al-'Azīz and 'Abd ar-Rahmān bin 'Abd al-Latīf Al-Mana' wrote to Nāsir bin Muhammad Al-Mani' to verify the sale of his slave women to Juma' Al-Somali. Juma', the men explained, made the best offer for the women and proved more reliable than other interested parties. Juma' paid one thousand rupees and $135 altogether for them, which was less than Nāsir expected, but they felt they had to accept his price because the women were causing problems. As the men explained, "If they were taken by some other person he would have kept them with him and then returned them as being unfit (for service). The reason was that whenever anyone wanted to buy them they used to show themselves to be unfit, which made the purchasers refrain from buying them. When Ibrahim Islam heard about them he asked us to send them to him and after seeing them he returned them without making any offer whatsoever."[35] 'Abd al-'Azīz and 'Abd ar-Rahmān did not want to lose the opportunity to sell to Juma' Al-Somali, since he planned to take the women with him by car right after he purchased them. How the women showed themselves to be "unfit" to their potential buyers is unknown. But the record allows for the possibility that they somehow found a way to negotiate their situation, perhaps by deliberately acting in a manner designed to discourage undesirable purchasers or reduce their sale price in order to, at the very least, harm their seller.

Enslaved African men and women in the Gulf faced challenging lives of hard work and strictly governed sexuality, but they often found ways to resist their conditions and negotiate some degree of sexual freedom. In this regard, their struggles mirror those of enslaved populations elsewhere and present the potential for comparison—a conversation that this volume and other recent works are beginning to make possible.

Notes

1. Statement of Faraj bin Said, slave of Bahrain lady, Bazza bint Sultan, wife of Khalifa bin Zaid al Jalahima, aged about 25 years (May 16, 1907), R/15/1/213, India Office Records (hereafter cited as IOR), British Library, London.

2. A. S. G. Jayakar, "Medical Topography of Muscat," *Administrative Report of the Persian Gulf Political Residency and Muscat Political Agency for the Year 1876–77*, ND 1/H, Centre for Documentation and Research, Abu Dhabi (hereafter CDR).

3. J. G. Lorimer, *Gazetteer of the Persian Gulf* (Calcutta: Superintendent Government Printing, 1915); Campbell Gibson and Kay Jung, "Historical Census Statistics on Population Totals by Race, 1790 to 1990," *U.S. Census Bureau Population Division Working Paper Series No. 56* (September 2002), accessed October 8, 2008, http://www.census.gov/population/www/documentation/twps0056/twps0056.html.

4. See, for example, Statement of slave Mubarak bin Othman, aged about 40 years, recorded at the Political Agency, Bahrain (April 25, 1931), R/15/1/205, IOR.

5. Statement made by Mubarak bin Nar, originally from Zanzibar, aged about 40 years (November 24, 1930), Residency Agent, Sharjah to Secretary to Political Resident, Persian Gulf (January 22, 1931), R/15/1/217, IOR.

6. Statement of Khadia bint Mabrook, aged about 35 years, recorded at the Political Agency, Bahrain (January 11, 1929), R/15/1/204, IOR.

7. Statement of Zubad bint (father unknown), aged about 20 years (February 19, 1937), R/15/1/219, IOR.

8. Matthew S. Hopper, "Imperialism and the Dilemma of Slavery in Eastern Arabia and the Gulf, 1873–1939," *Itinerario* 30, no. 3 (2006): 76–94.

9. Statement of Said bin Sanqur, born at Sharjah, aged about 25 years (August 13, 1938), R/15/1/211, IOR.

10. See, for example, Statement made by Sa'ad bin Mubarak, aged about 40 years (January 31, 1938), and Statement made by Farhan bin Sa'ud, aged about 60 years, born at Suwahil (January 31, 1938), R/15/1/210, IOR.

11. Statement of Mubarak bin Salmin, born in Shaqra of Nejd, aged about 50 years (April 13, 1940), R/15/1/212, IOR.

12. Statement made by Zainab bint Mubarak, aged about 30 years, place of birth Saibiyeh of Yemen (June 27, 1927), R/15/1/208, IOR.

13. Statement of slave Sadullah bin Salem, aged about 45 years (January 25, 1927), R/15/1/204, IOR.

14. See, for example, Statement of Marzook bin Hassan, aged about 27 years (October 22, 1927), R/15/1/204, IOR.

15. Statement of Sulaiman bin 'Abdullah, aged about 30 years (October 13, 1928), R/15/1/204, IOR.

16. Statement of slave Mabruk bin Ali aged about 30 years (October 29, 1928), R/15/1/204, IOR.

17. Statement of Zahruh bint Mubarak Swahili, aged about 30 years (December 2, 1929), R/15/1/208, IOR.

18. Statement made by Salhuh bint Ahmad, aged about 35 years (July 23, 1938), R/15/1/211, IOR.

19. Statement of Walaid (father's name unknown), aged about 50 years (May 15, 1929), R/15/1/204, IOR.

20. Statement of Hilaweh bint Rashid, born in Za'ab Island, aged about 35 years (February 18, 1942), R/15/1/207, IOR.

21. Statement made by Faraj bin Sulaiman, aged 34 years (October 10, 1939), R/15/1/207, IOR.

22. Senior Naval Officer in Persian Gulf (and Commander HMS *Vulture*) to Rear Admiral Arthur Cumming, Commander in Chief, East Indies (September 10, 1872), ADM 1/6230, National Archives (former Public Records Office), Kew, UK (hereafter PRO).; Lt. C. M. Gilbert Cooper, "Capture of a Slave Dhow: Or the Vulture and Its Prey" (n.d.), Lt. C. M. Gilbert-Cooper Papers, National Maritime Museum (Greenwich, UK), BGY/G/5.

23. Commander HMS *Philomel* to Commander in Chief, East Indies (October 15, 1884), ADM 1/6714, PRO.

24. Herbert W. Dowding, Commander HMS *Osprey*, to Rear Admiral Frederick W. Richards, Commander in Chief, East Indies (September 19, 1885), ADM 1/6758, PRO.

25. Unni Wikan, *Behind the Veil in Arabia: Women in Oman* (Baltimore, Md.: Johns Hopkins University Press, 1982); Unni Wikan, "Man Becomes Woman: Transsexualism in Oman as a Key to Gender Roles," *Man*, n.s. 12, no. 2 (August 1977): 304–19.

26. "News of the Trucial Coast, August 1–15, 1936," no. 15, "Local News," 306–7, Residency Agent, Sharjah, News Reports, vol. 2, 1935–36, R/15/2/1865, IOR.

27. Statement made by Khamīs bin Johar, born in Dubai, aged about 21 years (June 6, 1925), R/15/1/208, IOR.

28. Statement made by Maryami bint Jumah Swahili, aged about 30 years (May 17, 1931), R/15/1/209, IOR.

29. Statement made by Zainab bint Mubarak of Sabiyeh of Yemen, aged about 30 years (June 27, 1927), R/15/1/208, IOR.

30. Statement made by Rafia'h bint Marzuq Baluchi, aged about 25 years (October 21, 1925), R/15/1/208, IOR.

31. Statement made by Khamis bin Abdur Rahman, born at Dubai, aged about 34 years (July 27, 1933), R/15/1/218, IOR.

32. Residency Agent Sharjah to Secretary to Political Resident, Persian Gulf (September 30, 1933), R/15/1/218, IOR.

33. Statement made by Zamzam bint Wadh, originally from Dhohar, aged about 55 years (April 4, 1934), R/15/1/209, IOR.

34. Matthew S. Hopper, "Globalization and the Economics of African Slavery in Arabia in the Age of Empire," *Journal of African Development* 12, no. 1 (Spring 2010): 125–46.

35. 'Abd al-'Azīz and 'Abd ar-Rahmān bin 'Abd al-Latīf Al-Mana' to Nāsir bin Muhammad Al-Mani' (21 Muharram 1354, April 25, 1935), copy in attachment to Political Agent, Bahrain to Lt. Col. T. C. Fowle, Political Resident, Persian Gulf (May 2, 1935), R/15/1/226, IOR.

8

"I ASK FOR DIVORCE BECAUSE MY HUSBAND DOES NOT LET ME GO BACK TO MY COUNTRY OF ORIGIN WITH MY BROTHER"

Gender, Family, and the End of Slavery in the Region of Kayes, French Sudan, 1890–1920

MARIE RODET

In 1909, Makouroni D.[1] went to the provincial court of Médine, a town near Kayes,[2] to ask for a divorce because her husband did not want to let her return to her region of origin with her brother.[3] She declared her marriage was nullified, since Samba K. had never paid the bridewealth. They did, however, have a child. The court pronounced the divorce and granted custody of the child to the mother.

Some details in Makouroni D.'s case allow us to deduce the former slave status of at least one of the litigants. The fact that she asked to return to her country of origin is suggestive of a history of enslavement. Following the official abolition of slavery in 1905,[4] around 15 percent of the slave population left the region of Kayes between 1907 and 1910.[5] Some returned to the regions where their families originated. Makouroni D.

also mentioned that her husband never paid the bridewealth, which is another hint of her former slave status. Slave marriages or marriages between master and slave were rarely formalized by the payment of a bridewealth, or if they were, the bridewealth was likely to be very low.[6] Since in Makouroni D.'s case no bridewealth had ever been paid, the court ruled against the husband.

The transcripts of the court cases found in the Malian archives for the first decades of the twentieth century are often very brief and elusive on the precise context of the litigation. Nonetheless, they remain a precious source of information about gender conflicts taking place against the backdrop of the end of slavery in French Sudan. Increasing attention has been paid in recent scholarship to finding new sources in order to recover the voices of African slaves. The study of legal archives is part of this new endeavor. However, little research has been done on this issue from an explicitly gendered perspective, especially for the history of the former French West African colonies.[7] While reading records against the grain, this chapter aims to uncover slave women's sexual and migratory strategies, ignored by conventional historiography, in the region of Kayes at the time of emancipation.[8] A gender perspective on archival data will allow us to explore the ambiguities at the heart of slave women's condition. I will use complaints, petitions, court cases, and administrative correspondence to investigate the behavior of female slaves in the emancipation process.

This chapter is also an attempt to reexamine through the lens of carnal relations the categories of wife, concubine, and female slave as well as the tenuous and fluid borders between these three categories. Before the official end of slavery in French Sudan, the most common way for a slave woman to obtain her freedom was to marry her master or a nonslave man and to bear him a child.[9] With the beginning of the French colonization of the region, alternative opportunities for enslaved women to become free appeared. These new opportunities increased geographic as well as social mobility. In this chapter, I aim to assess the extent to which sex can be a useful category for the analysis of slave agency. I will look at how carnal relations were used and/or rejected by former slave women in order to enhance their mobility and to adapt to the new postabolition colonial environment.

Far from simply abolishing bonded labor, slave emancipation reshaped the relations between men and women and between the individual and society. The emancipation process was central to the destabilization and disruption of dominant discourses on slave and master identities. It also entailed the disorganization of supposedly fixed relations of gender and power hierarchies. Using carnal relations, (former) slave women developed spaces and locations that gave them the chance to disrupt not only gender hierarchies within their own communities but also the dominant colonial and local power structures within postabolition French Sudan. They were able to fluctuate between marginalized/subaltern positions within their own communities and to enhance their position within the colonial society. They therefore succeeded in constructing agency by favoring, depending on the circumstances, carnal, social, and/or family relations.

I will begin this chapter by analyzing the extent to which carnal relations were used or rejected or both by (former) female slaves in order to leave their masters and to adapt to a "moving" colonial environment. I will then examine how the end of slavery and the related slave exodus disrupted slave and master relationships and also, through the destabilization of gender relations, entailed the redefinition of marriage and family in postabolitionist French Sudan.

Wives, Concubines, and Mistresses: Carnal Relations and Emancipatory Strategies

Before the introduction of the colonial emancipatory policy, slave women in the region of Kayes resorted to different strategies to enhance their position in a society whose economy mainly relied on slave labor.[10] They tried to find new free or unfree "husbands" with better economic and social situations. They could run away from one master's house to attach themselves to another, more powerful master. A slave woman could also become the concubine or the wife of her master (when the master was a man) or marry a member of the master's family. However, it is very unlikely that a slave woman really had a choice when becoming the wife or the concubine of a freeborn man.[11] It might, in fact, be inappropriate to speak of strategy here. For a woman, slavery meant that her body became the property of her master; it was subjected to her master's will. In contrast, the sexuality and virginity of a free woman was tightly controlled.[12] In some parts of the region of Kayes, especially to the south, a nobleman could not marry a slave woman unless he freed her before doing so; otherwise, she would continue to be considered a slave as would her children. Several colonial legal customaries and reports on captivity mention that the children born from the concubinage between a female captive and a free man were free and that the mother acquired rights that were close to those of a free woman.[13] She could not be sold. However, she would never be considered at the same level as the legitimate wives. Bearing a child to her master could certainly allow her to belong, through blood ties, to the kinship and therefore, according to Igor Kopytoff and Suzanne Miers, to reduce her marginality.[14] In some regions, she became immediately free; in others, she became free when the master died. However, if the slave woman belonged to another master and her free husband did not ransom her, she would continue to belong to her master, as would her children. In any case, the life of a slave woman was largely determined by the status of her husband and by the protection he could win from a master or from a more powerful patron.

The rules mentioned here were, however, regularly violated, and their violation was rarely punished. Becoming the concubine of the master was therefore not a long-term protection nor a guarantee of freedom. In 1894, the commandant of the district of Kayes wrote to the governor of French Sudan to submit for his approbation five certificates of liberty.[15] One concerned Goundo C. who was married to Guy M., probably a *tirailleur*,[16] with whom she had a child. It is unclear under what conditions she married Guy M., but before joining the army column for the Bambouk, he ordered the chief of the liberty village in which she was living to sell her while he was absent. She was then sold to another tirailleur. On hearing of this, the commandant canceled the transaction. The buyer was reimbursed, and the seller was punished. Finally, Goundo C. asked for a liberty certificate in order to avoid being sold again by her husband. The commandant highlighted that she was in any case free, since she had been living in the liberty village for more than three months. She was also customarily free, since she was married to a free man and had borne him a child.

The liberty villages were funded by the French administration in the first years of the conquest of French Sudan. At the beginning of their existence, they took in, above all, the slaves of the defeated enemies of the French army. They also took in mistreated slaves, those threatened with sale by their masters, and those whose families had already been sold by the masters. The liberty villages were primarily an attempt by the French administration to control the increasing flight of slaves in the region and to create permanent, settled communities in the deserted surroundings of the colonial posts and along the main conquest and trade routes. The first attempts to restrict the slave trade in French Sudan began in 1895. Slave caravans crossing the colonial territory had to be seized and the slaves sent to the liberty villages, where they would be issued a liberty certificate after a three-month stay. However, up to 1901, slaves were systematically returned to their masters when those masters went to the commandant to claim them within three months from the date of entry in the liberty village.

The Goundo C. case highlights the confusion concerning the status of slave women that characterized the early years of colonization. A female slave was often simultaneously a concubine, a worker, and a commodity.[17] But this situation did not fit into French abolitionist categories. In theory, for the colonial administration, a woman could only be the slave or the wife (and therefore a free wife) of a free man. Confronted by cases such as the Goundo C.'s, in which the distinction between slave and wife tended to be blurred, the French administrators were reluctant to apply the categories they meant to set up: the question of slave women's liberation might challenge domestic and social stability in the newly conquered territories. Female slaves in the region of Kayes formed about 60 percent of the slave population. Moreover, they had a greater value than male slaves. They gave new dependents to their masters, but above all, female labor was predominant in production. The women's domestic labor was also essential to the family economy.[18]

The colonial officers often initially tried to prove that a woman was in any case free in order to justify the issuance of a liberty certificate—without questioning why she could have been sold in the first place. A similar ambiguity lay at the heart of the French abolitionist system of the liberty villages. The populations of these villages, where women were in the majority, could only enjoy a very limited "freedom."[19] Though the women were freed from their former masters, they had to serve the colonial administration as if they still were slaves. In addition, they were often abused by the colonial administration and systematically recruited for forced labor.[20]

Historian Denise Bouche assumes that slave women could leave the liberty villages only if they married tirailleurs or colonial agents.[21] It was certainly extremely difficult for women in patrilineal and patrilocal societies like those of the region of Kayes to remain unmarried because they would remain unprotected. This is probably why Goundo C. asked for a liberty certificate but not for a divorce. But the Goundo C. case also demonstrates the limits of this strategy, as these "marriages" were rarely long-standing ones in times of tremendous social and economical changes.

In 1894, the administrator of the district of Kayes wrote a report on the interrogation of Fatimata K., a *captive de case* (a slave born within the household), who complained that her master had threatened to correct her because she had again spent the night out.[22] The master denied this and affirmed that he had tried to correct her in the past but had had to abandon the attempt, as she never changed her behavior. Her mother confirmed that Fatimata always spent the night outside the house but said that she had not been beaten. Fatimata was asked in the presence of the administrator if she perhaps wished to get married, but she immediately refused this suggestion, declaring that she did not want to be under the guardianship of a husband. The administrator concluded that she seemed to have registered a complaint against her master in order to get freed and to be able to do whatever she wished during the night. The document does not reveal whether Fatimata was finally freed, but she probably was not because she could not prove the ill treatment of which she claimed to be a victim. As this case demonstrates, some female slaves were perfectly aware that marriage often simply added one more layer of control and restriction over their lives.

A few months earlier, the governor of French Sudan wrote to the commandant of the district of Nioro to advise him that while examining the liberty certificates he received for approbation, he had noticed the one for Cira S., a twenty-one-year-old slave woman, had to be corrected.[23] As she was an adult, she did not have to be left to somebody else's care. He further asked for an explanation concerning the people to whom former captives such as Cira S. were usually entrusted. The commandant of Nioro answered a few days later, saying that most of the people to whom these women were entrusted were their husbands or the chiefs of the liberty villages where they lived. They were therefore not entrusted as slaves to these people. In reality, however, this last remark had little chance of being true. The people to whom these women had been entrusted were likely to continue to consider them as slaves. The chiefs of the liberty villages were not of slave origin but had been granted their positions for services rendered to the administration. They often used their positions to increase their personal wealth. In 1895, the administrator of Médine wrote to the commandant of the district of Kayes to indicate that he had sent to prison all the section chiefs of the liberty village due to the misappropriation of funds: they had given the women of the liberty village in "marriage" and received the bridewealth themselves, and they also had given slaves back to their owners in exchange for gifts.[24]

In the same letter, the commandant of Nioro stated that based on the instructions sent by the governor relating to the establishment of the first liberty certificates, he believed that the issue of giving the names of the people to whom the former slaves were entrusted meant mentioning the names of the men with whom the female slaves were staying. Taking into account the governor's remark, he said he would henceforth no longer mention to whom these women would be entrusted. This latter comment shows that for the colonial administration, (former) slave women could only remain under the control of a male guardian. In this exchange of correspondence, the issue was whether the colonial administration had to mention administratively to whom these women had to be entrusted—not whether they had to be left in somebody else's care. It reveals the ambiguities of the colonial administration in the 1890s, which was reluctant to confront directly the issue of slavery except when it was necessary. These women were freed by the administration but entrusted to male guardians, and the administration was again unwilling to check with these guardians to determine whether the women were no longer considered as slaves. The introduction of an emancipatory politics did not mean the end of the circulation of slaves, especially female slaves. This issue also concerned freed slave children, who were left exactly in the same way in the care of Wolof traders and local notables, who continued to use them as servants.[25]

It is probably not a coincidence that the fourth section of the abolitionist decree of 1905 stated: "The preceding provisions are not prejudicial to the rights resulting from paternal, tutelary, and marital power over minors or married women, as long as the carried out acts do not constitute a temporary or definitive putting into bondage, to the benefit of a third party, of these minors or women."[26] The decree officially banned the slave trade, not slavery per se. This is probably why the fourth section stated that enslavement was only illegal if organized to the benefit of a third party. It therefore left intact bondage, such as domestic slavery ownership, and it left a good deal of room for the further circulation of bonded juvenile labor under the cover of guardianship and fosterage, as well as room for the trafficking of young girls under the guise of marriage.[27]

> Yet the colonial administrators at some point became aware of the inconsistencies of their abolitionist politics in practice. Less than a few months later, in a letter of instructions from 1906 specifying how the French legal system had to take into account the decree of December 12, 1905, the general prosecutor asked the French court personnel in French West Africa "to require from the accused all the written proof and all the documents issued by the administrative and municipal authorities which establish the veracity of their declarations." "Otherwise," he cautioned, "you would risk perpetuating, under cover of guardianship and, above all, of marriage, the actual sale of people, and if the law were to be got around this way, the repression [of slavery] would become impossible, or at least extremely difficult."[28]

Even if the colonial administration had difficulties in confronting the inconsistencies of its own abolitionist policy, it did not discourage female slaves from leaving their masters when they had the opportunity. Some female slaves seemed to have used the few niches opened by the new abolitionist context to leave their masters. The colonial administrators in the region regularly received complaints concerning female captives who had been sent by their masters to colonial cities or to railway building sites to sell food or to work but then never returned.[29] In 1902, the administrator of Kita received a complaint about a female slave named Fatimata who had been sent by her master to sell milk on the railway building site in Boudofo.[30] Due to the outbreak of yellow fever in the region, she had to stay on the site, for it had been put in quarantine. She finally decided to settle there, and she married the servant boy of an officer after having been the "mistress" of several French officers. Questioned by the commandant of Kita following the complaint lodged by her master, Mamadou D., she refused to return to the master's house, where she declared she was mistreated.

In 1906, J. H. Dufort, the manager of the bar at the station of Toukoto, sent a letter to the colonial administration in Kita asking for the liberation of two female captives, Goroko and her daughter Douélé (or Doualé), who had taken refuge at his place.[31] He had hired Goroko as a laundress. An investigation conducted by the administration clarified the circumstances of the flight of Douélé from her master's house.[32] Douélé's master, Diouldé D., had sent her and her mother, Goroko (called Kani D. in the correspondence by the administrator of Bafoulabé), to Toukoto in order to graze the herd. Douélé then became the mistress of Dufort, who encouraged her to go to Kita to ask for her freedom. Unfortunately, the archival record does not give us the outcome of the case.

The acquisition of a new source of "protection" through sexual relations was evidently one way by which slave women tried to enhance their social position. In the emancipatory process, carnal relations and marriage soon became other sources of protection for (former) slave women. Some of them tried to attach themselves to men linked to the colonial administration, who could secure for them, to a certain extent, a social protection. Scholars often estimate that it was easier for men than for women to leave their former masters, since the latter suffered under the double disability of being both female and slave.[33] The masters would not have let them go as easily as men. It is certainly difficult to determine the number of female slaves who effectively left their masters. However, the use of carnal relations to gain freedom seems to have been a very effective female strategy. Through concubinage or marriage, women easily found a new source of protection in order to rebuild their lives. Flight could therefore be less difficult for slave women than for slave men.

Following the colonial conquest of French Sudan and with the gradual introduction of the French emancipating legislation, the opportunities for slave women to seize their freedom increased, which, in turn, tended to complicate the relations between men and women in the region.

Female slaves did not always stay with their masters even when they were their concubines or their wives.

In September 1900, the representative in Kayes of the governor-general received a complaint from Beydy C. asking for the return of his three wives, who sought refuge in the liberty village of Kita.[34] In an earlier letter, the commandant in Kita had declared that these women were free, since they had left the liberty village after a three-month stay.[35] He thus considered that this case was a divorce case that had to be brought to the colonial court of necessity. In this instance, the so-called husband considered his wives to be free even if he might have bought them as slaves, whereas the wives declared themselves captives when entering the liberty village of Kita. Their slave status was then confirmed in a letter of September 1900 written by the commandant in Kita, explaining that these women had been abducted by the army columns of Samori.[36] These women therefore knew exactly how to use their status as "captives" to emancipate themselves from their husband with the help of the colonial administration. They had first left Médine, where they used to live with Beydy C., for the Kaarta, where they knew they could hide more easily. Had they initially gone to the liberty village of Médine, they would almost immediately have been returned to Beydy because he would have found them easily and quickly claimed them. The three women took refuge in the village of Labadéri.[37] While the commandant of the district of Kita was on an inspection tour in the region, the village chief of Labadéri went to him to declare that three women who escaped from Médine had been living at his place for one month. It is unclear why the village chief reported the women to the administration, but we can suppose that he did so to avoid administrative reprisals in case the commandant on tour had discovered there were three more inhabitants in the village who had not been declared for the census and the tax collection. The tours of inspection were mainly used for updating the data available on the region. They were often a violent demonstration of the presence and the power of the colonial administration in the region.

In considering the Beydy C. case, we are again at the heart of the ambiguities of the slave women's condition. In the process of emancipation, women attempted to prove that they were slaves whereas men tried to prove themselves to be the women's nominal husbands. This strategy is often found in the records of the native courts in the region of Kayes in the first decade of the twentieth century. As many other petitions addressed to the colonial administration tend to demonstrate, slave women tried to seize all kind of opportunities, not only carnal ones, to gain freedom for themselves and their families. The Beydy C. case further illustrates how some (former) slave women were able to make their case to the colonial administration in order to gain freedom, even when they were the concubines of their masters.

In September 1902, Oumarou L., from the district of Nioro, addressed a petition to the representative of the governor in Kayes concerning his wife, Fatimata N. He reported that she had run away after being advised by a policeman named Trebilé to seek him out him if she wanted his help in gaining her freedom from the colonial administration.[38] Oumarou went to the commandant of the district of Nioro, who refused to return his wife to him. He therefore asked for the help of the representative to get his wife back, as he was too old to work in order to acquire another one. Fatimata's mother and daughter were still living with him. In a telegram from the administration in Nioro to the representative in Kayes, we learn that Fatimata was a slave of Oumarou L., who made her his concubine.[39] She had run away earlier in the year, in May 1902, because her master mistreated her, and she took refuge at the liberty village of Nioro. The commandant of Nioro had then returned her to Oumarou on the condition that she would no longer be mistreated. But Fatimata returned to the administration on August 4, 1902, bearing marks of a beating. When her master went to the administration to claim her, she vigorously refused to go back to him. Considering the repetition of the alleged mistreatment as well as Fatimata's wish to go to the liberty village, the commandant of Nioro sent her there. Interestingly enough, this case happened in 1902, more than one year after the release of Circular 978, which prohibited the administration from returning slaves taking refuge at the liberty village to their masters.[40] Fatimata was granted access to the liberty village because she was allegedly mistreated by her so-called husband. The fact that she was the concubine of Oumarou L. surely interfered in the first administrative decision to return her to him. Once again, the administration did not seem to be willing to confront the ambiguous status of a slave woman: the administrators seem to have considered slave women who were "married" to their masters first and foremost as wives rather than as slaves, in order to avoid upheavals in the region. They therefore limited their action in regard to women's emancipation.

Despite this, women participated in the "slave exodus" to a great extent. In the liberty village of the region of Kayes, we can find the same imbalance between the number of men and women as existed in the total slave population of the region. On average, women made up 60 percent of the village population for the period from 1894 to 1911, the highest ratio of men to women being 75 men for 100 women in 1908 in the liberty village of Kayes. The figures for that liberty village clearly show that from 1908 onward, the overall increase of the population was largely due to the increase of the female population. The political reports confirm the predominant participation of women in the slave exodus. Further, twice as many women as men addressed requests for freedom to the colonial administration. Women were actually the first migrants to the city of Kayes, where they formed the majority of the "floating population."[41] Female slaves took advantage of a shifting landscape of economic and social opportunities to cross into new social positions in colonial towns.[42]

Numerous cases presented to the native courts of the region of Kayes in the first decade of the twentieth century demonstrate the different attempts of some (former) slave women to rebuild their lives "independent" from male guardianship.

The End of Slavery and the Redefinition of Marriage and Family

Slave women tried to take advantage of the end of slavery in order to emancipate themselves not only from their masters but also, with more or less success, from husbands they had rarely chosen. As the Makouroni D. case presented early in the chapter suggests, (former) slave women were able to go to the provincial courts of the region of Kayes to ask for a divorce when their husbands refused to allow them to take part in the slave exodus.[43] Some former slave women like Makouroni D. preferred following relatives and leaving husbands to staying in the region where they had been enslaved. They favored family ties over marital relations, since "they [could] not refuse the word of a brother."[44]

In the first years of the existence of the provincial courts, the judges in such cases were inclined to pronounce the divorce and to assign custody of the child or children to the mother. Women, whether free or slave, normally had no legal claims on their children in divorce,[45] and children of slaves customarily belonged to the master of the mother. But with the introduction of the new legal system in French West Africa in 1903,[46] followed by the abolition of slavery in 1905, the courts were urged by the colonial administration not to acknowledge slave status in their decisions. They were therefore inclined to give the custody of the children to the mother when no bridewealth had been paid, as was often the case in slave marriages. On April 16, 1910, Diamou D. went to the court of Yélimané to ask for his child. He explained that Awa D. and he were slaves of the same master.[47] They had married, and then he left for Yélimané-Refuge.[48] Awa, who was pregnant, refused to follow him. Diamou consequently asked for his child. Awa, however, declared to the court that she had never received any bridewealth, as witnesses confirmed. The court decided, therefore, that the child would stay with the mother.

Some other women, after having moved to a liberty village with their husbands, preferred staying in the colonial cities to following husbands who wished to return to their regions of origin. On April 23, 1910, Toumani S. explained to the civil court of Yélimané that he had settled in the liberty village of Yélimané with his wife, Assa D., a few years earlier.[49] Now, he wanted to return to his region of origin, but Assa refused to accompany him. Toumani therefore asked for his children. His wife declared that she had never received any bridewealth. The court acknowledged her declarations and decided that the children would stay with her.

This case, like others, shows that the struggle for control over the family life was a vital issue of emancipation. It also illustrates how central family and kinship were at the time of emancipation. Both female and male former slaves attempted to gain control in keeping their families together as a unit—whether by staying with their former masters or by leaving them. Contrary to what the colonial administration and, later, most scholars commonly presumed, slaves were not without connections and, above all, not without family ties. Even if slave family units were regularly dispatched between different regions and households because of wars, sales, and purchases, freed slaves often attempted to trace their still enslaved families, sometimes with the help of the colonial administration, in order to obtain their freedom. With emancipation, slaves acquired the right to create their own lineages. In May 1910, Alamboudou K., who settled in the district of Bafoulabé, went to the court of Yélimané to claim his children.[50] Boundia K., the mother, said she had never received any bridewealth and had had to provide for her children for seven years. Consequently, she refused to surrender them. Alamboudou's demand was nonsuited. In September 1910, Dakou D. declared to the court of Yélimané that he had left his two wives eight years earlier in order to gain his freedom in his country of origin.[51] He returned to get them, but his wives declared that they had already married again and had provided for their children during his absence. The court rejected Dakou D.'s demand. He appealed the judgment, but a few weeks later, the appeals court of Nioro affirmed the first judgment.

From the 1910s, the courts progressively increased their control over women by implementing a specific jurisprudence that forced women—no matter what their former status was—to go back to their husbands after they deserted and that also gradually made divorce more difficult for them to obtain.[52] In February 1911, Boïrik B. declared to the provincial court of Yélimané that he had married Boïlil M. seven years before, that they had gotten along well, and that they had had two children, one of whom was deceased.[53] However, he said, his wife had deserted him, taking their child, in order to live in Yélimané-Refuge. He asked for her to return with their child or for the reimbursement of the bridewealth as well as custody of the child. His wife claimed that she was not married to Boïrik and denied he was the father of her child, but she had no witness to back her declarations. The court ordered her to return to her husband because she had no valid reason to leave him. In another case, from June 1911, Mamadi K. went to the court of Nioro declaring that his wife, Sélé S., wished to divorce him after twenty-one years of marriage but without any valid reason.[54] The wife declared she wanted to return to the region her father was from. The court decided that Sélé had no legitimate reason for divorce and condemned her to stay with her husband.

Divorce cases linked to the issue of slavery increasingly followed the general pattern of the jurisprudence of nonslave marriages, in which children were considered to belong to their father. In 1912, Seikolo D. went to the court of Nioro in order to force his wife, Sountoura S., to return to him.[55] Sountoura declared to the court that she had been married to Seikolo by her master against her will and that she wanted to stay with her parents. Consequently, Seikolo asked the court to pronounce the divorce, which it did. Sountoura was not ordered to reimburse the bridewealth because she had never received one, but custody of the child was given to the father.

This progressive tightening of the jurisprudence in the 1910s can be directly linked with the aftermath of the end of slavery in the region and the precarious food situation that developed almost simultaneously. Between 1897 and 1915, the region of Kayes suffered fourteen years of bad harvests and food shortages, with the most severe crises occurring in 1905–7 and 1913–15.[56] The region again experienced serious food shortages in 1918–19. These crises encouraged the emancipation of the slaves, since their masters were not able to provide them with their daily sustenance. A 1912 report noted that the local population of the region of Kayes was discouraged by a succession of bad harvests; certain villages were completely deserted; and a large number of former slaves left for their regions of origin or resettled in more fertile areas, such as the Senegambian peanut basin.[57] Some women (both slave and free) tried to take advantage of the weakened power of family heads in times of severe food crises in order to free themselves from their male guardians/masters and husbands. No longer able to provide for his dependents, the head of the family often struggled to keep his family unit together and to arbitrate between the different members of the household. Confronted with a situation marked by the growing mobility of the population, both socially and geographically, the courts implicitly decided to increase control over women—and therefore over the main labor force of the region—by limiting their ability to get out of marriages.

The emancipation of slaves in the region of Kayes and the related exodus reveal numerous underlying tensions between matrimonial ties and family ties. Family ties tended to prevail over matrimonial ones when slaves decided to leave their masters at the turn of the twentieth century. From the 1910s on, however, the courts of the region, by forcing women to stay with their husbands although they wished to divorce, progressively obliged women to favor matrimonial ties over family ties. In September

1920, Sadio K. went to the court of Bafoulabé to register a complaint against his wife, Penda D., who had deserted him to go to her family of origin. He claimed her family members pushed her to ask for divorce.[58] He explained to the court that he had been married to Penda for more than twenty-five years and that they had four children. He added that his wife wanted to get divorced because he was old and almost blind. Penda declared to the court that she had decided to ask for a divorce after a quarrel during which her husband claimed he had bought her. Penda D. had, indeed, been a captive of Sambou D., chief of the village, and Sambou D. had received the bridewealth and used it for his own needs. Penda's brother confirmed that Sadio said he had bought her following a quarrel with her. The brother therefore also wanted this marriage to end. Nonetheless, the court ultimately ordered Penda to return to the marital home.

Social ties with former masters remained prominent, since the vast majority of former slaves in the end chose to stay with the masters. Former slaves did not always choose to follow their relatives who tried to convince them to leave the masters. In 1910, Macira T. from Yélimané summoned her children Coumba S. and Binta D. to the court of Yélimané, as they refused to accompany her when she went to settle in that city. Because the two daughters were of age to get married and had declared to the court that they lived well in Tambakara and wished to stay there, the court decided to nonsuit Macira's demand.

These different court cases demonstrate the real issues that family and matrimonial ties presented at the time of emancipation. The picture that emerges from the cases discussed in this chapter is far different from the colonial image of emancipated slaves who were without attachments and were likely to become vagrants if they did not stay in the liberty villages.[59]

One of the ways in which (former) slave women tried to enhance their social position in postabolitionist French Sudan was to use sexual relations to acquire a new source of "protection." Of course, some of these women also knew the limits of this strategy, which often simply added yet another layer of control over their existence. However, to assume that carnal relations were the only ties (former) slave women could develop in order to cross to new positions in a fluid colonial environment risks understating the role of family in the emancipation process. Former slaves, men and women alike, were not, as colonial political reports tended to suggest, without connections; above all, they were not without family ties. Depending on the circumstances, female and male slaves favored family, matrimonial, or/and social ties in the context of the end of slavery in the region of Kayes. These men and women had social and family networks that they tried, with more or less success, to preserve. For them, gaining control over the family and thus over the labor force was definitely one of the major issue of the emancipation process; at the same time, their former masters struggled to hang on to the control they had long exercised.

In order to overcome the male guardians' monopolization of control over the family, some women did not hesitate to turn to the colonial administration and the courts. But the colonial administration had an ambiguous policy toward the (former) slave women's emancipation. Since slave women as concubines, workers, and commodities were the cornerstone of the economy in the region, the colonial administrators preferred not to confront this ambiguous status and therefore the consequence of a true emancipation. As a result, they claimed that, as wives and daughters, women had to remain under the control of male guardians. Through the tightening of the jurisprudence of the courts concerning cases of divorce and female desertion of the marital home, the local and colonial powers thus implicitly agreed on forcing former slave women to favor matrimonial ties over family ties.

Notes

1. Due to privacy concerns raised by the regulation issued by the Republic of Mali in 2002 restricting the use of any records held by the National Archives of Mali that might "implicate the private lives of citizens," I use only the first name and the initial of the last name to identify a disputant in a court case and correspondence. For more information on court cases and privacy, see Richard Roberts, *Litigants and Households: Colonial Courts and African Disputes in the French Soudan, 1895–1912* (Portsmouth, N.H.: Heinemann, 2005), xi–xii.

2. Kayes was the first capital city of the colony of French Sudan and remained the capital up to 1904.

3. État des jugements rendus en matière civile et commerciale par le tribunal de province de Médine, 1st quarter 1909, 2 M 123 (Fonds ancien, hereafter cited as FA), Koulouba, Archives nationales du Mali (hereafter cited as ANM).

4. The Decree Roume of December 12, 1905, abolished the slave trade in French West Africa. If the decree as such did not seem to ban ownership of

domestic slaves, circulars of February 20, 1906, and April 24, 1908, clearly invited colonial administrators to ban all forms of slavery.

5. Marie Rodet, *Les migrantes ignorées du Haut-Sénégal (1900–1946)* (Paris: Karthala, 2009), 282–84.

6. Richard Roberts, "The End of Slavery, Colonial Courts, and Social Conflicts in Gumbu, 1908–1911," *Canadian Journal of African Studies / Revue canadienne des études africaines* 34, no. 3, special issue titled "Slavery and Islam in African History: A Tribute to Martin Klein" (2000): 702.

7. Exceptions certainly include the articles by Roberts, "End of Slavery," 684–713, and Emily S. Burrill, "'Wives of Circumstance': Gender and Slave Emancipation in Late Nineteenth-Century Senegal," *Slavery and Abolition* 29, no. 1 (2008): 49–64.

8. It refers in the French colonial archives to the *cercles* (districts) of Bafoulabé, Kayes, Kita, Nioro, and Satadougou.

9. Here, it did not seem to matter whether the child born to a slave concubine was a boy or a girl.

10. Slaves would have represented around 40 percent of the total population of the region of Kayes, but this number could be as high as 60 percent in some parts of the region.

11. According to Kopytoff and Miers, the most common fate of a young female slave was that her master or somebody from his family would take her as a concubine or wife. Igor Kopytoff and Suzanne Miers, "African 'Slavery' as an Institution of Marginality," in *Slavery in Africa: Historical and Anthropological Perspectives*, ed. Miers and Kopytoff (Madison: University of Wisconsin Press, 1977), 32. The advantage for the master was that the slave did not have parents to protect her or to take her back in case problems arose. If she refused, she risked being sold away by her master. Administrator of the Haute-Gambie to Administrator of the Cercle of Bakel, May 25, 1904, letter no. 27, 1 E 218 (FA), Koulouba, ANM.

12. Martin A. Klein, *Slavery and Colonial Rule in French West Africa* (Cambridge: Cambridge University Press, 1998), 247.

13. 1 G 229 (FA), Fonds du gouvernement général d'Afrique occidentale française (hereafter cited as GGAOF), Archives nationales du Sénégal (hereafter cited as ANS); K 14 (FA) GGAOF microfilm, Archives nationales d'Outre-mer (hereafter cited as ANOM).

14. Kopytoff and Miers, "African 'Slavery,'" 32.

15. Commandant of the district of Kayes to the Governor of French Soudan, March 17, 1894, letter no. 90, 1 E 161 (FA), Koulouba, ANM.

16. The tirailleurs were colonial soldiers recruited by the French army in the French African colonies from the nineteenth century.

17. Burrill, "Wives of Circumstance," 52.

18. Marie Rodet, "Migrants in French Sudan: Gender Biases in the Historiography," in *Trans-Atlantic Migration: The Paradoxes of Exile*, ed. Toyin Falola and Niyi Afolabi (New York: Routledge, 2008), 165–81.

19. Ibid.

20. Report on the captivity in Médine, undated (but probably 1894), K 14 (FA), GGAOF microfilm, ANOM; Excerpt of Maurice Gamon, "Kayes—Le village de liberté: 8 novembre 1904," *Au Soudan*, Poitiers Universitaires (1905), K 24 (FA), GGAOF microfilm, ANOM; see also Denise Bouche, "Les villages de liberté en A.O.F. (suite et fin)," *Extrait du Bulletin de l'Institut français d'Afrique noire* 12, no. 1 (January 1950): 183–84.

21. Bouche, "Villages de liberté," 155.

22. Administrator of Kayes to Délégué of the Governor in Kayes, letter of November 25, 1894, 1 E 201 (FA), Koulouba, ANM.

23. Governor of French Soudan to the Commandant of the district of Nioro, September 27, 1894, letter no. 693, 1 E 211 (FA), Koulouba, ANM.

24. Administrator of Médine to the Commandant of the district of Kayes, December 3, 1895, letter no. 140, 15 G 116 (FA), GGAOF, ANS.

25. Marie Rodet, "'Under the Guise of Guardianship and Marriage': Mobilizing Juvenile and Female Labor in the Aftermath of Slavery in Kayes, French Soudan, 1900–1939," in *Trafficking in Slavery's Wake: Law and the Experience of Women and Children in Africa*, ed. Benjamin N. Lawrance and Richard L. Roberts (Athens: Ohio University Press, 2012), 91–92.

26. In this chapter, the translations of the colonial archival documents from French into English are mine: "Les dispositions qui précèdent ne préjudicient point aux droits résultant de la puissance paternelle, tutélaire ou maritale sur les mineurs ou les femmes mariées, en tant que les actes accomplis ne constituent point mise en servitude temporaire ou définitive, au profit de tiers, de ces mineurs ou de ces femmes." Decree of December 5, 1905, relating to the repression of the slave trade in French West Africa and in French Congo, *Journal officiel de l'Afrique occidentale française* 53 (January 6, 1906): 17.

27. Rodet, "'Under the Guise of Guardianship,'" 86–100.

28. "Exiger des prévenus toutes les pièces justificatives et tous documents émanant des autorités administratives ou municipales et établissant l'exactitude de leurs déclarations.

"Autrement, vous risqueriez de laisser se perpétuer sous le couvert de tutelle et principalement de mariage, de véritables ventes de personnes, et, la loi ainsi tournée, la répression deviendrait sinon impossible, du moins extrêmement difficile." Circulaire du 7 février 1906, Procureur général p.i. à procureurs près des tribunaux et justices de paix à compétence étendue de l'Afrique occidentale française, 1906, K 24 (FA), GGAOF microfilm, ANOM.

29. Bafoulabé, monthly political report, June 1905, 1 E 17 (FA), Koulouba, ANM.

30. Commandant of the district of Kayes to the Délégué of the Governor in Kayes, March 19, 1902, letter no. 47, 15 G 140 (FA), GGAOF, ANS.

31. Letter from J. H. Dufort to the administrator of the district of Kita, July 16, 1906, 15 G 151 (FA), GGAOF, ANS.

32. Response to notice 325, Administrator of Bafoulabé to administrator of Kita, August 6, 1906, letter no. 176, 15 G 151 (FA), GGAOF, ANS.

33. For an account of the historiography sustaining this idea, see Richard Roberts and Suzanne Miers, "Introduction: The End of Slavery in Africa," in *The End of Slavery in Africa*, ed. Miers and Roberts (Madison: University of Wisconsin Press, 1988), 38–40.

34. Political Affairs, Correspondence Cercles, Kayes, 1882–1921, 1 E 201 (FA), Koulouba, ANM.

35. Commandant Kita to Médine, August 2, 1900, letter no. 164, 15 G 138 (FA), GGAOF, ANS.

36. Commandant Kita to Délégué, September 28, 1900, letter no. 222, 15 G 140 (FA), GGAOF, ANS.

37. 15 G 138 (FA), GGAOF, ANS; 1 E 203 (FA), Koulouba, ANM.

38. Oumarou Lamine to Délégué of the Governor in Kayes, letter of September 18, 1902, 1 E 212 (FA), Koulouba, ANM.

39. District of Nioro to Délégué in Kayes, September 18, 1902, telegram no. 961, 1 E 212 (FA), Koulouba, ANM.

40. Circular Ponty no. 978, February 1, 1901, K 15 (FA), GGAOF microfilm, ANOM.

41. Rodet, "Migrants in French Sudan."

42. Marie Rodet, "Disrupting Masculinist Discourse on African Migration: The Study of Neglected Forms of Female Migration," in *Crossing Places: New Research in African Studies*, ed. Charlotte Baker and Zoë Norridge (Cambridge: Cambridge Scholars Press, 2007), 28–38.

43. État des jugements, 1st quarter 1909.

44. Copy from 1907 of an undated letter (but probably from 1906) by the administrator of the Cercle of Kayes to the temporary lieutenant governor of Upper Senegal-Niger, 2 E 12 (FA), Koulouba, ANM.

45. Roberts, "End of Slavery," 701.

46. According to section 75 of the decree, the court had to enforce African customs for African subjects as long as these customs were not opposed to "the principles of French civilisation." This latter restriction directly concerned the issue of slavery, since the possession of others is opposed to the "principles of French civilisation." Masters could therefore no longer settle their conflicts with their slaves with the help of the local courts.

47. État des jugements rendus en matière civile par le tribunal de province de Yélimané, 2nd quarter 1910, 2 M 135 (FA), Koulouba, ANM.

48. Yélimané-Refuge is the name of the former liberty village of Yélimané.

49. État des jugements, 2nd quarter 1910.

50. État des jugements, rendus sur appel, en matière civile et commerciale par le tribunal de Cercle de Nioro, 2nd quarter 1910, 2 M 135 (FA), Koulouba, ANM.

51. État des jugements rendus en matière civile et commerciale par le tribunal de province de Yélimané, 3rd quarter 1910, 2 M 135 (FA), Koulouba, ANM.

52. Rodet, "Disrupting Masculinist Discourse."

53. État des jugements rendus en matière civile et commerciale par le tribunal de province de Yélimané, 1st quarter 1911, 2 M 135 (FA), Koulouba, ANM.

54. État des jugements rendus en matière civile et commerciale par le tribunal de province de Nioro, 2nd quarter 1911, 2 M 135 (FA), Koulouba, ANM.

55. État des jugements rendus en matière civile et commerciale par le tribunal de province de Nioro, 2nd quarter 1912, 2 M 135 (FA), Koulouba, ANM.

56. See the political reports for this period: 1 E 17, 1 E 44, 1 E 45, 1 E 48, 1 E 61, 1 E 69, (FA), Koulouba, ANM.

57. Rapport politique annuel, Haut-Sénégal-Niger, 1912, 2 G 12/13 (FA), GGAOF microfilm, ANOM.

58. État des jugements rendus en matière civile et commerciale par le tribunal de subdivision de Bafoulabé, September 1920, 2 M 103 (FA), Koulouba, ANM.

59. Commandant district of Bafoulabé to Délégué of the Governor in Kayes, April 29, 1900, letter no. 78, 1 E 186 (FA), Koulouba, ANM.

9

THE FATAL SORBET

An Account of Slavery, Jealousy, Pregnancy, and Murder in a Harem in Alexandria, Egypt, ca. 1850

George Michael La Rue

Charles Didier's *Les nuits du Caire* might initially appear to be an unlikely place to find one of the most detailed descriptions of the interplay between slavery, power, and sex in an Egyptian harem.[1] Didier's reputation—as a francophone poet who left Switzerland to live and write in Paris, as a novelist who was one of George Sand's lovers, and later as a travel writer—does not immediately inspire confidence in his account of the life of Menour, a sixteen- to eighteen-year-old slave woman from Kordofan, living in a moderately sized harem in Alexandria, Egypt, sometime between 1840 and 1858.[2] The book attempts to convey the atmosphere of Cairo during that period, using a structure inspired more by the legendary Persian queen Scheherezade in *The Thousand and One Nights* than the usual nineteenth-century traveler's account. However, though Didier's qualifications as a romantic novelist must be taken into consideration in evaluating this account, so must his reputation as a sharp-eyed travel writer.

Didier published a narrative involving a wealthy Egyptian man, his wife, and her young black female personal slave in Alexandria in the mid-nineteenth century. This chapter examines that narrative; assesses its usefulness as a historical source and its place among the medical descriptions of slavery in Egypt; and analyzes its insights into interpersonal relations in Egyptian harems, as well as the challenges it presents for those who have used reductionist theories to study harems in Muslim societies of the past.

Standard depictions of the Muslim harems in North Africa and the Middle East provide relatively little information about African slave women. Although scholarly writers on the harem have often focused on basic Muslim laws and practices governing polygamy and concubinage and although the more artistic set has portrayed the exotic, erotic, and sensual consequences of those practices,[3] critics of Western "orientalists" consider the use of tropes of harem women as one aspect of Western domination of the East. Thus, in *Orientalism*, Edward Said was silent on African slaves (male or female)—perhaps because his binary worldview of the dominant West and the subjected East left no room to comment on Egypt's imperial relationship with the Sudan or the presence of enslaved Africans in "oriental" societies.[4]

The Muslim harem and the significance of Western women's accounts of it have been much discussed and debated by both Muslim and non-Muslim feminists. For example, Billie Melman, a Western feminist critic of Said, analyzed anglophone female travel accounts of the Middle East between 1718 and 1918 and found their descriptions of harems differed from the conventional image projected by Western males. She examined Western feminine discourse on the Orient historically, without fully historicizing the Orient or even the feminine Orient. She concluded that "Europe's concept and representation of the Orient were not unified, that there was, indeed, a plurality of notions and images of the 'other'; that the discourses about things oriental was polyphonic and the experience of the eastern Mediterranean was heterogeneous and not, or not only, political."[5]

Some modern Western feminists view the harem and the veil as means of controlling women. By contrast, modern Muslim feminists see the same cultural practices as essentially liberating. They portray the harem as "women's space," a place for family life and for female solidarity. The harem constitutes a locus where domestic versions of Islam and Muslim culture have been preserved, sheltered from broader shifts in Islam as taught and preached in madrassas and mosques.[6] Some argue that Western women travel writers were simply female corollaries to their imperialist, orientalist, male counterparts and that their writing "foregrounds the complicity between orientalism and Western feminism."[7]

Other feminists take a more differentiated view, recognizing the Muslim harem as both an instrument of patriarchy and a space to resist that patriarchy. For example, Mervat Hatem holds that "the three gender institutions of eighteenth and nineteenth century Egypt, the family, slavery, and sexual segregation, served to cement ties among the patriarchs across class lines."[8] She emphasizes patriarchal control over women of all classes, as well as social segregation of middle- and upper-class men and women. At the same time, however, Hatem suggests that in separating women from men who were not their relatives, the harem could give women a place to resist the patriarchy—a theme that will be developed in this chapter.

Hatem also suggests that in eighteenth- and nineteenth-century Egypt, the harem was a terrain contested by females because of the hierarchies within that harem, based on the seniority of wives, the superiority of wives to concubines, and a ranking of concubines in a racial hierarchy. These divisions weakened females in their struggles with the patriarchs.[9] Hatem particularly points out the substantial difference in status between a wife and a concubine, and the means by which a concubine can change her status by bearing the master's child, thus becoming an *umm walad*, and often receiving manumission, and possibly becoming a wife. A wife had formal rights and duties, with the greatest benefits being support and shares in his estate for herself and her children. Women within a single harem were thus made rivals.[10]

Hatem provides a dynamic framework for thinking about the harem and slavery in Egypt, but her references to the impact on slave women focus on Turco-Circassian rather than African slaves.[11] Indeed, recent feminist writing on Egyptian harems generally says little specifically about African slave women and their interactions with free males, free wives, and African eunuchs in the household. Given that Turco-Circassian but not African slave sources were closed down under British pressure and that, as a consequence, the use of African eunuchs increased everywhere from Cairo to Istanbul to Mecca, one can readily imagine that the roles of African slave women also expanded.[12]

About Didier and His Source

In *Les nuits du Caire,* Didier provides an exceptionally insightful description of the dynamics of an Egyptian harem. The book details a wife's growing suspicion that her husband has become sexually involved with a black slave woman—a member of a large harem of female slaves and eunuchs—and describes the murderous consequences of their subsequent interactions. This narrative might be dismissed as an exotic harem fantasy, except that the Didier gives as his source for the information the apparently eyewitness account of a professional French midwife. Moreover, Didier, who lived for a time in Cairo, also traveled in Morocco, Sudan, and Arabia, and he wrote about those locations for reputable geographic journals. He had, in fact, already written four books on his travels in Muslim countries, and in at least three of them, he showed an interest in the fate of African slaves and African slave women in particular.[13]

In his travels, Didier had also met and discussed his experiences and observations with a range of interesting European observers, including Richard Burton, the famous explorer, and Alfred Peney, chief medical officer in the Sudan and a former protégé of Antoine Barteleme Clot (also known as Clot-Bey). Clot, a French surgeon, had entered the service of the Egyptian army in 1825; he quickly replaced Charles Dussap—an older French doctor who had arrived in Egypt as a nurse with the Napoleonic French Expedition—as head of the Egyptian Medical Service and went on to found the Egyptian Medical School.

Suzanne Voilquin, a Saint-Simonian feminist who arrived in Cairo and moved into the Dussap household in 1834, provides considerable detail about female slaves of the epoch. She recorded Dussap's account of his relationship with Halima, a Sudanese slave he had purchased and married and by whom he had two children. Halima died in 1833 on the eve of the plague epidemic of 1834–35. Voilquin also describes the household dynamics between Dussap, his two children by Halima, the various household slaves, and a series of Sudanese slave women afflicted by the plague who came into the household for care. Both his daughter and Voilquin took midwifery courses and assisted in his medical practice.[14]

Clot also had close contact with slave women. His initial attempts to open a midwifery school were frustrated by local male hostility to Egyptian women receiving instruction from European male physicians. Clot resolved the problem by purchasing Sudanese and Abyssinian slave women in the Cairo slave market in 1831–32 and training them as midwives.[15] Later, he recruited two French women midwives who had trained at La Maternité in Paris to be instructors in the Egyptian midwifery school.[16] One of these women was the main source for Didier's account.

Didier provides several clues about the identity of his source, who is unnamed in the text, but it has not yet been possible to identify her with certainty. The source is not Voilquin, who was neither recruited nor trained in midwifery in Paris and had left Egypt long before Didier arrived. Mlle Palmyre Gault and Mlle Féry, two of the French midwives whom Clot-Bey recruited from Paris to teach obstetrics in the Midwifery School in Egypt, are possible candidates.[17] Unfortunately, almost nothing about either appears in the usual sources on Clot, the midwifery school, and the slave midwives they instructed, nor are they mentioned in Didier's published material on his travels in Egypt, Sudan, and Arabia.[18] In 1847, Estefan Efendi led the negotiations to find a new Frenchwoman for the position of chief instructor in the Midwifery School at an annual salary of 1,500 piasters (approximately 15 British pounds). However, the archival records do not provide the name of this new doctor, who, by 1857, had been replaced by a local student.[19] Elsewhere, Clot-Bey refers to a "Mademoiselle Leweillion who won the first prize in the competition of the Faculty [of la Maternité de Paris?], and who in addition to possessing a superior intelligence, has a solid education and a remarkable aptitude for teaching."[20] Leweillion is the most likely candidate to be Didier's source, based on the timing of her career, and the fact that Didier's midwife stated that she had not taught since her marriage, a possible reason for "Mlle Leweillion's" apparent replacement in 1857.

Didier had already mentioned his source and her husband in an article on Khartoum and in his travel account *Cinq cents lieues sur le Nil*.[21] In *Nuits de Caire*, he cites his earlier works as he introduces the midwife. Didier provides additional confirmatory material, including the fact that Abd al-Rahman, the midwife's husband, was for a time governor of Suez and later an employee of the Transit Department. Research in Egyptian sources may reveal more about him, but it may not reveal the name of his French wife. Elsewhere, Didier notes that he saw his first slave for sale outside the office of the "Transit Administration," suggesting that he may have known al-Rahman while he was working there. Moreover, in the small world of francophone expatriates in Egypt, it is very likely that Didier met most of the French living in that country. He was acquainted with Alfred Peney, former assistant to Clot, who was a long-term resident of Egypt and the Sudan and who originated from the same part of Switzerland as Didier himself.[22] Peney could easily have introduced Didier into the medical circles in Egypt or directly to the narrator of Menour's tale. Another possible link between Didier and Abd al-Rahman, on the one hand, and the French medical circles, on the other, was that Abd al-Rahman was blind in one eye and Didier was going blind as he wrote *Les nuits du Caire.* Didier must have been seeking medical advice from the professionals in Cairo, and his plight may have increased the likelihood of an encounter with his reported source.

The Narrative and Setting

Didier's description of Menour differs from those he gave of other slave women he met on his journeys in Arabia and in Sudan. There is great economy in the description of the physical settings of the narrative. There are few medical details, but the observations of interactions between the characters involved, the style, and the point of view all fit well with Didier's reported source for the story—the French midwife.

The narrative is set in Alexandria. The primary setting is the harem of a "very wealthy *bey*, a regional governor, who occupied an important post in the civil administration."[23] The unnamed bey had only one wife, Hadilé, who was "Turkish by birth, young, fairly pretty, and of a well-endowed family. She was proud of her family, of the large dowry that she brought to her husband, and of the children she had given him." Hadilé was extremely jealous and constantly spied on her husband. The household's several eunuchs were also under her command. Initially, Hadilé ran the harem, described as "a large one, containing many slaves, most of whom were Abyssinians who worked in the kitchen, thanks to a special aptitude common to all the women of that country. The others were all purely negro women, more or less black in color, more or less dark, and all very ugly."[24] The sole exception was Menour, "a young girl of sixteen or eighteen years . . . who the jellabs had stolen at a young age on the southern frontier of Kordofan."[25] Even this brief description contrasted with the usual portrayal of slave women in the harem, typically seen as having no history and no biography. Menour was described as a beauty, emphasizing her face more than her body, the perfection of which was declared rather than fully inventoried:

> In spite of her quasi-equatorial origin, she had no negro features save color; and her skin, of the most pronounced black ebony, had the softness of velvet. Her long tresses were enviable to any European; her dainty, even teeth shone like twin rows of pearls. The whites of her eyes, which is yellow in nearly all negroes, had to them that azure tint of all beautiful eyes, rare even in Europe. Her round cheeks, her straight nose, her thin lips—all her traits had, in a word, the regularity of the Caucasian race. Her body, admirably modeled, was in complete harmony with her countenance. All her curves were pure: the chest, the shoulders, the arms, each perfection itself. And what hands! What feet! To paint her at one stroke, she was a Greek statue in black marble.[26]

Menour was also said to have a fine character and a natural sense of style, displayed in her tasteful dress and carefully arranged hair. Hadilé chose Menour to be her chambermaid.

The French professional midwife is the narrator of the story and a character in it as well. The other characters include an older slave woman who was later assigned to care for Menour, several eunuchs, and the kitchen staff.

Power Shifts in the Narrative

We learn at the beginning of the narrative that the bey found himself at a disadvantage at home. He had married well, and his wife now dominated the harem. She "possessed such jealousy that this passion, rare among women in the Orient, grew in her to the point of insanity."[27] In response, the bey removed himself and rarely stayed at home, which only increased her fears. The narrator challenged contemporary Western images of male domination over the harem: "In Europe it is generally believed that Muslim husbands flaunt their infidelities and shamelessly do as they will with the slaves of their household. This is an error. I do not say that they forgo;

merely that they hide these acts. . . . Disloyal husbands thus use great circumspection in this delicate chapter, and their caution redoubles if their wives, as in the case of Hadilé, belong to families that have great wealth and influence that the husband is interested in sharing."[28] At some point, Hadilé began to imagine "that her husband paid the beautiful slave an attention a bit too keen."[29]

Since the bey could leave the house and harem and stay away for long periods, Menour took the brunt of Hadilé's jealousy, as the midwife reported:

> One day, for example, when I visited them, I found the young slave sprawled, not only at the feet, but under the feet of her mistress, who made a footstool of her body. Lying on the ground, nearly nude, the poor child put up with hours of this intolerable torture, not daring to move for fear of being beaten. Moved with pity, I tried to reason with Hadilé. The bey, entering just moments after me, joined in my efforts. "I expected you to plead for her," Hadilé responded bitterly, without changing position or suffering her victim to move. "It's very simple that you take sides with this creature. A favorite always wins out over a legitimate wife.
>
> "I find it fitting," she added, pressing her feet on her living cushion, "since a slave should be proud and think herself happy that her mistress deigns to derive comfort from her." The poor husband, so sharply berated, beat his retreat without replying. I admit that, though less than eager to put my hand between the goose and the gander, I had already done as much, without repeating my lesson of humanity or interfering further in this domestic dispute.[30]

What was the basis of Hadilé's fears?[31] Menour's beauty coupled with a husband's legal right to have sex with any female slave in his household could easily have provoked a basic jealousy. But beyond that, Hadilé must have known that if a slave woman had a child by a free Muslim master, both the new umm walad (literally, mother of a child) and her child would be free and have rights to a share of the estate on the father's death. Thus, Hadilé was defending not only her own economic interests but also those of her children.[32] There was undoubtedly a racial component to the jealousy as well, for high-class Turkish women were at the top of the racial hierarchy of the harems, above Egyptian women, Circassians, Greeks, Abyssinians, and black women. To be displaced in her husband's affections by such a low-status rival was even more hurtful and must have heightened Hadilé's suspicions of Menour's economic motives.

Menour immediately suffered a sharp drop in status within the harem—from the enviable position of chambermaid, she was relegated to the lowest menial duties. Hadilé spat in Menour's face and had her beaten by the eunuchs on any pretext; the slave lived in fear of the lash. The entire harem saw her treatment as retribution for Menour having abused her beauty and former status within the harem. She had few options: "A slave pushed to the limit can in certain cases force his master to release him by going to the *qadi* [judge], but this desperate measure is fraught with such difficulties that it is nearly illusory, and nearly impracticable for a man; for a female slave it is completely so."[33] In the broader literature on slavery in Islam, there are references to black male slaves appealing to legal authorities, but it was much rarer for female slaves to do so.[34]

Up to that point, Hadilé largely controlled the harem, but that was about to change. The bey decided to summon help from the French midwife, and he personally went to fetch her. On arriving, he tells her:

> "I have come . . . to beg your assistance. Menour is pregnant, my wife has found out, and knowing her character as you do, I'll let you imagine the fine scene that she has made! All the demons of hell have been unleashed in the house. It is unbearable—I leave at dawn and only return home to sleep. At the same time I'm not gaining much by absence, and the devil loses nothing by it given that the night is no calmer than the day time. My wife spends the whole night heaping insults on me. It's impossible to close an eye. I have to barricade myself in the divan but her furious voice pierces through all the doors. If this uproar continues, I'll give the place up and flee to the ends of the earth."[35]

The bey begged the midwife to save Menour from the physical abuse heaped upon her by Hadilé, who had the household eunuchs beat her "evening and morning as punishment for her offence."[36] No other slave women attempted to shield Menour from physical harm at this point. Clearly, under Hadilé's rule, the harem was not a scene of either female or racial solidarity.

As the French midwife, in her professional capacity, hastily accompanied the bey to his house, she considered her position, for he had not admitted that he was the father of Menour's child: "But it was not my place as a foreigner, and less so given my profession, to force it out of him. I didn't doubt that he was the seducer of Menour, and that his wife's jealousy had made her much more clairvoyant than me for jealousy is the most clairvoyant of the passions. I kept my suspicions to myself, not to say my certainties, and we reached his door without having exchanged a single word."[37] At first, Menour—whom she had not seen for several months—appeared hopeless, in fact scarcely alive. According to the midwife:

> The bad treatment which she had undergone at such a critical moment and when so much care and tending were necessary, had thrown her into a depression which consumed her. She was so changed that I would not have recognized her if I hadn't known who she was. She was frightfully thin and all her lovely curves had disappeared. Her sunken cheeks, her withered lips—she no longer had a youthful appearance. A high fever burned in her beautiful black eyes, blood-shot and already nearly dazed by terror, were naturally very large and now seemed to fill her whole face. Add to this sorry picture that her poor body was furrowed in every direction by open and bloody wounds cut by the *courbache* (whip), and which no one had taken the trouble to dress.[38]

Immediately, the midwife became a powerful advocate for Menour and her pregnancy, with maternal health and a successful delivery of the child as her prime concerns. This, together with her general sympathy for the bey, placed her at odds with Hadilé.

The Frenchwoman proceeded to take control of the situation. First, she gave Hadilé a severe dressing down:

> So you want to kill her? But God has sent me to save her from death. Your rights over her do not go so far as to take her life away. My own duty is to give it back to her, and at the same time to save the innocent being which she carries in her body; because it is a double murder which you are committing there. I swear to you by my God and by yours that this crime will not be committed. Henceforth, this woman belongs to me by virtue of my official position, and due to the evil which is consuming her. If you so much as try to remove her from my care, the law will be on my side, and if it is necessary to go to His Highness, I will take that step. I'll denounce your conduct to him, and we'll see if he will allow a double assassination to be committed in his domains![39]

This blast of moral righteousness, combined with legal and political threats, reversed the balance of power between Hadilé and her husband and reestablished him as the dominant force in the harem. The midwife continued her narrative, relaying the bey's commanding words: "'I want the patient to be cared for as if she were my own daughter; that madame,' he added extending his hand towards me, 'should enter here at any time of day or night, whether I'm here or not, and that everyone should obey her as myself. I am the master after all, and only I have the right to give orders here. The first eunuch who dares (in the future) to touch Menour, even with a fingertip and by the order of anyone, will perish by the rod.'"[40] This edict and the vigilance of the midwife, who returned frequently to treat Menour, realigned power in the harem. The bey was in charge, the eunuchs and other slaves readily obeyed him, and Hadilé retreated to the farthest end of the harem.

At first, Menour was in very bad shape, and the midwife ensured that she had someone to care for her and protect her within the harem:

> At my request, the bey gave me an old intelligent slave woman as an assistant. She was to be the guardian, to obey only me and completely, to never leave the patient day or night, and was to answer for her well-being with her life. The poor child was so feeble, so exhausted, that she was nearly unaware of the

> unexpected change that had been made in her position. She had heard all that had been said without understanding that it was about her. Her eyes, haggard, animated by fever had only one expression, if they had any at all, and that was terror.[41]

Although the midwife was a professor of obstetrics at the Vice-regal School of Medicine, she refrained from giving a detailed medical report on Menour's physical state: "I don't intend to make you undergo an obstetrical course on Menour's condition. It will suffice to say that in a very little time the wounds of the patient scarred over, that their traces were erased, and that the healing was soon completed. Youth works miracles everywhere."[42]

As her patient recovered, the midwife grew fond of her and took some credit for her recovery: "Beauty returned to her with her health. Plumping up gave back to her body, once deformed, its roundness and fullness. Her eyes no longer expressed horror, but gratitude, the joy of loving, and all her facial features had been restored to their natural perfection. At term, she gave birth with my help to a large little mulatto, perfectly viable, whose café-au-lait skin suggested a very white paternity."[43] Aware of the tradition of remarking on a child's resemblance to its father, the midwife refrained in this instance. Nonetheless, the bey took a fatherly pride in the infant.

Hadilé had remained neutral toward the expectant mother while she was under the midwife's care, but her emotions were revealed shortly after the birth. The midwife reported:

> When I went to announce to her, as was my duty, that her slave had delivered, and to present her the newest resident of the harem, she didn't say a word, but gave the innocent creature a look which made me shiver, and later came back to my memory, never to be erased. Instead of expressing spite or anger which frankly would have been quite natural, her look was joyful, but mixed with a ferocity—the joy of a vindictive savage ready to savor her revenge.[44]

This moment of revelation soon passed, and the midwife turned to helping the mother and child. Given Menour's youth and easy delivery, "in a few days [she] was on her feet, and proud of her new status, drunk with joy, she nursed her child with such an exuberant prodigality, that without me she would have killed it through indigestion!"[45]

The mother was proud of her child and her status as a mother. The bey was also very pleased. The midwife's visits became less frequent. Several months later, however, the bey reappeared at the midwife's home with an urgent message. She recalled the event:

> "My son is dead!" he shouted, falling to the ground and removing his turban, which for true believers shows the height of despair. "Which one?" I asked, knowing that he had several by his wife. "Oh, Menour's," he answered letting out his secret with an explosion of tears and sobs, because paternal love is the foremost and strongest passion of Orientals. "So she killed him?" I asked imprudently. "She?" the bey repeated, looking at me in astonishment. "Who, she? Do you think that Menour . . . ?" "Are you a fool?" I interrupted quickly, delighted that he had picked up the scent, "because you are right to think that it is not Menour that I suspect, but another, Hadilé (since we must name her) who came immediately to mind. Is such a guess possible? I was simply asking what illness had killed your son." "I don't know. Last night he fell asleep in complete health in his mother's arms; this morning she found him dead at her side. But maybe not all hope is lost," he continued as he quickly got up, clinging onto that idea like a shipwrecked man to the first thing to come to hand. "You are a capable woman, nothing is beyond you. You saved the mother, why won't you save the infant? Come, I beg you, come quickly. Allah will help you and have pity on an unhappy father."[46]

Together, they rushed to his house and into the harem.

Immediately, the midwife saw that the infant had been smothered. She wrote: "Jealousy had pushed Hadilé to murder. The frightening look with which she had greeted the birth of her rival's child was now explained. She had found her vengeance, and her apparent calm had masked it until the fatal hour. Clearly she could be content as she had struck at her rival and her husband with this one blow."[47]

Egypt had a high infant mortality rate, particularly among the children of black slave women, due chiefly to malnutrition, diseases such as smallpox, and accidents. However, as the midwife carefully examined the baby in front of the distraught and grieving mother, she returned again and again to the visible imprints of fingers on the child's throat. As she watched the midwife, Menour suddenly understood her child's fate:

> She suddenly struck her forehead, as if a sudden clarity had lit it up. She gave a tigress' roar which moved me to my very core. She had figured it all out. "She strangled my child!" she yelled with a tone and look that had to be seen to be understood. "Hush, you," I told her, putting my hand over her mouth, "May God console you!" She quieted herself, but a complete transformation came over her—her shouting ceased, her tears stopped. A calm more terrible than her most violent outbursts, showed on her face, and in her whole being. She also had found her vengeance.[48]

As Didier wrote elsewhere: "Like all primitive peoples, the Sudanese did not understand murder as a crime when it is revenge for an outrage; they hold it rather to be a duty, and as they are always armed, blood frequently flows among them."[49] However, a slave woman in Alexandria would not use a man's weapon. The power of a slave woman resided in the trust placed in her. Complete trust gave her full possibilities. So Menour suppressed her feelings and bided her time.

Days passed before anything happened. This time, it was not the bey who rushed to the house of the midwife, who described what happened next:

> "My mistress is dying!!" shouted one of the bey's eunuchs as he suddenly arrived at my home. "My master didn't want to leave her, but he begs you to follow me without losing a minute." I ran, I arrived. It only took a glance to recognize the symptoms of a poisoning, and the remains of a sorbet, left at the dying woman's side, told me enough to know how she had met her death. I am not sufficiently versed in toxicology to tell you what

> poison killed her, but it matters little. It's enough for you to know that the poison was fatal, and the sign that first struck me was that the palms of the victim's hands were completely black. Hadilé passed away a few minutes after I arrived.[50]

Menour was not immediately suspected because only the midwife knew that she had a strong motive for killing Hadilé.

As slaves were generally blamed by their owners for anything that went wrong, from spoiled meals to house fires, the household slaves were alarmed. They feared that they would be suspected of Hadilé's murder. However, the midwife thought she could detect a slight trace of satisfaction on Menour's face, and she saw in the earlier murder a motive for this one. By contrast, the bey immediately plunged into deep grief. As the midwife recalled:

> By a common enough phenomenon, he mourned once dead, the wife who had in life so tormented him. Many relatives of the deceased—her father, her brothers, her uncles—had been called to witness her last living moments and had brought many doctors with them, including one European doctor. His talents were useless, but his stop could not be uncertain. He was the first to pronounce the word poison. By taking the initiative, I would have feared condemning Menour. Her crime was obvious to me; but surely a civilized jury would have found that there were extenuating circumstances?[51]

If Menour had intended to regain the attention of the bey, her plan was quickly ruined after an inquiry was launched. The Abyssinian women who worked in the kitchen were the first suspects. "But they exonerated themselves easily," the midwife reported, "by proving by solid testimony that the fatal sorbet, whose residue was still saturated with poison had not been prepared by them but by Menour."[52] When questioned, Menour soon admitted her action, as the midwife related: "'My mistress strangled my child,' she said in the most natural tone, 'I poisoned my mistress, what more is there to say?'"[53] Given the audience—the male relatives of the bey and Hadilé—this statement brought a cry of horror.

Public opinion favored Hadilé, an elite Turkish woman, over Menour, a young, black, kinless slave woman who had admitted killing her mistress and now challenged her good name. A leader of the murder inquiry summed up the family's view, and the midwife reported his words: "'How can one imagine, in effect, that a wife so devoted, so good, would have even the thought of wronging her husband, by depriving him of a slave who was his legitimate property, because the mother belonged to him? The black slander of this miserable one falls apart by itself, and is unworthy of examination.'"[54] Hadilé the respectable wife, mother, sister, and free woman was to be sanctified, and the slave was cast as a villain without any further consideration.

What about the man who had been terrified to stay home with the jealous Hadilé, who barricaded himself in his divan to get away from her scolding, who sought help for his secret lover only when she was on the point of death, who reasserted control of the harem after the midwife's righteous intervention, and who was the proud father of Menour's child? The bey did nothing to help Menour. He clearly saw that the males of the two families were going to revert to patriarchal societal norms, to sanctify the good free woman and blame the black slave woman.He knew that Hadilé's family would never allow Menour to go unpunished; the relatives would dismiss any extenuating circumstances and even seek their own revenge if they were not satisfied with the legal proceedings against her. Because Hadilé's family was still rich and powerful, the bey's economic interest lay in keeping in their good graces to claim a share of their wealth as her loyal spouse and heir. The midwife observed: "The bey himself turned against his child's mother. Always weak and passing from one domination to another, he fell now under the influence of his wife's relatives as he had fallen under hers."[55]

The French midwife, however, tried to help her young black patient. One can speculate on whether she was motivated by her European views of the appropriate judicial procedures to follow in such cases, by her professional responsibilities, or simply by feminine empathy. She arranged to have an audience with the viceroy, and her account of the case won his sympathy. Nonetheless, he refused to intervene, as she recounted: "'I do not intervene in private affairs,' he told me, showing me out politely. 'The crime is constant, the law is strict, public opinion is worked up, and if one did not make an example, all the slaves would start poisoning their mistresses.'"[56] The French midwife's valiant attempt to save Menour again had failed. She had relied on her own cultural sense of what was right and proper. She had appealed to political power in the hope of overcoming a legal and social system that in its actual workings was stacked in favor of the free and against the enslaved. The viceroy gave the classic argument of officials facing strong public opinion, citing the dangers of encouraging crime by the lower orders of society—in this case, by leaving the poisoning of a free woman by her African slave woman go unpunished.

By happenstance, the very next day the midwife was on the shore in the old port of Alexandria, where sharks were often seen in the nearby waters. There, she witnessed Menour's punishment: "I was not far away on the beach when I saw three eunuchs who I recognized as belonging to the bey. They were carrying a hermetically sealed leather sack in which something was moving. A *cawas* (official) accompanied them. All four got in a small boat which awaited them, and drew away from the shore, powered by oars. When they were some distance from land, I saw them balance their mysterious load in their arms for a time, and then throw it into the sea, which swallowed it up immediately. Thus perished poor Menour."[57] Drowning was a common way to get rid of troublesome slave women.

Didier's work provides one of the most detailed descriptions of the interplay between slavery, power, and sex in a nineteenth-century Egyptian harem. To grasp its full significance requires an understanding of normative Muslim laws and cultural practices pertaining to women and slaves and of the history of slavery in nineteenth-century Egypt and the Sudan. Beyond that, it requires an understanding of the expansion of the European medical presence in Egypt, specifically the introduction of French midwifery training and French professionally trained midwives.

The academic study of the Muslim harem is contested terrain, reflecting the very real struggles in the harems of earlier centuries. To develop a better understanding of how Muslim harems worked, not only in nineteenth-century Egypt but also in other times and places, scholars must first locate more narratives that illustrate common patterns of behavior in harems that included wives, concubines, slave women from various cultures, and eunuchs. Then, the theoretical models, such as those used and articulated by Mervat Hatem, need to be reworked to include a society that was patriarchal and that also encompassed a racial hierarchy of slaves and a social hierarchy of males of various nationalities, such as Egyptians and "Ottomans." Didier's narrative of the interactions between a Sudanese slave woman, a Turkish wife, and an Egyptian husband shows that their lives were not completely determined by what happened within the harem but were affected by broader social norms, conventions, and political structures.

The dynamics of the harem were determined, in part, by the actions of those within it, including each actor's sexual strategies for personal advancement and domestic power. They were also determined by broader societal norms and conventions, as well as the support each actor had from his or her kin group. When the sexual strategies of the bey and Menour coincided, they could temporarily displace the relative power of Hadilé, the Turkish wife. But she saw that Menour's rising position in the harem depended not on the bey's favor but on Menour's legal position as umm walad, the mother of a child by the master. Eliminating the child undercut the slave woman's position.

Menour's poisoning of Hadilé eliminated her as a rival within the harem but also brought larger forces into play. Most notable among them was Hadilé's powerful Turkish family, which outranked the bey's familial connections and left Menour defenseless as a kinless slave with no familial backers. Beyond that, the society reinforced the more generic social hierarchy in which a "good" wife outranked any slave woman, let alone one accused of murdering her social superior. Even the viceroy saw that he could not stand in the way of these overarching societal norms.

But the presence of the French midwife reveals that as more Europeans relocated to Egypt, Egyptian society changed in other ways as well. Egyptians came under increased pressure to conform to European sexual mores, feminist and other egalitarian ideas, and abolitionist forces. These European influences had their own disharmonies and contestations, and they further disrupted older Egyptian patterns. One reaction was to re-emphasize the patriarchal patterns and to reinforce the norms that kept African slave women from advancing within Egyptian harems or within society at large.

Notes

1. Charles Didier, *Les nuits du Caire* (Paris: L. Hachette, 1860), 185–201. My son, John A. La Rue, translated pages 187–91, and I did the rest.

2. For biographic information on Didier, see Philip Ward, "Charles Didier—Life and Works," in Didier, *Sojourn with the Grand Sharif of Makkah*, trans. Richard Boulind (New York: Oleander Press, 1985), vii–viii. See also John A. Sellards, "The Journals of Fontaney and of Didier," *PMLA* 51, no. 4 (1936): 1114–22. Sellards also wrote a biography of Didier, *Dans le sillage du romantisme* (Paris: Champion, 1933), which I have not yet seen.

3. For recent examples of focusing on the basic laws of Islam from the Africanist literature, see "Basic Texts on Slavery" and "Slavery and the Law," in John Hunwick and Eve Trout Powell, *African Diaspora in the Mediterranean Lands of Islam* (Princeton, N.J.: Markus Wiener, 2002), 1–9, 21–32. See also Humphrey J. Fisher, *Slavery in the History of Muslim Black Africa* (New York: New York University Press, 2001), 14–18.

4. Edward Said, *Orientalism* (New York: Vintage Books, 1979). Two important works critical of his views are Billie Melman, *Women's Orients: English Women and the Middle East, 1713–1918* (Ann Arbor: University of Michigan Press, 1992), and John MacKenzie, *Orientalism: History, Theory and the Arts* (Manchester, UK: Manchester University Press, 1995).

5. Melman, *Women's Orients*, 3.

6. Leila Ahmed, "Western Ethnocentrism and Perceptions of the Harem," *Feminist Studies* 8, no. 3 (1982): 521–34.

7. For a summary of this debate, see Teresa Heffernan, "Feminism against the East/West Divide: Lady Mary's Turkish Embassy Letters," *Eighteenth Century Studies* 33, no. 2 (1990), 201–15. See also Meyda Yegenolu, *Colonial Fantasies: Towards a Feminist Reading of Orientalism* (Cambridge: Cambridge University Press, 1998), 68–94.

8. Mervat Hatem, "The Politics of Sexuality and Gender in Segregated Patriarchical Systems: The Case of Eighteenth- and Nineteenth-Century Egypt," *Feminist Studies* 12, no. 2 (1986): 255.

9. Ibid., 258–59.

10. Ibid., 257–58.

11. Ibid., 268.

12. Ehud R. Toledano, "The Imperial Eunuchs of Istanbul: From Africa to the Heart of Islam," *Middle Eastern Studies* 20, no. 3 (1984): 379–90.

13. The most relevant works are the following by Charles Didier: *Séjour chez le Grand-Chérif de la Mekke* (Paris: Librairie de L. Hachette, 1857); *Cinquante jours au désert* (Paris: Hachette, 1857); *Cinq cents lieues sur le Nil* (Paris: Hachette, 1858); and "Khartoum," *Nouvelles annales des voyage* 2 (1858): 56–90.

14. See George Michael La Rue, "A Generation of African Slave Women in Egypt, from ca. 1820 to the Plague Epidemic of 1834–1835," in *Women and Slavery*, vol. 1, *Africa, the Indian Ocean World, and the Medieval North Atlantic*, ed. Gwyn Campbell, Suzanne Miers, and Joseph C. Miller (Athens: Ohio University Press, 2007), 168–89.

15. The purchase of Sudanese and Abyssinian slave women to become midwifery students has been widely reported, first by Antoine Barthelemy Clot-Bey, *Aperçu général sur l'Egypte* (Paris: Fortin, Mason, 1840), 2:427; John Bowring, *Report on Egypt and Candia*, in Great Britain, House of Commons, Sessional Papers, XXI (London: Her Majesty's Stationery Office, 1840), 138, 140; Baptistin Poujoulat, letter to Michaud dated April 2, 1838, in his *Voyage dans l'Asie Mineure* (Paris: Ducollet, 1840), 2:517–20. Later discussions include J. Heyworth-Dunne, *An Introduction to the History of Education in Modern Egypt* (London: Frank Cass, 1968), 132; Judith E. Tucker, *Women in Nineteenth-Century Egypt* (Cambridge: Cambridge University Press, 1985), 120; Amira al-Azhary Sonbol, *The Creation of a Medical Profession in Egypt, 1800–1922* (Syracuse, N.Y.: Syracuse University Press, 1991), 46; Ehud Toledano, *Slavery and Abolition in the Ottoman Middle East* (Seattle: University of Washington Press, 1998), 78; LaVerne Kuhnke, *Lives at Risk: Public Health in Nineteenth-Century Egypt* (Berkeley: University of California Press, 1990), 186–87, 268; Mervat F. Hatem, "The Professionalization of Health and the Control of Women's Bodies as Modern Governmentalities in Nineteenth Century Egypt," in *Women in the Ottoman Empire*, ed. M. C. Zilfi (Leiden: Brill, 1997), 66–80; Khalid Fahmy, "Women, Medicine, and Power in Nineteenth-Century Egypt," in *Remaking Women: Feminism and Modernity in the Middle East*, ed. Lila Abu Bughod (Princeton, N.J.: Princeton University Press, 1998), 47–48; and La Rue, "Generation of African Slave Women," 174–75.

16. Heyworth-Dunne, *Introduction*, 132; A. B. Clot, *Mémoires de A.-B. Clot Bey*, ed. Jacques Tagher (Cairo: Institut français d'archéologie orientale, 1949), 281.

17. Sonbol, *Creation*, 46.

18. Detailed in notes 6 and 7.

19. Fahmy, "Women," 48–49.

20. A.-B. Clot-Bey, *Compte rendu de l'état de l'enseignement médical et du service de santé civil et militaire de l'Égypte au commencement de mars 1849* (Paris: V. Masson, 1849), 19.

21. Didier, *Cinq cents lieues*, 38.

22. Ibid., 41–42.

23. Didier, *Nuits*, 187.

24. Ibid., 188.

25. Ibid. Jellabs were long-distance traders, usually from the northern Sudan. Kordofan was a region in central Sudan, west of the Nile.

26. Didier, *Nuits*, 188.

27. Ibid., 187.

28. Ibid., 189.

29. Ibid.

30. Ibid., 190.

31. This is not the only mention by Didier of a powerful woman using a black slave as a footstool. See Didier, *Cinq cents lieues*, 18, and compare Bayard Taylor, *A Journey to Central Africa* (New York: Putnam, 1862), 305. Didier may have heard of this incident in 1851 from Peney or the Austrian Vice-Consul Constantin Reitz.

32. On the status of umm walad, see Hunwick and Pouwell, *African Diaspora*, 28–30. For a literary description of the jealousy of an older Muslim woman in Senegal whose husband took a second, much younger wife, see Miriama Bâ, *So Long a Letter* (Portsmouth, N.H.: Heinemann, 1989).

33. Didier, *Nuits*, 191.

34. For references to male slaves having recourse to Muslim law in the face of abuse, see Fisher, *Slavery*, 146. For an interesting way for a slave to attract legal attention, see the discussion of slaves cutting the ear of a freeman's horse in Fisher, *Slavery*, 81.

35. Didier, *Nuits*, 191.

36. Ibid.

37. Ibid., 192.

38. Ibid.

39. Ibid., 193.

40. Ibid.

41. Ibid., 194.

42. Ibid.

43. Ibid., 195.

44. Ibid.

45. Ibid.

46. Ibid., 196–97.

47. Ibid., 198.

48. Ibid. These symptoms suggest a poison that was a peripheral vasoconstrictor; it could have been one of several available in Egypt at the time.

49. Didier, *Cinq cents lieues*, 36.

50. Didier, *Nuits*, 198–99.

51. Ibid., 199.

52. Ibid., 199–200.

53. Ibid., 200.

54. Ibid.

55. Ibid.

56. Ibid., 200–201.

57. Ibid., 201.

INTIMATE POWER

Sexuality and Slavery in the Households of the Atlantic World

10

Sexual Relations between the Enslaved and between Slaves and Nonslaves in Nineteenth-Century Cuba

Ulrike Schmieder

This chapter presents historical sources that contain information about the sexual life of Cuban slaves, who normally were illiterate and thus did not write letters or memoirs about their private affairs. It refers to slave couples and the relationships of masters and other freemen with slave women, integrating those relations in the economic, demographic, and social context of mass slavery in nineteenth-century Cuba. The chapter shows the victimization both of slave women through the sexual assaults of their owners and of all slaves by the intervention of masters in their private lives, as well as the various obstacles to forming couples and families. But it also attends to the everyday struggle of slaves to defend their personal lives and family ties against the hardships of the slavery system.

Before I comment on the issue of sexual relations in the Cuban slave society, I will give a short introduction to Cuban slavery and the historiography on sexual relations within the broader context of literature on gender and the family relations of enslaved people.

Cuban Slavery during the Sugar Boom

The first African slaves were transported to Spanish Cuba in 1526.[1] From the sixteenth century to the eighteenth century, slaves produced sugar, coffee, and tobacco on small and medium-sized farms in modest quantities. Slaves also worked in stock farming, mining, and urban crafts and services, in the ports as well as in the houses of rich and poor slaveholders. In the first three centuries of colonial Cuba, slavery was less harsh compared with the mass slavery of the nineteenth century, when on big plantations with hundreds of slaves bondsmen and bondswomen were so overworked that they often suffered premature death and only terror could maintain white domination. But mistreatment or material neglect of slaves also occurred in the close, patriarchal (often despotic and arbitrary, not "mild") master-slave relationship during the first three centuries of slavery.[2]

After Haiti ceased to be one of the largest producers of sugar in the world as a result of the slave revolution of 1791, Cuba underwent a boom in its sugar economy. Between 1780 and 1873, at least eight hundred and fifty thousand African men and women were displaced as slaves to Cuba, particularly from the Bight of Benin and the Congo.[3] Treaties with Britain about the abolition of the transatlantic slave trade dating from 1817 and 1835 did not end this trade. The last slave ship probably arrived at the island in 1873.[4]

During the middle of the nineteenth century, the Cuban sugar economy was industrialized and mechanized; the sugar was transported via railway. The traditional sugar mills—*ingenios*—were replaced by big sugar centrals—*centrales*—and the old sugar aristocracy of Havana lost many plantations to Spanish slave traders or US corporations, the only ones that could carry the costs of these technological changes. In the last decades of slavery, Chinese contract workers—semislaves—and poor Spanish immigrants worked alongside African and Creole slaves on the plantations.

Although Cubans lost the Ten Years' War against Spanish colonial rule and although the abolition of slavery by Cuban patriots (1869–70) was canceled with their defeat, the war dealt a hard blow to the slavery system because many plantations, particularly in eastern Cuba, were destroyed. Spaniards and Cubans had mobilized slaves as soldiers and helpers, subsequently freeing them. After the free womb law of 1870 (Ley Moret) and the introduction of the so-called *patronato* (patronage) in 1880, a period of transition from slavery to freedom, Cuban slavery was finally abolished in 1886.

Historiography of the Sexual Relations of Slaves in Cuba

Even classic early studies of Cuban slavery, such as *El Ingenio* by Manuel Moreno Fraginals,[5] deal with some aspects of gender relations and also mention sexuality under conditions of slavery. More recent books, such as Michael Zeuske's work on the history of the "Black Caribbean" and Rebecca Scott's research on slave emancipation, cover the topic more intensively, although sexuality is not a central theme in these studies.[6] Other works that discuss the sexual relations of the enslaved within a broader context are those of Digna Castañeda, Elsa Caprón, and Marrietta Morrissey, who write on women in slavery; María Carmen Barcía, Karen Morrison, and Aisnara Perera Díaz y María de los Angeles Meriño Fuentes, who write on the family life of slaves (including the long-ignored role of slaves as fathers); Gloria García Rodríguez, who addresses slave agency; and lastly, Camilla Cowling, who describes the strategies used by slave women to get their freedom.[7] A recent article by Karen Morrison analyzes cases where white slave owners recognized and freed their children with slave women (who often remained slaves) and developed family bonds with their progeny.[8] Studies of Cuban women's history or gender history, including studies about prostitution, by Verena Martínez Alier, María del Carmen Barcía, Juan Andreo García, and A. J. Gullón Abao and Sabrina Hepke also mention facets of relationships between masters and their female slaves, interethnic marriages, and forced prostitution. However, they focus mostly on the free population.[9]

Laws That Regulated the Sexuality and Marriage of Slaves

Old Spanish law, particularly the Leyes de Siete Partidas of the thirteenth century, offered certain safeguards for slaves against extreme physical abuse (murder, dismemberment) and total material neglect. In cases of mistreatment, slaves could ask a judge to order their sale to another master.[10] Slaves also had to be baptized according to old Spanish stipulations. And the Leyes de Siete Partidas prohibited the prostitution of female slaves. A slave woman whose owner forced her to prostitute herself could be manumitted. Royal orders of 1672, 1693, and 1710 forbade masters to send female slaves to the streets and demand money of them that could only have been received through prostitution.[11]

State and church law allowed the marriage of slaves (with other slaves and with free persons) and prohibited a forced separation of husband and wife—for example, by selling one of the partners far away.[12] The synods of Hispanic American dioceses often affirmed the right of slaves to marry because, in practice, the owners often denied it. In Cuba, the synod published such a declaration in 1680.[13] The protection of slave marriages was repeated in the enlightened "Instruction of the Treatment of Slaves" of 1789, but the instruction never went into effect due to the protests of slaveholders all over Spanish America.[14] Slavery legislation of 1842 and 1844 reduced the protective aspects of slave law, but it did not abolish the right to marry.[15] According to these laws, slaves were human beings who should live according to Christian morals. Unfortunately, there were no laws that forbade the abuse of female slaves, even minors. Homosexual relations were persecuted by the Inquisition and by the Crown judiciary, but they were not specifically mentioned in the laws concerning slaves.

Spanish law did not protect the relations between slave mothers and children before 1870; indeed, it was not uncommon for mother and child to be sold separately. It was preferable for children born of a Spaniard and a woman slave to be sold to their father.[16] In Spanish America, manumissions of slaves were not forbidden or restricted; they could be bought or were granted gratuitously. Many Cuban slaveholders manumitted slaves in their wills in gratitude for their services as wet nurses, mistresses, nurses, or faithful butlers.

Beginning in 1778 in Cuba, all Spanish American parents could forbid their minor children to enter into an unequal marriage, such as with a black or "colored" person. From 1805 onward, marriages between whites and nonwhites required a special license from state authorities. After 1830, it became even more difficult to marry a person from another ethnic group, and interracial matches were prohibited completely between 1864 and 1874. Only in 1881 did all legal barriers to interracial marriages fall away.[17] In the age of mass slavery, conjugal relations between blacks and whites were considered a menace to the social order, as the tolerances displayed in previous centuries disappeared. But interracial couples continued to be a common phenomenon. There was no vigilante "justice" in cases of sexual relationships between white women and colored men, such as the public lynching rituals in the US South. But such relationships could still provoke violent reactions from white fathers and other relatives, for they were seen as a loss of honor for the family of the white woman involved. The elite ideal was a marriage between social and racial equals.

Sources: What They Tell and What They Do Not Tell

To obtain accurate information about the sexual life of slaves requires reliable and adequate resources. It is easier to get information on what slaveholders or Cuban intellectuals thought about the sexuality of slaves than to get to know the slaves' version, since members of the upper class knew how to write and the slaves normally did not.

The only known Cuban slave narrative is the autobiography (presumably written between 1835 and 1839, published in 1840)[18] by the slave poet Juan Francisco Manzano, who had been bought and freed by the most famous Cuban journalist and abolitionist, Domingo Del Monte (1804–1853).[19] Estebán Montejo, a former slave and Maroon who told his story to Cuban author Miguel Barnet in 1963, gave some information about the sexual relations of slaves, which I will deal with later. Montejo perhaps told collective memories, not his own, because he was born later than Barnet thought.[20] Barnet constructed the Maroon as a pioneer of the Cuban Revolution, concealing the racism of the early Cuban Republic.

The *síndicos de esclavos* (advocates of slaves) were municipal functionaries who initially could only represent slaves in court and supervise *coartaciones* (gradual self-bought manumissions), but they became state authorities who defended the slaves against abuse by their masters and resolved many conflicts without trial.[21] Slave petitions to the síndicos de esclavos are very useful sources in providing a glimpse of the discourse and the agency of slaves. Files of criminal trials on murders, suicides, violations, and assaults in which slaves were involved as offenders, victims, or witnesses are of similar importance. However, one has to consider that the slaves spoke and acted vis-à-vis the authorities of a slaveholder state, where judges and officials themselves possessed slaves and/or were the friends of the proprietors of slaves. Moreover, recorders wrote down the words of the slaves in the language of the educated. But it is nearly impossible to come any closer to the slaves than in these documents (with the possible exception of songs and tales of Afro-Cuban origin).[22] Even though the emphasis on agency may risk underestimating the heteronomy of slave life,[23] the slaves' use of judicial and state authorities was itself a form of agency: the slaves were not passive sufferers when they complained about their living conditions, and they defended their humanity when they did so.

Notary records offer information about manumissions: who freed whom, with pay or for free. Cuban slaves were sometimes manumitted for the services, sexual and others, they provided to their masters. For some privileged groups, it was also possible to buy their freedom gradually in the system of *coartación*. Female slaves could use sexual relations with masters or with white men to get an unpaid manumission or to obtain the money needed to buy their own freedom and that of their children. But there was no right to manumission or any guarantee that such a sexual relationship would lead to emancipation. And slave complaints show that female slaves were often betrayed by owners who did not deliver the promised manumission. Notary records also reveal that female slaves were manumitted more often than male slaves. But a notary record does not say, "I give the slave X her freedom because she is my concubine"; it only mentions that the manumitted slave served "well and faithfully." This generic wording could refer to sexual services as well as to the services of a wet nurse, nurse, or housekeeper or, indeed, to any other services usually performed by female slaves.

Baptismal and marriage records contain information about slave couples and families. Sometimes, these records also mention the father of the slave child, even when he was not married to the child's mother, which could imply a consensual union. In wills or at the notary's office, white or black fathers—whether free, freedmen, or slaves after emancipation—sometimes recognized their children born out of wedlock.[24]

Travel accounts are also an important narrative source. Normally, such accounts present the view of outsiders or of persons who had no direct economic interest in slavery. Of course, that does not mean that they were free of racist or anti-Catholic prejudices or uninfluenced by the opinions of abolitionists or slaveholders. But many travelers described in detail what they saw in cane fields, barracks, and masters' houses; they knew that readers of travel accounts were interested in eyewitness information about slavery, the abolition of which was a broadly discussed topic in Europe at that time. In evaluating a travel account as a source, it is important to determine whether the traveler saw with his or her own eyes what he or she described or only heard it, from whom the information was obtained, how long the traveler was in the slaveholding colony, and if he or she understood Spanish.

In press advertisements that offered slaves for sale, there are sometimes also indications about interracial relationships. This was the case in an 1833 advertisement in *El noticiero y lucero de La Habana* that read: "A *mulatica* [mulatto girl] and a *chinito*, both 4 years old, and a *negrito* [Negro boy], one year old, are sold." (*Chinito* does not mean a small person from China but a person of a particular skin color.) Such an advertisement also shows that small children were separated from their mothers. Another 1833 advertisement from *El noticiero* said: "A black woman from the Kongo, about 22 years old, more than average laundress, ironer, and cook, of beautiful presence, and agile in mechanic service, is sold."[25] The indication of her "beautiful presence" suggests that the slave woman would also have had to perform services beyond regular domestic work.

Novels, as works of fiction, must be dealt with very prudently when used as sources. But *costumbrista* novels of Cuban writers often describe everyday life in *ingenios*, *cafetales* (coffee plantations), and slave owners' residences in Cuba in detail, so even novels can deliver useful information.

One should not forget statistics, especially those produced by state authorities using demographic data such as birth and death rates, infant mortality, and life expectancies for slaves. Demographic data on Cuban slavery, particularly the nineteenth-century mass slavery, reveal that the real living conditions of slaves bore no resemblance to the supposed general "mildness" of Iberian American slavery.[26] These figures also demonstrate another key fact for the analysis of the sexual relations of slaves. About two-thirds of the imported slaves were men, and on many plantations, there were far more men than women. For instance, in 1862 on the sugar plantations (where 47 percent of slaves lived), there were 174 men to every 100 women; on the coffee plantations (where 7 percent of the slaves lived), there were 124 men to 100 women. In the cities, where 21 percent of the slaves lived, the ratio of men to women was 95 to 100. On average, then, there were about 149 men to 100 women among the

Cuban slave population.[27] Of course, these general numbers tell us nothing about the situation on any specific plantation, which was what really influenced the life of an individual slave man or woman. But it can surely be appreciated that the sexual life of slaves was different for those possessed by Don Juan G. Cantero, who in 1858 owned 694 men and 58 women in Trinidad, and those owned by Don Gonzalo Alfonso, who in 1857 was the master of 178 male and 184 female slaves in Sagua La Grande.[28]

Sexual Relations in Slavery Explained by Slaves or Their Descendants

The slave author Juan Francisco Manzano (1797?–1854), mentioned earlier, was the son of a female house slave and a free domestic servant.[29] He does not directly mention sexual abuse in his book, but he does speak of the physical torture and constant fear he experienced in his youth under the hand of his second mistress, the Marchioness de Prado Ameno. He also makes mention of the harm caused by the intervention of masters in the private lives of slaves and what it did to their affective relationships and family life.[30] The autobiography of Manzano also reveals a problem with slave narratives as a source. Over the years, editors and translators alike have changed Manzano's text according to their own interpretations and to suit their own aims; as William Luis puts it: "The editors, as surely as slave masters, continue to mold and control Manzano's life."[31]

Former slave and Maroon Estebán Montejo speaks about sexuality as follows:

> As soon as the drums started on Sunday the Negroes went down to the stream to bathe—there was always a little stream near every plantation. It sometimes happened that a woman lingered behind and met a man just as he was about to go into the water. Then they would go off together and get down to business. If not, they would go to the reservoirs, which were the pools they dug to store water. They also used to play hide-and-seek there, chasing the women and trying to catch them. The women who were not involved in this little game stayed in the barracoons and washed themselves in a tube.[32] . . . In any event, life tended to be solitary because there were none too many women around.

> To have one of your own you had either to be over twenty-five or catch yourself one in the fields. The old men did not want the youths to have women. They said a man should wait until he was twenty-five to have experiences. Some men did not suffer much, being used to this life. Others had sex between themselves and did not want to know anything of women. This was their life—sodomy. The effeminate men washed the clothes and did the cooking too, if they had a "husband."[. . .]It was after Abolition that the term "effeminate" came to use, for the practise persisted. I don't think it can have come from Africa, because the old men hated it. They would have nothing to do with queers. To tell the truth, it never bothered me. I am of the opinion that a man can stick his arse where he wants.[33]

Summarizing, Montejo informs us that the slaves did not have a private space in which to have sexual relations. Further, women were not always asked if they wanted to have sex with a particular man (they were "caught") and thus were treated as objects of male sexual wishes. The elder men controlled the disposal of women and rejected homosexuality, but some men lived in homosexual partnerships that included not only sexual but also social relations, like a marriage.

From official reports, we know that some slaveholders allowed their slaves to be together as couples, in *bohíos* (small huts) or in small rooms in the barracks. These rooms were about 4 meters square and offered a little privacy to the couple to engage in intimate relations.[34]

Agency of Slaves vis-à-vis Authorities and in the Courtroom

In looking at recorded complaints of slaves, one has to take into account that only certain groups of slaves had access to the so-called *síndicos de esclavos* and that, in addition, even they seldom had their rights approved in these institutions. But the complaints to the síndicos show the everyday struggles slaves faced to improve their own situation and that of relatives and reveal their discourses on gender, sexuality, and honor.

In 1839, the slaves of the cafetal La Suerte, in possession of Don José de la Luz Piedra, complained to the *capitán* (captain) of Alacranes that there were no female slaves on the plantation. The authorities sent them back to the plantation with the promise that the slaveholder would buy women slaves before Christmas.[35] This incident is reported in a rare document in the Provincial Archive of Matanzas, and it shows that male slaves suffered from sexual deprivation and acted with the aim of overcoming this situation.

Another example involved Juana González, a freed "colored" woman who fought for fifteen years to achieve the manumission of her daughter María Quirina in 1836. The father of Juana's child was Francisco González, son of her master, Gerónimo González. Francisco forgot his promise to manumit his lover and his child. Juana was sold to another proprietor (Luisa Brito) but always kept a relationship with her daughter, who stayed in the house of the González family with her grandmother. After Juana could buy her own manumission, she went to the síndico in order to obtain daughter María Quirina's freedom. Her problem was that while she was pregnant with the child, she had been forced to marry a black slave (Juan de la Cruz), and he was officially recorded as the father of María Quirina. But Juana González dared to confront the síndico with the physical appearance of her light-skinned daughter, who could not be the child of her very dark-skinned husband, and she pointed out the similarity between her daughter and her white sisters and brothers. As a result, María Quirina was freed along with her own son, Rafael, the nine-month-old grandchild of Juana González. The father of Rafael, whose name was not recorded in the document of manumission, paid a "compensation" for the boy.[36]

When researching court records, one must take into consideration that colonial justice persecuted crimes committed by slaves (against free people or other slaves), as will be presented here, but left unpunished most of the crimes committed by slaveholders against slaves. In Havana, a case of murder and attempted suicide brought against a female slave, who was the property of Don Ramón Infiesta, illustrates some harsh realities of sexual relations between masters and female slaves in 1837.

Teresa, a twenty-year-old house *lucumí* (person from the Yoruba nation of West Africa) slave, asserted that she had not attempted to commit suicide and told the following story. Her mistress assumed a sexual relationship had developed between her husband and Teresa while the mistress had traveled to a spa. Teresa always denied this relationship, but her mistress did not believe her and whipped and mistreated her as a result. The paper that would have allowed Teresa to look for a new master was refused to her. One day, a slave child named Francisco observed the mistress dragging Teresa's three-year-old child to the chicken house. After being alerted by Francisco, Teresa found her child there. On seeing that the child had had its throat cut or been beheaded,[37] she began to scream. The master tried to kill her by cutting her throat.

Teresa's owners claimed that she murdered her own child, and according to their version, the lesions on Teresa's body were the result of an attempted suicide. The prosecutor and court believed the slaveholders, even though Teresa's advocate believed in her complete innocence. The prosecutor demanded a penalty of ten years in jail in chains, coerced labor (breaking stones for road construction), and one hundred lashes with the whip. The appellate court, taking into account the earlier mistreatment of Teresa, instead punished her with six years of confinement in chains in the women's hospital, as by this time, she had gone mad and therefore could not be punished as foreseen.[38] Due to differences in the recorded testimonies, we will never know what happened thereafter. What is obvious is that a young slave woman was treated cruelly because of the jealousy of her mistress and finally went mad because of the conditions of her life and the violent death of her child.

When a male slave had a wife or consensual partner, he had to deal with the humiliating fact that he could not prevent the master, the driver, or other men from sexually abusing her. Male slaves could not protect, control, or lock up their spouses as free men could. Sometimes, this led to violence against the slave woman by her husband or partner, as a case documented in the Cuban National Archive illustrates.

In 1868, Pedro Milanés, a twenty-six-year-old, illiterate plantation worker in the sugar plantation Tranquilidad in the jurisdiction of Manzanillo, who was a slave of Don Silverio Valerino, was sentenced to ten years in jail. In a jealous rage, he had beaten, strangled, and thus killed his pregnant female companion, Micaela, with whom he already had seven children, because he thought the new baby was not his. Lamentably, the document does not say whom he suspected of being the father, as he did not admit the crime to the judge (although he did to other slaves). With respect to the motive, he only said that she had been a *puta* (prostitute).[39]

Another trial involved a crime committed in 1867 by a slave in Ciudad de Nueva Paz, near Güines. A black slave named Carlos or Calixto, property of Don Juan Tomás Herrera, was accused of poisoning the two-month-old mulatico Gerardo, the son of Celia, by placing a caustic substance into the baby's mouth. Celia was a black slave belonging to Doña Ana Valladares. The crime was denounced by Don José María Aguilar, father of Doña Ana's husband, Don Ignacio Aguilar; the potentially lethal act had been committed in the latter's house. (Carlos worked on a stock farm but stayed overnight once a week with Celia in her owners' house.) Celia saw Carlos take the baby out, and she subsequently noticed a stinging smell as she tried to console the crying child. She later explained that Carlos was jealous because she had given birth to a colored baby who was not his. Therefore, he had threatened her twice with a knife and announced that he would kill her. Carlos was condemned to one year in prison because the child survived without further harm. The sentence was approved by the appellate court in Havana in 1868.[40]

From the court document on this case, we know that the proprietors of Carlos and Celia tolerated the couple's nonconjugal sexual relationship and were also aware that a white man in the house or in the neighborhood had impregnated her, knowing that she was in a consensual partnership. We do not know if physical violence was used to force Celia into the relationship with the white man, but carnal relations in a master-slave relationship were always related to coercion. Celia was under double pressure—first from her white lover or rapist and then from her black companion, who obviously thought, despite his own status as a dependent slave, that Celia was his property and that he could decide whether she or her baby lived or died if his male honor was hurt.

Jealousy was the main cause of violence committed by slave husbands against their wives, and in extreme cases, it led to the murder of an unfaithful wife. In 1836, the slave Macedonio Mandinga killed his wife Lucía Conga in the cafetal Santa Clara, located in the village San Antonio del Rio Blanco del Norte, because she denied him sexual intercourse. He related this refusal to her relationship with Juan Jose Gangá, a married slave of the plantation. He, too, was wounded by Macedonio.[41]

The Sexuality of Slaves in the Mirror of Travel Accounts

European travelers often painted a contradictory picture of the sexual relations of slaves. On the one hand, they viewed these relations as inconstant and shallow—only sex, not love. On the other hand, when they told stories of slaves they had come to know personally, the depictions differed greatly.

Fredrika Bremer (1801–1865),[42] a Swedish novelist, feminist, and abolitionist who nonetheless had some racist ideas, visited the United States and Cuba in 1851. She wrote this about slave couples she encountered: "In other respects the slaves live in the *bohea* (hut) very much like cattle. Men and women live together, and part again according to fancy and whim. If a couple, after having lived together some time, grow weary of each other, the one will give the other some cause of displeasure, and then they separate."[43] But she also told a story of a couple who had been together for their whole lives since leaving Africa,[44] and she mentioned another slave couple who met secretly for many years because their masters did not allow them to live together.[45]

In a very interesting paragraph, Bremer described an African dance on the ingenio Ariadne near Matanzas. Her description reflected not only the perceived eroticism between the slaves but also the abuse of power by the driver, who compelled women to dance with him instead of with the men of their choosing:

> The dance always requires a man and a woman, and always represents a series of courtship and coquetry; during which the lover expresses his feelings, partly by tremor in all his joints, so that he seems ready to fall to pieces as he turns round and round his fair one, like the planet around its sun, and partly by wonderful leaps and evolutions, often enfolding the lady with both his arms, but without touching her; yet still, as I said, this mode varied with the various nations. One negro, a Caraballis, threw one arm tenderly round the neck of his little lady during the dance, while with the other he placed a small silver coin in her mouth. And the black driver, an ugly little fellow (he under whose whip I saw the women at work), availed himself frequently of his rank, sometimes by kissing, during the dance, the prettiest

> of the girls that he danced with, and sometimes by interrupting the dancing of another man with a handsome young negro girl, or with one of the best dancers, and then taking his place; for it is the custom that if any one of the bystanders can thrust a stick or a hat between two dancers, they are parted, and he can take the man's place.[46]

María de las Mercedes Santa Cruz y Montalvo, the Countess of Merlin (1789–1852),[47] was a Cuban-born aristocratic woman. She was married to the Bonapartist general Christophe-Antoine Merlin,[48] a famous *salonnière* in *orléanist* Paris, and was an authoress and singer.[49] She visited her native country after many years in Europe and wrote about this trip,[50] in a book entitled *La Havane* (1844).[51] She wrote that Afro-Cubans seldom married because a husband and wife could be sold to different owners and be separated forever; moreover, their children did not belong to them. Because domestic happiness was forbidden for the slaves, she observed, their relations were characterized by "*une sensualité violente et désordonnée*" (a violent and orderless sensuality)—a prejudiced interpretation from a woman who condemned what did not correspond to the moral standards of her own class and did not know anything about Afro-Cuban family ties. According to the Countess Merlin, if a female slave became pregnant, her owner (if not her lover) would usually punish her by, for example, cutting her hair and sending her from town to work at a sugar plantation. Other masters gave slave women compensation for every child born, legitimate or not, and treated and fed pregnant women slaves better and perhaps manumitted them if they had borne a certain number of children.[52]

The Irish abolitionist Richard Madden (1798–1886) stayed in Cuba between 1836 and 1840. According to the 1835 treaty between England and Spain concerning the abolition of the transatlantic slave trade, Madden was responsible as superintendent for the so-called *emancipados*, Africans who were found on ships illegally continuing the slave trade from Africa. They were supposed to be freed on reaching Cuba but were held for many years in a slavelike system of coerced labor. Madden took this function very seriously and fought for the rights of the emancipados by promoting abolitionist literature. He even translated and published the autobiography and poems of the slave Juan Francisco Manzano.[53] In his book *The Island of Cuba*, Madden told the story of a North American woman who had chained and tortured a slave belonging to her Spanish lover, probably because of jealousy. The slave was liberated but later died of her injuries. The murderess could expect no more than banishment as punishment for her crime.[54] This story is typical, as the court records and slave complaints indicate. White women often took revenge on the slave concubines of their husbands or lovers because they could not prevent the men from having sexual relations with female slaves.

Cuban Novels

As mentioned, novels are a difficult source of history, since they are fiction and reflect the very subjective vision of the author, although the novels of the Cuban literary style known as costumbrismo pretended to be "realistic."[55] Most nineteenth-century Cuban authors came from upper- or middle-class, white, normally slave-owning backgrounds, and their novels show how people of these classes saw slavery and race relations. Often, the books reflected racial prejudices even if the writers were abolitionists.

The Cuban writer Gertrudis Gómez de Avallaneda (1814–1873), a feminist and moderate abolitionist, was the only author who dared to imagine, in her novel *Sab* (Madrid 1841),[56] the unfulfilled love of a slave, Sab, for a white woman, Carlota de B., of the planter aristocracy.[57] She tempered this break with a long-standing taboo by describing Sab as a light-skinned mulatto, son of an African princess who had fallen into slavery and a white man of the upper class. She painted a picture of romantic love that had little to do with the real social life of the slave society of Cuba, although she located the story in an ingenio (Bellavista) in a real village (Cubitas) in Puerto Príncipe (Camagüey); the town was a center of activities supporting independence and abolitionism and the place where her mother's family lived. Anselmo Suárez y Romero (1818–1878), a journalist and professor in Latin language and literature and a member of the *tertulia* (social circle) of Domingo Del Monte,[58] wrote *Francisco: El ingenio o las delicias del campo*, finished in 1839.[59] The novel, which describes the everyday life of Cuban slaves, was written for the abolitionist Richard Madden, who intended to use it for abolitionist propaganda. Madden took the manuscript to England but did not publish it.[60] Only decades later, around 1880, was the novel finally published, in New York.

Francisco tells of the love story between the slaves Francisco, a *calesero* (coachman), and Dorotea, a house slave, who are forbidden to marry by their capricious mistress (Sra. Mendizábal). When Dorotea gives birth to a baby by Francisco, he is sent to field labor and Dorotea to washerwoman's work in another house. Ricardo, the son of the mistress and *hermano de leche* (milk brother) of Dorotea, tortures Francisco because he wants Dorotea for himself and she has rejected him. Since the mistress wants to pardon both slaves and permit the marriage, her son accuses Francisco of crimes he never committed. Dorotea, fearing for the life of her Francisco, finally agrees to carnal relations with Ricardo. When she admits this to Francisco, he commits suicide. Dorotea dies of grief some years later.

Suárez y Romero addresses the custom of punishing disobedient house slaves by sending them to the cane field, where they will be subjected to the lash of the driver. The novel includes many details of plantation life and work. What is remarkable in this love story is that the author does not repeat the typical slaveholder's view that slave women have loose morals and masters are respectable persons; instead, he underlines the sexual abuse of Dorotea by her master and the suffering of the slave couple caused by the arbitrary actions of the female slave owner.

Behind the plot of a slave committing suicide was a sad reality. According to an official investigation with respect to the years 1839 and 1845, Cuban slaves committed suicide much more often than members of other segments of the Cuban population. This situation was attributed by the planter class to the slaves' lack of religious education,[61] but it was more likely related to the terrible living conditions slaves endured and, in some cases, to the bad treatment accorded them by sadistic masters. We do not know whether the high incidence of suicide among slaves was also a consequence of destroyed couple and family relations.

Félix Manuel Tanco y Bosmeniel (1796–1871) was a member of the tertulia of Domingo Del Monte of Colombian origin. Tanco had to escape to the United States for political reasons in 1848. A decade earlier, in 1838–39, he had written the antislavery trilogy *Escenas de la vida privada en la isla de Cuba*, in which he denounced the cruelties of slavery and the abuse of female slaves by their owners. His novel *Petrona y Rosalía* tells how the slave Petrona is violated by her owner, Don Antonio Malpica, and sent to the family's ingenio when the wife of the owner, Doña Concepción, detects the pregnancy that has resulted. After Don Antonio dies, his son Fernando impregnates Petrona's daughter Rosalía, who is also banished to the ingenio and later dies. The novel avoids an incest story by declaring that Fernando is the fruit of an adulterous relationship between his mother and the Marquess of Casanueva. In *El hombre misterioso,* Tanco recounts the story of Padre Salvador de Medina, who abducts and seduces the mulata daughter of a white plantation owner. The novel *Francisco o el locumí* seems to be lost.[62] All that is known of this novel suggests it concentrates on the sexual abuse of slave and free colored women by elite Cuban men, thus depicting slavery as a totally immoral institution that corrupts the whole society. The limits of Tanco's image of Afro-Cubans are also obvious, for in his work, slave women are presented only as victims, not as agents in the Cuban slave society.

The most famous novel of nineteenth-century Cuba is Cirilo Villaverde's (1812–1894) *Cecilia Valdés o La Loma del Angel* (written in 1839, rewritten in 1879–82, and published in 1882).[63] Villaverde was the son of a plantation doctor who was also a member of Del Monte's circle and a Cuban political refugee in the United States from 1849.[64] He tells the story of Cecilia Valdés, a young colored, nearly white woman—"the little bronze virgin." She is seduced by Leonardo Gamboa, a white man who, unknown to both of them, is also her half brother, for his father had a secret sexual relationship with her mother. When Cecilia becomes pregnant from her half brother, interracial sexual relations are connected with incest and rendered even more scandalous. At the end of the story, Leonardo is murdered by the colored musician José Dolores Pimienta, who loves Cecilia and wants to avenge her. He kills Leonardo (who has abandoned Cecilia) on the day of his marriage to a white woman of his own class, Isabel Ilincheta. Cecilia is condemned for complicity in the act and confined for one year to the Paula Hospital.

Villaverde describes how white men liked to have sexual relations with colored women but did not marry them and often abandoned them after dishonoring them. The "guilt" of illegitimate motherhood was assigned to the women, the seductive mulatas, by a society dominated by white slave owners. As Leonardo's father, Don Cándido, who himself keeps a colored mistress, says about Cecilia: "Since she is of mixed race, her virtue is none too reliable."[65] Villaverde's novel, affirming the cliché of the morally corrupt mulata, is full of racial prejudice, which is why it was criticized strongly by Afro-Cuban intellectuals such as Martín Morúa Delgado.[66] Yet in spite of its racist bias, the book reflects typical convictions and behaviors of Cuban people toward slavery and ethnic hierarchies. For example, Villaverde mentions the preference of black mothers for lighter-skinned children over darker-skinned ones because colored children symbolized the hope for freedom and social advancement whereas black children were connected with the hated status of a slave.[67]

In a long monologue, the slave María de Regla also shows that a white man knew, in spite of all the stories of seductive black and colored women, that a slave woman could be separated from her husband at any moment and that the man had no choice if an overseer or another white man insisted on having sex with her because the men simply used physical violence if they did not get what they wanted.[68]

The Afro-Cuban journalist and politician Martín Morúa Delgado (1857–1910), whose mother was a former slave of *gangá* origin,[69] wrote the novels *Sofía* (1891) and *La familia Unzúazu* (1901). Both are retrospective condemnations of slavery and the agency of slaveholders, particularly the moral double standard of mistresses who expected their female slaves to be chaste and yet ignored the sexual violence perpetrated by their own husbands and sons against these slaves. *Sofía* tells the story of a freeborn woman of Spanish Canarian origin who is wrongly held as a domestic slave and violated by her own brother because he does not know that they share the same father. She and her child eventually die due to mistreatment by the master. The revelation of her true identity comes too late to rescue her. *La familia Unzúazu* mentions the arbitrary separation of slave mothers from their children and the flogging of pregnant slaves. The narrative also, however, reflects the reality of violence breeding violence. Delgado tells the story of a slave named Liberato who violates his mistress, runs away, and becomes a Maroon. But hostility against slavery does not necessarily mean sympathy for the African heritage: Morúa Delgado also condemns African culture and religion as barbarous and considers them obstacles to the intellectual emancipation of Afro-Cubans.

In summary, all these male novelists describe the same phenomena—the sexual abuse of slave women by white men, the punishment of the victims instead of their rapists (often by the wives of the rapists) by sending female house slaves to sugar plantations, the hidden risks of incestuous liaisons because of the carnal relations between masters and women slaves, and the exploitative character of sexual relations between white men and free colored women.

Conclusion

The sexual exploitation of female slaves, their rape by masters and drivers, and their forced prostitution were integral parts of the Cuban slave society and common, everyday phenomena. Female slaves were blamed for the sin of concubinage whereas male violence was neglected. Furthermore, even "voluntary" sexual relations involved a hierarchy of power and domination. A woman's hope of gaining her freedom through intimate relations with her master was sometimes realized, but more often, it was not. In addition, when a slave woman had carnal relations with her owner, she often paid dearly by provoking the hatred and vengeance of the owner's wife. Yet slave women were not mere victims in every instance. The complaints they filed in the courts and the manumissions they bought demonstrated their agency and testified to the efforts they made to defend themselves (and their children) against different forms of abuse.

Male slaves had difficulties in living their heterosexuality on many plantations where there were very few or no women. They also suffered when they could not prevent theirs masters or drivers from raping their female partners. Some reacted with violent jealousy against their female companions; others tried to defend their partners, even when they knew they would get the heaviest punishment for doing so. Physical resistance to slaveholders and drivers was also intended to defend their masculinity.

The image painted by slave complaints and court records frequently varies significantly from the stereotype propagated by the white segment of the Cuban slave society. This is evident, for example, in novels where the stereotypical "sexy mulata" was used to illustrate how (white) men fell victim to the "lasciviousness" and "promiscuity" of colored woman. The depiction of the sexy mulata was intended to absolve white masters from the accusations of sexual violence that Cuban and foreign abolitionists made—with good reason.

Notes

1. Michael Zeuske, *Schwarze Karibik: Sklaven, Sklavereikultur und Emanzipation* (Zurich: Rotpunktverlag, 2004), 72. A total of 145 slaves from the Cape Verde Islands were introduced to Cuba.

2. Ibid., 111.

3. Michael Zeuske and Max Zeuske, *Kuba, 1492–1902: Kolonialgeschichte, Unabhängigkeitskriege und die erste Okkupation durch die USA* (Leipzig: Leipziger Univ.-Verl., 1998), 276.

4. Zeuske, *Schwarze Karibik*, 395.

5. Manuel Moreno Fraginals, *El ingenio: Complejo económico social cubano del azúcar*, 3 vols. (Havana: Ed. de Ciencias Sociales, 1978).

6. Zeuske, *Schwarze Karibik*; Rebecca J. Scott, *Slave Emancipation in Cuba: The Transition to Free Labour, 1860–1899* (Princeton, N.J.: Princeton University Press, 1985).

7. Digna Castañeda, "The Female Slave in Cuba during the First Half of the Nineteenth Century," in *Engendering History: Caribbean Women in Historical Perspective*, ed. Verene Shepherd, Bridget Brereton, and Barbara Bailey (London: James Currey, 1995), 141–54; Elsa Capron, "Les femmes esclaves à Cuba (1789–1886): Premières approches" vol. 2 (Ph.D. diss., Université Paris VIII–Vincennes-Saint-Denis, 2003), 423; Marietta Morrissey, *Slave Women in the New World: Gender Stratification in the Caribbean* (Lawrence: University of Kansas Press, 1989); María del Carmen Barcia Zequeira, *La otra familia: Parientes, redes y descendientes de los esclavos en Cuba* (Havana: Casa de las Américas, 2003); Karen Morrison, "Creating an Alternative Kinship: Slavery, Freedom, and Nineteenth-Century Afro-Cuban Hijos Naturales," *Journal of Social History* 41, no. 1 (2007): 55–80. Aisnara Perera Díaz and María de los Angeles Meriño Fuentes, *Esclavitud, familia y parroquia: Otra mirada desde la microhistoria* (Santiago de Cuba: Ed. Oriente, 2006), and *Matrimonio y familia en el ingenio: Una utopía posible–La Habana (1825–1886)* (Havana: Editorial Unicornio, 2007); Gloria García Rodríguez, *La esclavitud desde la esclavitud: La visión de los siervos* (Mexico City: Centro de Investigación Científica Ing. Jorge Y. Tamayo, 1996); Camillia Cowling, "Negotiating Freedom: Women of Colour and the Transition to Free Labour in Cuba, 1870–1886," in *Slavery & Abolition* 26, no. 3 (2005): 377–91. A good historiographical overview is Michael Zeuske, "Sklaverei, Postemanzipation und Gender: Ein Überblick," *Comparativ: Zeitschrift für Globalgeschichte und vergleichende Gesellschaftsforschung* 17, no. 1 (2007): 18–37.

8. Karen Morrison, "Slave Mothers and White Fathers: Defining Family and Status in Late Colonial Cuba, " *Slavery and Abolition* 31, no. 1 (2010): 29–55.

9. Verena Martínez Alier, *Marriage, Class and Colour in Nineteenth-Century Cuba: A Study of Racial Attitudes and Sexual Values in a Slave Society* (London: Cambridge University Press, 1974); María del Carmen Barcia Zequeira, "Entre

el poder y la crisis las prostitutas se defienden," *Contrastes: Revista de historia moderna* 7, no. 8 (1993): 7–18; Juan Andreo García and A. J. Gullón Abao, "'Vida y muerte de la mulata,' Crónica ilustrada de la prostitución en la Cuba del XIX," *Anuario de estudios americanos* 54, no. 1 (1997): 135–57; Sabrina Hepke, *"Amerikas schönste Geliebte": Prostitution und Frauenhandel in Havanna (1850–1925)* (Stuttgart: Heinz, 2009).

10. Samuel Parsons Scott, ed. and trans., *Las siete partidas: Published for the Comparative Law Bureau of the American Bar Association* (Chicago: Commerce Clearing House, 1931), 979.

11. Gwendolyn Midlo Hall, *Social Control in Slave Plantation Societies: A Comparison of St. Domingue and Cuba* (Baton Rouge: Louisiana State University Press, 1996), 91; Manuel Lucena Salmoral, *Regulación de la esclavitud negra en las colonias de América Española (1503–1886): Documentos para su estudio* (Alcalá de Henares, Spain: Universidad, 2005), 188, 210.

12. Parsons Scott, *Siete partidas*, 901–3.

13. Eduardo Torres-Cuevas and Eusebio Reyes Fernández, *Esclavitud y sociedad: Notas y documentos para la historia de la esclavitud negra en Cuba* (Havana: Ed. de Ciencias Sociales, 1986), 51–59, paragraph about slave marriages on p. 58; Lucena Salmoral, *Regulación*, 195: *Disposiciones del Sínodo Provincial sobre matrimonios y bautismos de esclavos*, Havana 1680: Slaves from Africa who wanted to marry had to be baptized first and taught the Christian doctrine. Slave owners were not allowed to forbid slaves to get married and live together. Also, slaveholders had to guarantee slaves continuous marital lives when selling them, and therefore, it was only allowed to sell married slaves within a certain distance.

14. Manuel Lucena Salmoral, *Los Códigos Negros de la América Española* (Alcalá de Henares: Ed. Unesco, Universidad, 1996), 108–23.

15. Ibid., 295–300; Manuel Barcia Paz, *Con el látigo de la ira: Legislación, represión, y control en las plantaciones cubanas, 1790–1870* (Havana: Ed. de Ciencias Sociales, 2000), 105–7, app. 3.

16. On the Law of 1870, see Roberto Mesa, *El colonialismo en la crisis del XIX español* (Madrid: Instituto de Cooperación Iberoamericana, 1990), 73–74; Lucena Salmoral, *Regulación*, 92: *Real cedula para que los padres sean preferidos cuando se vendan hijos de español y esclava*, 1563 ("Royal order that fathers should be preferred when children of a Spaniard and slave woman are sold").

17. Martínez Alier, *Marriage, Class and Colour*, 11–14, 31, 40.

18. Ivan A. Schulman, ed., *The Autobiography of a Slave by Juan Francisco Manzano: A Bilingual Edition* (Detroit: Wayne State University Press, 1996), 12–16.

19. Del Monte had to leave Cuba in 1842 because of his friendship with the Scottish abolitionist Consul David Turnbull and because he was accused of having been involved in the conspiracy of La Escalera by the poet Plácido (Gabriel de la Concepción Valdés). In Paris, Del Monte defended himself in a

letter to *Le Globe* and proposed to solve the labor question in Cuba with white workers. Biographic information is from Instituto de Literatura y Lingüística de la Academia de Ciencias de Cuba, *Diccionario de la literatura cubana,* vol. 2 (Havana: Ed. Letras Cubanas, 1984), 629–32.

20. According to Michael Zeuske, Esteban Montejo was born in 1868 instead of 1860. Zeuske, "The Cimarrón in the Archives: A Re-reading of Miguel Barnet´s Biography of Esteban Montejo," *New West Indian Guide/Nieuwe West-Indische Gids* 71, no. 3–4 (1997): 265–79.

21. About the proceedings of the sindicaturas de esclavos, see Scott, *Slave Emancipation in Cuba,* 74–76; Barcia Zequeira, *Otra familia,* 47–54.

22. Martin Lienhard, *Le discours des esclaves de l´Afrique à l´Amérique Latine* (Paris: Harmattan, 2001).

23. For a critique of the "agency" concept, see Walter Johnson, "On Agency," *Journal of Social History* 37, no. 1 (2003): 113–25.

24. Perera Díaz and Meriño Fuentes, *Esclavitud, familia y parroquia,* 149, 166, 169–71, 173.

25. *El Noticios y Lucero de La Habana,* February 13 and 14, 1833.

26. About the thesis of the "mildness" of Iberian American slavery initiated by Frank Tannenbaum, *Slave and Citizen: The Negro in the Americas* (New York: Random House, 1947); Alejandro de la Fuente, "Slave Law and Claims-Making in Cuba: The Tannenbaum Debate Revisited," *Law and History Review* 22, no. 2 (2004): 339–69; Ulrike Schmieder, "War die iberoamerikanische Sklaverei milde?" *Zeitschrift für Weltgeschichte* 4, no. 1 (2003): 115–32.

27. Scott, *Slave Emancipation in Cuba,* 12.

28. Archivo Histórico Nacional, Madrid (hereafter cited as AHN), Sección Ultramar, legajo [box] 3550, expediente [file] 5, no. 27, and exp. 4, no. 14.

29. Biographic data are from Michael Zeuske, "Epilogue," in Daisy Rubiera Castillo, *Ich Reyita: Ein kubanisches Leben* (Zurich: Rotpunktverlag, 2000), 229; Edward J. Mullen, *The Life and Poems of a Cuban Slave, Juan Francisco Manzano, 1797–1854* (Hamden, UK: Archon Books 1981); Gerda Burton, "Introduction," in *Ambivalence and the Postcolonial Subject: The Strategic Alliance of Juan Francisco Manzano and Richard Robert Madden* (New York: Lang, 2004), 22 (indicating 1853 as the year of death).

30. Schulman, *Autobiography of a Slave.*

31. William Luis, *Literary Bondage: Slavery in Cuban Narrative* (Austin: University of Texas Press, 1990), 82–100, quotation on p. 99.

32. Miguel Barnet, *The Autobiography of a Runaway Slave: Esteban Montejo* (London: Macmillan Caribbean, 1993), 51; originally published as Barnet, *Biografía de un cimarrón* (Havana: Inst. de Etnologia y Folklore, 1966).

33. Barnet, *Autobiography of a Runaway Slave,* 61.

34. Jean-Pierre Tardieu, "*Morir o dominar*": *En torno del reglamento de esclavos de Cuba (1841–1866)* (Frankfurt am Main: Vervuert, 2003), 208–57.

35. Archivo Histórico Provincial de Matanzas (hereafter cited as AHPM), Esclavos, September 16–18, 1839, leg. 23, exp. 30.

36. Barcia Zequeira, *Otra familia*, 51–53, 181–83 ("carta de libertad," September 10, 1836).

37. The Spanish word *degollar* could mean "to slaughter," "to behead," or "to cut through the throat," which is why the manner of death is not clear.

38. Archivo Nacional de Cuba, Havana (hereafter cited as ARNAC), Miscelánea de Expedientes (hereafter cited as MdE), May 6, 1837, box 2266, A. The case is also cited, with fewer details than given here, in Jorge L. Giovanetti and Camillia Cowling, "Hard Work with the Mare Magnum of the Past: Nineteenth-Century Cuban History and the Miscelánea de Expedientes Collection," *Cuban Studies* 39 (2008): 60–84, 90.

39. ARNAC, MdE, leg. 1137, B, June 27, 1868. The ethnic origin of the slave was used as the surname.

40. ARNAC, MdE, leg. 816, M, 1867. Capron cites the case: see Capron, *Femmes*, 2:478.

41. ARNAC, MdE, leg. 651, B, 1836. Macedonio was sentenced to ten years in jail (the advocate of the military commission that condemned him had excused the slave, arguing that he was "a savage" and "subject to his natural passions"). Juan José had to work one year in chains and got fifty lashes with the whip because he had disturbed the marriage of Macedonio. Capron cites the case: see Capron, *Femmes*, 2:423. Capron also describes another case of wife murder, involving the slave Miguel, who killed María Antonio in 1822 in the ingenio of the family Sotolongo because she would not follow him to the bohio as he wished (p. 425).

42. Biographic data are from Fredrika Bremer, *Cartas desde Cuba* (Havana: Ed. Arte y Literatura, 1981), prologue; Nara Araujo, ed., *Viajeras al Caribe* (Havana: Casa de las Américas, 1983), 181–82; Brita K. Stendahl, *The Education of a Self-Made Woman: Fredrika Bremer (1801–1865)* (Lewiston, N.Y.: E. Mellen Press, 1994).

43. Fredrika Bremer, *The Homes of the New World: Impressions of America*, vol. 2 (New York: Harper, 1853), 335, electronic version in the University of Michigan Library, accessed December 14, 2007, http://name.umdl.umich.edu/ABF6887.0002.001.

44. Ibid., 2:336.

45. Ibid., 2:385–86.

46. Ibid., 2:326–27.

47. Biographic data are from Araujo, *Viajeras al Caribe*, 113–16; José Luis Prieto Benavent, "Mercedes de Santa Cruz y Montalvo, Condesa de Merlin, 'une femme du monde,'" *Revista Hispano Cubana* 13 (2002): 83–96, accessed April 7, 2005, http://dialnet.unirioja.es/servlet/oaiart?codigo=257823; Jorge Yviricu, "Los misterios de la Condesa de Merlin," accessed April 7, 2005,

http://www.habanaelegante.com/Spring2003/Ronda.html; Ariana Méndez-Rodenas, *Gender and Nationalism in Colonial Cuba: The Travels of Santa Cruz de Montalvo, Condesa de Merlin* (Nashville, Tenn.: Vanderbilt University Press, 1998); Maria de Mercedes Santa Cruz y Montalvo, *Viaje a la Habana*, Introduction by Salvador Bueno (Havana: Ed. de Arte y Literatura, 1974), 7–60.

48. There are different versions of the identity of her husband in the historiography. I took the version of Yvirucu, "Misterios."

49. Maria de las Mercedes Santa Cruz y Montalvo, *Mes premières douze années* (Paris: Gaultier-Laguionie, 1831); *Histoire de la Soeur Inès* (Paris: Dupont & Laguionie, 1832); *Souvenirs et mémoires* (Paris: Charpentier, 1836); and *Madame Malinbran* (Brussels: Typographie Belge, 1838).

50. For further information about the trip, the travel account, and its reception in Cuba, see Ulrike Schmieder, "La Condesa de Merlin: Una mujer aristocrática e intelectual entre Francia y Cuba," in *Sin fronteras: Encuentros de mujeres y hombres entre Amèrica Latina y Europa (siglos XIX–XX)*, ed. Eugenia Scarzanella and Monica Raissa Schpun (Frankfurt am Main: Vervuert, 2008), 165–86.

51. Maria de Mercedes Santa Cruz y Montalvo, *La Havane*, 3 vols. (Paris: Librairie de Amyot, 1844).

52. I used this edition: Maria de Mercedes Santa Cruz y Montalvo, *La Havane*, vol. 2 (Brussels: Méline, Cans et Compagnie, 1844), 38–40.

53. Juan Francisco Manzano, *Poems by a Slave in the Island of Cuba, Recently Liberated; Translated from the Spanish, by R. R. Madden, M.D. with the History of the Early Life of the Negro Poet, Written by Himself; to Which Are Prefixed Two Pieces Descriptive of Cuban Slavery and the Slave-Traffic, by R. R. M.* (London: T. Ward, 1840). In his translation, Madden changed and omitted parts of Manzano's text in order to give it a more antislavery bias (Luis, *Literary Bondage*, 93–96) and also to protect Manzano, whose former mistress was still alive (Burton, *Ambivalence*, 50–51). On Madden's biography, see Otto Olivera, *Viajeros en Cuba (1800–1850)* (Miami: Ediciones Universal, 1998), 153; Mullen, *Life and the Poems*, 4–13; Burton, *Ambivalence*, 26–40. Before his stay in Cuba, Madden was special magistrate in Jamaica in 1834 and fought for the better treatment of former slaves and the immediate abolition of apprenticeship; see Burton, *Ambivalence*, 28–29.

54. Richard R. Madden, *The Island of Cuba, Its Resources, Progress, and Prospects, Considered in Relation Especially to the Influence of Its Prosperity on the Interests of the British West India Colonies* (London: Gilpin, 1849), 163–65. Capron located the case in the ARNAC (Capron, *Femmes*, 2:477), which proves its truth.

55. Costumbrismo is a form of "realistic" literature in Iberian countries that describes typical customs and manners in the everyday life of a society in exactly defined locations and landscapes. In Cuba, it was possible to cultivate *cubanismo* (Cubanism) and to form a Cuban identity without confronting the colonial power directly.

56. Gertrudis Gómez de Avallaneda, *Sab* (1841; Salamanca: Anaya, 1970). Biographic data are from Gómez de Avallaneda, *Sab*, Introduction by Catherine Davies (Manchester, UK: Manchester University Press, 2001), 1–33; Instituto de Literatura y Lingüística de la Academia de Ciencias de Cuba, *Diccionario de la literatura cubana*, 1:375–80; Sara Rosell, *La novela antiesclavista en Cuba y Brasil* (Madrid: Madrid, 1997), 61–70.

57. Sab dies on the wedding day of Carlota and Enrique Otway. The son of an English merchant, Otway only marries Carlota due to the wealth she has gained from the lottery winnings she received from Sab via an intermediary. Carlota does not know anything of Sab's love, nor does she know that the lottery ticket was a gift from him. Carlota is unhappy in her marriage and is consoled by a letter from Sab, written before his death, which reveals his love.

58. Biographic and bibliographic data are from Instituto de Literatura y Lingüística de la Academia de Ciencias de Cuba, *Diccionario de la literatura cubana*, 2:387–90.

59. About the author and his work, see Mario Cabrera Saqui, "Vida, pasión y gloria de Anselmo Suárez y Romero," Introduction to Suárez Romero, *Francisco*, 7–36; Antonio Zambrana (1846–1922), writer, lawyer, and member of the Assembly of Guáimaro, remade the novel under the title *El negro Francisco* (Santiago de Chile, 1875), giving Francisco a more African identity. The novel is less romantic but more racist. Biographic data from Zambrana, *El negro Francisco*, Prologue by Salvador Bueno (Havana: Editorial Letras Cubanas, 1979).

60. Luis, *Literary Bondage*, 97.

61. AHN, Ultramar, leg. 3550: "Secretaria del Gobierno Superior Civil de la Isla de Cuba," 1846, "File about the reasons which influence the frequent suicide of slaves and the instruments to implement in order to prevent this": The Audiencia Pretorial de la Habana asserts that from April 1839 to November 10, 1845, 115 whites, 51 free colored persons, and 1,171 slaves committed suicide. The reason for this, according to the attorney, was not the bad treatment of slaves (he thought that nowhere were slaves treated so kindly as in the Spanish Antilles) but that the slaves lacked instruction in Catholic religion and had "no idea of another life."

62. For information about Félix Tanco y Bosmeniel's novel *Petrona y Rosalía* (Barcelona: Linkgua, 2012) and biography, see Humberto Triana y Antorveza, "Dos colombianos en Cuba: José Fernández Madrid (1780–1830) y Félix Manuel Tanco y Bosmeniel (1796–1871)," *Boletín de historia y antigüidades* 92, no. 828 (March 2005): 55–94, esp. 80–93; Adriana Méndez Rodenas, "Tropics of Deceit, Desire and the Double in Cuban Antislavery Narrative," *Cuban Studies* 28 (1999): 83, 87.

63. I quote from Cirilo Villaverde, *Cecilia Valdés or the Angel Hill* (Oxford: Oxford University Press, 2005); the information about publication dates is in the introduction.

64. Biographic data are from Cirilo Villaverde, *Cecilia Valdés o La Loma del Angel* (Madrid: Cátedra, 1992), Introduction, 11–13; Instituto de Literatura y Lingüística de la Academia de Ciencias de Cuba, *Diccionario de la literatura cubana*, 2:1097–1102.

65. Villaverde, *Cecilia Valdés or the Angel Hill*, 454.

66. Ibid., 18.

67. See ibid., 206, about the slave Maria de Regla and her daughter Dolores (black) and son Tirso (mulatto).

68. Ibid., 378–84.

69. *Gangá* refers to an individual from an African nation from what is now southern Sierra Leone and northern Liberia. Biographical data are from Nicolás Guillén, *¿Quien fue . . . ? Martín Morúa Delgado* (Havana: Ed. Unión, 1984).

11

"THIS COMPLICATED INCEST"

Children, Sexuality, and Sexual Abuse during Slavery and the Apprenticeship Period in the British Caribbean, 1790–1838

TARA A. INNISS

Historians of slave societies in the Americas have defined the contours of gender, race, and class through discussions of sexuality.[1] However, only a handful of studies have looked at the role sexuality played in enslaved communities, and most of these have concentrated on gleaning sexual mores from the illicit or conjugal relationships that enslaved persons formed with their masters and one another.[2] Moreover, little research has been done on sexuality and its role in the socialization of enslaved and apprenticed children in plantation societies. This chapter uncovers some of the silences in the historical record relating to children, sexuality, and sexual abuse during slavery and the apprenticeship period. It also explores some of the social, political, medical, and legal aspects governing sexuality and sexual abuse in Barbadian plantation society.

It is difficult to define who was considered a child in the past, especially in enslaved populations. Few primary sources indicate the ages of the children they describe. Indeed, the exact age of any enslaved person is difficult to discern, as dates of birth were not usually recorded. However, the rigid stratification of the plantation gang labor system does offer some insight into when a child entered the plantation labor force. The gang labor system was commonly used by planters and managers to divide their labor force according to the difficulty of the task that needed to be performed. In Barbados, able-bodied adult men and women were organized into the first and second gangs and usually performed the most physically demanding jobs on the plantation.[3] As soon as they were able to work—usually at the age of four or five—enslaved children entered the third gang, commonly referred to as the "hog-meat gang" or "pot-gang."[4] Children's work was lighter than that of enslaved adults, but it included essential tasks such as picking grass and insects, or "hog-meat," for the plantation livestock. As they grew older, children were incorporated into the second or even first gangs. Enslaved children could also be found among the domestics and tradespeople on plantations and in urban households.

In the transition from slave to free labor during the apprenticeship period, children under the age of six were freed. After 1834, these children and those born on estates were generally referred to as free children. In the documents, the ages of other servile children are difficult to identify, for, even though estates had to keep more accurate records, they rarely specified the ages of "apprentices" except in surviving food allowance records that mark food rations according to age and type of labor performed. In other cases, age can sometimes be inferred from the activities in which children would have participated, such as attending infant and day schools established on some estates to promote religious instruction. For the purposes of this chapter, all those up to twelve years old—the age at which they were likely to be allocated adult tasks—are considered as children.

Sexual age, however, is more difficult to determine. Modern constructions of phases in childhood development, such as the period of preadolescence or adolescence, are not appropriate designators for populations involved in forced labor regimes where children performed the work of small adults and were largely regarded as such. The type of labor performed by youth generally reflected the different stages in their physical development from children to adults.[5] The onset of puberty, particularly among girls, signaled a shift in the type of labor the enslaved performed and the way they were viewed by plantation personnel and members of the enslaved community.

On Seawell plantation in Barbados, for example, all individuals under the age of twenty—the point when many young people graduated to the first gang and were considered adult members of the workforce—were designated ages. Although it appears that most of the enslaved working in the first gang were assigned approximate rather than exact ages, this does give us some idea of the relationship between the age and the role of enslaved youths. The records indicate that the "grown girls" employed in the second gang were between thirteen and twenty years old. Some women in the first gang were between eighteen and twenty, and as several of these were mothers to young children, there may be some correlation between first pregnancy and graduation to the first gang. By contrast, though "grown boys" in the second gang were between the ages of fourteen and eighteen, no male members of the first gang were younger than twenty.[6]

There were several perceptions or myths circulating in the planter community about the promiscuity of young enslaved girls and women, who were perceived to engage in premarital sex from the age of puberty.[7] Certainly, slave youths commonly engaged in premarital sex, but this did not reflect promiscuous behavior. Rather, premarital sexual liaisons were seen as trial relationships undertaken with the aim of securing the right partner for a monogamous marriage. Moreover, parents played a large role in preparing young people for conjugal or sexual relationships. In many West African societies, premarital sexual relations were permitted as part of the marriage process within communities. Trial marriage between two young persons, which was sanctioned by both sets of parents, was also practiced in the American South and in Jamaica and was not considered to entail promiscuous behavior. Therefore, it was not uncommon for children to be born of these unions prior to "formal" marriages.[8] Suzanne LaFont has related the development of sexual mores in the Afro-Jamaican enslaved society to those in the American South; there, as Eugene Genovese has noted, though mothers tried to prevent their young daughters from becoming sexually active and though a girl's virginity was valued as a "prize" to be taken, girls were not expected to remain virgins into womanhood.[9]

Indeed, enslaved parents protected girls and boys from entering too hastily into conjugal relationships. Anthony Parent and Susan Wallace report that in the American South, parents and communities chose partners and determined when young enslaved persons commenced relationships. The acceptable "courting" age was seventeen for men and twenty-one for women.[10] Although the planter-inspired rhetoric referenced much earlier sexual involvement for young slaves in the British Caribbean, the Newton estate records indicate that young women in Barbados likely entered into conjugal relationships around the age of twenty-one.[11]

Parent and Wallace argue that enslaved children in the Americas knew little of sexual functions or activities even if they were exposed to them in the close quarters of slave homes.[12] It was common for babies to sleep in the same bed with parents, where they would have been present during sexual intercourse, and even older children probably witnessed sexual encounters between parents, especially given the small one- or two-room slave huts in which they lived. But it is not clear in what context children interpreted these actions. For example, in Jamaica, when Thomas Thistlewood, a planter, caught Jimmy, one of his slaves, sleeping with Abba, he commented that "one of the children was upon the bed with them."[13]

Sexual Abuse in Historical Context

The term *sexual abuse* is currently used to describe incidents in which a child might be exposed "to sexual stimulation inappropriate for the child's age, level of psychosocial development, and role in the family."[14] However, Lloyd deMause contends that sexual abuse of children has historically been "humanity's most powerful and most successful ritual."[15] He argues further that "a childhood more or less free from adult sexual use is in fact a very late historical achievement, limited to a few fortunate children in a few modern nations."[16] Sexual abuse, therefore, must be given a context specific to time and space, but it should also be recognized as a pervasive concern throughout human history. The next few sections discuss some historical accounts of incest and other forms of sexual abuse involving boys and girls in Barbados during the slave and apprenticeship periods. The examples provided in these sections offer insight into the nature of child sexual abuse and some of the relationships children had with their abusers.

Incest

The historical record is relatively silent on the existence of incestuous encounters between enslaved parents and children in colonial Barbados.

In early nineteenth-century Britain, incest violated ecclesiastical law but not common law. In fact, it was not until the passage of the Punishment of Incest Act in 1908 that incest became a charge that could be prosecuted in secular courts in England and Wales.[17] Thus, individuals could not be held criminally responsible for sexually abusing members of their family within the degrees of consanguinity prohibited by the church. In their turn, English ecclesiastical courts "treated incest simply as a form of fornication or adultery, to be punished by a light penance."[18] Prohibitions against incest were meant to protect the institution of marriage and prevent inbreeding, not necessarily to protect women and children from sexual abuse.[19]

Taboos against sexual relations between kin, both consanguineous and affined (related through marriage or linked by a close relationship), exist in both European and African cultures. The incest taboo, it is argued, promotes marital alliances outside the nuclear family and between family groups, which provide the basis for social order.[20] In Afro-Caribbean cultures, sexual unions even among kin groups not related by blood, or "shipmates," were also subject to taboos. This was important for enslaved children who forged strong bonds with each other, especially when, as often occurred, they were purchased together from the same market. Although children did not make up a significant proportion of the manifests on slave ships, some found themselves in the New World with little or no family or kin relations for protection. These "virtual orphans" found refuge among others of similar ages or ethnic backgrounds, but they rarely permitted such attachments to become sexual. This point was underscored by William Sells, a Jamaican physician, who observed that though a boy and a girl he purchased in 1808 were brought up as house servants and "always took a most lively interest in each other's welfare, both in sickness and health," the common bonds forged in their experience as shipmates during the Middle Passage dissuaded them from forming sexual attachments after their arrival.[21]

However, the scarcity of reports of consanguinal incest in the historical record is probably due to underreporting—especially as incest was not a criminal charge in British possessions until 1908. Peter Bardaglio demonstrates that in the majority of cases heard in criminal courts in the American South, where incest was a criminal offense in most states by the 1850s, the crime committed was between father and daughter. Bardaglio argues that "if these cases were at all reflective of the kind of incest occurring in the population at large, then incest in the South had clear patriarchal overtones . . . incest usually took place in the context of an unequal distribution of power between parties in terms of their age and position in the family."[22] Although Bardaglio's case studies relate chiefly to white Southerners, his assertion about patriarchy and the unequal distribution of power among adult and child female victims provides a basis for understanding how incest was viewed throughout slave-based colonial societies.

The role patriarchy played in perpetrating incest in Barbados is exemplified in a reflection made by the traveling protagonist of a satirical novel entitled *The Adventures of Jonathan Corncob, Loyal American Refugee.* There is some debate regarding whether the author, who has remained anonymous, actually visited the island and whether his writing is informed by personal experience or by observations made by other travelers.[23] But the author's creative license does highlight some well-known perceptions about the power dynamics of interracial relations in Barbados. In one of his adventures, Corncob recounts a visit he paid to the home of a Barbadian slave owner, Mr. Winter. When Corncob entered Winter's parlor, he witnessed "an old negress, smoking her pipe; near her was an elderly mulatto woman; at a distance was a female still less tawny of complexion, called in this country, as I believe, a mestee; and at the other end of the room I observed a yellow quadroon giving suck to a child, which though a little sallow, was as white as children in Europe generally are."[24] When he inquired who the fathers were of all these women of different "gradation" of shades, his companion replied, "Mr. Winter himself is the father of them all . . . when he was very young he had the mulatto woman by the negress: when the mulatto was twelve years old, he took her for his mistress, and had by her the mestee. At about the same age his intimacy with the mestee produced the quadroon, who had by him a few months ago the white child you see in her arms." Corncob's companion went on to say that "this is what is called in this country washing a man's self white, and Mr. Winter had the credit of having washed himself white at a very early age, being at this time less than sixty years old."[25] In addition to explaining Winter's "complicated incest," Corncob's description intimates that male slave owners were socialized from early ages into viewing their young female chattel as sexual commodities.[26] Their premarital sexual education often began at young ages with enslaved concubines. Corncob was astonished by what he saw as incestuous miscegenation that had the desired effect of producing offspring who gradually removed the taint of Winter's initial sexual encounter with a black woman. In the colonial Caribbean, sexual relations with Winter's children/concubines were legitimized because these individuals were his sexual and paternal property. He was truly patriarch of his family and his slaves.

The Question of Pederasty

The sexual abuse of male children has been recognized by contemporary researchers as comprising a significant proportion of the larger number of reported sexual abuse cases among children today. But contemporary neglect of the incidence of male sexual abuse may also point to the marginalization of the male child victim in history. In 1980, Norman Ellerstein and J. William Canavan reported that medical case studies often promote the diagnosis and management of female victims of sexual abuse, with little mention of male victims; in turn, this has led to incidences of sexual abuse being perceived as involving male abusers and female victims exclusively.[27] In contemporary slavery, evidence demonstrates that a proportion of the girls and boys are used as sex slaves for pedophiles and pederasts.[28] The illicit trade in children today indicates that slavery and other forms of coerced labor or exploitation have concealed the activities of sexual predators in both past and present societies. However, the contemporary evidence that has been gathered can only demonstrate how forced labor systems accommodated sexual abusers of children and allowed abuse to persist. With few primary sources, historians have little insight into the nature of these relationships or how they operated in past societies.

It is difficult to impose modern definitions of human sexualities on past populations. But as Ronald Hyam has argued, the unequal power relations implicit in an imperial setting created sexual opportunities for authorities and other dominant parties.[29] Minimal surveillance of the actions of those in positions of power enabled them to engage in often unreported but illicit sexual relationships, not only with children but also with other men and local women. Since homosexual activity occurred in both European and African populations during the colonial period, it is likely that male-male sexual encounters also occurred in Caribbean colonial societies.[30] Certainly, colonial legislation against sodomy resembled imperial laws on the subject.[31] Yet it is much more difficult to historicize male-male sexual encounters and behavior, not to mention the incidence of pederasty in the region, when the historical record in the Caribbean is silent on these issues. Louise Jackson argues that the sexual abuse of boys was rarely discussed. Whereas the sexual abuse of girls was framed in the discourse of "seduction" and "prostitution" of young girls in public debates, sexual abuse of boys never received public attention.[32] Few medical or legal investigations were carried out into the nature of men's sexual relations with boys. By the mid-1850s, only a few physicians were investigating the physical signs of sexual abuse in male children.[33]

Despite the general silencing of male-male sexual relations in the historical record, there are a few allusions to the sexual exploitation of male adults and children by men in positions of authority on estates. Harriet Jacobs, for example, remembered the tyranny inflicted on one young slave named Luke in their owner's household in the American South. Wilma King writes, "Jacobs described the situation as the 'strangest freaks' which she found 'too filthy' to write about"—a strong indication that the description referred to pederasty.[34] Karl Watson also implied such a relationship on Newton estate between Yard, a plantation manager, and one of the grandsons of the enslaved matriarch Old Doll, Billy Thomas, who was Yard's confidant and "even lay in his chamber." When Billy Thomas was accused of stealing a key to the storehouse containing the estate's store of rum, sugar, and corn, Yard smuggled him off the island to Guyana. Although it was not uncommon for personal servants, particularly child servants, to sleep within the bedchambers of owners, Watson argues that by protecting Billy Thomas from prosecution, Yard set an unusual precedent in plantation society, where he could have also been subject to strict penalties for concealing a thief.[35] This unusual action may, therefore, hint at an intimate relationship between master and slave.

There has been little historical investigation into same-sex sexual relations in the Caribbean. Since primary sources tend not to report the issue, historians can only assume that same-sex sexual relations occurred in colonial societies. Given the power relations governing sexual relationships and sexuality in the Caribbean, historians can further surmise that same-sex sexual activity occurred among and between elites and the enslaved.[36] As LaFont writes, "It is difficult to imagine that male slaves were not sexually exploited by colonial men or that they were blind to the advantages of having sex with *Buckra* [coll.: white man]." Similarly, certain enslaved boys may have been groomed to participate in such relationships with older white men, much like some of their female counterparts.[37] Thus, despite the general lack of evidence, it is clear that predatory male-upon-male sexual relations involving adults and boys did occur during slavery and the apprenticeship period, although more research is called for to determine the nature of these relationships in a historical context.

Child Sexual Abuse and Medical Descriptions

Caribbean historians have done little work on children's sexual health. But three cases involving sexual assaults on children, found in Colonial Office correspondence records for Barbados after the end of slavery, offer insight into childhood sexual abuse as well as the legal protections that child sexual abuse victims and their families could access. Certainly, many incidences were not reported, and conclusions made here cannot be considered typical. They do, however, reflect how a child's sexual and physical health was perceived by parents, legal and medical professionals, and society at large.

Definitions of sexual abuse of female children posed several legal challenges for both colonial and imperial authorities. Prior to 1868, legal statutes indicated that "unlawful carnal knowledge" was a crime in both Barbados and other West Indian colonies, such as Jamaica. However, in the early and mid-nineteenth century, there was considerable legal debate over the definition of *consent*, with the emerging consensus being that offenses against younger victims should be seen as more serious and deserving of harsher sentencing. In early nineteenth-century imperial law, certain evidentiary requirements had to be satisfied to distinguish cases of statutory rape and unlawful carnal knowledge. Evidentiary requirements relied on the degree to which the child's hymen had been penetrated in order to prove actual penetration. In 1777, the decision in *Rex v. Russell* "established that, although some degree of penetration must be proved, the hymen could still be intact."[38] However, in 1832, another precedent was set: "If the hymen is not ruptured, there is not sufficient penetration to constitute this offense."[39] Jonathan Dalby reports that in Jamaica in 1837, a statute was enacted in regard to all sexual offense cases stipulating that "it shall not be necessary in any of those cases to prove actual emission of seed, in order to constitute a carnal knowledge, but that the carnal knowledge shall be complete upon proof of penetration only."[40]

How penetration was proven remains vague. The ambiguity of legal requirements pertaining to the sexual abuse of girls undoubtedly frustrated imperial and colonial authorities, not to mention child victims and their families. Medical investigators were aware that a girl could be born without a hymen and that in some children the hymen could be extremely elastic, hindering complete penetration. Controversies over the burden of proof persisted throughout the nineteenth century. It was not until the 1850s that "experts ... agreed that penetration of the vulva alone needed to be proved in order to establish that rape or unlawful carnal knowledge had been committed." Jackson writes that "lifting of the death penalty for crimes of rape in 1841 must have rendered this view more acceptable."[41]

In 1868 in Barbados, crimes against the person were consolidated into one act dealing with offenses such as abduction, indecent assault, and common assault. Under this act, "unlawfully and carnally" knowing a girl under the age of thirteen carried a penalty ranging from a minimum of three years to a maximum of life in penal servitude. If the victim was under the age of ten, sentencing also involved the private whipping of the assailant. In Jamaica, by contrast, the designation of carnal abuse was used for two categories of victims. For girls under the age of nine, the crime was defined as a felony. For girls between nine and eleven, it was a misdemeanor only.[42] In two of the cases under review here, the victims were girls under the age of ten. Their alleged perpetrators were older men with whom the girls had been acquainted. Both cases demonstrate that family members, particularly mothers, were ultimately responsible for seeking medical and legal assistance for their children.[43] The third case involved an assault on the infant daughter of a white couple. The crime was allegedly perpetrated by the child's black female nurse.

The two cases involving the sexual abuse of children reveal little about the racial dynamics of sexual abuse or whether black or white children were more likely to be victims of abuse. More investigations into sexual offenses involving children need to be carried out before any conclusions can be made. But at least one contemporary American study suggests that white girls are as vulnerable to sexual abuse as their black counterparts.[44]

Julianna

In February 1835, Lawrence Edwards, manager of the Searles estate in Christ Church, was accused of assaulting an apprenticed laborer named Julianna, "an Infant under the age of twelve years." To evade prosecution, Edwards reportedly boarded a merchant vessel and sailed to Liverpool within a week of the incident. Governor Lionel Smith asked Liverpool authorities to arrest Edwards upon arrival and send him back to the colony for trial; further, in case Edwards evaded the police, Smith also announced a £200 award for his capture and return.[45] The alacrity with which government officials acted is surprising. This was one of the few cases of child rape allegedly committed by a white man that were reported in local media.

Caroline Wilson

In December 1835, apprenticed laborer Mark George was charged with the rape of an eight-year-old named Caroline Wilson, a "colored" girl. George lived near or at times in the child's family home. This case, which involved detailed testimony from the child's mother, an apothecary, a physician, and Caroline herself, reveals much about the relationships between children, their parents, and other laborers, as well as the nature of medical intervention and observation in incidences of child sexual abuse.

Korine Eady, Caroline's mother, had left the girl in the care of her sister one day. When she returned home between seven and eight o'clock that evening, she found the child "in a dreadful state," bleeding profusely with "Pains in its Loins."[46] Caroline, crying, told her mother that George had hurt her. Her mother examined her linen—later used as evidence in court—and found it bloody. She also solicited medical advice and reported the incident to the authorities. Mothers were usually the first to suspect and report incidences of child sexual abuse.[47] That Eady had the presence of mind not only to report the incident but also to preserve evidence and solicit medical advice suggests that she was cognizant of the legal measures required to capture and convict her daughter's attacker.

It is rare to have testimony from a child victim of rape. For this reason, Caroline's testimony, albeit filtered through court transcripts, is of significance. She related that night had fallen and her mother had not yet returned home. As it was dark, it is unclear whether she could see the person who seized her in the yard, but she testified that she knew it was Mark George because he had been in that area: "He was in the Yard in the Evening, he came with a light, he took her into the Buttery and blew out the light, he then put her across his Lap, and extended her Legs, she felt something hard run up against her, which hurt her and burnt her very much. She screamed out. Her sisters were at the Shed Door when Prisoner took her into the back premises."[48]

When asked what Mark George "hurt" her with, she replied, "Sir, he hurt me with his nakedness."[49] Caroline's testimony was recorded with an air of detachment and very little emotion. There was no sense that she was reliving the very apparent trauma she suffered on the day of the alleged rape. She seemed to answer the questions directly. Jackson, however, argues that in such cases, it is very difficult to decipher from the transcripts who exactly was speaking. Clearly, the child was questioned by authorities, but the way in which the transcript was prepared reveals that the statements made were the result of a "collaborative effort" between authorities and family members.[50] The prisoner's counsel suggested that Caroline might have been lying when he cross-examined her. He asked her if she knew what would happen if she lied. She responded, "Yes Sir; I will go into everlasting Fire." Children in court cases were asked such questions to determine if they were telling the truth and if they knew the consequences of their statements.[51] Caroline insisted that it was George who assaulted her.

The documents of this case also include a description of one of the few recorded medical encounters between children and medical professionals during this period in Barbados. Discussions of the legal and medical investigations of child sexual abuse cases in nineteenth-century England suggest that both victims and their mothers were viewed with derision by legal and medical authorities even when evidence of violence and symptoms of venereal disease were present. In the later Victorian period, medical journals commonly published articles alleging that children simulated sexual abuse and rape.[52] As Jackson notes, "Doctors were extremely reluctant to diagnose sexual abuse and a whole battery of alternative explanations was found for suggestive signs including physiological disease, physical dirt, forgery and precocious imagination."[53]

Nevertheless, Korine immediately summoned an apothecary and later a physician—both males—to attend to Caroline. This indicates that she did not seem uncomfortable in reporting the incident to medical professionals. Presumably, she was aware that a medical examination would be needed to prove Caroline's case in court. The medical testimonies are candid and detailed, and—unusually for the time—they confirm Caroline's story.[54] After noting the girl's bloody clothing and feet, the apothecary, Mandeville, examined the child and reportedly "found nothing but the Hymen Injured, told the Mother on ascertaining this, and not to make herself uneasy, that it would not kill her this time. This he said to relieve the Mother's mind. The Mouth of the Vagina was distended. The Hymen was ruptured a little." He then instructed Korine to call the police.

Three days later, William Clarke, a physician, was called to examine Caroline. The authorities might have required a formally trained physician to conduct an examination that would hold up in court. Certainly, in the nineteenth century, it was common for British physicians to examine children several days after a reported rape—although delays could compromise medical evidence.[55] The physician confirmed the apothecary's observations, and he noted that the wound still had not healed. It is unclear how reliable Barbadian medical professionals were in such cases, and few doctors at the time were experts on rape, although most were familiar with debates about cases of physical and sexual abuse.[56] However, both the medical men in Caroline's case appear to have been competent. The counsel for the prisoner, in his cross-examination, asked Mandeville about the nature of the child's injury and whether it was done by a sharp or blunt instrument; he asked the physician if he could prove conclusively when the wounds were inflicted and if there were any injuries to the rest of Caroline's vaginal area. Both men authenticated the girl's story, Clarke insisting that "the Child bore evident marks of having been violated."

Infant "Waith"

In 1836, a capital charge was brought against a nurse named Mary Jane, who was accused of assaulting and violently wounding the ten-month-old daughter of Mr. and Mrs. Thomas H. Waith. Mary Jane had reportedly worked in the Waith household for a number of years and was, to a certain extent, considered part of the family. It is unclear whether she was apprenticed to the family or a hired servant. Although she had a bad temper, Mary Jane had apparently cared for the child's elder siblings without any hint of physical abuse. That changed, however, on April 17, 1836, when the infant was in Mary Jane's care. After visiting some friends, the Waiths returned home to find their infant daughter crying and screaming while being held in Mary Jane's lap. When Mrs. Waith took the child from the nurse, she found the child's clothes wet and bloody; the garments would be produced in court as evidence. When the parents asked Mary Jane what had happened, she replied, "The Child must have got a fall" and insisted that she had done the child no harm. Unsatisfied, the Waiths examined their daughter's body to discover the source of the blood. They "found to their Horror that the private parts of the Child had been injured and were bleeding." They sent immediately for Stephen H. Walcott, a physician and apothecary. Upon examining the infant, he confirmed that the injuries, which were life threatening, were not the result of a fall but were caused by a sharp instrument—although he did not know how deeply it had been inserted. The following day, the girl was examined by Dr. King, a surgeon, who concluded that the wound was about 1 inch deep and that the parts of her body around her pelvis had become "much inflamed, irritated, and swollen, and were much discoloured."[57]

Philly Ann, a neighboring servant, confirmed that Mary Jane had abused the child. In her testimony, she asserted that she had never quarreled with Mary Jane prior to the alleged incident and therefore had no reason to lie. She stated that she had met the nurse and the child on the road as they were returning from town. As the child was screaming and crying, Philly Ann endeavored to take the child from Mary Jane. The child, however, would not leave her, even though Mary Jane told the girl that she would give her good reason to cry later. Philly Ann saw that a pin or needle may have been pricking the child. She asked what reason Mary Jane had for inflicting such pain on the infant. Mary Jane said she "did not want to go Home with the Child that Night she wanted to remain in Town." When asked whether she saw the infant bleeding, Philly Ann replied that she had not: the infant might have been bleeding, but she could not see because it was getting dark. At the end of the trial, Mary Jane was sentenced to death. Of course, given the burden of blame levied on emancipated workers at this time, it is unclear whether the evidence was as convincing as prosecutors related. Did she, in fact, injure her charge knowingly or was it an accident caused by the diaper fastener?

This particular case raises several questions in relation to the nature of abuse as well as characterizations of abusers. Cases of sexual abuse in England overwhelmingly involved male assailants, prompting Jackson to suggest that "explanations for abuse must lie in the constructions of masculinity and male sexuality in this period."[58] The implication was that women had a "weaker sex drive" and therefore were unlikely to engage in illegal sexual behavior.[59] However, there was no indication that Mary Jane derived sexual pleasure from injuring the Waiths' baby.[60] Her actions were clearly uncommon, and they raise important questions for historians who conventionally define sexual abuse and abusers in terms of the quest for sexual gratification.

Certainly, the case was not regarded as a sexual abuse case. Although she did harm the infant's private parts, Mary Jane was charged with "violent Assault and Wounding with Intention to cause some bodily Harm."[61] Philly Ann's testimony suggests that Mary Jane punished the child for preventing her from remaining in town. As deMause notes, children are often "expected to 'absorb' the bad feelings of their caretakers."[62] The Waith infant could neither name her attacker nor defend herself, so she could have been the perfect receptacle for Mary Jane's frustration.

Reports of Sexual Misconduct in the Apprenticeship Period

Interestingly, all the cases discussed in this chapter (and another involving an apprentice and a bestiality charge) were reported after 1835—immediately after emancipation—whereas during slavery, sexual assaults on the enslaved never appeared in court records, for "rape as a form, or degree, of sexual violation perpetrated against enslaved women by males—black, white, free or enslaved—was not considered a legal offense."[63] By contrast, after emancipation, colonial and imperial officials took an interest in cases involving sexual "deviance" or "perversion." Thus, in Jamaica, whereas cases of sexual abuse rarely came to official attention before the 1830s, prosecutions of such cases rose sharply after emancipation.[64]

Dalby notes that from that time on, the authorities suddenly developed a concern for the "sexual habits of the masses" and became less concerned with their "capacity for larceny and violence."[65] Legal authorities may have been trying to demonstrate the moral decay of the laboring population through charges and cases that depicted the sexual depravity of newly emancipated workers. Increasingly concerned with their civilizing mission through Christianity and education, colonial officials could now command the moral authority to impose their ideologies on the emancipated population.

It is clear from the few examples in the historical record that children's sexuality and sexual experiences were closely monitored and guarded by family and community members during the eras of slavery and apprenticeship. Enslaved children were exposed to sexual difference and sexual activity early in life. They observed both loving and exploitative relationships, and they probably understood from very young ages that such relationships played key roles in establishing social and racial hierarchies. Contrary to the planter rhetoric, the majority of young slaves did not enter promiscuous relationships. They did engage in conjugal relationships or "trial marriages," but these were inevitably condoned and supported by parents and community members. Such relationships helped to stabilize the family and the wider community.

When sexual mores were violated through abuse, enslaved victims could not access legal protections. As slaves, they did not possess the civil rights that offered free people legal protection against such abuse. Only after emancipation did they, too, acquire such rights, and only then did the authorities begin to grant them legal redress.

Notes

1. Catherine Clinton, "'Southern Dishonor': Flesh, Blood, Race, and Bondage," in *In Joy and Sorrow: Women, Family, and Marriage in the Victorian South, 1830–1900*, ed. Carol Bleser (New York: Oxford University Press, 1991), 53.

2. Steven E. Brown, "Sexuality and the Slave Community," *Phylon* 42 (Spring 1981): 1–10.

3. Henry Drax, "Instructions for the Management of Drax-Hall, and the Irish-Hope Plantations: To Archibald Johnson by Henry Drax Esq," in *A Treatise upon Husbandry or Planting*, ed. William Belgrave (Boston: D. Fowle, 1755), 65.

4. William Dickson, *Letters on Slavery* (Westport, Conn.: Negro University Press, 1970), 12; Richard Dunn, "A Tale of Two Plantations: Slave Life at Mesopotamia in Jamaica and Mount Airy in Virginia, 1799 to 1828," *William and Mary Quarterly* 34, no. 1 (1977): 47.

5. Vivian C. Fox, "Is Adolescence a Phenomenon of Modern Times?," *Journal of Psychohistory* 5, no. 2 (1977): 279.

6. Newton Plantation Records MS 523/288 1796 List and Report of Negroes at Seawell.

7. Barbara Bush, *Slave Women in Caribbean Society, 1650–1838* (Kingston, Jamaica: Heinemann Caribbean, 1990), 94.

8. Ibid.

9. Suzanne LaFont, "Very Straight Sex: The Development of Sexual Mores in Jamaica," *Journal of Colonialism and Colonial History* 2, no. 3 (2001): 48; Eugene Genovese, *Roll, Jordan, Roll: The World the Slaves Made* (New York: Vintage, 1976), 465–66.

10. Ibid.

11. Bush, *Slave Women in Caribbean Society*, 94. For those women on Newton estate who were listed by age (together with the age of their first surviving child), we know that their average age was 23.5 years; see MS 523/288 List of and report on negroes at Newton 1796.

12. Anthony S. Parent and Susan Brown Wallace, "Childhood and Sexual Identity under Slavery," *Journal of the History of Sexuality* 3, no. 3 (1993); 391.

13. Douglas Hall, *In Miserable Slavery: Thomas Thistlewood in Jamaica, 1750–1786* (London: Macmillan, 1989).

14. Norman S. Ellerstein and J. William Canavan, "Sexual Abuse of Boys," *American Journal of Disease of Children* 134, no. 3 (1980): 255.

15. Lloyd deMause, "The History of Child Abuse," *Journal of Psychohistory* 25, no. 3 (1998): 217.

16. Ibid., 218.

17. Peter Bardaglio, "'An Outrage upon Nature': Incest and the Law in the Nineteenth-Century South," in Bleser, *In Joy and Sorrow*, 38.

18. Adam Kuper, "Incest, Cousin Marriage, and the Origin of the Human Sciences in Nineteenth-Century England," *Past and Present* 174, no. 1 (2002): 160.

19. Bardaglio, "'Outrage upon Nature,'" 39.

20. Ibid., 35.

21. William Sells, *Remarks on the Condition of the Slaves in the Island of Jamaica* (London: J. M. Richardson, Cornhill and Ridgways, 1823).

22. Bardaglio, "'Outrage upon Nature,'" 40.

23. Jerome Handler and Francesca Brady, "Jonathan Corncob Visits Barbados: Excerpts from a Late 18th Century Novel," *Journal of the Barbados Museum and Historical Society* 52 (2006): 29–30.

24. Jonathan Corncob, *Adventures of Jonathan Corncob, Loyal American Refugee Written by Himself* (London: G. G. J. and G. Robinson, 1787), 126.

25. Ibid., 127.

26. Ronald Hyam, "Empire and Sexual Opportunity," *Journal of Imperial and Commonwealth History* 14, no. 2 (1986): 55.

27. Ellerstein and Canavan, "Sexual Abuse of Boys," 256.

28. Save the Children UK, "The Small Hands of Slavery: Modern Day Child Slavery—A Report by Save the Children" (2007), http://www.humantrafficking.org/uploads/publications/ChildSlaveryBrieffinal.pdf.

29. Hyam, "Empire and Sexual Opportunity."

30. LaFont, "Very Straight Sex," 35.

31. Sodomy was considered an ecclesiastical offense, but it was later made a common-law felony by English statute: "'Sodomy' is a generic term including both 'bestiality' and 'buggery'" *Black's Law Dictionary*, ed. Bryan Garner (Eagan, Minn.: West Group, 2004).

32. Louise A. Jackson, *Child Sexual Abuse in Victorian England* (London: Routledge, 2000), 100.

33. Ibid., 71.

34. Wilma King, *Stolen Childhood: Slave Youth in Nineteenth-Century America* (Bloomington: Indiana University Press, 1995), 110.

35. Karl Watson, *A Kind of Right to Be Idle: Old Doll Matriarch of Newton Plantation* (Bridgetown: Department of History, Cave Hill Campus, University of the West Indies and the Barbados Museum and Historical Society, 2000), 21. Old Doll was an older enslaved matriarch at Newton who had gained favor with the plantation owners.

36. LaFont, "Very Straight Sex," 36. *Buckra* was a colloquial term used among Africans in some English-speaking territories in the Caribbean meaning "white man."

37. Ibid.

38. Jackson, *Child Sexual Abuse*, 74.

39. Ibid., 75.

40. Jonathan Dalby, *Crime and Punishment in Jamaica: A Quantitative Analysis of the Assize Court Records, 1756–1856* (Kingston, Jamaica: Social History Project, Department of History, University of the West Indies, Mona Campus, 2000), 45.

41. Jackson, *Child Sexual Abuse*, 75.

42. Dalby, *Crime and Punishment in Jamaica*, 45.

43. Jackson, *Child Sexual Abuse*, 33.

44. Gail Elizabeth Wyatt, "The Aftermath of Child Sexual Abuse of African American and White American Women: The Victims' Experience," *Journal of Family Violence* 5, no. 1 (1990): 63.

45. CO 28/115 #11, February 13, 1835.

46. CO 28/116, September 11, 1835.
47. Jackson, *Child Sexual Abuse*, 33.
48. CO 28/116, September 11, 1835.
49. Ibid.
50. Jackson, *Child Sexual Abuse*, 93.
51. Ibid.
52. Pamela Paradis Tice, Doris Georgiou, and Dorothy Lemmey, "Victorian Children and Sex: The Reality Ignored by Proponents of Child Sexual Rights," *Journal of Psychohistory* 30, no. 4 (2003): 401.
53. Jackson, *Child Sexual Abuse*, 73.
54. In fact, the only time when any modesty was evident was when Caroline's mother called on the apothecary late that night. Since his wife was present, Korine only mentioned that her child was bleeding. She did not want to offend the sensibilities of a respectable gentlewoman in her home with the abhorrent details of her daughter's trauma. It was not until she and the apothecary were on the road that she fully explained what had happened.
55. Jackson, *Child Sexual Abuse*, 78.
56. Ibid., 78.
57. CO 28/119 #10, January 22, 1837, Mary Jane Assaults and Infant.
58. Jackson, *Child Sexual Abuse*, 59.
59. James Kincaid, *Child-Loving: The Erotic Child and Victorian Culture* (New York: Routledge, 1992), 190.
60. Jackson, *Child Sexual Abuse*, 110.
61. CO 28/119 #10, January 22, 1837, Mary Jane Assaults and Infant.
62. DeMause, "History of Child Abuse," 222.
63. Hilary Beckles, "Property Rights in Pleasure: The Marketing of Slave Women's Sexuality in the West Indies," in *West Indian Accounts: Essays on the History of the British Caribbean and the Atlantic Economy in Honor of Richard Sheridan*, ed. Roderick A. MacDonald (Bloomington: Indiana University Press, 1996), 170.
64. Dalby, *Crime and Punishment in Jamaica*, 45.
65. Ibid.

12

STRATEGIES FOR SOCIAL MOBILITY

Liaisons between Foreign Men and Enslaved Women in Benguela, ca. 1770–1850

MARIANA P. CANDIDO

The focus of this chapter is the relationship between foreign men and slave women in Benguela, in west central Africa, during the late eighteenth and early nineteenth centuries.[1] At that time, Benguela was a relatively small town, with a population that fluctuated between 1,500 and 3,000 inhabitants, excluding slaves in transit.[2] Yet despite its small size, Benguela was one of the most important ports for the Atlantic slave trade, to which, between 1695 and 1850, it furnished at least 764,000 slaves.[3] From the mid-eighteenth century, foreign merchants began to settle in Benguela in search of captives for export to the Americas. Most of these merchants, including those who had left wives at home, formed stable relationships with local women, both free and enslaved. They thereby established complex transatlantic family links, a pattern that lasted until at least 1850, when, with the closure of the Brazilian market, the Atlantic slave trade came to an end.

The use of enslaved women as sexual objects by their owners was common in slave regimes. This was more evident in places, such as Benguela, where few white females were available. Even slaveholders who were accompanied by wives sexually abused their female slaves.[4] Indeed, white men viewed all nonwhite females, whether free or servile, as available to service their sexual needs, and they systematically asserted their sexual dominance especially over enslaved women,[5] who were in control of neither their bodies nor their sexuality.[6] In fact, sexual abuse was recognized as one of the mechanisms through which white male power, dominance, and control were exercised over the slave population.[7]

At the same time, enslaved women used sex and relationships with foreign men as means to acquire freedom. In Benguela as in other slave societies, manumission was a gendered process in which slave women could use sex to their advantage, and some slave women who bore the children of their masters thereby secured manumission for themselves or their children. Others were able to gain economic benefits. Some enslaved women apparently were even able to turn rape to their advantage.[8] Through an examination of archival documents, wills, nominal lists, and letters from Benguela between 1770 and 1850, when the transatlantic slave trade was at its height, this chapter explores the complexity of the relationships established by foreign traders in Benguela and, notably, the ways in which slave women sought to achieve freedom. The Benguela case allows a better understanding of gendered questions of slavery and the possibility for social mobility in an African port during the transatlantic slave trade.

Foreigners in Benguela

Despite being a notoriously unhealthy locale, Benguela was a major supplier of slaves for the Atlantic trade, and its permanent population of under 3,000 was augmented by temporary influxes of people from the interior, via caravans, and from Brazil and Portugal, via the sea. The result was a continuous interaction of different peoples, both local and foreign.

A small core of mixed-race and whites—Europeans, Brazilians, and their descendants—occupied most administrative and military positions in Benguela.[9] The number of white male inhabitants fluctuated but remained below 100 from 1797 until 1844, when they numbered a mere 37, only to rise sharply thereafter to reach 137 in 1850—probably due to official encouragement of poor peasant immigration from Brazil and Portugal.[10] However, the white female inhabitants of Benguela were considerably fewer, their numbers falling from 9 in 1797 to between 1 and 7 from 1800 to 1850.

Benguela's white population included exiled individuals, especially convicted criminals, from other parts of the Portuguese Empire.[11] As Charles Boxer has stressed, "The notoriously unhealthy or ill-famed regions, such as Benguela . . . hardly received anyone else save these exiles and government officials after the mid-seventeenth century."[12] In 1792, for example, five men condemned for treason in the failed 1788–89 Inconfidência Mineira, or Conspiracy of Minas Gerais in Brazil, were sent to Benguela.[13] For some, exile offered the possibility of economic prosperity, particularly for those engaged in slaving activities. Yet for most, exile translated into an unrewarding and exacting work regime, and for some, it was a death sentence. Benguela was notorious for its high mortality rates among Europeans,[14] and access to the town's hospital was a privilege reserved for the elites (and even they suffered from the institution's lack of equipment and trained personnel).[15]

Color classification should not be taken at face value. As Joseph Miller has noted with respect to the white women listed in the 1797 Luanda census, "The racial distinction carefully recorded in this census certainly reflected wealth and local prestige more than the physical features of these women. . . . [They] were probably the influential daughters of Luso-African families evident in other sources, whose wealth lightened their social and legal complexions no less than in Brazil."[16] Indeed, it can be said that in Benguela, as elsewhere in the South Atlantic world, "money whitened." Classification into white, *mulato*, and black categories was based on subjective ascriptions, including economic activity, place of residence, language skills, social behavior, access to land, and appearance—as characterized by hairstyle, clothing, and body language.[17]

Portuguese officials commented on what they considered to be the reprehensible sexual and moral conduct of white and Luso-African residents in Benguela. In 1760, the Marquis of Pombal, the prime minister of King Dom João I, was outraged by reports of the behavior of white men in Benguela,[18] and in 1769, Francisco Inocêncio de Sousa Coutinho, the governor of Angola, wrote: "Some white men forget the respect and fidelity to the saint religion [Christianity] . . . [they are] in a Christian capital, conquered for God Almighty."[19] For single men and for unaccompanied married white men, it was difficult to resist the temptations of a place that was reputedly exotic and mysterious.[20] A few were motivated by patriotism and ambition to travel to Benguela; others were motivated by the desire to experience sexual freedom, for as Anne McClintock has put it, "Africa . . . had become what can be called a porno-tropics for the European imagination—a fantastic magic lantern of the mind onto which Europe projected its forbidden sexual desires and fears."[21] Black women were the "forbidden fruit" with whom white men could realize all their fantasies. Some of these European men maintained long-term relationships with local women, whereas others had sporadic sexual encounters, consensual or not. In all, European men in Benguela generated a large number of descendants. In 1795, for example, João Pedro Barbosa, a single soldier stationed in the town, recognized four daughters from three different free women.[22]

In the Portuguese colonies, in contrast to the French, Spanish, and British Empires, no code of laws was formulated, but there nevertheless existed a series of social regulations that created barriers between whites and "others"—meaning the black population.[23] High-ranking officials were expected to bring their families to Benguela and live a "decent" lifestyle, respecting Christian values.[24] Local administrators also tried to control the behavior of European males of lower status, threatening to imprison those who did not follow a "religious, justifiable, and industrial way of life."[25] However, the Lisbon administration expected lower-ranking officials to marry local women. In fact, in 1716, a charter was issued preventing soldiers who had established families in Angola from abandoning the territory without governmental approval.[26] Again, poor whites could mingle with blacks in their social and sexual spheres. Moreover, the lack of white women inevitably meant that European males sought slave women. In this, Benguela was no different from other slave societies where white men perceived sexual access to black slave women as a right.[27]

Slave Women

Though the white population of Benguela remained predominantly male, the sex balance of its slave population changed over time. At the end of the eighteenth century, between 60 and 75 percent of the slave population of Benguela was female, but within a few years, the balance had altered, and from 1804 to 1811, 55 percent of the town's slaves were male.[28] The shift in gender may have been related to changing demands for labor, which reflected a decline in agricultural production—a sphere dominated by women.[29] However, after 1811, the balance again shifted, and in 1813, women represented 60 percent of Benguela's slave population (670 women as opposed to 471 men), a proportion also reported for 1815. In 1826, women still formed the majority of slaves (54 percent, with 663 females and 566 males). Variations in the sex distribution of Benguela's slave population from 1811 were intimately related to the transatlantic slave trade. As a whole and especially for the period of this study, west central Africa exported more males than females. Male slaves constituted 69 percent of all slaves exported during the eighteenth century, increasing to 72 percent in the nineteenth century.[30] Because the transatlantic demand for male captives remained high, it is probable that many female captives were kept locally in Benguela,[31] which indicates there was an internal demand for enslaved females related to their productive and reproductive capacities.[32]

In the preabolition era, female slave labor was fundamental to Benguela's economy. Women slaves could be found throughout the town engaged in "female tasks": they prepared food to sell in the streets, sold agricultural produce in the markets, worked as seamstresses and hairdressers, did laundry, ironed clothes, and cultivated fields. These activities benefited the slave masters who profited from their vendor work but also generated some income for the slaves themselves. A major activity of slave women was to supply food and water to a population that was in constant movement. Throughout Angola, enslaved women worked as *quitandeiras* (street vendors),[33] selling their products on the streets, in public markets (*terreiro public*), and in private shops. Many quitandeiras concentrated their business in the public market, selling crops (notably beans, manioc flour, and corn) that private cultivators produced outside Benguela. They were so important to the market's functioning that the government, which established the market in the 1760s, changed its location several times at their request.[34] Ownership of the quitandeiras was concentrated in the hands of a small group of Benguela slave owners, who thereby dominated the urban market in agricultural produce. One such slave owner was António da Costa Covelo, who, in the 1850s, possessed thirty slaves, two-thirds of whom were women. Covelo employed his male slaves mainly in fishing and copper activities, but most of his female slaves (eighteen out of twenty) were street vendors. Only two of his female slaves were not quitandeiras:

Sebastiana, an eight-year-old girl, and Joaquina, a one-year-old toddler.[35] Other West African Atlantic ports had similar gender-specific work profiles. In all, marketers were predominantly female slaves.

However, most slave women cultivated gardens around the town or performed domestic tasks, and thus, they had less opportunity than quitandeiras or most male slaves—fewer of whom were engaged in domestic labor—to engage in urban commercial activities.[36] Female domestic slaves performed a large variety of tasks. Some cultivated backyard plots, chased off unwelcome animals, or maintained fires to keep mosquitoes at bay.[37] Others cleaned, cooked, acted as nurses, and performed many other tasks, including fanning—to keep the interior of the dwellings cool and to protect guests from mosquitoes at night.[38] Because they lived in their owners' houses, domestic slaves in Benguela had only limited geographic mobility. But most had the opportunity to engage in independent activities within the town, and some accumulated sufficient money to buy their freedom through selling food or other products on the streets.

Strategies for Social Mobility: Slavery and Sex

The scholarship on female slavery in Africa has emphasized the role of women in agricultural and domestic labor, although Claude Meillassoux has suggested that if "there was no a priori preference for one sex over the other, it was because slaves were sought as *asexual agents of work*."[39] However, the dimension of sex in female slave labor is usually neglected in the literature.[40] As noted, there is no doubt that the labor of female slaves was important in agricultural production in the lands surrounding Benguela, and female slaves also worked as street vendors, seamstresses, washers, and cooks. Nevertheless, the evidence indicates that in Benguela, slave masters preferred female over male slaves because, in addition to being able to use them for domestic and economically productive purposes, they could exploit them sexually.[41]

This was particularly the case with female slaves employed within the slave-owning household. Domestic slave labor created varying degrees of intimacy with members of the slave-owning family, which, in turn, offered female domestic slaves the possibility of developing acquaintanceships and friendships with free people; it also enabled them to build social networks that could prove extremely important in helping them improve their social standing and even achieve freedom. Of great importance here were sexual relationships. Slave masters considered themselves sovereign within the household. Many viewed female housekeepers as available sexual partners and forced them to also perform sexual services for them.[42] Such abuses were characteristic of all slave societies. Indeed, although the Portuguese administration did not officially sanction such practices, it openly tolerated them.[43]

Thus, for female slaves, concubinage and domestic servitude were closely related. However, some slave women were able to manipulate their masters' desire for sexual services in order to enhance their own lifestyle and status.[44] Throughout Portuguese overseas settlements, as, for example, in Brazil[45] and Luanda,[46] some female slave concubines were able to obtain manumission for themselves or their children.[47] This process and the complex relations between masters and their slave concubines is, in part, reflected in the wills left by individual slave owners in Benguela. One such case is that of Antonio José de Barros. In 1797, three years before his death, Barros was a sergeant in Benguela's army. He was also a trader with strong links to Rio de Janeiro. When the residential list was collected, Barros was in Rio de Janeiro on a business trip.[48] He died when the *Pensamento Feliz*, the ship on which he was returning to Benguela (from this or another visit to Brazil), sank off the Cabo Negro coast. In his will, drawn up before leaving Benguela,[49] he stipulated that eight days after his death, Vitória and Francisca, two domestic slaves who had given birth to three of his daughters, should be given letters of manumission in return for providing him with "good service"; thus, they were liberated from future servitude to his family or to anyone else. They were also to receive 20,000 reis worth of textiles—the major commodity in and around Benguela. Thereby, Barros ensured that Vitória and Francisca could engage in business and survive as freed women.[50]

Moreover, Barros had probably maintained relationships with his five other female slaves: Feliciana, Rosaria, Mariana, Micaela, and Joana—a seamstress. His will stipulated that, upon his death, any slave woman who had a newborn baby recognized by him or who alleged to be pregnant by him should be freed and receive textiles. He noted in his will that although he had no child by Joana, she should receive the same "reward" for services rendered as Vitória and Francisca: manumission and 20,000 reis worth of textiles, indicating that Joana was also called upon to satisfy Barros's sexual desires.

Some masters, in addition to granting their female slave concubines their freedom and capital—in the form of textiles—with which to trade, also set them up as slave owners themselves. For instance, in the first decade of the nineteenth century, António de Carvalho, another Benguela trader, stipulated in his will that Bibiana, a household slave with whom he had had three daughters, should receive not only her manumission but also textiles and two slave girls. Another domestic slave, Josefa, also received her freedom, textiles, and—after she had served Carvalho's daughters for six years—a young slave girl named Mariana. Josefa would probably have employed Mariana in farming, preparing food for local trade, or even selling food in the streets. For former slave concubines, owning a slave represented more than a chance to increase productivity and to profit from the slave labor generated. It also represented prestige: slaves were displayed when slave owners went out or when they needed moral and physical support. In other words, they enhanced the status of their owners.[51]

Carvalho also possessed a slave woman, Beba, who lived in the hinterland in the *libata* (house) of Kingolo and gave birth to a boy recognized by Carvalho as his son. In Carvalho's will, Beba was granted her freedom in addition to some pieces of textiles, and her son was granted a young slave—as were all five of Carvalho's children.

Indeed, through his will, Carvalho influenced the destiny of each of his slaves. Male slaves José Catimba, Manoel, Joaquim (a fishermen), José (a cooper), and Cabindalala (an old man located in Kingolo) all received manumission letters, as did Catumbo, an enslaved woman and José. By contrast, Carvalho stressed that Catarina, the first slave he had bought, should not receive her freedom. She was supposed to serve his sons and daughters until they decided her destiny.[52]

In another example, Francisco Xavier willed that upon his death, Mariana Benguela, who lived in Bahia and was the mother of his daughter, Martinha, should be freed. Xavier also freed two of his male slaves, Mateus and Lourenço. Other slaves of his did not fare so well. Joaquim Benguela and António had probably been born into slavery. Classified as "*ladino*"—indicating that they spoke Portuguese and were acculturated—they had also received religious instruction, and they were skilled laborers. However, Xavier willed that upon his death, they were to be taken to the Benguela slave market and sold—a trauma they had probably experienced before.[53]

Barro, Carvalho, and Xavier were by no means exceptions. It was publicly recognized that slave masters often had a large number of children by different women. Most white Benguelan merchants freed children they fathered with black woman, and most did so through their wills.[54] The intersection between violence and power was particularly significant for slave women who had borne children for their slaveholders.[55] In Catholic society, the will was the last means available for individuals to make peace with God and thus guarantee the salvation of their souls. Slave owners freed their slaves in order to redeem their sins and cleanse their souls—that is, they did so for fear of hell and eternal damnation, rather than from piety or remorse. A concubine therefore only achieved freedom after the master's death. This procedure might be related to the religious belief in moral expiation, similar to practices in the Muslim world.

Nevertheless, having children with her master also granted the female slave significant benefits during his lifetime because, generally, the children enjoyed free status from birth. Thus, Barros had recognized Rita and Rosa, Vitória's daughters, as his progeny and thereby acknowledged their free status from the moment they were born. The young Rita had been sent to Rio de Janeiro to be educated by Frutuoso José da Cruz, a trader from Rio de Janeiro related to Barros, whereas Rosa had remained in Benguela in the company of her parents. Francisca had also had a daughter with Barros, a girl named Joana, whom Barros likewise had freed at birth by recognizing her as his biological daughter.[56]

In his will, Barros recognized six children as his heirs. Two of them, João and Feliciana, like Rita (his daughter with Vitória), lived in Rio de Janeiro with some of his business partners. Two others, Joana and Rosa, lived with him in Benguela. The sixth was Feliciano, who was born from an affair Barros had in Rio with Ana, a mulatto slave woman owned by Domingos Rebelo Pereira, a Rio de Janeiro trader. When Pereira learned of her pregnancy, he asked Barros to buy Ana's freedom in the name of the unborn child she was carrying. Barros was initially reluctant, as Ana had other children, but under continued pressure from Pereira and fearing possible social condemnation, he eventually agreed to free Ana and her child who, when he was born, was baptized Feliciano in the Candelária parish.[57] Recognized as Barros's natural son, Feliciano was entitled to part of his father's estate.

In another case from the first decade of the nineteenth century, Francisco Dias, also a trader in Benguela, freed Ana, Josefa, and Joaquina, three of his slaves identified as "Benguela." These three women had given birth to three children, all of them recognized by Dias as his offspring. A fourth slave woman, Francisca Benguela, was pregnant when he wrote his will. Afraid that Francisca's baby was not his, Dias came up with a solution to determine paternity. If the unborn baby was mixed-race, then the baby was his, and Francisca and the baby were to be freed. If the baby was black, then the baby was not his, and Francisca and the baby were to be sold to anyone who offered a good price.[58] Carvalho was more exacting: his will recorded that only if his pregnant domestic slave give birth to a white baby would he recognize it as his own.

In slave regimes such as that in Benguela, white slave masters often had many different kinds of relationships with their female slaves. Most slave owners used their power sexually to exploit female slaves. That said, concubinage could provide a means for a slave woman to improve her status.[59] Unlike in Muslim societies, bearing the child of her master did not guarantee that a slave woman in a Portuguese settlement would acquire freedom automatically after her master's death. However, in the Portuguese colonies—though not in Portugal itself—it could improve her chances of gaining manumission. This was the case for Benguela, where in most of the wills I have located, slave owners freed women with whom they had had children and/or long relationships.

Such relationships were nominally taboo, but Portuguese authorities and the church largely turned a blind eye toward them, and slave masters saw them as a legitimate benefit of slavery—a way to maintain their social control, notably within the domain of the patriarchal household.[60] Although enslaved women entered such relationships involuntarily, some were able to turn them to their own advantage. Of course, this does not excuse the violence implicit in the relationship. These women experienced racism and sexual violence in an intense and unique way. However, the fact that white men demanded sexual favors from enslaved females gave these women the opportunity to frequent spaces that were otherwise exclusive to white people, as well as the intimate spheres of the slaveholding men. As a consequence, slave concubines had a dual role—as oppressed slave workers, on one hand, and as sexual partners with intimate knowledge of their masters' lives, on the other. This duality offered them a chance to exert control over their destiny; as concubines, they gained special privileges that gave them the possibility of using their sexuality to forge new ways of resisting oppression and bargaining to enhance their status. Slave concubines could anticipate some recompense, perhaps even manumission for themselves or their children. Through these relationships, slave women had easier access to manumission upon their masters' death than slave men did. In this sense, slave women used their sexuality consciously as a tool to resist enslavement, improve social mobility, and even achieve freedom.

Notes

1. I would like to thank Paul Lovejoy, Mariza de Carvalho Soares, Beatrix Heintze, Ana Lucia Araujo, Stacey Sommerdyk, and Yacine Daddi Addoun for their comments on this essay.

2. Mariana P. Candido, "Enslaving Frontiers: Slavery, Trade and Identity in the Benguela Hinterland, 1780–1850" (Ph.D. diss., York University, 2006), 128–54.

3. David Eltis and David Richardson, *Atlas of the Transatlantic Slave Trade* (New Haven, Conn.: Yale University Press, 2010), 151; David Eltis, "The Volume and Structure of the Transatlantic Slave Trade: A Reassessment," *William and Mary Quarterly* 58, no. 1 (2001): 17–46; José Curto, "The Legal Portuguese Slave Trade from Benguela, Angola, 1730–1828: A Quantitative Re-appraisal," *África* 17, no. 1 (1993–94): 113–15; Curto, "Luso-Brazilian Alcohol and the Legal Slave Trade at Benguela and Its Hinterland (1617–1830)," in *Négoce blanc en Afrique noire: L'évolution du 18e au 20e siècles*, ed. H. Bonin and M. Cahen (Paris: Publications de la Société Française d'Histoire d'Outre-Mer, 2001), 367; David Eltis, Stephen Beherendt, David Richardson, and Herbert Klein, *The Transatlantic Slave Trade: A Database on CD-ROM* (Cambridge: Cambridge University Press, 1999); and David Eltis, Paul E. Lovejoy, and David Richardson, "Slave-Trading Ports: Towards an Atlantic-Wide Perspective," in *Ports of the Slave Trade (Bights of Benin and Biafra)*, ed. Robin Law and Silke Strickrodt (Stirling, UK: Centre of Commonwealth Studies, University of Stirling, 1999).

4. José Curto, "As If from a Free Womb: Baptismal Manumissions in the Conceição Parish, Luanda, 1778–1807," *Portuguese Studies Review* 10, no. 1 (2002): 42–46.

5. *Busha's Mistress, or Catherine the Fugitive: A Stirring Romance of the Days of Slavery in Jamaica*, ed. Paul Lovejoy, Verene Shepard, and David Trotman (Kingston, Jamaica: Ian Randle Publishers, 2003); Paul Lovejoy, "Concubinage and the Status of Women Slaves in Early Colonial Northern Nigeria," *Journal of African History* 29, no. 2 (1988): 245–66.

6. Martin Klein, "Women and Slavery in Western Sudan," in *Women and Slavery in Africa*, ed. Claire Robertson and Martin Klein (Portsmouth, N.H.: Heinemann, 1997), 87.

7. Jacquelyn Down Hall, "The Mind That Burns in Each Body: Women, Rape, and Racial Violence," in *Powers of Desire: The Politics of Sexuality*, ed. Ann Snitow, Christine Stansell, and Sharon Thompson (London: Virago, 1983), 339–60. See also Mary C. Karasch, "From Porterage to Proprietorship: African Occupations in Rio de Janeiro, 1880–1850," in *Race and Slavery in the Western Hemisphere: Quantitative Studies*, ed. Stanley L. Engerman and Eugene G. Genovese (Princeton, N.J.: Princeton University Press, 1975), 383–85; Douglas Hall, *In Miserable Slavery: Thomas Thistlewood in Jamaica, 1750–1786* (London: Macmillan, 1989); Paul Lovejoy, "Concubinage in the Sokoto Caliphate (1804–1903)," *Slavery and Abolition* 11, no. 2 (1990): 159–89.

8. See the examples provided in Pamela Scully and Diana Patons, eds., *Gender and Slave Emancipation in the Atlantic World* (Durham, N.C.: Duke University Press, 2005).

9. Candido, "Enslaving Frontiers," 101–13.

10. Valentim Alexandre and Jill Dias, *O império africano, 1825–1890* (Lisbon: Estampa, 1998), 441–54; William Gervase Clarence-Smith, "Capital Accumulation and Class Formation in Angola," in *History of Central Africa*, ed. David Birmingham and Phyllis Martin (New York: Longman, 1986), 2:163–99; and W. G. Clarence-Smith, *Slaves, Peasants, and Capitalists in Southern Angola, 1840–1926* (Cambridge: Cambridge University Press, 1979), 49–51.

11. For criminals from different parts of the Portuguese Empire, see AHU, Angola, box 87, document (doc.) 77, 1798; AHU, Paraiba, box 6, doc. 452; AHU, Pernambuco, doc. 213, doc. 14477; Biblioteca Municipal Pública do Porto (hereafter cited as BMPP), volume (vol.). 437, Francisco Inocêncio de Sousa Coutinho, "Memoria do Reino de Angola e suas Conquistas," Arquivo Histórico Nacional de Angola (hereafter cited as AHNA), vol. 442, folio (fl.) 134v, September 17, 1800; AHNA, vol. 447, fl. 151–52, September 11, 1820; and AHNA, vol. 448, fl. 29, August 10, 1822.

12. C. R. Boxer, *The Portuguese Seaborne Empire, 1415–1825* (London: Hutchinson, 1969), 312.

13. AHU, Angola, vol. 1629, fl. 73v, October 14, 1792; Instituto Histórico Geográfico Brasileiro, Rio de Janeiro, Brazil (hereafter cited as IHGB), doc. DL 86, 07.08, May 29, 1792.

14. Joseph Miller, "Significance of Drought, Disease and Famine in the Agriculturally Marginal Zones of West Central Africa," *Journal of African History*

23, no. 1 (1982): 17–61, and Jill Dias, "Famine and Disease in the History of Angola, c. 1830–1930," *Journal of African History* 22, no. 3 (1981). See also AHU, Angola, box 45, doc. 94, September 18, 1762; AHU, Angola, box 54, doc. 72, August 18, 1770; AHU, Angola, box 73, doc. 44, October 12, 1788; AHU, box 82, doc. 62, December 2, 1795; AHU, Angola, box 103, doc. 55, March 23, 1802; AHU, Angola, box 122, doc. 75, July 15, 1811; AHU, Angola, box 131, doc. 2, 1815; AHU, Angola, box 144, doc. 2, January 4, 1824; AHU, Angola, box 153, doc. 61, December 20, 1826; AHU, Correspondência dos Governadores, folder 1, March 23, 1835; AHU, Correspondência dos Governadores, folder 10A, March 18, 1846; AHU, Correspondência dos Governadores, folder 10B, July 1, 1846; AHNA, vol. 447, fl. 90, November 26, 1819; AHNA, vol. 448, fl. 15v, March 30, 1822; AHNA, vol. 457, fl. 3v, April 23, 1845.

15. J. C. Feo Cardoso de Castello e Branco e Torres, *Memórias contendo a biographia do vice almirante Luiz da Motta Feo e Torres* (Paris: Fantin Livreiro, 1825), 263; AHU, Angola, box 36, doc. 7, March 16, 1748; AHU, Angola, box 78, doc. 16, January 23, 1793; AHU, Angola, box 82, unnumbered doc., June 15, 1795; AHU, Angola, box 88, doc. 46, March 28, 1798; AHU, Angola, box 103, doc. 55, March 23, 1802.

16. Joseph Miller, *Way of Death: Merchant Capitalism and the Angolan Slave Trade* (Madison: University of Wisconsin Press, 1988), 192.

17. For more on color as a concept of social construction, see Deborah Posel, "Race as Common Sense: Racial Classification in Twentieth-Century South Africa," *African Studies Review* 44, no. 2 (2001): 87–113; Robert H. Jackson, *Race, Caste and Status: Indians in Colonial Spanish America* (Albuquerque: University of New Mexico Press, 1999); and Mara Loveman, "Nation-State Building, 'Race' and the Production of Official Statistics: Brazil in Comparative Perspective" (Ph.D. diss., University of California–Los Angeles, 2001).

18. AHU, Angola, box 43, doc. 111, November 20, 1760.

19. AHU, Angola, box 53, doc. 1, January 10, 1769.

20. For the interpretation that Portuguese men had relationships with local women because of the lack of white women, see Ivana Elbl, "Men without Wives: Sexual Arrangements in the Early Portuguese Expansion in West Africa," in *Desire and Discipline: Sex and Sexuality in Postmodern West*, ed. Jacqueline Murray and Konrad Eisenbichler (Toronto: University of Toronto Press, 1996), 61–87. For the idea that Portuguese men were also motivated by the sexual opportunities that the empire expansion offered, see Ronald Hyam, *Empire and Sexuality: The British Experience* (Manchester, UK: Manchester University Press, 1992), esp. chap. 4.

21. Anne McClintock, *Imperial Leather: Race, Gender and Sexuality in the Colonial Contest* (New York: Routledge, 1995), 22. See also Barbara Bush, *Slave Women in Caribbean Society, 1650–1838* (Kingston, Jamaica: Heinemann Publishers, 1990).

22. AHU, Angola, box 83, doc. 37, April 10, 1795.

23. See A. J. R. Russell-Wood, "Iberian Expansion and the Issues of Black Slavery: Changing Portuguese Attitudes, 1440–1770," *American Historical Review* 83, no. 1 (1978): 16–42.

24. AHU, Angola, box 43, doc. 111, November 20, 1760.

25. "Não estivessem sujeitos a viver unidos em sociedade em religião, em justiça, e em indústria, será imediatamente preso e remetido para esta capital," *Arquivo de Angola* 1, no. 1 (1936): 178.

26. AHU, Angola, box 26, doc. 38, October 9, 1717.

27. Hilary Beckles, *Natural Rebels: A Social History of Enslaved Black Women in Barbados* (New Brunswick, N.J.: Rutgers University Press, 1989), 60.

28. The 1804, 1805, 1806, 1808, and 1809 censuses are at, respectively, AHU, Angola, box 113, doc. 6; AHU, Angola, box 116, doc. 87; AHU, Angola, box 118, doc. 21; AHU, Angola, box 120. doc. 21, and AHU, Angola, box 121, doc. 32. The 1811 census is at AHU, Angola, box 124, doc. 59.

29. For comments on agricultural decline, see AHU, Angola, box 181, doc. 28, 1812.

30. Eltis et al., *Transatlantic Slave Trade.*

31. Eltis and Engerman, "Fluctuations in Sex and Age Ratios," 310; David Eltis and Stanley L. Engerman, "Was the Slave Trade Dominated by Men?," *Journal of Interdisciplinary History* 23, no. 2 (1992): 252.

32. George Tams, *Visita as possessões Portuguesas na costa occidental d'Africa*, vol. 1 (Porto, Portugal: Tipografia do Calvario, 1850), 144. See also Paul Lovejoy and David Richardson, "The Initial Crisis of Adaptation: The Impact of British Abolition on the Atlantic Slave Trade in West Africa, 1808–1820," in *From Slave Trade to "Legitimate" Commerce: The Commercial Transition in the Nineteenth-Century West Africa*, ed. Robin Law (Cambridge: Cambridge University Press, 1995), 33, and Linda Heywood, "Slavery and Forced Labour in the Changing Political Economy of Central Angola, 1850–1949," in *The End of Slavery in Africa*, ed. Suzanne Miers and Richard Robert (Madison: University of Wisconsin Press, 1988), 417.

33. For more on quitandeiras, see Selma Pantoja, "A dimensão atlântica das quitandeiras" in *Diálogos Oceânicos: Minas Gerais e as Novas Abordagens para uma História do Império Ultramarino Português*, ed. Júnia F. Furtado (Belo Horizonte, Brazil: UFMG, 2001), 45–68. For women as food producers elsewhere, see Robert Harms, "Sustaining the System: Trading Towns along the Middle Zaire," in *Women and Slavery in Africa*, ed. Claire Robertson and Martin Klein (Portsmouth, N.H.: Heinemann, 1997), 95–110.

34. See Ralph Delgado, *Ao sul do Cuanza, Ocupação e aproveitamento do antigo reino de Benguela*, vol. 1 (Lisbon: n.p., 1944), 71–75; Elías Alexandre da Silva Correa, *Historia de Angola*, vol. 1 (1799; repr., Lisbon: n.p., 1937), 80; and José Carlos Venâncio, *A economia de Luanda e Hinterland no século XVII: um estudo de sociologia histórica* (Lisbon: Estampa, 1996), 63–70.

35. AHNA, vol. 3160.

36. See Selma Pantoja, "As fontes escritas do século XVII e o estudo da representação do feminino em Luanda," in *Construindo o passado angolano: As fontes e a sua interpretação. Actas do II, seminário internacional sobre a história de Angola* (Lisbon: Comissão Nacional para as Comemorações dos Descobrimentos Portugueses, 2000), 583–96.

37. Arquivo Histórico Militar, Lisbon, Portugal (hereafter cited as AHM), 2-2-3-d. 14, "Lopes: Descrição da Catumbela," 1847, fl. 5.

38. Tams, *Visita as possessões Portuguesas*, 1:125.

39. Claude Meillassoux, "Female Slavery," in *Women and Slavery*, Claire Robertson and Martin Klein (Portsmouth, N.H.: Heinemann, 1997), 58 (emphasis added).

40. Igor Kopytoff and Suzanne Miers, "Introduction," in *Slavery in Africa: Historical and Anthropological Perspectives*, ed. Miers and Kopytoff (Madison: University of Wisconsin Press, 1977), 29–34; Klein, "Women in Slavery in the Western Sudan," 87–88; Meillassoux, "Female Slavery," 49–66.

41. Paul Lovejoy, *Slavery, Commerce and Production in the Sokoto Caliphate of West Africa* (Trenton, N.J.: Africa World Press, 2005), 117–52. See also Patricia Romero, "Laboratory for the Oral History of Slavery: The Island of Lamu," *American Historical Review* 88, no. 1 (1983):,858–82, and Frederick Cooper, *Plantation Slavery on the East Coast of Africa* (New Haven, Conn.: Yale University Press, 1977).

42. Ladislau Magyar, "A nação dos quimbundos e seus costumes," chap. 7, also available in German in *Reisen in Süd-Afrika in den Jahren 1849 bis 1857* (Pest and Leipzig: Lauffer and Stolp); Magyar, "Estadia em Benguela," chap. 1, *Reisen in Süd-Afrika*, 10 (I would like to express my gratitude to Maria da Conceição Neto, who kindly made her Portuguese translation available to me); Beckles, *Natural Rebels*, 141–43.

43. The Luso-Tropicalista idea is a result of this, asserting that slavery in the Portuguese world was mild. See Gilberto Freyre, *Casa Grande e Senzala: Formação da família brasileira sob o regime de economia patriarcal* (Rio de Janeiro: Funarte, 1985).

44. Camillia Cowling, "Negociando a liberdade: mulheres de cor e a transição para o trabalho livre em Cuba e no Brasil, 1870–1888," in *Trabalho livre, trabalho escravo, Brasil e Europea, séculos XVIII e XIX*, ed. Douglas C. Libby and Júnia Ferreira (São Paulo, Brazil: AnnaBlume, 2006), 166; Sandra Lauderdale Graham, "Slavery's Impasse: Slave Prostitites, Small-Time Mistresses, and the Brazilian Law of 1871," *Comparative Studies in Society and History* 33, no. 4 (1991): 669–94; Bush, *Slave Women in Caribbean Society*, 111.

45. Sweet stresses that slave masters in Rio de Janeiro made use of certain expressions, such as "for the love I have for her," in manumission letters. See James Sweet, "Manumission in Rio de Janeiro, 1749–54: An African Perspective," *Slavery and Abolition* 24, no. 1 (2003): 59.

46. Curto, "As If from a Free Womb," 26–57.

47. Ibid., 27–54. Law stresses women's economic independence; see Robin Law, "Legitimate Trade and Gender Relations in Yorubaland and Dahomey," in *From Slave Trade to "Legitimate" Commerce: The Commercial Transition in the Nineteenth-Century West Africa*, ed. Robin Law (Cambridge: Cambridge University Press, 1995), 207, and Karasch, "From Porterage to Proprietorship," 384.

48. IHGB, DL 32,02.02, "Relação de Manuel José de Silveira Teixeira sobre os moradores da cidade de São Felipe de Benguela separados por raça, idade, emprego, título de habitação, oficios mecânicos e quantos mestres e aprendizes existem," fl. 7.

49. Arquivos Nacionais da Torre do Tombo, Lisbon, Portugal (hereafter cited as ANTT), Feitos Findos (hereafter cited as FF), Junta Ultramarina (hereafter cited as JU) Africa, mç. 2, n. 3 A, 1800.

50. Biblioteca da Sociedade de Geografia de Lisboa, Lisbon, Portugal, Res-1--E-2, "Memoria de Mucanos," August 13, 1841; see also Roquinaldo Amaral Ferreira, "Transforming Atlantic Slaving: Trade, Warfare and Territorial Control in Angola, 1650–1800" (Ph.D. diss., University of California–Los Angeles, 2003), 116; Miller, *Way of Death*, 310–11.

51. Adam Jones, "Female Slave-Owners on the Gold Coast: Just a Matter of Money?," in *Slave Cultures and the Cultures of Slavery*, ed. Stephan Palmie (Knoxville: University of Tennessee Press, 1995), 100–111.

52. ANTT, FF, JU, Africa, mc. 22, n. 5, 1803; AHU, Angola, box 74, doc. 49, February 20, 1789.

53. ANTT, FF, JU, Africa, mc 24, n. 17, 1800; for the protection of and reticence about selling ladino slaves, see Martin Klein and Paul Lovejoy, "Slavery in West Africa," in *The Uncommon Market: Essays in the Economic History of the Atlantic Slave Trade*, ed. Henry Gemery and Jan Hogendorn (New York: Academic Press, 1979), 187; Miller, *Way of Death*, 52 and 270–71; Beatrix Heintze, *Asilo ameaçado: oportunidades e consequências da fuga de escravos em Angola no século XVIII* (Luanda, Angola: Ministério da Cultura, 1995), 8; Ira Berlin and Philip Morgan, "Labor and the Shaping of Slave Life in the Americas," in *Cultivation and Culture: Labor and the Shaping of Slave Life in the Americas*, eds.Ira Berlin and Philip Morgan (Charlottesville: University Press of Virginia, 1993), 21.

54. Ferreira, *Transforming Atlantic Slaving*, 169. For more on mixed-race individuals' easier access to manumission, see Curto, "As If from a Free Womb," 26–57; Ira Berlin, *Slaves without the Masters: The Free Negros in the Antebellum South* (Oxford: Oxford University Press, 1981), 178–79.

55. Klein and Lovejoy, "Slavery in West Africa," 191; John Hunwick and Eve Troutt Powell, *The African Diaspora in the Mediterranean Lands of Islam* (Princeton, N.J.: Markus Wiener Publisher, 2002), 27–29; Curto, "As If from a Free Womb," 26–57.

56. ANTT, FF, JU, Africa, mç. 2, n. 3 A, 1800.

57. I was not able to locate Feliciano's baptism record in Candelária parish in Rio de Janeiro. The lack of information on his age makes it more difficult to track his baptism. However, the existence of some registers for slave children born to slave mothers and free fathers suggests that cases such as Feliciano's may not have been unusual in eighteenth-century Rio. See Arquivo da Cúria do Rio de Janeiro, Rio de Janeiro, Brazil, Registro de Batismo de Escravos, 1770–1802.

58. ANTT, FF, JU, Africa, mc. 19, n. 13, 1809.

59. Romero, "Laboratory for the Oral History," 858–82; Lovejoy, "Concubinage and the Status of Women Slaves," 246.

60. Stuart B. Schwartz, *Sugar Plantations in the Formation of the Brazilian Society: Bahia, 1550–1835* (Cambridge: Cambridge University Press, 1985).

SEX TRAFFICKING AND PROSTITUTION

13

JAPANESE BROTHEL PROSTITUTION, DAILY LIFE, AND THE CLIENT

Colonial Singapore, 1870–1940

JAMES FRANCIS WARREN

POVERTY, PATRIARCHY, AND PROSTITUTION

Between the Meiji Restoration of 1868 and the advent of World War II, prostitution in Singapore was tightly linked to economic factors in rural Japan. Extreme poverty, weak family economies, and rising economic expectations were all part of a set of prevailing conditions that created a huge supply of Japanese women and girls for international traffic. These startling economic conditions due to Japan's modernization are brought into sharp relief when attention is focused on regional demography and the lack of occupational choices for the rural daughters of destitute fishing and farming families of southern Japan, who were trafficked for brothel prostitution.

Poor village girls and women were either abducted or sold by *zegen* (traffickers) or pimps involved in the "flesh trade" through an international network of Japanese brothels in China and Southeast Asia, including Singapore. The brothel owners used the idea of the national good to enslave the girls, who were told that their bodies belonged to the state and that as a group they constituted a form of female army. They were also told that participating in the trade was their chance to serve the emperor and their country, to pay off their debts, and to become decent citizens. Their numbers swelled when Japan went to war against China in 1894 and again in 1905 in the conflict with Russia. By the late 1890s, there were already two thousand of these girls and women in Singapore. They were transported in coal or cargo ships inside boxes, barrels, and crates (they sometimes did not see daylight for twenty days), and when they arrived at the port, they were auctioned off like cattle to the highest bidder. In Singapore, they were resettled in brothels along Malay, Hylam, Trengganu, and Sago Streets. In order to pay off their debts to the brothel owner, the women and young girls had to service about two thousand men over several years. Other migrant workers, *dekasegi rodasha*, predominately single males, also left Japan to work abroad, and they too were to bear much of the burden and social cost of the early industrialization and urbanization of Japan's modern century.[1]

Extreme conditions of agrarian poverty, overcrowding, and falling levels of productivity became intolerable for many ordinary Japanese as their nation faced west in the latter decades of the nineteenth century. One of the few ways such wretched rural conditions could be mitigated was for individuals to leave Japan in search of work abroad. Work and job prospects were advertised by emigration agents and shipping companies. At this time, all those (both men and women) who left western and northern Kyushu to work in another country were called *karayuki-san* (one who goes to China), *kara* being the word used for China at that time.[2] Only after World War II did the meaning of karuyuki-san change, to specifically describe those women and young girls, primarily from Kyushu, who became prostitutes abroad.[3]

The Shimabara Peninsula, which is located in Nagasaki Prefecture, and the arid and mountainous Amakusa Island, which faces the peninsula from across the Kayosaki Strait in Kumamoto Prefecture, produced the largest number of karayuki-san. The fishing and farming areas of northern Kyushu were among the most impoverished in Japan. From a detailed analysis of village registers and population and taxation records, Mori Katsumi has shown that between 1651 and 1856, the population of Amakusa rose dramatically, more than trebling in size, but rice production lagged behind, increasing by a factor of only 1.08.[4] Because of the island's poor fertility, the growth in population led to an intensification of poverty.[5] Population continued to increase in the three decades after 1868 (during which infanticide was considered a capital crime), further exacerbating agrarian poverty. With mounting overpopulation, Amakusa villagers realized that to make gains in the face of modernization, they would have to leave their homes to seek work, turning in hope to overseas emigration. The geographic proximity of Amakusa Island and Shimabara Peninsula to the Chinese mainland and the countries of the *Nanyo*—the "south lands"—or the tropics, as well as to the port of Nagasaki, greatly facilitated the exodus of Kyushu women and girls, many of whom were forced to migrate or were sold by their parents into prostitution.

Japanese agriculture was backbreakingly labor intensive, and in calamitous times, every bowl of rice meant a personal struggle of some sort. For rural farmers and fishers, survival was a primary social and individual goal. In many cases, the exchange of a daughter was the only hope for a possible future. Patriarchy in traditional Japanese culture was responsible for the exploitation of women—financially, physically, sexually, and emotionally.

In many cases, karayuki-san entered prostitution to obtain much-needed financial assistance for parents and kin. The appeal to an ill-fed daughter's filial devotion by starving or irresponsible parents during periods of pestilence or famine often resulted in her going abroad under the compromise of debt.[6] Ironically, in a case where either parents or other relatives had received the amount of the pledge upon her entry into a Singapore brothel, the unselfish motive of filial piety often compelled the young karayuki-san to respect the contractual obligation and honor the debt. Parents took full advantage of this ideology of duty to raise money against the exchange value of their filial daughters, much as they would with any other negotiable asset or property. In one such case, an Amakusa villager applied at the local police station for a passport for his daughter so she could emigrate. Thereafter, a police officer was sent to dissuade the father from pursuing such a rash course of action. Upon discovering the family's miserable lot, however, the officer felt he had no choice but to assist the family in sending their child to Southeast Asia:

> Besides the fact that the parents were ill, there were eight children, including the eighteen-year-old daughter, freezing and starving in a dilapidated shack. The money which the young girl might have earned as textile-mill worker would not have been nearly enough to feed nine mouths. If she had become a prostitute in Japan, she would have only earned enough to support them for half a year. So the daughter with the policeman's help went to Singapore. She became one of the most popular prostitutes in the brothel quarter, and was able to send home regularly seventy dollars a month over a six-year period.[7]

The traditional concept of filial piety placed the female child at a severe disadvantage. If an ordinary Japanese family had to part with a child because of agrarian poverty or overpopulation, it was to their daughters that the parents first turned. Female children of eleven or under were often sold to procurers to save the rest of the family. In such circumstances, it was not unusual for the parents to consent to the unconditional transfer of their daughters to anyone who claimed to be in a position to feed and clothe them. Thus, the Japanese patriarchal system constantly produced women and young girls for prostitution abroad; these females were either sold or pawned to total strangers by poverty-stricken families. The purchasers, after having paid the usual indemnity money to the parents or other relative, had the right to transfer the child or young woman against the same kind of indemnity to a brothel keeper in Singapore or elsewhere in Asia.

International Traffic and Brothel Prostitution

The international traffic in Japanese women for brothel prostitution occurred at a time when there was a vigorous market for prostitutes in the colonial port towns of Southeast Asia. Brothel districts in major cities such as Singapore were sanctioned by colonial governments to cater to the sexual needs of tens of thousands of migrant bachelor laborers. By 1880, due to the British colonial policy on single male immigration to Singapore, there was a generation of bachelors in the city unable to marry because of the scarcity of women. The flood of *singkeh*, or bachelor coolies arriving from China to work in Singapore, had created a massive gender imbalance in the port's population, and the relentless demand for prostitutes by these migrant laborers was largely responsible for the extensive and organized traffic in young Japanese women and girls.[8] At the end of the nineteenth century, brothel prostitution had become a multimillion-dollar network, linking remote villages in rural Japan, ports such as Nagasaki and Kobe, the dockside in Hong Kong, and the brothels in Singapore.

Hence, traffic in women and children from Japan and licensed brothel prostitution in Singapore were inextricably linked. The primary incentive for this trade that made Singapore a major destination for Japanese women and young girls was the existence of organized houses of prostitution from which women could be sold.[9] Consequently, these places became major sources of supply for the zegen, the procurers and traffickers—the flesh traders. The trade in karayuki-san was extremely lucrative. At the turn of the century, so great was the demand for Japanese women that it could not be fully met, and large sums of money were involved in human trafficking. Karayuki-san were sought after not only in Singapore but also throughout Asia, including in India, Burma, Thailand, and the Netherland Indies, as well as in the French colonial city of Saigon and in American-controlled Manila. The Malayan tin-mining center of Ipoh, the Sumatran tobacco plantations in Medan, and the rubber estates in Johor also had established brothels. Some girls were sent by zegen to work at the far-flung economic margins of the region, to places such as the pearling center of Broome in northwestern Australia and to the tiny port of Sandakan on the east coast of British North Borneo.[10]

The karayuki-san played an important pioneering role in establishing a bridgehead for Japanese economic expansion into many of these colonial cities. Once firmly established, the overseas brothels created an economic wedge—an opening for the development of other Japanese entrepreneurs (such as kimono sellers, florists, photographers, hoteliers, and restaurateurs) associated with the sexual economy and catering to the needs of the prostitutes and their clients. Singapore, which offered practically unrestricted possibilities to traffickers, thus became the hub for the movement of Japanese women intended for brothel prostitution in Southeast Asia.

A contemporary, sorrowful song sung to the chords of the samisen informs historians about the demand, spread of destinations, and ultimate fate of many karayuki-san from Kyushu.

Carried on the drifting currents
Her destination will be
In the west, Siberia:
Or in the east, Java.
Which country will be her grave?
Lovers' chatter
Is like the dust
Of any country.[11]

The increasing complexity of this traffic for international brothel prostitution was reflected in the fact that by 1912, Japanese girls were being labeled in sets, according to destinations and demand, as being bound "for Korea," "for Siberia," or "for America." Many of them were thus sold and transported in batches by zegen as "Chosen *yuki*," "Siberia *yuki*," or "*Ameyuki-san*."[12]

It was zegen such as Muroaka Iheiji and his henchmen who went to the stricken northern prefectures and the Kyushu countryside and neighboring islands in search of young, uneducated girls to purchase for the Singapore market. These traffickers were directly involved with brothel owners in Singapore in a highly organized vice network. Ginji Shibuya, Gajero Nihonda, and Tambaya were the kingpins in the organization that trafficked women and children and controlled brothels in turn-of-the-century Singapore.[13] And with the steady rise in the number of karayuki-san in Singapore, even more zegen arrived and preyed upon them. Tomojiro Onda, an eighty-year-old prewar barber who lived most of his life in Singapore, told Yamazaki Tomoko that the influential traffickers included Akijiro Kusasa and his brother from Shimabara Peninsula, the Shimada family from Isahaya, the Naka family from Fukuoka, and the Meyosaki family from Nagasaki.[14] Muroaka Iheiji even wrote about his activities as a zegen. Between 1890 and 1894, he claimed, in somewhat exaggerated fashion, to have presided over the smuggling from Japan to Singapore of more than thirty-two hundred women destined to become karayuki-san. Muroaka dispatched them as far west as Mauritius and as far east as the northern fringe of Australia, for anywhere from four hundred to two thousand yen.[15]

But the sale of Kyushu's daughters from impoverished rural areas into overseas brothels, as opposed to textile mills and factories, was never a solely male-run trade. In Kyushu and elsewhere in Japan, it was not uncommon for older women to sell their female relatives or to act as procurers for international vice rings. In particular, elderly karayuki-san who had returned to their rural villages in Japan from the Nanyo sometimes attempted to persuade destitute parents to sell their daughters or to lure young women abroad from famine-prone farm areas with promises of newness and change—distant lands to the south with glittering neon signs, white rice three times a day, and enough water to drink. The promises of white rice and good food were not always exaggerated. As one young prostitute, Osaki, recounted:

> We were able to eat white rice morning noon and night. That's more than we could have done in Amakusa, where eating rice was limited to New Year's and to certain festivals. And for an orphan like me to have enough to eat in those days was something in itself. But we ate, night and day. The rice wasn't the same as Japanese rice: it was Siamese. . . . It wasn't sticky: it was loose, and when you cooked it, instead of being white, it was a little pink. We were still only children and when we saw the rice we clapped our hands for joy and shouted, "red rice, red rice!" [and] we even had fish to go with the rice. Amakusa is surrounded on all sides by water, and our village is right near the harbor of Sakitsu: yet we never ate fish. My father had died and my mother gone off. On the other hand, Ohana had been adopted into the Ahoda family and the whole year long had to swallow what they dished out—and that was her food. I ask you, which do you think she liked best, living like that, or with rice and fish on her tray?[16]

The exact number of Japanese prostitutes imported to Singapore during the latter part of the nineteenth century is not known. But several sources suggest there was a dramatic increase in the number of karayuki-san between the late 1870s and 1914. The social and demographic data in the Japanese consular records for Singapore and other parts of Southeast Asia indicate a high degree of underregistration.[17] In most tabulations of female occupations, the categories "others" and "special" tacitly meant "prostitution" in the consul's brief, as a large proportion of the women who had not registered with the consulate had been smuggled out of Japan. As a consequence, the number of karayuki-san cited in the Japanese consular records for various Southeast Asian countries were, at best, conservative estimates.

Japan's victory over Russia in 1905 reinforced a crucial lesson about the need for a strong country to expand economically, and as a result, many new Japanese businesses were opened in Singapore. In the immediate aftermath of the Russo-Japanese War, many karayuki-san were repatriated from Vladivostok and the interior of Siberia to Japan. Unable to adjust and settle down to village life, they again left Japan, going south to seek work in Singapore, Sumatra, Borneo, and Australia. The traffic continued to grow and peaked during the Taisho era (1912–26).[18] There were over 300,000 Japanese working overseas in 1906, and almost 10 percent of them, more than 22,000, were karayuki-san.[19] Singapore had not only become the focal point for Japan's supply of prostitutes to the region by that time; it was also reputed to have the largest number of karayuki-san, which can be seen by the following figures mentioned in a 1906 Japanese Ministry of Foreign Affairs report: Singapore, 2,086; Vladivostok, 1,087; Batavia, 970; Shanghai, 747; Hong Kong, 485; Manila, 393; and Saigon, 192.[20] The following year, 1907, Singapore's karayuki population markedly increased, assisted by the invasion from the north of Siberia-yuki, although the brothel registry in the Office of the Chinese Protectorate showed only 620 Japanese prostitutes on the books![21] In addition to those listed, there were many unregistered prostitutes, particularly among the newly arriving women from Russia.

Prostitution in Singapore was carried on by karayuki-san in public brothels registered under the Contagious Diseases Ordinance in two parts of the city that were recognized as brothel areas; in public brothels in the city outside these two areas; and in private brothels, which were unregistered and not recognized by the Chinese Protectorate and which were generally known as sly brothels. At the same time, some karayuki-san did not live in brothels, and other Japanese women and young girls who lived in lodging houses and who were not professional prostitutes occasionally sold their bodies.[22] Some "salt-water" prostitutes frequented ships and wharves, waterfront taverns, and hotel lounges, or they solicited on nearby streets.

The Brothel Family
"Mothers" and "Daughters"

Organized Japanese brothel prostitution in Singapore was located around the brothels of Malay Street and Trengannu Street, and waves of karayuki-san operated through them. The available sources tell us something about the people who owned and managed these brothels. Most madams or brothel keepers (*okāsan, mamasan*) tended to be older women, often ex-prostitutes or brothel servants with money and "background." Although many Japanese women were merely managers of brothels, some were independent proprietors.[23] It was only the skillful, farsighted women who made the transition from being inmates of brothels to being mamasan or okāsan; it was these women who went from forfeiting a portion of their earnings in a previous career as a prostitute to charging their "girls" or boarders as owners or housekeepers.[24]

Apart from regional and ethnic identities, keepers and other members of a brothel shared distinct titles signifying kinship ties within the traditional Japanese family structure.[25] The vocabulary of these fictive kinship relations was not just confined to the women and men of a brothel but was also utilized professionally to express specific kinds of associations with keepers and prostitutes in neighboring houses. Inside a Japanese brothel, the common values of the social group or fictional "family"—the prostitutes, the keeper, and the owner—shaped the karayuki-san's actions and thoughts, as well as their divergent sexual identities.

Most karayuki-san were single women or girls, working far away from home. This isolation helps to explain the family cult of belonging and the social significance of the fictive relationships between the keepers and prostitutes—or "mothers" and "daughters" in the brothel context. Some girls were only eight years old when they left their hometowns and their families for Singapore, Sandakan, or Vladivostok. The fictive terms *mother* and *daughter*—and the specific values and enduring features signified in such ritualized language and kinship networks—provided many of these young girls with some sense of belonging to a family. Occasionally, genuine bonds of affection developed between the "pocket mothers" and keepers and their "adopted daughters." That said, the kinship terminology pragmatically masked the harsh indifference of the social and business relations in the name of profit ordinarily associated with Japanese brothel prostitution in Singapore. The karayuki-san were often the okāsan's property. At any time, the keeper could command their sexual services or labor, routinely transfer them, or trade them as commodities. The fictive kinship language, which linked them together in traffic and bondage as so-called mothers and daughters, was more influential than gender in veiling the significant differences in status and wealth that set them apart from one another.

It is difficult to determine just how far fictive family identity and a shared sense of womanhood and life experiences could bridge conflicting interests and status differences among prostitutes. Ideally, the kinship terms and rituals associated with the fictive family were meant to reinforce a sense of cohesion and signify a genuine concern by the brothel keeper for the well-being and personal conduct of her filial and obedient daughters. However, cases in colonial files and newspaper columns pertaining to suicide and flight, together with oral recollections of discipline and punishment, suggest that the idiom of kinship was not always successful in linking members of a house together through a sense of social duty and obligation as a "family."

Despite the daily use of such familial language, the fundamental oppression of women by women continued on a twenty-four-hour-a-day basis inside Japanese brothels. Eyewitness accounts of the sharp discrepancy between a karayuki-san's fictive role as a daughter with a quasi-familial status and her actual condition and treatment in the brothel are especially telling. Because the karayuki-san lacked basic rights-in-self, they could readily be subjected to emotional and physical violence by mamasan and okāsan. Though the treatment of karayuki-san by their keepers does not appear to have been unduly harsh in general, there were occasional reports of extreme cruelty. Long hours of work, bad food, inadequate health facilities, and the threat of punishment made life and work miserable for some Japanese prostitutes in lower-class houses. In such places, brothel owners who had acquired the debt of a young woman for five years logically considered the value of their purchase to diminish by one-fifth per annum. Hence, it was in their self-interest to extract the maximum amount of surplus value from their "daughter's" labor in that period of time. It did not matter to such keepers if, at the end of several years, the young woman was already exhausted or extremely ill. Karayuki-san everywhere were expected to earn a daily income, and there was no letup from work. A prostitute's income was affected if she became ill, contracted a venereal disease, or failed to serve customers during menstruation. The risk of having no income fostered situations of absolute dependency in which keepers, through excessive intimidation or violence, sometimes transgressed the limits of the so-called moral economy of power that they held over the quasi-fictional family in the brothel. Some okāsan or mamasan cursed and abused those who worked for them and were not concerned if a karayuki-san was pregnant.[26]

Nevertheless, a purely selfish, antagonistic relationship generally would not benefit an okāsan's self-interest, if only because the successful exploitation of a human being—as a woman and as a sexual commodity—hinged, ultimately, on the goodwill and cooperation of the prostitute and her "sisters."[27] The brothel keeper had to have courage, shrewd judgment of character, and physical stamina to run a good brothel in Singapore in 1900. Knowledge of first aid and do-it-yourself gynecology together with skills in self-defense were also necessary, as well as extreme tact and the capacity and ruthlessness to keep the karayuki-san in line, in order to avoid conflict among the women and clients in her house.

Between "Sister" and "Sister"

Mother-daughter symbolism expressed the fictive relationship between brothel keeper and prostitute, but the notion of sisterhood was basic to fostering a sense of community among the karayuki-san. The fictional web of family relationships implied hierarchy, fraternity, empathy, and compatibility. Such relationships among "sisters" were specifically expressed in differential kin terms and deferential obligations between a new girl and a more experienced prostitute, as *imouto san* (younger) and *onee san* (older) sisters.[28] These kinship terms, which defined the hierarchical, stratified relationship between prostitutes, were meant to establish harmony within the brothel family, to reduce competition, and to foster a sense of affinity between the supposed sisters.

The following example from a Sandakan brothel in northeast Borneo is a case in point. Osaki (then age ten) and her closest friends, Ohana and Otsuji, had been forcibly emigrated from Amakusa in the second decade of the twentieth century on the promise that they would do domestic work abroad. In a very genuine sense, these girls bonded as sisters after they were shipped to Sandakan via Singapore. From Osaki's account (as reported in Tomoko Yamasaki's pioneering work, *Sandakan Brothel No. 8: An Episode in the History of Lower-Class Japanese Women*), we learn that several years later, as a child of thirteen, Osaki put up stiff resistance to working as a prostitute and argued with the male keeper, Tarozo. Her opposition was supported by her sisters; she recalled: "Otsuji, Ohana and I stood up to him. We're not taking any men. Say what you like, we're not doing it."[29] Shortly afterward, the three girls confronted the keeper's tyranny again, still united: "We would rather die than do what we did last night. We're through."[30] In those difficult early days, Osaki particularly remembered Ofumi, as an older sister and friend: "It was only the two senior girls who treated the three of us like real sisters. This was especially true of Ofumi, who stuck up for us whenever Tarozo or his wife yelled at us. 'You three are from Amakusa, just like me,' she said."[31]

Clients

The prostitute cannot be understood in isolation. A social analysis of the nature of the economic and cultural transaction between the prostitute and the client reveals salient aspects of their society in turn-of-the-century Singapore. The men who patronized the city's karayuki-san are the most difficult group to resurrect, for there is only fragmentary evidence in the Coroner's Records and some source material in accounts drawn from oral history. Nevertheless, the firsthand data obtained from the Coroner's Inquests and Inquiries enable a study of the clients of the Japanese brothels. When calamity struck, brothel keepers and prostitutes often told the coroner everything they knew about their clients, including ethnicity, age, occupation, marital status, and personal habits and preferences.

The Coroner's Records indicate that the clients who therein lost their anonymity were a diverse collection of humanity. There were, among others, hard-bitten rickshaw pullers, stevedores, and coal coolies; wealthy teenage schoolboys in search of carnal opportunities; pleasure-seeking soldiers; white-collar workers; and the unemployed. Even after the abolition of brothel registration in 1894, the Singapore government had continued unofficially encouraging Japanese brothel prostitution, especially to service the troops from the garrisoned military and naval bases in the city.

The power and security of the colony as a British fortress in Southeast Asia depended partially on having satisfied soldiers and sailors.

At the start of the twentieth century, Chinese men, especially hard laborers, constituted the majority of the population in Singapore. In the latter half of the nineteenth century, one immediate effect of the colonial policy on single male immigration was that the gender ratio slipped out of balance, and major social problems were created as a result of the acute shortage of females. By 1890, there was already a generation of unattached men in the city—bachelors unable to marry because of the scarcity of women. These men tended to escape the pressures of monotonous work and the loneliness of the port city's twilight landscape by seeking commercial sexual services. Inside the brothel quarter, away from the crushing misery and tedium of daily life, they found a hint of intimacy, excitement, and good humor with the karayuki-san.

The karayuki-san, who spent a good part of their lives dealing with sailors, had preferences for particular nationalities. They reported that European, Japanese, and Chinese men who had spent long periods at sea without women were the most generous. Malay and Indonesian fishers and trading crews with poor wage levels were the least desirable customers, as their sailing *prahu* (Malay sailing craft) frequently did not provide good food and accommodation. Sikhs and Tamils were the least popular, as they were physically large and dark skinned. Malays were also known to use aphrodisiacs and were considered potentially dangerous customers. Rather than relying on capricious destiny, some karayuki-san, took matters into their own hands. For example, Kikuyo Zendo explained in graphic detail to filmmaker Imamura Shohei how she and others smeared pork fat on their door frames and bedposts to deter Malays who liked "messing around with love potions."[32]

In the late 1890s, men from the Japanese Imperial Navy provided a steady source of clients for the karayuki-san. Groups of Japanese mariners onboard dreadnoughts showing the flag in Singapore had been at sea for months and desired female companionship. Given the size of the fleet that dropped anchor, these sailors could number in the thousands, and brothel owners were overwhelmed by the sailors' demands for sexual gratification, which was twenty to thirty times greater than the supply of women. The brothel keepers solved this problem by pressing every available woman into service. Before the fall of Singapore, all the karayuki-san in Singapore, many of whom had a portrait of the emperor hanging on the wall above their beds, were prepared to surrender themselves to the large annual invasion of their compatriots.

The sailors on shore leave were so numerous that they marched in ranks toward the brothels and formed lines outside to await their turn. On command, two lines of blue-jacketed sailors and marines entered, one through each swinging door, and drew to a halt. The impatient fellows were checked to see whether they had venereal diseases, and when a karayuki-san became available, the second order was given, "Enter!" The men went in one by one, trousers lowered. For the karayuki-san, the work was exhausting, emotionally as well as physically, but the women aimed for maximum income. In the 1970s, some elderly repatriated Kyushu women still remembered that time of extraordinary prosperity and patriotic fervor when it was not uncommon for them to receive twenty to thirty clients a night.[33]

Excluding sailors, the stream of customers who sought the services of the karayuki-san came primarily from the pool of bachelors with meager wages who worked all over the city;[34] wealthier patrons (Chinese businessmen, European and Japanese naval officers, and Western diplomats) brought large salaries with them and were able to improve the standard of living of certain Japanese prostitutes. Some of the *ichiban bijin* (the most beautiful girls) in the brothels lived extravagant lives as a result of their profession, but for most, the prosperity did not last. In terms of improving the women's social and economic prospects, the Chinese were the most welcome customers. They were not only the most frequent visitors but also among the most eager to redeem the debt of a karayuki-san. Except for visiting naval officers, regular ranks, and merchant seamen, the karayuki-san rarely catered to their own compatriots before 1914. However, by the end of World War I, a sizable number of Japanese trading companies had been established in Singapore and rubber plantations had opened up in nearby Johor, which resulted in an influx of male Japanese migrants.[35] By 1918, these men loomed larger on the social scene in the Malay Street quarter.

Just prior to and shortly after World War I, Europeans were regular patrons of the karayuki-san, who were versed in Western ways. In order to pass the time of day, soldiers serving king and country considered it proper to spend their money on Japanese women and alcohol. This was a way of life in the city before the last post was sounded in the Tanglin Barracks and at Fort Canning.[36] In Singapore, karayuki-san knew that tourists would not offer even the illusion of a possible long-term relationship, nor could some of the seedy British barflies—sad expatriate planters and accountants—left over from Rudyard Kipling's era. Only clerks in city offices with four-year terms and servicemen in the Tanglin lines with two-year tours of duty could offer them a chance of becoming mistresses or possibly, in rare cases, escaping from debt and poverty.[37]

The Carnival of the Night

Karayuki-san worked every night from six in the evening to five in the morning. When it was dark, each brothel lit the gas globe lantern under its eaves on which a number was painted. Japanese girls, six or seven in a house, sat around the vestibule or under the veranda waiting for the first customers. At the bidding of the okāsan, they sometimes went out into the street and hustled customers into the house by tugging on the sleeve or shirt of any passing European. In order for the girls to remit money to their kin in Japan and pay off their debts, the scene was repeated thousands of times nightly among the crowded brothels and bars. Osaki, one of the women who began her career as a prostitute at thirteen years of age, explained how she paid off her two thousand yen debt: "Money wasn't worth then what it is now. . . . Two thousand yen in the Taisho period was big stuff. We were only thirteen, and that debt of two thousand yen weighed heavily on us. We were to use our bodies to pay it back. Our fee was, if the man left straight away, two yen; if he stayed the night, then ten. We divided the money in half with Tarozo. He was supposed to provide room and board, and the women were supposed to provide their own clothes and cosmetics."[38]

Some okāsan compelled prostitutes to have sex with as many as a dozen customers per night. Imamura Shohei interviewed an elderly repatriated Kyushu woman named Kikuyo Zendo, who told him that she serviced as many as eight clients per day and then added, "I didn't like sleeping with men. I had to do it all the time, every day."[39] Osaki also recalled the excessive number of customers she had to entertain and the direct link with indebtedness: "The girls who were thus made into karayuki-san had to receive visitors, at times as many as thirty a night, but their debts—the money the brothel-owner paid the pimp and what the girl borrowed from the brothel-owner in order to help her parents' poor household—could not be cleared easily. Half of what the girl earned was the brothel's profit, and the interest on the debts were [*sic*] not small either. Such was the system adopted by brothels so that girls would not be able to pay off their debts for some time."[40]

Before the beginning of the Russo-Japanese War in 1905, girls as young as ten or eleven became apprentice karayuki-san. Some, sold into the profession by impoverished parents, began as brothel maids at even earlier ages. Several years of training in sexual techniques and how to please a man, traditional etiquette, proper posture, and the art of conversation were prerequisites in upper-class brothels. With such skills, a karayuki-san was often able to break down a customer's reserve, satisfy his fantasies, and help him pour out his woes. Morisaki Kazue's message, based on an oral history of such lived experiences, is that the source of the karayuki-san's vital presence and charm originated in the moral character of their village-based values and traditions. The Amakusa and Shimabara insistence on early sex education and self-reliance later enabled these rural girls to be magnanimous and nurturing in their relationships with clients. The relative freedom and outspokenness of adolescent village girls, which included salacious joking, drinking, singing obscene songs, and engaging in premarital sex, created young karayuki-san who could be remarkably sensual, while often possessing social graces and homespun restraint as well. Village life in Kyushu was not devoid of sexuality, and Amakusa and Shimabara girls were resilient and warmhearted. Many karayuki-san understood that in the emergent bustling atmosphere and character of Singapore, as a port city, their emotional work, supported by traditional values, specific training, and a set of recognized cultural rules, enabled them to help lonely, hardworking men feel at ease. One client commented on these striking qualities, which generally typified the personal demeanor of the karayuki-san in the brothels of Malay Street.

> They received me graciously, with many bows . . . and made a place for me at the table. Their faces, seen in the glow of a

> hanging lamp, showed signs of middle age, and neither of them were, I guessed, under forty. The elder of the two set beer and cigarettes on the table, and engaged me in lively conversation about the picture theatres of Singapore. Both women treated me rather as an honoured guest than as a potential customer. . . . They were neither beautiful nor pretty, yet they were pleasant companions, and their infectious laughter would have wrung a smile from the most unyielding of social reformers. They made no coarse jests, no lewd advances, and not once during my visit did either of them insist that I should choose a bed-partner for the night. There was nothing sordid, furtive or ugly about those women or their surroundings. Indeed, I was impressed by the obvious decency (no other word adequately describes it) of everything I saw and heard in that brothel. . . . [A]s the women of a country where courtesans have a definite social status they paid due attention to traditional forms and ceremonies. Merely by exercising their feminine charm they created an atmosphere in which their patrons could find not only physical but mental relaxation.[41]

Although the prostitutes were solicitous about the welfare of their clients, they also needed to be cautious regarding their own health and well-being. In the late 1890s, it took only a few weeks for a newly arrived karayuki-san to realize that the most devastating and widespread epidemic after homesickness was venereal disease. Clients soon learned that in the karayuki-san houses in Malay Street, all men had to be checked, and if gonorrhea or syphilis were detected, they were simply dismissed. The rules had to be obeyed. The primary motive for this command was a recognition of the crucial practice of social hygiene over the drive for personal profit. A secondary motive was to retain the patronage of mainstay customers who might stop coming if it became known that the karayuki-san were servicing skinny, feverish, diseased clients. In an interview in 1987, an elderly male resident of Kreta Ayer explained the cleanliness of the karayuki-san. "The Japanese prostitutes wanted money for their country but they also taught us how to check for venereal disease," he said. Pointing in the direction of Spring Street, he continued: "Those Japanese women were very careful, very strict. They would examine a client first for any signs of ill health before accepting him. The woman would do this by herself in her room. She would tell the client to undress. If he was filthy, then he was asked to take a shower first. If he had VD she did not want his custom and would chase the man out."[42] Another old Chinatown resident mentioned a different precautionary practice: "The Japanese women were very clean . . . she brings you a basin [that] contained potassium permanganate, what they called 'medicine water.' Everybody must wash in it."[43]

The Other Side of Midnight

Violence and physical abuse were also grave dangers confronting the karayuki-san in Singapore. Among the thousands registered in brothels in 1900, some were victims of homicide because of personal or professional complications in their lives—or simply fate. The specter of violent death always haunted the karayuki-san. How they faced it and evaded it, how they tragically embraced it, and how they were granted temporary reprieve from it—these were matters that shadowed their everyday lives and dreams, no matter what their other preoccupations.

Crime was a way of life in the congested streets of turn-of-the-century Singapore, but slayings of particular prostitutes shocked many at the time. The direct testimony preserved in the Coroner's Records and provided by former prostitutes exposes the system that institutionalized this violence. The murder of a licensed prostitute had to be reported to the coroner, and no burial was allowed without a certificate signed by him.[44] Usually, the main complaint made by Japanese prostitutes to colonial surgeons involved the nature of assaults perpetrated by men visiting brothels on the women residing in them.[45]

The Coroner's Records offer a glimpse into the darker side of Singapore's history—into the malevolent pathological operations of individual physical violence and sexual assault. The coroner was most interested in the chinks between inhumanity and everyday life, the surreal dimension where danger exists and life goes on. The fragmentary records of those occasions when private, institutional, and personal sexual conflict came under official notice can be used to explore the brutal consequences of the gender asymmetry of Singaporean life after 1870. The hitherto neglected evidence of the gruesome and the tragic gives this historical rendering of the relationship between Japanese brothel prostitution and violent sexual assaults and suicide a chilling, compelling quality.

Even so, gaps in the police statistics and records—the undetected offenses—make the available evidence somewhat incomplete.[46] On the basis of past experience, one can assume that police records tended to minimize both the prevalence of male violence against Japanese prostitutes and the instances of abuse by okāsan. Surviving police charge books underreport the extent of sexual assault and prostitute battering. The silence—the lack of evidence in the files—and the low arrest rates raise serious questions about the levels and types of violence ignored by the Singapore authorities.[47] Though the police department attempted to arrest guilty offenders and bring them to trial, its resources were limited, and at least half the assaults and slayings of karayuki-san in the Coroner's Records were unsolved.

Some of the most disturbing but important discoveries in the records pertain to the pervasiveness of crimes of passion and the use of emotional violence in pursuit of power. Such violence, the coroner noted, was conveyed through verbal abuse, threats, intimidation, and physically aggressive behavior. Some prostitutes complained that vulnerable, emotionally damaged men who became tense at times communicated with them in vulgar language that indicated dangerous, judgmental attitudes and behaviors.

An example from the Malay Street quarter of the 1920s highlights the intensity of feelings in a triangular love affair between paramours of different social status and a karayuki-san by the name of Duya Hadachi, who also had the Malay nickname "Panjang." When she was found dead in a pool of congealed blood in the second-floor room of the brothel, her long blue-black hair had been released from its tight bun and the tropical climate had added a layer of moisture to her makeup and blood-spattered corpse.[48] From the coroner's inquest, it is apparent that a steady stream of Japanese, Malay, Chinese, and Indian clients had visited her on a daily basis. However, several clients fell in love with her simultaneously, and forbidden feelings and tensions surfaced and were expressed. It seems that Duya had breached the rules of the sensuous, ambivalent play that was the ideal in the world of the Japanese brothels.[49]

The protagonists in this passionate triangle were Shindo, Yukichi Nonaka, and Duya herself. Shindo worked as a carpenter's apprentice.

He was described as a good worker who never gave Benji Watanabe, his senior, any trouble. The master carpenter knew Duya, for she used to visit his house in Waterloo Street to see Shindo. Watanabe described the karayuki-san as being on intimate terms with his apprentice, even taking his dirty clothing away and washing it for him: "They were lovers, at least I took them to be so. I have often seen them together in Shindo's room but I don't know if she ever slept there."[50] He had never heard them quarrel and told the coroner that Duya usually went to Shindo's room about once a week. The okāsan, Oyoka Michikawa, mentioned that Shindo visited Duya in the daytime every third day and that the other protagonist, Yukichi Nonaka, also visited Duya regularly—at least fifteen times in the space of a month. This information provides a clue as to why the carpenter's apprentice became consumed by jealousy and insecurity.

Nonaka did not know the carpenter's apprentice and met him only once—in Duya's room on the day of the murder. What follows next in the testimony provided by Nonaka depicts a rare, frank conversation between two men caught in a sexual entanglement over a beautiful prostitute:

> Shindo sent Duya to call me. I was at No. 12 Malay Street about 4:00 p.m. when Duya came and said that Shindo wanted to see me in her room. I did not ask her who Shindo was or what he wanted me for. I went with her to her room and saw Shindo there. Shindo spoke to me first and said, "I am very sorry for troubling you but I should like to speak to you [about] something." He then said, "I am Shindo. I have made up my mind to leave Duya Hadachi." I replied that it was a very good idea even if he was not in a position to come so often. Shindo then said "If you say so then I am very sorry for you." Then I told him I had a wife and children in Japan and I promised him I would never come and see Duya again. He seemed pleased and said, "Let us have a drink." Duya then brought two bottles of beer and we three drank the beer. Then I left the house. Duya and Shindo remained there. I left about 5:00 p.m. I have not been there since. Everything was quiet when I left. Duya seemed quite satisfied with the arrangement.[51]

Although Yukichi Nonakahe clearly stated his intention to give up Duya, what is so striking in his testimony is just how badly he misunderstood Shindo's real intention, with its tragic outcome. Shindo thought that the karayuki-san was cheating on him. It is obvious from the sequence of events that he wanted her to quit seeing Yukichi Nonaka; he saw her as his property. In the end, the carpenter's apprentice stabbed the woman he loved out of jealousy and then killed himself as the ultimate gesture of owning another person; she was his property, and killing her was his right. In his mind, the frightening act signified real possession, and it offered the illusion of power.

Naka Kawata, a karayuki-san who had been in the brothel for only a month, described how Duya died before her eyes: "Shindo used to visit the house sometimes. Came to see 'Panjang' who lived in the room next to me. She died in my room. About 7:30 p.m. on 8 November she suddenly ran into my room and fell down. She did not speak. She just laid still, groaned and then died. I was very frightened and ran downstairs. I did not see anyone else there. I looked into Panjang's room through the door which was open. I saw Shindo standing there with this knife held in his hand. I ran downstairs and gave the alarm."[52] The alluring Duya had broken the fundamental rule of the demimonde; play and reality had become blurred in her life and work. She refused to acknowledge the fact that love was forbidden in the houses of the Malay Street quarter.[53]

The testimony in the records shows that the coroner, police, and brothel keepers often had little knowledge of the strong emotions that churned in alienated men who were not regular customers. They knew about theft, love triangles, and other such things but not necessarily about the nature of the quiet desperation that led some men to rape and murder. Often, when a Japanese prostitute met death at the hands of a stranger, the sexual abuse and premeditated violence were horrific. Most of the victims of this form of violence were young karayuki-san, who rarely had access to any means to save themselves.

Even though hardworking laborers or handicapped or elderly men did not have to fear rejection with the karayuki-san, a lot of anger and violence was often dumped on these women. Many clients who were emotionally cared for by the prostitutes were experiencing extreme denial and bitterness in their lives. The impression gained from the witness testimony preserved in official records suggests that from the point of view of unknown assailants, the murdered Japanese prostitutes were expendable; after all, there were so many girls, and any female body could provide the required sexual release. To the killer, the dead prostitute was simply an object to be taught a lesson.

Some Japanese prostitutes wanted to leave particular parts of the city because of the increasing prevalence of crime and drugs and the lack of safety both in the brothels and on the streets. Karayuki-san frequently wanted to tell their okāsan that they were going to get out of the business and do something else because of the slayings. But the testimony in the coroner and police records reveals that most prostitutes had no choice but to continue to work because they had impoverished families to support and debts to clear.

To add to a karayuki-san's insecurity, she was prohibited by the brothel keeper from either carrying a weapon on her person or hiding a small knife or razor under her pillow. Some girls hid their valuables in different places in their rooms so they did not lose everything if a client turned out to be a thief. At night, some slept with their hands folded over their throats in case an assailant came at them with a sharp blade in the dark.

What comes across strongly in the testimony about violent encounters is that the events drew people in the brothel together. Furthermore, each attack or death was liable to spark panic, and prostitutes sometimes refused to work for a night or two in a house that had just experienced a chilling murder. Yet, because of the socially managed nature of sexual labor, karayuki-san frequently had to suppress their emotions in the aftermath of frightening events; for example, they might have to laugh and perfect a smile with a client even when they were aching with fear. But Japanese prostitutes rarely went through terrifying, tragic situations such as those found in the Coroner's Records without being emotionally scarred. In many cases, not talking about such horrific events and suppressing feelings caused subsequent emotional and psychological difficulties for them in terms of coming to grips with their past experiences in Singapore.

The unsolved murder of a Japanese prostitute frequently left the brothel districts coping with fearful women and a jumpy public. Every idle stranger looked suspicious to the karayuki-san, and the impact of a killer's actions on the brothels and the businesses adjacent to them was all too clear. Several thousand laborers, shopkeepers, and dependents lived in and around the brothel districts, and normally, the brothel customers kept the abacuses of the Trengganu and Malay Street houses clicking. The callous slaying of a young karayuki-san by an unknown client emptied the bars, restaurants, teahouses, and neighboring shops with amazing rapidity.

Apart from the haunting reminders of physical abuse and scenes of murder, Japanese prostitutes were also exposed to several other kinds of violence and mayhem, especially as the death toll among visitors unexpectedly climbed. Around 1900, coal heavers, merchant seamen, soldiers, and tourists flocked to the Japanese houses. Laborers regularly worked to exhaustion. Coolies, stevedores, and rickshawmen were often sick, and they were always tired after working twelve to fourteen hours a day. In the damp months, many caught diseases associated with overcrowding and poverty, such as influenza and tuberculosis, and in the hot weather, cholera and typhoid fever took their toll. The bleakness of these men's lives led many to alcohol and opium.

The lower-grade karayuki-san attracted poor laborers, sailors, drunkards, and drug addicts. The archival descriptions of conditions in many lower-class brothels indicate that the prostitutes worked in rows, with thin partitions between their cubicles offering little privacy. The women themselves were emotionally shocked by an intoxicated customer's unexpected demise. The Malay seaman Mayassan, for example, was a prodigious drinker. He had become completely drunk before he went to visit Oseki at a Japanese brothel in Malabar Street, and he arrived in a deplorable state. The karayuki-san described to the coroner how the thin, hard-drinking sailor who had passed the night with her was ill and unable to communicate.

> The Malay man whose corpse is in my room came to this brothel last night alone. He came in a rickshaw. He was very drunk, but could speak. He undressed and put on some clothes of mine, and went upstairs, he gave me $3. It was about midnight. He went to bed with me and we did not wake till 5:00 a.m. He was then all shaking and could not speak. I called to him, but he gave no answer. He passed his water in the bed and

> I lifted him and laid him on the floor. I waited by him until 9:00 a.m., thinking he would get better. Sometimes he was quiet sometimes he was shaking. Then I went and called the mistress [O'Ahye]. Dr Boon Keng came soon after 10:00 a.m., and said the man was dead. I never saw him before last night.[54]

The coroner surmised that the cause of Mayassen's death at the age of only twenty-six was alcohol poisoning.

Several major factors contributed to rural Japanese women and girls becoming overseas prostitutes (karayuki-san) or otherwise falling victim to the traffic destined for the international brothel market. These factors included dire poverty, the ideology of the imperial state, and the patriarchal family system. The demand for prostitutes was exacerbated by an economically burgeoning Singapore, with its vast number of single coolies, and the lack of alternative employment opportunities closer to home. To lure girls into such enslavement, brothel owners explained that, in the interest of Japan's national good, their bodies belonged to the state and that they and others like them constituted a kind of female army to serve the emperor.

The presence of the karayuki-san was indispensable in maintaining the singkeh or coolie labor force that was so necessary for Singapore's economic growth. Equally important was the fact that large profits were to be extracted from the earnings of prostitutes—profits that would enable Japanese families to pay off their debts; Japanese entrepreneurs to accumulate capital and diversify their economic interests overseas; and Japanese women to send back remittances, in the name of economic and political gain, to patriotically support Japan's wars against China and Russia. The lucrative network of overseas brothels reflected, on the one hand, the economic dynamism of tidewater colonial ports such as Singapore and, on the other hand, the social disintegration of the old agrarian world of northern Kyushu in the face of Japan's rapid economic growth. In all the big port cities of Asia—Seoul, Shanghai, Hong Kong, Manila, Batavia, and Rangoon—brothels were major destinations for the karayuki-san and critical links in the chain of international traffic in Japanese women and girls. But by the early 1890s, Singapore emerged as a key redistributive hub for this illicit web of human traffic in the East Asian region.

Impoverished rural families in northern Kyushu often survived economically because they were financed by the contributions of former farm women and girls who were now working as prostitutes overseas. This organized traffic was so extensive that by 1910, it was estimated there were more than twenty-two thousand karayuki-san working in brothels, bars, and restaurants from the huge ports of Singapore and Vladivostok to the frozen wastelands of booming mining towns and timber camps in Siberia and British Columbia. The daughters of Japanese peasants who worked in the overseas brothels and lower-class boardinghouses in Singapore, like their "sisters" scattered around the globe, were subjected to physical and emotional abuse and coerced labor.

The karayuki-san's life inside the brothel was typified by the use of fictive kinship terms that created a quasi-familial environment. This pragmatically masked the brutal indifference of the social and business relations ordinarily associated with brothel prostitution in colonial Singapore—patterns of dominance and relations of debt and enslavement that mirrored practices among trafficked women and children around the globe at that point in time. The lives of the karayuki-san were controlled by both the procurers and the brothel keepers, but it was the clients who all too often exhibited the extreme aggression and sometimes utterly terrible violence that was perpetrated against prostitutes. The deep-seated hostility of these clients had its roots in the grinding physical labor that typified the lives of Singapore's underclass of migrant coolies, and it was further fueled by alcohol and opium abuse and by racial prejudice. Under such circumstances, only those women who possessed balance and strength had any chance of surviving unscathed the paradoxes of both Japan's and Singapore's emerging, entangled economic and political development in the early twentieth century.

Notes

1. Morisake Kazue, *Karayuki-san* (Tokyo: Asahi Shinbunsha, 1976), 17–18; Yamazaki Tomoko, *Sandakan Hachiban Shookan Tehihen Joseishi Joshoo* (Tokyo: Chikuma Shoboo, 1972), 60; Mikiso Hane, *Peasants, Rebels and Outcasts: The Underside of Modern Japan* (New York: Pantheon Books, 1982), 218; Motoe

Terami-Wada, "*Karayuki-san* of Manila, 1880–1920," in *Philippine Studies* 34, no. 3 (1986): 287–306, 303.

2. Kazue, *Karayuki-san,* 17–18; Yamazaki Tomoko, "Sandakan No. 8 Brothel," *Bulletin of Concerned Asian Scholars* 7, no. 4 (1975): 52–60, 52. Yamazaki Tomoko, *Sandahan Brothel No 8: An Episode in the History of Lower-class Japanese Women*, trans. Karen Colligan-Taylor (New York: M.E. Sharpe, 1999).

3. Yano Tooru, *Nippon–no Nanyo Shikan* (Tokyo: Chuukou Shinsho, Chuuo o Koo ron, 1979), 131–33.

4. Hane, *Peasants, Rebels and Outcasts,* 218; Yamazaki, "Sandakan No. 8 Brothel," 56–57; Terami-Wada, "*Karayuki-san* of Manila."

5. Yamazaki, "Sandakan No. 8 Brothel," 56–57.

6. League of Nations, *Report of the Commission of Inquiry into the Traffic in Women and Children in the East* (New York: CETWCE, 1933), 44, 73.

7. Nanyo Oyobi Nipponjinsha, *Nanyo no Gojunen Shingaporu o Chusin ni Doho Katsuyaku* (Tokyo: Shokasha, 1937), 156.

8. James Francis Warren, *Rickshaw Coolie: A People's History of Singapore* (Singapore: Oxford University Press, 1986), 14–19, 161–65, 249; Joyce Ee, "Chinese Migration to Singapore, 1869–1941," in *Journal of Southeast Asian Studies* 2, no. 1 (1961): 37; Lucie Cheng Hirata, "Free, Indentured, Enslaved: Chinese Prostitutes in Nineteenth-Century America," *Signs: Journal of Women in Culture and Society* 5, no. 1 (1979): 3–29, 5–7.

9. League of Nations, *Report of the Commission,* 21–22, 51, 96; Nanyo Oyobi Nipponjinsha, *Nanyo no Gojunen,* 160.

10. See Yamazaki, "Sandakan No. 8 Brothel"; Yamazaki Tomoko, *Sandakan no Haka* (Tokyo: Bungei Shunjuu, 1977); D. C. Sissons, "*Karayuki-san:* Japanese Prostitutes in Australia, 1887–1916, Part I," *Historical Studies* 17, no. 68 (1977): 323–41.

11. Sissons, "*Karayuki-san,*" 323.

12. Kazue, *Karayuki-san,* 18.

13. Nanyo Oyobi Nipponjinsha, *Nanyo no Gojunen,* 152–53; Yamazaki, *Sandakan no Haka,* 48.

14. Yamazaki, *Sandakan no Haka,* 48.

15. See Iheiji Muroaka, *Muroaka Iheiji Jiden* (Tokyo: Nanposha, 1960).

16. Yamazaki, "Sandakan No. 8 Brothel," 55.

17. Terami-Wada, "*Karayuki-san* of Manila," 293, 303.

18. Hane, *Peasants, Rebels and Outcasts,* 218.

19. Yamamuro Gunpei, *A Theory of Social Purification* (Tokyo: Chuo Koron, 1977), 252–55.

20. Ibid.

21. Ibid., 144.

22. Sir Arthur Young to Walter Lord, July 13, 1917, no. 60716, 273/457, Colonial Office London (hereafter cited as CO).

23. Susan Gronewald, *Beautiful Merchandise: Prostitution in China, 1860–1936* (New York: Haworth Press, 1982), 12, 16; Gail Herschatter, "The Hierarchy of Shanghai Prostitution," *Modern China* 15, no. 4 (October 1989): 478–79.

24. Joel Best, "Careers in Brothel Prostitution in St. Paul, 1865–1883," *Journal of Interdisciplinary History* 12, no. 4 (Spring 1982): 614.

25. Gronewald, *Beautiful Merchandise*, 9.

26. Memorandum by E. O. A. Travers for Acting Governor Sir J. H. Swettenham to Mr. Chamberlain, September 8, 1898, no. 25, 882/6, CO.

27. Lt-Colonel Anson to the Earl of Carnarvon, April 21, 1877, no. 132, 273/91, CO; Memorandum by E. O. A. Travers, State Surgeon, for Acting Governor Sir J. H. Swettenham to Mr. Chamberlain, September 8, 1898, no. 227, 882/6, CO.

28. On geisha living and working in a social group defined traditionally by kinship terms, see Liza Crihfield Dalby, *Geisha* (Berkeley: University of California Press, 1983), 39–40.

29. Yamazaki, "Sandakan No. 8 Brothel," 55.

30. Ibid.

31. Ibid.

32. Kikuyo Zendo, interview by Shohei Imamura in producing the film *Karayuki-san*, Malaysia, 1970.

33. Ibid.

34. Nanyo Oyobi Nipponjinsha, *Nanyo no Gojunen*, 157.

35. Ibid., 161.

36. Singapore Coroners' Inquest and Inquiry (SCII) Subordinate Court, of Albert Chacksfield, November 8, 1912, no. 178.

37. Ibid.

38. Yamazaki, "Sandakan No. 8 Brothel," 55.

39. Zendo interview.

40. Yamazaki, "Sandakan No. 8 Brothel," 50.

41. A. Dixon, *Singapore Patrol* (London: Harrap, 1935), 212–13.

42. Yip Cheong Fung, interview by author with the assistance of Tan Beng Luan, Singapore, October 1, 1987.

43. Sng Choon Yee, interview by Daniel Chew, reel 1, Oral History Department, Singapore Government, Singapore, March 5, 1981.

44. Anson to the Earl of Carnarvon.

45. Ibid.

46. See Judith Allen, "Evidence and Silence: Feminism and the Limits of History," in *Feminist Challenges: Social and Political Theory*, ed. Carole Pateman and Elizabeth Gross (Sydney, Australia: Allen and Unwin, 1986), 184–85.

47. Ibid.

48. SCII Subordinate Court, of Duya Hadachi, November 8, 1924, no. 452.

49. Ian Buruma, *A Japanese Mirror: Heroes and Villains of Japanese Culture* (London: Penguin, 1984), 50.

50. Ibid.

51. Ibid.

52. Ibid.

53. Ibid., 81–82.

54. SCII Subordinate Court, of Mayassen, October 23, 1905, no. 187.

14

BODY-PRICE

Ambiguities in the Sale of Women at the End of the Qing Dynasty

JOHANNA RANSMEIER

Over the past two hundred years, the trade in women has remained one of the most persistent forms of exploitation in China. Today, trafficked women most commonly find themselves sold as wives or to supply brothels. The degree of deception employed by traffickers varies widely. As was true in the past, Chinese women sometimes accede to these sales in order to help their own families or because they perceive they have no other option. Some women agree to one arrangement only to find themselves bound by another. Criminal brokers manipulate women, obtaining their complicity in order to facilitate their trade. Because of the nature of trafficking, it is often hard to determine whether the term *slavery* is suitable to describe the situation of women sold for their services *as women* or if the analytical legacies of scholarship on slavery in other contexts have any bearing at all upon the forms of servitude historically endured by women in China.[1] By the late Qing period, most forms of enslavement in China served to enhance the status of slave owners or to expand their leisure time, rather than to enrich them economically. In some cases, the acquisition and maintenance of a slave could be quite costly. And as was the case throughout the Indian Ocean world, women were bought and sold with significantly greater frequency than men.

This chapter examines the intersection of the traditional marriage market with the coerced sale of women in the final decades of the Qing dynasty (1644–1911). By first outlining some of the differences between the ideal marriage arrangements aspired to by elites, on the one hand, and more commonplace marriage practices, on the other, I show how Confucian family structure, poverty, and the perception of tainted virtue combined to justify the routine sale of women. These women were sold not only as wives, concubines, or prostitutes—roles that transferred an explicit sexual obligation to a woman's purchaser—but also as domestics, "slave girls" (*binü* 婢女, or sometimes simply *bi* 婢) who waited upon their mistresses and were vulnerable to the sexual predations of their masters. This term, which combines the character for a female slave with the character for woman, was commonly used to describe women and girls who had been purchased or inherited by more affluent households. Because I am specifically interested in fleshing out the connection between family tolerance of these practices and the perpetuation of a market for women, my argument here will focus more on arrangements made within households rather than on the brothel trade.[2] To better understand what it meant for struggling households that their wives and daughters could be profitably transformed into chattel, the latter half of the chapter presents examples from the judicial archive. These cases, drawn from the Qing criminal archives, help illustrate the ambiguous position of sold women. We will see the tension between women's complicity, often motivated by a filial desire to help their families, and the exploitative nature of a system from which traffickers and kidnappers profited.

It is especially revealing to consider the marketability of Chinese women in the late nineteenth and early twentieth centuries, an era when the adherents of Confucianism strained to justify traditional practices in a changing society that was increasingly concerned with modernity. Patriarchal ideas still dictated the distribution of power in most Chinese households, but the upheaval of the Taiping and Nian rebellions, the Opium Wars, and the growing presence of foreigners in treaty ports along the coast and up the Yangzi River began to dislodge conservative customs. In turbulent times, men often left their families for long periods; as a result, senior women found themselves adopting the role of head of household with greater frequency.[3] Growing prospects for women to earn money in the textile industry reduced their reliance upon husbands and parents.[4] Western missionaries brought unfamiliar educational opportunities for men and women alike, and by the early twentieth century, local Chinese communities sponsored secondary schools for young women. Around this time, a small number of determined female students even found their way to universities in Japan.

Despite these expanding horizons, women continued to be bought and sold, sometimes willingly, sometimes under duress. A legitimate marriage market coexisted with a thriving illicit trade in women. Transactions in which a husband's family paid a bride-price in exchange for the promise of marriage were legal and commonplace. Although Chinese anthropologists draw some comfort from describing marriage practices in terms of ritual, nineteenth-century archival records indicate these payments were frequently discussed with commercial language. Terms for buying, selling, price, deposit, and expense were common. As we will see, this situation provided traffickers, intermediaries, and even husbands and neighbors with an ideal cover for more nefarious arrangements. Moreover, responsibility for the continuation of the practice of selling women did not reside with men alone. Though elite women occasionally took up the plight of their less fortunate sisters as a social cause, it was just as common for privileged women to act as consumers in this market. Wives procured concubines for their husbands, bought slaves for their kitchens, and leased wet nurses from their neighbors. By taking a leadership role in staffing their households, elite wives managed to secure a modicum of liberty for themselves.[5] The gap between the exceptional women for whom China's cosmopolitanism had introduced new opportunities and the vast majority of Chinese women only widened.[6]

As other scholars in this volume have noted, throughout the greater Asian region slavery exists not as half of a binary system in which individuals are either free or enslaved but as part of a spectrum of varied and highly contingent statuses. The place of women in Chinese society was defined both by the language of property and by the language of obligation. Money was routinely exchanged as part of establishing a marriage or concubinage and women were often simultaneously considered kin and property. This makes it extremely difficult to unravel when a woman's situation went from one of traditional obligation to exploitation and servitude. Yet any consideration of sex and slavery during the late Qing must also acknowledge the common practices used to acquire wives as part of an overall societal context in which more coercive sales continued to be tolerated. The division of responsibility within the Confucian marriage during the Qing dynasty might be understood as follows: Men and women had mutual obligations to one another, but women's duties were greater. Above all, men valued women as providers of sexual, reproductive, childrearing, and domestic services. A woman was fortunate indeed if companionship could be added to this list.

During the Qing dynasty, most women—whether they were skilled at embroidery, good conversationalists, instructive mothers, adept lovers, or wise housekeepers—lived with an awareness of the price on their heads. No matter how invaluable she made herself, a married woman remained part of her husband's estate. If their material circumstances changed, society at large might pity him, but peoplewould not rebuke a husband should he choose someday to sell his wife. Were she to be widowed, the rest of his family could conspire to sell her for cash. Her husband's family was also entitled to make plans for her remarriage and to receive a bride-price. But a widow could not be forced to marry against her will. Violation of this rule was punishable by eighty blows with the heavy bamboo.[7] The crime was even greater if the widow was forced to interrupt the three years of mourning ritually due to a deceased husband. Despite these laws, however, the temptation for relatives to plot against a widow could be particularly strong if the husband had accumulated substantial property. If a widow remained chastely devoted to her late husband, she was entitled to a share of his wealth for the remainder of her lifetime; if she remarried (or began another intimate relationship), she forfeited all claims to her share of his fortune.[8]

Young, fertile women had significant value, and widows had a stake in their household finances. Infant girls possessed neither advantage. Girls were a notorious liability to a poor family.[9] (And even a rich household might view the birth of a baby girl with ambivalence.) The traditional patrilocal marriage patterns that were typical throughout most of China meant that (at least in theory) resources spent in raising a girl drained her family permanently when she departed from her natal household as a young woman to join her husband's family. Because struggling families resorted to infanticide, abandonment, or selling off their infant girls to traffickers bound for the cities, men significantly outnumbered women throughout the countryside. In other parts of the world, labor shortages became the driving force behind systems of chattel slavery, but in China, a shortage of marriageable young women can be partially blamed for the persistence of a coercive and profitable trade in women.

In the abstract, the wife in the ideal Chinese marriage was not purchased. Instead, the elite bride brought into marriage a dowry that substantially *exceeded* the traditional gift the groom's family had presented to her family as part of their engagement ritual. But for most families, practice could not conform with ritual ideals. Female children were already considered an unnecessary burden for a struggling family, and the obligation of the dowry only exacerbated this situation. The perceived expense of raising a girl grew exponentially in the imagination of socially ambitious households. In reality, however, a dowry-based engagement was unattainable for most families. As a result, the traditional ideal was upheld only in a minority of marriage arrangements. More typically, the groom's family paid a more generous bride-price as part of a tacit acknowledgment of the expense of raising a girl.

Even for those who did not directly engage in these transactions, the practice colored the overall cultural ethos and household hierarchy. It became a point of pride for wealthy families that they did not sell their daughters in marriage, and some vocal literati families lauded themselves for choosing to educate their female offspring.[10] Few families could afford to flaunt this kind of cultural capital. When young women did bring a dowry to their marriages, that dowry served to ensure a small measure of financial independence for the new couple. In some communities, tradition dictated that dowry wealth be retained for the *fang*, the term for the immediate conjugal unit of the bride and her husband.[11] Households that were able to do so exercised their superiority by providing their wives and daughters with maidservants, further emphasizing their considerable means as compared with their less fortunate neighbors. If one raised a "bookish" daughter or married a "talented" wife, then someone had to be acquired to do her chores. This status discrepancy between marriages entered through dowry and those entered through the payment of a bride-price sheds light upon how women became transferable property, especially for households at the bottom of society. Families perceived women from different social strata as having fundamentally different values. The distinction between those who could be sold and those who could not came down to perceived sexual availability and economic desperation.

The interaction between the routine and accepted sale of women as wives and the illicit trafficking of women was complicated.[12] The Qing government could reasonably set as a goal the prosecution of kidnapping or the prohibition of prostitution, but the elimination of practices that supplied wives and, perhaps more important, mothers (essential biological building blocks of the Chinese family) proved impossible. That these practices also supplied domestic slaves, short-term surrogate mothers, and sexual companions often seemed beyond the power of the state to control. An overview of relevant contradictions within the late Qing legal environment may help to explain why.

The legal statutes of the Qing dynasty forbade the sale of honorable commoners (*liangmin* 良民) as slaves, whether male or female.[13] People who were already considered debased (*jian* 賤) could be sold, but the number of people to whom this category could be unambiguously applied had decreased by the nineteenth century.[14] During the first century of Qing rule, debased, or *jian*, status passed from parents to children, but by the middle of the eighteenth century, hereditary practices began to change.[15] Moreover, as Matthew Sommer has shown, over the course of the Qing dynasty the connotation of the terms *jian* and *liang* evolved. The terms shifted from being hierarchical status distinctions to designating an individual's morality.[16] Examples from case books suggest that purely status-based claims rarely appeared in late Qing courts.[17] According to the Code, ordinary people were not entitled to own slaves, although they were permitted to indenture workers to till their land and extract labor for debt. The Qing Code had once stipulated that men were not supposed to purchase concubines unless they had reached the age of forty without begetting an heir, but in 1740, the Qianlong emperor realized the futility of enforcing this age limit and repealed the statute.[18] Despite various prohibitions, however, a wide array of substatutes extended permission and exceptions to the statutory laws. A Qing official was allowed to hold a certain number of slaves depending upon his rank and the location of his post.[19] Officials regarded most restrictions on the acquisition of concubines as mere suggestions, and they tended to ignore such laws, dismissing them as outdated or anachronistic.

The law supposedly barring commoners from slaveholding came to be interpreted as applying only to slaves working outside the domestic sphere; merchant households that could afford to purchase domestic help found a ready supply of poor families willing to commend themselves into service. Poverty was considered an acceptable reason to sell oneself, a wife, or a child. The Qing Board of Punishments formally established a precedent of leniency with its handling of wife-selling cases during the first three decades of the nineteenth century.[20] These precedents are evident in sample casebooks that were intended to offer guidance to magistrates on controversial decisions. In some communities, these sales were reversible and accordingly may have seemed more palatable to their executors. Local magistrates drew an analogy to substatutes on land sales carried out in times of desperate poverty; these sales could be redeemed if the sellers' circumstances changed. The law permitted sellers to buy back their family members if they could save some money after weathering the worst of a drought or famine. Surviving judicial records confirm this tension between the laws prohibiting trafficking and polices of compassion and leniency for the poor: in Qing investigations and court cases prosecuting the sale of people, poverty became the most commonly employed defense.

Consistent with past justifications for slavery the world over, when faced with starvation or enslavement many people chose to survive as slaves rather than die at liberty. Qing jurists accepted the survival defense as legitimate, though court cases include ample evidence that defendants were asked to demonstrate the extent of their poverty. This requirement helps to explain why both buyers and sellers insisted upon the creation of bills of sale to document an otherwise illegal activity. These sale contracts usually opened with an evocative preamble describing the pathetic misfortune of the seller: grain prices had become too high, crops had failed, parents had become ill or addicted to opium, their villages had been beset by bandits, or their fields were plagued by locusts.[21]

During the most severe famines, however, laws were effectively suspended. Understandably, local officials were more concerned with coordinating the supply of grain or monetary aid to crisis areas and fighting the corruption that accompanied relief efforts than they were with prosecuting traffickers. Late Qing relief workers looked on as the fastest-moving carts on the road seemed to be those bearing women and young girls away from their homes.[22] Most of these women were destined to serve in brothels in more urban areas.[23] This trade offered an escape route for women even as it further skewed the sex ratio in parts of the country where men outnumbered women even in prosperous times. This, in turn, exacerbated the situation for poor, unmarried men, who would have to resort to buying brides. In the short term, the practice of selling women moved at least one portion of the population out of a blighted region, and in such times, the trade was tolerated as criminally sponsored welfare.

The statutes prohibited husbands from selling their wives without just cause. Poverty was only one acceptable motivation. When a wife proved adulterous, her husband was also entitled to sell her.[24] In contentious cases, the magistrate's office itself took the lead in selling off adulterous women, and many yamens retained official matchmakers (*guanmei* 管媒) to accommodate just such situations. (The yamen compound contained the offices, court, and residence of the magistrate.) The yamen facilitated a new match, as either a wife or a concubine, for an adulterous woman. Her partner in adultery was not permitted to purchase her, nor were the parties concerned allowed to profit by her resale. Official matchmakers were in the curious position of being legally authorized to relocate and sell women, carrying out an otherwise illegal practice. Moreover, because their official tasks placed them in regular contact with criminals, they had the opportunity to establish lucrative sideline businesses as traffickers themselves. Some professional matchmakers implicitly trusted a husband's accusation of infidelity and, relying upon his word alone, began to make arrangements to sell off his wife. Others looked for physical evidence. To provide just one example: the guanmei Gao, who lived by the temple to the medicine god north of Beijing's Andingmen gate, examined the body of a young girl to see if she had been "spoiled" before agreeing to sell her.[25] Although Gao was employed by the yamen, the matchmaker leveraged her official position to sell and introduce clients independently. By committing adultery, a woman activated the property aspect of her relationship with her husband. She became lost property when she strayed, and she could be treated as such. In effect, she went from being an honorable commoner (*liangmin*) to being someone whom the law would now treat as salable (*jianmin*).[26]

If the court decided that a woman had been seduced or enticed to run away, her partner in adultery faced a beating of from eighty to one hundred blows, depending upon the circumstances of those concerned. The textual geography of the categories in the Qing Code offers a clear metaphor for the ambiguous kin-as-property position of women in their husbands' homes. In the Qing Code, the statute addressing wives who ran away with their partners in adultery appeared in the section dedicated to burglary and theft.[27] Women—and specifically sexual access to their bodies—properly belonged under the proprietary control of men.

Another substatute gave husbands permission to sell wives who had run away, although a husband was only allowed to do so if he had done nothing to instigate her flight. (The notion that a woman might have a sound reason to seek refuge from her husband appears to be raised by this substatute, but women were rarely able to demonstrate that flight was justified. The evidentiary bar was too high; wives were expected to display broken limbs and missing teeth to the magistrate as proof of maltreatment.)[28] A wife who had run away without a legitimate reason could be given one hundred blows by the magistrate and sold.

Women, if they did not live too far away, often ran back to their natal families for protection. Indeed, disputes seem to have been almost as likely to erupt between a protective brother and an abusive husband as between a jealous husband and an absconding lover.[29] The richest available descriptions of these intimate family confrontations appear in the judicial archives generated by local magistrates and in the records of the Qing Board of Punishments. Because the board concerned itself primarily with capital cases, this surviving record of domestic disagreements tends to be especially violent. The challenge of reading these cases is to identify ongoing accepted practices in the background investigation of the often bloody crimes being prosecuted by the Board. To be perceived as resellable placed a woman at considerable physical risk. As part of the routine review of the facts in these cases, investigators often learned the amount of the *shenjia* 身價, or body-price, paid for access to a woman's sexual and domestic labor. The unofficial scribes who helped draft contracts applied this term liberally, whether stating the acquisition price of a bride, a concubine, or a servant. The sale of women appeared incidental to more serious offenses described in the judicial record. Thus, it was not the act of selling a woman itself that placed a case before the Board for review but rather the bloodshed that accompanied conflicts erupting in a chaotic transaction. In the following description of a case from Zhili (modern Hebei Province), a negotiation that began as an amicable arrangement for a second marriage ended with kidnapping and violence.[30]

Shortly after his new wife arrived at his home in early 1881, Yan Shu'er realized that he and his wife, née Men, would never get along. He drafted a marriage severance document for her natal family, explaining the situation. Graciously acknowledging that it took "mutual cooperation to make a successful marriage," Yan did not press the Men household to return his bride-price, and he willingly sent the Men daughter home "so that she could be affianced to someone else." If Yan anticipated a commission on this future arrangement, he did not express that in writing.[31] Miss Men's maternal aunt watched all this with interest. An older man named Ma Yimei had confided to her that he hoped to acquire a concubine, and she agreed to approach her niece with his offer. Miss Men acquiesced, in part because her mother had been ill for several years and the Men family needed the money to pay for medical consultation. The aunt drew up a contract with Ma Yimei, setting a *shenjia* of seventeen hundred strings of copper cash. They agreed that Ma Yimei's brother, Ma Yishan, would deliver the money when he arrived with a donkey cart to fetch Miss Men. It was a long day's journey across the dusty Quyang countryside not far from the Baoding county seat. Ma Yishan stopped with his brother's newly purchased concubine near a house belonging to an acquaintance, Zhang Sanmeng.

Zhang caught a glimpse of the weary young woman resting in the cart tethered by his gate, and this aroused his interest. He proposed that Ma Yishan sell her to him on the sly rather than taking her back to his elder brother, Ma Yimei. The two men argued. Zhang Sanmeng struggled to separate Miss Men from Ma Yishan, forcing her into his house at knifepoint. He pushed her into an empty room and bolted the door. Despite his attraction to the young woman, he decided not to rape her. (The record states that he did not "actually pollute her with illicit sex.") Instead, Zhang Sanmeng began to plan to sell her himself.

Ma Yishan was forced to drive his cart home and inform his brother that the concubine he had just paid for had been stolen. Ma Yimei was furious. He summoned his nephews, Ma Hengwei and Ma Hengyu, and they set out together to try to persuade Zhang Sanmeng to return the young concubine.

When the four men arrived at Zhang Sanmeng's property, they found the front gate barred. The older man, Ma Yimei, called out to Miss Men. Zhang Sanmeng taunted him from inside the house, telling him that the only way to retrieve his concubine would be to pay a ransom. Ma Yimei and his two nephews could hear the young woman moving about in the house. They forced their way to the door. Zhang Sanmeng attempted to the block the entryway with a long, sharp staff. One of the nephews tried to knock the staff from his hands. Zhang struck out at the three men, and one of the younger nephews pulled out a knife. In the ensuing struggle, Zhang Sanmeng received fatal wounds. Ma Yimei had grown weak in his old age, and although the blows might not have killed a younger man, he also died. Miss Men managed to run away.

The magistrate's yamen gathered these facts from one of Zhang's younger cousins and from interrogating one of the Ma nephews. When weighing the fate of the young concubine, the property contested in this dispute, the magistrate considered three options: she could stay with the Ma household; she could return to her family, the Men clan; or she could stay with Zhang's cousin. (This third option may have been included merely to demonstrate thoroughness, but it is curious that the law would bother to consider the claim of a kidnapper's family.) Miss Men was instructed to return to her family.

This court case complicates our expectations of divorce negotiations and concubine sales. Conflict entered this case from the roadside, not from any dispute in the arrangements themselves. The young woman was released from her first unhappy marriage without argument. The initial arrangements to sell her as a concubine were made by an older female relative, who was in regular contact with neighbors. In the world where these people lived, women were not confined solely to ritually prescribed separate spheres; the matchmaking aunt did not have to venture out of a Confucian "inner chamber" to find a buyer for her niece. She was already a public person involved in conversations with male and female neighbors. The young woman herself consented to becoming a concubine in order to help her family; indeed, her matchmaking aunt discussed the situation with her at some length, describing her buyer's age and expectations. Here, the case offers the tiniest glimpse into a young woman's sense of her own value and obligations; when she agreed to be sold as a concubine to Ma Yimei, Miss Men exploited her own marketability. The body-price paid for medical care for her ailing mother.

What was Miss Men's value to the men who fought over her? Zhang Sanmeng seized upon the opportunity to kidnap her because he saw her as a potential commodity, a pretty thing he could ransom now or sell later. His audacity at grabbing a young woman from the roadside speaks to just how ubiquitous the market for women had become during this period. Kidnapping normally required some planning, but this particular kidnapping, as described to the court, seems haphazard. The circumstances suggest that Zhang's decision to snatch Miss Men was somewhat spontaneous. Even along a well-traveled road, it would have been strange for a professional kidnapper to wait for a victim to show up at the gate.[32] Although Zhang Sanmeng owned a plot of land, he was probably not as well-off as the Ma household. The date of this case also reveals something about Zhang's situation. In 1881, small landholders in southern Zhili would not yet have recovered fully from the severe drought of the late 1870s. Zhang might naturally have been on the lookout for criminal ways to augment his livelihood. If he were willing to transport Miss Men from Zhili to Shanghai, he could have sold her to a brothel for several times the body-price Ma Yimei had paid to the Men family; he would thus earn enough money to live more comfortably when the next famine came.

For the Ma family, Miss Men represented a chance for Yimei to establish his own descent line. Ma Yimei's younger brother and nephews supported his decision to bring a concubine into the household. The Board of Punishment record does not state that Ma Yimei had a wife, but he probably did. Had he been unmarried, Miss Men's matchmaking aunt might have considered pressuring the older man to buy her niece as a wife rather than as a concubine.[33] There were other reasons Yimei might not have wished to bring Miss Men into his household as a wife. Under the law, after her husband's death a wife was entitled to a portion of his property during her remaining years—provided she did not remarry. A concubine did not share this privilege. As a concubine sold after an unsuccessful first marriage, the young woman was more likely to be sold a third time. Furthermore, because she had been sold as a concubine, it was unlikely that Miss Men would ever regain the status of primary wife (except perhaps to a very poor man). All record of Miss Men ends with the Qing Board of Punishment's decision to send her back to her natal household. Given the family's strapped circumstances, her matchmaking aunt probably began gossiping and searching for another childless man to purchase Miss Men almost before she had returned home. But the young woman's involvement in the deadly affray on the Zhang property certainly would have made any potential buyer think twice. Miss Men had narrowly escaped being sold as a prostitute by Zhang Sanmeng; to what lengths would her natal family go to turn a profit for a third time?

As Matthew Sommer has demonstrated, prostitution, as a form of illicit sex outside of marriage, had been illegal since the Yongzheng "emancipation edicts" of 1723.[34] Accordingly, it was against the law to sell a young woman of an honorable background to be a prostitute or courtesan.[35] Vibrant pleasure quarters for the consumption of sexual entertainment in Beijing, Shanghai, and other growing cities belied the effectiveness of the Qing law at the end of the nineteenth century, although the vice was certainly most rampant in treaty ports where the Qing only had partial jurisdiction. For Qing jurists, sexual availability made a woman more readily commodified. Ordinary people shared this perception. Zhang Sanmeng could easily have assumed that a kidnapped concubine would not be difficult to resell and that if he were caught, the punishment he would face for selling a woman such as Miss Men would be less than that for selling a chaste wife or an unmarried young woman.

Inequality under the law was an inherent component of the Qing legal system. For subjects of China's last dynasty, this inequality did not equal injustice. Instead, justice depended integrally upon the relationship between the victim of a crime and its perpetrator. For a son to strike his father was a capital office, whereas a father could raise his hand against his own son with relative impunity. The importance of relationship principles in the execution of Chinese justice had a direct bearing on the position of women under the Qing criminal code as well. Crimes committed between husbands and wives were subject to status-based distinctions. Furthermore, status distinctions in the law meant that though a man would be punished for abducting his neighbor's wife, the punishment for abducting the neighbor's slave girl or concubine was less severe. The rape of a chaste woman was a greater crime than having sex by force with a known adulteress or a prostitute. Thus, a woman's virtue became a deciding factor in the prosecution of her abductor.

The trade in women could be exploited by those on both sides of a transaction. It was not always as simple as a buyer taking advantage of an impoverished family's difficulty. At times, even the woman being sold stood to benefit. To be sold as a slave or to a brothel meant a difficult life and loss of status, and accordingly, it left a woman especially vulnerable to resale. Yet sometimes, poorer families sought to improve their station by creating an alliance with a more economically stable household. These households dared not hope that a man of stature would make their daughter his wife, but such a man *might* be persuaded to take a poor but pretty girl as his concubine. A family that was willing to make this compromise gambled that as a concubine, their daughter might outlive the man's wife, bear sons for the family, or otherwise obtain some influence in her new patron's home.

A concubine who bore sons could expect greater respect in the household, and if she were allowed to maintain a close relationship with these sons, this could ensure her an unofficial improvement in her status. Under the law, however, her sons were considered the children of the patriarch's primary wife. Consequently, their primary ritual relationship and mourning obligations were to their legal mother rather than their biological mother. Quite naturally, sentiment could find a way to prevail under such circumstances, and some men maintained close relationships with their biological concubine mothers. A husband might choose to promote a concubine to the position of wife if his first wife should die, and providing sons made such a promotion more likely. Similarly, slave girls (bi) who became pregnant after assignations with their masters attained a kind of "lower concubine" status.[36] They could no longer be dismissed or disposed of so easily and were considered members of the family, albeit with low status. In a prosperous household, bearing male children might improve a woman's status; for poorer families, however, successful childbearing could place a fertile wife or concubine at risk for a different kind of arrangement. Such a promising woman might find her womb leased for surrogacy.

The Qing Code also forbade leasing women through a form of mortgage known as *dian* 典. The term was borrowed from a semilegal type of redeemable land transfer. Whether the object to be leased was a woman or a piece of land, the written justification sellers provided in the dian contract was almost always poverty. Through dian, the buyer borrowed a married woman from her husband for a fixed period, usually for three years. In exchange, the legal husband received a prearranged payment, and the wife joined the buyer's household. Any children born during this time became part of the family of the dian-holder and bore his surname. The woman's status in her secondary household was below that of a wife or a concubine. Substatutes promulgated in 1740, 1772, and 1802 to prosecute this practice attest to the Qing government's concern about eliminating these short-term arrangements.[37] If confronted by the magistrate, most purchasers of dian rights to a woman deployed the language of tradition to justify their disregard of the law.

One commonly cited maxim asserted that there was no worse way to offend one's ancestors than to fail to guarantee their posterity: Confucian values required that a male heir and patrilineal descendants had to ritually tend ancestral tablets. With a choice between the possibility of a reprimand from the state or the certainty of ancestral wrath, a childless man might not balk at the chance to borrow a fertile wife from his neighbor. Only in this way could he guarantee that his ancestors—and later his own spirit—would be appeased. Stories praising self-sacrificing wives who, acknowledging their own failure to conceive male children, helped their husbands acquire surrogates (sometimes even through well-intentioned deception) circulated and shaped popular opinion. The lack of shared interests among women across economic circumstances or across disparate social statuses ensured that domestic forms of sexual exploitation prevailed in Qing homes.

The practice of keeping slave girls to carry out domestic chores was itself not illegal. Almost all means of acquiring them, however, operated at the edge of the law. The legal codes were more permissive when it came to regulating the purchase of concubines, but even here, in theory, there were some restrictions. Wife sales also transpired in an ambiguous realm; though it was illegal to sell a married woman, officials were sympathetic to men whose circumstances demanded this as a solution. Women, whether wives or concubines, represented a significant investment, and family members did not always agree on how to manage their human capital. The knowledge that women could be turned into cash sometimes tore families apart, as a local investigation from Shuntian Prefecture in Hebei Province shows.

In 1882, Chu Fuzhong struck an agreement with his younger brother Chu Fukui. The crops on their small plot of land had not been bountiful for several years, and what little had recovered from successive droughts had already been harvested. After taking stock of the family's limited provisions for the coming winter, Fuzhong decided that he had better find work as a hired laborer helping to bring in the remaining harvest in a more fertile village. Fuzhong left his wife and two children—a son, age four, and a daughter, age seven—in his brother's care and set out to try to earn some money for additional grain.

Fuzhong returned several months later to find that all four had left the village. The magistrate questioned his neighbors and learned that Fukui had intended to sell Fuzhong's wife to a widower who lived in a town several days' walk from Chu Family Village. Fukui had hoped to sell both the children as well, the young girl as a courtesan's slave girl and her brother to a family lacking a male child. Fuzhong learned that while traveling in the winter months, his wife and children had taken ill on the road and died. When he petitioned the magistrate to charge his brother with causing their deaths, Fukui brought a countercharge. The younger brother claimed that it was originally Fuzhong's idea to sell off the wife and children and that he had only been acting on his brother's behalf. In the end, the magistrate dismissed the case, warning the two men that they were in danger of becoming the town laughingstock. The deaths and the plans to sell Fuzhong's wife and children went unprosecuted.[38]

Throughout the Qing dynasty and well into the Republican period, widespread social acceptance of the trafficking of women and children persisted despite a general awareness of the violence that sometimes accompanied the trade. Late Qing society fully acknowledged that kidnapping was a growing crime; newspapers regularly described recent local abductions. Indeed, editorial articles intended to forewarn an expanding readership listed the strategies a kidnapper might use to entice an unsuspecting child, and they gave stern warnings directed at women about the dangers of traveling alone by steamship. Serialized articles dramatized the arrest and resulting prosecution of particularly notorious kidnappers, sometimes quoting the criminals' unrepentant admissions about their thwarted schemes. For the most part, however, this cautionary literature did not take into account the simple truth that the majority of traffickers were relatives and friends.

Although literacy in China was increasing throughout the late nineteenth and early twentieth centuries, newspapers such as the *Shenbao* and the *Minli Ribao* and even the growing number of newspapers intended for a female readership, among them the *Funü Zazhi* and its competitors, were consumed primarily by the most educated and affluent readers. Many of the men and women who leafed through the *Shenbao*'s news reports and warnings about kidnapping were born into families that regularly negotiated with neighborhood brokers to purchase their domestic staff. They tended to assume that servitude as it occurred in their own homes was a justifiable, indeed noble, act of charity and that they were providing the maids or household retainers who were fortunate enough to serve them with food, shelter, and a meaningful occupation. For affluent urbanites, a wide chasm existed between their own devoted domestics and the illicit trade in people. Most could not see beyond their own charitable impulses to a broader pattern of exploitation and coercion.

Elite households may have been perfectly correct in their assessment of the positive role they played as benevolent providers for their domestic staff. Certainly, affection developed between wet nurses and their charges, between ladies' maids and their mistresses, between shopkeepers and apprentices, and between successful merchants and their chauffeurs. Literati memoirs reflect upon annual efforts to express affection and appreciation for domestics: special red envelopes at the New Year, inclusion in festival activities, an honorary opportunity to offer sacrifices to the family's ancestors as one of their own. When a member of the household's domestic staff declined to take a leave to return home, this was typically interpreted as devotion to the master's family (rather than the equally likely possibility that conditions at home were less comfortable or that, after a long period of absence, the servant had become estranged from his or her own family).[39]

Many domestic relationships initiated with a sales transaction did not function as slavery. Ordinary marriages began with the exchange of a bride-price. Concubines fell in love with their buyers. Wet nurses were allowed to send money home. And indentured laborers could leave—and often did, confident that despite their debts, most magistrates were too overextended to pursue them. For many runaway servants, the arm of the local magistrate was not long enough to reach them in another district. Moreover, at least according to the law, masters were not given free rein in disciplining their domestics. Purchased people could be fully integrated into family life. Yet in other ways, they remained property. In practice, serving maids were sexually available to their masters, and men frequently traded concubines among themselves.

Occasionally, women could be involved in shaping the conditions of their servitude. Some women willingly chose brothel life over other hardships; others were forced into the sex trade through kidnapping. Wives purchased concubines for their husbands, sometimes in order to extricate themselves from an excessively demanding or unpleasant sexual relationship; sometimes motivated by affection; and sometimes merely to find the husband a more fertile, childbearing partner.

Late Qing society struggled to reconcile the reliance of households of all social strata upon an unsavory trade in people, on the one hand, with a desire for a clear Confucian moral hierarchy, on the other. An article from the *Shenbao* newspaper, dated September 12, 1880, captured this ambivalence perfectly. The anonymous author began by stating that "the distinction between master and slave lies outside the five cardinal relationships of the Confucian system," and then he embarked on a historical analysis that traced the evolution of the hierarchical relationship between master and slave back nearly two millennia. This served as his long-winded preamble to reflections on a more immediate problem: the chronic abuse of slave girls by cruel mistresses. Too much suffering, he felt, had been inflicted under the guise of "educating" or "giving instruction" to household slaves. He blamed the Qing Code for its failure to issue explicit restrictions on the methods masters could use to "educate and instruct" their menials. Mistresses were particularly to blame, he observed, as they often splashed their maids with scalding water to punish them, occasionally causing fatal burns. (Indeed, this practice was so common that the Board of Punishments was forced to promulgate a new substatute on the matter.)[40]

The *Shenbao* writer was acutely aware that female slaves and indentured servants were vulnerable to lecherous advances from their masters and any of their masters' friends. To rebuff these advances was dangerous. He continued, "If a woman is taken as a concubine by the master, and she is not debased [*jian*] and has not been for some time, even though her status has now fallen, should she still be subject to the fury of her master? . . . Household heads have the power to make the days delightful or to pass miserably for the women and children in their homes." His critique exhibited some awareness that these situations eroded not only the humanity of those whom they exploited but also the moral authority of the master. Yet he fell far short of calling for broad social change. Instead, he implored elites to adopt a proper Confucian approach to managing their homes.

Women who joined a household as concubines or as slave girls were especially vulnerable to sexual advances from their masters and also from neighbors and visitors to the home. As in adultery cases, the prosecution of a man for seducing the purchased woman of another was essentially assessed as a matter of theft. And like all crimes in Qing China, the status difference between the man and the slave girl or concubine had an impact on the potential sentence that the thief (or rapist) would receive. It was a greater crime to sexually assault a wife than a slave girl, but in either case, the law considered the crime to be an affront against the master of the house at least as much as a crime against the reluctant object of the lecherous affection or violence. Assailants came to believe that women who were considered debased (or jian) due to their family background or the circumstances through which they had entered a household could be imposed upon with greater impunity. Young women whose status was in any way ambiguous were especially vulnerable.

A 1896 report from the Board of Punishments offers a view of this predatory environment.[41] In the winter of that year, in Shuyang Prefecture in Jiangsu Province, a middle-aged man named Jiang Fang frequently passed a house where a young girl known throughout the village as "Xiao's small yatou" lived with her father, Xiao Qilong. (*Yatou*, part of the girl's nickname, was a generic term typically used to refer to very young girls, slave girls, and unmarried women who worked as domestics.) From observing the house, Jiang Fang was able to determine in which section of the building the girl usually slept. He watched carefully, taking note of when she was alone with her chores and when she retreated by herself to the southwest corner of the house, where she kept her woven sleeping mat. One evening after she had gone to bed, Jiang Fang crept up to the house intent upon raping Xiao Yatou. He carried a rough stick with him and under the cover of darkness pushed his way into her quarters, knocking things over. He then proceeded to try to violate the girl with his stick. Neighbors heard cries from Xiao Yatou's corner of the house. Jiang Fang threw open the door and fled, dropping his bloody stick as he ran.

The rape attempt came to the attention of the Shuyang district magistrate only after Xiao Yatou, again left alone at the house, took a rope and hanged herself a day later. The magistrate's investigation attributed the hanging to her great distress and shame after surviving the assault. This was no simple postmortem conviction. Under the Qing Code, to cause a suicide was a crime equivalent to murder, and Jiang Fang could have been banished or even executed. The Board of Punishments reviewed the case and concurred with the magistrate, sentencing Jiang to beating and banishment. The Board showed him considerable leniency. For causing a young woman of good background to kill herself, he might have faced a sentence of strangulation after the autumn assizes,[42] though even sentences scheduled for after the assizes could sometimes be deferred indefinitely. Would Xiao Yatou have been disappointed with this outcome? No archival record allows the historian to see into the mind of a young suicide. Nonetheless, her death raises intriguing questions about how much a young girl might have known about legal precedents. Living in Jiangsu, Xiao Yatou might well have been familiar with the practice of inscribing the names of those who resisted rape (as well as the names of chaste widows) on memorial arches.[43] She had grown up in a world in which many people believed that the ghosts of suicides would haunt those who had wronged them. Did she also know that the Qing Code could potentially condemn to death the man who had tried to rape her?

We have slightly more insight into the mind of the Widow Song (née Tang). In 1876, she learned that the family of her deceased husband intended to sell her to an acquaintance, to be his concubine.[44] After her husband's death, Widow Song had managed his fields in the Sichuan basin valleys in Tongliao County, northwest of the provincial seat of Chongqing. An investor from Yunnan sought to buy the land from her husband's clan, and because Widow Song was still rather young, he pressed them to make arrangements through a matchmaker to sell her as a concubine. When Widow Song learned of the scheme, she talked the situation over with her young son, who later tearfully spoke with the magistrate on her behalf; he explained that his mother could not cope with the shame of being sold to another man and that she had been willing to die to preserve her chaste widowhood. She chose to cut her own throat rather than face a concubine's fate. Widow Song may have known that her husband's family could be punished for pressuring her to violate her vows, but she did not trust that her chaste widowhood would receive sufficient protection had she instead turned to the local magistrate.

At the end of the Qing dynasty, the practice of purchasing young women as household slaves (binü) and as concubines was symptomatic of a growing tension between changing legal ideas and more conservative impulses. Ironically, improved inheritance rights for widows during the Qing placed women who outlived their husbands at increased risk of being pressured or even sold into remarriage or concubinage.[45] In Guangzhou and Hong Kong, affluent households continued to purchase *mui-tsai*, a Cantonese term for young girls who were sold by their parents and would devote themselves to providing domestic service to elite households until such time as they might marry.[46] British officials in Hong Kong struggled over whether to outlaw this system. They were especially confounded by the contradiction between Cantonese locals' reassurances that the term *mui-tsai* meant "little younger sister" and the obvious exploitation many of these girls faced in their purchasers' homes as vulnerable domestic laborers. Was this exploitation disguised as charity? Although the laws would change when the dynasty came to an end, several decades would pass before popular practices throughout the country adapted to Republican China's new laws.

Conditions of enslavement worked in subtle ways in Qing households. The protection promised by legal codes offered women scant shelter and instead ensured that, for the most part, exploitative transactions occurred beyond the purview of the law. Violations of the prohibition against selling women tended to appear in court proceedings only when a far worse crime had been committed as well. Trafficking became a mitigating circumstance in assessing guilt, rather than a crime prosecuted on its own terms. That women were sold in China did not, of itself, make them slaves; money was exchanged to establish most relationships between men and women. Whether a sold woman might be considered to be enslaved very much depended upon the treatment she received after the initial transaction and to what extent she might be subjected to further, unanticipated transactions. Some women played an active part in shaping their own sales and in making arrangements to provide for their families. Yet the agency of these enterprising women overshadows the abusive environment in which many women inevitably found themselves. We should not let their apparent complicity obscure broader patterns in accepted forms of domestic and sexual exploitation. The ambiguities in these sales themselves reveal competing ideas about the place of women as simultaneously family and property at the end of the Qing dynasty.

Notes

1. Given the long expanse of China's history, surprisingly little scholarship has scrutinized the processes of slavery. Work on the subject seems particularly thin on the ground not only because of significant changes over dynastic periods but also due to dramatic variation across different regional contexts. Only a handful of monographs and articles have been devoted to the subject in any period or region. For the Qing period, Wei Qingyuan's slim volume *Qingdai nubi zhidu* [System of slavery during the Qing dynasty] (Beijing: Zhongguo renmin daxue chubanshe, 1982), remains the only book exclusively dedicated to slavery in the Qing. Angela Shottenhammer also provides a brief introduction to Chinese slavery in "Slaves and Forms of Slavery in Late Imperial China," in *Conference Volume on Slavery in the Modern and Premodern Worlds*, ed. Gwyn Campbell (Avignon, France: Frank Cass Publishers, 2003), 143–54. Clarence Martin Wilber's 1943 study discusses slavery two millennia ago: see Wilber, *Slavery in China during the Former Han Dynasty: 206 B.C.–A.D. 25* (Chicago: Anthropological Series, Field Museum of Natural History, 1943). Robin Yates has also written an article on slavery during the early period: "Slavery in Early China: A Socio-cultural Approach," *Journal of East Asian Archaeology* 3, no. 1–2 (2002): 283–331. For the twentieth century, anthropologists and ethnographers have done regional studies of practices in southern China. James Watson describes the regional practice of selling men known as *ximin* or *sai-man* into hereditary servitude among the Man lineage located in a village in Hong Kong's New Territories, in "Chattel Slavery in Chinese Peasant Society, a Comparative Analysis," *Ethnology* 15, no. 4 (October 1976): 561–75. Watson demonstrates that in contrast with many slave societies, in the lineages of South China chattel slaveholding did not serve a direct economic function. Hereditary slaves

offered social status but at great economic expense. Watson emphasizes the difference between the logic of slavery in the context he studies and forms of slavery described elsewhere.

2. Prostitution, especially in Shanghai, has been written about extensively by Christian Henriot and Gail Hershatter. See Henriot, *Belles de Shanghai: Prostitution and sexualité en Chine aux XIXe–XXe siècles* (Paris: Editions du CNRS, 1997), and *Prostitution and Sexuality in Shanghai, 1849–1949* (Cambridge: Cambridge University Press, 2001). Also see Hershatter, *Dangerous Pleasures: Prostitution and Modernity in Twentieth-Century Shanghai* (Berkeley: University of California Press, 1997).

3. For an example of how one elite household relied upon the determined ingenuity of female household heads, see Susan Mann, *The Talented Women of the Zhang Family* (Berkeley: University of California Press, 2007).

4. Emily Honig, *Sisters and Strangers: Women in the Shanghai Cotton Mills, 1919–1949* (Stanford, Calif.: Stanford University Press, 1992).

5. Sometimes, this position of responsibility also proved a burden and cause for considerable anxiety. The women of Susan Mann's Zhang family balanced their anxieties and responsibilities with aplomb: see Mann, *Talented Women.*

6. For a sense of this gap, see studies of rural women such as Margery Wolf's *Women and the Family in Rural Taiwan* (Stanford, Calif.: Stanford University Press, 1972).

7. This punishment is prescribed in the first substatute under statute 105. Statutes for the Qing Code in this article are based on their appearance in Xue Yunsheng's 1905 *Duli cunyi* 讀例存疑 [Doubts upon reading the substatutes], punctuated and edited by Huang Tsing-chia 黃靜嘉, 5 vols. (1905; repr., Taipei: Chinese Materials and Research Aids Service Center, 1970), (hereafter cited as DLCY).

8. For the most significant discussion of transforming attitudes and Qing policies on chastity, see Janet Theiss, *Disgraceful Matters: The Politics of Chastity in Eighteenth Century China* (Berkeley: University of California Press, 2002).

9. For a glimpse of the lengths to which some families went to ease their burden, see Michelle King, "Drowning Daughters: A Cultural History of Female Infanticide in Late 19th Century China" (Ph.D. diss., University of California, Berkeley, 2007).

10. This was by no means new. The female scholar Ban Zhao's treatise on women's education, *Nüjie*, or *Admonitions for Women*, dates to the first century CE. Susan Mann describes the value of a classical education in "Learned Women in the Eighteenth Century," in *Engendering China: Women, Culture, and the State*, ed. Christina K. Gilmartin, Gail Hershatter, Lisa Rofel, and Tyrene White (Cambridge, Mass.: Harvard University Press, 1994), 27–46. As Mann emphasizes, debates in imperial China over women's education focused not on whether elite women ought to be educated but on what the content of

that education should be. See also Dorothy Ko, *Teachers of the Inner Chambers: Women and Culture in 17th Century China* (Stanford, Calif.: Stanford University Press, 1995). By the early twentieth century, the radical revolutionary Confucian scholar Kang Youwei took particular pride in providing his daughters with a worldly and wide-ranging education.

11. Myron Cohen, *Kinship, Contract, Community and State* (Stanford, Calif.: Stanford University Press, 2005).

12. Influential literati families had been forming important alliances through marriage for many centuries, and at the level of national and provincial elites, the stakes both in terms of honor and ritual dowry payments could be high. Payment of the bride-price as well as the dowry traditionally indicated that an engagement had been locked in place.

13. Statute 275 prohibited the "abduction of people and the abduction for sale of people." This statute appears in the section of the Qing Code for theft and robbery.

14. Jing Junjian, *Qing dai shehui de jianmin dengji* 清代社會的賤民等級 [Debased legal status in Qing society] (Hangzhou: Zhejiang renmin chubanshe, 1980).

15. For a detailed study of the origins of the diverse category of jian, see Anders Hansson, *Chinese Outcasts: Discrimination and Emancipation in Late Imperial China* (Leiden: Brill, 1996). By the Qing, people belonging to the debased or mean category included slaves or bond servants, prostitutes, musicians, actors, and yamen runners employed by the government to serve as the "muscle" behind the office of the magistrate. Honorable men and women came from peasant farming families, scholarly literati households, or artisan and merchant households (p. 1).

16. Matthew Sommer, *Sex, Law and Society in Late Imperial China* (Stanford, Calif.: Stanford University Press, 2000).

17. One example from 1822 involving a fatal struggle between self-identified commoners and a young man descended from a family of former funerary musicians appeared in the *Xing'an Huilan* 刑案慧蘭 [Conspectus of penal cases] (Beijing: Tushu jicheng ju, 1886), 39:1. In this instance, the magistrate weighed the status difference of the men involved in order to determine an appropriate sentence. The Qing Board of Punishments overruled his decision, remarking that "they ought to be punished, not as slaves who have attacked their masters, but as free common men who have been made equal." Pierre Hoang also discusses this conflict in *Mélanges sur l'administration* (Shanghai: Imprimerie de la Mission Catholique, 1902), 129–30.

18. Shen Jiaben, *Shen Jiaben weike shujicuan* 沈家本未刻書集纂, repr. ed. (Beijing: Zhongguo shehui kexue chubanshe, 1996), 348. Cited in Hsieh Baohua, "The Market in Concubines in Jiangnan during Ming-Qing China," *Journal of Family History* 33, no. 3 (2008): 262–90.

19. Wei Qingyuan, *Qingdai nubi zhidu* 清代奴婢制 (Beijing: Zhongguo renmin daxue chubanshe, 1981), 1–6.

20. One example dates from 1818 in the *Xing'an Huilan.* Matthew Sommer points to this example in *Sex, Law and Society.*

21. Examples of these common excuses in action during the Qing can be found throughout the archives of the Baodi County magistrate in the Shuntian Prefecture archives held at China's Number One Historical Archive in Beijing. I have described these contracts in further detail in "Transactions on the Margins of Legality: Secret Contracts for Sale and Indenture in Republican China," paper presented at the New York Association for Asian Studies, 2008, and currently in preparation for publication.

22. See descriptions in Kathryn Edgerton-Tarply, *Tears from Iron: Cultural Responses to Famine in Nineteenth-Century China* (Berkeley: University of California Press, 2008).

23. Hershatter, *Dangerous Pleasures.*

24. Wu Tan, *Da Qing lüli tongkao jiaozhu* 大清律例通考交主 [Thorough examination of the Qing Code Statutes and Sub-statutes], ed. Ma Jianshi and Yang Yutang (Beijing: Zhongguo zhengfa daxue chubanshe, 1992), 951.

25. *Xingke tiben,* 3991, reel 11, microfilm 2050–83, Qing Number One Historical Archive, Beijing.

26. The most important book on all forms of illicit sex during the Qing, including adultery, rape, and prostitution, is Sommer, *Sex, Law, and Society.*

27. Philip Huang, *Code, Custom, and Legal Practice in China: The Qing and the Republic Compared* (Stanford, Calif.: Stanford University Press, 2001), 159.

28. DLCY, vol. 4, juan 36, p. 929.

29. Theiss, *Disgraceful Matters.*

30. *Xingke tiben,* Board of Punishments Archive, reel 22, 1393–1405, GX 6.4.15, Number One Historical Archive, Beijing.

31. Yan also neglected to include the standard phrases renouncing all claim to any future bride-price her family might obtain, so it is possible that he had not ruled out the possibility that he might receive a small commission for his earlier courtesy.

32. The road was known to be dangerous; reports from contemporary newspapers indicate that some innkeepers facilitated the kidnappings.

33. However, it is conceivable that Ma Yimei was a widower and that his younger brother and nephews might have discouraged him from remarriage. A wife would have gained a claim on his property that a concubine would never have. Chinese law and cultural practice permitted men to take only one wife. His other spouses were considered concubines, unless promoted after the death of the primary wife.

34. Sommer, *Sex, Law and Society,* 260–304.

35. "To sell a young woman of an honorable background to be a prostitute or courtesan": *mai liangnü wei chang* 賣良女為娼.

36. Matthew Sommer concludes that Qing judicial decisions suggest that "sexual intercourse with a female domestic slave amounted to the consummation of some sort of secondary spousal relationship." See Sommer, *Sex, Law and Society*, 50.

37. See statute 102 forbidding *diangu qinü*, or "the leasing out of a wife or daughter," DLCY, vol. 2, p. 292.

38. Reel 73, 61–96, Shuntian Prefecture Archive, Qing Number One Historical Archive, Beijing.

39. This motif plays out particularly poignantly in fiction. Possibly the most famous example, Ba Jin's popular novel *The Family*, set in 1920s Chengdu, dramatizes the fates of two bonded girls who have been left in the hands of the waning patriarch. One of these two commits suicide rather than marry and be forced to leave the household she has served since childhood. Local conflicts depicted in the Republican period archive make it clear that as systems of slavery were dismantled, former servants and slaves did not always know where to turn. For a contrast between elite notions of the position of the slave girl and reality, the Beijing Municipal Archive (file J181-19-10044) contains a 1919 description of one such servant who had nowhere else to go.

40. "Titled Ladies Ill-Treating Their Slave Girls," from the *Xingbu zouding zhangcheng* [Regulations established through memorials of the Board of Punishments], Guangxi, Section 1:76a–80b. Abridged and translated in Marinus J. Meijer, "Slavery at the End of the Ch'ing Dynasty," in *China's Legal Tradition*, ed. Jerome Cohen (Princeton, N.J.: Princeton University Press, 1979), 348–52.

41. *Xingke tiben*, Board of Punishments Archive, reel 81, 4245-5, GX 21.12.12, Number One Historical Archives, Beijing.

42. DLCY, vol. 4, p. 881.

43. To understand the legacy of Qing rule for conceptions of virtue and chastity, see the thorough study on evolving meanings of chastity and patriarchy during the eighteenth century in Theiss, *Disgraceful Matters*.

44. *Xingke Tiben*, Board of Punishments Archive, reel 11, 3991-19, GX 3.4.29, Number One Historical Archive, Beijing.

45. Theiss, *Disgraceful Matters*. Also see Kathryn Bernhardt, *Women and Property in China, 960–1940* (Stanford, Calif.: Stanford University Press, 1994).

46. For an ethnographic study of the life experience and work conditions of several mui-tsai, see Maria Jaschok, *Concubines and Bondservants: A Social History* (London: Zed Books, 1988).

15

SEX SLAVERY AND HUMAN TRAFFICKING IN NIGERIA—AN OVERVIEW

Roseline Uyanga with Marie-Luise Ermisch

West Africa's involvement in the sale of people has a long history. From the tenth century to the fourteenth, there was an active trade in people across the Sahara that, in turn, fed into the transatlantic slave trade, which lasted from the late fifteenth century to the mid-nineteenth century.[1] Historians have estimated that during the transalantic slave trade, 12.5 million slaves were shipped across the Atlantic Ocean from sub-Saharan Africa, with a significant number originating from or passing through what is now Nigeria.[2] In 1807, however, Britain outlawed the slave trade and, in 1833, it abolished slavery completely throughout its empire. The gradual enforcement of British and later international antislavery policy led to the refocusing of West Africa's export trade on "legitimate" products, such as petroleum, machinery, palm oil, palm kernel, cocoa, and cotton, as well as entertainment. Many people have thus come to assume that, with the end of the transatlantic slave trade, the trade in human beings has ceased in Nigeria. However, the selling of people has not only continued but, in the age of globalization, has also taken on new dimensions and characteristics. Now called human trafficking, it is a multibillion-dollar industry that is facilitated by inequality, poverty, crime, corruption, and violence, together with low-cost transportation and communication.[3] Though human trafficking affects men, women, and children and can lead to many forms of coerced labor, a disproportionately high percentage of victims are girls and women who are used for sexual purposes. Nigeria is a major source, transit route, and destination country for such trafficking victims. It is therefore crucial to understand the dynamics that facilitate this trade so that more effective policies and initiatives can be developed to help prevent trafficking, protect its victims, and prosecute its perpetrators.

Although the Nigerian government has made serious efforts to curtail human trafficking through the signing of the Palermo Protocol,[4] the establishment of the National Agency for the Prohibition of Traffic in Persons (NAPTIP) in 2003, and participation in regional initiatives such as the 2000 Libreville Declaration and 2001 Economic Community of West African States (ECOWAS) Interim Plan for Action, it still serves as a major supplier of women and children used for sexual exploitation in Europe, especially in Italy.[5] The American government has recognized these efforts by assigning Nigeria a Tier 1 status in its 2010 *Trafficking in Persons Report*, demonstrating that the Nigerian government is fully complying with the minimum standards of the American Trafficking Victims Protection Act (2000) in regard to protection, prevention, and prosecution.[6] The Nigerian government is also addressing the factors that predispose many women and girls to become involved in human trafficking, such as poverty, illiteracy, and gender inequality, through its commitment to the UN Millennium Development Goals (MDGS) and the Beijing Plus 10, among other national and international initiatives. Yet despite all these efforts, human trafficking, especially for sexual purposes, persists in Nigeria and is even flourishing.

Within this context, this chapter addresses characteristics that are deeply ingrained in human trafficking and the sexual exploitation of women and girls in Nigeria. The discussion that follows is based on investigations of the sex trade and human trafficking in the country, the factors that push certain Nigerians to engage in these risky ventures, the effects of such ventures on society, and strategies that can be used to combat them. For this purpose, Roseline Uyanga carried out an interview-based study in the states of Kaduna and Adamawa in northern Nigeria and Edo and Akwa

Ibom in southern Nigeria. The interviews she conducted with a hundred women involved in the sex trade and human trafficking shed important light on the relationship between sex, power, and the oppressive structures that lead to sex slavery or a dependence on prostitution.

Sex slavery, a central feature of modern-day slavery, is a global phenomenon that is facilitated by human trafficking.[7] Slavery, of course, is a situation in which one is held captive by a person or persons of superior power and is stripped of all rights and privileges, including the freedom to make decisions. Modern slavery is often equated with human trafficking. Kate Manzo, however, argues that slavery and trafficking should be examined as two different kinds of exploitation. She contends that though the two are closely related, looking at them as distinct processes allows different actors and power dynamics to emerge; in turn, this allows for the development of more nuanced approaches to combating them. Thus, Manzo sees human trafficking as a facilitating factor for sex slavery.[8] Nonetheless, the two are intrinsically linked because it is the structures created by human trafficking that make the victims of sex slavery powerless and oppressed. Human trafficking establishes this vulnerability by removing people from their familiar environments, creating dependence on the traffickers and/or those who buy the victims, exposing the victims to physical and psychological violence as a form of control, and often establishing a situation of debt bondage.[9] Consequently, sex slavery and human trafficking, though not the same, are fundamentally linked.

Sex slavery chiefly involves the trafficking of girls and young women from poor and often rural regions to markets characterized by a high demand for commercial sex. The trade can occur within the same country or between different countries. In the latter case, victims are often tricked into cross-border travel by experienced traffickers masquerading as labor recruiters. Once the women have reached their assigned destination, they are handed over to their purchasers (commonly known as "madams"), who sometimes belong to the same crime syndicate as the trafficker. The trafficked women or children are then physically secluded and forced into sexual exploitation, pornography, prostitution, or sex tourism. Their earnings, if any, are taken by their owners as payment for their recruitment, travel, accommodation, and upkeep costs, with only a small allowance returned to them. All financial gains accruing from by-products, such as videos, go directly to the victims' owners. The money the women are allowed to keep is often sent to their families or spent on drugs and alcohol, which become common coping mechanisms that reinforce the women's need to sexually exploit themselves in order to afford them.[10]

Many studies examine the international dimensions of human trafficking and sex slavery, but few give voice to the women who work within this orbit. To remedy this, Uyanga interviewed women and girls working in four of Nigeria's seven geopolitical zones, focusing on brothels and hotels located in the capital cities of the selected states: Uyo (Akwa Ibom State), Yola (Adamawa State), Kaduna (Kaduna State), and Benin (Edo State). Prior to the interviews, permission was obtained from the brothel and hotel managers in each of the cities. Both participants and the hotel and brothel managers were financially motivated to participate in the study. The interview content was designed to explore the respondents' background information, factors that led them to the sex trade, and their attitudes toward the trade; the interviews were administered by Uyanga personally. Twenty-five respondents were carefully chosen in each city, resulting in a total of one hundred participants. In conducting these interviews, Uyanga obtained valuable information on patterns, trends, and attitudes concerning sex slavery, trafficking, and prostitution.

Her findings demonstrate that sex slavery in Nigeria is not a localized affair. Though Edo State is often associated with sex slavery and is, in fact, the place of origin for many internationally trafficked women and girls, sex workers in Nigeria come from all over the country and even from neighboring nations, such as Niger. Some of the women may have relocated of their own volition, hoping to find a better future elsewhere in the country; others may have been internally trafficked. It should also be noted that Nigerian women who choose to work in the sex trade often prefer to operate outside their local communities to avoid detection. The states of origin of the survey participants are as follows (in descending order): Edo (12), Akwa Ibom (9), Benue (8), Cross River (8), Delta (8), Lagos (8), Rivers (8), Bayelsa (7), Kaduna (7), Imo (6), Abia (4), Adamawa (3), Kano (3), Kwara (3), Niger (3), and Ondo (3).

The age of commercial sex workers is also not uniform, although certain trends are evident. For example, only 2 percent of the respondents were 40 and above, whereas the majority, at 41 percent, were 18–25 years of age. Some 20 percent were children as defined by Nigeria's Child's Rights Act, which designates anyone under the age of 18 as a child.[11] Yet even though the act criminalizes the trafficking and sexual exploitation of children, as of 2010 only 23 out of Nigeria's 36 states had enacted the measure, thus limiting the act's potential.[12] In sum, 20 of the respondents were between the ages of 13 and 17, 41 were 18–25, 32 were 26–32, 5 were 33–39, and 2 were 40 or older.

Of these women and girls, 79 percent indicated that they were tricked into the sex trade, whereas 21 percent said they ventured into it due to financial hardship. Through her research, Uyanga identified poverty (linked to a get-rich-quick syndrome), illiteracy, poor parenting, patronage of the sex trade by the wealthy, societal corruption, the low status of women, and ineffective law enforcement as some of the determining factors that led many into sex slavery. As this list demonstrates, the factors behind trafficking and forced prostitution are many and varied, and the choice to participate in the process is sometimes made by the victim. Unfortunately, the woman then becomes the victim of traffickers and, later, of her "owner." As Jørgen Carling points out, many women are aware that they will be prostitutes but are unaware of the appalling conditions that they will work in, conditions that result in the loss of their independence and dignity.[13] Other women are tricked into the trade—by family members, friends, or recruiters—with false promises of better life opportunities elsewhere. However, in discussing whether or not women choose to participate in human trafficking and sexual exploitation, it must be remembered that trafficking is a criminal offense and a violation of human rights.[14] Trafficked women do not choose to be abused, and thus, they deserve protection and reintegration opportunities as necessary.

The abusive conditions the women work in are reflected in the reasons given by interviewees in this study for not quitting the trade: 28 percent were afraid of the consequences of breaking the oath they took not to quit without paying off their debt, 25 percent believed that their madams would not let them go easily, 20 percent were able to solve their family problems through participating in the sex trade, 17 percent were already stigmatized and had tested positive for HIV,[15] and 10 percent had no hope for a better job in Nigeria. Thus, alongside the violence inherent in the sex trade itself, trafficked women also face psychological and physical abuse that pressures them to remain in the sex industry.

Debt bondage is the most common coercive method used by traffickers and the madams. The debt obligation occurs once a woman (or someone acting on her behalf) pledges her future earnings to a trafficker in exchange for safe passage to a foreign destination.[16] This contract is often reinforced by religious means. Traffickers visit shrines and use juju to bind their victims to the repayment of their travel debts before they can be freed from the chains of sex slavery. Some take blood oaths; others leave pubic hairs, fingernails, underwear, hair from their heads, and similar items with juju priests or witches, whom they believe can always trace them or their families if they fail to fulfill their promises to their madams. Some also swear oaths never to expose or disobey their madams once their destination is reached. After the trafficked women arrive at the appointed destination, they are responsible to their madams, who threaten them not only with violence but also with supernatural harm.[17] Often the women's debts are skillfully manipulated by the madams, extending the period of sex slavery and further entrenching the women in an oppressive system. In addition, the pressure to provide for their families and the fear of violent reprisals against family members should their debts not be repaid are other coercive methods applied to keep women in sex slavery. This constant threat is facilitated by criminal networks in Nigeria, to which many madams have access. Thus, families in Nigeria may be threatened, beaten, or have their property destroyed if their women do not meet their obligations.[18]

It is not only traffickers and madams who profit from the vulnerability of others. Sometimes, sex slavery even occurs within one's own home. This was found to be the case for thirteen-year-old Idara John, whom Uyanga interviewed while she was lying sick in a private clinic in Uyo, Akwa Ibom State. The patient was interviewed with the permission of the medical director, who at the same time asked for assistance, financial and otherwise, for the patient. Idara's story is a common one in Nigeria. She lost her mother at the age of five and was living with her father, a fisherman, and her stepmother. In the translated version of her interview (from Ibibio to English), Idara recalled:

> Each time papa goes fishing, he spends a minimum of two weeks in the creeks where he fishes, smokes and returns to sell his ware. During his absence, my stepmother arranges and forces me to sleep with different men; else I would not eat or enter the house. She threatens that I must never disclose this to my father, or I would face a more difficult time when he returns to the creeks. I still did, but papa did not believe me. I received nothing from the men, but I must not tell anyone, except my stepmother who would treat me with a hot water bath. See, I am now pregnant even before my first menstruation, very sick and also HIV positive. I don't ever want to see them again.[19]

Idara, who had been taken to the hospital by personnel from the Akwa Ibom State Women Commission, did not pull through the pregnancy. She died in the hospital, and all efforts to see her stepmother failed, as she had absconded. As noted, Idara's story is not uncommon in Nigeria. She was enslaved, traumatized, and abused by a heartless stepmother who took advantage of her youth and innocence; the woman knew that her husband would always disregard the girl's complaints while believing her own version of events. In other words, Idara's story demonstrates the complicity of family members in sex slavery. The father's response to her pleas for help is not easily explained, however. It can be ascribed either to the low status of the girl child in Nigeria, which would have predisposed her father to disregard her voice, or perhaps to the fact that, as Kate Manzo argues, "it can be difficult to alert West African parents to the dangers of trafficking when the idea of adults harming children—especially when those adults are relatives or friends—is an alien concept."[20] Whatever caused this disassociation with the situation, it demonstrates a critical need for raising awareness of sex slavery and human trafficking in Nigeria.

In Yola in Adamawa State, Uyanga interviewed three sex workers as a group. These respondents, who chose to remain anonymous, were randomly selected from a set of eight women who practiced their trade at the Embassy Hotel. When asked why they worked in prostitution, the ultimate answer indicated it was for practical purposes. As the first respondent stated, "No be say we like am o-o, but we choose to do *ashawo* work for reasons."[21] The other two women provided more specific answers: one said it helped them look after themselves and their families, and the other said that she did not have other work alternatives.[22] Clearly, then, the lack of economic opportunities is one of the reasons why these women do not leave the commercial sex trade. They are not sex slaves, as they themselves chose to enter the trade, but it is because of their grim economic reality that they are forced to sell their bodies. Yet even though the sex trade seems to offer some financial benefits, it also puts the women at risk of contracting sexually transmitted diseases. Uyanga asked them if they knew what HIV/AIDS was and that it could kill. The first woman responded by laughing and saying, "Yes ma, but everyone go die one day now. You fit die of accident, hunger, AIDS or anything."[23] This casual attitude toward HIV/AIDS and sexual health was only reinforced by customers who were willing to pay more for sex without the use of a condom, as was made clear by the third respondent: "Ah! Some customers no dey like use condom sam sam. Those ones de pay higher sha, and we, ma, we dey take capsules."[24] The tragic consequences of such attitudes—and often a sex worker's inability to control her sexual health—are evidenced by the fact that 17 percent of the survey participants stated they had tested positive for HIV.

Psychological and emotional trauma is also associated with human trafficking and sex slavery. This unhappy reality is demonstrated by the story of twenty-seven-year-old Pat of Zaira, Kaduna State, who was tricked into a fake marriage with a young, wealthy Nigerian who then exposed her to international sex slavery. In September 1987, Pat joined her husband in Italy and was surprised to discover that he was a kingpin in the sex trade. She was then forced into prostitution, without which she would not have had a roof over her head. Having married him without the consent of her family, Pat believed that she could not complain. "What could I do?" she asked herself. She was dehumanized and raped at will. She is now back in Nigeria, devastated and too psychologically damaged to think of ever remarrying. What may be surprising about Pat's story is that she has a West African Senior School Certificate (equivalent to a US or UK high school certificate), is a trained hairdresser, and even used to own her own salon.[25] Her situation is not uncommon. Rasheed Olanyiyi points out that 55 percent of sex workers in Nigeria have a secondary school education.[26] Another survey, carried out under the auspices of the Nigerian government, puts the number as high as 70 percent.[27] Pat's story demonstrates that even education could not secure her future, as false promises of marriage and perhaps the desire for a better future in Italy exposed her to the devastating effects of human trafficking and sex slavery abroad.

However, as stated previously, not everyone is tricked into such a situation. In Benin City, Edo State, Uyanga came into contact with a thirty-two-year-old woman who chose to go to Italy to earn money through prostitution. After some time in Italy, she was found out and deported back to Nigeria. During the interview, she provided a clear narrative of her story:

> I was not forced into the sex trade; I went on my volition to Italy, because I thought I was going to make a lot of money within a short time, then return to Nigeria to start a fruitful living. I was not properly briefed by my friend Rosa, who recruited me and other young girls of my age to Italy. When we arrived in Italy, our travel documents which were with "Madam Rosa" were no longer released to us. Madam informed us that we were brought to Italy for prostitution. Having had foreknowledge of this, I was not worried, but the other girls who were tricked into coming were heart-broken.
>
> We were handed over to a syndicate of sex slavers, who tortured and even raped those that refused to cooperate. They used weapons and threatened that we would be reported to the immigration as illegal aliens in Italy. . . . I cooperated because I needed the money; but I found none. . . . I returned to Nigeria penniless. I made money for the slavers and returned sick, broken and devastated. I am now HIV-positive and so also is this my baby. My family is ashamed of me, and so does not care for me. Can I blame them? They would always say—"Oh she went to Italy and returned with nothing. Can't she see what others did for their families? Iyabo built chains of flats and bought cars for her family. Benita is sponsoring her junior ones to Italy and is virtually living there herself."[28]

In this case, the victim gave her consent to be trafficked into Italy and knew that she would be working as a prostitute. Rather than seeing Rosa as an agent of exploitation, this respondent saw her friend as a valuable service provider who could give her access to a richer country and thus better life opportunities and even wealth.[29] In addition, the illegality of the enterprise may not have been clear to her, as many human trafficking victims often cannot distinguish between legal and illegal work opportunities abroad.[30] As the story demonstrates, the respondent's trust in her "friend Rosa" was abused, and as a result, she found herself in a position of powerlessness due to physical and psychological abuse.

Another important element in this story is the respondent's relationship with her family. Though she did not provide her reasons for going to Italy directly (and most likely they were varied), her description of her relationship with her family suggests that they expected financial support from her. Such expectations are common and are based on the fact that, despite the stark realities of most trafficked women and girls, some have been able to provide support to their families through the sex trade, as exemplified by the three women working at the Embassy Hotel in Yola. A more striking example is the fact that in 2003, some 80 percent of privately owned public transportation in Benin City was reported to be owned by women and girls who had been trafficked and worked in prostitution.[31] Such examples are widely touted by recruiters to lure poor and ambitious women into sex slavery with the promise of wealth.[32] Contributing to this is the fact that poverty and inequality have forced many women to become contributors to the family income while simultaneously turning them into marketable sexual commodities on the global market.[33] These factors combine to make a temporary stint in the sex trade appear to be a lucrative option.

The need to succeed makes family ties an integral aspect of human trafficking and the sex trade, in terms of expectations and support (or lack thereof). For instance, community health workers in Benin City have reported that women are internationally trafficked with the consent of their families, even their husbands;[34] moreover, Carling argues that families are favorably disposed to women emigrating because they show more consideration than men for their families back in Nigeria.[35] This was evidenced in Uyanga's conversation with the pastor of a Pentecostal church in Benin City in 2003. The pastor related his encounter with a desperate mother who approached him for prayers over a pair of white pants that she intended to send to her daughter in Italy. The prayer request was for good luck and for increased patronage of her daughter's business. The priest told Uyanga that "when asked to name her daughter's line of business in Italy for specificity of prayer points, mama was not forthcoming as she found it hard to expose her daughter's line of business."[36] Such discretion led both Uyanga and the pastor to conclude that the daughter was active in the sex trade and that her mother supported this.

Although the encounter with the mother left the pastor praying for the girl's release from bondage, many Nigerians do not see sex trafficking as such "a terrible crime against humanity and a grievous sin in the sight of God."[37] The normalization of the sex trade in areas where it is common, such as Edo State, also encourages young women and girls to participate. In the 1980s, Nigeria established structural adjustment programs in the wake of the oil crisis. The increased inequality and poverty that ensued gradually made prostitution acceptable and even welcome as a method for dealing with financial uncertainty.[38] Consequently, girls and women from Benin City have been involved in the international sex trade for decades, and every year the successful ones recruit scores of others to follow them, perpetuating the cycle. For them, prostitution has become an acceptable trade, a situation that makes the fight against sex traffickers a difficult one in Nigeria.

However, Uyanga's interviews demonstrate that many women do not become rich through the sex trade. And a failure to provide for their families, alongside the emotional, physical, and psychological harm that human trafficking and the sex trade can cause, feeds into the sexual stigmatization of sex workers who do not strike it rich. These women are further victimized by being "sexually stereotyped as immoral, insatiable, perverse and carriers of HIV/AIDS" by both society and their relatives.[39] Grace Osakue, the director of a Nigerian nonprofit called Girls Power Initiative, reiterates this point: "They are selling a product for which there is a market. . . . It's not a stigma anymore, as long as money comes with it. If they come back with money, they are respected. If they come back poor, they are sex workers, they are failures."[40] However, these "failed" women are now finding a voice, with a mounting number of returnees warning others of the dangers of trafficking and sex slavery.[41] Their voices are supported by government initiatives, such as NAPTIP's Public Enlightenment Unit, which focuses on local and national awareness-raising efforts.[42]

But changing the public image of human trafficking and the sex trade and illuminating how the trade affects its participants will have little impact without also raising the status of the girl child and the woman in Nigeria. The birth of a boy to a Nigerian family generates much happiness; society places a heavy premium on the boy child, on whose shoulders rests the task of propagating the family lineage. His status as the future head of the family is not contestable. An example of the extreme deference required of some Nigerian women toward their husbands can be found among the Fulanis, where wives, as a mark of respect, must never call their husbands or first sons by their names. And, among the Tivs of northern Nigeria, a man will express his appreciation, love, and acceptance of a male visitor by handing over his wife (who has no choice in the matter) to the guest so that he can spend the night with her. Both examples demonstrate the inequality between men and women in parts of Nigeria, with the latter even exhibiting the commodification of women as possessions to be shared with male visitors.

Although the birth of a boy is much celebrated, the reverse is true for the birth of a girl. In fact, a girl child's birth may spell doom for a mother, particularly one who has given birth to two or three daughters previously. A girl's status in society is tied to the gains that her family can derive from her. As Uyanga has argued elsewhere, the girl child is a victim of societal degradation, which is demonstrated by the way males speak about her and also by the value the society and family place on her. She is a housekeeper, a family cook, a babysitter, and an instrument for improving her family's income through marriage.[43] Should there be a choice between a boy or girl child pursuing an education, the burden of illiteracy will always fall on the shoulders of the girl. She is the one to go hawking, engage in petty trading, or serve as domestic help in order to generate income for her family and education for the boys. The girl child has grown to accept this role, a situation that greatly influences her psyche and fosters her zeal to constantly seek ways of improving her family's economic status. Indeed, her perceived value in society is a causal factor in her involvement in human trafficking and sex slavery or prostitution. As Ursula Biemann writes, "The automatic channeling of . . . women into sex work is an index of their status under national rule but it also speaks of the place of sex in that national space where law protects the flourishing sexual life of male citizens as a privilege and a source of power."[44] This guarding of male prestige is reflected in the Nigerian government's failure to domesticate the UN Convention on the Elimination of All Forms of Discrimination against Women (CEDAW, ratified by Nigeria in 1985) and the Protocol to the African Charter on Human and Peoples' Rights on the Rights of Women in Africa (signed by Nigeria in 2003). Though the government adopted a gender policy in 2007 and has established development centers for women in the country's thirty-six states, among other initiatives, it has failed to enact appropriate legislation that encompasses all aspects of these instruments of international and regional law.[45] As one Nigerian government representative stated at the forty-first session of the Committee on the Elimination of All Forms of Discrimination against Women in 2008, "The CEDAW domestication bill was presented in 2007 but was not passed by Parliament owing to a lack of advocacy."[46] At the time this book went to press, in June 2014, the bill had still not passed.

However, the Nigerian government has been much more active in domesticating and enacting the 2000 Palermo Protocol. The protocol defines human trafficking in terms of movement (in regard to recruitment, transportation, transfer, harboring, and receipt) and coercion (through threats, force, fraud, and so forth) for the purposes of exploitation (forced labor, sexual and otherwise); it focuses on combating trafficking through prevention, protection of the victims, and prosecution of its perpetrators.[47] In 2003, the Nigerian government domesticated this protocol by passing the Trafficking in Persons (Prohibition) Law Enforcement and Administration Act, which gave birth to the National Agency for the Prohibition of Traffic in Persons. NAPTIP actively pursues the prevention, protection, and prosecution strategies outlined in the Palermo Protocol. In terms of prevention, NAPTIP's Public Enlightenment Unit raises awareness of human trafficking in innovative ways. In 2009, for instance, it convened a model UN conference for secondary school students with the theme of combating human trafficking. It also held its first annual race against human trafficking in Edo State that same year.[48] NAPTIP is improving its human rights approach to victim protection as well. Among other things, it set up the Victim's Trust Fund in 2009 to assist victims seeking judicial redress against traffickers by channeling the confiscated assets of traffickers to the victims. The government also took a stronger stance toward prosecution by raising the jail term for sex traffickers to ten years in 2005.[49] Finally, in 2009, the Nigerian government identified and provided assistance to 1,109 victims and conducted 149 investigations into trafficking cases, which resulted in 26 prosecutions and 25 convictions.[50]

Though NAPTIP embodies the Nigerian government's efforts to domesticate the Palermo Protocol, it also demonstrates how problematic it is to adapt international law to a national context. This issue was discussed at NAPTIP's International Conference on Human Trafficking in 2010. At this conference, Aondoaver Ayuhwa Kuttuh, assistant director of NAPTIP's Investigation and Monitoring Department, pointed out that NAPTIP cannot prosecute offenses that, though integral to human trafficking in the Nigerian context, are not covered by the agency's act; one example would be the oath of debt bondage. He also stated that the discrepancy between the legal definition of trafficking and what the public understands exploitation to be creates difficulties for the prosecution of the crime. Sola Ehindero, regarded as one of Nigeria's leading experts on human trafficking, agreed, emphasizing that the role of the media and politics in sensationalizing, misrepresenting, and oversimplifying issues of human trafficking is a great challenge for the fight against this crime.[51] For instance, human trafficking by definition encompasses all kinds of forced labor, yet such distinctions are often not acknowledged, especially because in Nigeria human trafficking is commonly conflated with prostitution.[52] This misunderstanding of the legal definition of human trafficking has led to the feminization of trafficking (since sex trafficking victims are predominantly female) and the neglect of trafficking cases where the victim is male or cases that are not linked to the sex trade.

In addition to the laws and initiatives enacted by the government, a number of nongovernmental organizations (NGOs) are fighting this scandalous trade. One is the Women Trafficking and Child Labour Eradication Foundation (WOTCLEF), an NGO that is headquartered in Abuja and led by Titi Abubakar Atiku, the wife of Nigeria's former vice president. This organization is dedicated to the eradication of trafficking in persons, child labor, and the abuse of women's rights through advocacy, international cooperation, educational initiatives, and victims' assistance programs. WOTCLEF's dedication to women's and children's rights even extends beyond the borders of Nigeria—it now also has an office in Florida, as the United States is a major destination for many trafficking victims.

Despite the fact that the Nigerian government and its people are making explicit efforts to combat human trafficking and sex slavery, those involved in the trade are rarely apprehended and successfully prosecuted, as the scant twenty-five human trafficking convictions of 2009 prove. Traffickers are continuing to perfect their trade by taking advantage of Nigeria's weak and compromising law enforcement strategies, its corrupt immigration authorities, and its long and porous borders. And as the previous examples have proven, this situation is only worsened by women's low status in society, their lack of economic empowerment, the misperceptions and allure surrounding human trafficking and sex slavery, and the abuse of power by family members and recruiters. As a result, the fight is a slow and seemingly unsuccessful one at this point. Yet major advances were made since the early 2000s in regard to sex slavery and human trafficking, and Nigeria can and must continue to find sustainable strategies to combat this evil.

Increased international and regional cooperation, a balanced approach to human trafficking and sex slavery that considers both the victims and the perpetrators, a more nuanced definition of the crime, and the design of appropriate legal measures to deal with it would comprise a good start, and, indeed, the Nigerian government has already committed itself to these efforts. However, these are reactive measures that do not address the source of human trafficking and sex slavery, which is female vulnerability in Nigeria. Thus, there is no tool more powerful than the empowerment of women for the combating of human trafficking and sex slavery. This chapter posits that there ought to be workable economic empowerment and development strategies for women in Africa and Nigeria in particular, which should include the empowerment of women through education and mass enlightenment about the realities of prostitution, HIV/AIDS, different kinds of abuse, and women's political rights. This approach can be broken down into three components: economic, social, and political empowerment.

Economic empowerment involves job creation and the provision of gainful employment to young females after leaving school. Yet even though the education of girls is expanding, women are deliberately kept within low-paying sectors of the economy. They therefore find employment in low-paid positions as, for instance, teachers, nurses, typists, customer service representatives, and telephone operators.[53] Female employment in the government shows that there are limited opportunities for women generally, even for those who are educated. Not only should women be gainfully employed, they should also be given access to credit facilities to enable them to engage in lucrative businesses and allow them financial independence. Traditional barriers and laws that prevent women from owning and/or inheriting land should be abrogated so that they can own collateral securities for credit purposes. As the World Bank has rightly pointed out, "The uncertainty of women's legal and financial status is a factor that is consistently reducing their potential credit worthiness."[54] Surely, better employment prospects and income-generating opportunities for young Nigerian women within their own country would dissuade them from venturing into bleak and risky business opportunities, such as prostitution, both in Nigeria and abroad.

Social empowerment involves providing women with greater access to education, health care, and basic services such as water, light, and sanitation, among others, so that they can make the most of their potential. It should also include campaigns, in both urban and rural areas, that raise awareness of the dangerous realities of the sex trade and human trafficking. These campaigns should target children, women, and men in order to serve both as a mechanism of prevention and as a weapon against stigmatization. In this regard, national orientation agencies and NGOs, churches, mosques, and other community organizations should be encouraged to serve as grassroots social and education engineers. Also, the establishment of a "parent antitrafficking league" would be useful in combating trafficking and sex slavery, as its efforts could minimize the enticement of risky work abroad.

Related to the education of women is political empowerment. This involves placing women in positions of authority to implement government decisions, especially those pertaining to women. It is one thing to promulgate a law, another to enforce it. The use of women as ministers of women's affairs, as judges, and in other positions to enforce laws against the trafficking of girls and women and sex slavery would go a long way in ameliorating the situation, as women provide different insights into the problem and have different ways of interacting with victims compared to men. In 2005, the Nigerian government took important steps toward this end by establishing desk officers on gender issues in police stations, while also training police officers in law enforcement and human rights as well as in gender issues and access to justice.[55] However, it is not only in the government and civil service that women must find a voice and take action. They must also become more visible within their communities and in civil society in order to advocate on issues that concern them. Atiku's establishment of WOTCLEF is but one example, and it ought to be replicated.

Human trafficking and sex slavery has many faces, is experienced in myriad ways, and is legally and socially complex. The increased commodification of women's bodies and the ability for these bodies to be sold in a global market, coupled with the high numbers of women who live in poverty and inequality, who lack socioeconomic advancement, and who dream of a better future, will continue to facilitate this crime. To combat this, governments must work with individuals, communities, NGOs, businesses, state officials, and other countries to heighten awareness and to build the capacity of communities at the local, national, and international levels to fight this crime and empower the people most vulnerable to it.

Notes

1. Patience Elabor-Idemudia, "Migration, Trafficking and the African Woman," *Agenda*, no. 58 (2003): 104.

2. David Eltis, "A Brief Overview of the Trans-Atlantic Slave Trade," Emory University, http://www.slavevoyages.org/tast/index.faces.

3. Jørgen Carling calls these push, pull, and facilitating factors. See Carling, *Corruption and Human Trafficking: The Nigerian Case* (IOM—International Organization for Migration, 2006), 7. Also see Ann D. Jordan, "Human Rights or Wrongs? The Struggle for a Rights-Based Response to Trafficking in Human Beings," *Gender and Development* 10, no. 1 (2002): 28.

4. The Palermo Protocol is a UN initiative that addresses human trafficking. It was signed in Palermo, Italy, in 2000. Formally, it is known as the Protocol to Prevent, Suppress and Punish Trafficking in Persons, Especially Women and Children, supplementing the UN Convention against Transnational Organized Crime. Nigeria was one of the first countries of sub-Saharan Africa to sign and then ratify the protocol (in 2000 and 2001, respectively), demonstrating its commitment to combating human trafficking. In 2003, the government

domesticated the protocol into national law, through the Trafficking in Persons (Prohibition) Law Enforcement and Administration Act.

5. Other major European destinations include Belgium, the Czech Republic, France, the Netherlands, Spain, and Sweden. It is important to note that human trafficking in Nigeria can and does lead to kinds of coerced labor other than sexual exploitation. For example, women and young girls are also trafficked from West, East, and Central Africa to Europe and the Middle East for agricultural and domestic labor purposes. See Elabor-Idemudia, "Migration, Trafficking and the African Woman," 106; Bisi Olateru-Olagbegi and Anne Ikpeme, "Review of Legislation and Policies in Nigeria on Human Trafficking and Forced Labour: Action Programme against Trafficking and Forced Labour in West Africa" (*International Labour Organization, Special Programme to Combat Forced Labour Working Paper* [2006], accessed December 14, 2011, http://www.ilo.org/wcmsp5/groups/public/---ed_norm/---declaration/documents/publication/wcms_083149.pdf 46.

6. From 2001 to 2003 and 2005 to 2008, Nigeria had a Tier 2 ranking, in 2004 Tier 3, and from 2009 onward Tier 1 These rankings are significant because countries with low rankings may face sanctions from the US government. That said, some see this ranking system as problematic, since it can be construed as the American government imposing its standards and values on other nations in an inappropriate way. See Office to Monitor and Combat Trafficking in Persons, *Trafficking in Persons Report*, 10th ed. (US State Department, June 2010), 48, 256–57 accessed December 12, 2011, http://www.state.gov/j/tip/rls/tiprpt/2010/index.htm.

7. Kate Manzo, "Exploiting West Africa's Children: Trafficking, Slavery and Uneven Development," *Area* 37, no. 4 (2005): 393–401.

8. Ibid.

9. Human trafficking and human smuggling should not be confused. Human trafficking is characterized by elements of coercion and forced labor, whereas human smuggling involves a contractual agreement between the smuggler and the customer that terminates upon arrival at the destination. This distinction has important legal ramifications in many countries because smuggling is considered a crime for all parties involved, whereas in cases of human trafficking, a distinction is made between traffickers as criminals and the trafficked as victims.

10. Jeffrey Cole, "Reducing the Damage: Dilemmas of Anti-trafficking Efforts among Nigerian Prostitutes in Palermo," *Anthropologica* 48, no. 2 (2006): 220.

11. The Child's Rights Act specifically states that "buying, selling, hiring or otherwise dealing in children for the purpose of begging, hawking, prostitution or for unlawful immoral purposes are made punishable by long terms of imprisonment. Other offenses considered grave include sexual abuse, general exploitation which is prejudicial to the welfare of the child . . . and the

importation/exposure of children to harmful publications." See UNICEF, "Information Sheet: The Child's Rights Act" (2007), 2.

12. Office to Monitor and Combat Trafficking in Persons, *Trafficking in Persons Report*, 256.

13. Carling, "Corruption and Human Trafficking," 30.

14. Ibid.

15. This number could be higher, as not all the women were aware of their current HIV status.

16. Cole, "Reducing the Damage," 221.

17. Ibid., 220.

18. Ibid., 221.

19. Idara John, interview by Roseline Uyanga, Dammy Clinic, Uyo, Nigeria, 2001.

20. Manzo, "Exploiting West Africa's Children," 398.

21. I.e., "We do not like to work as prostitutes but we choose to do prostitution for certain reasons." Three commercial sex workers interviewed by Roseline Uyanga, Embassy Hotel, Yola, Nigeria, 2001.

22. Respondent II: "Ide help us look after ourselves and our families. Me, as I dey so, I get pikin wey de wid my mama for village, I dey feed am." Respondent III: "Doctor, make government give us another work now. . . . If I get another work me-o, I go leave *ashawo* work." Ibid.

23. Ibid.

24. I.e., "Ah! Some customers do not like to use condoms at all. However, such customers usually pay higher for services rendered; also we usually place ourselves on pills." Ibid.

25. Patricia, interview by Roseline Uyanga, Kaduna, Nigeria, 2001.

26. Rasheed Olaniyi, "No Way Out: The Trafficking of Women in Nigeria," *Agenda*, no. 55 (2003): 47.

27. Anthony Hodges, *Children's and Women's Rights in Nigeria: A Wake-Up Call, Situation Assessment and Analysis 2001* (Lagos: National Planning Commission and UNICEF, 2001), 210–12.

28. Personal discussion with a returnee from Italy, held by Roseline Uyanga, Benin, Nigeria, November 23, 2000.

29. Ursula Biemann, "Remotely Sensed: A Topography of the Global Sex Trade," *Feminist Review*, no. 80 (2005): 193.

30. Olaniyi, "No Way Out," 48.

31. Elabor-Idemudia, "Migration, Trafficking and the African Woman," 106.

32. Cole, "Reducing the Damage," 221.

33. Elabor-Idemudia, "Migration, Trafficking and the African Woman," 103–4.

34. S. Sengupta, "Sex Trade in Nigeria," *New York Times*, November 5, 2006.

35. Carling, "Corruption and Human Trafficking," 24.

36. Pentecostal pastor's report, in discussion with Roseline Uyanga, Benin City, Nigeria, November 5, 2003.

37. The priest said that once he realized what kind of business the daughter was in, he "began to pray for God's intervention concerning her release from whatever bondage she had found herself, and for God's forgiveness of the sins of mankind. The body is the temple of God, and must not be defiled. Sex trafficking is a terrible crime against humanity and a grievous sin in the sight of God." Ibid.

38. Cole, "Reducing the Damage," 222.

39. Olaniyi, "No Way Out," 50.

40. As quoted in Sengupta, "Sex Trade in Nigeria."

41. Osita Agbu, "Corruption and Human Trafficking: The Nigerian Case," *West Africa Review* 4, no. 1 (2003): 51.

42. Office to Monitor and Combat Trafficking in Persons, *Trafficking in Persons Report*, 257.

43. Roseline Uyanga, "Gender Stereotyping, Biased Language Use and Female Education in North Eastern Nigeria," *International Journal of Scholarly and Scientific Research*, no. 1 (Fall 2004): 146.

44. Biemann, "Remotely Sensed," 190.

45. Omoyemen Odigie-Emmanuel, "Assessing Women's Rights in Nigeria," *Pambazuka News*, November 24, 2010, accessed December 12, 2011, http://pambazuka.org/en/category/features/69028

46. Committee on the Elimination of Discrimination against Women, "Summary Record of the 836th Meeting–Sixth Periodic Report of Nigeria" (August 6, 2008), accessed December 12, 2011, http://www.iwraw-ap.org / resources/pdf/41_official_documents/nigeriaSR836.pdf, 3.

47. UN Protocol to Prevent, Suppress and Punish Trafficking in Persons, Especially Women and Children, Supplementing the United Nations Convention against Transnational Organized Crime, 2000. Vidyamali Samarasinghe and Barbara Burton, "Strategising Prevention: A Critical Review of Local Initiatives to Prevent Female Sex Trafficking," *Development in Practice* 17, no. 1 (2007): 53.

48. Office to Monitor and Combat Trafficking in Persons, *Trafficking in Persons Report*, 257.

49. Ibid.

50. Ibid., 256.

51. National Agency for Prohibition of Traffic in Persons and Other Related Matters (NAPTIP), "Report of the 3 Day International Conference on Human Trafficking," paper presented at the Providing an African Initiative to the Global War against Human Trafficking Conference, Abuja, Nigeria, November 30–December 2, 2010, 6, 16.

52. Olateru-Olagbegi and Ikpeme, "Review of Legislation and Policies in Nigeria," 7.

53. National Planning Commission, "Children's and Women's Rights," 212.

54. World Bank, *A Continent in Transition: Sub-Saharan Africa in the Mid 1990s* (Washington, D.C.: World Bank, 1995), 212.

55. Committee on the Elimination of Discrimination against Women, "Summary Record of the 836th Meeting," 4.

16

THE REALITIES AND RISE OF FEMALE SEX TRAFFICKING IN THAILAND AND CAMBODIA, 1960–PRESENT

Francesca Ann Louise Mitchell

It is a popular assumption in many societies around the world that slavery ended during the nineteenth century. However, in reality, huge numbers of people across the globe live in conditions of modern slavery, as victims of human trafficking. Human trafficking has been illegal under international law since 1933, but the latter half of the twentieth century and the early years of the present century have nonetheless witnessed a significant rise in the trafficking of women and girls for sexual exploitation, hereafter referred to as "female sex trafficking." This process can be defined as the recruitment, transportation, transfer, or receipt of women or girls for purposes of sexual exploitation, primarily but not necessarily limited to prostitution. The UN Palermo Protocol on human trafficking states that trafficking in people can be constituted as "the recruitment, transportation, transfer, harbouring or receipt of persons, by means of threat or use of force or other forms of coercion, of abduction, of fraud, of deception, of the abuse of power or of a position of vulnerability or of the giving or receiving of payments of benefits to achieve the consent of a person having control over another person for the purposes of exploitation. 'Exploitation' shall include . . . the exploitation of the prostitution of others or other forms of sexual exploitation, forced labour or services, [or] slavery."[1]

In this chapter, I will maintain that female sex trafficking is a form of modern slavery because it incorporates the denial of free will, including the right to leave; it deprives its victims of civil rights; and it often involves the use of physical restraint, captivity, violence, or coercion. In this context, the violence and coercion encompass personal, physical violence; psychological or financial coercion; and the wider phenomenon of "social violence," such as poverty.

Current estimates indicate that between two hundred thousand and three hundred thousand women are trafficked into Thailand annually for sexual exploitation.[2] Yet the number of females who have fallen victim to sex trafficking is almost impossible to calculate, partly due to the underground and illegal nature of the trafficking trade but also due to historiographical issues of definition; not all sex workers can be considered trafficking victims because many actively choose to enter the sex trade, often out of familial obligation or poverty. Moreover, a discussion of the tourist industry alone is insufficient in a study of the rise of sex trafficking, since many females working in this sector of the industry have chosen to undertake sex work and hence cannot be defined as trafficking victims. However, this by no means applies to all sex workers: widespread reports suggest that many prostitutes working in the tourism industry are indeed trafficked or coerced into this type of work. Nonetheless, it should be acknowledged that sex trafficking is far more prevalent in the (much larger) "domestic" sex industry that caters to local men, and given its severely limited earning potential, girls are much less likely to participate in this trade of their own free will. This distinction between "slave" and "free" in the sex industry is further complicated by the question of when a sex worker becomes enslaved. This may occur at the point of acquisition by a trafficker, or it might occur later—that is, a girl may choose freely to enter the trade but later find herself personally or financially coerced into remaining there. In this way, a girl's status as a so-called sex slave can be acquired at varying points in her "career," which makes it all the more difficult to both define and accurately estimate how many sex slaves or trafficked sex workers operate in Thailand and Cambodia. For the purpose of this essay, only those women or girls who can be defined as trafficked—as opposed to all prostitutes in the region or those who have later become sex slaves—will be discussed.

As a study of the rise of female sex trafficking in Thailand and Cambodia from the latter half of the twentieth century, this essay will examine the conditions, realities, and contexts of the sex slave trade, on the one hand, and the reasons for the rise of trafficking for sexual exploitation in this particular locale and era, on the other. The principal factors to be discussed are the increase in demand for female prostitutes with the greater foreign military presence in the region in the 1960s, 1970s, and 1990s, and the influx of migrant workers from the 1970s; the growth of the tourism—and, simultaneously, sex tourism—industry in both countries but especially Thailand; the impact of economic developments such as globalization on the populations that supply the industry; and the role of official complicity and corruption. What will become apparent is that at the heart of all these factors lies a possibility for profit for those actively or complicitly involved, ultimately resulting in large-scale socioeconomic systems built on this trade in and exploitation of human beings.

The Practicalities of Sex Trafficking in Thailand and Cambodia

Sex trafficking became big business in the Greater Mekong Subregion in the latter half of the twentieth century, and various trafficking routes continue to exist throughout Thailand and Cambodia. Despite having been a labor-exporting country in the 1970s, Thailand has been importing labor since the 1990s due to its economic growth,[3] and the country has become a common destination for trafficking victims. Females are trafficked to the urban centers, such as Bangkok, Chiang Mai, and Pattaya, from both inside and outside of the Thai borders. Internal sex trafficking largely affects poor females from rural areas, such as the hill tribe peoples in the north of the country. In addition, girls from Cambodia, Burma (Myanmar), Laos, China, and Vietnam are frequently trafficked into Thailand, and Siddharth Kara even reports that prostitutes from as far away as Nigeria are working in Bangkok,[4] suggesting the magnitude of Thailand's position as an importer of trafficked sexual labor. However,

Thailand is not merely a country of destination for trafficked sex workers: it also frequently serves as a transit point for women trafficked from China, Cambodia, or Laos to Malaysia.[5] Meanwhile, Thai females are also trafficked out of the country to Japan, Malaysia, Hong Kong, Europe, the United States, and Australia for exploitation both in the sex industry and as mail-order brides.

In Cambodia, there are far fewer notable instances of the country serving as a point of transit for trafficking victims, although some Vietnamese females are taken to Cambodia while en route to other destinations.[6] Internal trafficking is common in Cambodia, with girls from impoverished rural areas frequently destined for the urbanized and tourist areas of Phnom Penh, Siem Reap, and Battambang. Others are trafficked from nearby countries for exploitation in Cambodia's sex industry, notably from Thailand, China, Malaysia, and Vietnam. Trafficking from Thailand is most prevalent in border towns such as Poipet,[7] and trafficking from Vietnam is especially common, with one red-light area of Phnom Penh, Sway Pak, often called Little Saigon.[8] However, Cambodia is also an exporter of sex workers, who are trafficked into Thailand and Malaysia for prostitution and into Taiwan for "false marriages,"[9] whereby girls are transported on promises of marriage, only to be forced into sexual exploitation. It is clear that the web of trafficking routes across the region and beyond is very complex, sometimes coordinated across great distances. The obvious willingness of the traffickers or brothel owners to transport sex workers suggests a great deal of potential profit; otherwise, it is highly unlikely that they would stand to bear the effort, risk, and expense of trafficking them so far.

There is a common assumption, due to the comparatively large body of work on the subject, that the chief destination for females trafficked into the sex industry is the highly visible foreign tourist market. However, there are actually far greater numbers of trafficked sex workers in the domestic sex markets of both countries,[10] as suggested earlier. Most local men cannot afford to pay the high prices demanded in the foreign sex tourism industry, and so the services of women and girls prostituted in the local brothels are sold at much lower prices than in the more conspicuous tourist areas. Consequently, a large number of trafficking victims live and work in the lower-end institutions, where the brothel owner may only demand a low price from the customers and hence keep a larger profit. For example, although a foreign tourist might pay US$300 for sex with a virgin, the standard charge for a prostitute for a local man was only $1 in 2003.[11]

The Supply: The Realities of Life for a Trafficked Sex Worker and Conditions of Modern-Day Slavery

The victims of sex trafficking in Thailand and Cambodia are, as intimated earlier, sometimes difficult to identify. Yet the basic profile of a trafficked sex worker is fairly distinctive. She will generally be young: most girls in the industry begin sex work between the ages of ten and sixteen.[12] There is evidence of girls as young as six being trafficked into the industry,[13] and older girls and women may also be involved, especially if deemed physically attractive. The girls tend to have a similar economic background, usually coming either from rural areas that have grown increasingly impoverished with the advent of economic liberalization or from marginalized or disadvantaged communities such as Thailand's northern hill tribes. These areas have been economically neglected, leaving individuals and families with few other income options, as will be discussed later in this chapter. The stream of females trafficked for sexual exploitation from the hill tribes reached such a peak in the 1990s that the Thai government felt obliged to intervene and take special preventative measures, such as implementing education schemes, in order to stem the flow.[14]

In addition, refugee populations have been prone to targeting by traffickers. In Cambodia, there was a large influx of 350,000 returning refugees in the 1990s,[15] after the 1991 peace resolution that ended almost three decades of conflict in the country. These returnees became especially marginalized and disadvantaged because of the lack of viable agricultural land available to them, due to prior ownership, and wartime environmental damage such as land mines. This situation presented few options for making a living, thus rendering the refugees more vulnerable to deception and trafficking as they looked for alternative forms of income. In Thailand, members of the Karen refugee population from neighboring Burma, who began fleeing the Than Shwe regime in 1989, were frequently trafficked from refugee camps.[16] The camps are situated only eight hours from Chiang Mai and twelve hours from Bangkok, providing a perfect hunting ground for potential trafficking procurers.[17] As refugees, the Karen are unable to work legally in Thailand, but their dislocation and disenfranchisement make then highly susceptible to false job offers from traffickers.

False job offers are merely one of the many means used by sex traffickers to target vulnerable women and girls. In such cases of deception, girls and often their families are led to believe that they will be undertaking legitimate wage labor in a city—for example, in a factory or hotel—that will help them to provide financially for their families. (In Thai society in particular, it was traditionally the role of the unmarried daughter to provide for her parents, largely due to the matrilineal inheritance system and the desire for sons to enter monasteries.)[18] Other victims may be aware that they will be required to carry out sex work but unaware of the exact status or conditions under which they will be forced to live and work.[19]

In many cases, victims are sold by family members, for example by parents or aunts, either out of the desperation of acute poverty or, increasingly since the 1990s, out of a desire to escape a condition of "relative deprivation."[20] This process sometimes constitutes a direct sale to the brothels, but more commonly, trafficked sex workers will be sold to a procurer and rarely paid for outright. The worker's family is usually given an advance on the girl's earnings, and thus the exchange is not universally considered a straightforward sale. Traffickers have also adapted the agricultural practice of "green harvesting," whereby a farmer pledged unharvested rice crops in return for a loan. In the late twentieth century, as trafficking became more sophisticated, this system was increasingly applied to girls: an agent placed a deposit on a girl as she hit puberty and, in return, the girl was pledged to the sex industry.[21] In addition, other girls are sold by their boyfriends, and still others are raped by procurers in order to prevent their being able to marry in societies that value female chastity, severely limiting their options in life. In some, albeit rarer, instances, the girl might even be kidnapped.

In certain scenarios, the trafficker may be a freestanding individual agent. He or she may be a relative or another person closely connected to the victim, who sells her directly to a brothel. However, in many cases, it appears that the initial procurer is just one in a much larger network of sex traffickers. Many trafficking victims who have been interviewed for academic studies report having been sold multiple times between agents before being sold to the brothels in which they currently work.[22] One particular interviewee stated that in her experience, trafficking networks are indeed large and complex and that "the big fish are in Thailand."[23] Although concrete information on these networks is scarce due to the illegal and furtive nature of their operation, it has been noted that they are fairly sophisticated, often adapting drug-smuggling routes in the region for human trafficking,[24] and that they have the ability to procure false immigration documentation. Using fake documents actually facilitates sex trafficking, in that traffickers can ensure their victims will not report them to authorities either by giving them invalid documents or by otherwise withholding or failing to procure documents for them at all. If a victim reports her trafficker, she will be exposed as an illegal immigrant and face potential deportation or arrest.

Victims of trafficking are often subjected to living and working conditions that are tantamount to slavery. Living quarters may be cramped and dirty, and workers are often required to sleep with multiple men per day. Drug use is common, with many prostitutes often being fed methamphetamine, among other drugs.[25] The rate of HIV infection in some areas is high: in 1997, an estimated 40 percent of Cambodian prostitutes were thought to have HIV.[26]

Naturally, there are large variations between individual cases, but several trends are common to the experiences of many trafficked sex workers. First, upon initially arriving in a brothel, many girls are forced to undergo a process of conditioning to overcome their unwillingness to perform sex work. Some will be raped into submission; others may be locked inside the brothel and denied food until they become compliant. Such a process is sometimes referred to as "social death,"[27] in that, as Julia O'Connell Davidson argues, the victim loses power over her own life and becomes unable to make reciprocal demands on her clients. She will lose her natality in her objectification, and she may lose her sense of honor in being degraded to the status of a whore.[28] O'Connell Davidson's thesis may not be relevant to all prostitutes, as was her original intention,[29] but the application of the concept of social death in this sense does seem significant as regards the conditioning of a trafficked sex worker. Furthermore, this process of social death may leave the victim with very few emotional relationships—typically only with the sex workers with whom she lives and with the brothel owner or madam. This is especially the case among younger trafficking victims: many madams are called *mama-sans*, or "respected mothers." Such emotional and psychological bonds may well pressure an otherwise "socially dead" victim to remain in a condition of slavery.

Another fundamental aspect of life for modern trafficked sex workers is debt bondage. Many girls are effectively sold by their families, who are given an advance on their earnings, a debt which the girls must then repay at the brothels. In addition, they will usually be forced to repay the cost of their purchase and travel expenses, and they will owe a monthly fee for their accommodation, food, clothing, and any medical bills they may incur. Kara gives the example of a trafficking victim named Panadda, who was held against her will under debt bondage. She was told that in addition to the debt of 35,000 baht (US$875) for the cost of purchasing her, upon which she was charged a variable monthly interest, she owed a debt of 500 baht ($16) to her parents each month. She was then charged a monthly room-and-board rate of 10,000 baht ($250). To pay for that room and board, she would have to have sex with fifty men every month, before even beginning to repay her debt.[30]

Moreover, since many trafficked sex workers are never given access to their earnings, they become dependent on the brothel owner for food, shelter, clothing, and medication, making leaving the trade virtually impossible. In combination with the aforementioned bonds that many victims share with their mama-sans, this arrangement provides a strong incentive for girls to remain in the brothels. To do otherwise would be to risk destitution and falling into the same cycles of vulnerability that led them to be trafficked in the first place. (In some cases when girls have left their brothels, the problems they confronted have led to their retrafficking.) Since many girls are trafficked over large distances, they face inherent difficulties in attempting to return home, and if they are from conservative communities, they may face severe social stigma if they succeed in going back. The sense of shame coupled with the effects of the "social death" keep some girls from trying to escape their conditions. It should be noted, though, that not all trafficking victims will face such stigma should they return to their homes, as some communities increasingly view sex work as a legitimate profession. This has been especially true in Thailand since the 1990s.[31]

The Demand: Clientele, Profitability, and the Rise of Sex Trafficking

Of course, none of the preceding concerns would exist without a significant and profitable demand side of the sex trafficking equation. Such demand stems, in part, from foreigners such as tourists as well as military personnel in the 1960s in Thailand and the 1990s in Cambodia. But to a large extent, the demand comes from local men and migrant workers who are increasingly able to afford prostitutes. In order to keep the price of these sex workers' services low enough for most clients to afford them, the cost of the worker to the brothel owner likewise must remain low. Therefore, the procurement of workers through trafficking is perceived as necessary. Indeed, in Thailand, as Louise Brown has shown, trafficked females from neighboring countries are often preferred by brothel owners to Thai girls, many of whom are now able to navigate the sex market more independently and have hence become "too assertive."[32]

In addition, in both countries—although most notably in Cambodia—there has been an increase in pedophilia among both tourists and local men,[33] leading to a burgeoning demand for child prostitutes. The onset of the AIDS crisis in 1989 aggravated this trend, as it brought about the rise of the "cult of virgin sex,"[34] whereby men preferred to have sex, especially unprotected sex, with young virgins. This was due to either a belief that they were less likely to contract HIV if having intercourse with a virgin or—primarily among local men—a belief that having sex with a virgin could actually cure HIV/AIDS. The increase in the demand for children for sexual exploitation may reflect a wider reality, in that virtually all children in the sex industry have been trafficked because they are too young to make a conscious decision to enter this line of work. Thus, it is possible to see the way in which a growth in the demand for prostitutes and sex workers, whether children or adults, inevitably requires a greater and ready supply.

Therefore, in examining the rise of sex trafficking in the region from the latter half of the twentieth century, it is necessary to investigate the increase in demand and the principal reasons behind it. The most commonly touted reason for the greater demand is the presence of foreign military troops. During the Vietnam War, with the deployment of US servicemen to Southeast Asia, a much more institutionalized form of military prostitution arose, most prominently in Thailand. US troops went to Thailand in 1962 for Rest and Recreation (R & R), during which they frequented the ever-more-numerous go-go bars, massage parlors, nightclubs, and brothels built to cater to their demands. Indeed, Rest and Recreation was commonly referred to as "Intercourse and Intoxication."[35] A 1967 article stated that Bangkok had become the "liveliest, the loudest, and probably the most licentious city in South East Asia,"[36] a place where "new restaurants, bars, night clubs and so-called 'massage parlours' are opening every week."[37] Since US personnel were comparatively very big spenders—spending by US military personnel in Thailand exceeded $20 million by 1970[38]—there was a perceived opportunity to make a large profit by meeting this demand.

Moreover, the Thai authorities and US officials who were coordinating the soldiers' Rest and Recreation, such as Secretary of State Robert McNamara, knew that a fundamental component of R & R was the availability of female prostitutes. According to Kathleen Barry's figures, an estimated 100,000 prostitutes were "recruited" for the military in Thailand.[39] Meanwhile, the police believed there were 426,908 "special service girls" involved in military sex work in 1964.[40] It is widely acknowledged that trafficking was resorted to in order to meet the huge demand. Years later, with the end of the US military presence in the region, authorities expected the recruitment of females for prostitution in the newly established institutions would end. Yet sex trafficking in the region continued despite the withdrawal of troops, as those profiting from the trade began to seek a new market, as shall be discussed.

A similar situation was seen in Cambodia in the 1990s, where the UN Transitional Authority in Cambodia (UNTAC) mission is identified as the principle reason for the rise of sex trafficking. Cambodia had been a site of conflict since the 1960s, when many parts of the country were bombed by the United States during the Vietnam War. Then, almost one-third of the population was killed in the extreme communist experiment of Pol Pot's Khmer Rouge regime of 1975–79, which was ended by a Vietnamese invasion and occupation. The occupation lasted until the Paris Peace Accords of 1991 and the deployment of international UNTAC peacekeeping forces in 1992.

The UNTAC mission was generally considered a huge success, with great developments for human rights in Cambodia.[41] However, the presence of 23,000 UN personnel, including 17,000 soldiers,[42] increased the demand for prostitution, which was reportedly viewed by the in-country UN leadership as a necessary part of soldiering.[43] Men were only cautioned about involvement in the sex industry when using official vehicles, and additional condoms were shipped to Cambodia during the UNTAC mission. Like the US troops in Thailand in the 1960s, these military personnel were comparatively high-spending and would pay an average of US$10 per night for a prostitute, compared to the $4 paid by Cambodian men.[44] This signaled a clear boost in profit potential for brothel owners and traffickers.

Therefore, it seems clear that the arrival of UNTAC troops, which brought a greater demand for prostitution and enhanced profitability in the trade, created a space for the coercion of local women into the sex industry. According to the Cambodian Women's Development Association (CWDA), the number of prostitutes in Cambodia grew from 6,000 in 1992 to 25,000 at the height of the UNTAC mission.[45] This number reportedly fell to 17,000 with the departure of UNTAC,[46] demonstrating a significant net increase in the number of sex workers from the UNTAC mission onward. There are numerous discrepancies in statistics on the number of prostitutes in Cambodia in this period: another source estimated that by 1995, there were 56,000.[47] It would be an oversimplification to state that all of these sex workers were trafficking victims, but given such heavy fluxes in supply and demand, a level of trafficking seems an inevitable scenario. Indeed, a study by the Cambodian Women's Crisis Centre (CWCC), an NGO, found that 64.5 percent of female sex workers in Cambodia had been forced into prostitution.[48] Moreover, given that there were only 17,000 UNTAC soldiers stationed in Cambodia, it seems unlikely that such large numbers of sex workers as mentioned here were recruited or trafficked exclusively to cater to military personnel. Therefore, it is important to consider other aspects of the demand side of the sex industry in examining the rise of sex trafficking in this period.

As mentioned previously, the most conspicuous aspect of the sex industry in Thailand and Cambodia—especially in Thailand—is the foreign tourist market. Despite the illegality of prostitution in both countries, attitudes toward buying sex are fairly casual, particularly in tourist areas. Many researchers working in-country report being told by taxi drivers as a matter of course where they could go for sexual services,[49] demonstrating the presence of a thriving and highly visible industry. Tourism and, simultaneously, sex tourism in Thailand grew phenomenally in the latter half of the twentieth century. After the decline in the number of American soldiers and sailors going to Thailand from 1971 and the final departure of troops in 1975, the sex industry needed a new market to prevent a large drop in profitability. The void left by the departing troops was increasingly filled by sex tourism. Foreign tourists were now lured by advertisements for "super sexy tours,"[50] which included a vacation to Thailand with the opportunity to "buy a wife"[51] for between US$1,500 and $3,000.[52]

Moreover, according to Thai economic planning as approved by the World Bank, tourism was to become a significant source of the country's income, and indeed, by 1982, it had overtaken rice exports as Thailand's largest earner of foreign revenue.[53] However, the country was not advertised as a family destination, and until as late as 2009, two-thirds of all tourists in Thailand were unaccompanied males.[54] When the economic planning began in the 1960s and 1970s, it seemed unlikely that a region with such a tumultuous recent history would have favorable prospects for mass family or honeymoon tourism. Instead, it was thought that unaccompanied male travelers with disposable incomes would be more effectively targeted. Moreover, the R & R facilities established under the US military presence arguably represented the sort of travel experience Thailand was willing and able to offer. The World Bank's agreement on Thai development initiatives was negotiated by Robert McNamara, who had previously overseen the R & R contracts in Thailand. Thus, one might argue, as Ryan Bishop has, that it was virtually a foregone conclusion that the tourism envisaged in the World Bank plan would include sex tourism.[55] From the 1970s, consumers were targeted with advertising messages featuring young, beautiful, submissive, and cheap Thai girls who were ready and willing to cater to their desires. In addition, the 1980s saw the rise of Thai sex tours carried out by Japanese businesses as company perks, in which a large proportion of the predominantly male workforce participated. The advertising was effective, and foreign tourists arrived in their millions,[56] especially in 1987 and 1988 after the Tourism Authority of Thailand (TAT) organized the 1987 "Visit Thailand Year." In that year, for example, the number of Japanese tourists in Thailand jumped by 33.7

percent over the previous year.[57] Many of the main tourist areas of the country are now famous for highly visible sex tourism, notably including Pattaya, Chiang Mai, and Bangkok's Patpong and Taniya Alley.

A similar, albeit less dramatic trend became visible after the departure of UNTAC personnel from Cambodia in 1993. The departure meant a loss of business and alternative economic opportunities for many of those who had been involved in the sex industry. As in Thailand, although on a much smaller scale, tourism became the first industry to flourish in Cambodia after the Paris Peace Accords of 1991.[58] For example, from 2000 to 2001, there was a 28 percent increase in tourists visiting Cambodia.[59] Sex tourism featured heavily in this: areas of Battambang, Poipet, Siem Reap, Sihanoukville, and Phnom Penh (primarily in Sway Pak and Tuol Kork) became strongly connected with the sex trade for foreign tourists. Siem Reap clearly demonstrates the nexus between tourism and sex tourism—it is a high-profile tourist destination, due to its proximity to the Angkor Wat temple complex, in which a thriving commercial sex industry has simultaneously risen with the arrival of increasing numbers of tourists.

It should also be noted that beginning in the 1990s and continuing into the twenty-first century, the Internet has been a dynamic venue for advertising sex tourism, expanding the trade's publicity on a global scale and giving a major new impetus to the sector. The Internet has encouraged client anonymity and instant online payment, facilitating links between clients and brothels. Since the late 1990s, more and more Internet sites have been devoted to the Cambodian sex industry,[60] and many of these sites were reportedly tied to Thai and Filipino sites,[61] suggesting a degree of connectivity between sexual "establishments" across borders.

The demand that fueled the growth of the sex tourism industry has inevitably required a constant and expanding supply of sex workers. Although it is evident that some females enter this comparatively high-end side of the sex industry of their own free will, it is also important to note that the industry could not be steadily supplied with sex workers without recourse to trafficking. Moreover, since tourism—and, within this, sex tourism—is so fundamental to the economies of both Thailand and Cambodia (but especially Thailand), it might well be argued that the economic plans implemented in these countries not only created space for but also contributed to the entrenchment of sex trafficking in the socioeconomic systems that underpin these nations.

However, even though the sex tourism industry continues to be the most conspicuous aspect of the sex trade, various researchers highlight that the domestic sex market is actually much larger and more significant in the rise of sex trafficking. Local men generally cannot afford to pay the high prices foreign tourists are charged for sexual services; thus they demand lower-cost sex workers. As noted earlier, these workers are more frequently trafficking victims. It can be presumed that local prostitutes have been working in the region since time immemorial: Vidyamali Samarasinghe describes what she deems to be a "popular assumption" that men must inevitably want to purchase sex, accounting for the acceptance of the sex industry in general.[62] That said, large-scale, profitable sex trafficking is a much more recent phenomenon; it can largely be dated from the implementation of the economic liberalization and development plans in Thailand and Cambodia in the 1960s and the 1990s, respectively. The advent of widespread wage labor in these reforms contributed to a growth in consumer demand because more men became able to afford the service of a prostitute and to afford it more often. This trend was exacerbated by the use of trafficked individuals, including many of those originally trafficked for R & R and UNTAC prostitution, since this meant that brothel owners could expand the market for their "product" by lowering the price of their workers' services. Furthermore, the increase in migrant labor forces in Thailand, especially during the economic boom of the 1990s, also led to a heightened demand for cheap prostitutes. It should also be noted that this applies even to manual laborers (for example, in Chiang Mai) who had themselves been trafficked.[63] The provision of trafficked sex workers for trafficked laborers arguably suggests the scale and sophistication of the human trafficking business.

Socioeconomic Changes and the Increased Availability of a Supply?

As noted previously, the mounting demand for sex workers undeniably contributed to the rise of sex trafficking. However, it is unlikely that the trafficking of females for sexual exploitation would have grown to such an extent had social and economic changes in both countries not created spaces in which women and girls were vulnerable to traffickers. Feminist writers believe that the policies of economic liberalization adopted in both countries in the late twentieth century gave a new impetus to the sex industry. Brown argues that prostitution and sexual exploitation can be seen as the rawest form of capitalism,[64] in that the perpetrators seek to profit from the vulnerability of others. Meanwhile, Samarasinghe claims that economic liberalization led to an influx of predatory entrepreneurs profiting from the sexual exploitation of trafficked females.[65] Further, she argues that market forces released by globalization resulted in a greater sense of female vulnerability, creating more spaces globally for augmenting female sex trafficking.[66]

Economic liberalization and development in Thailand began with the first five-year plan in 1961 but were pursued more vigorously from the 1970s. Until the onset of the Asian Economic Crisis in 1997, the overall aims of the plans were to transform the nation's industrial structure from an agrarian system to a combination of manufacturing for export and earning foreign currency, primarily through tourism, to sustain import orientation. The development plans succeeded in dramatically increasing the per capita gross national product (GNP): by 2009, Thailand was ranked 87th among 182 countries in the United Nations Development Programme Human Development Index (UNDP HDI).[67]

Cambodia followed similar policies of economic development from the beginning of peace in the 1990s onward, although this country arguably had much more to recover from both socially and economically. Paul Leung claims that society was devitalized to such an extent that development seemed virtually impossible,[68] and Cambodia remains one of the poorest countries in the world. The average Cambodian is poorer and less educated than his or her neighbors in surrounding countries,[69] as indicated by Cambodia's ranking in 137th place on the UNDP HDI.[70] During the decades of conflict in the country, traditional political, social, and familial relationships were broken down, and much agricultural land was destroyed or became unavailable for use due to the continued presence of land mines. This situation seriously affected the production of rice crops and thus severely impacted the lives of the largely agrarian rural population.

The effects of the economic developments are very significant in the rise of sex trafficking. In both countries, the development initiatives neglected the agricultural sector and brought about a widening gap between rich and poor in the countryside, leading to the impoverishment of rural communities. In Thailand in 1971, 79 percent of the labor force was employed in the primary sector, yet this sector accounted for only 28 percent of Thai gross domestic product (GDP),[71] and the percentage has continued to decrease ever since. Some families were directly and negatively affected by policies focused on foreign-currency earning, whereby the government provided loans to encourage rice growers to switch to multi-crop farming and to adapt to agroindustries such as food processing for export. However, some could not pay back the loans and became debt bound. Furthermore, the needs of the rural poor, as gleaned from their recent experiences and insights, were not incorporated in Thailand's development plans until, at the earliest, the eighth development plan (1997–2001). A World Bank report in 1975 showed that poverty was 500 percent higher in rural areas than urban areas in Thailand, with 89 percent of the country's poor living in rural areas.[72] Meanwhile, in Cambodia, 35.9 percent of the population was living below the poverty line in 1999.[73] The average life expectancy was only 54.4 years,[74] and infant mortality rates were the highest in Southeast Asia, with 106 fatalities for every 1,000 live births.[75]

Such rural impoverishment contributed significantly to the greater vulnerability of rural girls and women to sex trafficking. Of a sample of Thai sex workers interviewed in 2009, 82 percent stated that extreme poverty was a "prominent precondition" in their being forced into prostitution.[76] The neglect of the primary sector decreased employment opportunities in the countryside and, where there was work, it was poorly paid, pushing the younger generation to search for alternative employment in urban areas in order to financially support their elders. Indeed, a 1993 survey found that the average remittance from a commercial sex worker was 3,000 baht (US$150) per month, almost triple the average monthly wage available in agriculture in 1991.[77] As Bishop states, the inability of many families to survive purely from farming in the wake of the economic changes assured a constant and ever-expanding supply of young female migrants, who would be particularly vulnerable to trafficking agents offering them work or other "help."[78]

Trafficking victims are, according to scholars such as Samarasinghe, especially susceptible to such offers due to another facet of economic liberalization and globalization: the feminization of labor and migration that began in the late twentieth century.[79] With the advent of more wage labor, traditional women's work was seen as less profitable, and so more women began to search for alternative employment than ever before, and they looked across wider geographic areas. Globalization has created a perception that work is readily available for poorer women—for instance, in Cambodia in 2005, 20 percent of the female population aged between eighteen and twenty-five was employed in the garment industry.[80] This perception means that the number of individuals looking for legitimate wage work is often higher than the number of jobs available and that women or girls with no formally recognized skills or education have become more vulnerable to enticement or coercion into sex trafficking.

Such trends were aggravated in the Asian Economic Crisis of 1997. During this crisis, unemployment in Thailand tripled and the price of basic sustenance rose by between 50 and 80 percent,[81] leading to a sudden surge in rural poverty and mass migration to the cities by desperate individuals. Many of the unemployed and desperate women and girls who had moved to the cities were particularly vulnerable to false offers of employment and trafficking. A similar, albeit less dramatic situation was seen in Cambodia in 2005, during the garment industry crisis. After the Multi-Fibre Agreement of 2005, the Cambodian garment industry was put in direct and unsustainable competition with its Chinese counterpart, resulting in large-scale job losses in Cambodia. Within just two months, fifteen thousand predominantly female Cambodian garment workers lost their jobs, and the creation of new jobs did not come close to matching this total,[82] resulting in a large pool of at-risk women with few alternative employment options. This, in turn, increased the likelihood of sex trafficking in these areas.

Thus, difficult and changing economic conditions virtually guarantee a plentiful supply of vulnerable females for the sex trafficking business. At the same time, the dire economic conditions so prevalent in the rural areas, especially in Cambodia, ensure that the cost customers pay for trafficked prostitutes is low, which sustains the demand for sex workers. In turn, sex trafficking is deemed necessary to fulfill this demand. In this sense, there is a vicious cycle to the sex trade in Cambodia and Thailand. However, such a supply-and-demand system in the illegal trafficking of human beings would be less able to function had its development or continued existence been more effectively hindered by authorities and law enforcement.

An Unstemmed Tide: Official Complicity and Ineffectual Law Enforcement as Aids to the Rise of Sex Trafficking

One of the most prominent aspects of the rise of sex trafficking in recent decades has been the lack of effective legal or official reaction. There are instances of ineffectual responses to the issue, and corruption has been confirmed at many levels—local, regional, national, and international—demonstrating the depth and scope of the sex trafficking problem. Of course, this situation is connected with the immense profitability of the industry, whether for a complicit or corrupt individual, for organized crime networks, or for the tourist-reliant economies of both countries. Wathinee Boonchalaski and Philip Guest highlight the way in which the profits of the sex industry impact not only the owners, managers, or other employees in the sector but also those working in tourism-related industries and public officials who receive payments from the sector.[83] As an illustration, the Thai sex industry is worth an estimated US$22.5billion to US$27billion annually.[84]

In some cases, the failure of national or local authorities to successfully implement anti-trafficking laws created an atmosphere in which traffickers could practice with a degree of freedom, as the likelihood of severe punishment was not great. Conviction rates in both countries have been low: of 165 people arrested in Cambodia in relation to trafficking in 2005, only 24 were successfully prosecuted,[85] and in Thailand in the same year, there were a mere 8 convictions.[86] In Cambodia, this was partially facilitated by the lack of a comprehensive law on human trafficking. The Draft Law of 1999–2002 attempted to address this problem, but concerns were raised regarding inconsistencies with both international trafficking laws and current domestic criminal laws.[87] This effectively undermined the rule of law, and it facilitated corruption within the criminal justice system. Moreover, under Cambodian law, confiscation of the proceeds of trafficking offenses is provided for only after conviction for such offenses; no provisions are made for freezing or seizing proceeds prior to that point.[88] Given the low rate of convictions, it would appear that the industry's profitability remains unchallenged by the legislation currently in place.

In addition, enforcement efforts, such as the Cambodian government's 2003 crackdown on Vietnamese prostitution in Sway Pak, tend to be ineffective in the long term, as profitable businesses quickly resume once the government's attention turns elsewhere. In the case of Sway Pak, despite the sealing off of fifty brothels and the ordered closure of karaoke bars and discos,[89] activity in the area continued, and today, Sway Pak still has a thriving business. There is also a significant shortage of qualified and experienced judges, lawyers, and prosecutors able to work on sex trafficking cases.[90] In light of all this, it appears that public officials and other authorities have not created an atmosphere in which trafficking is actively discouraged or prohibited, which indirectly contributes to the continued existence and propagation of sex trafficking.

The corruption and direct complicity of officials in sex trafficking has furthered this message. Bribery at national borders is widespread, facilitating the trafficking of sex workers between countries. For example, at the Mae Sai crossing between Thailand and Burma, a $25 bribe per person is sufficient to secure passage.[91] It has also been observed that it is common for local pedophiles to buy their way out of trouble with the authorities,[92] so the demand for trafficked child sex workers has not decreased, despite its illegality. Moreover, there are documented cases of exposed corruption among officials of both countries. In 2000, Thailand's Pattaya police chief admitted that corruption within his ranks had posed a barrier to cleanup operations in the area, which is known to harbor international crime syndicates.[93] In Cambodia, four police officials associated with anti-trafficking work were arrested and prosecuted in 2006, and six other officials, including the former deputy director of the police's Anti-trafficking and Juvenile Protection Department, were convicted for complicity in trafficking in 2007.[94]

Officials have also been criticized on an international level. The CWCC has highlighted a form of diplomatic complicity in the continuation of the sex industry, in that embassies in Cambodia are prone to indirectly ensuring that charges against foreign nationals are dropped, asking authorities to take into account their desire to protect their citizen, and reportedly use aid as leverage.[95] Embassies are said to be anxious to avoid the bad press that the prosecution of their citizens would receive, and local authorities generally wish to maintain good diplomatic relations with the countries of those involved, especially if they are major humanitarian donors. Hence, many offenders, such as pedophiles, will be released without charge. Such actions do little to deter potential customers of trafficked women and children. As a consequence, there is no reduction in demand, and sex trafficking to meet this demand continues.

From all of the above, several key points should be underscored. First, given the conditions of trafficked sex workers in Thailand and Cambodia—including their limited agency, their lack of access to their own earnings, their social death, and the physically, psychologically, or socially violent treatment or coercion they often endure—there can be little question that these girls and women live in a form of contemporary slavery, despite the inherent difficulties of defining and identifying these females. Second, it appears that the fundamental reason behind the operations and rise of sex trafficking—and, indeed, the sex industry—is the potential for profitability in the context of an economy ruled by the laws of supply and demand. This profitability drives the involvement of organized crime networks and implicates corrupt officials. In addition, one can reasonably argue that the implementation of economic liberalization, which immediately followed the initial growth of the commercial sex industry with the foreign military presence, is fundamental to understanding the rise in sex trafficking. The profitability of the industry directly coincided with two distinct developments: the advent of widespread wage labor and growth of the tourist sector, which provided a new market demand for sex workers, and the impoverishment and mass migration of the rural population, which provided a supply of females vulnerable to trafficking. In this way, sex trafficking became deeply entrenched in the socioeconomic systems of the two countries. As a result, effectively tackling the problem will not only require an elimination of the corruption and organized crime networks that facilitate it but also a profound reorientation of local and national economies, both of which will require enormous amounts of resources.

Notes

1. Vidyamali Samarasinghe, *Female Sex Trafficking in Asia: The Resilience of Patriarchy in a Changing* World (New York: Routledge, 2008), 21.

2. Julie Debeljak and Susan Kneebone, "Combating Transnational Crime in the Greater Mekong Subregion: The Cases of Laos and Cambodia," in

Trafficking and Human Rights: European and Asian Perspectives, ed. Leslie Holmes (Cheltenham, UK: Edwin Elgar Publishing, 2010), 137.

3. Ibid., 134.

4. Siddharth Kara, *Sex Trafficking: Inside the Business of Modern Slavery* (New York: Columbia University Press, 2009), 156.

5. Debeljak and Kneebone, "Combating Transnational Crime," 134.

6. Ibid., 139.

7. Ibid.

8. Samarasinghe, *Female Sex Trafficking in Asia*, 102.

9. Debeljak and Kneebone, "Combating Transnational Crime," 139.

10. Louise Brown, *Sex Slaves: The Trafficking of Women in Asia* (London: Virago Press, 2001).

11. Paul Leung, "Sex Tourism: The Case of Cambodia," in *Sex and Tourism: Journeys of Romance, Love and Lust*, ed. Thomas G. Bauer and Bob McKercher (New York: Haworth Hospitality Press, 2003), 189.

12. Ibid., 181.

13. Samarasinghe, *Female Sex Trafficking in Asia*, 103.

14. Brown, *Sex Slaves*, 49.

15. Caroline Hughes, *UNTAC in Cambodia: The Impact on Human Rights*, Occasional Paper, Institute of Southeast Asian Studies, no. 92 (Singapore: Institute of Southeast Asian Studies, 1996), 75.

16. Kara, *Sex Trafficking*, 171.

17. Ibid., 172.

18. Karou Aoyama, *Thai Migrant Sex Workers: From Modernisation to Globalisation* (New York: Palgrave Macmillan, 2009), 42.

19. Ronald Weitzer, "The Social Construction of Sex Trafficking: Ideology and Institutionalisation of a Moral Crusade," *Politics and Society* 35, no. 3 (September 2007): 453.

20. Aoyama, *Thai Migrant Sex Workers*, 69.

21. Brown, *Sex Slaves*, 54.

22. Kara, *Sex Trafficking*, 159–60.

23. Debeljak and Kneebone, "Combating Transnational Crime," 138.

24. Christine Beddoe, Michael Hall, Michael Ryan, and Chris Ryan, *The Incidence of Sexual Exploitation of Children in Tourism* (Madrid: World Tourism Organization, 2001), 31.

25. Ibid., 38.

26. Leung, *Sex Tourism*, 182.

27. Orlando Patterson, *Slavery and Social Death: A Comparative Study* (Cambridge, Mass.: Harvard University Press, 1982), 38.

28. Julia O'Connell Davidson, cited in Aoyama, *Thai Migrant Sex Workers*, 35.

29. Aoyama, *Thai Migrant Sex Workers*, 35.

30. Kara, *Sex Trafficking*, 159–60.

31. Brown, *Sex Slaves*, 53.
32. Ibid., 48.
33. Debeljak and Kneebone, "Combating Transnational Crime," 135.
34. Ibid., 140.
35. Brown, *Sex Slaves*, 9.
36. Ryan Bishop and Lillian S. Robinson, *Night Market: Sexual Cultures and the Thai Economic Miracle* (New York: Routledge, 1998), 35.
37. Ibid.
38. Jeremy Seabrook, *Travels in the Skin Trade: Tourism and the Sex Industry*, 2nd ed. (London: Pluto Press, 1996), 7.
39. Kathleen Barry, *Female Sexual Slavery* (New York: New York University Press, 1984), 108.
40. Leslie Ann Jeffrey, *Sex and Borders: Gender, National Identity, and Prostitution Policy in Thailand* (Vancouver: University of British Columbia Press, 2002), xii.
41. Hughes, *UNTAC In Cambodia*.
42. Samarasinghe, *Female Sex Trafficking in Asia*, 100.
43. Ibid., 101.
44. Ibid., 100.
45. Ibid., 101.
46. Ibid.
47. Kang and Phally (1995), cited in Samarasinghe, *Female Sex Trafficking in Asia*, 101.
48. Samarasinghe, *Female Sex Trafficking in Asia*, 90.
49. Kara, *Sex Trafficking*, 153.
50. Barry, *Female Sexual Slavery*, 108.
51. Ibid.
52. Ibid.
53. Bishop and Robinson, *Night Market*, 98.
54. Kara, *Sex Trafficking*, 76.
55. Bishop and Robinson, *Night Market*, 98.
56. Brown, *Sex Slaves*, 9.
57. Aoyama, *Thai Migrant Sex Workers*, 50.
58. Leung, *Sex Tourism*, 181.
59. Beddoe et al., *Incidence of Sexual Exploitation of Children*, 37.
60. Samarasinghe, *Female Sex Trafficking in Asia*, 54.
61. Ibid.
62. Ibid., 24.
63. Kara, *Sex Trafficking*, 159.
64. Brown, *Sex Slaves*, 45.
65. Samarasinghe, *Female Sex Trafficking in Asia*, 101.
66. Ibid.

67. Debeljak and Kneebone, "Combating Transnational Crime," 134.
68. Leung, "Sex Tourism," 181.
69. Debeljak and Kneebone, "Combating Transnational Crime," 139.
70. Ibid., 134.
71. Aoyama, *Thai Migrant Sex Workers*, 59.
72. Ibid., 60.
73. Leung, "Sex Tourism," 186.
74. Ibid.
75. Ibid.
76. Aoyama, *Thai Migrant Sex Workers*, 57.
77. Wathinee Boonchalaksi and Philip Guest, "Prostitution in Thailand," in *The Sex Sector: The Economic and Social Bases of Prostitution in Southeast Asia*, ed. Lin Lean Lim (Geneva: International Labour Office, 1998), 162.
78. Bishop and Robinson, *Night Market*, 94.
79. Samarasinghe, *Female Sex Trafficking in Asia*, 98.
80. Ibid.
81. Kara, *Sex Trafficking*, 29.
82. Samarasinghe, *Female Sex Trafficking in Asia*, 98.
83. Boonchalaski and Guest, "Prostitution in Thailand," 162.
84. Paola Monzini, *Sex Traffic: Prostitution, Crime and Exploitation* (Black Point, Nova Scotia: Fernwood Publishing, 2005), 26.
85. Debeljak and Kneebone, "Combating Transnational Crime," 149.
86. Sandeep Chawla, Angela Me, and Thibault Le Pichon, *UNODC Global Report on Trafficking in Persons* (United Nations Office on Drugs and Crime, February 2009), 184, http://www.unodc.org/documents/Global_Report_on_TIP.pdf.
87. Debeljak and Kneebone, "Combating Transnational Crime," 146.
88. Fiona David, Anne Gallagher, Paul Holmes, and Albert Moscowitz, *Progress Report on Criminal Justice Responses to Trafficking in Persons in the ASEAN Region* (Jakarta: Association of Southeast Asian Nations, 2011), 18.
89. Samarasinghe, *Female Sex Trafficking in Asia*, 103.
90. Debeljak and Kneebone, "Combating Transnational Crime," 142–43.
91. Kara, *Sex Trafficking*, 162.
92. Beddoe et al., *Incidence of Sexual Exploitation of Children*, 32.
93. Debeljak and Kneebone, "Combating Transnational Crime," 150.
94. Ibid.
95. Beddoe et al., *Incidence of Sexual Exploitation of Children*, 43.

17

THE JAPANESE ARMY AND COMFORT WOMEN IN WORLD WAR II

Shigeru Sato

In December 1991, a group of thirty-five Koreans appealed to the Tokyo District Court seeking an apology and compensation from the Japanese government for damages they suffered during World War II. This group consisted of four war veterans, twenty-two former civilian employees of the military, sixteen bereaved family members, and three elderly women who had been forced to provide sexual services to the soldiers as "comfort women." It was known that Japanese soldiers had used comfort women, but little publicity had previously been given to them.

The court case immediately captured national and international attention and evoked widespread and fierce controversy over forced prostitution used by the Japanese military. Over the next fifteen years, almost a hundred Japanese books appeared with the term *ianfu* (comfort women) in the title. They formed the literary core of a debate focused on key issues such as the number of ianfu; their origins, methods of "recruitment," and working conditions; and the role the Japanese state played in establishing and maintaining the ianfu system.

The involvement of the state was clarified in 1992 when the Japanese government admitted responsibility and officially apologized to former ianfu in South Korea and the Philippines. Further, the government established the Asian Women's Fund that, from 1994 to 2007, issued an official letter of apology as well as monetary compensation to each authenticated former ianfu. The Asian Women's Fund also created the bilingual Digital Museum website dedicated to the history of the ianfu and made basic information about them available to the international community.[1] Despite such measures, however, it is still conventional wisdom that the Japanese government has never truly apologized for abuses committed during World War II. This, in turn, is related to historical relations between Japan and other Asian countries, as well as the postcolonial rise of Asian nationalism.

For some Southeast Asian countries, the experience of being invaded by the Japanese helped crystallize local independence movements against European colonialism. In India, where the Japanese occupation was limited to the Andaman and the Nicobar Islands and where Japanese authorities promoted anti-British nationalist movements, many of those attracted to the movements developed strong pro-Japanese sentiments. By contrast, in China and Korea, invasion by the Japanese was a much more harrowing experience. Moreover, the history of humiliation suffered by these countries at the hands of the Japanese antedates World War II. The Chinese, for example, recall the Sino-Japanese War (1894–95); Japanese colonization of Taiwan; Japan's "twenty-one demands" during World War I, which, if accepted, would have undermined Chinese sovereignty; and Japan's invasion, occupation, and creation of puppet states in northern China after 1931. Korean perceptions of Japan are largely shaped by the Japanese annexation of 1910, as well as Tokyo's attempt toward the end of World War II to make Koreans Japanese citizens and crush their cultural and linguistic identity.[2]

Thus, in China and Korea, occupation during World War II served to accentuate anti-Japanese nationalism. In both these countries, the Japanese government's apologies to and compensation of comfort women has only refreshed memories of older humiliations and encourage demands for more extensive apologies.

With this background in mind, this chapter examines the origins and functioning of the *ianjo* (comfort stations) during World War II in Japanese-occupied territory.

Comfort Women

Because of the lack of comprehensive statistical records, the number of comfort women is unknown—estimates vary widely, ranging from 20,000 to 410,000. These numbers have been inferred from the number of soldiers. Chinese scholar Su Zhiliang argued for 410,000 on the basis that 3 million Japanese soldiers had access to comfort stations, that there was at any given time an average of 1 ianfu per 30 soldiers, and that each ianfu was replaced three times during the course of the war for reasons such as death, illness, or escape. Japanese military historian Hata Ikuhiko argued for the lowest estimate of 20,000 comfort women on the basis that 2.5 million soldiers had access to ianjo, the ratio of ianfu to soldiers was 1 to 150, and 50 percent of comfort women were replaced.[3] By contrast, Yoshimi Yoshiaki estimated the number of comfort women at between 45,000 and 200,000. The lower estimate reflected a possible ratio of 1 ianfu to every 100 soldiers and an ianfu replacement rate of 50 percent; the higher estimate was based on a ratio of 1 woman to every 30 soldiers and an ianfu replacement rate of 100 percent.[4]

On busy days, an ianfu might service 30 "clients." Theoretically, therefore, had there been 410,000 comfort women, each soldier could have paid a daily visit to a comfort station. However, soldiers were usually permitted access to ianjo only on the weekly payday and on days immediately preceding and following major military expeditions. Otherwise, they were restricted to their barracks. In locations with many military divisions, smaller units alternated days off. The ianfu, too, regularly took days off. They needed to. Before and after major military operations, long queues of soldiers would form outside the ianjo, some of which had no partitions, which meant there was no privacy. Soldiers waiting in line often shouted at the man engaged with an ianfu to urge him to make haste; sometimes, they even kicked his buttocks. Most customers completed their business with minimal fuss and left the place swiftly. On a busy day, an ianfu spent on average a little less than ten minutes with each customer.[5]

Our knowledge of the origins and ethnic composition of the comfort women is equally imprecise. The ianfu lawsuit presented the issue essentially as a case of abuse of one nation by another, thereby discounting the numerous Japanese ianfu. However, the Japanese military transported comfort women from Japan as well as from Korea and Taiwan to the remotest parts of the war theater—from the Andaman Islands in the west to Rabaul in the east. In the Philippines, Indonesia, New Guinea, and other occupied territories, local women were also used.[6]

Taiwan and Korea were Japanese colonies from 1895 and 1910, respectively, until Japan's surrender in 1945. Some Koreans, including the plaintiffs in the ianfu lawsuit, argued that the majority (up to 90 percent) of comfort women were Korean. However, they *included* in their estimates Korean girls mobilized as *teishintai* (dedication corps)—a considerably larger form of wartime labor mobilization for ammunition production and related industries.[7] It is clear that Koreans comprised the majority of ianfu in certain comfort stations, but there is insufficient evidence to sustain the argument that most ianfu were Korean. Of the few detailed extant records, one shows that of the 1,883 comfort women sent to China between November 1943 and December 1944 via (or from) Taiwan, 938 (49.8 percent) were Japanese, 561 (29.8 percent) were Korean, and 384 (20.4 percent) were Taiwanese. In another document, a male Korean who was a civilian employee on the Chuuk Islands during the war testified that about 250 Korean and 500 Japanese ianfu were sent there and subdivided into groups of 20 or 30 women—and each group was allocated to a military unit.[8]

Recruitment

The most controversial issue is whether the Japanese government was responsible for the coercive recruitment of ianfu. Protagonists of the plaintiffs in the lawsuit argue that the military authorities approved the establishment of ianjo and that most of the women were deceived into becoming ianfu and subsequently forced to provide sexual services to soldiers; consequently, the ultimate responsibility lay with the Japanese state. Others contend that although the central authorities approved the use of comfort women, each military unit commissioned licensed brothel managers to provide its soldiers with the service. As registered prostitution was legal at the time, it is argued that if there was any abuse of the system, those military units or the brothel operators involved were the responsible parties, rather than the state.

The plaintiffs' testimonies revealed the complex socioeconomic background to the case. Only one of the three Korean women plaintiffs, Kim Hak-Sun, used her own name in the initial lawsuit; the other two remained anonymous. Kim testified that her parents were so poor that they were obliged to give her up for adoption. Her foster father sent her for three years to a prostitute training school, from which she graduated in 1939 at the age of seventeen. Informing her that he had found a "good job" for her in China, he then escorted Kim and another girl by truck and train through Pyongyang and Beijing to a small village in northern China where a Japanese army unit was stationed. There, Kim was locked up in a house and made to serve ten to thirty soldiers daily. Subsequently, alongside four other women, she was obliged to accompany a unit of some three hundred soldiers that moved around northern China. Eventually, she ran away with a Korean man to the French concession in Shanghai, where she had a daughter in 1942 and a son in 1945.[9]

An anonymous witness, Plaintiff A, testified that one day in 1942, she left home to see the first elevator in a Japanese department store in Pusan. Two men, one Korean and the other Japanese, approached her in the street and asked if she was interested in going to Japan to work in a textile factory. She was hesitant but accompanied them to the wharf, where they took her onto a ship. Once aboard, she expressed her wish to return home, but she was forcibly detained. The ship sailed to Hiroshima, from where she was taken to Rabaul; there, she joined about twenty other women working as ianfu in a church building.[10]

The other anonymous witness, Plaintiff B, stated that a Korean man came to her village with the offer of work in Shanghai and showed thirty or forty yen as advance payment. She accepted willingly, gave the money to her mother, and accompanied him to an inn in a nearby town, where fifteen other Korean women had already been assembled. The man escorted them by train to Shanghai, and from there, a Japanese soldier drove them in a military truck to an ianjo (where each woman had a military tent) in a garrison on the outskirts of the city; it was run by an elderly Japanese couple called *Otosan* and *Okasan* (Mum and Dad).

The lawsuit involving these three cases led to an extensive search for additional evidence about comfort women and induced many other former ianfu from Korea, Taiwan, the Philippines, and Indonesia to testify. In Indonesia, however, so many false reports were made by women hoping to be awarded damages that the acceptance of testimonies there was curtailed.[11]

The investigation revealed considerable variation in the methods used by the Japanese military to obtain women. Notably, not a single Japanese woman has presented herself as a victim of the ianjo system—although there were significant numbers of Japanese ianfu, many of whom, like their Korean counterparts, had been compelled by their parents or their socioeconomic circumstances to become prostitutes. Moreover, whereas conscripted Japanese men and war widows received pensions after the war, ianfu (like company employees who went to war zones) received nothing, despite the fact that many no doubt suffered from physical and psychological trauma, disease, and sexual and social discrimination.

The reluctance of Japanese ianfu to come forward may be linked to the fact that most were already professional prostitutes—members of large and officially registered brothels that had been operating from the prewar years. The Japanese authorities avoided recruiting nonprofessional Japanese women because they feared the reaction of their soldiers should they learn that their own sisters or daughters had been mobilized by the state as ianfu.

Japanese former ianfu and brothel managers who have been interviewed tend not to perceive themselves as victims or perpetrators, respectively. Since they had been working at large brothels, they may have felt that being sent to the war theater was inevitable in the context of the national wartime mobilization.[12] Also, Japanese ianfu generally enjoyed superior status and better working conditions than comfort women of other nationalities. Many catered only to officers, and some of the more popular women from reputed Japanese brothels earned more money than army generals.[13]

The Japanese authorities did not exercise the same caution with regard to non-Japanese women. In Korea, for instance, they mobilized women as ianfu often as a part of the teishintai, using local government officials, police agents, brothel managers, and human traffickers as their "recruiters." This created a situation in which some Korean brothers, recruited as soldiers, and their sisters, recruited as ianfu, found themselves serving in the same war zone. Japanese law prohibited prostitution by women under the age of twenty-one, but many Korean comfort women appear to have been younger than that, although precise figures are impossible to find because, at that time, there was no birth registration for women in Korea.

Origins of the Ianjo System

The Rape of Nanjing in China, from late 1937 to early 1938, when Japanese soldiers indulged in unrestrained rape and killing, inflamed the anger of local people and aroused widespread international condemnation. The reaction alarmed the Japanese authorities. In response, they decided that to avoid similar incidents in the future, they needed to provide a safe outlet for the sexual frustration of Japanese troops. Hence, they established a network of ianjo throughout Japanese-dominated territory, run by professional brothel managers and commissioned and supervised by the military.

In the terms *ianfu* and *ianjo*, *ian* means "comfort," "consolation," or "entertainment"—usually presented to a group of people as an expression of gratitude for their prolonged hard work. Other forms of ian included performances (called *imon*, meaning "visit for ian") for troops in war zones by singers and actors as well as the provision by women's associations of bags containing small gifts (*imon bukuro*) for soldiers.

However, the military provision of ian for soldiers was sporadic. Indeed, the Japanese provided far fewer wartime recreational activities for their citizens than their European allies did. In the 1920s, Fascist Italy created the organization Dopolavoro (meaning "After Work") and Nazi Germany the Kracht durch Freude (or "Strength through Joy")—nationwide organizations offering affordable forms of entertainment, comfort, and leisure for the working classes that helped create a sense of national unity and pride. In Germany, these efforts included the provision of the Volkswagen Beetle and pompous festivals such as the 1936 Berlin Olympics.[14]

By contrast, following the outbreak of the war in China in July 1937, when the Japanese government instituted mass mobilization for the war effort it also enacted a stringent sumptuary law and banned Anglo-American forms of entertainment, such as Hollywood movies and jazz. The authorities had intended to grant soldiers furloughs, but transport and manpower shortages prevented the systematic implementation of such plans, and when troops returned home from the war zones, it was to a largely joyless environment.

Comfort stations were designed to compensate for these shortfalls and, through the provision of easy and safe sex, both to control the spread of sexually transmitted diseases (STDs) among Japanese troops and to minimize friction between soldiers and local communities. The ianjo thus marked a turning point in the Japanese system of military prostitution.

The Japanese method of managing the soldiers' sexual behavior contrasted with the centralized economic management of occupied territory. After its military conquest of Southeast Asia, the Japanese government commissioned almost five hundred Japanese companies to dispatch staff to manage the economies of occupied territories in line with a central government plan. However, to run the ianjo, the military commissioned managers of licensed brothels in Japan, and they were not subject to centralized supervision.

As a result, there was considerable variation in the way Japanese brothel managers procured women. Brothels already existed throughout the territories overrun by Japanese forces, but since the military authorities considered that a large proportion of local prostitutes were suffering from disease, they often preferred to procure nonprofessional local women or import prostitutes from Japan and its colonies. Even when the ianjo were idle or infrequently used because of the absence of troops, they were barred to local men, for authorities feared they would infect the ianfu. In officially supervised ianjo, the women were subject to weekly medical checks, and visiting soldiers were required to use condoms and disinfectants. If an ianfu failed an examination, she was declared unsuitable, released, and sent home.[15]

The ianjo proved immensely popular with the troops. By providing comfort stations, the military transformed over a million Japanese boy virgins into regular users of the comfort stations. Most conscripts felt that their lives might soon end, and those who were sexually inexperienced commonly wished to "become real men" by experiencing sex before they died. Ianjo managers usually barred drunken men from the comfort stations, but on their weekly payday most soldiers fell into a routine of spending time at the local pub before visiting the ianjo.

High-ranking Japanese officers in occupied territory, who lived in houses rather than barracks, often not only visited comfort stations but also, in common with Japanese civilians in occupied territory, sought local women as mistresses. They frequently installed these mistresses—mostly European or Eurasian women whom they termed *only-san* (Miss Only, a woman who provided sexual services to only one man)–in their own homes. This practice was particularly common in Indonesia, where Japanese officers redeemed some of these women from high-class brothels, called "white horse clubs," that were frequently run by nationals from Axis and neutral countries, such as Germany and Switzerland. Other so-called mistresses were recruited from among the local, mostly Eurasian female population (offspring of Dutch fathers and Indonesian mothers). As time progressed, supplies of such mistresses ran so short that Japanese officers started to select Dutch women from internment camps. Many only-san had children, but at the end of the war, they were barred from accompanying their Japanese partners back to Japan.[16]

Indeed, liberation ushered in difficult times for only-san and ianfu. Even if they had been coerced into prostitution, many were severely punished by local men for having had sexual relations with the Japanese. In late 1945 in the city of Tebingtinggi, Sumatra, a group of local radical youths seized former ianfu who had been imported from Java, stripped them naked, and paraded the sobbing and wailing women through the streets in order to humiliate them publicly.[17]

Warfare and Sexual Stress

In war zones, a combination of sex and violence formed a potent concoction. Many soldiers did become sex addicts, and their desire for sex led them to turn to women outside the ianjo as well. Throughout areas they occupied, the fact that they were agents of the conquering power helped remove soldiers' inhibitions about approaching unknown women for sex. In the city of Medan in Sumatra, women who had relations with Japanese men were termed *gadis san-yaru*—a mixture of Indonesian and Japanese words as used in the phrase "*Gadis-san, yaru?*" meaning "Miss, [shall we] do it?"—indicating the approach of drunken Japanese soldiers who offered local women money for a one-off liaison.[18]

Despite the availability of comfort stations, some soldiers continued to violate local women. In peacetime, rapists usually acted secretively. In war zones, soldiers often raped women in public, even in front of their families, in order to demonstrate their power over local people. Gang rape was also common, reflecting a collective sense of military superiority.

Plaintiffs in the lawsuit who came from areas where Japanese forces encountered guerrilla resistance (as in China) and those who came from the Philippines (where ianfu were imported rather than locally recruited) were actually not ianfu but rather local rape victims.[19] The use of rape during the war was part of a widespread and vicious campaign of abuse and intimidation. Female captives were often repeatedly raped and mutilated and sometimes even murdered.[20]

In areas of little resistance, such as most of Indonesia, where local people generally cooperated with the Japanese occupation forces, sexual assaults occurred but were generally less vicious. Typically, a group of soldiers would spot an attractive woman, locate her house, and a few days later pay a visit, meet her parents, and say to them in faulty Indonesian, "*Pinjam cewek*" ("We'll borrow the girl"). They would then carry her away to a nearby building that the military had commandeered and gang-rape her. Sometimes, they would then release the victim, but just as often, they would keep her for a week or so before releasing her or sending her to a comfort station.[21]

Rapists often went unpunished, both because the military officers considered that sexually aggressive men would be militarily aggressive on the battlefield and because few victims or their relatives lodged official complaints. Some girls appealed or protested when they were taken, and their relatives sometimes attempted to recover them. One father whose daughter was abducted by a group of Japanese troops later spotted one of the responsible soldiers in the street, approached him, and shouted, "Return my daughter!" The solder retorted, "Get lost!" The man persisted, ran up to the solder, and clung to him, repeating, "Return my daughter! Return my daughter!" The soldier drew his sword and cut down the man with one stroke. What happened after that to this rapist and murderer is unknown.[22]

Thus, many Japanese soldiers who regularly visited ianjo also frequented local prostitutes and accosted nonprostitutes as well—despite an increasing awareness of the dangers of unprotected sex. Married soldiers gave their sexually inexperienced colleagues informal advice about STDs and preventive measures. Japanese-language newspapers published in the occupied lands also provided information, although it was designed more to scare young soldiers away from unregulated sex rather than to educate them.[23] For example, one article warned soldiers of "candle disease," a peculiar STD that caused the penis to wither from the tip down, causing excruciating pain to the sufferer and eventually leaving only the urethra, like the wick of a candle. Other articles published medical statistics showing that virtually all unlicensed local prostitutes were suffering from diseases.[24]

Newspaper campaigns were largely ineffective, as was the policy adopted by the military authorities of handing out free condoms for use at the comfort stations. Many soldiers used their condoms outside the designated ianjo and continued to have unprotected sex with both ianfu and local women. As a result, some of them inevitably contracted diseases and spread them in the comfort stations, which thus became notorious STD centers.[25] It should be emphasized, however, that this was not a uniquely Japanese problem. A comparative study of the spread of STDs in India demonstrates that the situation in the British-occupied territory there was much worse than in Japanese-occupied zones.[26]

There is another side to the history of war stress and sex. Many soldiers suffering from the stress of warfare and the imminence of death, coupled with separation from loved ones, sought emotional comfort from the ianfu. This was almost impossible to achieve, of course, as the comfort stations were designed to provide quick sexual relief for soldiers, not humane interactions between the sexes. Yet despite this, some men and women attempted to bond. Significant numbers of soldiers became emotionally disturbed, and some of them begged the women to elope with them, commit double suicide with them, or leave the stations and find other jobs. Some men tried to befriend an individual ianfu (particularly if she reminded them of a daughter, sister, girlfriend, or wife) and ease her work by buying up to five tickets and staying with her for the maximum allotment of five hours, without demanding sex. Such behavior often touched the heart of the ianfu, who recalled such incidents long after the war had ended. A minority of soldiers and ianfu forged meaningful bonds.[27]

Aftermath

At the end of the war, some soldiers even succeeded in taking their ianfu sweethearts to Japan and marrying them there—despite often stiff opposition from their relatives.[28] However, in general, the story played out differently. The idea that women exist primarily to satisfy a primordial male desire for sex, coupled with the narrow equation of ian with sex and alcohol, was so firmly rooted in Japanese mentality that the Japanese even established brothels for foreigners they employed, such as the Chinese sent involuntarily to Japan and forced to work in coal mines and the local auxiliary soldiers the Japanese hired in Burma.[29] Moreover, in Tokyo immediately after Emperor Hirohito surrendered, ultranationalist groups that had been strongly anti-American until the surrender founded the Tokubetsu ian shisetsu kyokai (Association of Special Comfort Facilities, called in English the Recreation and Amusement Association [RAA]) with the aim of recruiting five thousand ianfu to service the Allied occupation forces. On August 28, 1945, the day the first Allied troops arrived, several hundred American soldiers visited its facilities. Over one thousand of the planned five thousand ianfu were present, but no beds or futons had been assembled and no room partitions had been erected, so sex occurred publicly.[30] It was, in many ways, a ritual demonstration of the power of the victor over the vanquished. However, as there was a sudden surge of STD infections among their troops, American authorities decided to close the RAA facilities. There followed almost half a century of silence about the role of the ianjo—until the court case of 1991–92.

Just as the Japanese kept providing comfort women to the Allied occupation forces, the Koreans provided their women to the Allied troops during the Allied occupation from 1945 and through the Korean War (1950–53), using the preexisting social system for managing prostitution. These issues are deeply rooted in the history of prostitution and gender relations in both countries.

The academic debate about comfort women continues. Military historian Yuki Tanaka condemned the Japanese crimes against the comfort women in the first half of his 2002 book but went on to reveal in the second half that the Allied occupation forces also committed crimes against Japanese women.[31] This prompted an Australian scholar to respond that "the equation of the Allied nations and Japan's sexual ideologies predisposes this volume to the impression that it is partially an apologia for the 'comfort' women system."[32]

At a conference in Beijing in 1995, when feminist scholar Chizuko Ueno expressed her view that feminism ought to transcend nationalism, a Korean feminist replied that Koreans, as a subjugated people, had to assert nationalism because the historical issues of the Japanese invasion and occupation were part of a wider and ongoing context of Japanese racism against Koreans.[33]

It is apparent that the history of the comfort stations cannot be understood without also analyzing the profound historical roots of both racism and sexism, not only in Japan but also in Korea and China. Moreover, it is evident from the history of the sexual behavior of European troops that such issues are universal and thus need to form an integral part of historical studies of wartime activities elsewhere.

Notes

1. See Digital Museum, http://www.awf.or.jp.

2. Carter J. Eckert, Ki-baik Lee, Young Ick Lew, Michael Robinson, and Edward W. Wagner, *Korea Old and New: A History* (Seoul: Ilchokak Publishers for Korea Institute, Harvard University, 1990), 199–326.

3. For more detailed statistical surveys, see "Number of Comfort Stations and Comfort Women," Digital Museum, http://www.awf.or.jp/e1/facts-07.html.

4. Yoshiaki Yoshimi, *Jugun ianfu* [Military comfort women] (Tokyo: Iwanami, 1995), 78–84.

5. Similar situations existed elsewhere. During World War I at a German military brothel in the city of Mitau, Russia, one woman had thirty-two visitors between the hours of four and nine, the regular business hours for the brothel; see Magnus Hirschfeld, *The Sexual History of the World War* (Honolulu: University Press of the Pacific, 2006), 150.

6. For information about Japanese, Korean, and Chinese comfort women in the Andaman Islands, see T. S. Sareen, *Sharing the Blame: Subhas Chandra Bose and the Japanese Occupation of the Andamans, 1942–45* (Delhi: S. S. Publishers, 2002), 149–60.

7. Teishintai were formed throughout Japan and its colonies during the war. This three-syllable word literally means "body-dedicating corps." Pronounced the Korean way, it sounds like "corps of forced prostitutes," which seems to be the cause of this misunderstanding. Apparently, there were cases where girls who mobilized to join a teishintai were, in fact, made to become comfort women.

8. "Sojo" (Petition), 22, http://www.awf.or.jp/pdf/195-k1.pdf.

9. Ibid., 51, and Hata, Ikuhiko, *Ianfu to senjo no sei* [Comfort women and sex in the theater of war] (Tokyo: Shinchosha, 1999), 179-82.

10. This and the following paragraphs are based on ibid., 47–50.

11. A. Budi Hartono and Dadang Juliantoro, *Derita paksa perempuan: Kisah jugun ianfu pada masa pendudukan jepang, 1942–1945* [Sufferings of forced women: Stories of the military comfort women during the Japanese occupation, 1942–1945] (Jakarta: Sinar Harapan, 1997).

12. For one case, see Rumiko Nishino, *Jugun ianfu to jugo nen senso: Biruma ianjo keieisha no shogen* [Military comfort women and the Fifteen Year War: Testimonies of a manager of a comfort station in Burma] (Tokyo: Akashi Shoten, 1993).

13. Payment was part of the system. Every visitor of an ianjo had to buy a ticket, and part of the money was paid to the ianfu. Tipping was also common among the officers. Where there were post offices, the women were able to deposit the money or remit it to their families. Women sent to remote areas have testified that they received no payment. Some men also witnessed comfort women retreating together with soldiers from the jungles of Burma, carrying heavy backpacks filled with money.

14. Victoria de Grazia, *The Culture of Consent: Mass Organization of Leisure in Fascist Italy* (Cambridge: Cambridge University Press, 2002), and Kristin Semmens, *Seeing Hitler's Germany: Tourism in the Third Reich* (New York: Palgrave Macmillan, 2005).

15. Yoshiaki Yoshimi, ed., *Jugun ianfu mondai shiryoshu* [Compiled documents on the issue of comfort women] (Tokyo: Otsuki Shoten, 1992), document nos. 2, 34, and 70.

16. About the European and Eurasian comfort women, see Bart van Poelgest, "Report of a Study of Dutch Government Documents on the Forced Prostitution of Dutch Women in the Dutch East Indies during the Japanese Occupation," Office of the Ministry of Interior, the Netherlands, unofficial translation, January 24, 1994, accessed August 31, 2010, http://www.awf.or.jp/pdf/0205.pdf.

17. Takao Fusayama, *Sumatora no yoake* [Dawn in Sumatra] (Tokyo: Kodansha, 1981), 95–96.

18. Shigeru Sato, "Various Terms for a Comfort Woman," in *The Encyclopedia of Indonesia in the Pacific War*, ed. Peter Post, William H. Frederick, Shigaru Sato, and Iris Heidebrink (Leiden: Brill, 2009), 195–96.

19. Nelia Sancho, ed., *War Crimes on Asian Women: Military Sexual Slavery by Japan during World War II–The Case of the Filipino Comfort Women* (Manila: Asian Women Human Rights Council, 1994).

20. Ibid.

21. Fumiko Kawata, *Indoneshia no "ianfu"* [Indonesian "comfort women"] (Tokyo: Akashi Shoten, 1997), 51–90.

22. Ibid., 111–14.

23. See *Jawa Shinbun* [Java Daily] for a series of boxed features on health and hygiene in the tropics, from January 4 to February 5, 1943.

24. Ibid., October 25, 1942.

25. Kentaro Minegishi, *Kogun ianjo to onna tachi* [The imperial forces' comfort stations and the women] (Tokyo: Yoshikawa Kobunkan, 2000), 67–89.

26. Sareen, *Sharing the Blame*, 149–59.

27. Nishino, *Jugun ianfu to jugo nen senso*, 49–62 and 116–21.

28. Ibid., 175.

29. Yoshimi, *Jugun ianfu*, 76 and 80.

30. John Dower, *Embracing Defeat: Japan in the Aftermath of World War II* (London: Allen Lane, 1999), 123–32. The Allied occupation forces included women. There is testimony by Japanese men that some of the women employed Japanese men as their sex slaves and ordered them to make love to them, without showing any sign of affection toward these slaves.

31. Yuki Tanaka, *Japan's Comfort Women: Sexual Slavery and Prostitution during World War II and the US Occupation* (New York: Routledge, 2002).

32. Narrelle Morris, review of *Japan's Comfort Women: Sexual Slavery and Prostitution during World War II and the US Occupation*, by Yuki Tanaka, in *Intersections: Gender, History and Culture in the Asian Context* 9 (August 2003), http://wwwsshe.murdoch.edu.au/intersections/issue9/morris_review.htm.

33. Chizuko Ueno, *Nationalism and Gender* (Melbourne: Trans Pacific Press, 2004), xi and 137–48.

ART, SEXUALITY, AND SLAVERY

18

HIDDEN GEOGRAPHIES OF THE CAPE

Shifting Representations of Slavery and Sexuality in South African Art and Fiction

GABEBA BADEROON

THE BODY IS A LANDSCAPE ON WHICH HISTORY IS WRITTEN

In nineteenth-century landscape paintings and travel writing, the city of Cape Town was portrayed as ordered and domesticated. Landscape paintings of the city, with its iconic mountain and neat streets, often featured finely dressed colonists in the foreground and "Malay" slaves placed near the edges of the canvas, as though they marked the boundary of the domesticated space of the city. Malays had been brought to the Cape at the founding of the colony in the mid-seventeenth century from territories around the Indian Ocean, and their depiction as quaint, colorful figures anchored a view of Cape Town as an aesthetically pleasing and urbane space. Such picturesque representations elided the signs of violence and sexual exploitation that characterized slaveholding society at the Cape. In contrast to this picturesque tradition, recent work by the award-winning South African visual artist Berni Searle and novels such as *The Slave Book* by Rayda Jacobs and *Unconfessed* by Yvette Christansë, radically reenvision Cape Town and its subsumed tropes of slavery.[1] In this chapter, I analyze South African art and fiction that recover the traumatic history of slavery and sexual subjection hidden within the picturesque colonial landscape and that also craft images of the resilience and interiority of enslaved people.

Slavery in South Africa

In 1652, the Dutch East India Company (Verenigde Oostindische compagnie, or VOC) established a refueling station at the Cape, at first focused solely on provisioning ships engaged in the Dutch trade in spices from the East.[2] The Cape settlement was distinguished from those in the New World by the fact that it was not initially aimed at colonial expansion (though it later became the first of the colonies that would constitute South Africa). The reach of activities by the Dutch soon encroached on the land of the Khoisan, the indigenous people of the Cape, who resisted Dutch attempts to conscript them as labor for the company. Because the VOC forbade the enslavement of indigenous people, the company resorted to the use of slave labor imported at first from West Africa and subsequently from territories around the Indian Ocean.[3] During the Napoleonic Wars, control of the Cape passed to the British in 1795, and the colony became a permanent British possession in 1806.

The slave population at the Cape never reached more than forty thousand,[4] and studies of the city's history before the 1980s assumed that the role of slavery in the Cape was minor and its character relatively "mild."[5] Popular cultural texts such as cookbooks and landscape paintings also reflected this benign view of the colony's system of labor. It was only in the 1980s that significant new scholarship on slavery in South Africa began to counter these assumptions to demonstrate that, in fact, slave labor was critical to the Cape Colony. Nigel Worden points out that during the colonial period, slavery structured the entire society of the Cape and its hinterland, and slaves at times constituted the majority of the population of the colony.[6] Moreover, because the Dutch colony depended on slave labor for its survival and because of the high proportion of male slaves in relation to colonists, control over slaves was exercised through "the massive use of judicial force,"[7] and slaves owned by private burghers were subjected to punishments that were often "violent and extreme."[8] Furthermore, given the high ratio of slaves in the colony and the proportion of male slaves in relation to male colonists, colonial society showed an intense fear of slave resistance (which was manifested most commonly through desertion); the colonists also feared rebellion, poisoning, and theft.[9] Such anxieties helped to shape social relations as well as the built environment of the colony. The historical archaeologist Martin Hall conducted an "archaeology of silences" into colonial Cape architecture, including many extant colonial-era farms and their slave quarters.[10] He showed that the architecture was shaped by the intimate presence of slaves and Khoisan serfs, as well as the fear of arson by runaway slaves. This was evident in the placement of trees and rocks and the structure of the slave quarters in colonial houses.[11]

Given that slaves came to constitute the majority of the population of the Cape and that their labor was crucial to the survival of the colony, the impact of slavery on the subsequent history of South Africa has been profound. Social relations formed in the slaveholding society at the Cape under the Dutch from 1658 to 1795 and 1803 to 1806 and under permanent British control from 1806 laid the foundation for the later emphasis during apartheid on racial hierarchy as the basis of economic and political power in South Africa. I will also show that slavery generated ideas about race and sexuality in South Africa that continue to influence perspectives in the country today.

Slavery and Islam are intricately connected in the colonial history of the Cape. The name given to enslaved people transported to the Cape by the Dutch was Malays, and even today, the descendants of slaves at the Cape are often called (and some name themselves) Cape Malays. This name suggests that their geographic origin lay in Southeast Asia, but, in fact, slaves were brought from a number of regions in Africa and Asia, including Angola, Mozambique, Madagascar, India, and Southeast Asia.[12] Melayu was a lingua franca in the eastern Indian Ocean region and among slaves in the Cape, hence the name Malay for slave and, after the abolition of slavery, for Muslim. Many slaves were Muslim, and, in addition, there was a high rate of conversion to Islam among indigenous people at the Cape. This conversion occurred, in part, because Islam offered its adherents a spiritual and communal world unconnected to that of the slave owners. Worden argues that Islam offered "a degree of independent slave culture" separate from slave owners.[13] The owners also encouraged conversion of their slaves to Islam because the law of matrilineal descent allowed the enslavement of the children of Muslim slaves, unlike Christian ones, and because Muslim slaves were deemed to be more reliable workers due to Islam's prohibition on consuming alcohol.[14] Since Islam offered enslaved people the possibility of an interior life and a communal space beyond the control of slave owners, it was regarded with ambivalence by the Dutch. Under the Statutes of India—the set of laws governing the VOC possessions in Batavia, which were also implemented in the colony in 1715—Islam was tacitly tolerated at the Cape (as the encouragement of conversion shows), but the *public* practice of Islam was punishable by death.[15] The presence of Islam in the colonial context must thus be read in oblique ways, partly due to the highly conventional tradition of representing slavery at the Cape.

The critical importance of slave labor for the Cape Colony had implications for the way in which slavery—and consequently Islam—has historically been represented in South Africa. As noted earlier, the dominant style of such portrayals is the mode of the picturesque, in which the violence of the slaveholding colony is transformed into a pleasing, domesticated view of the Cape and its environs. Since landscape is the main theme of such paintings, the colonial picturesque tradition has had to accommodate the deep contradictions of South Africa's systems of exploitative labor in working the land. From the colonial period, the portrayal of landscape in South Africa has been haunted by a profound ambivalence about the representation of black labor.[16] This stems from the Protestant belief in the necessity of work and the inherent sinfulness of being idle, yet to apply such a view in colonies that were dependent on slave labor led to unsettling implications. As J. M. Coetzee points out, "If the work of hands on a particular path of earth, digging, plowing, planting, building, is what inscribes it as the property of its occupiers *by right*, then the hands of black serfs doing the work had better not be seen."[17] In other words, the visibility of black labor disturbed the colonists' claims to "occupation by right." However, a particular view of Malay slaves in colonial representations of the land—as passive and compliant—helped to resolve the contradiction of black labor and settler belonging by portraying a picturesque view of slave labor *in the service* of white colonists. This is manifested in the perennial deployment of hardworking Malay figures in paintings of the Cape landscape. Such representations underplayed evidence of resistance by slaves and the use of violence by slave owners, and they produced a picturesque view of a benign slaveholding society at the Cape that has persisted to the present day. This happened despite the fact that "resistance, not acquiescence, is the heart of the history of human slavery," as Robert Ross notes in his groundbreaking 1983 study of Cape slavery, *Cape of Torments: Slavery and Resistance in South Africa.*[18]

Because of these contradictions, representations of the domesticated and picturesque landscape at the Cape are shadowed with hidden meaning. From the Tulbagh Code that compelled slaves to carry a torch at night to the picturesque Malay figures often found on the edges of nineteenth-century landscape paintings of the Cape, a highly structured visibility of Islam—the representation of Muslims at the Cape as compliant with the desires of white colonists—was crucial to the conventional portrayal of a pleasing colonial cityscape. The picturesque tradition led to a heightened but ambiguous visibility for Muslims in the Cape, recognizable through a circumscribed set of tropes.[19] In contrast to indigenous people, who resisted forced labor and were consequently portrayed as prone to "idleness" and "volatility," Malay slaves were depicted by settlers as skilled, reliable, and compliant, if also entertaining and exotic.[20] This picturesque tradition, which continued into the mid-twentieth century, consistently staged Muslims in paintings, stories, and news articles about wedding feasts and funerals as "quiet, kind, slow-speaking, fatalistic and passive."[21] Because the terms *slave* and *Malay* were seen as largely coterminous, such conventions have played a significant part in portraying Islam in South Africa into the contemporary era.

Gender is crucially implicated in these conventions of benign representations of slavery. Gender (and sex) was a central factor in South African slavery. By the 1830s, providing domestic labor was the primary role carried out by two-thirds of the slaves in the Cape.[22] In addition, due to the gender imbalance among settlers, slave women and free black women were a source of marriage partners for settlers, and the Slave Lodge, which housed company-owned slaves, effectively acted as "Cape Town's main brothel."[23] Slavery thus generated fulsome discourses about black bodies, whether Khoi, San, or slave, and this has had a lingering impact on subsequent notions of sexuality and race in South Africa.[24] In nineteenth-century Cape Town, popular paintings and cartoons depicted enslaved men as passive and feminized,[25] and slave women were shown as physically alluring and compliant.[26] However, because the picturesque tradition has suppressed attention to the violence of slavery at the Cape, the topic of sexuality and slavery suffers from "the problem of silence."[27]

Attending to the connection between slavery and sexuality reveals a hidden sexual geography at work in Cape Town. Indeed, the very name of the city implicates it in the history of sexual slavery, to which slave women were subjected under Dutch rule. The phrase *Van de Kaap* (Dutch for "of the Cape"), when used as the last name of a slave, indicated the individual was born at the Cape of mixed-race parentage.[28] In the rest of this chapter, I will draw on the historiography of slavery at the Cape to analyze shifting representations of Cape slavery and sexuality in recent South African visual art and fiction.

Why is it important to look at the relationship between sexuality and slavery? Sexuality and race were crucially linked in European colonial territories, where control over sex was central to definitions of *race*. Thus, according to Philippa Levine, European beliefs about the perverse sexuality of colonized people were used to justify imperialism, and notions of the "naturalized prostitution, promiscuity, and homosexuality claimed to be central to Chinese, Indian, Arabic, 'Oriental,' and Aboriginal societies were definitive of what made these places ripe for colonial governance, unworthy of self-rule, and inferior to their colonial masters."[29] In her study of the Dutch Empire in Indonesia, Ann Laura Stoler argues that "the very categories 'colonizer' and 'colonized' were secured through forms of sexual control."[30] Because of low ratios of European women in the Cape, sexual license over the bodies of slave women and indigenous women was granted to European colonists and slave owners during the Dutch period, resulting in systemic sexual violence and the enforced prostitution of enslaved women owned by the VOC.[31] This system of sexual violence at the founding of the colony led to a high level of racial heterogeneity at the Cape. The racial implications of systemic sexual violence, together with the anxiety felt in colonial society about the effects of miscegenation on white racial identity, led to increasingly detailed meanings based on skin color in the British era. Levine writes that in the British colonies, "all 'native' women had the potential to be prostitutes," and, in fact, practices that regulated sex in the colonies led to "the merging of blacks and prostitutes as a category."[32] With the legacy of this foundational period in South African history, the concepts of race and sexuality that emerged from the systemic sexual violence of the colonial period have had lasting and damaging effects on contemporary notions of sexuality and gender; these are manifested in continuing patterns of sexual violence as well as derogatory portrayals of black bodies and sexual identities.

The possibility of sexual and therefore racial transgression haunted the colonies. As Stoler notes, "The obsession with white prestige was a basic feature of colonial thinking."[33] In her study of prostitution and race in the British Empire, Levine points out that in the colonies, "fears around racial difference . . . were often represented in sexual terms."[34] Supporting this, Stoler contends that "through the policing of sex . . . racial boundaries were maintained."[35] Yet, as Levine observes, colonial culture was defined by "sex out of place," or sexual relations that crossed racial boundaries and therefore destabilized racial categories themselves.[36] Transgressions of permitted sexual relations between Europeans and indigenous people, ranging from marriage to concubinage and sexual slavery, posed an intolerable threat to the racial status of whites, as examples from the British colonies show (specific sexual cultures arose in French, Dutch, Portuguese, and British colonial territories).[37] According to Carmel Schrire, the sexual exploitation of enslaved women and consequent racial heterogeneity of the population was so widespread that "it was hard to distinguish Cape-born slaves from settlers on outward appearance."[38] This idea is explored in *The Slave Book*,[39] a historical novel about Cape slavery, when the protagonist, Somiela, finds that her appearance poses a fundamental threat to slave owners because "you're a slave and you dare to look white."[40] One can track the creation of gendered white identities in the colonies through panics about a "black peril" and the need to protect white women from predatory slave sexuality. In South Africa, steps taken by the British colonial authorities to moderate the power of slave owners before abolition led to a response from Dutch slave owners in Stellenbosch that was framed in immediately recognizable terms of racial and sexual panic. Thus, a letter to local officials emphasized the need to defend white women and children "from the danger of incited slaves. Not alone our Wives and Daughters, but also yours, will in a libidinous manner be prosecuted by our Slaves with rape and defloration."[41]

A comparison of representations of enslaved women in different imperial territories shows the commonalities in depictions of sexuality and slavery. Stoler notes that "Asian women [were] centerfolds for the imperial voyeur,"[42] and the historian John Mason points out that "the erotic allure of young slave women was explicit in the accounts of the Cape that white men composed."[43] As he observes, the transgression of permitted sexual boundaries motivated much of the appeal of the women in these accounts: "The eroticism of their writing depended as much on taboo . . . as on the exotic beauty of the women."[44] Demonstrating how resilient this pattern of images is, when I did archival research into the nineteenth- and early twentieth-century newspaper archives in the Cape, I found that the attractiveness of "Malay girls" was frequently referenced.[45] As Mason notes, there was a subtext to the constant testimony about the allure of the Malay women: "Commentators on the Cape stereotyped slave women as sensual and abandoned, in much the same way that slave women were described in the Caribbean and the American South. As in the New World, these stereotypes served to legitimate sexual exploitation."[46] Mason's research into the records of the Office of the Protector of Slaves reveals the many cases of sexual abuse that slave women brought against the owners. Indeed, as the feminist historian Gerda Lerner states, "for women, sexual exploitation marked the very definition of enslavement, as it did *not* for men."[47] At the same time, the depiction of certain male slaves as feminized and passive indicates that male slaves, too, could be subjected to sexual violence, as Rayda Jacobs displays through incidents of male rape in her novel *The Slave Book*.[48]

Intimacy

Because of the repressed record of the impact of slavery both in historical accounts and in the memories of descendants of slaves, probing the silences around sex and slavery raises issues of trauma. Some historians of colonialism have introduced a new term in discussing sexuality and slavery: *intimacy*. In their introduction to the collection *Senses of Culture*, editors Sarah Nuttall and Cheryl-Ann Michael propose a hermeneutics of South African history based on an "intimacy" predicated on a set of continuing, if uneven, exchanges, and they argue against "the over-determination of the political, the inflation of resistance and the fixation on race" that have marked previous approaches to South African culture.[49] In support of their thesis, they cite Tony Morphet's writing on architecture in Durban that shows stylistic continuities with other African port cities,[50] as well as David Bunn's study of poison, in which he points to a degree of mutual influence in the ideas about poison that circulated between the Khoisan, on the one hand, and Dutch and British settlers, on the other. Though intermittent and uneven, these exchanges "gesture toward the beginnings of an ambivalently shared knowledge of medicines and herbs."[51] Most important, Nuttall and Michael refer to Robert Shell's work on the subtle and profound transactions between slaves and slave owners at the Cape, which are reflected in South African food, language, architecture, and music.[52] Shell observes that the paternalistic and often violent space of the slaveholding household was also a space of continual and intimate encounters between slaves and their owners, which would have a permanent impact on the food, languages, and cultures of South Africa. Using such writing by Bunn, Morphet, and Shell, Nuttall and Michael envision the movement of South African studies of culture away from a preoccupation with "closure" and "borders"—tropes that they say have overdetermined the country's intellectual and cultural production because of apartheid—to "intimacies and connectivities."[53]

What is the nature of the intimacy that Nuttall and Michael propose? The authors draw strongly from Shell's *Children of Bondage*,[54] in which he identifies "intimacies" in the context of the physical proximity of domestic slavery as sites of cultural remaking. There, Shell argues, "slave ancestors injected diversity and challenge into an oppressive settler culture, bending and finally changing it, creolising it into a new culture. But it is toward this amalgam of human relationships, however difficult it may seem, that the historian must force readers to focus their thoughts. Another generation might find the trace elements, no matter how small, of a single domestic creole culture, within the otherwise starkly stratified and bifurcated slave society of early Africa."[55] He notes further: "Slavery brought different people together, not across the sights of a gun, as on the frontier, but in the setting of a home. Each slave was exposed to each owner and each settler to each slave on a very intimate footing. There was, in fact, a common reciprocal legacy . . . this legacy was the as yet unexamined Creole culture of South Africa, with its new cuisine, its new architecture, its new music, its melodious, forthright and poetic language, Afrikaans, first expressed in the Arabic script of the slaves' religion and written literature."[56] In these passages, Shell argues that slaves "injected" new elements of "diversity and challenge" into the dominant slave-owning culture, eventually "bending," "changing," and "creolising" it, leading to a new "amalgamated" culture.

This is a compelling and, in many ways, an important vision. Little attention has been paid to the impact of slavery and enslaved people on contemporary culture, partly as a result of the portrayal of the latter as passive and compliant figures on the side of the main currents of history. Studies by historians such as Shell, Worden, Pam Scully, Andrew Bank, and Shamil Jeppie, as well as recent work by the literary scholar Pumla Gqola,[57] balance the general absence of discussion about the impact of slavery on South African culture. However, does giving attention to such intimacies run the danger of displacing the reality of slavery—the "blood, sweat and tears" of colonialism?[58] Sean Jacobs contends that Nuttall and Michael's argument about foundational intimacies runs the risk of "hastily abandoning class and race, domination and resistance" in studies of South Africa.[59] This is a necessary caution. However, Nuttall and Michael make a key point about the need for nuanced theories on the intersections, silences, and complexities of South African history and culture. Precisely because the exclusion and silences in the archives mean that slaves' lives are absent except in highly constricted forms, if we read intimacy against the grain—as uncanny nearness, as charged silence and displacement, as trauma writing its meanings in elusive ways, much as Lisa Lowe does in "The Intimacies of Four Continents," an essay on the reverberating effects of colonialism and slavery on the modernity of the New World—we can attend to the absences of history that must be saved from erasure.[60]

This would allow us to read the charged silence in the archive about the violence of slavery in illuminating ways. In this vein (and unlike Shell), Andrew Bank argues that slaves at the Cape found the slave-owning household a dangerous and constricted space and that it was *outside* the paternalistic household that enslaved people were able to exercise a kind of agency, including through the practice of Islam.[61] In the early nineteenth century, such spaces—which lay beyond the control of slave owners except as viewers of compelling but unsettling sights such as the *ratiep*, a ritual exhibition of imperviousness to pain by adepts as their skin is pierced—enabled a reimagining of picturesque images of Islam. For instance, ratiep could be read as "an active expression of control over the body through denial of physical pain" and "a rejection of their owners' claims over their bodies."[62] Bank's analysis illustrates the idea that opened this chapter—that is, the ways in which history is written on the body.

Another instance of meaningful absences in the archives is slave naming. Mason notes that "the absence of slave family names in the records . . . tells us more about the enslaving society than about the slaves."[63] In this absence, the literary scholar Zoe Wicomb reads signs of shame about sex and slavery. In her important article "Shame and Identity, the Case of the Coloured in South Africa," Wicomb analyzes the meaning behind the use of European names by the descendants of slaves (who became known as "coloureds" in the postemancipation period). In the structures of slaveholding colonial society and in the development of a racial hierarchy that solidified into apartheid in the mid-twentieth century, coloured people in South Africa were made to feel "shame for our origins of slavery, shame for the miscegenation, and shame, as colonial racism became institutionalized, for being black, so that with the help of our European names we have lost all knowledge of our Xhosa, Indonesian, East African, or Khoi origins."[64] Wicomb argues that this suppressed knowledge, or "amnesia," is the result of "the shame of having had our bodies stared at, but also the shame invested in those (females) who mated with the colonizer."[65] This intense, internalized shame generated a powerful form of forgetting—"the total erasure of slavery from folk memory."[66] Thus, discussions about sex and particularly the systemic sexual violence that accompanied slavery at the Cape were manifested long after emancipation by particular kinds of historical silences, gendered shames, and internal psychological mechanisms that alluded to slavery by never naming it. For instance, Wicomb writes about the contradictory valuing of light skin and light eyes among the descendants of slaves, while at the same time these physical features testify to the "shame" imposed on the women who "mated with the colonizer."

As Wicomb's analysis shows, one can read in the portrayal of the body some of the unspoken elements of history. Her use of the word *mated* calls attention to the association of black women with animal-like sex and complicity with their dehumanization during slavery. The systematic scale of the sexual violence imposed on enslaved and enserfed women was so comprehensive, Wicomb contends, that it produced a social amnesia for the shamed victims and the valuing of the culture of the violators over their own. In effect, the sexual shame associated with slavery has erased memories of slavery itself, which has had the further effect of overwriting Xhosa, Malay, and Khoi histories in the Cape. It is also vital to note the gender of sexual shame in Wicomb's analysis. It is clear that the responsibility for promiscuity was attached to black women particularly, so that they fell even below black men in the colonial measure of humanity. My analysis in this chapter proposes to uncover the impact of slavery despite erasure and to conduct an archaeology of memory by reading the body.

I will now turn to a detailed analysis of three contemporary works of art in South Africa that engage with the legacy of a picturesque view of slavery at the Cape.

Visual Art, *Colour Me*, and Staging the Skin

> Skin . . . is the most visible of fetishes . . . and plays a public part in the racial drama that is enacted every day in colonial societies. . . . Skin, as a signifier of discrimination, must be produced or processed as visible.[67]

Berni Searle is a visual artist based in Cape Town. In 1999, her photographic installation *Colour Me*, which featured the naked body of the artist covered in red, brown, and yellow spices, attracted widespread public attention and critical acclaim.[68] The depth of color in the photographs is immediately engaging. Some photographs document the whole body of the artist. In others, only parts of her body appear. In both instances, her body is covered by spices, and the sensuous colors and textures of the spices are crafted into works of arresting visual power that are simultaneously weighted with history. I argue that *Colour Me* creates a new way of looking at spices in South Africa by calling attention to the enforced sexual availability of black women during slavery.

Searle's work uses spices—elements that are familiar, domestic, and seemingly innocuous—and inflects them with radically different meanings. The poet C. Louis Leipoldt famously referred to Malay women's "free, almost heroic" use of spices.[69] *Colour Me* revises familiar tropes of that type. Spices drove the Indian Ocean slave trade, the plantation system of the West Indies, and therefore also the transatlantic slave trade.[70] Slaves from East Africa, India, and Southeast Asia were transported in ships that called at the Cape on the same routes as the trade in commodities, such as spices. Therefore, in the notions of "exotic" spices and "exotic" skin, the memory of the brutal trades in human beings and commodities lingers. The sight of spice in *Colour Me* therefore indexes a violent history.

Searle's body in these images is both naked and covered by spices. This element of the installation evokes the history of uncovering and gazing at naked, vulnerable bodies in the Cape Colony. European colonists and the scientists who drew on their descriptions and traffic in biological samples based theories of human hierarchy on the bodies of colonized people. And the construction of "hypersexualized" images of indigenous and enslaved women and men at the Cape provided "key moral justification for genocide and slavery."[71] In the *Colour Me* installation, the naked body of the artist covered in spices articulates the role of the spice trade in driving the slave trade at the Cape as well as the sexual exploitation of slave women's bodies. The artist's prone form alludes to images of compliant Malay women in nineteenth-century paintings but subversively so, in that the figure in the photographs, though masked by spices, looks directly at the viewer.

In the photographs, Searle appears not adorned with the spices but almost stifled by them—they cover her mouth and eyes. The spectator feels the pleasure but also the compulsion of looking. Under the mesmerizingly rich colors of the spices, the unsettling availability of Searle's body reminds the spectator that the opportunity to look has been deliberately created. In being looked at, the artist presents viewers with the act of looking itself. The installation enacts the desire to look and also creates the sense of being caught in the act of looking. In *Colour Me*, Searle's body does not so much physically return the gaze as ask, by staging the occasion of gazing, who is being looked at and what object draws the gaze.

Searle's naked and prone body recalls colonial images of the insistent visibility of slave women and men in the Cape, such as the "undressed Khoekhoe women" whose bodies were a source of European popular and scientific fascination.[72] Yet Searle's body appears stiff rather than alluring, insistently corporeal rather than ethereal. In this mode, her body indexes the layered meanings of spice and of skin, showing how artifice is present in our perception of the "naked" body. In the photographs, there is a play between surface and covering, availability and excess. In one sense, the spices obscure the body. In another sense, they intensify attention to its outlines. Despite its nakedness, Searle's body is actually laden with meanings.

Though the nakedness of the body in the work seems to offer untrammeled access, the photographs in *Colour Me* perform a series of receding meanings. Searle's body encodes a lack of volition, yet her stillness also suggests absence and subtraction of the self. The very withdrawal by the self into an inaccessible space inside the body intensifies the effect of the gaze, and this desire for the receding subject becomes part of the experience of the artwork. The gaze becomes the invisible object of the work. *Colour Me* is a series of stagings: "the act of looking, the to-be-looked-at-ness"[73] of the body, the history of spice, and the skin as a fetish that promises to resolve all these unstable meanings.

Fiction

The slow awakening to the role of slavery in understandings of "race" and sexuality in South Africa means that one has to look obliquely at the topic. In this section, I will explore the impact of slavery on discourses of sexuality in the occurrence of sexual virtuousness and licentiousness in two novels about slavery in South Africa, *The Slave Book* and *Unconfessed*. I will also analyze *Disgrace*, a work of fiction that engages with the topic of sexuality and slavery in ways that are formally and thematically complex and evoke the country's history of representation.

The title of Rayda Jacobs's historical novel *The Slave Book* is taken from the name of the ledger in which the sales of slaves in the Cape were recorded. The novel's heroine is a beautiful, light-skinned, sexually virtuous slave woman who eventually marries a convert to Islam. *The Slave Book*, which until *Unconfessed* was the most prominent historical novel about slavery in South Africa, portrays black and Muslim female characters as obedient, selfless, and redemptive figures. South African literature did not have the kind of formal or thematic innovation of Toni Morrison's *Beloved*, which dares to imagine a protagonist whose actions and interior life are complex and troubling, until the publication of *Unconfessed*, a novel inspired by the trial records in the Cape archives of an enslaved woman who was convicted of murdering her child and imprisoned on Robben Island. *Unconfessed* uses a poetic, nonlinear narrative structure that mirrors the psychic disruptions of the protagonist's life. In fiction, as in the historical record, the body is the site where slavery exercised its visible authority. I will turn now to a portrayal of sexuality and slavery in the novel *Disgrace*. Thereafter, I will analyze *The Slave Book* and *Unconfessed* in greater detail.

Disgrace

In its story of the fall into disgrace of a university professor named David Lurie, *Disgrace*, a novel by the Nobel Prize–winning author J. M. Coetzee, touches on the legacy of colonialism for contemporary ideas about race and sex in South Africa. From its opening pages, *Disgrace* maps the geography of Cape Town as a sexual space. We see the city through Lurie's eyes, and it is through his perspective that the events in *Disgrace* are conveyed. Although Lurie focalizes the story for readers, he is nonetheless a coolly distant protagonist, and the novel constructs him through third-person narration as an abstracted, watchful, and largely unsympathetic figure.

In the opening pages of the novel, we learn how Lurie navigates the city as a sexualized space. Walking through Cape Town, he is "at home amid the flux of bodies where eros stalks and glances flash like arrows."[74] Beneath the language of romance, *Disgrace* maps a city that traffics in sex amid the bustle of its streets. Though Lurie speaks of "eros" stalking the streets, we learn that he pays for sex with a prostitute named Soraya. "On Thursday afternoons he drives to Green Point,"[75] we are told. This reference to a suburb just outside the center of Cape Town that is notorious for prostitution also evokes the strict demarcation of space along racial lines during the apartheid era. Interracial sex was forbidden by the Immorality Act during apartheid, and coloured bodies such as Soraya's were a particular focus of both revulsion and attraction, for they signaled the history of forbidden and desired sex between white and black bodies that long preceded apartheid. During apartheid, Green Point was a place where black and white people interacted and even lived with one another in transgression of the prohibitions of the period. Such "grey" areas were seen as spaces of racial and also sexual transgression. *Disgrace*'s opening scenes thus refer to hidden spatial relations in Cape Town, and through the figure of a Muslim prostitute, I argue, the novel alludes to the submerged history of sexual exploitation in the urban spaces of the city.

A visual economy holds bodies in relation to each other in the city. Lurie views the landscape through the bodies of women. The first woman we see through his eyes is Soroya, with her "honey-brown body" and "long black hair and dark, liquid eyes."[76] Through the body of Soraya, the city is rendered explicable, "contented," and "lulling."[77] With these signifiers, Soraya can be seen as a deliberate literary summoning of the placid and picturesque Malay figure placed near the edge of the frame to mark the boundary of domesticated space. The familiar but unstable strategy of using a picturesque Muslim figure outlines the secret sexual geography of Cape Town in the opening pages of *Disgrace.* Yet the strategy is always shadowed by instability and signals an ultimately fragile hold over space. Eventually, Lurie's relationship with Soraya suffers precisely this fate, and his place in the city changes irrevocably.

As noted earlier, the very name of Cape Town had a sexual meaning. In the colonial period, the last name Van de Kaap (of the Cape) was given to a slave born at the Cape.[78] Due to the enforced prostitution of enslaved women, the Cape Colony was known as one of the most racially heterogeneous places in the world.[79] The name Van de Kaap therefore indexes a widespread and brutal system of sexual violence. The issue of names is important in the novel because Coetzee refuses to name race in the narrative. Instead, he uses names such as Isaacs to indicate slave ancestry, since many slaves were given biblical names, and Soraya, which means "Princess" in Farsi and is a common name for Muslim women in the Cape. Thus, the author is showing that the historical meanings of race and sex are imprinted on spaces and bodies. In a charged reference to the geography of the city, Lurie speculates that aside from their weekly assignation, Soraya lives "a respectable life in the suburbs, in Rylands or Athlone," areas designated as "Indian" and "coloured," respectively, under apartheid.[80] Lurie carelessly conflates the two areas, though their separate existence was part of apartheid's obsessively detailed attempts to name and fix race in place.

Another way in which the novel alludes to the hidden sexual history of the Cape occurs during the disciplinary hearings to which Lurie is summoned after his affair with a student is made public. While discussing Lurie's actions, a black female administrator named Farodia Rassool notes the "long history of exploitation" of black female bodies as a factor in the committee's deliberations.[81] As readers, we see with discomforting closeness the effect of that history on the unequal relationship between Lurie and his student Melani. Their last sexual encounter is described from Lurie's perspective as "not rape, not quite that, but undesired nevertheless, undesired to the core."[82] Yet, as readers, we also see that Melani's inert body contradicts what Lurie insists is "not rape, not quite that," and we understand what his repetition of "not . . . not" unconsciously conveys. The novel appeared in the same year as Searle's *Colour Me* exhibition, and the unmoving body of Melani testifies, like Searle's images, to a "long history of exploitation" that is usually unspoken.

The novel's unblinking testimony to sexual violence in this scene—despite Lurie's self-serving denial—is recalled in a second and deliberately paralleled instance of violence. After refusing to cooperate with the university's disciplinary committee, Lurie is dismissed, and he leaves Cape Town to join his daughter, Lucy, on her farm in Grahamstown in the Eastern Cape. The second part of the novel tells of Lucy's rape by three men. Again, the novel signals that it has deliberately called on the historical sensitivity about this theme. Coetzee has written elsewhere that the rape of a white woman is "the *ne plus ultra* of colonial horror-fantasies."[83] Lucy's rape and its implications for representations of race and sexual violence in contemporary South Africa has led to great controversy about *Disgrace*, but it is clear that Coetzee has deliberately invoked a parallel between the "not rape, not quite that" of Melani and the rape of Lucy. By its twinned and doubled structure, the novel connects the "strangeness" in Cape Town to the violence in the Eastern Cape.[84] The encounters between Lurie and Soraya at the beginning of the novel, far from being simply a prelude to the real substance of the novel, prefigure the "strangeness" that follows.

Perhaps it is through Soraya that *Disgrace* suggests most clearly the ongoing salience of colonial discourses about sexuality for contemporary South Africa. Soraya appears in the familiar language of the picturesque—as "pliant,"[85] "exotic,"[86] and "docile,"[87]—and sex between Lurie and Soraya is described as leisurely and "complacent."[88] Referring to the owners of the flat in which he meets Soraya every week, Lurie muses, "In a sense they own Soraya too, this part of her, this function."[89] Seen in these terms, Soraya recalls the enforced prostitution of Muslim slaves in the Cape Colony. I contend that through reference to the leisurely possession of bodies in these scenes at the beginning of the novel, *Disgrace* alludes to the complex impact of slavery on discourses of sexuality and race in South Africa.

The Slave Book

The Slave Book is set in 1832, two years before the British would abolish slavery at the Cape. The British had taken control of the colony from the Dutch in 1806, and relations between Dutch and British settlers and between Dutch settlers and the British administration were filled with tension and contestation. In 1823, to curb the excessive abuse of slaves, the British instituted the Office of the Protector of Slaves, which gave enslaved people a narrow public space in which to bring complaints against their masters. At the opening of *The Slave Book*, Jacobs reprints the Tulbagh Slave Code of 1754, a revealing list of regulations that specify punishments for slaves at the Cape:

> Slaves
> Are to be indoors after 10 PM or carry a lantern
> Are not to ride horses or wagons in streets
> Are not to sing, whistle or make any other sound at night
> Are not to meet in bars, buy alcohol, or form groups on public holidays
> Are not to stop in the street to talk to other slaves
> Who insulted or falsely accused a freeman, would be flogged
> Who struck a slaveholder–put to death
> Are not permitted to own or to carry guns
> Free Blacks aren't equal to free white burghers
> Freed slave women are not to wear coloured silk or hoop skirts, fine lace, or any decoration on their hats, or earrings made of gems or imitation gems.[90]

Throughout the novel, Jacobs also incorporates quotations from travel writing by European visitors to the Cape to show the continuity between the events that occur in *The Slave Book* and in the historical record.

The novel succeeds in creating a sympathetic protagonist in Somiela, as well as pointing to the connections between settler abuses of slaves and indigenous Khoisan people, who were subjected to genocidal practices and conditions similar to enslavement by the settlers. In *The Slave Book*, the slave owner's wife, Marieta, insults Somiela by using a common term for sexual promiscuity: "We can see alright what she is. A naai-mandje."[91] This crude sexual jibe—implying that Somiela, the visible result of interracial sex, was guilty of licentiousness—exemplifies the brutal logic that blamed slave women for their sexual exploitation by their owners. Yet Jacobs ensures that we know that Somiela is an expressly virtuous heroine, proven by the extent of the slave mistress's violent reaction to her husband's apparent interest in the young woman. The latter's hair is cut off; she is whipped; and her jewelry and dress, made by the mother from whom she has been separated since they were sold to different masters, are confiscated.

However, along with its determinedly sympathetic heroine, the novel also replicates some of the regressive tropes through which slavery had been represented at the Cape, where an emphasis on phenotype and physical attractiveness colluded with the commodification of slaves' bodies. Somiela, for instance, is described as having "a tawny complexion, with green eyes and brown hair; a half-breed. The half-breeds were the favoured slaves, and the price . . . would be high."[92] Furthermore, Kananga, the Mozambican slave who is the overseer on the farm where Somiela lives, is shown to be violent and animal-like through the sexual abuse of male slaves. His malevolence and uncontrollable violence toward other slaves makes him an almost inhuman character. Worryingly, Kananga's dark skin and his sexual proclivity toward men seem to prompt the most revulsion in the novel, more so even than the slave owners do.[93]

However, *The Slave Book* also points to more subtle anxieties behind the contradictory valuing of mixed-race slaves and contempt for naai-mandjies. Such conflicting views and the fact that freed slave women were forbidden by the Tulbagh Slave Code from wearing "coloured silk or hoop skirts, fine lace, or any decoration on their hats, or earrings made of gems or imitation gems" indicated the severe anxiety about the purity of whiteness in the colony.[94] Because of the extent of sexual relations across racial boundaries in the Cape due to the enforced prostitution of slave women, whiteness was not self-evident. Moreover, skin color was not a reliable indicator of who was a slave and who a slave owner, which was the reason for the detailed policing of the body evident in the Tulbagh Code. Because of the anxiety generated by the indeterminacy of whiteness, an extensive and complex set of relations developed around skin color, citizenship, and social status at the Cape. Harman, the man with whom Somiela falls in love, who converts to Islam in order to marry her, exemplifies these anxieties surrounding race. Harman is not, it emerges in the novel, white, though he is accepted as such by the slave owner, Andries de Villiers, and is even pursued by one of the latter's daughters.

These complexities, as well as its status as one of the first South African novels to recount slavery from the perspective of the enslaved, make *The Slave Book* a vital contribution to its genre. Ultimately, however, this contribution is limited by the constraints of the virtuous heroine and the format of the historical romance. As a result, *The Slave Book* remains an early incarnation of the South Africa novel about slavery. Jacobs's later novel, *Confessions of a Gambler*, moves beyond these limitations to create a complex, morally ambiguous, sexually adventurous heroine who is not so easily redeemable and who also happens to be Muslim.[95]

Unconfessed

Unconfessed, the novel about slavery by Yvette Christiansë published eight years after *The Slave Book*, is a groundbreaking novel in both form and power. The only words the protagonist, Sila, writes before her forbidden writing lessons are stopped are "My name is Sila van Mozambique."[96] When the novel opens, we learn that she is known by the authorities as "Sila van den Kaap, slave woman of Jacobus Stephanus Van der Wat of Plettenberg Bay in the District of George. A woman moved from master to master, farm to farm, from the district's prison, to the big town's prison. A woman fit for a hanging. Child murderer."[97] Her change of name is due to the fact that Sila had been granted her freedom by a former owner, Hendrina Jansen. However, Jansen's will was stolen by her son, who pretended that Sila was a Cape-born slave and sold her to another farmer. Sila was sold from farm to farm, until she eventually arrived in Cape Town. The fact that she killed her child seems to consign her to the trope of monstrous black mother. However, the novel recounts that after her son, Baro, was grievously injured by her slave owner, Sila chose to murder him rather than allow him to continue to live as a slave.

Memories of slavery among the descendants of slaves have been largely suppressed or obliquely remembered, and *Unconfessed* is remarkable both for recounting Sila's memory of her childhood in Mozambique before the slave raiders arrived and for creating scenes of a "middle passage" in her journey from Mozambique. This is recalled in the scenes of moving across the water to Robben Island, the infamous piece of land that has been used as a prison since the earliest days of the colony. Sila narrates what she sees: "Sometimes I set myself the task of staring at the ships. . . . And some days I make my eyes reach far, further still, and I tell you I see the anchors splash into the water off that coast, there, that Cape of Tears, Cape of Death, Cape of Struggles."[98] This passage directly engages with the way in which slavery has been subsumed behind the representation of the Cape as a place of leisure and beauty. The novel notes the cruel erasures of this aesthetic discourse through the contemptuous words of a visitor to the prison on Robben Island on seeing the imprisoned slave women: "It is such a shame that such wretched creatures should be in such a place of beauty."[99]

The starkest difference between *The Slave Book* and *Unconfessed* is the latter's attention to the sexual abuse of women slaves. Sila's children are the result of rape by her owners and by the men who pay the prison guards for sex with imprisoned female slaves. In the opening pages of the novel, when the new prison superintendent visits her cell, Sila thinks at first that he has paid to have sex with her before realizing that he believes her story. She says, "This time would be different from all the other times, all the other visitors. . . . There would be no quick counting of coins, or the rough laugh he gave as the visitor ran to wash himself."[100] This recounting of sexual slavery does not try to counter the stereotype of black female licentiousness by creating a virginal heroine but testifies to the brutality of repeated sexual abuse to which slave women were subjected.

The novel ends with scenes of both beauty and loss. Amid the brutality of prison life, Sila finds a transcendent and healing love with a fellow prisoner on Robben Island, Lys, an indigenous woman from the Cape. The relationship between Sila and Lys creates a different view of the body than has been possible in Sila's life until that point. She, Lys, and the other women prisoners on the island share their food, take care of one another's ill and damaged bodies, look after the children born of sexual abuse, and speak to one another in languages that they share with no one else. Despite their imprisonment, Sila and Lys create an intimacy that cannot be imagined by the guards and therefore remains invisible to them. Sila recounts that "we reach out and we are there. Being woman is enough here."[101] The completeness of their relationship acts as a language that cannot be read by the wardens and guards. Their bodies become sources of comfort, love, and sexual pleasure to each other. Within the institution of slavery, their relationship is a form of rebellion and resilience. This sanctuary takes shape through poetic language, in which Sila repeats the name "Lys. Lys."[102] Upon the latter's death, Sila envisages the prison of Robben Island as scattered with the names of everyone she has lost. This legacy of names seeds the island with memories that will be felt by all subsequent generations. The relationship between the two women therefore reclaims their bodies, their pasts, their languages, and their futures from imprisonment and slavery.

Reading the Body in the Landscape

In this chapter, I have shown that widespread sexual violence during the period of slavery in South Africa has an ongoing salience for contemporary attitudes about race and sexuality in the country. The absence of a broad public discussion on slavery and sexuality is countered by increasingly visible themes about slavery and identity in contemporary South African fiction and art. I have analyzed novels such as *The Slave Book*, *Unconfessed*, and *Disgrace* and the visual art installation *Colour Me*, all of which revisit elements of the history of slavery that otherwise remain untouched. *Unconfessed*, I argue, reframes South African discourses on slavery and sexuality by drawing on archival material to convey in complex and resonant ways the interior psychic reality of the life of its enslaved protagonist. The novel replaces the conventional portrayals of the Cape as a leisured and privileged space by recalling that the city was built with slave labor. For Sila, the novel's protagonist, even the ocean, usually shown as a beautiful background to the cityscape, reminds her of what she has lost since being stolen as a child from Mozambique. The city may be an Edenic sight for some, but viewed from Robben Island, its aesthetics have a different meaning. Portrayed through the cruelties of sexual slavery and physical abuse, the city of beauty is renamed "Cape of Tears, Cape of Death, Cape of Struggles."[103] The novels and visual art discussed in this chapter reinsert the body into a Cape landscape from which the record of slavery and sexual exploitation had been elided. Instead, these texts show the profound and lingering impact of slavery on contemporary discourses of race and sexuality in South Africa. They unsettle the stubbornly picturesque mode that has shaped perspectives of the Cape since the colonial period, and in doing so, they uncover the hidden sexual geography of the city.

Notes

1. Rayda Jacobs, *The Slave Book* (Cape Town: Kwela, 1998), and Yvette Christiansë, *Unconfessed* (Cape Town: Kwela, 2007).

2. N. Worden, *The Making of Modern South Africa: Conquest, Segregation and Apartheid* (Oxford: Blackwell, 1994), 9.

3. N. Worden, *Slavery in Dutch South Africa* (Cambridge: Cambridge University Press, 1985), 7.

4. N. Worden and C. Crais, eds., *Breaking the Chains: Slavery and Its Legacy in the Nineteenth-Century Cape Colony* (Johannesburg: Wits University Press, 1994).

5. T. Keegan, *Colonial South Africa and the Origins of the Racial Order* (Charlottesville: University Press of Virginia, 1996), 16.

6. Worden, *Slavery in Dutch South Africa*, and Wayne Dooling, *Slavery, Emancipation and Colonial Rule in South Africa* (Athens: Ohio University Press, with UKZN Press, 2008), 7.

7. Robert Ross, *Cape of Torments: Slavery and Resistance in South Africa* (London: Routledge and Kegan Paul, 1983), 2, and J. Mason, *Social Death and Resurrection: Slavery and Emancipation in South Africa* (Charlottesville: University of Virginia Press, 2003).

8. Worden, *Slavery in Dutch South Africa*, 4.

9. Dooling, *Slavery, Emancipation and Colonial Rule*, 12.

10. M. Hall, *An Archaeology of the Modern World* (London: Routledge, 2000), 198.

11. Ibid.

12. Robert Shell, *Children of Bondage: A Social History of the Slave Society at the Cape of Good Hope, 1652–1838* (Hanover, Conn.: Wesleyan University Press, 1994); F. R. Bradlow and M. Cairns, *The Early Cape Muslims: A Study of Their Mosques, Genealogy and Origins* (Cape Town: A. A. Balkema, 1978).

13. Worden, *Slavery in Dutch South Africa*, 4.

14. Robert Shell, "Between Christ and Mohammed: Conversion, Slavery and Gender in the Urban Western Cape," in *Christianity in South Africa: A*

Political, Social, and Cultural History, ed. Richard Elphick and Rodney Davenport (Oxford: James Currey, 1997), 268–85, 272.

15. George McCall Theal, *Records of the Cape Colony from February 1793*, vol. 34, *By Cape of Good Hope (South Africa)* (London: Public Record Office, 1905), 1–2.

16. J. M. Coetzee, *White Writing* (New Haven, Conn.: Yale University Press, 1988), 5.

17. Ibid.

18. Ross, *Cape of Torments*, 3.

19. See G. Baderoon, "Ambiguous Visibility: Islam and the Making of a South African Landscape," *Arab World Geographer* 8, no. 1–2 (2005): 90–103.

20. Coetzee, *White Writing*, 28.

21. Shamil Jeppie, "I. D. du Plessis and the 'Re-invention' of the 'Malay,' c. 1935–1952" ([Cape Town]: unpublished seminar paper, Centre for African Studies, University of Cape Town, [1988]), 3.

22. Mason, *Social Death and Resurrection.*

23. Keegan, *Colonial South Africa*, 20.

24. P. D. Gqola, "'Slaves don't have opinions': Inscriptions of Slave Bodies and the Denial of Agency in Rayda Jacobs' *The Slave Book*," in *Coloured by History, Shaped by Place*, ed. Z. Erasmus (Cape Town: Kwela, 2001), 45–63.

25. Pam Scully, *Liberating the Family?: Gender and British Slave Emancipation in the Rural Western Cape, South Africa, 1823–1853* (Portsmouth, N.H.: David Philip, 1997), 36, and Baderoon, "Ambiguous Visibility."

26. Baderoon, "Ambiguous Visibility."

27. J. D. Wrathall, "Provenance as Text: Reading the Silences around Sexuality in Manuscript Collections," *Journal of American History* 79, no. 1 (1992): 165–78.

28. Frank R. Bradlow, "Islam at the Cape of Good Hope," *South African Historical Journal* 13, no. 1 (1981): 12–19.

29. P. Levine, *Prostitution, Race and Politics: Policing Venereal Disease in the British Empire* (New York: Routledge, 2003), 325.

30. A. L. Stoler, *Carnal Knowledge and Imperial Power: Race and the Intimate in Colonial Rule* (Berkeley: University of California Press, 2002), 42.

31. Keegan, *Colonial South Africa*, 20.

32. Levine, *Prostitution, Race and Politics*, 182.

33. Stoler, *Carnal Knowledge*, 54.

34. Levine, *Prostitution, Race and Politics*, 324.

35. Stoler, *Carnal Knowledge*, 54.

36. Levine, *Prostitution, Race and Politics*, 179.

37. See Stoler, *Carnal Knowledge*; Anne McLintock, *Imperial Leather: Race, Gender and Sexuality in the Colonial Contest* (New York: Routledge, 1995).

38. Carmel Schrire, *Tigers in Africa: Stalking the Past at the Cape of Good Hope* (Lansdowne: University of Cape Town Press, 2002), 36.

39. Jacobs, *Slave Book.*
40. Ibid., 33.
41. Mason, *Social Death and Resurrection,* 72.
42. Stoler, *Carnal Knowledge,* 44.
43. Mason, *Social Death and Resurrection,* 93.
44. Ibid.
45. Baderoon, "Ambiguous Visibility."
46. Mason, *Social Death and Resurrection,* 95.
47. Gerda Lerner quoted in ibid., 101.
48. Jacobs, *Slave Book,* 53.
49. S. Nuttall and C. Michael, eds., "Introduction," in *Senses of Culture, South African Culture Studies* (Cape Town: Oxford University Press, 2000), 1.
50. Ibid., 4.
51. Ibid., 8.
52. Robert Shell, *Children of Bondage: A Social History of the Slave Society at the Cape of Good Hope, 1652–1838* (Hanover, Conn.: Wesleyan University Press, 1994); also see Nuttall and Michael, "Introduction," 5–8.
53. Nuttall and Michael, "Introduction," 5.
54. Shell, *Children of Bondage.*
55. Ibid., 415, quoted in Nuttall and Michael, "Introduction," 5.
56. Ibid.
57. Pumla Dineo Gqola, *What Is Slavery to Me?: Postcolonial Memory in Post-apartheid South Africa* (Johannesburg: Wits University Press, 2010).
58. Gutierrez quoted in Stoler, *Carnal Knowledge,* 14.
59. S. H. Jacobs, review of *Senses of Culture, South African Culture Studies,* ed. Sarah Nuttall and Cheryl Ann Michael, H-SAfrica, H-Net Reviews (September 2002); http://www.h-net.org/reviews/showrev.php?id=6731.
60. Lisa Lowe, "The Intimacies of Four Continents," in *Haunted by Empire: Geographies of Intimacy in North American History,* ed. A. L. Stoler (Durham, N.C.: Duke University Press, 2006): 191–212, 192–93.
61. Andrew Bank, "Slavery without Slaves: Robert Shell's *Social History of Cape Slave Society,*" *South African Historical Journal* 33, no. 1 (1995): 184.
62. Ibid.
63. Mason, *Social Death and Resurrection,* 86.
64. Zoe Wicomb, "Shame and Identity: The Case of the Coloured in South Africa," in *Writing South Africa: Literature, Apartheid and Democracy, 1970–1995,* ed. D. Attridge and R. Jolly (Cambridge: Cambridge University Press, 1998), 100.
65. Ibid., 92.
66. Ibid., 100.
67. Homi Bhabha, *The Location of Culture* (London: Routledge, 1994), 78–79.

68. My earlier writing on *Colour Me* appears in Gabeba Baderoon, "The African Oceans—Tracing the Sea as Memory of Slavery in South African Literature and Culture," *Research in African Literatures* 40, no. 4 (2009): 89–107.

69. C. Louis Leipoldt, *Leipoldt's Cape Cookery* (Cape Town: W. J. Fleisch, 1976), 11.

70. T. Morton, *The Poetics of Spice: Romantic Consumerism and the Exotic* (Cambridge: Cambridge University Press, 2000), 172.

71. Elaine Salo and Pumla Gqola, "Editorial: Subaltern Sexualities," *Feminist Africa*, no. 6 (2006): 1.

72. Ibid.

73. Laura Mulvey quoted in D. Lewis, "The Conceptual Art of Berni Searle," *Agenda*, no. 50 (2001): 108.

74. J. M. Coetzee, *Disgrace* (London : Vintage, 1999), 6.

75. Ibid., 1.

76. Ibid.

77. Ibid., 8

78. Jacobs, *Slave Book*, 25.

79. C. Hendricks, "Ominous Liaisons: Tracing the Interface between 'Race' and Sex at the Cape," in *Coloured by History, Shaped by Place*, ed. Z. Erasmus (Cape Town: Kwela, 2001), 37.

80. Coetzee, *Disgrace*, 3.

81. Ibid., 53.

82. Ibid., 25.

83. Coetzee quoted in D. Attwell, "Race in *Disgrace*," *Interventions: International Journal of Postcolonial Studies* 4, no. 3 (2002): 331–41, 336.

84. Coetzee, *Disgrace*, 6.

85. Ibid., 5.

86. Ibid., 7.

87. Ibid., 1.

88. Ibid.

89. Ibid., 2.

90. Jacobs, *Slave Book*, unpaginated.

91. Ibid., 25. *Naai-mandje* literally means "sewing basket" in Dutch, but the word *naai* (in both Dutch and, later, Afrikaans) is also a crude term for sex. Therefore, Somiela is accused here of being a promiscuous woman or someone defined solely by her sexual function.

92. Ibid., 16.

93. Ibid., 53.

94. Ibid., unpaginated.

95. Rayda Jacobs, *Confessions of a Gambler* (Cape Town: Kwela, 2003).

96. Christiansë, *Unconfessed*, 12.

97. Ibid.

98. Ibid., 66.
99. Ibid., 73
100. Ibid., 19.
101. Ibid., 334.
102. Ibid.
103. Ibid., 66.

19

INNOCENCE CURTAILED

Reading Maternity and Sexuality as Labor in Canadian Representations of Black Girls

Charmaine Nelson

It is commonly said that no girl or woman receives a certain kind of insult unless she invites it. That does not apply to a colored girl and woman in the South. The color of her face alone is sufficient invitation to the Southern white man—these same men who profess horror that a white gentleman can entertain a colored one at his table.[1]

As we went out in the morning, I observed several women, who carried their young children in their arms to the field. These mothers laid their children at the side of the fence, or under the shade of the cotton plants, whilst they were at work; and when the rest of us went to get water, they would go to give suck to their children, requesting someone to bring them water in gourds, which they were careful to carry to the field with them. One young woman did not, like the others, leave her child at the end of the row, but had contrived a sort of rude knapsack, made of a piece of coarse linen cloth, in which she fastened her child, which was very young, upon her back; and in this way carried it all day, and performed her task at the hoe with the other people.[2]

Both of these quotations draw attention to the social status and value of black women within and shortly after slavery in America. The connection between them is sexuality and its racialization in colonial societies. In the first quotation, the southern colored woman laments the hypersexualization of black women by white men, the very men who are unwilling to participate in legitimate social exchange and interaction with the same colored people they daily assault with libidinous advances. In the latter (but historically earlier) quotation, the results of this ongoing hypersexualization are evoked, if not directly elaborated. Within the colonial context of transatlantic slavery, black female slaves became mothers through sexual coercion or outright rape in many cases; through sex with other black slaves or free men; and, significantly, often through their exploitative sexual contact with the white men who owned them or wielded power over them. The fact that the female slaves' status as laborers was not disrupted by their maternal duties (they are suckling their babies in the fields) underscores the extent to which the humane care of black slave children and the postpartum care of black slave mothers were generally not priorities for white owners, beyond a concern for their own profit and accumulation of wealth. Clearly, too, the suckling of the infants and the rearing of a new generation of slaves were also seen as part of the labor they performed for their owners. Indeed, the sexuality and the related "breeding" functions of female slaves within the context of so-called natural increase were among a range of labors that black women were expected to provide to their white masters and mistresses. I would argue, then, that the racialization of sexuality as "black" and abject and the strategic exploitation of this black female sexuality for pleasure and profit were core elements of the "proper" practice of transatlantic slavery.

As I have posited elsewhere, the racialization of sexuality was, in part, a material practice, intrinsic to the literal daily lives and exchanges between human subjects and their environments within the institution of slavery. But it was also a product of representation—how a white-dominated artistic and cultural realm *represented* black subjects in ways that conflated blackness with the status of slave, visualized ideals of black sexual excess, normalized white supremacy, and authorized white access to black bodies.[3]

But since this sweeping sexual exploitation led deliberately to the production of more slaves (the children who became property of the slave mothers' white owners, regardless of race and the social status of the father), it behooves us to ask questions not only about the histories of female slave sexuality and slave maternity but also about the slave children themselves. In this chapter, I hope to enhance our understanding of the lives and experiences of these black children, specifically enslaved black girls, by investigating, on the one hand, their material realities and, on the other, how they were visually represented in Western art both during and after slavery.

Although the term *transatlantic slavery* generally conjures up images of tropical or semitropical locations such as the American South or the Caribbean, not all sites of slavery featured fields of sugarcane or cotton or swaying palm trees. Certainly, this was not true for northern sites of slavery, many of which have been strategically sanitized and erased from larger scholarly and lay discussions, aligned instead with abolitionism; northern liberalism; and, as in Canada, the Underground Railroad. However, this erasure is indeed retroactive, a failure caused by academic blind spots and a political strategy that has effectively worked to read nations such as Canada out of histories of transatlantic slavery and, connectedly, triangular trade and the black diaspora.[4]

This chapter is an attempt to check this retroactive elision. To carry out this undertaking, I must first challenge the absence of race in Childhood Studies, especially the erasure of the study of black children from Canadian Studies. But I must also reconceptualize sexuality itself, for what the context of slavery reveals is that enslaved black females were strategically initiated into sexuality, materially and within representation, earlier than their enslaved black male and free white counterparts. For the female slave, the centrality of their sexuality for the pleasure and economic gain of their white masters and mistresses rendered age largely insignificant with regard to their strategic sexual exploitation.

Defining Childhood

The term *childhood* marks a specific temporal and social designation of assumed human development. But the equation of childhood with a time of innocence and protection is and has been an experience of those whose identities have afforded them access to necessary forms of protection.[5] Childhood is not an essential or universal category; it is not an automatic benefit of one's age or time of life but rather the product of a discursive structure that both empowers and marginalizes subjects on the basis of markers of identity such as class, race, sex, and gender.

Early Western scholars of childhood often forged their ideas through the repeated alienation and othering of subjects who were not white and upper class. To examine race and childhood is to call for a postcolonial reading capable of scrutinizing the ways in which the Western scholarship of Childhood Studies has neglected the bodies and subjectivities of Native children and children of color and centralized the white child as the universal paradigm upon which explorations should be based. To examine race, class, sex, and gender simultaneously is to acknowledge the necessity of black/postcolonial feminist practice and to account for distinctions between male and female subjects. For the purposes of this investigation, I am considering childhood to be from infancy into the early to middle teen years, in part because of the socialization and developmental processes that every human must undergo over the course of years and in part because of the standard age of the start of menarche (globally seen as a girl's right of passage) in black slave girls; James Trussell and Richard Steckel have calculated this as age fifteen.[6]

It is my contention that representations of black children, especially historical ones, in the Canadian context and in other locations of the diaspora demand an understanding of the construction of childhood (or perhaps it is better to call this an erasure) within transatlantic slavery. As an institution that literally changed the world over the course of some four hundred years, slavery is no little consideration. Rather, it should be thought of as the very foundational ground upon which notions of personhood and childhood became racialized and black children were effectively marked off from white children in biology, appearance, behavior, and experience. Although this chapter is an attempt to recuperate the social, cultural, and psychic contexts of black girls' lives historically in Canada by examining the ways that they were represented in Canadian art, the task cannot be rigorously accomplished without also examining relevant information about and artworks representing slave populations and free black subjects in other contexts.

For one thing, the scant historical scholarship on black children in Canada compels us to look beyond national borders for relevant methodological models and data. But besides being a way to fill research gaps fundamentally caused by scholarly neglect and academic racism, the need to also look outward stems from a specific migratory reality: many black child slaves who ended up in Canada were either born abroad and forcibly migrated to settlements such as Montreal and Halifax or were born to slave parents who themselves were not native to Canada. Therefore, the scholarship on the daily lives, labors, and health of black slave women and children in locations such as the Caribbean and the American South is directly relevant to black slave children in Canada.

Slavery's context is deeply paradoxical and poignant. Slavery was a profoundly conflicted and grotesque institution comprising mind-boggling events and practices that seem today to make impossible bedfellows. It necessitated a constant and coerced physical, sexual, and biological intimacy between whites and blacks. This *perverse intimacy*—wherein black bodies were a necessity of white power, society, sexuality, economy, and family—led not to the liberation of black subjects but rather to their further marginalization and abuse. Black slave children inhabited this world, and their production through visual representation is the necessary foundation for an understanding of later twentieth-century representations in the Canadian context.

Putting Race into Childhood Studies

Writing in 1904, a woman described as southern and colored lamented her helplessness as a mother who was incapable of protecting her children: "I dread to see my children grow. I know not their fate. Where the white girl has one temptation, mine will have many. Where the white boy has every opportunity and protection, mine will have few opportunities and no protection. It does not matter how good or wise my children may be, they are colored. When I have said that, all is said."[7] This mother's heartbreak was prompted by a deep understanding of the nature of racism and the ways that it fractured the romantic Eurocentric ideal of childhood innocence. This innocence, she understood, was not available to her black children. What is interesting is the multifaceted nature of the problem of race or blackness for her children. Temptation, opportunity, and protection were the dimensions through which she expressed the unequal and potentially disastrous consequences for them. The overdetermined signifier of black skin, in its conflation with colonial stereotypes of pathology, immorality, social deviance, and so on, was a burden that would precede her children throughout their lives and allow for their premature condemnation. Thus, it is crucial to note how transatlantic slavery made race a matter of class; the blackness of the black body was seen as a stain that not only placed blacks on the lowest rungs of society but effectively denied them the right to aspire to higher class positions.

Although scholars focusing on childhood have recently explored the ways in which children were molded—physically, emotionally, mentally, and socially—such scholarship has concentrated on issues of child labor as a problem of class structures.[8] Meanwhile, the usually unstated racial focus (whiteness) overlooks an endemic problem: the naturalization of black child labor and exploitation in the colonial territories of these vast European empires where slavery flourished. Ironically, at the moment when Western disciplines began to liken white children to savages or primitives, black people were being infantilized and likened to children; both groups were seen as requiring civilization, which would be best delivered by socially and economically elite white adults.[9]

Black Female Slaves, Reproduction, and Labor

The racial abuses of slavery confounded traditional Western notions of gender, sex, and age. What were given boundaries and expectations *off* the plantations were perverted and disfigured practices and ideologies *on* them. Thus, although Marilyn R. Brown has argued that "both then and now, childhood has been primarily a cultural invention and site of emotional projection by adults,"[10] the imaginary potential of this invention for the white subject far outdistanced that for the black in the colonial West.[11] Therefore, a black/postcolonial feminist analysis of the representations of black girls and the lives that black girls historically led, under slavery and under prolific colonial regimes of race, serves to rupture the romantic cult of childhood.

It is clear that the health of all slaves was compromised by slavery across all locations of the diaspora. From most critical accounts, we know that malnutrition and overwork were commonplace and had immediate and long-lasting detrimental impacts on generations of Africans and their descendants, starting in the womb. Kenneth and Virginia Kiple have argued that although a fetus will draw from a mother's skeletal stores to satisfy its mineral requirements, the maternal deficiencies of slave women, combined with their high fertility, made for a progressive "bankruptcy" of those stores. Accordingly, they claim, "some slave babies then must have entered the world with serious mineral deficiencies."[12]

Steckel has compiled significant data on slave nutrition, health, growth, and mortality in the context of the United States.[13] Commenting on the small stature of black slave children that the data revealed, he has argued that "the origins of poor health can be traced to difficult periods of fetal and infant growth. Slave newborns probably weighed on average fewer than 5.5 pounds or 2.500 grams compared with modern standards of 3.450 grams."[14] And these slave children were the "lucky" ones, in that they were able to survive at all. The problem of infant mortality among slaves in the diaspora was largely attributable to the health and well-being (nutrition, labor, and so forth) of the slave mothers. Nutritional deficiencies (as in a lack of calcium, magnesium, and iron) that slave children inherited from their mothers at birth would continue through nursing, since the quality of the breast milk was affected by the slave mothers' health. But weaning could be even worse for slave children, for a diet composed mainly of hominy, cornbread, and fat and deliberately short on lean protein and vegetables was the norm in the southern United States.[15] This racialized nutritional deferential would, of course, have had severe negative impacts on slave populations over the course of individuals' lives and across generations.[16]

The ability of slaves to reproduce themselves (what slave owners called "natural increase") had much to do with their overall and reproductive health and differed in distinct locations of the diaspora. Herbert Klein and Stanley Engerman debunk the idea that attitudes toward slave treatment and material provisions were the key determinants in the disproportionate natural increase of slaves in the United States when compared to Brazilian and West Indian slave societies.[17] Instead, they argue, the lower average length of lactation in the United States played a pivotal role in the comparatively higher fertility of black female slaves.[18]

But female labor practices also had much to do with reproductive health and viability. In most tropical locations of the diaspora, agricultural commercial interests dominated and dictated the practices and patterns of colonization, settlement, and resource extraction. Caribbean colonies such as Jamaica became prized for the production of sugar,[19] but they also produced other crops for export.[20] Meanwhile, the American South became famous for crops such as cotton and rice. The engine driving much of tropical plantation slavery then was monocrop agricultural production, fueled by the labor of mainly black male *and* female slaves. Lucille Mair's research on women fieldworkers in Jamaica has revealed that "in 1832, sugar employed 49.5 per cent of the slave work force. The majority of those workers were women, the ratio being 920 males to 1,000 females."[21] In the case of Jamaica, therefore, the dominance of the sugar industry "dictated a conscious policy of job allocation which concentrated black enslaved women in the fields in the most menial and least versatile areas of cultivation in excess of men, and in excess of all persons, male and female, who were not black."[22] In other words, black slave women did not do "women's work" as defined by white bourgeois standards but were regularly forced to perform hard labor, in grueling physical, environmental, and climatic conditions. Furthermore, they worked mostly with crude and dangerous technology, and they had substandard nutrition and little access to medicine or other health and welfare care. Compared to the nutrition of whites (especially wealthy whites), the nutrition of slaves in the diaspora was substandard not only in terms of the quantity of food but also in terms of quality and, as Kiple and Kiple have pointed out, with regard to three key bioclimatic factors that affected slaves as West African descendants.[23]

Given the arduous field labor performed by the average plantation slave, male or female, slave children received dramatically different care and attention than white children. And the health and welfare of the pregnant slave was often at odds with the slave owner's economic bottom line. Shortly after giving birth, female slaves were ordered back to the fields, to the obvious detriment of their infants. Field slaves sometimes took their small children to the fields with them, carrying them on their backs or leaving them nearby while they labored.[24] But ultimate control of their ability to take care of their children resided with their enslavers, who dictated the amount of attention and even the frequency of feedings that slave children could receive.[25]

Black slave women regularly and throughout their lives did "men's work"; put another way, the lives and labors of black female slaves give the lie to the Eurocentric ideal of the gendered separation of labor. In the Canadian context, too, the needs of the white owners seemed to override any normative upper-class gender ideals when it came to black female slaves and labor. In a Halifax slave sale ad from January 1779, a Negro woman of twenty-one years was described as "capable of performing both town and country work and an exceedingly good cook."[26] The mention of "town work" referenced her experience with domestic labor, but "country work" most likely indicated that this woman knew her way around a farm and was skilled at various agricultural and field tasks.

White demands for black labor often had detrimental impacts on slave women and on their children as well. A slave woman in Georgia described the labor performed by nursing black female slaves: "Women with little babies would have to go to work in de mornings with the rest, come back, nurse their children and go back to the field, stay two or three hours, then go back and eat dinner; after dinner dey would have to go to de field and stay two or three more hours and go and nurse the chillun again, go back to the field and stay till night."[27] This grueling schedule would have taken a severe toll on even the most hearty slave woman. But it is equally important to note that given the consistent absence of the slave mother and, as a consequence, the absence of the black baby's only or main source of nourishment, slave children were *socialized into deprivation* at a very early stage.

This deprivation was about more than the inability of their mothers to provide sufficient nutrition[28] through the quantity and quality of their milk or through the number of feedings.[29] Absence and inconsistency must also be seen as key modalities of the black mother-child relationship within slavery, modalities that had profound psychic as well as physical repercussions for mothers and children alike. A chilling recollection that illustrates the psychic and psychological dimensions of this trauma comes from William Wells Brown, who recalled that, as a slave child, he was the "cause of his mother's whippings."[30] It is hard to fathom the emotional burden that black slave children would have felt when they reached an age at which they connected their mother's loving attention to her violent abuse at the hands of white enslavers. In regard to black girls and their representation in Western art, this socialized deprivation and its various burdens must be seriously considered not just within the immediate context of slavery but also within its aftermath in terms of the inherited racial traumas that became its legacy.

Slavery, "Breeding," and the Sexualization of Black Slave Girls

The practice of "breeding" female slaves, in order to replenish the labor on one's plantation and increase one's wealth and/or property, was not commonplace until the middle of the eighteenth century.[31] After that point, all aspects of a female slave's life came under invasive scrutiny from the slave owner, including her marital status, her workload, and her diet.[32] As I have discussed elsewhere, the exposed breast of the enslaved black female depicted in *Portrait of a Negro Slave* (1786) (see figure 19.1) by the Canadian artist François Malepart de Beaucourt indexes the slave woman's sexual labor and so-called breeding potential as active considerations in her value and exchange.[33] Deborah Gray White has argued that a pregnant slave woman's care was provided at the discretion of the slave owner and was generally poor.[34] The benefit, if any, of reproduction for such a woman was the comfort of being assisted during pregnancy, delivery, and the postpartum period by a community of caring black females, including a midwife.[35] However, the lower standard of care for black slave women was decidedly racialized and linked to the endemic and strategic animalization of blacks in general. It was this view of the black slave as animal/chattel that led to the mistaken belief that "slave women gave birth more easily and quickly than white women."[36]

It is a grave irony of slavery that black female slaves often performed a tandem maternal duty—caring for the white master's children even as they cared for their own. The psychic burden of this coerced responsibility cannot be underestimated, for several reasons.

First, in various locations of the diaspora, the rearing of the white master's children, which sometimes included serving as a wet nurse, was largely done at the expense of the slave woman's own offspring, in terms of time, attention, and resources.[37] Some of these resources were biological (breast milk), and fulfilling this extramaternal responsibility was obviously to the detriment of the slave's own babies.[38] Steckel has noted that children born to slave mothers were often, due to the demands of white owners, weaned too early and introduced to food sources that were frequently contaminated or unsanitary, which increased the postneonatal infant mortality rate.[39]

Second, the rearing of white children was literally tantamount to the

FIGURE 19.1 François Malepart de Beaucourt, *Portrait of a Negro Slave, or The Negress* (1786), oil on canvas (*courtesy of McCord Museum of Canadian History, Montreal*, M12067)

rearing of the slave's future master/mistress/oppressor. Raising the children of the people who daily humiliated, controlled, and demeaned you would be traumatic enough without the added torment of believing you might live long enough to suffer the same treatment at the hands of your "white children."

Third and finally, a large percentage of the children born to slave women would have been of mixed race, usually the product of coerced sexual relations (sometimes through outright rape and sometimes through psychological or economic manipulation). The mental damage suffered by these black slave mothers who were forced to carry and bear the interracial children of their enslavers/rapists is difficult to quantify, but it must be considered another endemic and catastrophic dimension of the racialized trauma of slavery.

There are many examples in the nineteenth-century photographic tradition of black women pictured as the primary caregivers or nurses of their white child charges. *Mrs. Wilson's Nurse* (ca. 1890s), created by an unknown American photographer, is a compelling example, notable for the ways in which it celebrates and naturalizes these problematic cross-racial and cross-class relationships. The image's proximity to slavery is obvious. In it, a stout black woman who appears to be past middle age wears a stiff white apron and a checked, long-sleeve blouse as she lifts aloft a large, naked white infant. The heftiness of the white child speaks to the parents' upper-class status and their ability to provide abundant nutrition. The face of the black nurse exudes pride and devotion. Her gaze is one of motherly love; for all intents and purposes, such black women were indeed the mothers of their white charges. However, the white child in this image does not meet the black nurse's gaze. Instead, the baby looks off to the right, not even toward the camera. Of course, a child of this age would not be in control of his or her responses and actions. But the implication of another presence in the room, likely that of the white biological mother whose signaling or noisemaking has drawn the child's attention away from the black mother/nurse, can be read as an ominous prediction of things to come.

Another Canadian example of the representation of black woman as nurse to white children is William H. Buckley's *Nanny with Children in Her Care, Guysborough* (ca. 1900) (see figure 19.2). Again, the black female is anonymized by the absence of her name in the title. Her erasure from the family record is paradoxical given the role she likely had as primary caregiver to the two white children in the image, one standing at her left and the other being pushed by her in a carriage. The group's position evokes the idea of a Sunday stroll. The black nanny has most likely been summoned to walk, to pose, and to look at the command of the photographer, Buckley. The two children also gaze dutifully at the camera.

FIGURE 19.2 William H. Buckley, *Nanny with the Children in Her Care, Guysborough* (c. 1900), photograph (*courtesy of Nova Scotia Archives, Halifax, Buckley family NSARM acc. no. 1985-386/216*)

The black woman's polished clothing, consisting of a long skirt, pleated blouse, and decorated hat, mark her as being in the employ of an upper-class family. Consequently, it is quite likely that she was a live-in nanny and that her service came at a very high price for her own family, if indeed she was able to create and sustain one. It is interesting to note that black children are generally absent from such photographs. At the same time, however, they seem to haunt the photos through their very absence.

Even if white children were raised, loved, nourished, and even breast-fed by their black nurses, they were still white, and their education into white supremacy was an integral part of the way in which whites reproduced their social power. As photographs such as *Mrs. Wilson's Nurse* reveal, black female sexuality and fertility were intimately tied to white power and control both during and after slavery.

Although the history of the Americas is arguably the history of black women (enslaved and free) raising white children, the reactions to a recent photograph should alert us to the fact that this legacy is prolifically denied and repressed in the Western collective consciousness. The Benetton advertisement that featured Oliviero Toscani's *Breast Feeding* (1989)—showing a white child strategically placed in front of a dark-skinned black woman with breast exposed, implying that the child was breast-feeding—caused much controversy, largely because it triggered recollections of precisely these same exploitative histories within slavery.

In the realm of "high" art, contemporary American artist Kara Walker's much-celebrated and much-loathed dreamscapes, which narrate plantation life in the American South, are partially targeted for such extreme criticism because of her representation of children, black and enslaved and white and free. In works such as *The Legend of Uncle Tom* (1995), *African't* (1996), and *The Means to an End–A Shadow Drama in Five Acts* (1995), Walker recounts the horrific abuse, sexual and otherwise, perpetrated by white slavers, male and female, against black children. But she also empowers her children with agency, which they use to humiliate and torture others.

In *The Battle of Atlanta: Being a Narrative of a Negress in the Flames of Desire–A Reconstruction* (1995), the white children, identified by their dress, physiognomy, scale, and the fact that they are "at play," sneak up on a black female slave. Slumped over and tied to a tree by her neck, the slave is perhaps unaware that a young boy intends to penetrate her with his sword. The horrific nature of the phallicized toy prophesies the generations of violent miscegenating abuse that has been visited upon black female bodies by white males. Further, the work reminds us of the speed with which the white children of slave owners turned on their black mothers.

As White has argued in the American slave context, once black female slaves came to be seen as breeders, they were economically positioned as possessing, in the biological sense, the potential for an extremely lucrative payoff for their owners. In White's words, "Young *girls* therefore were valuable for their progeny as well as for the labor they would be expected to do in the field. If handled properly, females made for their masters a 'mine of wealth.'"[40] Thus, the exploitation was not only about mastering black adult females but also about the strategic sexual cultivation of black girls from a very young age. The burden of sexual reproducing for the production of wealth marked a fundamental distinction between the lives of black girls and white girls, and it was the colonial licentiousness of the white slave owners that was projected onto the bodies of the black female slaves.

White has argued that slave owners made it a point to sexually initiate adolescent female slaves quite quickly because they "practiced a passive, but insidious kind of breeding"—they encouraged young slaves to create relationships by granting black males access to their young female slaves.[41] Female slaves who were "breeding" were sometimes given additional "payoffs" by their happy masters, above and beyond the usual incentives of additional food and less arduous labor.[42] However, biological data on female slaves demonstrate that they clearly resisted the slave owners' coercive breeding strategies, drawing out the time between menarche (mean age of 15, as noted earlier) and their first birth (mean age of 20.6).[43] But due to the extreme social and economic value of reproductively healthy female slaves, to be deemed barren was to suffer marginalization and potential public humiliation linked to infertility, even if it also meant a reprieve from potential sexual abuse motivated by the "natural increase" imperative.[44]

Slave owners in the American South as well as other diasporic locations celebrated their "breeding wenches" and their capacity for the so-called natural increase that sustained their colonial economic enterprises. But for the slave woman, the ability to give birth to future slaves had detrimental impacts on her chances to pursue freedom. In particular, studies of fugitive slaves largely between the ages of sixteen and thirty-five indicate that the vast majority of the runaways were male. The mobility of female slaves within this age bracket was severely hindered by childbearing.[45]

Black Motherhood and Black Children in Western Art

The Western visual archive of black children is quite large but unusual in some aspects. White, black, and other races of children can easily be found in portraiture and in genre scenes, but it is how and when black children appear that make for a disturbing reminder of Western colonial histories. Black children seem overtly present in some specifically articulated trends, yet they are almost utterly absent in others. I will explore some of these Western and specifically Canadian visual art objects, paying careful attention to the representation of the cross-racial interaction of black and white subjects and the intra-racial representation of black subjects. Arguably, an understanding of how visual representation helped to produce the category of black children hinges not only upon images of that discrete group but also upon images of their parents, masters, mistresses, and fellow children who were both black and nonblack.

Strategically deployed for their ability to suggest exotic locations and to mobilize references to the white bodies' colonial reach, wealth, and privilege, black children were often present only as slaves or servants within white family portraits produced in various areas, including the United

States, Europe, and the Caribbean.[46] Although black children were often depicted with white children, their representation in service visualized the concrete relations of servant and master. Robert Street's *Children of Commodore John Daniel Danels* (ca. 1826) is a rare example of a portrait in which the black boy at play with the white children can be read as an equalizing gesture. However, most often, it was the black slave children's labor and service that ensured the white subject's childhood.

Black children's subservient status was generally noted both compositionally and directly on their bodies. In placement and activity, they were often shown as being below the white family, in terms of what they were doing (which was labor) and in terms of how they were dressed and positioned (usually on a lower compositional register and at the outskirts of the central action). Due to their "exotic" potential as slave bodies—personal property with literal monetary value—slaves were often dressed up in exoticizing (often orientalizing) garb to further emphasize that they were "foreign" luxury objects possessed by their owners. (Equally, though, slave children were pictured in tattered, worn, and substandard clothing, which more aptly captured the impoverished state of most black slaves.) As for the common use of exoticizing dress, the black slave children who were represented in such ways were not always foreign of course. Rather, many, especially in the nineteenth century, would have been born in the West and would even have had parents who were similarly removed generationally from their African heritage. I should also point out the obvious here: some of the slave children's parents *were* white Europeans. Thus, such portraits and their treatment of black slave children were a means for white Europeans, white Creoles, and white Euro-Americans (and here I use the word *American* in the broadest "New World" sense) to erase the ever-increasing "European-ness" of their black slaves, even as their continuing investments in imperialism produced it.

As the histories of slavery and the mistreatment of black women and children have revealed, black girls were likely to have serious illnesses, to suffer from malnutrition, to be the victims of sexual and racial abuse, and to bear the weight of consistent social surveillance and manipulation by whites. All this was simply the norm. Given the histories of slave labor, sexuality, and motherhood across various locations of the diaspora, certain trends in the historical representation of black subjects are not surprising. One of these trends pertains to the general absence of representations of black mothers with their own black children, especially works whose focus is a romanticized view of the mother-child bond. A second, related trend is the extreme rarity of images of pregnant black women or black women giving birth or nursing. Of course, this second absence was due, in part, to social taboos that positioned the topic of women's fertility and reproduction as outside appropriate social decorum. However, given the stereotypical view of black women as sexually licentious and excessive, one might have expected greater representation of these otherwise off-limit subjects featuring black women as opposed to white females. The casual nature of the sale and enslavement of black bodies worked against the black family and black female maternal rights. One American bill of sale detailed Abraham Van Vleek's purchases for October 28, 1811. Listed alongside "1 Red face Cow," "1 Yearling Calf," "1 Plough," "8 Fancy Chairs," and various kitchen wares were "1 Wench Nam[ed] Eve & Child."[47]

Canadian Henrietta Shore's *Negro Woman and Two Children* (ca. 1916) is a rare example in that it depicts a black woman in a maternal role in reference to black children. The woman gazes directly and warily out at the viewers, her arms draped protectively down around the seated children. Her body language connotes an awareness of white antagonism to the black family and the various abuses—psychic, emotional, sexual, and physical—that this implies. Although she is not explicitly named as a mother, her body language marks her as a protector. All three figures are dressed rather finely in good, clean, and pretty-looking garments. The infant, seated in the woman's lap, wears a white dress, white bonnet with blue ribbon, white socks, and black shoes. Her dress and the rattle that she absently grips seem further to indicate the attentiveness, love, and care provided by her black mother. The little girl seated in the immediate left foreground meets the viewer's gaze directly with her own, a bright smile indicating that her childhood innocence might not yet have been stolen.

Black child subjects, like black adult subjects, rarely appear in finished individual historical portraits. The elitist and historically inaccessible nature of portraiture made independent access for blacks virtually impossible. Throughout the time of slavery, when oil-painted or marble-sculpted portraits were the norm for the wealthy and privileged, and prior to the invention of photography, blacks, many of whom were slaves, simply did not have the money—or the requisite social independence or cultural knowledge—to commission portraits of themselves or their loved ones. Instead, black subjects were a frequent presence in the portraits of aristocratic and bourgeois white families. On rare occasions when black females posed alone, the works were often problematically commissioned by their owners or employers, and the women have remained unnamed, as in *Mrs. Cowan's Nurse* (1871) by the Canadian photographer William Notman (see figure 19.3).

FIGURE 19.3 William Notman, *Mrs. Cowan's Nurse* (1871), photograph (*courtesy of McCord Museum of Canadian History, Montreal, I-66067.1*)

Mrs. Cowan's Nurse, *Mrs. Wilson's Nurse*, and *Nanny with the Children in Her Care, Guysborough* all remind us that black women continued to raise white children (and care for white adults) well after the end of slavery. Although the young black female's white charge is absent in *Mrs. Cowan's Nurse*, white power and authority are mapped onto the image through the process of naming, whereby the black nurse's name is replaced with that of her white female employer. As such, even though they are a century removed from Malepart de Beaucourt's *Portrait of a Negro Slave*, photographs of this type are similarly structured by the same racialized power imbalances of the much earlier oil portrait—with the white owner/master/mistress/employer as the initiator of the commission or image and the black female slave/nurse as a considerably restricted agent in her own representation.

Representing Black Children in Slavery

The equation of black child bodies with property is driven home by the brutal efficiency with which one Mrs. Blankenship related her desire to purchase a slave child to Mr. E. H. Stokes: "I am anxious to buy a small healthy negro girl—ten or twelve years old, and would like to know if you could let me have one—I will pay you cash in State money—and you allowing the per centage on it—I will take her on trial of a few weeks—please let me hear from you as soon as possible (—I would like a dark Mulatto)."[48] As with any other commodity, Blankenship laid out the specifications for her purchase, citing the condition, the age, the sex, and even the complexion and race mixture of the child slave that she hoped to purchase.[49] Most alarming is the fact that this black child was commodified as an object for which one could request a trial period. The potential buyer's blasé attitude toward the "trial of a few weeks" demonstrates how little compassion whites had for the suffering of black children who were regularly separated from their parents and loved ones, due to white participation in and reliance upon slavery. That Blankenship requested a healthy girl of ten or twelve years of age should also alert us to her potential interest in "breeding" her new slave when the time came.

European slavers did not spare children when purchasing their human cargo.[50] African children were a part of the horrific practices of the Middle Passage. Enslaved children might have been sold into slavery or born into it, since within most colonial regimes, any child born to a slave woman became the property of her master and mistress, regardless of the race or social status of the father. As I have already discussed in detail, this colonial logic supported the endemic sexual exploitation and abuse of black female slaves, who had no direct recourse under the law to protect them from this specifically sexual oppression. To a large extent, the ability of all slaves to form and protect their own familial units was inherently contradictory to slave practices—or at least to their owners' overriding economic interests.

But once again, slavery in the Canadian context was largely not agriculturally driven because the temperate climate, which made for harsh winters, was not conducive to a monocrop plantation society. Instead, slaves in Canada, *panis* (Native) and black, worked in fisheries, for example, and in industries such as mining, lumbering, and fur trading; they also worked as domestics for middle- or upper-class whites, including military personnel of all ranks, clergy, lawyers, hairdressers, and merchants (goldsmiths, butchers, and the like).

As yet, there are few publicly owned artworks that represent black slave girls in Canada; at least, few have been thoroughly cataloged in a way that would allow them to enter public or even scholarly consciousness.[51] However, enslaved black girls are represented in significant numbers in another archive that is primarily textual, although abundantly visual. The archive to which I refer is that of the slave sale and fugitive slave advertisements that were posted in newspapers and produced as broadsheets. Slave sales were also documented in the legislation of Upper and Lower Canada and the Maritimes and witnessed by notaries or colonial administrators. As Marcus Wood has argued, "For the slave-owner the presentation of the runaway through advertising was outwardly straightforward, and constituted the announcement, within the terms of an established legal code, of an act of theft, albeit a paradoxical self-theft."[52] According to Wood, runaway slave ads became a staple of eighteenth- and nineteenth-century print culture in locations such as Brazil, the Caribbean, and the southern United States; to that list, I would add Canada.[53]

Some ads featured text that was accompanied by typecast or woodcut images, but many others relied solely on the verbal description of the slave's supposed physical characteristic and behaviors. But we must be cautious in using such ads and documents as authoritative descriptions of what a slave "really looked like," keeping in mind that the visual language of description (created by whites) was meant to reinforce the status of blacks as property. Slavery in Canada was not only about whites needing or desiring labor; it was also about the profits that could be made in the exchange of human beings. As advertised in the *Halifax Gazette* on May 15, 1752, six Negro slaves were "just imported and to be sold" at Major Lockman's store in Halifax.[54] The rapid turnaround implied by the word *just* signaled that the slaves' current owner, Joshua Mauger, was intent on the quick disposal of his "property" for profit.

Canadian slave advertisements, whether regarding sales or runaways, have enormous commonalities with their American (continental South and North) and Caribbean counterparts. The bulk of any such description was focused upon the anatomy and physiognomy of the slave, detailing specific or extraordinary facial or bodily features. Not surprisingly, many of these descriptions, especially in slave sale ads, were devised to suggest the good health and strength of the slave's body, for who would want to buy a slave who was sickly or infirm? As such, slave sale ads often featured descriptors such "well-made," "well built," "strong," "stout," and (despite the widespread malnutrition and the premature mortality rates across the diaspora) "healthy." But whites were equally interested in the personality and attitude of a potential slave. Consequently, adjectives such as "industrious," "obedient," "orderly," "sober," and "honest" were also common elements of slave sale advertisements.

In the case of the group sale in Halifax, the two younger Negro boys (aged twelve and thirteen) were described as "likely, healthy, and well-shaped," most probably referring to their muscle tone; this would be read as a sign of their strength and endurance. Meanwhile, the eighteen-year-olds in the group were described as being "healthy" and as possessing "agreeable tempers."[55] Another sale at Halifax in 1769 was advertised as offering "two hogsheads of rum, three of sugar and two *well-grown* negro girls aged 14 and 12" to be sold to the highest bidder, clearly, as noted by William Riddell, "a consignment from the West Indies."[56]

But slave ads also featured other descriptors, including physical anomalies, details about a slave's temperament, or special skills or talents the slave possessed. These details also shed light on the daily lives and experiences of slaves in Canada, particularly in regard to what they suffered and survived. For instance, in 1773, Jacob Hurd of Halifax offered a five-pound reward for the apprehension of a fugitive slave, a Negro man named Cromwell. According to Riddell, Hurd described him as a "'short thick set strong fellow' strongly pock marked 'especially on the nose' and wearing a green cloth jacket and a cocked hat."[57] Hurd's description not only conveyed the strength and power of the black man's body but also recalled a past illness, the smallpox that Cromwell must have survived, which had scarred his face. Finally, in addition to enlightening us about the value of slaves in these sites, details on the individuals' skills and strengths also help to debunk the retroactive lie that slaves were uneducated and helpless, needing slavery as a "civilizing mission."

Canadian ads typically described the race of the slave, a facet of identification that was extremely important given that both blacks and Natives were enslaved. It seems the Native slaves were given no other racial indicator but were commonly listed merely as male (*panis*) or female (*panise*). Black slaves, however, were regularly subdivided further through descriptions of the complexion or a specific racial heritage or mixture. Such descriptions normally incorporated terms such as *mulatto* or *quadroon*—indicating that Euro-Canadians were well aware of the interracial status of many slaves and the "miscegenating sex" that had created this population. A case in point was the sale in Halifax by Charles Proctor of a "Mulatta girl" to Mary Wood of Annapolis.[58] The texts also reveal other disturbing information about the standard treatment of enslaved black girls in Canada. First, they show that these girls, as well as young black boys, were regularly sold separately from their parents or any older relatives. Two cases in 1802, for example, mention a three-year-old boy named Simon and a five-year-old girl named Catherine, both described as mulattoes, who were sold in Prince Edward Island.[59] Second, the ads provide evidence that enslaved black girls experienced an accelerated "childhood," being considered women in their middle to late teens, whereas comparably aged black male slaves were still listed as boys. Of course, these two issues were related, since it was, in part, the forced separation of slave girls from their mothers that accelerated their development into womanhood—if not biologically, then at least socially.[60]

Riddell documented a thirty-five-year-old Negro woman who was said by her seller to be skilled at "needle-work of all sorts and in the best manner; also washing, ironing, cooking, and every other thing that can be expected from such a slave."[61] With skills like these, many enslaved black girls in their teen years would have been running the households of their white owners, solely or with the help of other slaves or servants. Louison and Isabella were two black slave girls who were very likely in just such a position, and each was sold alone. Louison was described as "a negro woman" of about seventeen years and Isabella, or Bell, as a "mulatto slave" of about fifteen.[62] Both were sold to male buyers, Louison to a captain in the navy in the Montreal garrison on June 6, 1749, and Isabella to the lieutenant governor of Quebec, Hector-Theophile Cramahé, on November 14, 1778.[63]

Isabella's case also highlights the normality of upheaval in a slave girl's life. Over the course of several years, Isabella was sold at least four times.[64] The prospect of having four different male owners was extraordinarily destabilizing for any slave in terms of relocation, separation from loved ones and a familiar environment, climate, food sources, and so on, coupled with potentially dramatic changes in lifestyle.[65] But it was especially dangerous for female slaves, for whom sexual exploitation and abuse were part of their daily reality. That danger would have been heightened for the eleven-year-old girl who was advertised for sale along with a boy of the same age in a public auction at Halifax on November 3, 1760. The fact that the youngsters were listed for sale along with "a puncheon of choice cherry brandy with sundry other articles" says much about the nature of black slavery in Canada: these children were merely two commodities among others, much the same as the two Negro girls discussed earlier who were sold with puncheons of rum and sugar.[66]

As suggested earlier, black slave girls seemed to have been codified differently than their black male counterparts of the same age, being constituted as women while still in their teens whereas many males in their teens were being identified as boys. In three cases involving the sale of black males in Lower Canada—a fifteen-year-old Negro named Kitts, a sixteen-year-old Negro named Tanno, and a sixteen-year-old mulatto named Pierre—the youths were all described as boys, not men.[67] The practice also existed in other parts of the country. On March 27, 1775, the *Nova Scotia Gazette and Weekly Chronicle* advertised the sale of a "negro boy about 16 year old."[68] In contrast, the black female slave Louison, discussed previously, was described as a woman even though she was just seventeen years old. The issue of childhood in naming is also, of course, racialized, since the practice of whites calling grown black men "boys" was institutionalized through slavery as a form of public humiliation and psychic castration. To call a black man, slave or free, "boy" was to attempt to deny him his manhood and to create a category or cult of "true manhood" solely around the bodies of white men. To disenfranchise adult black males in this way obviously served a strategic purpose in terms of enforcing white control and power over black male labor and action. It was also a means to psychologically strip black males of their role as protectors (fathers, uncles, brothers, husbands) of black females by "breaking" them. Within this context, whites had very good reason to want to infantilize their male slaves even as they accelerated the maturation of their female ones.

The frequent international movement of slaves into Lower Canada and other parts of the country also indexes the extraordinary diversity of black Canadian slave populations.[69] Obviously, in our discussion of enslaved black girls in Canada (and of enslaved blacks in general), we are dealing with African, African Canadian, African American, and African Caribbean slaves (and possibly even others, such as African South American slaves). And indeed, this heterogeneity *within* blackness may actually be one key mark of the distinctiveness of black slaves and the practice of transatlantic slavery in Canada when compared to other locations of the diaspora.[70] As such and given the dominant trade in black slaves between the islands of the Caribbean and Canada's internationally networked port settlements such as Halifax and Montreal, I would propose that it would be a worthy historical and theoretical endeavor to conceptualize a *second Middle Passage between the shores of the Caribbean and Canada*—secondary only in historical context but no less tumultuous a journey across perilous waters, this time between two New World ports.[71]

Black Girls in Canadian Art

Black children's legacy of vulnerability to racialized poverty and abuse is evident in the works of Canadian painters Prudence Heward and Louis Muhlstock, both based in Montreal. Although Heward's *Clytie* (1938) shows a little black girl in her "Sunday best," her frozen pose and unemotive expression seems at odds with twentieth-century ideals of childhood. Clytie stands erect in her pretty pink dress with blue waist-high bow, her hair neatly coiled and held in place by a pink accessory. Her white-gloved hands, white stockings, and clean white shoes also signal that she is dressed up for a special occasion. But who is Clytie? Why is she alone in this street? And for whom does she pose? Heward's own identity as a white female artist provides one layer of initial viewership that allows us to recall the actual act of her creating the portrait. If, indeed, Clytie was a friend of the Heward family cook, then a power imbalance based on race and another based on age are both at play in the painting.[72]

Meanwhile, the pensive and sorrowful expression of the black girl in Muhlstock's *Evelyn Pleasant, St. Famille Street* (1937) marks a convergence of the artist's interest in black subjects, poverty, and social oppression. The young Evelyn stands alone, peering through the dirty window of what we may assume is her home. The interior behind her is impenetrable, an ominous darkness enveloping her like a heavy gloom that we are not allowed to penetrate. Thus, the painting does not allow us to enter Evelyn's world, which, unlike that in representations of her white contemporaries, does not appear too childlike. The smudge to her right on the windowpane has taken on the distinctive outline of her four small fingers and thumb; she has been pressing her hand against the window, suggesting her bid to escape or at least to see beyond her gloomy room.

Canadian Dorothy Stevens's *Amy, Piccanniny* (ca. 1930)[73] represents a little black girl who is just as stoic and melancholy as the aforementioned pair (see figure 19.4). Her hold on the white doll that she cradles in her lap is disturbing on at least two levels. First, it calls up the infamous American social science studies of black children and black and white dolls, which revealed the process of play as racial socialization and the early stages at which black children were brainwashed into racial self-loathing and DuBoisian double consciousness. And second, it prophesized this girl's likely later station in life as yet another caregiver to white children.[74] The representation of black women mothering white children helped to produce a hierarchy of family, parental duty, childhood, and care in which the black family and black children were forever at the bottom; the preciousness of the white child enabled the abuse and neglect of the black. This configuration was also emasculating for black male slaves, who were effectively denied access to the patriarchal authority and legitimacy that would have let them protect and provide for their wives and children.[75]

FIGURE 19.4 Dorothy Stevens, *Amy, Piccanniny* (c.1930), oil on canvas (© *Dorothy Stevens; reproduced by permission of Jeff Stevens; courtesy of National Gallery of Canada, acc. # 3983; photograph © National Gallery of Canada)*

As with Clytie and perhaps even more so, Amy has been posed. The awkwardness of the chair, turned to the child's right, and the child's body in that chair (also facing to her right as her head is turned back to her left, toward the viewer/artist) convey a staged look. Perhaps unconsciously, then, all three of these white Canadian artists have produced paintings in which black girls are decidedly unchildlike in demeanor. It is odd that none of the three girls, not even Amy with her doll in hand, is actually in the act of play. Rather, each portrait in its own way is melancholy, again perhaps unconsciously capturing the malaise of childhood for black girls in the first half of the twentieth century.

As I have discussed in detail, black girls were particularly vulnerable to all manner of abuse and exploitation throughout the period of transatlantic slavery and well beyond it. As slave children, they were disadvantaged from the womb. And even when they were little girls, whites sought, through force and manipulation, to accelerate their progress into adulthood in order to both shape and exploit their sexuality and reproductive capacity. This prolific sexual exploitation of black girls and women did not, of course, die out with abolition. Rather, it was maintained through institutional racism and patriarchal social obstacles that continue, even today, to align black femaleness with a lower-class status.

For example, as black women transitioned historically from the fields into domestic and other blue-collar labor, the legal sexual exploitation of the plantation was replaced by their illegal exploitation within the white home or workplace; in either case, the exploitation was rendered invisible behind the white picket fences of the suburbs or the hard factory walls of cities. Due to the prolific nature of black female exploitation and the cross-generational trauma of slavery, we must interrogate the artworks and who and what they represent; beyond that, we must also pose questions about *how* such representations of black girls came into being. To ask how is to be attentive to the process of cultural production and the extreme differential in power between white adult artists and their young and vulnerable black female sitters or subjects.

The history of the representation of black children and girls in particular in Western art in many ways follows a parallel trajectory to that of black adults and women. However, in other ways, the roles and function of the black girl have prophesied the racialized and gendered identifications and status of the black female adult subject. Although there are examples of black children experiencing the modern ideals of a protected, beloved Western childhood, many artworks represent the exact opposite, that is, the social, cultural, and psychic displacement of black girls as "other" to the paradigmatic ideal of white girls. The colonial discourses that enabled transatlantic slavery to flourish for four hundred years are crucial to an understanding of the disparate experiences and representations of childhood, which are always racialized. I have demonstrated that our attention to race in the field of Childhood Studies should not be an afterthought but a primary and urgent consideration. At the same time, I have sought to reveal and to contextualize the strategic hypersexualization of black female subjects within transatlantic slavery, not only as it applied to black women but, sadly, as it was invested in the accelerated sexual initiation of black girls.

Notes

1. "The Race Problem—An Autobiography, by a Southern Colored Woman," *Independent* 56, no. 2885 (1904): 587, 589.

2. Charles Ball, *Slavery in the United States: A Narrative of the Life and Adventures of Charles Ball, a Black Man* (Lewistown, Pa.: J. W. Shugert, 1836), 150–51.

3. See Charmaine Nelson, *Representing the Black Female Subject in Western Art* (New York: Routledge, 2010).

4. See Charmaine Nelson, *Ebony Roots, Northern Soil: Perspectives on Blackness in Canada* (Newcastle upon Tyne, UK: Cambridge Scholars Press, 2010).

5. See Ellen Ross, *Love and Toil: Motherhood in Outcast London, 1870–1918* (New York: Oxford University Press, 1993); Carol Duncan, "Happy Mothers and Other New Ideas in Eighteenth-Century French Art," in *Feminism and Art History: Questioning the Litany*, ed. Norma Broude and Mary D. Garrard (New York: Harper and Row, 1982), 201–20.

6. See James Trussell and Richard Steckel, "The Age of Slaves at Menarche and First Birth," *Journal of Interdisciplinary History* 8, no. 3 (1978): 492, cited in Deborah Gray White, *Ar'n't I a Woman? Female Slaves in the Plantation South* (New York: W. W. Norton, 1999), 104.

7. "Race Problem—An Autobiography."

8. Linda A. Pollock, "Foreword," in *Picturing Children: Constructions of Childhood between Rousseau and Freud*, ed. Marilyn Brown (Aldershot, UK: Ashgate, 2002), xv–xix.

9. Marilyn R. Brown, "Introduction: Baudelaire between Rousseau and Freud," in Brown, *Picturing Children*, 3.

10. Ibid., 1.

11. According to Brown, this cult is thought to have begun in literature with Jean-Jacques Rousseau's *Émile* (1762) and visually in British portraiture. See ibid., 3.

12. Kenneth F. Kiple and Virginia H. Kiple, "Slave Child Mortality: Some Nutritional Answers to a Perennial Puzzle," *Journal of Social History* 10, no. 3 (1977): 287–88.

13. Steckel has drawn from slave manifests (lodged both at embarkation and final destination between 1820 and 1860), legislated by the US Congress in 1807, that required ships' captains to produce lists detailing the name, age, sex, color, and height of each slave. See Richard H. Steckel, "A Peculiar Population: The Nutrition, Health and Mortality of American Slaves, from Childhood to Maturity," *Journal of Economic History* 46, no. 3 (1986): 722–23.

14. Ibid., 732.

15. Kiple and Kiple, "Slave Child Mortality," 288. Hominy is dried corn that has gone through a process of nixtamalization, which involves soaking it in sodium or potassium hydroxide (i.e., limewater).

16. Kiple and Kiple detail a host of ailments, including deformed bones, blindness, lameness, skin lesions, and dental problems. They also calculate that black slave children, aged zero to nine, most commonly died from convulsions, teething, tetanus, lockjaw, suffocation, and worms, and they were four times more likely to die from these ailments than their white counterparts. See ibid., 289–91.

17. Herbert S. Klein and Stanley L. Engerman, "Fertility Differentials between Slaves in the United States and the British West Indies: A Note on Lactation Practices and Their Possible Implications," *William and Mary Quarterly* 35, no. 2 (1978): 357.

18. Ibid., 358. Klein and Engerman argue that a key factor in the distinction in reproduction between slave women in the United States and in the West Indies was the length of lactation. Though the American slaves generally breast-fed for one year, their West Indian counterparts did so for two, effectively, whether deliberately or not, using lactation as a contraceptive. Treckel concurs with the idea of breast-feeding as contraception and has written that a nursing woman's return to fecundity, signaled by the return of her menstrual cycle, is a matter of the *type* of breast-feeding that she practices. See Paula A. Treckel, "Breastfeeding and Maternal Sexuality in Colonial America," *Journal of Interdisciplinary History* 20, no. 1 (1989): 39.

19. Jamaica became the jewel of Britain's imperial crown, largely for its sugar production, and from a very early moment in its colonization, it was identified (even before British possession) as a "gallant plantation" with enormous agricultural productive capacities. According to Mair, Jamaica was the world's largest sugar producer in 1805, and for most of the nineteenth century, its production commanded most of the island's natural, human, and economic resources. See Lucille Mathurin Mair, "Women Field Workers in Jamaica during Slavery," in *Caribbean Slavery in the Atlantic World: A Student Reader*, ed. Verene Shepherd and Hilary McD. Beckles (Kingston, Jamaica: Ian Randle, 2000), 390.

20. Islands such as Jamaica were extremely fertile. One nineteenth-century source lists the following natural products among the islands exports from

September 29, 1820, until September 29, 1821: sugar, rum, molasses, coffee, ginger, pimento, cocoa, cotton, indigo, hides, logwood, fustic, nicawood, lignum, mahogany, cedar, and lancewood. See James Hakewill, *A Picturesque Tour of the Island of Jamaica, from Drawings Made in the Years 1820 and 1821* (London: Hurst and Robinson, 1825), n.p.

21. Mair, "Women Field Workers," 390.

22. Ibid., 390–91.

23. First, Kiple and Kiple argue that the sickling trait that protected West Africans from malaria in their original environment became the origin of potential illness—sickle cell anemia—in the diaspora. The trait also increased the person's need for iron and folic acid. Second, the high frequency of lactose intolerance (affecting 70 to 77 percent of blacks in the United States in the 1970s), caused by the absence of the lactase enzyme that metabolizes milk sugars, meant that many slaves likely eliminated milk from their diet (if they were provided it at all). This, of course, would have resulted in calcium deficiencies. And third, the darker pigmentation of black slaves, which helped to cool their bodies in Africa, would have resulted in vitamin D deficiencies in some North American contexts (such as the more northern states and Canada). See Kiple and Kiple, "Slave Child Mortality," 285–86.

24. Philip D. Morgan, "The Significance of Kin," in *The Slavery Reader*, ed. Gad Heuman and James Walvin (London: Routledge, 2003), 338.

25. Ibid., 340.

26. William Renwick Riddell, "Slavery in the Maritime Provinces," *Journal of Negro History* 5, no. 3 (1920): 363.

27. Ulrich B. Phillips, *Plantation and Frontier: Documents, 1649–1863* (Cleveland, Ohio: Arthur H. Clarke, 1909), 1:27, cited in White, *Ar'n't I a Woman?*, 113.

28. Throughout the seventeenth and eighteenth centuries, Western medicine commonly defined breast milk as diverted menstrual blood. Accordingly, many medical texts advised lactating women against any sexual activity, and some even cautioned against sexual thought, due to the fear that sexual stimulation would turn the milk back into blood. Such manuals also advised that the resumption of menses marked the time for mothers to wean their children. See Treckel, "Breastfeeding and Maternal Sexuality," 32.

29. Even when slave children grew older, their nutrition was largely determined by the policy of their owners. In the American South, Steckel has argued, slave owners often discussed the care and feeding of slaves among themselves in agricultural journals. Their goal was to determine the ideal quantity of food necessary to extract the maximum labor potential from a slave at minimum cost. As standard practice, a slave child's nutrition was to be "proportionately less" than that of an adult slave (proportional in reference to their work effort). Steckel argues that the plump bellies, shiny bodies, and glistening ribs of

slave children, reported by travelers as signs of the good health of slaves, were actually signs of malnutrition and protein deficiency. See Steckel, "Peculiar Population," 733–34.

30. White, *Ar'n't I a Woman?*, 113. Brown's mother would take him to the field with her, and she was whipped for taking time away from her work to nurse him.

31. Ibid., 67.

32. Ibid., 68.

33. Charmaine Nelson, "Slavery, Portraiture and the Colonial Limits of Canadian Art History," in *Representing the Black Female Subject in Western Art* (New York: Routledge, 2010), 63–75.

34. White, *Ar'n't I a Woman?*, 111.

35. Ibid. White also claims that the white slave mistress was sometimes present at the delivery of new slave children. But this can easily be read as the female slave owner's desire to watch over her economic investment.

36. Ibid., 112. This belief not only led to various preventable ailments such as backaches, uterine pain, and hernias but also in some cases led to the death of the slave. White notes that within the first two to three weeks after giving birth, slave women were put back to work spinning, weaving, and sewing. But further damage was often done to their bodies by this hasty return to work before their bodies were given sufficient time to recuperate. Additionally, slave owners were quick to use physical punishment, such as whipping, if slave women lagged behind their expectations. See ibid., 112–13.

37. Treckel has argued that the normalcy of the custom of employing black female slaves as wet nurses for white children in the American South is hard to pinpoint. She speculates that this is, in part, due to the biological racism of whites, who feared that such intimate contact and transfer of bodily fluid might result in the racial degeneration of white children. See Treckel, "Breastfeeding and Maternal Sexuality," 47–50.

38. Paula Treckel has noted the dominance of wet nurses for upper-class white English children in the 1700s and among the white American elite in the same period. This was part fashion and part the state of Western medicine, since throughout the seventeenth and eighteenth centuries, various medical texts instructed women to avoid initiating breast-feeding too early. The fear was that the colostrum, the initial secretion that is a potent immunological defense, was instead toxic and fatal. See Treckel, "Breastfeeding and Maternal Sexuality," 26–27.

39. Steckel, "Peculiar Population," 732. For more on the plantation records upon which Steckel based his research, see Richard H. Steckel, "Birth Weights and Infant Mortality among American Slaves," *Explorations in Economic History* 23, no. 2 (1986): 173–98.

40. White, *Ar'n't I a Woman?*, 201 (emphasis added).

41. Ibid., 98–99.

42. Ibid., 99–100. White mentions one Major Wallon who bestowed a calico dress and a silver dollar upon female slaves each time they produced a child. In the American South, White points out, pregnant female slaves were often moved to the "trash gang" as they neared delivery, performing a job that was less arduous than other field duties.

43. Ibid., 104. Given the estimated period of sterility following menarche of 2.6 years, slave women were able to delay childbirth by at least two years. These findings were based upon the height, weight, and age data derived from slave ship manifests. See Trussell and Steckel, "Age of Slaves at Menarche."

44. White, *Ar'n't I a Woman?*, 101. White mentions lawsuits wherein buyers were refunded their money due to the reproductive "defect" of slave women who were unable to "breed." Reasons for poor reproductive health included sexually transmitted diseases such as syphilis and gonorrhea and gynecological problems such as uterine infections. I mention the element of public humiliation because these buyers were able to recoup their money through the public legal documentation of the female slave as "defective."

45. Ibid., 70. White points out that women in this age group were often pregnant, nursing, or caring for small children and less likely than male parents to abandon their children. One sound example of the indelible bond and commitment of slave mothers to their children is the fact that of the 151 fugitive women included in advertisements in New Orleans newspapers of 1850, none was listed as having run away without her children. See ibid., 71.

46. See, for example, Bartholomew Dandridge, *The Price Family* (ca. 1730); Jacob Huysmans, *Edward Henry Lee, 1st Earl of Litchfield and His Wife Charlotte Fitzroy as Children* (ca. 1676–77); Justus Englwhardt Kuhn, *Henry Darnall III as a Child* (ca. 1710); Sir Peter Lely, *Elizabeth Murray Countess of Drysart* (ca. 1651–52); Antonis Mor, *Joanna of Austria with a Slave* (mid-sixteenth century); Jean Francois de Troy, *Presumed Portrait of Madame de Franqueville and Her Children* (1712); and Phillip Wickstead, *Richard and Jane Pusey* (ca. 1775).

47. "Bill of Sale of Abraham Van Vleek," in *Black Women in White America: A Documentary History*, ed. Gerda Lerner (New York: Vintage Books, 1992), 7.

48. "Mrs. Blankenship Wishes to Buy a Slave Girl," in Lerner, *Black Women in White America*, 8.

49. The term *mulatto* was used to define a person who was half black and half white. Generally, such persons were seen as visually embodying both white and black racial characteristics (i.e., hair that was neither straight nor "kinky," complexions that were neither white nor brown, and similarly in-between physiognomic features). Yet, of course, vast differences existed in what mulattoes looked like.

50. David Eltis and David Richardson, "West Africa and the Trans Atlantic Slave Trade," in Heuman and Walvin, *Slavery Reader*, 52–53.

51. Historically, in Western museums and likely to an even greater extent in Canada due to Canada's national delusion of a race-blind multiculturalism, collections have been endemically racially miscataloged. These archival mistakes have largely resulted from the error of omission, whereby well-meaning white museum staff excluded details of the race of the sitter/subject or artist/producer, helping to create the illusion of a universal whiteness. Due to these compiled absences and sanitizations, there is no way to know how many important works representing or produced by black Canadians exist and simply cannot at present be identified as such.

52. Marcus Wood, "Rhetoric and the Runaway: The Iconography of Slave Escape in England and America," in *Blind Memory: Visual Representations of Slavery in England and America, 1780–1865* (Manchester, UK: Manchester University Press, 2000), 79.

53. Ibid., 80.

54. The slaves were listed as a woman of 35, a boy of 12, a boy of 13, two boys of 18, and a man of 30. Riddell gives no indication if the members of the group were related, nor does he indicate from where they were migrated. See Riddell, "Slavery in the Maritime Provinces," 360.

55. Ibid.

56. Ibid., 362 (emphasis added).

57. Ibid., 363.

58. The slave girl was sold for fifteen pounds Halifax currency and after a year was assigned to the purchaser's daughter, Mary Day. See ibid., 361–62.

59. Ibid., 373.

60. I deliberately say mothers here, as opposed to parents, because in most cases of "miscegenating sex" (due to the nature of the sexual abuse of black female slaves), the mothers of slave children would have been dominantly black females.

61. Riddell, "Slavery in the Maritime Provinces," 360.

62. See Riddell, "Notes on the Slave in Nouvelle-France," *Journal of Negro History* 8, no. 3 (1923): 319, 323–24.

63. Ibid., 318–19.

64. Riddell documented Isabella as first being sold by Capt. Thomas Venture to George Hipps at auction, but he gave no date. Hipps, described as a merchant butcher, then sold Isabella to the lieutenant governor on November 14, 1778, who later sold her to Peter Napier, a captain in the British navy, on April 20, 1779. See ibid., 324.

65. The fact that many of the slave owners in Lower Canada were military men of various ranks (cadets, captains, and other officers) increased the vulnerability and forced mobility of the slaves they owned, since the soldiers' postings were largely not within their own control. But slaves owned by people of non-military backgrounds also experienced the same upheaval. Riddell documents

the "hiring out" of a Negro male slave known as Louis Lepage by Jean Baptiste Valleé of Quebec on December 27, 1744, to François de Chalet, inspector general of the Compagnie des Indes, "to serve him as a sailor for the remaining term of de Chalet's tenure of the Ports of Cataraqui (Katarakouye, i.e., now Kingston, Ontario) and Niagara." Other cases include a Negro female slave named Flora who was relocated from L'Assomption to Montreal (both in Lower Canada, now Quebec) when she was sold along with a Negro male named Caesar to Solomon Levy by James McGill, acting on behalf of Thomas Curry. A Negro woman named Sarah was moved from Saratoga to Montreal when she was sent by her owner, Hugh McAdam, to be sold by his friend John Brown to James Morrison of Montreal on February 20, 1785. Three Negro slaves (Tobi, aged twenty-six; Sarah, aged twenty-one; and a child) were sold on the open market at Montreal by William Ward of Vermont; he had purchased them, along with a fourth Negro (Joseph, aged twenty-two), from Elijah Cady of Albany, New York. And finally, a Negro female slave named Nancy Morton had been moved from "Mary Land" to New Brunswick by her owner, Caleb Jones. See ibid., 322–23, 327–28, and Riddell, "Slavery in the Maritime Provinces," 370–71.

66. Riddell, "Slavery in the Maritime Provinces," 361.

67. Kitts was sold on August 10, 1792; Tanno was gifted on July 27, 1793; and Pierre was sold on July 11, 1793. See Riddell, "Notes on the Slave in Nouvelle-France," 329.

68. Riddell, "Slavery in the Maritime Provinces," 363.

69. See Riddell, "Notes on the Slave in Nouvelle-France," 327–28, and Riddell, "Slavery in the Maritime Provinces," 360, 362. Not only were the black slaves within Canada international but white Canadian slave owners also owned slaves who lived outside Canada. In one such case, the executors of the estate of John Margerum of Halifax, who was deceased, noted a credit of £29.9.4.½ (i.e., almost thirty pounds) for the sale of a Negro boy at Carolina. See Riddell, "Slavery in the Maritime Provinces," 362.

70. Another mark would, of course, be the lack of monocrop plantations as the economic fuel (as opposed to other types) of slavery.

71. The Middle Passage, of course, has been theoretically and historically discussed only as the Atlantic crossings that took place between the coasts of Africa and the "New World" ports of the Americas and the Caribbean. To my knowledge, scholars have yet to research, theorize, or conceptualize the secondary transatlantic crossings through which ships departed from more southern New World ports and landed at northern ones, such as those in Canada and the northeastern United States. The black female slave represented in Malepart de Beaucourt's *Portrait of a Negro Slave* might have been just such a survivor.

72. Letter from Colonel R. S. McLaughlin to H. O. McCurry, Director of the National Gallery of Canada, July 19, 1948, cited in Michelle A. Jacques,

"A Reassessment of Prudence Heward's Black Nudes" (master's thesis, York University, Downsview, 1995), 9.

73. Dorothy Stevens, *Amy* (ca. 1930), oil on canvas, 86.8 x 76.4 cm, National Gallery of Canada, Ottawa. Photo copyright National Gallery of Canada.

74. The normalcy of using racist language to describe black bodies is evidenced in the fact that this painting was exhibited under the title *Piccaninny* throughout Ontario in the *Exhibition of Pictures by Canadian Artists*, under the auspices of The Art Association of Canadian Service Clubs and the Ontario Society of Artists, Winter 1930–31.

75. I do not wish to glamorize or glorify patriarchal authority, but we must honestly consider the ramifications of the fact that this historical means of supporting, protecting, and providing for one's family was denied black male slaves.

20

GENDER, SEX, AND POWER

Images of Enslaved Women's Bodies

Ana Lucia Araujo

Over the twentieth century, the work of European artists who traveled to Brazil during the nineteenth century greatly influenced the reconstruction and renewal of the memory of slavery among Europeans, Africans, and Brazilians. The representations of slavery and slaves developed by European artists, especially French painters Jean-Baptiste Debret (1768–1848), Johann Moritz Rugendas (1802–1858), and François-Auguste Biard (1799–1882)—whose works are specifically examined in this chapter—are still considered as important sources of historical and ethnographic data today. Although these paintings and engravings do not always offer an accurate portrait of the life of enslaved men and women in Brazil, the watercolors, wood engravings, and lithographs the artists produced allow us to understand certain dimensions of the experiences and living conditions of Brazil's enslaved Africans, as well as how Brazilians and Europeans perceived slavery at the time.

Although these works were originally intended for a European audience, their scope is much broader today. The images have circulated and still circulate not only in South America and North America but also in Africa. In Brazil, representations of enslaved Africans and slavery in the work of Debret and Rugendas have become significant points of reference for historians and anthropologists. In the nineteenth century, however, Debret's work was criticized by the Brazilian monarchy and local elites, who did not appreciate the attention that slavery and slaves thus received, especially the few plates representing physical punishments endured by the enslaved population.[1] At the time, it was unusual to see these subjects represented in either European or Brazilian academic painting. Biard's work was criticized by the local elites as well because in his book *Deux années au Brésil* (1862), he provided a negative portrait of Brazilian slave society. Little known in Brazil, Biard's representations of Brazilian daily life and slavery were a source of shame for Brazilian expatriates living in France.[2] His caricatural representations of the Brazilian court and the scenes of Rio de Janeiro urban daily life helped to disseminate through France a very negative and sometimes humorous image of Brazil.

Wide reproduction of these artists' works popularized the images, and today, we find them illustrating websites, textbooks, museum facades, posters, and book covers. Reappropriated and reinterpreted, they have helped not only to develop a specific vision of Afro-Brazilians in Europe and Africa but also to reinforce or transform the vision Brazilians have of themselves today.

This chapter focuses on how wood engravings and lithographs published in the travel accounts of Debret, Rugendas, and Biard reveal the vision that male European artists had of black and mulatto women.[3] I seek to understand how their representations of black women's bodies express both gender relations and the sometimes subtle, sometimes explicit power relations between masters and female slaves. The first part of this chapter establishes a preliminary genealogy of these images, in which nudity clearly shown or subtly evoked reminds us of the ways in which European travelers have exhaustively represented Brazilian indigenous women's bodies since the sixteenth century. The second part gives a brief overview of the biographies of Debret, Rugendas, and Biard in order to introduce the analysis of some lithographs and wood engravings published in the travel accounts and albums produced by the three artists. I explain how their representations of the cordial relations between masters, slaves, and *feitores* (overseers) helped to nourish the idea of Brazil as a country of racial harmony. Finally, the chapter demonstrates that these images are part of a larger trend visible in films and television series focusing on slavery in the Americas in general and Brazil in particular. I argue that the contemporary images of Brazilian black and mulatto women have a close association with these early representations of enslaved African women.

First European Images of Enslaved Women's Bodies

The texts and illustrations of the first European travel accounts in Brazil, especially those by Jean de Léry, André Thevet, and Hans Staden in the sixteenth century, repeatedly described and depicted the naked bodies of the native populations.[4] The woodcuts illustrating these first travel accounts very often showed scenes of daily life and described the Brazilian natural landscape, fauna, and flora. In these representations, the indigenous men and women appeared with well-built bodies and were completely integrated into the natural setting. The representation of their bodies was idealized and frequently inspired by classical tradition. These early depictions of indigenous peoples tell us far more about Europe than about the Americas.

At the time, the traveler was often not the artist who produced the images illustrating the travel accounts. Instead, an artist who likely had never visited the Americas would draw the sketch according to the oral description given by the traveler. The same artist or an illustrator would then transfer the sketch to the block of wood, carving the areas that should be white and leaving at the original level the areas to show in black. Following this stage, the block of wood was covered with ink, which would then be removed from the surface to appear in white. The image was sometimes printed separately or along with the block containing the text. In other print techniques, such as lithography—which emerged at the end of the eigthteenth century and was extensively used during the nineteenth century to reproduce artistic works—the process of reproducing images was similar. Initially, the artist or the traveler would draw the first sketches or watercolors. Then, typically, another individual would redraw these sketches on lithographic limestone by using an oil-based medium. The printer would then cover the lithograph limestone with a solution containing substances such as gum arabic, in order to coat the pores of the stone in all the zones that should not absorb ink. After this preparation process, the surface that was drawn with greasy material, which was to form the image, absorbed the ink; the parts that were covered with gum arabic, to appear in white, rejected it. This long and complex process, which relied on the collaboration of traveler, artist, illustrators, engravers, and printers—most of whom knew nothing or very little about the American continent—gave rise to idealized representations of the Americas. As a result, it is not surprising that in the different stages of the process, the various individuals in charge of producing these images sometimes intervened by adding or removing elements from the original drawings. Particularly in the images produced in the sixteenth century, it was not uncommon for illustrators depicting landscapes and peoples they had never seen to make analogies between the Americas and its populations, on one hand, and the paradise described in the Bible, on the other. Moreover, because Europeans sailed the West African coast and were in contact with Africans before conquering the Americas, the first images representing Brazilian native peoples and enslaved Africans in European travel accounts of the sixteenth and seventeenth centuries often contained very similar features.

The Dutch artist Albert Eckhout (1607–1666) lived in Brazil from 1637 to 1644, during the Dutch occupation of Pernambuco (1630–1654). While in Brazil, Eckhout produced dozens of sketches that gave birth to still-life paintings depicting the fruits and vegetables found in Brazil. Eckhout also produced large-scale oil paintings representing Brazilian landscapes, as well as portraits of Brazilian natives, enslaved Africans, and even African ambassadors from the Kingdom of Congo who were visiting the northeastern region to negotiate the terms of the Atlantic slave trade. Housed in the National Museum of Denmark in Copenhagen, these full-body portraits of Brazilian inhabitants remain rare examples in which enslaved Africans are portrayed as primary characters in painting. Over the next two centuries, Europeans who traveled to Brazil represented the slave world through watercolors, drawings, lithographs, and wood engravings, but slavery was not considered a noble enough subject to be represented in oil painting. Indeed, the collections of French museums, such as the Louvre and the Museum of the Château de Versailles, confirm that French painters privileged European landscapes, official portraits, and historical themes.

Albert Eckhout's first paintings of enslaved Africans in Brazil, in the seventeenth century, were very similar to the portraits of native Brazilians that he produced during the same period. In the two full-body portraits,

African Woman and Child (figure 20.1) and *Tupinamba/Brazilian Woman and Child* (figure 20.2), both the indigenous woman and the African enslaved woman are bare-breasted. Both are also set in the exotic space of the sugarcane plantation, and both carry a straw basket containing calabashes, yams, and tropical fruits that evoke the luxuriance of nature, the fertility of the soil, and female sexuality. Reinforcing the exoticism of

FIGURE 20.1 Albert Eckhout, *African Woman and Child* (1641), oil painting *(courtesy of Nationalmuseet, Copenhagen)*

FIGURE 20.2 Albert Eckhout, *Tupinamba/Brazilian Woman and Child* (1641), oil painting *(courtesy of Nationalmuseet, Copenhagen)*

the scene, to the left of the enslaved woman one can see a large palm tree, and to the right of the Brazilian woman is a huge banana tree. Unlike the indigenous woman's body, the body of the enslaved African woman is very strong, with well-defined muscles, indicating that she performs hard physical work. Each woman holds her child, but the skin color of the enslaved African woman's young child is much lighter than that of his mother. The difference between the boy's skin color and his mother's is an explicit reference to the miscegenation resulting from sexual intercourse, usually forced, between African female slaves and the masters of sugarcane plantations and sugar mills. As with other images of children during this period, the young boy is represented as an adult in miniature form. In one hand, he holds a small parrot, and in the other, an ear of corn. The pale, phallic-looking corn pointed toward his mother's vagina can be seen as a clear reference to the sexual role of female slaves in the plantation and in the Brazilian slave society.[5]

In the next centuries, representations of naked breasts were widely disseminated in the imaginary surrounding African and Afro-Brazilian enslaved women. Very often, these women were employed as wet nurses in the families of white masters because of the belief that black women were physically stronger than white women and could better endure Brazil's hot tropical weather.[6]

After the Portuguese expelled the Dutch from northeastern Brazil in 1654, few European travelers left illustrated travel accounts.[7] This context would change in 1808, when the Portuguese court moved to Rio de Janeiro, encouraging European travelers to visit Brazil. Representations of the female's or male's enslaved body developed by artists such as Debret, Rugendas, and Biard are, to some extent, indebted to the first images of native Brazilians made by European travelers beginning in the sixteenth century. In the majority of the images of the nineteenth century, the bodies of the enslaved men and women continue to be completely idealized. However, these engravings tell us much more about the gender relations in the Brazilian slave society than the images produced in the previous centuries.

Debret, Rugendas, and Biard

Jean-Baptiste Debret was a cousin of Jacques-Louis David (1748–1825).[8] He studied at the Collège Louis-le-Grand, and after attending David's classes, he followed the illustrious artist to Italy to help him execute the painting *Le serment des Horaces*.[9] From 1785 to 1789, Debret attended the Fine Arts Academy of Paris. In the Prix de Rome competition, his painting *Regulus partant pour Carthage* received the second prize. During the French Revolution, he abandoned painting in order to attend civil engineering classes at the École de ponts et chaussées, the future École polytechnique, where he was later appointed professor of drawing, replacing François Gérard. He took up his artistic activities again at the time of the Salon of 1798, in which he received a new prize. Under the empire (1804–14), he accepted several official commissions and participated regularly in the Salons, showing historical paintings that featured Napoleon Bonaparte as the main character. After the fall of Napoleon and the death of Debret's only son, the official commissions decreased, and he accepted Joachim Lebreton's invitation to participate in a French artistic mission to Brazil, commanded by Dom João VI. In Rio de Janeiro, Debret taught historical painting at the Academy of Fine Arts. He continued to develop his own work in the genre and produced numerous portraits of the Portuguese court. He returned to France in 1831, at a time when the regulations of the Fine Arts Academy were undergoing reform and a series of political crises provoked the abdication of Dom Pedro I.

From 1834 to 1839, Debret published in Paris, at Firmin Didot Frères, the three volumes of *Voyage pittoresque et historique au Brésil*. Charles Pradier, his former colleague on the French artistic mission, made the lithographs (based on Debret's watercolors), which were later printed by Thierry Frères.[10] Historians, art historians, and anthropologists developed an interest in the *Voyage pittoresque*, especially because of its representations of Brazilian native populations as well as enslaved Africans and Afro-Brazilians.[11]

Johann Moritz Rugendas was born in Augsburg into a family of artists. He studied at the Academy of Munich and became a disciple of Lorenzo Quaglio (1792–1869). He traveled to Brazil in 1822 with the Langsdorff expedition but soon abandoned it to pursue his journey alone, accumulating sketches of the Brazilian inhabitants and landscape. When he returned to Augsburg, he published his *Voyage pittoresque dans le Brésil* between 1827 and 1835.[12] This illustrated travel account includes one hundred lithographs based on his drawings. The text was probably written by Victor-Aimé Huber,[13] who developed his descriptions from Rugendas's accounts.[14]

François-Auguste Biard studied at the School of Fine Arts of Lyon before becoming a professor of drawing in the French navy. Between 1827 and 1828, he traveled to Cyprus, Malta, Syria, and Egypt. After leaving the navy, he visited England, Scotland, Germany, Switzerland, Spain, Italy, and North Africa. In 1834, he established his studio in Paris and became an official painter under the July Monarchy (1830–48). In 1839, he was in charge of decorating the Palace of Versailles, and his work became very popular. Between 1839 and 1840, Biard and his young wife, Léonie d'Aunet, participated in a French expedition to the Arctic in the corvette *La Recherche*. From these several travels, he accumulated a number of sketches that led to the paintings he exhibited in the Salon in Paris. As an official artist, Biard largely relied on the revenue obtained from the paintings commissioned by King Louis Philippe. As a result, the end of the July Monarchy had a significant negative impact on his career. In 1858, when he was almost sixty years old, he traveled to Brazil using his own resources, and he remained in the country until the beginning of 1860. He was a former official artist, and once he was in Rio de Janeiro, the Emperor Dom Pedro II sponsored his work. Yet despite the support of the Brazilian monarchy, the artist decided to leave the urban environment to undertake an adventure in the jungle. He went first to Espírito Santo and later to Amazonia. During his journey from Rio de Janeiro to the distant regions of Amazonia, Biard produced many portraits of Brazilian native populations but also of people of African descent, enslaved, freed, and free. In 1861, he published a short version of his travel account in the illustrated journal *Le tour du monde*. One year later, the book *Deux années au Brésil* was published by Hachette in Paris. His account, illustrated with 180 wood engravings drawn by Édouard Riou and made by different engravers, is marked by its humorous vision of Brazilian daily life.[15]

Enslaved Bodies

European travelers who went to Brazil during the nineteenth century saw the country as the black continent of the Americas. Africans and their descendants were regarded as the engine of a society that relied entirely on slave labor. In this context, Brazilian exoticism was perceived by

Europeans primarily as African exoticism.[16] And quite often, this exoticism was associated with the almost-naked bodies of enslaved women. Portuguese officials and European travelers frequently referred to the presence of bare-breasted female slaves in the streets of cities such as Rio de Janeiro and Salvador. The Count of Resende wrote a letter, reproduced by Silvia Hunold Lara, describing Rio de Janeiro urban daily life, and he mentioned that enslaved women remained in the streets idling or selling "insignificant things." Even worse for Resende was the behavior of the mulatto women. According to him, these freedwomen, who lived close to the households of their former masters, became pernicious because of their bad behavior and gossip. However, according to Resende, it was worse still when they resided alone or with other mulatto women because they lived scandalous and libertine lives.[17] Before becoming a renowned painter, Édouard Manet traveled to Brazil in 1848 aboard the *Havre-et-Guadeloupe*, and he spent some months in Rio de Janeiro.[18] In his letters to his mother, the young man described the city as follows:

> In the streets one only meets male and female negroes; Brazilian men don't go often outside and Brazilian women even less. . . . In this country where all negroes are slaves; all these unfortunate men seem stupid; it is extraordinary the power that the white exert on them; I saw a slave market, it is a revolting spectacle for us; the negroes wear pants, sometimes a jacket in fabric, but as slaves they are not allowed to wear shoes. The majority of female negroes are naked to the belt, some wear neck scarves falling to the chest, they are generally ugly, however I saw some pretty ones; they dress very gracefully. The ones make turbans, the others arrange their crisp hair very skilfully and almost all of them wear underskirts decorated with ugly flounces.[19]

Travelers were ambivalent about the almost-naked bodies of enslaved women they saw in Brazil, sometimes expressing admiration, sometimes expressing repulsion. Although Manet initially perceived the exoticism of women of African descent as a "hideous" spectacle, he was also able to identify some beautiful "negro women." His attraction for black women was justified not only because of their stylishness and their naked breasts but also because they were the only women "available" in the streets of Rio de Janeiro. Indeed, so-called Brazilian women—which in the nineteenth-century travel accounts meant white women of Portuguese origin—did not go outside very often.

But the presence of Africans and people of African descent on the streets of the Brazilian cities such as Salvador and Rio de Janeiro was frequently a source of disappointment, especially for those travelers who went to the country in search of Amerindian exoticism. After arriving in Brazil, François-Auguste Biard clearly expressed a desire to go to the rain forest in order to paint indigenous groups: "I wanted to have some by any means; I had already seen negroes in Africa."[20] When he arrived in Bahia,[21] he noticed the massive presence of slaves and people of African descent in the streets of the city. In the engraving *Une rue de Bahia* (A street in Bahia) (figure 20.3), based on a Biard sketch, one can identify the narrow streets of Salvador's lower town. In the foreground, five black men are seated at the bottom of the staircase, in a position expressing a certain lassitude. In the middle ground, another man wearing a hat descends the staircase, and in the background, at the top of the staircase, are two women. The cut and pattern of their clothes are represented in detail. In the background, a palm tree announces the stereotypical "tropicality" of the landscape in the city's neighborhoods. One can observe a certain orientalizing tendency in the manner in which the architecture and the Brazilian inhabitants are represented.

In the accompanying text, the painter, despite expressing a certain dislike, remarks on the beauty of the African and Afro-Brazilian women:

> Arrived at the ground, nothing picturesque: the negroes, always the negroes, shouting, pushing; their costumes were not unexpected, dirty trousers, dirty shirts, grubby feet, often enormous, the sad result of this dreadful disease named elephantiasis, caused almost always by depravity. I have heard that if you want to see beautiful female negroes you must go to Bahia. Indeed, I saw several who were not bad, but all them were swarming in the narrow streets of the low town, where French, English, Portuguese, Jewish and Catholic merchants lived in an insalubrious atmosphere. I hastened to leave this anthill, while climbing with difficulty, as in Lisbon, the main street that leads to the high town.[22]

FIGURE 20.3 François-Auguste Biard, *Une rue de Bahia* (A street in Bahia), lithograph from *Deux années au Brésil* (1862), 39

The comment about the beauty of black women in Bahia is followed by a warning concerning the city's ambience of depravity. For Biard, as for other European travelers, the image of slaves was almost always associated with degeneracy, explicit sexuality, and consequent disease, even though the elephantiasis mentioned in this excerpt is transmitted by mosquitoes rather than by sexual contact. However, the association between disease and degeneracy did not emerge solely from the travelers' prejudices. As Gilberto Freyre points out, it was in the "voluptuous environment of the master's house, full of children, baby negroes, small female negroes, *mucamas*, that the venereal diseases were easily disseminated, by the domestic prostitution—always less hygienic than that of the brothels."[23]

Usually, enslaved women in the domestic urban environment had better living and work conditions than enslaved women who performed other kinds of work in the plantation environment. However, sexual abuse by the masters was not excluded. These enslaved female maids, often mulatto women, performed domestic services in their masters' households. As Mieko Nishida explains, they were "mistresses or common-law wives of the owners, served as supervisors of other slaves, washerwomen, cooks, housekeepers, and wet nurses (*amas de leite*) for the owners' legitimate children."[24] The French traveler Charles Expilly observed that owning a wet nurse was also an indicator of social status: "The luxury of the wet nurse indicates how prosperous is the household."[25] This idea is confirmed by Sandra Lauderdale Graham, who explains that especially the mucamas, who were in permanent contact with their masters and mistresses, "could expect finer clothes, perhaps a more varied or ample diet gleaned from the family's table, earlier attention to illness, and the small, sought-after protections a proper mistress or master was supposed to provide."[26] Expilly described the wet nurse as a woman who was able to manipulate her masters sexually: "She [the wet nurse] enabled them to satisfy their sensuality and momentarily to live according to their fantasies without fearing being punished."[27] However, as Graham notes, enslaved domestic servants such as the mucamas were expected to be loyal, and they lived under constant surveillance. In this context, loyalty also meant passive acceptance of sexual abuse, often beginning in childhood and sometimes under the promise of receiving manumission by their masters.[28]

FIGURE 20.4
François-Auguste Biard, *La Mulâtresse* (The Mulatto woman), engraving from *Deux années au Brésil* (1862), 348

Apart from ethnographic portraits representing "civilized" Brazilian natives, Biard produced only one engraving of a young female whom he clearly identified as a mulatto. The portrait *La mulâtresse* (The mulatto woman) (figure 20.4) is based on a drawing he produced when he was in Manaus (Amazonas). It emphasizes the model's beauty and delicate physiognomy. She has dark skin and curly hair, she is naked above the waist, and she is giving a sensual glance to the spectator.

This close-cropped portrait is different from the other compositions depicting indigenous women. Here, the artist's model is represented alone. To emphasize that she is not an indigenous woman living in the wilds or an enslaved African woman recently arrived in Brazil, Biard identifies her as a *mulato,* a word that designated a Brazilian-born slave, free, or freed person of white and African ancestry. In some cases, the adjective *mulato* was also employed to differentiate the status of a free or freed black person from that of an enslaved individual. Portraying the mulatto woman as bare-breasted is not naturalistic but part of the mise-en-scène intended to convey exoticism. The image suggests the painter has developed a more intimate relationship with his model. If the engraving accentuates the beauty of the mulatto woman, the text insists on her vivacity and her lack of integrity. During a walk, some thorns stuck in the bottom of Biard's feet. The mulatto woman represented in the image helped him to remove them: "A female mulatto did the operation correctly; only one of the fifty thorns inserted under the skin of my feet remained. Little by little she pulled them out without making me suffer. I regret having to add that this mulatto woman who was so skillful, was also a little robber. Few days afterwards, I had the pain to see her being whipped while the other women of color, less pretty than she, applauded. She was probably used to this kind of situation and it did not affect her very much. Two hours later she came to my room to pose, with all her talents and with flowers in her hair."[29] Explaining the differences between black and mulatto women, Biard assumes that miscegenation is a positive feature, at least from his aesthetic point of view. At the same time, he considers the mulatto woman as the "degenerate" portion of the white and black "races." Not only was she a thief, she also accepted physical punishment as something natural, and once her whippings were over, she was ready to adorn herself to take part in the posing sessions organized by the painter.

Images emphasizing the sexuality and sensuality of Afro-Brazilian women were widely disseminated in nineteenth-century travel accounts. In *Casa-grande & senzala*, Gilberto Freyre refers to a libidinous mulatto woman "who initiated us into physical love and transmitted to us . . . the first complete feeling of being a man."[30] He reveals how young Brazilian men of Portuguese origin developed what he calls a genuine "obsession" for black women during the colonial period. He reports that these white men, always surrounded by "easy mulatto women," could come to orgasm only with black women. In the description of these sexual relations between masters and female slaves, violence is totally evacuated.

Gender relations between masters, mistresses, and slaves are also visible in several nineteenth-century engravings. In one, the only lithograph in which Debret uses humor, a government employee is shown taking a walk with his family. The text accompanying *Un employé du gouvernement sortant de chez lui avec sa famille* (A government employee leaving his house with his family) (figure 20.5) reminds the reader that the streets of Rio de Janeiro were full of people of African descent but that it was uncommon to see white women outside the domestic space. The point is unsurprising.

FIGURE 20.5 Jean-Baptiste Debret, *Un employé du gouvernement sortant de chez lui avec sa famille* (A government employee leaving his house with his family), lithograph from *Voyage pittoresque et historique au Brésil* (1834–39), vol. 2, plate 5

In 1823, the slave population of Rio de Janeiro was 150,549, and the free population (including freedmen and freedwomen) was 301,009.[31] Further, Debret states that Brazilian white women did not have any taste; they dressed in an odd way and wore colored clothing according to the Anglo-Portuguese fashion.

Describing his lithograph, the artist explains that the line is led by the husband, the head of the family, followed by the children, from the youngest to the oldest, and then his pregnant wife. After that, one sees a mucama, a domestic enslaved woman, the black wet nurse, a younger female slave, the master's male slave (who is wearing a top hat and holding an umbrella), and finally a young male slave. At the end of the line comes a new "negro," who has recently been bought and who is "the slave of all the others, whose intelligence, more or less vivid, will be developed by blows of whip."[32] The satirical engraving illustrates in a simple manner how complex Brazilian society was. Owning slaves was more than an economic need; it was an issue of social prestige. The position of each character in the line and their sizes in relation to one another show the gender and hierarchical relations inside the family and among slaves themselves. If the domestic slave seems to be integrated into the family, the new slave's position is that of a commodity. The white male master, dressed in black, is visibly distinct from the other members of the group. The two young girls are dressed exactly like their mother, and their hairstyles are identical. The mucama, who is usually a mulatto enslaved woman and has a form of intimate contact with the mistress and obviously with the master, occupies a prominent position in the family's hierarchy. She wears a dress and a coat very similar to those of her mistress. However, as slaves, both the mucama and the wet nurse wear no shoes. Toward the end of the line, the slaves have darker skin and are younger. Their clothing and attitude are more modest than those of the slaves who precede them.

Debret's line constitutes a precise portrait of the nineteenth-century Brazilian family and slave society. Male white masters and female white mistresses have the highest position. A free male mulatto has a more important position than a free female mulatto, and both have more rights than freed mulatto men and women. Lower in the social and racial hierarchy, one can find mulatto female and male slaves and then black female and male slaves. Female and male Africans who had bought their freedom continued to be considered foreigners. In this socially and racially hierarchized society, skin color and physical features have a major impact on social mobility.

The wood engraving *Dames brésiliennes à Rio de Janeiro* (Brazilian ladies in Rio de Janeiro) (figure 20.6), published in Biard's travel account, was probably inspired by *Un employé du gouvernement sortant de chez lui avec sa famille* (figure 20.5). It shows a Brazilian white woman walking in the street, followed by a line of slaves. In the text, Biard simultaneously exalts the French fashion in evidence in Rio streets and criticizes Brazilian women both for their dress and for their custom of always being accompanied by slaves:

> I still didn't go walk in the splendid street of Ouvidor; however, it seems that this street is the meeting place of all the most elegant people spreading out their toilets in the lights of the shops. One can see the beautiful Brazilian women, who according to the custom are always followed by one or two mulattos, two or three

FIGURE 20.6. François-Auguste Biard, *Dames brésiliennes à Rio de Janeiro* (Brazilian ladies in Rio de Janeiro), engraving from *Deux années au Brésil* (1862), 85

> negro women, some young female and male negroes. The group walks gravely, the husband at the head of the line. In these colorful costumes, I could have recognized the spirit of economy and order that our Frenchwomen don't have all the time.[33]

Biard ridicules Brazilian women in the text and the image. The Brazilian white lady, her son, and the slaves who follow her are represented as caricatures: their physical features are deformed, and their traits are exaggerated. To complete the comical quality of the scene, the painter has added a dog at the end of the line, reminding the reader that the living conditions of slaves in Brazil are very close to those of animals.

Some ten years earlier, before visiting Brazil, Biard had painted *Traite d'esclaves dans la côte ouest de l'Afrique* (Slave trade in the West Coast of Africa), *Capture d'un bâtiment négrier par un navire français* (Capture of a slave ship by a French vessel), *Proclamation de la liberté des Noirs aux colonies (1848)* (Abolition of slavery in the colonies [1848]), and *Emménagement d'esclaves à bord d'un négrier sur la côte d'Afrique* (Slaves' transportation in a slave ship on the African coast).[34] Although he emphasized not only the horrors of the slave trade and the physical punishment associated with it but also the role played by France in that commerce, the painter was far from being an abolitionist. As a result, because of his relations with the Brazilian monarchy, the only possible way he would criticize Brazilian slave society was by using a humorous approach. Biard is careful in his text never to condemn slavery directly: "The life of a negro in Brazil is much far preferable to that of the most part of the unfortunate European immigrants. The authorities never fulfill the promises they made to them."[35]

This kind of discourse distorted the atrocious living conditions of slaves in Brazil and later corroborated the idea that Brazilian slavery was mild, especially in comparison to that of the United States. Today, even though 45 percent of the Brazilian population self-identifies as black (*negro*) or brown (*pardo*), the idea that slaves and nineteenth-century European immigrants to the country were in some way comparable still circulates in Brazilian society, especially among those opposed to affirmative action projects.[36]

Debret's idealization of black bodies is related to the neoclassical ethics that marks his work. Such an idealized image of slaves is present in his lithograph *Marchand de fleurs, à la porte d'une église* ("Flower Vendor at the Door of a Church") (figure 20.7), representing urban slavery in Rio de

FIGURE 20.7 Jean-Baptiste Debret, *Marchand de fleurs, à la porte d'une église* (Flower vendor at the door of a church), lithograph from *Voyage pittoresque et historique au Brésil* (1834–39), vol. 3, plate 6

Janeiro. It shows an enslaved man in front of a church, selling flowers to a Brazilian lady who is followed by a line of women slaves. The main character of this scene is the wage-earning slave, a street vendor who makes his living selling flowers and fruits and who, despite his greater autonomy, must give a large portion of his income to his master. The body of the enslaved man is drawn according to neoclassical conceptions of balance and proportion. He is well proportioned, and his stance is statuelike. Despite being barefoot, the character looks like a dandy because of the refined appearance of his clothes. The dresses of the women slaves in the image are embroidered, and their hairstyles combine aspects of local fashion with the French and Portuguese styles of the time. Although female slaves wore clothing that was modest in comparison to that of their mistresses, slave owners were concerned about the way their domestic slaves were dressed.[37] Owning slaves who wore refined clothes in European fashion and sometimes even jewelry was one way to show wealth.

Despite the theatrical poses of the Brazilian lady and the male slave in the lithograph, Debret insists in his text that his portrayal is realistic. Even if his intention of being objective can be questioned, the artist depicts in detail the clothing, the hairstyles, and even the specific location where the scene takes place. Nevertheless, the image has a symbolic dimension as well. The gesture of the slave in offering a carnation to the white lady underlines the gender relations between blacks and whites in nineteenth-century Brazilian slave society, at the same time suggesting that these relations are cordial. The image is almost the only one in existence to show a white woman in the street having direct contact with a black man. Hence, the slave's gesture evokes for the first time sexuality expressed between a black man and a white woman.

Representations of enslaved Africans inside slave ships, in the streets, and in the slave markets almost always refer to promiscuity, but European artists such as Debret and Rugendas also portray the slave family. These images depicting the daily lives of couples of enslaved men and women, expressing affection, contest the idea that Brazilian slaves did not follow the social norms of family and sexual life.[38] Debret depicts many scenes of slave labor and the daily life of slaves, but these images rarely evoke sexual relations between masters and women slaves—an issue obviously relegated to a zone of denial.

Violence, rape, and the control exerted by slave owners over the bodies of female slaves are nevertheless evoked in a few lithographs of Rugendas's travel account, in which he shows the sensuality of female slaves through nudity. The lithograph *Préparation de la racine de mendiocca* ("Preparation of the Manioc Root") (figure 20.8) presents a group of three women slaves preparing cassava. Another bare-breasted female slave has her back turned to the spectator, and a fifth is giving attention to her child. In the background, one sees the silhouette of two slaves enveloped by smoke. In the foreground, seated on the ground, are two male slaves and one female slave peeling manioc roots. Behind them, a male slave on his knees is trying to protect his face from the smoke coming from the cauldron in which the roots are being cooked.

But the two central elements of this image are a slave woman in profile and the *feitor*, or overseer. The *feitor* is the only white character in this scene. Dressed in pants, a white shirt, and a vest, he wears a hat and a scarf around his neck. He is in the position of an inspector: his right hand is behind his back, and his left arm rests on his left thigh. He is slightly

FIGURE 20.8 Johann Moritz Rugendas, *Préparation de la racine de mendiocca* (Preparation of the manioc root), lithograph from *Voyage dans le Brésil* (Paris: Engelman, 1835), 4e division, plate 7

turned to the woman slave, at whom he looks with interest as he talks. The woman slave, whose shoulders and back are revealed, holds a basket with both hands. She is looking at the *feitor* with wide-open eyes. Here, the relations of gender and power are expressed not through explicit hostility but through the suggestion of control and the threat of violence. Although the *feitor* is neither gesticulating nor punishing the enslaved woman, his glance indicates that he is in control of the situation.

In the beginning of the eighteenth century, authors such as André João Antonil mentioned the abuses perpetrated by the *feitor* against enslaved women. According to him, "they could "attach and whip with a liana until running blood, and putting in the *tronco*[39] or attached in a chain for months (when the master is in the city), the slave woman who did not agree to commit the sin."[40]

In the plantation environment, where women were numerically inferior, enslaved women were subjected to harder work conditions than men and to sexual abuse as well. A similar situation is depicted in the engraving *Nouveaux nègres* ("New Negroes") (figure 20.9). The scene is set in the slave quarter of a Brazilian plantation. The work portrays the nostalgia of three Africans who have just arrived from their homeland. At the center of the composition is a bare-breasted slave woman wearing a hat and earrings. Standing up and looking directly at the spectator, she appears unashamed, but she covers the bottom of her body with a shirt, probably influenced by the glance of the *feitor*, who is observing the scene with a mixture of interest and reprobation. Once again, the image reinforces the idea that the *feitor* controls the situation, as his role was to "break" the new slaves from Africa. Especially in the large plantations where the masters were not able to exert close control over the slaves' activities, one can suppose the *feitor* was also in charge of sexually "domesticating" the African female slaves.[41]

Moving Images, Renewed Memories

Slavery was abolished in Brazil in 1888. However, representations of the slave past continued to be disseminated throughout the twentieth century, especially in films and on television. In the early 1900s, a wave of films was inaugurated with *Uncle Tom's Cabin*,[42] and since the 1960s, many Brazilian and North American films and telefilms have depicted slavery. Among Brazilian productions are the films *Sinhá moça* (1953),

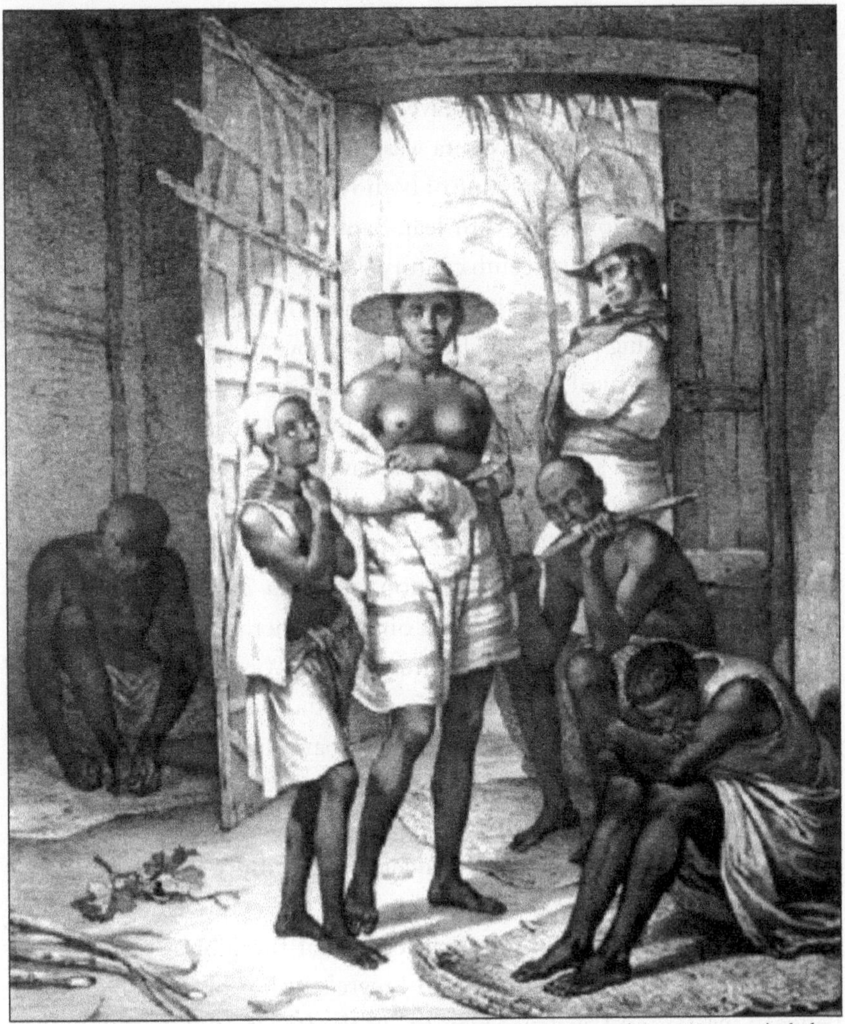

FIGURE 20.9 Johann Moritz Rugendas, *Nouveaux Nègres* (New Negroes), lithograph from *Voyage dans le Brésil*, 2e division, plate 16

Ganga Zumba (1963), *Xica da Silva* (1976), and *Quilombo* (1984) as well as the soap operas *A cabana do Pai Tomás* ("Uncle Tom's Cabin," 1969); *A escrava Isaura* ("The Slave Isaura," 1976), produced by the Globo television network; *A escrava Anastácia* ("The Slave Anastácia," 1990), screened at Rede Manchete; and *Xica da Silva* (1996), screened at SBT (Sistema Brasileiro de Televisão).

A cabana do pai Tomás—which was broadcast from July 7, 1969, to March 1, 1970, during the military dictatorship (1964–85)—was based on the novel

Uncle Tom's Cabin. Sérgio Cardoso (1925–1972), a white actor, played the role of Uncle Tom by using blackface theatrical makeup. In the soap opera *A escrava Isaura*, the main female slave character was also a white actress.[43] A second version of this soap opera was produced in 2004 by the Record television network. In the opening of both versions of this production, one sees an animation conceived with Jean-Baptiste Debret's watercolors, representing slave life in nineteenth-century Rio de Janeiro.[44] *A escrava Isaura* was a huge success not only in Brazil but also in eighty countries across the world, including Romania, Hungary, the Soviet Union, China, Cuba, Israel, Nigeria, Portugal, Kenya, Ghana, Mozambique, and South Africa. By watching the soap opera's opening, the international audience became familiar with Debret's representations of slavery.

These Brazilian television and film productions showed various elements of slave life in Brazil: resistance, punishments, *quilombos*, marriages, and manumissions. With the exception of *Ganga Zumba* and *Quilombo*, most of these productions shed light on the numerous strategies used by enslaved women to try to get their freedom. In *Xica da Silva*,[45] a former slave, Francisca da Silva (played by Zezé Motta), uses her sexual appeal to ascend socially. As Mariza de Carvalho Soares has pointed out, Xica's story gave a new interpretation to the work of Gilberto Freyre.[46]

In 1987, Werner Herzog directed *Cobra Verde*, an adaptation of Bruce Chatwin's novel *The Viceroy of Ouidah*.[47] The film depicts the life of Francisco Félix de Souza, a Brazilian slave merchant who settled in the Bight of Benin during the first decades of the nineteenth century. Herzog added a humorous touch to Freyre's vision of the relationship between masters and enslaved women. In the first part of the film, set in a sugarcane plantation in Pernambuco, the slave owner proudly affirms that he maintains sexual relations with the young enslaved women and that he likes when they become pregnant (figures 20.10 and 20.11). In the film, the beautiful domestic slaves do not give the impression of having a violent or conflictual relationship with their master. In one scene, a beautiful slave woman with bare shoulders walks slowly, slightly swinging her hips, toward the bedroom of her aged master. This caricatural and humorous vision of the master-slave relationship is largely attributable to the idea that slavery was milder in Brazil than in the United States.[48]

How very strange. I haven't bred
any children yet today.

FIGURES 20.10 AND 11 From the film *Cobra Verde*

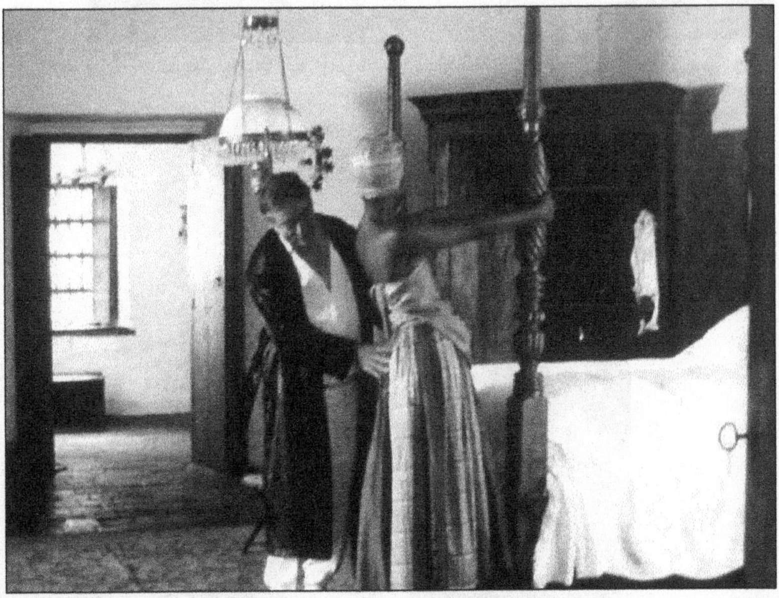

The notion that libidinous enslaved women enjoyed sex with their elderly and hideous masters is absent from the North American films and television programs. In the telefilm *Roots* (1977), an adaptation of Alex Haley's novel of the same name, published one year earlier, the slave Kunta Kinte has a young daughter named Kizzy. Separated from her family and sold to a master who beats and rapes her (figures 20.12 and 20.13), she never succeeds in having a family as her parents had done. Unlike the lascivious slave woman of *Cobra Verde*, Kizzy has no pleasure in

FIGURES 20.12 AND 13 From *Roots*

sexual relations with her master and never takes advantage of her sexual qualities to obtain better living conditions or win her freedom. In North American films, the potential threat presented in Rugendas's image of the *feitor* who looks attentively at the female slave (figure 20.8 and figure 20.9) is now a violent and accomplished act.

The images in the travel accounts of Debret, Rugendas, and Biard that represent the bodies of enslaved women and the gender and sexual relations between masters and slaves are indebted to the first European representations of Brazilian native women. Those sixteenth-and seventeenth-century works showed bare-breasted women living in harmony with nature. They also conveyed an idealized image of a cordial relationship between masters and slaves. That said, by including mulatto children in the images or evoking the control exerted on the female slaves by the *feitor*, Eckhout, Debret, Rugendas, and Biard also suggest the existence of violence and sexual relations between white men and enslaved women. However, in many of the illustrations and accompanying texts, Brazilian enslaved women seem to be completely integrated into the master's family. These representations of Brazil's slave society, later confirmed by Gilberto Freyre's work, therefore helped to produce and disseminate an unrealistically "generous" interpretation of Brazilian slavery.

Over the past thirty years, Brazilian and North American historians have deconstructed the myth of Brazilian slavery as somehow softer than that in the United States, but depictions of the female slave and the black domestic servant still persist. The cultural production developed over the last fifty years through advertising, films, and soap operas has helped to propagate a certain image of Afro-Brazilian women associated with nudity and heightened sexuality. At the same time, however, it has also helped to perpetuate the myth that Brazil is a country where one can find racial harmony.

Notes

This chapter relies on the research I developed in "Le romantisme tropical: Les illustrations de la relation de voyage *Deux années au Brésil* (1862) de François-Auguste Biard (1799–1882)" (Ph.D. diss., Université Laval, 2004). This work also gave rise to two articles and one book I authored: "Encontros difíceis: O artista-herói e os índios corrompidos no relato de viagem *Deux années au Brésil* (1862)," *Luso-Brazilian Review* 42, no. 2 (2005): 15–39; "Les représentations de l'esclavage dans les gravures des relations *Voyage pittoresque et historique au Brésil* (1834) de Jean-Baptiste Debret (1768–1848) et *Deux années au Brésil* (1862) de François-Auguste Biard (1799–1882)," *Canadian Journal of Latin American and Caribbean Studies* 30, no. 59 (2005): 161–83; and *Romantisme tropical: L'aventure illustrée d'un peintre français au Brésil* (Quebec: Presses de l'Université Laval, 2008). I wish to thank Elizabeth Elbourne for her enlightening comments and for carefully editing the chapter.

1. More information about the reception and the impact of Debret's work in Brazil can be found in Daryle Williams, *Culture Wars in Brazil: The First Vargas Regime, 1930–1945* (Durham, N.C.: Duke University Press, 2001), 165–76.

2. "Folhetim do Jornal do Comércio," *Jornal do comércio* 199 (July 19, 1882): 1.

3. In Brazil, a mulatto is usually considered to be a person of both Portuguese white and African ancestry. The word *mulato* constantly appears in nineteenth-century sources and is still widely used in Brazil.

4. For more recent editions of these travel accounts, see Jean de Léry, *Histoire d'un voyage fait en la terre du Brésil*, 1557, preface and epilogue by Frank Lestringant (Montpellier, France: Max Chaleil, 1992); André Thevet, *Le Brésil d'André Thevet: Les singularités de la France antarctique (1557)* (Paris: Chandeigne, 1997); Hans Staden, *Véritable histoire et description d'un pays habité par des hommes sauvages, nus, féroces et anthropophages* (Marbourg: André Kolben, 1557); and Staden, *Nus, féroces et anthropophages* (Paris: A. M. Métailié, 1979).

5. See Rebecca Parker Brienen, *Visions of Savage Paradise: Albert Eckhout, Court Painter in Colonial Dutch Brazil* (Amsterdam: Amsterdam University Press, 2007), 34. Zacharias Wagener (1614–1668) made annotated copies of Eckhout's paintings for his *Thierbuch* that includes a watercolor depicting this painting entitled "Molher negra" (ca. 1641). See Brienen, *Visions of Savage Paradise*, 134.

6. Robert Conrad, *Children of God's Fire: A Documentary History of Black Slavery in Brazil* (Princeton, N.J.: Princeton University Press, 1997), 133–40.

7. One of the few exceptions is Carlos Julião (1740–1811). Born in Piedmont (modern-day Italy), he was employed by the Portuguese army. Julião traveled to Brazil in the second half of the eighteenth century. Later, the watercolors he produced during his stay there were published in an album titled *Noticia summaria do gentilismo da Asia com dez riscos illuminados: Ditos de Figurinhos de Brancos e Negros dos Uzos do Rio de Janeiro e Serro do Frio: Ditos de Vazos e Tecidos Peruvianos*. About Julião's work, see Silvia Hunold Lara, "Customs and Costumes: Carlos Julião and the Image of Black Slaves in Late Eighteenth-Century Brazil," *Slavery & Aboliton* 23, no. 2 (2002): 125–46.

8. Marie-Monique Bernard, "Jean-Baptiste Debret, *Voyage pittoresque et historique au Brésil* (1834)," in *L'œil aux aguets ou l'artiste en voyage*, ed. François Moreau (Paris: Klincksieck, 1995), 167, and Alfonso de E. Taunay, *A missão artistica de 1816* (Brasilia: Editora da Universidade de Brasilia, 1983), 217.

9. Mario Carelli, *Cultures croisées: Histoire des échanges culturels entre la France et le Brésil de la découverte aux temps modernes* (Paris: Nathan, 1993), 62–63.

10. Wilson Coutinho, "Et les Français arrivèrent . . . ," in *Missão artística francesa e pintores viajantes: França-Brasil no século XIX, la mission artistique française et les peintres voyageurs: France Brésil au XIXe siècle*, ed. Jean Boghici (Rio de Janeiro: Secretaria de Cultura do Estado do Rio de Janeiro, Instituto Cultural Brasil-França, Fundação Casa França-Brasil, 1990), 48. But according to Carelli, Debret drew the lithographs with the assistance of the Viscountess of Portes. See Carelli, *Cultures croisées*, 67.

11. See Bernard, "Jean-Baptiste Debret," 167–76; Jeanine Potelet, *Le Brésil, vu par les voyageurs et les marins français, 1816–1840: Témoignages et images* (Paris: L'Harmattan, 1991); Xavier-Philippe Guiochon, "Le Brésil face au regard artistique français: Debret et la mission artistique de 1816," *Cahiers du Brésil contemporain* 23–24 (1994): 39–58; Rodrigo Naves, "Debret, o neoclassicismo e a escravidão," in Rodrigo, *A forma difícil–Ensaios sobre a arte Brasileira* (São Paulo: Ática, 1996); and Alejandra Mailhe, "Les limites du visible: Réflexions sur la représentation picturale de l'esclavage dans l'œuvre de Rugendas et de Debret," *Conserveries mémorielles* 2, no. 3, "Passé colonial et modalités de mise en mémoire de l'esclavage," special issue edited by Ana Lucia Araujo and Anna Seiderer (2007), http://www.celat.ulaval.ca/histoire.memoire/no_3.htm.

12. See Johann Moritz Rugendas, *Voyage dans le Brésil* (Paris: Engelman, 1835). The first edition was published in the same year both in French and German and comprises six parts.

13. See Tekla Hartmann, *A contribuição da iconografia para o conhecimento de Índios Brasileiros do século XIX* (São Paulo: Fundo de Pesquisas do Museu Paulista da Universidade de São Paulo, 1975), 75.

14. Unlike Debret's travel account, few studies were developed about Rugendas's travel account. The recent scholarly works about Rugendas include Robert W. Slenes, "African Abrahams, Lucretias and Men Sorrows in the Brazilian Anti-slavery Lithographs (1827-1835) of Johann Moritz Rugendas," *Slavery and Abolition* 23 (2002): 147-68.

15. See Araujo, "Romantisme tropical"; Araujo, "Encontros difíceis"; Araujo, "Représentations de l'esclavage"; and Araujo, *Romantisme tropical: L'aventure illustrée.*

16. Jeanine Potelet, *Le Brésil*, 166.

17. Letter from the Count of Resende to Luis Pinto de Souza Coutinho, April 11, 1796, cod. 69, vol. 13, fol. 39–42v, Correspondência do vice-reinado para a corte, Arquivo nacional do Rio de Janeiro, quoted in Silvia Hunold Lara, *Fragmentos setecentistas: Escravidão, cultura e poder na América Portuguesa* (São Paulo: Companhia das Letras, 2007), 13–14.

18. Manet left the Havre on December 9, 1848, and returned to France on June 3, 1849.

19. Édouard Manet, *Lettres du siège de Paris: Précédées des lettres du voyage à Rio de Janeiro* (Paris: Éditions de l'Amateur, 1996), 23–24. All translations from French are mine.

20. François-Auguste Biard, *Deux années au Brésil* (Paris: Hachette, 1862), 114.

21. Called "Bahia" by many travelers, the city of Salvador in the province of Bahia was founded in 1549 and was the capital of Brazil until 1763.

22. Biard, *Deux années au Brésil*, 38.

23. Gilberto Freyre, *Casa Grande & Senzala* (São Paulo: Global, 2003), 401. All translations from Portuguese are mine.

24. Mieko Nishida, *Slavery and Identity: Ethnicity, Gender and Race in Salvador, Brazil, 1808–1888* (Bloomington: Indiana University Press, 2003), 19.

25. "Le luxe de la nourrice dira la prospérité de la maison." Charles Expilly, *Le Brésil tel qu'il est* (Paris: Arnauld de Vresse, 1863), 204.

26. See Sandra Lauderdale Graham, *Caetana Says No: Women's Stories from a Brazilian Slave Society* (New York: Cambridge University Press, 2006), 25.

27. "Elle leur permet de satisfaire leur sensualité, et de vivre momentanément à leur fantaisie, sans avoir à redouter une dure répression." Expilly, *Le Brésil*, 206.

28. See the case of Rosa Egipciaca, an African enslaved girl bought when she was six years old and molested by her master until the age of fourteen, discussed in Luiz Mott, *Rosa Egipciaca: Uma santa africana no Brasil* (Rio de Janeiro: Bertrand do Brasil, 1993), and Mott, "Rosa Egipcíaca: De escrava da Costa da Mina a Flor do Rio de Janeiro, in *Rotas atlânticas da diáspora africana: Da Baía do Benim ao Rio de Janeiro,* ed. Mariza de Carvalho Soares (Rio de Janeiro: Editora da Universidade Federal Fluminense, 2007), 135–55. See also the story of the enslaved girl Liberata examined in Keila Grinberg, "Manumission, Gender, and the Law in Nineteenth-Century Brazil: Liberata's Legal Suit for Freedom," in *Paths to Freedom: Manumission in the Atlantic World,* ed. Rosemary Brana-Shute and Randy J. Sparks (Columbia: University of South Carolina Press, 2209), 219–34. In addition, see the case of Honorata, a young slave girl raped by her master at the age of ten, described in Conrad, *Children of God's Fire*, 273–80.

29. Biard, *Deux années au Brésil*, 348.

30. Freyre, *Casa-grande & senzala*, 367.

31. See Katia M. de Queiros Mattoso, *Être esclave au Brésil, XVIe–XIXe siècle* (Paris: Hachette, 1979), 70.

32. Debret, *Voyage pittoresque et historique*, 129.

33. Biard, *Deux années au Brésil*, 83–84.

34. See the paintings titled *Traite d'esclaves dans la côte ouest de l'Afrique*, exhibited at the Salon of 1835; *Capture d'un bâtiment négrier par un navire français*, exhibited at the Salon of 1846; *Proclamation de la liberté des Noirs aux colonies* (1848), exhibited at the Salon of 1849 (Musée national du château de

Versailles); and *Emménagement d'esclaves à bord d'un négrier sur la côte d'Afrique*, exhibited at the Salon of 1861.

35. Biard, *Deux années au Brésil*, 98.

36. According to the Instituto brasileiro de geografia e estatística, 45 percent of Brazilians identify themselves as negro (black) or pardo (brown). See Abdias do Nascimento and Elisa Larkin Nascimento, "Dance of Deception: Race Relations in Brazil," in *Beyond Racism: Race and Inequality in Brazil, South Africa and the United States*, ed. Charles V. Hamilton et al. (Boulder, Colo.: Lynne Rienner, 2001), 109.

37. See Juliana Monteiro, Luiza Gomes Ferreira, and Joseania Miranda Freitas, "As roupas de crioula no século XIX e o traje da beca na contemporaneidade: Símbolos de identidade e memória," *Mneme: Revista de humanidades* 7, no. 18, "Cultura, Tradição e Patrimônio Imaterial," special issue edited by Helder Alexandre Medeiros de Macedo (2005): 395–414.

38. See Robert W. Slenes, *Na Senzala uma flor: Esperanças e recordações na formação da família escrava–Brasil Sudeste, século XIX* (Rio de Janeiro: Nova Fronteira, 2000), 29.

39. The *tronco* (trunk) is a wood stem with holes for the neck and wrists.

40. André João Antonil, *Cultura e opulência do Brasil por suas drogas e minas* (1711; São Paulo: Editora da Universidade de São Paulo, 2007), 91.

41. Ibid.

42. Based on the Harriet Beecher Stowe's novel *Uncle Tom's Cabin, or Life among the Lowly* (Boston: John P. Jewett, 1852), the first version of the film is from 1903. Other versions followed until 1927.

43. The soap opera *A escrava Isaura* was based on the abolitionist novel by Bernardo Guimarães, *A escrava Isaura* (Rio de Janeiro: Casa Garnier, 1875).

44. The opening of the telenovela *A escrava Isaura* (1976) is available on YouTube, http://www.youtube.com/watch?v=c7XpRLtc9wo.

45. The film was based on João Felício dos Santos's novel *Xica da Silva: O romance* (Rio de Janeiro: Civilização Brasileira, 1976), inspired by the book written by his great-uncle, Joaquim Felício dos Santos, entitled *Memórias do distrito diamantino da comarca do Serro Frio*, in 1868. For a more recent work on Chica da Silva, see Júnia Ferreira Furtado, *Chica da Silva: A Brazilian Slave of the Eighteenth Century* (New York: Cambridge University Press, 2008).

46. Mariza de Carvalho Soares, "As três faces de Xica," in *A história vai ao cinema*, ed. Mariza de Carvalho Soares and Jorge Ferreira (Rio de Janeiro: Record, 2001), 61.

47. Bruce Chatwin, *The Viceroy of Ouidah* (London: Jonathan Cape, 1980).

48. See Manolo Florentino, *Em costas negras: Uma história do tráfico de escravos entre a África e o Rio de Janeiro* (São Paulo: Companhia das Letras, 1997), 51–52.

QUEERING THE STUDY OF SLAVERY

21

"TO LEVER'S ON SOAP!"

Roger Casement, Slavery, and Sexual Imperialism

BRIAN LEWIS

In his 1911 cash ledger, Sir Roger Casement recorded in jumbled form his activities, observations, and expenditures for Saturday, July 22: "Glorious day and morning. Ricudo suit 1/7/6 . . . (To Lever's on Soap!) (Notting Hill—Huge!) Busses on to M. Arch &c &c 1/3. Dinner Marguerite. (Lovely Italian.) Cab(s) 3/2. Cigarettes 2d. Many types. One showed big red head. Hard stiff wagging H. Park Corner." To put it less cryptically: on this splendid summer's day, Casement bought a suit for Ricudo, one of two "Amazon Indians" he had brought to Britain to help in his antislavery campaign; visited the soap magnate William Hesketh Lever; spotted a man with a very large penis at Notting Hill; took omnibuses to Marble Arch and elsewhere, which cost him 1 shilling 3 pence; had dinner at Marguerite's restaurant, where he was captivated by a very fine-looking Italian waiter; spent 3 shillings 2 pence on cabs and 2 pence on cigarettes; and saw many sexually available or desirable men as he skulked around his favorite cruising grounds (such as the toilets at Marble Arch), including one in an unspecified location who exposed a large red glans and another with an erection in the shadows around Hyde Park Corner.[1] It is the comment "(To Lever's on Soap!)" that is of principal interest for us here; we shall return to the cruising later.

This entry fragment is tantalizingly inconclusive. It could admit of an alternative interpretation (a visit to the company rather than the man himself, perhaps?); if the two men did, in fact, meet, it fails to specify where (was it Lever's London residence, The Hill, on the edge of Hampstead Heath, or was it Lever Brothers' London headquarters?); and it gives no hint as to what they talked about. There are no indications in the ledger or Casement's diaries or Lever's correspondence that they ever met on any other occasion.[2] "(To Lever's on Soap!)" seems rather dismissive, so perhaps, if they did meet, Casement was not impressed by his host. Yet E. D. Morel, the man who brought or tried to bring them together, was certain that Casement would impress Lever.

The three men were linked by the Congo. Casement, as British consul, had produced the 1904 report that gave widespread publicity to the quasi-genocidal nature of the pursuit of rubber in Leopold II's Congo Free State. Morel, the founder and driving force behind the Congo Reform Association, led the crusade to expose Leopold's crimes against humanity. Lever, to ensure more secure supplies of palm oil for his soaps, was negotiating with the Belgian government in 1910–11 for huge concessions in the post-Leopoldian colony of Belgian Congo. During this period, Morel and Lever carried on an extensive correspondence and met a number of times.[3]

In April 1911, Morel wrote to Lever, "I wish you could meet my friend Mr. Roger Casement, who knows more about the Congo than any man living and who is one of the finest men that God ever made. He could give you any number of hints and suggestions. In fact I don't hesitate to say that it is a privilege to anyone to have the opportunity of conversing with such a man as is Mr. Casement who combines with his other qualities twenty years' experience of the African tropics." Accordingly, Lever invited them both to dinner.[4] But Casement had recently left for Northern Ireland and spent most of the next month in Belfast. Given this plus Lever's immensely busy schedule micromanaging his vast concerns, perhaps July 22 was the first occasion they could arrange to meet. By then, both had been rewarded in George V's coronation honors list: Lever with a baronetcy for services to industry and politics, Casement with a knighthood for producing a second landmark report on slavery-like conditions, his 1911 exposé of atrocities perpetrated under the auspices of the Anglo-Peruvian Rubber Company in the Putumayo River region of Peru.[5]

The meeting, real or imaginary, between Sir William and Sir Roger is my entry point to a discussion about masculinity, sexuality, and slavery. Unlike most of the contributions in this volume, my focus is not on the multifarious sexual experiences of slaves and slave owners. Rather, it is on the gender constructions and sexual identities of two men—one straight, one gay; one English, one Irish—and how these roles and assumptions may have influenced their beliefs about forced labor and imperialism. I use Lever as a foil for the more problematic figure of Casement. Some have trumpeted Casement as a leading human rights advocate, others have denounced him as a sexual imperialist and predator, and yet others have tried to reconcile the two portrayals. In exploring the tension between Casement the antislavery crusader and Casement the enjoyer of young male bodies, this chapter dissects a particularly flagrant example of the ways in which our contemporary concerns influence how we understand and write history.

Sir William Lever, later the first Viscount Leverhulme, was all man. In posing as "the Chief" or "the Old Man"—the father figure of his company and of his subject African workers—he played his role on this conventional stage with aplomb. He was a coil of energy with more than a hint of megalomania; commentators described him as "a bit of human granite"[6] and "a whirlwind of a man."[7] He expressed admiration for men of action such as Theodore Roosevelt, Henry Ford, David Lloyd George, and Cecil Rhodes.[8] (He met Rhodes in Cape Town in 1895. "In later years the one has often been likened to the other," Lever's son wrote, "and in many ways their characters and achievements were similar. Courage, organizing ability and breadth of vision were their outstanding qualities, and each did a great work for Africa."[9]) But the most frequently recurring comparison was with Napoleon Bonaparte. If he had not built up the Lever Brothers' soap business, wrote A. G. Gardiner, the radical journalist and editor of the *Daily News*, in 1914, "he would have been the Napoleon of tea or of oil or of sugar. For he is of the Napoleon breed, born to marshal big battalions and win empires, if not in war, then in peace."[10] Lever himself admired Napoleon, and in collecting Napoleonic memorabilia, which he put on display in a special Napoleon Room in the Lady Lever Art Gallery in his factory village of Port Sunlight on the River Mersey, he invited the comparison.

Roger Casement, too, was usually represented as another irrefutably masculine figure: recall Morel's comment that he was "one of the finest men that God ever made." His "princely bearing more than confirmed his manhood," wrote the poet Alfred Noyes.[11] Tall and bearded, he reminded friends and acquaintances of a courtly, chivalric figure: a knight-errant, someone who had stepped out from a Velásquez painting.[12] On another occasion, Morel wrote that Casement had "a long lean, swarthy Vandyke type of face, graven with power and withal of great gentleness," and he concluded, lest anyone be in any doubt, "Here was a man indeed."[13]

Casement never married. Lever met his future wife, Elizabeth, at elementary school; they married young, and he apparently remained devoted to her for the rest of his life. They had one child, a son. There is no hint in the historical record of any other women at any time. (He had close male friendships. One was even described by Lever's son as "play[ing] 'Jonathan' to my father's 'David' all his life,"[14] a reference to passages in the Book of Samuel telling of the love between David and Jonathan, notably David saying to the slain Jonathan (2 Samuel 1:26), "Thy love to me was wonderful, passing the love of women." Nothing, however, suggests that these relationships were anything other than platonic.) A director of the company described Elizabeth as "a gracious, kindly and gentle little woman."[15] She gave Lever sympathy and understanding—"an unquestioning belief in the rightness of all that her husband undertook"—rather than counsel. After she died in 1913, he buried her under the west window at Christ Church, the church he had built at Port Sunlight, and after his own death in 1925, he was to join her in a recumbent bronze effigy in the manner of a medieval knight and his lady. The stained glass he added to the west window included "The Good Housewife" and "Ruth and Naomi" with its text, one of her favorite quotations, "Whither thou goest, I will go."[16]

There was no such devoted, domesticated spouse for Casement. Without the so-called black diaries, this enigmatic bachelor's archival traces would indicate a passionate commitment to certain causes—first the antislavery crusade, then Irish nationalism—and a peripatetic existence, living out of lodgings, in pursuit of his consular career or his crusades, with no time for conjugal bliss and settled domesticity. But the diaries change the picture quite markedly. These black diaries—for 1903, 1910, and 1911, together with the 1911 cash ledger—reveal that Casement liked having casual sex with men; in particular, he had a predilection for being sodomized by well-endowed youths. Since the diaries only came to light after he was arrested in 1916 for attempting to recruit Irish soldiers and smuggle German arms for the Easter Rising in Dublin, many of Casement's admirers at the time and ever since have denounced them as vicious British forgeries. And indeed, after he was sentenced to hang for high treason, judicious circulation of some of the more salacious pages to leading politicians and churchmen, especially in the United States, muted the appeal for clemency and helped seal his fate. But nearly a century of debate and extensive forensic analysis have persuaded all but the most die-hard of forgery theorists that the diaries are, in fact, genuine.[17]

The diaries—later named "black" (those with sexual content) and "white" (those without)—describe in detail Casement's daily activities and thoughts, sometimes in note form, sometimes more discursively. Buried amid all this innocuous information in the black diaries is the sexual material, which tells us a great deal about cruising patterns and cross-class and cross-cultural encounters but reveals almost nothing about Casement's subjective understanding of his sexuality. Only in some intriguing diary entries for 1903, which are mired in negativity, does he broach the topic. These reflect on the suicide of Sir Hector MacDonald, the commander of British troops in Ceylon, who took his own life after being accused of having sex with scores of male youths.[18] Casement commented in response on April 17, "The reasons given are pitiably sad. The most distressing case this surely of its kind and one that may awake the national mind to saner methods of curing a terrible disease than by criminal legislation." The suicide continued to weigh on his mind: two days later, he added, "Very sorry at Hector Macdonald's terrible end," and on April 30, he wrote, "Hector Macdonald's death very sad."[19]

Historians and sociologists working within a broadly social constructionist paradigm have long argued that a recognizably modern homosexual identity was created largely through the power of new medical and legal categorization in the late nineteenth century. Sexology and medical science classified the distinctive categories of the newly coined *heterosexual* and *homosexual* (which eventually beat out competing terms such as *invert, pervert, intersex, Uranian,* and *similisexual*), and legislative and moral codes (notably the notorious Labouchère Amendment of 1885 and the Vagrancy Act of 1898) policed the boundaries between "normality" and "deviancy" as never before. Much debate has centered on the negative or positive consequences of the imposition of sexological ideas: the extent to which homosexuals could use these new constructions to their advantage or to which they were controlled by them and trapped within them.[20]

More recent scholarship, picking up on many of the leads, themes, and nuances of these pioneers, has helped complicate our picture of this new homosexual. These proponents of the "new gay history" or the "new queer history" point to the late and partial reception of continental sexological ideas in Britain and downplay the significance of legal changes and high-profile court cases. They emphasize not so much Michel Foucault's famous sexual invert as a new "species" with a distinct identity, psychology, and pathology[21] but rather overlapping and colliding discursive formations and social types—multiple ways for men who had sex with men and women who had sex with women to understand themselves and be understood. Thus, scholars have devoted much attention not only to the sexologists and their reception but also to the significance of the Classical tradition; to the impact of the virile homoeroticism of Walt Whitman, especially the Calamus poems of *The Leaves of Grass*; and to the emancipatory potential of socialism to describe some of the principal building blocks of male homosexual identity from the late nineteenth century.[22]

One of the most intriguing claims is that the notion of distinct, binary opposite, "homosexual" and "heterosexual" identities did not take firm hold, in Britain as elsewhere, until the quarter century after World War II. Before then, according, for example, to Matt Houlbrook's account, "queers" could be roughly divided into three main groupings: the "queens" or "queans," who adopted effeminate mannerisms or drag or other markers of their "inversion"; higher-class men whose gender identification was strictly masculine and who tended to despise the queans; and working-class "trade," who did not identify as queer, who did not think their masculinity was compromised by having sex with men, and who often had sex with women as well.[23]

As this division between queans, queers, and trade suggests, class, gender, and representations of masculinity are central to any discussion of this period. Cross-class sexual intercourse, whether disrupting or confirming ordered, hierarchical social relations, is a recurring theme. It was, for instance, at the heart of the Cleveland Street scandal of 1889, which involved post office messenger boys supplementing their income in a male brothel catering to upper-class clientele, and of Oscar Wilde's self-described "feasting with panthers," his sex with working-class youths that landed him in court. Evidently, it was part of the fabric of male prostitution and cruising in public spaces, often involving soldiers from the Guards who had a long-standing reputation for augmenting their wages by selling their bodies. More idealistically, Edward Carpenter and his working-class lover, George Merrill, in their self-sustaining commune at Millthorpe near Sheffield, made crossing the classes integral to their sense of socialism—a relationship drawn on by E. M. Forster in his novel *Maurice* (1917) to depict the love between an upper-middle-class Cambridge man and an undergamekeeper.[24]

There was little that was idealistic about Roger Casement's sexual habits. He never "came out" (to use an anachronism) in the manner of Carpenter or to close friends and to posterity in the manner of Forster. He never campaigned for "gay rights" (ditto); his only confirmed comments relating to the subject (the Sir Hector Macdonald saga) indicate a quasi-progressive wish for tolerance, couched in a fashionable discourse of sexual deviance as sickness requiring understanding and treatment rather than criminalization. He left no sense that he had constructed a positive homosexual self-image out of a sexological, Classical, or Whitmanesque bricolage. Instead, on the surface, he lived a life of unblemished moral rectitude. His masculinity enabled him to pass as straight with ease ("Here was a man indeed"!), especially since the equation of the sodomite or the homosexual with effeminacy—scarcely a new equivalency—had been supposedly cemented in the popular imagination by the ambiguous figure of Wilde at the time of his trial.[25]

Family, friends, colleagues, and superiors apparently had no inkling that Casement made it a habit to acquire a knowledge of and explore the sexual geography of the cities, towns, and ports he lived in or visited in Europe, Africa, and Latin America. He seems to have made little effort to cultivate enduring relationships and recorded only a smattering of repeat partners; most of his sexual experiences fit neatly into the category of the masculine, higher-class queer in pursuit of lower-class, noneffeminate trade who gave and took sexual pleasure in exchange for money. (The economy of cruising is complex, and the motivations of the young men—financial or pleasurable or maybe both—are difficult to pin down with any certainty. But the sums given appear to be more in the way of [often substantial] tips from a wealthier, older man to a younger man rather than negotiated fees for prostitution.) Here is an example from New Year's Day 1911: "In Paris all day. Went Av. du Bois and met Denis and then to Prefecture and Quai d'Orleans to lunch. Back to Hotel and out to Boulevards. Met Pierre and to Gare du Nord. Enormous and fine. Back and turned in—'Oui! Msieur. Je suis bien servi!' Took in mouth with much groaning and struggle and moans of love."[26] The cash ledger records that he gave Denis 30 francs and Pierre 40 francs.[27] A second example is the entry for October 1, 1911, in Manaos, Brazil, the most concentrated burst of sexual activity that he recorded:

> Dr Dickey to breakfast and Schully. Then at 2 out and saw young sailor apprendez. Pure Indian boy only 16 I should say—to Kiosque and agreed meet at 7. Met at 7 to old Palace where I put it in mouth. It got huge and curved down and thick and stiff as iron—Said he wanted to enter and so did—he took off boots and trousers and gave a tremendous one. Then darkie sailor at corner. Lovely neck and asked—said yes and followed to Palace and <u>in</u> twice—kissing on neck and hugging—awfully strong, huge arms and stiff one. Then a *huge Darky* 9 inches long and thick and stiff but no chance beyond a feeling and then Agostinho of Madeira and home with him all night.
>
> *Huge one* on caboclo clerk. Stiff and said laughing he wanted to spend night "con rapaz" [with a guy]. Up at five stars cooling the sky. Took shower bath and Agostinho in again awfully kind—*three* times he did it and three from the two sailors—in all <u>six</u> times tonight.[28]

The cash ledger records very generous payments of 12$000 (12 mil reis) for the Indian boy, 15$000 for the sailor, and 40$000 for Agostinho—a total, in Casement's calculation, of £4 9s. 4d.[29]

How did the two contrasting "all man" performances I have outlined—the first by William Lever, conventional and transparent; the second by Roger Casement, conventional on the surface (if, as a bachelor, eccentric) but disguising dramatic transgressions of sexual and gendered norms beneath—influence their perceptions and practices?

Lever's understanding of colonization rested on and justified a familiar imperialist trope: the colonial power as masculine, dominant, protective, and penetrating and the colonized peoples as feminine, childlike, submissive, and penetrated.[30] His deal with the Belgian government in 1911 allowed him to gather palm-oil fruit for his soaps in five vast concessionary circles in the Congo. The Belgians, in the wake of the international outcry against the Leopoldian "red rubber" regime and anxious to repair the damage to their battered image, were delighted to attract foreign investment from such a leading industrialist noted for his enlightened paternalism.[31] According to popular legend, Lever then set about cementing his humanitarian reputation by—in the words of one panegyrist—bringing sunlight "to the darkest forests. Steaming swamps were drained; malaria and other diseases stamped out; roads, schools, and hospitals were built; villages were constructed and new meaning and purpose brought into the lives of primitive and aimless savages."[32]

The reality was rather more complex and less flattering. Lever Brothers' subsidiary, Les huileries du Congo Belge, just like the other large European employers of labor in the Congo and in many parts of Africa, came to rely extensively on slavery's stepchild—forced labor. The common problem for big business and colonial governments in the aftermath of antislavery conventions was to find a workforce to grow, harvest, or extract raw materials or to build the colonial infrastructure when the factors that had tamed European workforces (the fear of starvation or of the workhouse and/or the lure of material goods) operated sporadically at best. Rule by terror, the preferred method in the Congo Free State and the Putumayo, was scarcely an option in the wake of the humanitarian campaigns of Morel, Casement, and others. The thinly disguised slavery in the production of Cadbury Brothers' cocoa on the Portuguese islands of São Tomé and Príncipe similarly fell victim to the crusaders' onslaught.[33] But there were much more subtle ways of proletarianizing Africans, including forms of taxation that served the dual function of generating government revenue and forcing the "natives" into the cash economy to find the money to pay the tax.[34] This is how things worked in the post-Leopoldian Congo.[35]

The colonizers justified forced labor as part of the "civilizing mission." A committee convened by Portugal's Overseas Ministry in 1898 to investigate the problems of Portuguese Africa put it in unvarnished terms: "The state, not only as a sovereign of semi-barbaric populations, but also as a depository of social authority, should have no scruples in *obliging* and, if necessary, *forcing* these rude Negroes in Africa, these ignorant Pariahs in Asia, these half-savages from Oceania, to work, that is to better themselves by work, to acquire through work the happiest means of existence, to civilize themselves through work."[36] A piece in the *Gazette Coloniale* in the Congo Free State was just as forthright:

> The atrocity stories that are spread around originate in the fact that each white man who works in the Congo has to force the Negro to provide his labour power. . . . Those closet colonizers who deplore this state of affairs, implicitly proclaim the immortal right of the blacks to do absolutely nothing. We protest against this view. The idleness of the Negro should not stop us in trying to overcome or to get round it. . . . His unwillingness must not cause the non-utilization of the resources of that country. . . . Our own workers [in Belgium], who are forced to work for twelve hours or more each day on penalty of starvation, would find it very strange if they should accidentally learn of the absurd protection that some people would provide to the natives of the Congo. The law of work applies to the blacks as well as to ourselves. If they think they do not have to submit to it, we have the right and even the duty to force them to do so.[37]

Lever had drunk deeply from the waters of the civilizing mission. In his letters to Morel and consistently in all his correspondence and speeches over the years, he harped on its main tenets: the need for Africans to learn the value of work, and the need for Europeans to teach them to be industrious, productive *men.* Morel tried to persuade him of the virtues of an African yeomanry, whose members were cultivating their own land.

No doubt, something similar would have been part of a conversation between Lever and Casement. As Casement put it in a letter to Travers Buxton of the Anti-Slavery Society in 1911 in reference to the "Amazon Indians," "The expropriation of the Indians and barefaced denial of all rights in land of the Indians is at the bottom of the whole system of slavery that undoubtedly exists in those regions. If the Indians were protected in their land ownership they would not be the easy prey they are today to the exploiter. . . . If you root the natives in the soil—African or Indian, Polynesian or whatever band of native he may be—you free him."[38] Like Morel, however, Casement thought that Lever could possibly be a means to an end: "Who knows but *his* land concessions might not be the beginning of a true rooting of the people in their soil. Lever might create the Congo peasant proprietor."[39]

Yet Lever's language suggested he had no intention of doing any such thing. "It would serve no useful purpose for the white man to go and try to reverse the Divine order under which intellect and mental power rules and develops, protects and benefits inferior nations," he wrote to Morel. "I think that your advocacy of the black man's interest can be made more helpful to the black man if whilst fighting with all your power against brutal and inhuman and inconsiderate treatment for the black man you do not build a halo round the black man and convert him into a kind of being which it will take him hundreds of years of intercourse with the white man to become." Since blacks had never, anywhere, shown the necessary organizational skills to use land profitably, he continued, "the land of the world, in any part of the world ought to be in the possession of those people who can develop it and its resources."[40]

Lever was impressed by the African male body, the "black-bronze Hercules" paddling a canoe on the Congo River[41]—in passing noting with dismay, like missionaries for generations before him, what he saw as black men's failure to observe European norms of Christian, bourgeois respectability: "You might think that they could dress their wives and children more."[42] But he infantilized the African laborer: "He is a child, and a willing child, but he wants training and handling with patience."[43] Advertisements for Lever Brothers soaps reflected these notions by depicting African males as babies and children and African females as contented slaves for white women.[44]

Several members of Lever's African staff, in a petition to him on his last visit to West Africa in 1925, called for better housing, medical services, and pay, as well as improved prospects for promotion. They adopted (at least for rhetorical purposes) and tried to use to their own advantage the infantilizing and effeminizing discourse imposed upon them: "The simple and childlike Negro is as much a lady as he is a lad. He is a lad on account of his primitive simplicity; he is a lady on account of his womanly defencelessness and his motherly ownership; for he is the natural owner of the immense natural wealth deposited in the bosom and surface of his lands, without the means of protecting them himself, and yet, with the natural right of ownership of them. . . . We require the judicious and moral protection of the great White Race who, on account of that protection, is the foster-father of our wealth; and upon whom the onus of development rests."[45]

The "great White Race" built its rationale for the civilizing mission on a powerful sense of moral superiority grounded in the fixity of gender roles and sexual identities. Homosexuality was utterly subversive of this divine and scientific order. Casement not only transgressed heterosexual domesticity, he breached boundaries of race, gender, class, and age by allowing himself to be anally penetrated by working-class lads, by Guardsmen, and by African and Latin American youths—the quintessentially effeminizing experience in contemporary discourse.[46] No wonder, then, that at the time of the trial and the revelation of his secret life, some thought him mad. Sir John Harris, secretary to the Aborigines Protection Society and an ally since the Congo days, saw the diaries as "the unfolding of a life which for years had been poisoned by disease." He wrote to the archbishop of Canterbury, "I must admit with the most painful reluctance that the Roger Casement revealed in this evidence is a very different man from the one up to whom I have looked as an ideal character for over fifteen years." The archbishop, in turn, commented that it was further evidence of a man who had become mentally unhinged.[47]

In contrast to Lever, where the link between his understanding of the natural order and his resort to forced labor is reasonably straightforward, the connection between Casement's secret sex life and his antislavery advocacy is more speculative. Can we, for example, make anything of his writings and conversations that reveal a profound respect for the indigenous body in terms of maintaining its integrity against white predations? Here, complete with a hint of the sadomasochistic, is Morel's description of Casement's monologue about his Congo experiences at their initial meeting in December 1903: "The daily agony of an entire people unrolled itself in all the repulsive terrifying details. I verily believe I *saw* those hunted women clutching their children and flying panic-stricken to the bush; the blood flowing from those quivering black bodies as the hippopotamus hide whip struck and struck again; the savage soldiery rushing hither and thither amid burning villages; the ghastly tally of severed hands."[48] Was there a psychosexual connection between Casement's wish to stop the flogging and the severing and his appreciation of the erotic potential of the young male body? Imaginative re-creations of Casement have certainly suggested as much. Michael Carson, in his 1995 novel *The Knight of the Flaming Heart*, portrays Casement returning to Ireland and the Congo as a modern gay saint performing miracles on Africans and gay men with AIDS. Michael Eaton, in a 1999 screenplay, imagines Casement hallucinating in the Tower of London in 1916 after he has poisoned himself with curare: "Then suddenly, in Roger's mind's eye, he appears among the maimed. And as he touches the broken bodies they are miraculously healed. As he puts his hands on the scars on the Indian boys' backs they are miraculously erased. They are returned to a state of innocence—re-membered after all this dis-memberment."[49]

This is interesting speculation, but we are perhaps on firmer ground with the oft-repeated suggestion that gay people, because they realize their own divergence from conventional norms, often view the world at an angle and are therefore more likely to challenge the orthodox and mainstream. This is not something that Casement himself articulated, of course. He explained his conversion to anti-imperialism and Irish nationalism in terms of his reaction to the South African War and to what he had seen in the Congo. In a famous passage written to Alice Stopford Green in 1907, he stated,

> I had accepted Imperialism—British rule was to be extended at all costs, because it was the best for everyone under the sun. . . . Well the War gave me qualms at the end—the

> concentration camps bigger ones—and finally when up in those lonely Congo forests where I found Leopold I found also myself—the incorrigible Irishman. . . . I realized then that I was looking at this tragedy with the eyes of another race—of a people once hunted themselves, whose hearts were based on affection as the root principle of contact with their fellow men and whose estimate of life was not of some thing eternally to be appraised at its market "price." And I said to myself, then, far up the Lulongo River, that I would do my part as an Irishman, wherever it might lead me to personally.[50]

It is perfectly possible to follow this logic and map out a genealogy of Casement's thought without reference to sex. This tendency to "de-queer" him and/or to ignore his private life as irrelevant is alive and well, as we shall see. But it has been swimming against a strong current since the 1970s, one that accepts that a connection needs to be made. The heavyweight biographies of the seventies and eighties tapped into a fashionable Freudianism suggesting that sex maketh the man and could help explain many of Casement's contradictions and neuroses. To borrow Angus Mitchell's phrase, "the sexual subtext was tailored discreetly into the biographical suit of Casement's life to produce the 'whole man.'"[51] Then, in the new, more progressive Ireland of the 1990s, liberal voices reached something of a consensus that Casement's sexuality was the key to all the laudable aspects of his life.[52] "Perhaps it was his very homosexuality," posited the novelist Colm Tóibín in 1997, "which made him into the humanitarian he was, made him so appalled. Unlike everyone around him, he took nothing for granted. His moral courage . . . came perhaps from his understanding of what it meant to be despised."[53] The German writer W. G. Sebald concurred in 1998, saying that "it was precisely Casement's homosexuality that sensitized him to the continuing oppression, exploitation, enslavement and destruction, across the borders of social class and race, of those who were furthest from the centers of power."[54] Róisín McAuley, who reported on the authenticity of the diaries for the BBC Radio 4 series *Document* in 1993, rounds out this line of thinking with her comment, "He can now be claimed by us all. He couldn't have been Sir Roger Casement humanitarian hero if he hadn't believed in an enlightened role for the

British Empire. He wouldn't have been Roger Casement republican hero if he hadn't seen the oppression of Empire abroad. And if he hadn't been homosexual, knowing what it was like to feel oppressed and marginalized, he might not have been a hero to anyone."[55]

But other commentators resist such a beguiling equation and are deeply troubled by Casement's sexual exploits. If most can now handle the concept of a gay Casement, they would much prefer a well-mannered, monogamous, domesticated homosexual nurturing a loving relationship in his own private space. Though many gay men and historians of queer sexuality have no difficulty at all in recognizing and relating to Casement's cruising habits and register no surprise that he could operate right under the nose of polite society,[56] other investigators shrink in disbelief from the "moral degenerate" they see revealed in the diaries or the Jekyll-and-Hyde mismatch between Casement's public persona and the sex jottings.[57]

The youthfulness of Casement's sexual partners adds fuel to the debate. He liked them to be sexually mature (indeed "huge!" or even "enormous!") and in their middle to late teens or early twenties; but he did ogle younger boys and admit his desire for them. "Saw small mestizo boy of about 9 (tall and slim, perhaps 10) tossing himself off in street," he wrote in Iquitos in 1911. "It was fully 7" long and sticking out half a foot—a huge one and a very nice looking boy indeed, but quite a child."[58] He drew a boundary in this case, but did he when he went to the seaside park of Hastings Rocks, Barbados, in August 1911, to scrutinize boys? He encountered "Budds"—"lovely and huge one too. Only 11 years old on 17th July"—and made him a present of five shillings for reasons unspecified.[59]

One strategy employed when faced with the "dirty diaries"[60] is exemplified by Angus Mitchell, the foremost recent exponent of the diaries-are-fake thesis. Though not perturbed by the thought of a queer Casement, he believes that the sexual elements in the diaries are homophobic forgeries. He has been working hard to refocus interest on Casement's importance in a developing language of human rights, and for him, this is emphatically not linked to the furtive, promiscuous sex, the voyeurism, and all the other elements of alienation, repression, and loneliness that he detects in the diaries. Far from being the key to understanding Casement and far from liberating him sexually, Mitchell asserts, the black diaries have helped silence his real significance: "They destroy his mystical role as both imperial knight and the moral standard-bearer of advanced nationalism. He is turned from being the investigator of the system into the exploiter, the sexual colonizer, the crude fantasist. . . . Casement as sexual subordinate has come to dominate his 'other' positions as 'African,' 'Amazindian' or 'Irish rebel' or his spiritual/mystic dimension. In these suppressed voices his deeper meaning can be found."[61] Mitchell contends that the essence of the man and the importance of what he accomplished can and should be recaptured without reference to his alleged sexual practices.[62]

A second strategy is to ignore the diaries or to "accept and get over them," questioning the relevance of Casement's private life to any understanding of his public actions. "These diaries have no literary, and now little historical value," writes John Bruton, the former Taoiseach, in a review of the 2002 biography and new edition of the diaries by Northern Irish gay activist Jeff Dudgeon, "and should not have been given so much space in an otherwise stimulating, fair and well-written book."[63] Roger Sawyer, though acknowledging with some regret that the diaries are genuine, also believes that we should simply accept the fact that they exist and "move on to the more worthwhile issues which worried Roger Casement and for which he was willing to sacrifice his own life. From now on, that should be our priority."[64]

A third strategy is to accept the diaries but register disquiet. The writer Charles Nicholl, for example, believes them to be genuine but is left with a queasy feeling: "Casement's homosexuality is, of course, no longer any bar to admiring his great achievements as a champion of human rights, a one-man Amnesty International. . . . But there is none the less something unsettling about the constant overheated sexual machinations." He adds, in a reversal of the more positive psychosexual linkages noted previously, "There seems a collusion between his deep concern for the welfare of the slaves and his obsessive interest in their bodies."[65] Christopher Andrew condemns Dudgeon's upbeat and noncensorious take on Casement's sexual practices as special pleading: "During Casement's lifetime, there was of course no age of consent for homosexual sex, since it was wholly illegal at any age. But—though there is no doubt about the selfless bravery with which Casement fought for Irish independence and campaigned for human rights in the Third World—he was also a sexual predator among the young and sometimes vulnerable on at least two continents."[66]

The rush to moral judgment—to sanctify or to condemn—is all rather peculiar. William Lever expressed the racial and gender prejudices of his time and made use of some of the coercive tools routinely deployed by big business in Africa, and historians carefully chronicle and contextualize his behavior. But any measured depiction of Roger Casement and his work struggles against current gay politics and moral qualms about promiscuous homosexuality, prostitution, and pederasty or intergenerational sex. Canonizing him as a gay saint or fashioning him as a gay icon makes little sense, since his restless pursuit of casual sex was human and hardly heroic and his contribution to gay rights has only been posthumous and inadvertent. But even though reductive attempts to discover in his sexuality the roots of his compassion for suffering and exploited peoples are likely to be as unconvincing as the attempts to "de-queer" him, "whiting out" his sex life is as futile as it is misleading.[67]

In his admirable book on colonialism and homosexuality, Robert Aldrich notes that many European homosexuals took advantage of their power in the colonial situation "to extract sexual favors from foreign men or subaltern Europeans." All were, to some degree, complicit with imperialism, and some known or suspected homosexuals, such as Cecil Rhodes and H. M. Stanley, were enthusiastic imperialists. But others involved in or writing on empire, from Casement through André Gide, Edward Carpenter, and E. M. Forster to Jean Genet, were not, and the gay liberation movement of the 1960s and 1970s linked sexual with political revolution and anti-imperialism. As Aldrich puts it,

> A significant number of European homosexuals overseas displayed an ambivalent attitude towards imperialism, or took an avowedly critical stance on European rule. Their renegade position as sexual heretics at home had led them to sexual opportunities in foreign countries, yet cast them in an ambiguous position. Although representatives of the "master race" and imperial power, they did not fit into the mould of heterosexual married life . . . and child rearing. They trespassed across boundaries of propriety by being intimate with foreign men, and sometimes making too close friends of them. Liaisons with such men could inspire a contrary perspective on the colonial world.[68]

Aldrich makes no direct link between the genitals and a particular pattern of thought, but he is quite rightly persuaded that sexual orientation is a critical part of the equation. In a similar fashion, to understand the dynamics of sex, power, and slavery, the complex subjectivities of all the slavers or imposers of forced labor or the antislavery advocates need to be reconstructed in all their contradictory, unsettling, unvarnished humanity from out of the remaining historical fragments. Casement, just like Lever, needs to be normalized and contextualized, not feted or demonized.

Notes

1. Diaries of Roger Casement, Home Office Records, HO 161/5, National Archives, Kew, London, UK (hereafter cited as NA); Jeffrey Dudgeon, *Roger Casement: The Black Diaries–With a Study of His Background, Sexuality, and Irish Political Life* (Belfast: Belfast Press, 2002), 294. All the black diary excerpts quoted in this chapter are taken from Dudgeon's edition.

2. Séamas Ó Siocháin, *Roger Casement: Imperialist, Rebel, Revolutionary* (Dublin: Lilliput Press, 2008), 545n148, notes that a Lever Brothers representative wrote to Casement to set up a meeting *after* this diary entry (July 25 and 26, 1911, MS 13073 [10/i], National Library of Ireland, Dublin), but there is no evidence that anything came of it.

3. See Adam Hochschild, *King Leopold's Ghost: A Story of Greed, Terror, and Heroism in Colonial Africa* (London: Macmillan, 2000); Jules Marchal, *E. D. Morel contre Léopold II: L'histoire du Congo 1900–1910*, vol. 2 (Paris: Éditions L'Harmattan, 1996); Wm. Roger Louis and Jean Stengers, eds., *E. D. Morel's History of the Congo Reform Movement* (Oxford: Clarendon Press, 1967); Wm. Roger Louis, "Roger Casement and the Congo," *Journal of African History* 5, no. 1 (1964): 99–120; Neal Ascherson, *The King Incorporated: Leopold II in the Age of Trusts* (London: George Allen and Unwin, 1963).

4. Morel to Lever, April 12, 1911, and Lever to Morel, April 18, 1911, file 100, F8, Morel Papers, London School of Economics, London, UK (hereafter cited as LSE).

5. Dudgeon, *Roger Casement*, 254, 286–87; William Hulme Lever [Second Viscount Leverhulme], *Viscount Leverhulme* (Boston: Houghton Mifflin, 1927), 151.

6. Sydney Walton in the *Yorkshire Evening News*, quoted in an article in the Lever Brothers magazine: "In Memoriam: William Hesketh Lever Viscount Leverhulme," *Progress* 25, no. 168 (July 1925): 145.

7. Earl of Birkenhead [F. E. Smith], *Contemporary Personalities* (London: Cassell, 1924), 284.

8. See Brian Lewis, *So Clean: Lord Leverhulme, Soap and Civilization* (Manchester, UK: Manchester University Press, 2008), chap. 1.

9. Lever, *Viscount Leverhulme*, 67.

10. A. G. Gardiner, *Pillars of Society* (London: James Nisbet, 1914), 199.

11. Quoted in Lucy McDiarmid, *The Irish Art of Controversy* (Ithaca, N.Y.: Cornell University Press, 2005), 194.

12. Stephen Gwynn, quoted in Alfred Noyes, *The Accusing Ghost or Justice for Casement* (London: Victor Gollancz, 1957), 118; Louis McQuilland, *Sunday Herald*, April 30, 1916, quoted in L. G. Redmond-Howard, *Sir Roger Casement: A Character Sketch without Prejudice* (Dublin: Hodges, Figgis, 1916), 8.

13. Quoted in Catherine Ann Cline, *E. D. Morel, 1873–1924: The Strategies of Protest* (Belfast: Blackstaff Press, 1980), 38.

14. Lever, *Viscount Leverhulme*, 15.

15. Andrew M. Knox, *Coming Clean: A Postscript after Retirement from Unilever* (London: Heinemann, 1976), 45.

16. Lever, *Viscount Leverhulme*, 30, 177–78.

17. For biographies of Casement and/or discussions of the diaries, see Dudgeon, *Roger Casement*; Benjamin Lawrence Reid, *The Lives of Roger Casement* (New Haven, Conn.: Yale University Press, 1976); Roger Sawyer, *Casement: The Flawed Hero* (London: Routledge and Kegan Paul, 1984); Brian Inglis, *Roger Casement* (London: Hodder and Stoughton, 1973); W. J. McCormack, *Roger Casement in Death: or, Haunting the Free State* (Dublin: University College Dublin Press, 2002); Ó Siocháin, *Roger Casement*; Angus Mitchell, *Casement* (London: Haus Publishing, 2003); William Bryant, *Roger Casement: A Biography* (Lincoln, Neb.: iUniverse, 2007); Brian Lewis, "The Queer Life and Afterlife of Roger Casement," *Journal of the History of Sexuality* 14, no. 4 (October 2005): 363–82.

18. See Ronald Hyam, *Empire and Sexuality: The British Experience* (Manchester, UK: Manchester University Press, 1991), 33–35.

19. Quoted in Dudgeon, *Roger Casement*, 121, 124–25. See also McDiarmid, *Irish Art of Controversy*, 176.

20. The classic text is Jeffrey Weeks, *Coming Out: Homosexual Politics in Britain from the Nineteenth Century to the Present* (London: Quartet Books, 1977).

21. Michel Foucault, *The History of Sexuality*, vol. 1, *An Introduction* (London: Penguin, 1978), 43.

22. For a useful overview, see Joseph Bristow, "Remapping the Sites of Modern Gay History: Legal Reform, Medico-legal Thought, Homosexual Scandal, Erotic Geography," *Journal of British Studies* 46 (January 2007): 116–42. See also Brian Lewis, ed., *British Queer History: New Approaches and Perspectives* (Manchester, UK: Manchester University Press, 2013).

23. Matt Houlbrook, *Queer London: Perils and Pleasures in the Sexual Metropolis, 1918–1957* (Chicago: University of Chicago Press, 2005), 7–8.

24. See, for example, Xavier Mayne [Edward Irenaeus Prime Stevenson], *The Intersexes: A History of Similisexualism as a Problem in Social Life* (1908; repr., New York: Arno Press, 1975); Jeffrey Weeks, "Inverts, Perverts and Mary-Annes:

Male Prostitution and the Regulation of Homosexuality in England in the Nineteenth and Early Twentieth Centuries," *Journal of Homosexuality* 6, no. 1–2 (Fall–Winter 1980–81): 113–34; Matt Cook, *London and the Culture of Homosexuality, 1885–1914* (Cambridge: Cambridge University Press, 2003); Morris B. Kaplan, *Sodom on the Thames: Sex, Love, and Scandal in Wilde Times* (Ithaca, N.Y.: Cornell University Press, 2005); Sheila Rowbotham and Jeffrey Weeks, *Socialism and the New Life: The Personal and Sexual Politics of Edward Carpenter and Havelock Ellis* (London: Pluto Press, 1977).

25. Alan Sinfield, *The Wilde Century: Effeminacy, Oscar Wilde and the Queer Moment* (New York: Columbia University Press, 1994), chap. 1; Joseph Bristow, *Effeminate England: Homoerotic Writing after 1885* (New York: Columbia University Press, 1995).

26. Casement Diaries, HO 161/4, NA; Dudgeon, *Roger Casement*, 322.

27. Casement Diaries, HO 161/5, NA; Dudgeon, *Roger Casement*, 257.

28. Casement Diaries, HO 161/4, NA; Dudgeon, *Roger Casement*, 339–40.

29. Casement Diaries, HO 161/5, NA; Dudgeon, *Roger Casement*, 315. I am grateful to Marc Herold and Roderick Barman for clarification on this point.

30. See Philippa Levine, "Introduction: Why Gender and Empire?" in *Gender and Empire*, ed. Philippa Levine (Oxford: Oxford University Press, 2004), 6–7.

31. See Charles Wilson, *The History of Unilever: A Study in Economic Growth and Social Change*, vol. 1 (London: Cassell, 1954); D. K. Fieldhouse, *Unilever Overseas: The Anatomy of a Multinational, 1895–1965* (London: Croom Helm, 1978); Lewis, *So Clean*, chap. 4.

32. Jervis J. Babb, *The Human Relations Philosophy of William Hesketh Lever* (New York: Newcomen Society in North America, 1952), 13–14.

33. Lowell J. Satre, *Chocolate on Trial: Slavery, Politics, and the Ethics of Business* (Athens: Ohio University Press, 2005).

34. The literature on forced labor is summarized in Lewis, *So Clean*, chap. 4.

35. Jules Marchal, *L'histoire du Congo 1910–1945*, vol. 1, *Travail forcé pour le cuivre et l'or*, vol. 2, *Travail forcé pour le rail*, and vol. 3, *Travail forcé pour l'huile de palme de Lord Leverhulme* (Borgloon, Belgium: Éditions Paula Bellings, 1999–2001).

36. From a section of the "Relatório da Comissão" published in *Antologia colonial portuguesa* (Lisbon: Agência Geral das Colónias, 1946), 25ff., quoted in James Duffy, *Portuguese Africa* (Cambridge, Mass.: Harvard University Press, 1959), 155.

37. Quoted in A. M. Delathuy [Jules Marchal], *E. D. Morel tegen Leopold II en de Kongostaat* (Antwerp: EPO, 1985), 57–58, quoted in James Breman, "Primitive Racism in a Colonial Context," in *Imperial Monkey Business: Racial Supremacy in Social Darwinist Theory and Colonial Practice*, ed. James Breman (Amsterdam: Vu University Press, 1990), 117.

38. S 19 D2/2, Mss. Brit. Emp., Anti-Slavery Society Papers, Rhodes House, Oxford University, UK; Casement to Travers Buxton, April 18, 1911, quoted in Séamas Ó Siocháin, "Roger Casement's Vision of Freedom," in *Roger Casement in Irish and World History*, ed. Mary E. Daly (Dublin: Royal Irish Academy, 2005), 10.

39. Casement to Morel, April 13, 1911, F5/3, Morel Papers, LSE, quoted in Ó Siocháin, *Roger Casement*, 209.

40. Lever to Morel, April 18, 1911, file 100, F8, Morel Papers, LSE.

41. Lever to Myrtle Huband, October 27, 1924, Lever Business Correspondence, LBC 4271, Unilever Archives and Records Management, Port Sunlight, UK (hereafter cited as UARM).

42. Lever to Annie and D'Arcy Lever, November 12, 1924, LBC 4506, UARM; see also Philippa Levine, "Sexuality, Gender, and Empire," in Levine, *Gender and Empire*, 135.

43. Quoted in W. P. Jolly, *Lord Leverhulme: A Biography* (London: Constable, 1976), 125.

44. Anandi Ramamurthy, *Imperial Persuaders: Images of Africa and Asia in British Advertising* (Manchester, UK: Manchester University Press, 2003), 56, 60, 89.

45. Letter of twenty-three African employees to Lever, January 5, 1925, LBC 5677, UARM.

46. See Levine, "Sexuality, Gender, and Empire," 151–53; Barbara Bush, "Gender and Empire: The Twentieth Century," in Levine, *Gender and Empire*, 84–85; Mrinalini Sinha, "Nations in an Imperial Crucible," in Levine, *Gender and Empire*, 188–89; Philippa Levine, *The British Empire: Sunrise to Sunset* (Edinburgh: Pearson, 2007), chap. 9.

47. Unpublished autobiography, quoted in H. Montgomery Hyde, *Trial of Sir Roger Casement* (London: William Hodge, 1960), cxxi; Harris to archbishop of Canterbury, July 20, 1916, and archbishop to Herbert Samuel (Home Secretary), July 14, 1916, HO 144/1636/311643/49, NA.

48. Unpublished history of the CRA, Morel Papers, quoted in Wm. Roger Louis, "Roger Casement and the Congo," *Journal of African History* 5, no. 1 (1964): 114.

49. Michael Carson, *The Knight of the Flaming Heart* (London: Doubleday, 1995); Michael Eaton, "Ruling Passions: The Story of Roger Casement," *Critical Quarterly* 41, no. 1 (Spring 1999): 89–90.

50. Casement to Alice Stopford Green, April 20, 1907, MS 10464(5), National Library of Ireland, quoted in Séamas Ó Siocháin and Michael O'Sullivan, eds., *The Eyes of Another Race: Roger Casement's Congo Report and 1903 Diary* (Dublin: University College Dublin Press, 2003), vi.

51. Angus Mitchell, "The Riddle of the Two Casements?" in Daly, *Roger Casement*, 104. For the biographies, see Inglis, *Roger Casement*; Reid, *Lives of Roger Casement*; and Sawyer, *Casement*.

52. See Lucy McDiarmid, "The Posthumous Life of Roger Casement," in *Gender and Sexuality in Modern Ireland*, eds. Anthony Bradley and Maryann Gialanella Valiulis (Amherst: University of Massachusetts Press, 1997), 127–58; Eibhear Walshe, "Oscar's Mirror," in *Lesbian and Gay Visions of Ireland: Towards the Twenty-First Century*, ed. Íde O'Carroll and Eoin Collins (London: Cassell, 1995), 150.

53. Colm Tóibín, "A Whale of a Time," *London Review of Books* 19, no. 19 (October 2, 1997): 26.

54. W. G. Sebald, *The Rings of Saturn* (New York: New Directions Books, 1998), 134.

55. Letter to editor, *Guardian* (London), March 16, 2002.

56. Dudgeon, *Roger Casement*, 357–58; Lewis, "Queer Life": 380–81.

57. Eoin Ó Máille and Michael Payne, *The Vindication of Roger Casement—Computer Analysis and Comparisons* (privately printed, 1994), quoted in McCormack, *Roger Casement*, 209; Martin Mansergh, "Roger Casement and the Idea of a Broader Nationalist Tradition: His Impact on Anglo-Irish Relations," in Daly, *Roger Casement*, 189, 192–93.

58. Casement Diaries, November 7, 1911, HO 161/4, NA; Dudgeon, *Roger Casement*, 353.

59. Casement Dairies, August 30, 1911, HO 161/5, NA; Dudgeon, *Roger Casement*, 307.

60. This was the term used by Owen Dudley Edwards, "The Trial of Roger Casement: A Study in Theatre Management," in Daly, *Roger Casement*, 149–77.

61. Mitchell, "Riddle of the Two Casements?" 112–13. See also Roger Casement, *The Amazon Journal of Roger Casement*, ed. Angus Mitchell (London: Anaconda Editions, 1997), 9. For a good discussion of the "two Casements," see Ó Siocháin, *Roger Casement*, 486–89.

62. This is what he has attempted in, for example, his brief biography, *Casement*, and in "Roger Casement: The Evolution of an Enemy of Empire–I," in *Enemies of Empire: New Perspectives on Imperialism, Literature and Historiography*, ed. Eóin Flannery and Angus Mitchell (Dublin: Four Courts Press, 2007), 40–57. See also Séamas Ó Siocháin, "Roger Casement's Vision of Freedom," 1–10; Margaret O'Callaghan, "'With the Eyes of Another Race, of a People Once Hunted Themselves': Casement, Colonialism and a Remembered Past," in Daly, *Roger Casement*, 46–63.

63. John Bruton, "Emotionalism Undid Him," *Daily Telegraph* (London), January 6, 2003.

64. Roger Sawyer, "The Black Diaries: A Question of Authenticity," in Daly, *Roger Casement*, 98.

65. Charles Nicholl, "Into the Dark Heart," *Times Literary Supplement*, 4945 (January 9, 1998): 32.

66. Christopher Andrew, review of Dudgeon, *Roger Casement*, in *Sunday Telegraph*, January 5, 2003.

67. See Michael Cronin, "Romantic Ireland Revisited: Sexuality, Masculinity and Nationalism in Some Recent Irish Texts" (master's thesis, University of Sussex, 2003).

68. Robert Aldrich, *Colonialism and Homosexuality* (London: Routledge, 2003), 367–68.

22

SODOMY, LOVE, AND SLAVERY IN COLONIAL BRAZIL

A Case Study of Minas Gerais during the Eighteenth Century

Ronaldo Vainfas

> Whoever went beyond the Amantiqueira ridge left his conscience there, either hanging or buried.
>
> —Father André João Antonil, 1711

In his 1805 book *Informação da capitania de Minas Geraes,* Basilio Teixeira de Saavedra stated that in this region, "the marriages, and even more so, the affairs of the masters with black and mulatto women had produced over three quarters of the free population, destitute of education, means of support, and good behavior."[1] Many others had similar notions regarding the Minas region of colonial Brazil—colonial authorities, travelers, moralists, and priests alike. The region was portrayed as a miserable land, despite the gold and diamonds it held. Worse still, it was a sinful land where, aside from the famine and hard living conditions, the prevailing sexual and moral conditions were most disorderly: concubinage, prostitution, and illicit love affairs of all sorts were common, contesting the truly Christian way of life that the Portuguese Crown and the Catholic Church intended to enforce in Brazil.

For the sake of truthfulness, it must be said that this sinful image was not exclusive to the Minas Gerais captaincy. Father André João Antonil stated, in his well-known 1711 book *Cultura e opulência do Brasil por suas drogas e minas*, that those who went beyond the Mantiqueira ridge left their consciences there, "hanging or buried,"[2] and Jorge Benci, likewise a Jesuit, would describe all of Portuguese America in similar fashion: "Oh, if the streets and alleys of the Brazilian towns and villages could speak! How many sins would they disclose, that the night covers and the day does not uncover . . . and that the pen trembles and shudders just by spelling them out."[3]

Undoubtedly, the image of the colony as a land of sin and turpitude was very much inspired by the state of mind of the literate persons who described it, especially the priests. Administrators were no exception—Pedro Miguel de Almeida Portugal, the Count of Assumar who governed Minas between 1717 and 1721, was relentless in pointing out the moral deficiency of his domain, linking it to the tense and rebellious environment that was indeed prevalent throughout Minas Gerais.[4] Either motivated by the Counter-Reformation or by a true obsession with moral and social order, all of these commentators emphasized these aspects while describing the everyday lives of the population in those days. Much of the region's image, which made such an impression at the time and is still mentioned in the work of current historians, was partially based on facts, such as the barriers the colonial state set for marriages; the racial prejudice that prevented many white men from marrying their black or mulatto lovers; and the colonial Catholic Church's laxity until at least the second half of the eighteenth century.

It should be kept in mind, though, that Minas Gerais was inserted into the colonial system of the Portuguese Empire under very peculiar conditions. Populated in the eighteenth century, this captaincy entered the colonial scenario just when the church's reinforcement of its institutions in Brazil was at its peak. The First Constitution of the Bahia Archbishopric was enacted in 1707, providing the colonial church with its own ecclesiastic code for the first time, and that was soon followed by the creation of the dioceses of Mariana and São Paulo and the prelacies or vicariates of Goiás and Cuiabá. Even before the bishopric of Mariana was established, still in the early eighteenth century, the Rio de Janeiro bishop sent visitors to Minas Gerais to examine the clerics' conduct, provide guidelines for Catholic pastoral activities, and inspect the religiosity and behavior of the inhabitants of the new captaincy. The analysis of these visits has already served as a basis for magnificent research into family life and deviant behavior patterns in Minas Gerais during the first half of the eighteenth century, such as the classic writing of Laura de Mello e Souza,[5] as well as the foundational works by Luciano Figueiredo.[6] Through these visits, we can trace the policing exerted by the church over the population, including the fearfulness that was instilled and even the use of physical punishments in the worst cases, such as the scandalous concubinages that were the favorite targets of this ecclesiastic activity.

Like the church, the Inquisition also seemed to structure itself best in eighteenth-century Brazil, including in Minas Gerais: it greatly increased the number of Holy Office agents (*familiares*), appointed several commissaries, and even asked for the support of the ecclesiastical justice commanded by the bishop, whose *Regimento do Auditório Eclesiástico* covered faults also pertaining to the Inquisitional jurisdiction.[7]

It is noteworthy that several defendants sentenced in Lisbon for sexual misconduct and moral deviation, coming from Minas Gerais or other captaincies, originated from the diocesan visits ordered by the bishops and conducted by diocesan judges or inspectors. Individuals were denounced, arrested, sent to the Holy Office commissaries, and from there boarded onto ships bound for Lisbon, where they would be sent to the secret prisons of the Inquisition.[8]

As noted, Minas Gerais was populated at the same time that the church was becoming strong throughout Portuguese America, in comparison to the two previous centuries, despite the fact that the ill-prepared secular clerics and the indigent parish structure continued to be barriers to the strict enactment of the guidelines of the Council of Trent in Brazil. To compensate for these deficiencies and for the virtual absence of religious orders in the captaincy, Minas Gerais saw extraordinary activity by the lay brotherhoods that, according to Caio Boschi, were the main tools shaping Catholicism in the captaincy.[9]

However, the means by which Minas Gerais was occupied in the wake of the gold prospecting that attracted thousands of individuals, whether Portuguese or born in other captaincies and all in search of instant wealth, turned Vila Rica, São João del Rei, Mariana, Vila do Príncipe, Sabará, and many other villages into unstable and transitory places of passage and adventure. The Minas Gerais town "looks like a road, a passage," said João Camilo de Oliveira Torres,[10] capturing with precision the style of occupation of the region that created illusions and lost fortunes, a style contrary to the church's spiritual ambitions in the colony. In short, it was an *alluvial society* as described by Sérgio Buarque de Holanda in his beautiful text "Metais e pedras preciosas."[11]

As expected, prospecting for gold and diamonds required a gigantic proportion of black slaves in the region. In the mid-eighteenth century, slaves made up 70 percent of the population of 266,668 inhabitants. As a captaincy with a massive concentration of slaves, Minas Gerais manifested many of the most troubling aspects of life in the slavery regions at that time: violence against black people, upheavals, seditions, and sexual abuse of all sorts.

In Minas Gerais, the slaves and the impoverished population were subject to the most precarious conditions and haphazard living arrangements. Moral rules were excessively slack in the eyes of the church. The proportion of illegitimate children born between 1719 and 1723 reached 90 percent, while the society was still settling, and then fell to 60 percent between the years of 1759 and 1763, when the demographic standard acquired its typical shape. It is unquestionable that many residents in Minas married, as demonstrated by the lengthy bibliography dedicated to this topic over recent years, beginning with Iraci Del Nero's work,[12] but most of the population lived in concubinage, as indicated by the summaries of the ecclesiastic inquests. In Minas, notwithstanding the multitude of brotherhoods and an increased ecclesiastic surveillance, moral and sexual transgressions were always numerous and most varied, encompassing all social strata without excluding any acts against the Sixth Commandment.

Based on the records of the clerical inquests and visits, Laura de Mello e Souza has painted a portrait of the true reign of lust that existed in the Minas towns during the eighteenth century, especially when she deals with the "protagonists of misery"[13]—powerful or minor lords living in concubinage with their slaves; priests in love with poor white or mulatto girls; husbands pimping their wives in exchange for money; men who lived with two women, and women who lived with two men; as well as prostitution of all kinds and innumerable brothels. In short, the variety of transgressions in Minas Gerais made concubinage the most amenable and unostentatious sin in the captaincy.

In the eyes of divine law, the worst of all the sins of the flesh and the most serious, since it could result in death by burning, was the "loathsome and heinous sin of sodomy," and this sin was very common in Minas Gerais. Preachers did not speak of sodomy from the pulpit because it was a heinous sin and therefore could not be mentioned or pronounced. Nor did the historians who based their work on the records from ecclesiastic visits mention it, although sodomy was included in the list of crimes published by the visitants at the townships they toured. The summary of indictments in such cases was usually sent directly to the Holy Church commissioners because, as of the second half of the sixteenth century, sodomy was a crime over which only the Inquisition had jurisdiction.

We are aware of the world of sodomy at Minas Gerais through Inquisition records and through the *Cadernos do nefando*,[14] logs that listed all accusations against so-called sodomites in the Portuguese realm and colonies overseas. We surmise from these Inquisitorial sources, as previously stated, that many suspects were originally accused by the ecclesiastic inquests and then sent to the Holy Office, although others were directly accused by the local population to the Inquisition authorities themselves without any ecclesiastic visitors' intermediation.

It is worthwhile to delve into the world of these *fanchonos* and *somítigos* of Minas Gerais—words of the popular Portuguese language used to describe the sodomites and homosexuals. We should ask, first of all, whether they formed some sort of analogous subculture to the one that existed in Lisbon or other European cities, that is, a semiclandestine world, cowed by imminent repression and endowed with its own codes, gestures, hairdos, and even a vocabulary specific to the fanchono way of being. This is a pertinent issue, as pointed out by Rafael Carrasco, a historian of the Valencia sodomites, because sodomy, as a mentality, was an essentially urban phenomenon. Only a town could provide the necessary secrecy, the defensive barriers, and the relative anonymity needed by those who, as a way of life, chose to disregard the official moral code and enjoy homoerotic pleasures.[15] This may be observed in the work of Carrasco, who was able to reenact the subculture of homosexuals in Valencia during the seventeenth and eighteenth centuries; of Maurice Lever, in Paris during the same period;[16] and of Luiz Mott, in seventeenth-century Lisbon.[17]

In his article entitled "Pagode Português," Mott reconstitutes in detail the usual places where the Lisbon somítigos met—the inns and taverns they frequented the most, together with meeting points such as the wall of the Chagas Church, the stairs of the Rua Nova,, and the Arco do Rocio. Mott states that some houses were actual homosexual brothels, such as the house of Father Santos de Almeida, himself the king's chaplain during the early seventeenth century; the neighbors called it "a school and brothel for *fanchonos*" due to the traffic of extravagant young men that characterized the place. Another priest who was a regular at this minimonastery jokingly called it "a synagogue of homosexuals," a free and libertine association between Father Santos's "Sodoma" and the presumed Judaism practiced by the newly converted Portuguese Christians in their "esnogas."[18] It was common practice to use code names or nicknames suggestive of the deviant sex that pleased those who attended these places. This was sex secretly enjoyed by men of different ages and social status, some of whom seemed to employ, with a degree of irony and debauchery, the stigmatizing vocabulary used by the population to ridicule the more brazen homosexuals. Father Pedro Furtado, a well-known preacher, was known among his pleasure companions as Dona Paula of Lisbon, and, like him, others were also called by curious names: one was secretly known as Isabel do Porto, another was Cardosa, and a third one Turca. Among this group, one had the extraordinary nickname of the Archsynagogue, more than likely because he was some sort of a rabbi in this school of homosexuals that shocked the town. The use of lip color, long hair and well-groomed bangs, the *gadelhas* (full hair)—all of these traits were found in seventeenth-century Lisbon's *bas-fond* (underworld).

If we look for similar examples of the homosexual world in the colonial areas, the best case would be Mexico City, again in the seventeenth century, which is the subject of an excellent article by Serge Gruzinski.[19] The capital of New Spain suffered from no lack of *maricones* and *sométicos* (insulting terms for homosexual men) who went to the *pulquería* and *temascale*, which were copies of the taverns and public baths of European cities. Nor was there a shortage of periodic orgies that brought reputation to certain places and were held even on religious holidays. During the orgies, young boys, elderly men, transvestites, and male prostitutes drank chocolate, talked about their amorous conquests, became intimate, and even fought over lovers. And then there were the mysterious and sassy nicknames among the participants, such as La Luna, La Martina de los Cielos, and Las Rosas.

Something similar existed in eighteenth-century Minas Gerais, a captaincy characterized by an intense urban life (although the towns were small) and by the constant coming and going of people that was so typical of mining areas. But the homosexual subculture in Minas did not come close to what several authors describe in other towns of those times. Perhaps because the villages in Minas were quite small in comparison to the main European or Hispano-American cities or perhaps because sodomy in Brazil was never persecuted as rigorously as elsewhere, the fact is that neither in Vila Rica nor in Mariana did homosexual relationships give rise to any type of nefarious conventicle. Casual sex, circumstantial love affairs in any place where such encounters could be held, this is how the "nefarious" life went on in Minas, just as in other parts of the Portuguese colony, where only in very rare cases is it possible to perceive more consistent and organized groups of homosexuals.[20]

In Minas Gerais, everyday sodomy was just as nonspecific as throughout the rest of Portuguese America, and the nefarious relationships merged with other types of social relationships, especially between masters and slaves. Nevertheless, it should be pointed out that male same-sex activities in Minas Gerais were neither few nor of little interest. Among many noteworthy examples, we find the confession of a miner who lived in Congonhas and organized real orgies toward the end of the eighteenth century: "To excite my flesh—Manuel Pereira confessed later—I sinned against the sixth commandment with my slave Ventura, ordering him to touch the dishonest parts of my body while he also touched the parts of a woman, as when we did it with the black women Vitoriana, Mariana, Ana Gonçalves and Felícia and with the she-goats Maria Tereza, Letícia, Maria Lopes, Rosa and others. Aside from the referred slave, I also committed the same sin with other men whom I called and to some of which I paid money." Untiring and insatiable, this man instigated his slaves to engage in oral sex, and he forced them to have intercourse with the said black women and she-goats in front of him while he frenetically masturbated.[21]

Orgies aside, Minas Gerais had some romances and love affairs among the thirty-five instances of sodomy entered in the Holy Office records, involving approximately one hundred individuals. Among the more or less lasting romances, some reached the point where they were effectively homoerotic concubinage, based on explicit affection and a certain constancy and duration of the relationships, including cases involving masters and slaves. A certain Corporal Giraldes, for example, had an affair with his black man Anselmo that lasted years in Tijuco, where diamonds were mined in the village. He was so possessive that he went as far as putting Anselmo in chains because he saw him in a suspicious conversation with another soldier.[22] Captain José de Lima Noronha Lobo, an important and married man in São João del Rei, had an affair that lasted eighteen consecutive years with the Angolan Antônio; they would meet very frequently in his own backyard, especially near the banana plantation, where he could hide his affair with this Angolan negro from his wife.[23] But perhaps the most interesting case is the one involving teacher João Pereira de Carvalho—a young man who taught Portuguese and Latin to the sons of neighbors at Lavras da Lagoa, also in São João del Rei. João fell madly in love with one of his students, Luis, to whom he would send written messages: "Luís, my little love, my life! Come to the banana plantation because I am already going there with a little bottle of alcoholic beverage."[24]

Contrary to what is stated by Rafael Carrasco, who says that sodomites in the past were men who seemed only to be concerned with casual sex and a variety of partners, we find some cases, in Minas Gerais and elsewhere, in which homosexuals had relationships full of passion and affection. These relationships were little different from heterosexual concubinages, the product of impossible or forbidden love affairs. If such cases appear in a much smaller number and if love is rarely mentioned in the records of the Holy Office, this is due mostly to the fact that, in determining guilt or innocence, the Inquisition was interested not in the existence of affection and passion but in the occurrence of consummated anal intercourse—that is, the release of semen *intra vas*, to apply the Inquisitional words—and this took up the great majority of the pages devoted to this type of suit.

In fact, everyday sodomy in Minas Gerais was not very different from the colony's overall standard or from that of the ancien régime in general, according to several papers written on the subject. Contrary to some interpretations, like that of Luiz Mott, who idealized homosexual relationships in the past, the typical relationship—far from being happy and affectionate—was primarily based on the exploitation of misery and on violence of various kinds. More or less powerful men—or those who were believed to be so—seduced young men in exchange for money, food, drink, and even opium. In return for lodging for a few days or even only one night, they demanded or insinuated sodomistic lust or, as the Inquisitors would state, carried out acts propitious to sodomistic practice, such as masturbation or oral sex. What seems to have been prevalent in Minas Gerais and in other regions of Portuguese America was an intertwining of sodomy and slavery, whereby the masters or free men forced black slaves into homosexual intercourse as passive or active participants, depending on the preference of whoever had the higher social ranking; if necessary, physical coercion was used to achieve their intent.

João Durão, who lived in São João del Rei, seduced his neighbors' slaves and (sometimes in the woods, sometimes in huts) sodomized them in exchange for nothing.[25] The same tactic was used by surgeon Lucas da Costa Pereira, a resident of Paracatú and an adept of sodomy since living in the Madeira islands, where he had a relationship with a Carmelite friar in a convent cell, according to what he stated to the Inquisitor. In Minas, he did the same with many young men, some free, others slaves, including a fourteen-year-old mulatto whom he got drunk and on whom he used physical force after unsuccessfully tempting him with presents.[26] The miner Manuel Álvares Cabral, a resident of Mariana, confessed in 1739 that, on many occasions, defeated by temptation, he had practiced the "nefarious acts" with seven of his "negroes, all of which were his slaves, either forced or almost forced to do so." And to protect himself from the Inquisition, he would send five partners, all of them his slaves, to confess such acts in the presence of the Holy Office Commissary, although some of them stated that they only consented to sodomy out of fear of being punished.[27]

Some masters not only coerced their slaves or servants to take part in sexual activity, using various forms of intimidation, but also reached the point of raping them. In rare cases, it was the slaves themselves who sought out an official of the Holy Office to accuse their masters and thus free themselves from violent harassment. Francisco, a Mozambican slave of Jacinto Ferreira dos Campos in Vila Rica, provides a good example of this. Around 1758, "he repeated ten times the Holy Name of Jesus, saying that he was not a woman to satisfy his master's sexual wishes." And he was given advice by a freed black woman that he should take the accusations to the white men because "they knew the means to punish such a sin."[28]

One of the most prominent cases is that of Father José Ribeiro Dias, a man who, despite being a priest, had made a good fortune in the mines of Paracatú. He had twenty-seven slaves who would be worth, "if well sold, two hundred eights of gold each"; three *datas* in Sabará,[29] worth 520,000 reis each; a small plantation worth 60,000 reis; several houses in the village of Paracatú totaling "ninety some eights of gold"; fifteen pieces of cutlery; and a silver platter. He was a habitual practitioner of sodomy with partners of varied social status, most of them young men and many just children from among his slaves; some partners participated actively, others passively. In the whole history of the Inquisition, Father José was one of the few men to pay a high price for being accused by a slave he had sodomized. In this case, however, it was the mulatto Felipe de Santiago who, in 1743, presented himself to Bishop Dom João da Cruz, an ecclesiastic visitor, accusing the priest of having forced him to perform acts of malice and sodomy, despite his refusal and determination not to consent. As eloquent evidence that he was fully aware that masters in fact had the power to sexually use and abuse their slaves, he stated that he ended up consenting to such acts because the priest "raped him with the power and commandeering respect of a master" while he, Felipe, "obeyed him out of fear because of his condition as of a slave." Father José was arrested by the Inquisition and sent to the galleys for ten years, ending his days in terrible conditions.[30]

In eighteenth-century Minas Gerais, where it was hard to distinguish the oppression that ordinarily afflicted the poor, the free men, and the slaves, wealthy masters or mere miners deemed themselves entitled to sexually abuse poor young men, whether their own slaves or those of others. Sometimes, they offered small gifts to their partners, but they did not always keep their promises of other rewards, and they often used physical coercion. The brutality found in many relationships between masters and slaves in Minas Gerais shows the other side of the violence traditionally linked to slavery in this captaincy. But we should not forget that violence and exploitation of the poor were not exclusive to the male homoerotic world; they were common in heterosexual relationships as well, including those between masters and female slaves. The Holy Office records contain, in fact, several accusations against masters for sodomizing their black and mulatto slaves in Paracatú, Sabará, Mariana, and elsewhere.[31]

The Inquisition's stance regarding accusations of sodomy, whether made by slaves or free men, was, once again, effectively characterized by indifference. In Minas Gerais, over one hundred individuals were accused to the Holy Office's commissaries or ecclesiastic visitors during the eighteenth century, yet only four were prosecuted. Most of the accused were not incarcerated in the feared Inquisition prisons, on the customary grounds cited by the Holy Office—a lack of conclusive evidence. The authorities then ordered their release. In addition, there were numerous instances in which, based on its internal regulations, the Holy Office was satisfied by the accuseds' detailed and voluntary confessions of their faults.

However, in those few cases where the Holy Office chose to arrest and prosecute the accused, it took a most rigorous stance, albeit never condemning any of the perpetrators to the maximum penalty of death by burning. It did confiscate assets and send the defendants to the king's galleys for ten years, as in the previously mentioned case of Father José—a penalty that was, in reality, equivalent to being sentenced to a slow death. Therefore, the men who did not report to the Holy Office commissioners to confess their wrongdoings fell into the Inquisition's web. They ended their days mutilated and disfigured by scurvy or by galley disease, all pleading that their provisional penalty should be suspended, after years of suffering, for the sake of Christ—or at least be commuted from galley to exile.[32]

To the relief of the Minas Gerais homosexuals, whether they were tender lovers or brutal masters, only four of them, as mentioned, met the tragic destiny of the galleys. This was a very small number, it should be stressed, as compared with the volume of charges of sodomy in this captaincy. But it is a number that should not be dismissed either, if we consider that only nine men were prosecuted in all of Brazil during the eighteenth century on charges of sodomy, some of whom were acquitted. Such modest figures actually do not suggest a decline of the Inquisitional activities in Brazil during the 1700s, as evidenced by recent research. This research has brought to light the great number of new Christians sentenced on charges of Judaism during the first half of the century, many of whom originated from Minas Gerais. It speaks for itself that, during the entire colonial period, about 51 percent of the prisoners residing in the colony were prosecuted during the first half of the eighteenth century, which marked the peak of the Portuguese Inquisitorial activity.[33]

Yet one should not take for granted that the Holy Office was lenient in its moralizing crusade. For example, bigamous individuals were never more prosecuted in Brazil than during the eighteenth century. A total of 74 individuals were charged with this crime (compared to 22 during the previous century), 11 of whom lived in Minas Gerais. There was a similar increase in prosecutions of those charged with the *solicitantes*[34] (although in lower absolute numbers: 18 prosecuted out of a total of 21), 85 percent of whom were caught in the Inquisition's web during the eighteenth century.[35]

The small quantity of sodomy prosecutions in Minas Gerais and throughout Portuguese America in comparison to the large number of charges followed the general decline in prosecutions against homoerotic practitioners in all the dominions of the Portuguese Empire, including Portugal itself. This trend was also evident in other European countries where there had been a relentless prosecution against sodomites during the sixteenth and especially the seventeenth centuries. According to Maurice Lever, the prosecution of sodomites gradually lost its sacredness in the 1700s, shedding its heretic tints during the Enlightenment, which coincided with the extinguishing of the fires and a decrease in the traditional persecutory frenzy. To a certain extent, the prosecution of sodomites in Brazil was never as intense as in Portugal, not even at its height during the seventeenth century. The Inquisitorial machine, assembled to prosecute Jewry, never seemed to earnestly pursue prosecution of the crime of sodomy, especially in the colony, where the court's employees were few, the distances were immense, and lust was everywhere.

The small number of persons actually sentenced for committing sodomy in Brazil is also explained by a tacit agreement between the Inquisitors and the colonial masters. The Holy Office seemed to follow the advice given by the colonial authorities in the 1500s—that Brazil would only be populated at the expense of many pardons. Although the Inquisitors considered the practice of sodomy totally abominable, they were also aware of the fact that it was impossible to separate the institution of slavery from sexual abuse. It was impossible to rigorously prosecute the *nefarious sin* without defying the arrogance of the colonial potentates. For this reason, since the sixteenth century, the Inquisition had chosen not to punish masters or slaves involved in the infamous crime, apart from a few exceptions. It constrained itself to punishing, from time to time, modest and simple men, the dominant social status among those sentenced by the famous Tribunal.

Minas Gerais was no exception in this regard, and it assimilated the sodomites here and there as just another of its many perditions, to the despair of the church. And as a consequence, the everyday life of homosexuals and sodomites in Minas Gerais continued amid the reproach of the gossiping population and the sexual desire of the practitioners, the loving notes from the teacher in São João del Rei and the brutal lust of the masters of the golden captaincy.

Notes

1. Basilio T. de Saavedra, "Informação da capitania de Minas Gerais (1805)," *Revista do Arquivo Público Mineiro* 2 (1897): 677.

2. "O que passou a serra da Amantiqueira aí deixou dependurada ou sepultada a consiciência," in André João Antonil, *Cultura e opulência do Brasil por suas drogas e minas* (1711; repr., São Paulo: Companhia Editora Nacional, 1976), 286.

3. "Oh, se pudessem falar as ruas e becos das cidades e povoações do Brasil! Quantos pecados publicariam, que encobre a noite e não descobre o dia . . . e a que a pena treme e pasma de os escrever," in Jorge Benci, *Economia cristã dos senhores no governo dos escravos* (1700; repr., São Paulo: Grijalbo, 1977), 118.

4. Pedro de Almeida, *Discurso histórico e político que nas Minas houve no ano de 1720*, with a critical introduction by Laura de Mello e Souza (Belo Horizonte: Fundação João Pinheiro, 1994).

5. Laura de Mello e Souza, *Desclassificados do ouro: A pobreza mineira no século XVIII* (Rio de Janeiro: Graal, 1983).

6. Luciano Figueiredo, *Barrocas familias: Vida familiar em Minas Gerais no século XVIII* (São Paulo: Hucitec, 1997). See also Luciano Figueiredo, *O avesso da memória: Estudo do papel, participação e condição social da mulher no século XVIII mineiro* (São Paulo: Hucitec, 1996).

7. The *familiares* of the Inquisition were those who had police power in the Inquisitorial structure. The *Regimento do Auditório Eclesiástico* contained the list of the religious or moral crimes that the visitors should investigate.

8. Caio Boschi, "As visitas diocesanas e a Inquisição na Colônia," *Revista brasileira de história*, no. 14 (1987): 151–87.

9. Caio Boschi, *Os leigos e o poder: Irmandades leigas e política colonizadora em Minas Gerais* (São Paulo: Ática, 1986).

10. Ibid., 32.

11. This translates as "Metal and Precious Stones." See Sérgio Buarque de Holanda, "Metais e pedras preciosas," in *História geral da civilização brasileira*, 4th ed. (São Paulo: DIFEL, 1977), 259–310.

12. Iraci del Nero Costa, *Vila Rica: População (1719–1826)* (São Paulo: IPE/USP, 1975).

13. de Mello e Souza, *Desclassificados*, 141–214.

14. This translates as *Nefarious Notebooks*.

15. Rafael Carrasco, *Inquisición y represión sexual en Valencia: História de los sodomitas (1565–1785)* (Barcelona: Laertes Ediciones, 1986).

16. Maurice Lever, *Les bûchers de Sodome: Histoire des "infâmes"* (Paris: Fayard, 1985).

17. Luiz Mott, "Pagode português: A subcultura gay em Portugal nos tempos inquisitoriais," *Ciência e cultura* 40, no. 2 (1988): 120–39.

18. The word meant "synagogue" in the popular language.

19. Serge Gruzinsky, "Las cenizas del deseo: Homosexuales novohispanos a mediados del siglo XVII," in *De la santitad a la perversión*, ed. S. Ortega (Mexico City: Grijalbo, 1985), 255–81.

20. See Ronaldo Vainfas, "O nefando e a colônia," in *Trópico dos pecados*, 2nd ed. (Rio de Janeiro: Nova Fronteira, 1997), 151–93. This text was recently published in English. See Harold Johnson and Francis Dutra, eds., *Pelo vaso traseiro: Sodomy and Sodomites in Luso-Brazilian History* (Tucson, Ariz.: Fenestra Books, 2007), 337–68. See also Luiz Mott, "Cripto-sodomitas em Pernambuco colonial," *Revista antropológicas* 13, no. 2 (2002): 7–38.

21. Luiz Mott, "O sexo cativo: Alternativas eróticas dos africanos e seus descendentes no Brasil escravista," in *O sexo proibido: Virgens, gays e escravos nas garras da Inquisição* (Campinas, Brazil: Papirus, 1980), 57.

22. Ibid., 44.

23. Ibid., 45.

24. "Luis, meu amorzinho, minha vidinha! Vinde para o bananal que eu já lá vou com a garrafinha de aguardente," in Luiz Mott, "Cupido na sala de aula: Pedofilia e pederastia no Brasil antigo," in *Cadernos de pesquisa* 69 (May 1989): 34.

25. Processo 5708, Inquisição de Lisboa, Arquivo Nacional da Torre do Tombo, Lisbon, Portugal (hereafter cited as ANTT).

26. Processo 205, Inquisição de Lisboa, ANTT.

27. Caderno do Nefando, n. 20, fl. 439, ANTT.

28. N. 20, fl. 364, ANTT.

29. A *data* was a plot of land of approximately 3,000 square meters.

30. Processo 10426, Inquisição de Lisboa, ANTT.

31. Mott, "O sexo cativo," 55–56.

32. They were Padre José Ribeiro Dias, Paracatú, processo 10426; João Durão, Paracatú, processo 5708; Lucas da Costa Pereira, São João del Rey, processo 205; and Antônio José Ribeiro ou José Peixoto Sampaio, Vila Rica, processo 280, Inquisição de Lisboa, ANTT.

33. Anita Novinsky, *Inquisição: Prisioneiros do Brasil* (Rio de Janeiro: Expressão e Cultura, 2002), 28.

34. Solicitantes were the priests who tried to seduce or did seduce persons through the sacramental confession. For the persecution of the solicitantes, see Lana Lage da Gama Lima, *O avesso da confissão: O crime de solicitação no Brasil Colonial* (Ph.D. diss., University of São Paolo, 1991).

35. Novinsky, *Inquisição*, 28.

23

EUNUCHS, POWER, AND SLAVERY IN THE EARLY ISLAMIC WORLD

Salah Trabelsi

Scholarship on the phenomenon of eunuch slavery has primarily concentrated on the Greco-Byzantine world, but in fact, this was without a doubt one of the most unique forms of slavery in the Islamic world. Historians highlight the presence of large numbers of black and white slaves who were recruited from the first quarter of the ninth century on to form an elite group of subaltern soldiers. Historical studies often lack depth, however, because they do not provide much information on the structure of this phenomenon or its social and cultural aspects. The reasons for this silence have not always been easy to explain, especially since it is possible to find documents from the period that include snippets and stories recounting the lives of certain eunuchs.

Generally speaking, the history of eunuchs is not very well known because our sources do not allow us to determine this institution's origin. The little information they give is often too short or imprecise. Most data concern the Abbasid and post-Abbasid dynasties. The most obvious difficulty for earlier periods is the lack of documents. But in spite of their fragmented and parsimonious nature, accounts written by historians and chroniclers are the most precious and reliable written material available.

Apart from data provided by annals, narrative literature, and legal treaties, the journals of geographers and travelers deserve special attention. They often give us vital accounts. Taking full advantage of this rich and varied corpus will allow us to grasp in minute detail the background and richness of historical events. They will also help us to be extra vigilant regarding a tradition of forgeries and exaggerations, by sorting out and eliminating events that do not seem particularly credible or accurate.

Arabic texts from the early Islamic world are full of rich and detailed stories that provide much information. The most common terms for eunuchs and castrated men in such texts are *ghilmān*, *mamālīk*, *fitiyān*, *tawāshī*, and *ʿabīd*.[1] In general, the words *khādim* and *ghulām* can be categorized as meaning eunuchs, but *ghulām* does not always have that meaning and *ghilmān* does not describe all castrated men. as the word *khādim* was sometimes used as a euphemism.[2]

The term *khasī* does not describe the actual state of the person. Some khadam were called *khisiyān*, which indicated they had had the scrotum removal without having the phallus cut off.[3] The phrase *madjbūb al-dhakar*[4] or *madjbūb* refers to slaves who had all of their organs removed. Arab authors were not unanimous when evaluating the eunuch's gender and attributes. In many places, the texts emphasize that the castrated slave was not categorized as a lesser man. His status did not exclude him from taking up arms and being brave on the battlefield. In fact, many eunuchs rose to positions in the upper echelons of the military.

Many of the sources that remain are literary or biographical texts that, through detailed eyewitness accounts or enlightening anecdotes, give us a look at aspects of social life that are often forgotten. These texts offer vignettes that evoke the ethnicity, personality, and life experience of humble servants and distinguished slaves such as Kafūr al-Ikhsīdī, a Nubian eunuch in Egypt, or Djawdhar al-Siqillī, of Slavic descent in North Africa, who proved to have exceptional skills in exercising authority and control caliphal power. Many Arabic documents demonstrate that during the Abbasid dynasty, caliphate courts such as those at Baghdad and Samarra brought together large groups of men and women who had been bought and trained in special schools at a very young age.

The Abbasid period is often associated with the development of the institution of slavery. The eviction of the Umayyads and the establishment of a new dynasty in the mid-eighth century no doubt caused great changes. These changes affected mentalities in particular and amplified the universal vocation of the new empire, particularly once the capital had been moved to Iraq, the cradle of the ancient cultures. New urban settlements flourished along the routes linking the Mediterranean, the Middle East, and the Far East. The city of Baghdad, epicenter of a glittering cultural and artistic life, was an enormous metropolis of over 1 million souls: tradesmen, members of the bourgeoisie, officials, plebeians, slaves, soldiers, and many others, with a multitude of different origins and religions.

The first two centuries saw the birth of what scholars often describe as a "golden age" during which pleasure and courtesy were raised to the level of supreme values and elites praised sensuality and freedom from constraints. It would not be quite true to claim that these golden age centuries were the summit of a licentious culture free from the influence of Islamic standards. Of course, it is sometimes said that extolling the pleasures of this world is an ephemeral vanity, but this notion is normally put forward as prefiguring the delights of eternal life. It should be pointed out that for most Muslim exegetes, the love of women, in the same way as gallantry is often magnified or even raised to the level of prayer or asceticism.

The splendor of the princely courts and bourgeois residences seemed to revolve around young slaves celebrated in surviving texts for their extraordinary beauty and their intellectual and artistic talents. Meetings of high society—bacchanalian and punctuated by poetry extolling love—were the favorite pastimes of the upper classes. At some of the meetings, there were more slaves than free people. For high-society women, there was a far greater value to such household staff. The possession of young male slaves was perfectly in line with the women's desire for extensive freedom and for easy access to masculinity. Their attachment to slaves who might be talented, discreet, and, even more important, more or less ambiguously virile enabled them to increase their influence and be involved in the affairs of the world and the plots being hatched therein.

This attraction of the adolescent slaves must be associated with male sexual interest in young women. There are some accounts that give us access to female homosexuality, such as that attributed to Al-Maqrīzī,[5] which describes a princess who went to a Cairo market to purchase a young Berber woman, apparently for sexual purposes.

Texts that survive emphasize the diverse backgrounds of the enslaved women, describing Greek, Slav, African, Indian, Turkish, or Russian domestic servants who, just as much as the male slaves, played a leading role in the mixture of ethnic and cultural identities. They greatly contributed to interracial marriages and to the creation of a completely crossbred population and culture—theirs was a resounding presence. Some documents concentrate on the physical characteristics, origins, and artistic talents of the favorites and of concubines of very diverse backgrounds.

The brief biographic details available about the Sultana Al-Khayzurān (d. 789)[6] tell of her meteoric rise and describe her as a beautiful and gifted woman of rare wisdom and indefatigable energy: she is portrayed as a great seductress who was also educated. Her journey began in Yemen, at the home of a Master Thaqafite of the Shuraysh tribe. She was then sold to someone from Mecca who took her to the Al-Mansūr palace. The caliph was seduced by her charm and vivacity and gave her to his son Al-Mahdī. Al-Khayzurān captured the heart and mind of the young prince and rose to the rank of concubine and then from mother to free woman.

The emirs were subjugated by her charisma and showed her boundless respect. If the laudatory accounts are to be believed, her sanctum was the scene of a permanent throng. She got the better of all her Arab-blood rivals, cheerfully surpassing Rita, Al-Mahdī's legitimate wife and daughter of As-Saffāh, the founder of the Abbasid dynasty. Military chiefs and ambitious dignitaries bustled around her door. With such support behind her, she managed to have her two sons crowned when the caliph died—first the elder, Mūsa Al-Hādī, and then, in August 785, her younger son, Hārūn. It was then that she seized real, absolute power, which she exercised until her death in 173/789. The example of Al-Khayzurān left a deep mark on history. Apart from As-Saffāh, Al-Mahdī, and Al-Amīn, all the Abbasid caliphs were sons of slaves. The same was true of Al-Muqtadir, who ascended the throne at the age of thirteen. It was his mother, a slave of Greek origin, who governed the empire, steadfastly braving threats and military insurrections.

The Arab chronicles also tell us that the caliph Al-Mu'tasim (218–230/833–844) was behind a royal office for recruiting young slaves, the *diwān al-ghilmān.* Although most militia personnel were of Turkish or Caucasian origin, the slaves also came from Ethiopia, Sudan, the Maghreb, and the Slavic world. Such ethnic and national diversity was designed to maintain discipline among the various militias and, if necessary, pit one against the other. The recruits were first entrusted to the senior eunuchs responsible for their training. Once this was complete, they were enfranchised and given a pension. They were installed in quarters depending on their nation of origin and were forbidden to visit Arab families; they were allowed only to marry women of the same status and origin as their own.

They were recruited to work in harems, in inner circles, or in government offices. Many of them were promoted into the upper echelons of the state and the military.[7] It seems clear that part of the slave population, often the most marginal and least powerful, managed to rise up to become symbols of political and cultural authority. Examples of certain biographies of uprooted slaves, who were sometimes mutilated and destined to be shunned by others, inspire reflection on personal responsibility and the uncertainties of life. The power of some of them to become decision makers endows history with a very unique dimension.

Eunuchs were close to the caliph and acted as guardians of state power and glory. They quickly became the system's linchpins, but they were also the main cause of instability and fragility in the regimes. This was true in prosperous times as well as during periods of decline. Eunuchs were put under the authority of the master of ceremonies, a slave-intendant. And they followed rules of etiquette to the letter and were in charge of the powerful and not-so-powerful alike. These slaves were aware of all schemes and conspiracies and were even accomplices and instigators themselves. Opportunities for promotion varied according to the position held. But obviously, the most fortunate eunuchs were those whose exceptional talents led them to the court. In addition to working in the ladies' apartments, many young male slaves were bought and trained to satisfy the sexual desires of their masters.

According to historical sources, during the apogee of Abbasid power (750–936), a flourishing new culture emerged from the simplicity and austerity of old Arab culture. From this era onward, attitudes in old Middle Eastern and Mediterranean societies were transformed progressively and harmoniously. The splendor and radiance of the caliphal court marked the epitome of this transformation. Intellectual and artistic activities were supported by a growing market economy and fed by a large movement of ideas and people that allowed the court to attain the highest level of refinement. Little by little, a new atmosphere permeated all levels of society, inspired by a fertile combination of Arab traditions and foreign influences. This golden age was also marked by a relative relaxation of the moral code. It prefigured the rise of a kind of lifestyle based on libertinage and pleasure, which encouraged the virtues of drunkenness and carnal love. A major character appeared in aristocratic society: the eunuch, the cupbearer, the singing slave full of wit, charm, and seductive power.[8] From then on, in the narratives of this courtly society, the enslaved person emerged as the key that unlocked a passionate quest for power and the enjoyment of sensual pleasures.

Eunuch slavery seems to have been a residual phenomenon of the splendor of princely households. The eunuch as object was the star of the court. The prince showed him off with pride and ostentation. Eunuchs and other very sumptuous gifts were given to honor kings and important dignitaries. For example, in 904, Ziyādat Allah III (d. 909), an Aghlabid emir, sent a diplomatic mission to Baghdad to present very expensive gifts to al-Muktafī billah, the Abbasid caliph (d. 908). In addition to silver, fine perfume, and expensive fabrics, there were two hundred rare-breed horses that were harnessed and two hundred eunuchs. He also gave the head of the mission the sum of 30,000 dinars in order to purchase slaves raised and educated in Baghdad.[9]

Ziyādat Allah III's grandfather, Emir Ibrāhīm b. al-Aghlab II (d. 902) had a large number of eunuchs. He owned sixty young enslaved men, who were obliged to provide sexual services when demanded. They were watched over by an adult eunuch in a dormitory set up just for them.[10]

Ziyādat Allah III's reign lasted six years, during which there were sporadic revolts and unrest. It ended in a humiliating escape. Fatimid propaganda spread quickly, forcing him to flee Tunisia and go to Baghdad with his treasure and court dignitaries. According to the Egyptian chronicler, he was accompanied by one thousand eunuch slaves who each wore a belt containing one thousand gold coins.[11] In June 909, he stopped in Egypt and then tried to get to Iraq. But along the way,

> Abbasid officials became interested in his possessions. So they offered to buy two young eunuchs in particular, whose charm appealed to everyone. Ziyādat Allah III refused to give them up. When he arrived in al-Raqqa, a Muhtasib was waiting to investigate his morals. He was dragged before the cadi and went on trial. Witnesses testified and denounced his immorality. The judge ordered that the eunuchs, who were at the center of the lawsuit, be sold in the name of virtue. Public morality was satisfied, as well as the Abbasid officials, by the purchase of these two charming boys.[12]

It is difficult to put the castrated slaves into a single occupational category because they had very different tasks and responsibilities, according to the texts. But we need to focus on one area within the extreme diversity of jobs assigned to eunuchs.[13] In particular, they were entrusted with espionage missions inside and outside the palace. And in addition, they commanded militias that would spy on rebellious emirs and princes if needed. These slaves were also able to arrest or eliminate any suspect, regardless of his rank or title.[14] Usually, certain responsibilities ensured them real promotions. They sometimes managed to rise to prestigious positions within the hierarchy.

It has often been wrongfully said that the young boys called ghilmān were rarely mentioned at the Umayyed caliphs' courts. However, certain texts later show that this was not the case.[15] Caliph Mu'āwiya (d. 680) was, in all probability, one of the first who had eunuchs in the royal palace. According to a chronicler named al-Mas'ūdī,[16] a group of these ghilmān was made up of slaves who worked for the caliphal cabinet. They were under the authority of Sardjūn, a freed slave. And these young, educated slaves were trained as secretaries to compile treatises of wisdom. These were put together in volumes on world history. Every day upon waking, the caliph would have these books brought to him, so that he could hear about kings and kingdoms of the past. Some eunuchs were responsible for reading these stories in order to entertain him and teach him good behavior.

Aside from these office assistants, Caliph Mu'āwiya also appreciated the company of young, attractive male slaves.[17] It appears that the number of ceremonial slaves grew considerably during the reign of his son Yazīd I

(d. 683). Arab sources who wrote about this prince and Shiite chroniclers in particular provided fragmented and often contradictory information. In general, their observations are so severe that it is difficult to trust them completely. They widely elaborate on Yazīd's weaknesses and mostly described him as a young, sadistic man who lived a life of debauchery. The chroniclers emphasized his tyranny and overindulgence. But they also wrote of his refined taste and love of pleasure, music, and erotic poetry. During his short reign, he emerged as an extravagant prince who was preoccupied with the satisfaction of his carnal desires. He enjoyed being surrounded by young, beautiful, and expensive eunuchs at all times. They came to every banquet and party. At this time, musical instruments were popular in Mecca and Medina, and singing and poetic jousts became widespread. This was also a period when artistic and literary groups were formed in the Hejaz, sponsored by wealthy city dwellers.[18]

Narrative sources give us one of the most comprehensive looks at the caliphal court through a series of vignettes. In a tradition given by al-Mas'ūdī,[19] eunuchs would wander freely in palace pavilions, and they served as intermediaries between the monarch, his wives, and his courtesans. Princess 'Atīka, Yazīd I's daughter and the wife of Caliph 'Abd al-Malik (d. 705), had many eunuchs of her own, and they took care of her living quarters. This same tradition shows us the central role played by eunuchs in the inner workings of the royal household. One day, the caliph admitted to one of his courtesans that he thought he had hurt his wife's feelings. In order to get back into her good graces and to calm her down, he asked the courtesan to intervene on his behalf.

Eunuchs and wet nurses went in to the queen's living quarters and succeeded in calming her nerves. Thanks to the slaves' and courtesans' intervention, the royal couple was able to reconcile their differences and, as we are told by al-Mas'ūdī (d. 956), a prolific writer in various disciplines, to give each other "passionate hugs."[20] To show his gratitude, the caliph gave his courtesan one thousand dinars, a group of slaves, and a large piece of land.

Still on the subject of eunuchs, Ibn 'Abd Rabbih, a panegyrist from Cordoba, wrote much praise for Prince 'Abd al-'Azīz (d. 720), and in his famous anthology, he boasted of the compassion the castrated slaves showed while mourning the loss of their master,[21] al-Walīd b. 'Abd al-Malik (d. 715).

Abbasid caliphs also enjoyed young slaves and cupbearers and spent large sums of money in order to purchase slaves. Judging from source documents, Caliph Harūn al-Rashīd (d. 809) owned a multitude of slaves. He was particularly fond of pleasure parties, where he had fun drinking and was surrounded by his wives, eunuchs, and musicians. His successor, al-Amīn (d. 813), allocated part of his fortune to the purchase of castrated slaves, which he enjoyed showing off. According to al-Mas'ūdī,[22] as soon as he acceded to the throne, al-Amīn quickly showed his appreciation for them. His passion for boys was so strong that he chose a eunuch named Kawthar as his favorite. His mother, Harūn al-Rashīd's wife, who was no doubt annoyed that her son neglected the empire for boys, decided to buy him some gracious and charming girls. She had their hair combed like boys and put turbans on their heads: "She had their bangs pulled back and their hair lifted up off their necks. The girls were then dressed in qabās, tunics, and belts that emphasized their waistlines." She then took them to her son and had them walk around him. He was so charmed and captivated by these disturbing creatures that he showed them off in public. This is why the tomboy style—inspired by young, female slaves with short hair, named *ghulāmiyyāt*, or tomboys[23]—spread to all social classes. The custom continued. Arab chronicles are full of stories showing that royal palaces and bourgeois homes were still full of beautiful slaves a century later. Referring to the life of Caliph al-Qāhir (d. 934), these texts describe him as an energetic and harsh monarch but also as someone who was impulsive and overcome by his passions. The authors paint the portrait of a court that exemplified the splendor and radiance of royal inner circles.

They describe the caliph as surrounded by his relatives, his cupbearers, and many enslaved young women who were "all the same size and looked like young male slaves. They were dressed in tunics, with a forelock on their foreheads and they wore their hair in braids and gold and silver belts." The author added: "When the Caliph lifted the cup to his mouth, I admired the pureness of its crystal, the brilliant color of the wine which sparkled. And I enjoyed the beauty of those young girls."[24]

In literary and historical sources concerning the reign of Caliph Harūn al-Rashīd, Queen Mother Zubayda Bint Dja'far was legendary. She singlehandedly owned more than a thousand slaves, whom writers at the time celebrated for their beauty.[25] The texts praise her wisdom and, above all, her political notoriety, which she gained while fighting to have her son al-Amīn named heir to the throne. They describe her as a very beautiful and clever woman who maintained privileged links with palace eunuchs. They also emphasize how much she hated the grand vizier and describe her close friendship with Yāsir,[26] her favorite eunuch. Because of his dedication and support, she was able to set up a network of followers determined to ruin the political ambitions of Vizier Yahya b. Khālid al-Barmakī. Her interference in governmental affairs left a long-lasting mark on caliphal history.

As far as daily life was concerned, a writer named Al-Djāhiz claims that castrated slaves could get married and have courtesans.[27] He also adds that women enjoyed them very much. This writer observes that women at the time took pleasure in having sex with eunuch men and appreciated the fact that they could not get pregnant from such encounters. The historian Ibn al-Athīr mentioned ʻAdūd al-Dawla (d. 983), a eunuch who was married to an Ethiopian slave.[28] In a passage about castrated slaves, al-Mas'ūdī wrote: "There have been a lot of discussions on castrated slaves. Some think there is a difference between those who have been mutilated by amputation and those by wrenching. Others claim that they are men when they are with men and women when they are with women. This idea is completely unfounded. The truth is the eunuch is still a man. Depriving him of a single organ is not enough to classify him in a hybrid gender. Not having a beard does not mean he is no longer part of the masculine gender . . , because the operation he underwent does not change who he is inside."[29]

This is probably why Caliph Mu'āwiya would only let old eunuchs into his harem, adds al-Mas'ūdī.[30] Yahya b. Khālid, vizier and palace-intendant, used to insist on having the harem doors locked at night. He would take the keys home with him and "put the Caliph's wives under surveillance. He forbade them from being waited on by the eunuch of their choice. This rule exasperated Zubayda, Caliph Harūn al-Rashīd's wife. One day, she found him and said, 'Prince of Believers, why does the palace intendant deprive me of my eunuchs' services and treat me as if he were royalty?'"[31]

Texts point out the presence of people who specialized in supplying castrated slaves in Medina and Mecca. Apparently, Caliph Hishām b. 'Abd al-Malik (d. 743) sent a decree to the governor of Medina ordering him to have young people who enjoyed debauchery mutilated to serve as an example.[32] This suggests that the Arabs knew about human mutilation procedures.[33] If the chronicles make reference to licensed torturers,[34] they also specify that some masters did not hesitate to mutilate their servants' bodies out of jealousy. However, it seems that most castration workshops were located outside the Islamic world.

Al-Djāhiz affirms that eunuchs were used by the Byzantines and Sabians as a religious institution.[35] Genitally mutilated children were intended to serve the church and temples. The same tradition also prevailed at Islamic holy sites. Nūr al-dīn (d. 1174), a Zengid Atabeg (governor), established a group of intendants made up of Slavic and Ethiopian eunuchs who worked in the mosque and sacred funeral chamber in Medina.[36] This pious institution continued afterward because Emir Saladin (d. 1193) decided to double the number of intendants. In his description of the Medina Mosque two centuries later, the traveler Ibn Battūta states that it was guarded by Abyssinian eunuchs who were richly adorned, beautiful, and elegant.[37] A grand eunuch called the *shaykh al-khuddām* was in charge of them, and he looked like a great emir.

The information given by al-Ya'qūbī and Hilāl al-Sābī sheds some light on another institution.[38] Young soldiers were born and raised outside the Arab world. Once their training was completed, they were obliged to avoid conflicts of interest that troubled Arab lands. They had to prove an unwavering commitment and an undying loyalty to the leader who put them under his command. Serving with self-sacrifice and obeying faithfully were these young slaves' unrelenting duties. Pulled from their homelands and their families, they were bound to a life of devotion to satisfy their masters and their ambitions for power. These troops were privately bought by Muslim leaders and were part of a group of reservists. The longevity of the system required a large turnover. Merchants were responsible for satisfying the palace's needs in terms of human merchandise, and they played the central role in this regard.

These young slaves would undergo training to improve their skills and learn the rudiments of their professions—all the better because the slave–civil servant was considered to be a jewel in the state's crown and a reflection of the grandeur of its leader. This training was designed to develop their capacities and talents before fine-tuning their skills. The prerequisites to be admitted into this kind of training were based, in principle, on two criteria: being born outside the Arab world and belonging to a eunuch contingent, some of the men having been castrated. Nizām al-Mulk (d. 1092), a famous vizier of Saljūkīd Sultans Alp Arslān and his son Malik Shāh, claimed this group of slaves was unique because they knew how to sabotage the status quo and would use strategies to gain access to decision-making bodies. Armed with solid training and possessing an acute perception of power distribution rules, they managed to adapt to changing circumstances with each power struggle.[39]

The same phenomenon existed in western Muslim provinces. Slave eunuchs sent to work in the palace in Andalusia were called fityān or ghilmān.[40] Some of them succeeded in controlling the reins of power and in founding small, local dynasties. Fityān were often placed under the authority of two superior officers who likely had been slaves themselves and brought up as great eunuchs. In North Africa, almost all monarchs had owned black guards, called *'abīd*, since the time of the Aghlabides. In addition to these African slaves, there were also troops from eastern and central Europe and Russia. Under the Aghlabid dynasty, the militias were led by black or Slavic generals. The Fatimid's arrival increased the number of Slavic slaves considerably.

Constant turmoil and threats of a major revolt in particular strengthened the Fatimidleaders' desire to have an army made up of foreign slaves capable of staying out of alliances with Arab and Berber forces. According to al-Maqrīzī,[41] Caliph al-Mu'izz li-Dīn-Allah (d. 975) learned how to speak the languages and dialects of his Slavic, Greek, and Sudanese slaves. During his reign, some domestic slaves held the positions of chamberlain and vizier.[42]

It was rare to see a slave attain supreme power, but Mudjāhid is an example of a slave who seized power in the province of Denia and the Balearic Islands and succeeded in declaring his autonomy.[43] His was not an isolated case. Egyptian history during the Tulunid, Ikhshidid, and Mamlūk dynasties as well as the Fatimid tradition concerning the political and military accomplishments of two famous slave eunuchs named Djawdhar and Djawhar al-Siqillī (d. 991)[44] represent a unique phenomenon whose protagonists were exceptionally rare men. Djawhar al-Siqillī, a eunuch of Sicilian or Greek origin who belonged to Caliph al-Mansūr, became a great general of the Fatimid army and proved that he was the most talented administrator the Fatimids ever had. In 969, he conquered Egypt and founded a new capital, Cairo. During four years, he stayed in power as the sole prince regent of Egypt.

Al-Ikhshīd (d. 946),[45] who would follow in his predecessor Ibn Tūlūn's footsteps, was the grandson of a Turkish slave who went to Iraq during the reign of al-Mu'tasim. In addition to his ghilmān troops, Al-Ikhshīd possessed a castrated Nubian slave named Abū al-Misk Kāfūr.[46] This slave was bought in 924–925 when he was ten years old for the meager sum of eighteen dinars. He was given an outstanding education and studied several fields of knowledge. After being in charge of the ablution fountain and then being named tutor for his master's sons, he quickly rose to become an adviser and eventually minister.[47]

After his master, Muhammad ibn Tughdj al-Ikhshīd, died, a eunuch of Nubian descent named Abū al-Misk Kāfūr al-Ikhshīdī (d. 968) ruled Egypt, which regained its brilliance and splendor during the twenty-two years of his reign. In the beginning (in 946), he was a regent, and he quickly became an absolute monarch. The government of Kafūr is generally regarded as the apogee of Ikhshīdī's power.

His court became a meeting place for talented men seeking wealth and power. They thought he personified the ideal monarch: a generous and noble patron. Because he wanted Kafūr to name him governor of Sidon in present-day Syria, al-Mutanabbī, the greatest Arab panegyric, dedicated plays to him that praised his magnificence. After his dreams went up in smoke, al-Mutanabbī wrote a violent satire mocking Kafūr's gloominess and powerlessness.[48]

There are numerous other examples of political and social successes among eunuchs. Many tales found in Arab chronicles show how slaves gained prestigious positions, and they confirm the importance of this phenomenon of the eunuch. Early on, some top subaltern officers decided to follow their masters' example and put together their own slave battalions. Their interference in succession scandals and their ethnic and political rivalries caused numerous officers to be put to death on multiple occasions. But caliphs ended up being powerless to stop their threat completely. These slaves quickly realized the importance of their political and social roles. Well before the Mamlūk dynasty was clearly established, this awareness would leave its mark on the foundations of the exercise and management of power in the Muslim world.

Unlike those servants who were crushed by difficult living and working conditions, the ceremonial slaves could enjoy high positions. These differing destinies raise questions about the criteria that normally determined the status of servant. What really was the status of slaves in the Islamic world? Were these elite servants exceptional, or did they express a particular characteristic of slavery in Arab-Muslim society as compared to other nations?

It would be difficult to give a positive reply, particularly because the number of the slaves' statuses and the variety of their economic and social conditions prevent us from imagining a context identical to all the categories of slaves in the Muslim countries.

Notes

1. Ibn Manzūr, *Lisān-l-'Arab* (Beirut: Dār Ihiyā' al-Turāth al-'Arabī, 1992), 4:41–42.

2. Al-Djāhiz, *Kitāb al-Hayawān*, ed. A. S. Hārūn (Beirut: Dār Ihiyā' al-Turāth al-'Arabī, 1969), 1:106–8, 111, 112–14, 116–29.

3. Ibid., 1:123.

4. Ibid., 1:129, 166.

5. Al-Maqrīzī, *Itti'āz al-Hunafā' biakhbār al-Aimma al-Fatimiyyīn* (Cairo: al-Hay'a al-'Amma Liqusūr al-Thaqāfa, 1967), 1:100.

6. Al-Zereklī, *Al-A'lām* (Beirut: Dār El-'Ilm Lilmalāyyīn, 1982), 2:328.

7. D. Ayalon, "The Mamluks: The Mainstay of Islam's Military Might," in *Slavery in the Islamic Middle East*, ed. Shaun E. Marmon (Princeton, N.J.: Princeton University Press 1998), 89–117; D. Ayalon, "Aspects of the Mamlūk Phenomenon," in *Der Islam* 53–54 (1976–77): 196–225 and 1–32; D. Ayalon, "The Eunuchs in the Mamlūk Sultanate," in *Studies in Memory of Gaston Wiet*, ed. Myriam Rosen-Ayalon (Jerusalem: Institute of Asian and African Studies, Hebrew University of Jerusalem, 1977), 267–95; D. Ayalon, "The Military Reforms of the Caliph al-Mu'tasim—Their Background and Consequences," in D. Ayalon, *Islam and the Abode of War* (London: Variorum Reprints, 1994); J. L. Bacharach, "African Military Slaves in the Medieval Middle East: The Cases of Iraq (869–955) and Egypt (868–1171)," *International Journal of Middle East Studies* (hereafter cited as *IJMES*) 13, no. 4 (1981): 471–95; C. E. Bosworth, "Armies of the Prophet," in *Islam and the Arab World*, ed. B. Lewis (New York:

Alfred A. Knopf, 1976), 201–12; P. Crone, *Slaves on Horses: The Evolution of the Islamic Polity* (Cambridge: Cambridge University Press, 1980); J. Dakhlia, "Les eunuques-soldats: Repères maghrébins et histoire islamique," in *D'esclaves à soldats: Miliciens et soldats d'origine servile* XIIIe–XXIe *siècles*, ed. C. Bernard and A. Stella (Paris: l'Harmattan, 2006), 53–66; S. Denoix, "La servilité, une condition nécessaire pour devenir prince: Les Mamlūks (Egypte, Syrie, 1250–1517)," in Bernard and Stella, *D'esclaves à soldats*, 38–52; M. Meouac, "Slaves, noirs et affranchis dans les armées fatimides d'Ifriqiya," in Bernard and Stella, *D'esclaves à soldats*, 15–37; P. G. Forand, *The Development of Military Slavery under the Abbasid Caliphs of the Ninth Century A.D. (Third Century A.H.), with Special Reference to the Reigns of Mu'tasim and Mu'tamid* (Princeton, N.J.: Princeton University Press, 1962); "The Relation of the Slave and the Client to the Master or Patron in the Medieval Islam," *IJMES* 2 (1971): 59–66; Osman S. A. Ismail, "Mu'tasim and the Turks," *Bulletin of the School of Oriental and African Studies* 29 (1966): 12–24; B. Lewis, *Race and Slavery in the Middle East* (Oxford: Oxford University Press, 1990); Huns Muller, "Zur Erforschung des islamischer Sklavenwesens," *Zeitschrift des Deutschen morgenländischen Gesellschaft*, suppl. 1 (1969): 611–22; F. Rosenthal, *The Muslim Concept of Freedom prior to the Nineteenth Century* (Leiden: E. J. Brill, 1960); Shaun E. Marmon, "Domestic Slavery in the Mamluk Empire: A Preliminary Sketch," in *Slavery in the Islamic Middle East*, ed. S. Marmon (Princeton, N.J.: Markus Wienner Publishers, 1999), 1–23; M. A. Shaban, *Islamic History: A New Interpretation* (Cambridge: Cambridge University Press, 1976); H. Yūsuf Fadl, *The Arab and the Sudan from the Seventh to the Early Sixteenth Century* (Edinburgh: Edinburgh University Press, 1967).

8. Al-Djāhiz, "Kitāb Mufākharat al-Djawārī wa-l-Ghilmān," in *Rasā'il al-Djāhiz*, ed. A. S. Harūn (Cairo: al-Matb'a al-'Arabiyya al-Hadītha, 1979), 164, 86–137; Al-Djāhiz, "Kitāb al-Qiyān," in Harūn, *Rasā'il al-Djāhiz*, 138–82; S. D. Goitein, "Slaves and Slave Girls in Cairo Geniza Records," *Arabica* 4, no. 1 (1962): 1–20; A. Cheikh Moussa, "Jāhiz et les eunuques ou la confusion du même et de l'autre," *Arabica* 24, no. 2 (1982): 184–214; A. Cheikh Moussa, "Figures de l'esclave chanteuse," in *Figures de l'esclave au Moyen-Âge et dans le monde moderne*, ed. H. Bresc (Paris: l'Harmattan, 1996), 31–78.

9. Ibn 'Asâkir, *Târikh madīnat Dimashq*, vol. 5, ed. S. al-Dīn. al-Munajjid (Damascus: Dār Ibn Kāthīr, 1914), 396; H. H. 'Abd al-Wahāb, *Waraqāt*, ed. al-Manār (Tunis: Maktabat al-Manār, 1965), 2:196.

10. M. Talbi, *L'emirat aghlabide* (Paris: Adrien-Maisonneuve, 1966), 306.

11. Ibn 'Idhārī, *al-Bayān al-Mughrib*, ed. E. Levi-Provençal (Beirut: Dār al-Thaqāfa, 1983), 1:162.

12. Al-Nuwayrī, "Conquête de l'Ifrikiya par les Musulmans," in *Appendice à l'histoire des Berbères et des dynasties musulmanes de l'Afrique septentrionale*, ed. Ibn Khaldūn, trans. Par de Slane and P. Casanova (Paris: P. Geuthner S. A., 1968), 1:446; Talbi, *Emirat aghlabide*, 690.

13. Nizām al-Mulk, *Traité de gouvernement*, trans. Ch. Schefer (Paris: Sindbad, 1984), 133–34.
14. Ibid.
15. Al-Tabarī, *Tārīkh al-Umama wa-l-Mulūk* (Beirut: Dār al-Kutub, 1991), 3:249.
16. Al-Mas'ūdī, *Murūdj al-Dhahab* (Beirut: Dār al-Fikr, 1973), 3:40–41.
17. Al-Tawhīdī, *al-Basā'ir wa-l-Ddhakhā'ir* (Damascus: Dār al-Fikr, 1964), 2:15.
18. Al-Isfahānī, *Kitāb al-Aghānī*, vol. 1 (Cairo: al-Hay'a al-Misriyya al-'Āmma lil-kitāb, 1992).
19. Al-Mas'ūdī, *Murūdj al-Dhahab*, 3:125–26.
20. Ibid.
21. Ibn 'Abd Rabbih, *al-'Iqd al-Farīd* (Beirut: Dār Sādir, 2001), 3:183.
22. Al-Mas'ūdī, *Murūdj al-Dhahab*, 4:318.
23. Ibid.
24. Ibid.
25. Al-Isfahānī, *Kitāb al-Aghānī* (Cairo: al-Hay'a al-Misriyya al-'Āmma lil-kitāb, 1992), 10:172.
26. Al-Mas'ūdī, *Murūdj al-Dhahab*, 3:386.
27. Ibid., 3:123, 166–67.
28. Ibn al-Athīr, *al-Kāmil fi-l-Tārīkh* (Leiden: Ed. Tornberg, 1851–76), 11:39.
29. Al-Mas'ūdī, *Murūdj al-Dhahab*, 4:247.
30. Ibid.
31. Ibid., 3:386.
32. Ibid., 1:121–22.
33. Ibid.
34. Al-Maqrīzī, *al-Khitat al-Maqrīziyya*, 3:222–23.
35. Al-Djāhiz, "Kitāb Mufākharat," 1:124, 125.
36. Ibn Djubayr, *Rihla* (Beirut: Dār Sadir, 1989), 168–72; N. Elisséeff, *Nūr al-Dīn: Un grand prince musulman de Syrie au temps des Croisades* (511–569/1118–1174) (Damascus: Adrien Maisonneuve, 1967), 2:559.
37. Ibn Battūta, *Voyages*, trans. C. Defremy and B. R. Sanguinetti, (Paris: La Découverte, 1990), 1:269.
38. Hilāl al-Sābī, *Rusūm Dār al-khilāfa*, 8, 11–17.
39. Nizām al-Mulk, *Traité de gouvernement, Siyast-Name*, trans. Française de Ch. Schfer (Paris: Sindbad, 1984), 133, 177–95.
40. Ibn Hawqal, *Kitāb Sūrat al-Ard* (Leiden: Brill, 1967), 1:97, 110.
41. Al-Maqrīzī, *al-Khitat al-Maqrīziyya*, 2:164, 166.
42. Ibid.
43. Lévi-Provençal, *Histoire de l'Espagne musulmane* (Paris: Maisonneuve et Larose, 1999), 2:279, 326, 337.
44. Al-Maqrīzī, *al-Khitat al-Maqrīziyya*, 2:164, 167.

45. Ibid., 2:127–28.

46. Ibn Saʿīd al-Andalusī, *al-Mughrib fi Huliyyi al-Maghrib*, ed. Z. M. Hasan and Sh. Dayf (Cairo, 2003), 199–201; al-Maqrīzī, *al-Khitat al-Maqrīziyy*, 3:41–42.

47. Al-Maqrīzī, *al-Khitat al-Maqrīziyya*, 3:41.

48. Ibid.

LEGACIES

Discourse, Dishonor, and Labor

24

SLAVES, COOLIES, AND GARRISON WHORES

A Colonial Discourse of "Unfreedom" in the Dutch East Indies

Joost Coté

This chapter approaches the theme of sex, power, and slavery from the perspective of discourse to focus on the function of the powerful metaphor contributed by the antislavery campaign in legitimating the more general condition of "unfreedom" that was colonialism. More specifically, it locates the image of the "unfree nyai/concubine/'sex slave'" in an evolving discourse on European identity in the Dutch East Indies. I will argue that the discourse on "her" condition had its origins in earlier concerns and formed part of a broader discourse on colonial identity.

Approaching the historical condition of slavery in this way is not to downplay the tragedy of the lived human condition of slavery and its equivalent conditions. It is a response to what Suzanne Miers has noted as the recent exponential expansion in the understanding of what constitutes slavery, on the one hand, and a recognition that, historically, the politics of defining slavery has played a central role in disguising its existence, on the other.[1] This chapter explores the genealogy of the nyai/concubine/sex slave image to trace the way in which various colonial political interests at various moments defined specific colonial relationships as forms of unfreedom and linked this to their own political or self-interested agendas for colonial policy reform. The critical delineation of certain kinds of colonial relationships at certain times as slavery was motivated by, and intended as, a critical reflection upon the quality of European civilization as manifested in the colony. Further, I will argue that over time, periodic campaigns against aspects of colonial policy typically recycled motifs, language, and images to exploit the emotive image of enslavement as a central trope. In the long gestation of a "reformist discourse" in the Dutch East Indies during the nineteenth century, concern with concubinage and the enslavement of women in traditional societies can best be represented as the final stage in the process of attempting to modernize East Indies colonial society, rather than as an altruistic campaign against the condition of unfreedom of the colonized native.

The chapter is divided into three parts: an overview of the colonial discourse on colonial labor relations to 1900; an examination of the late nineteenth-century concern with concubinage and "sex slavery"; and the extension of this internal colonial critique outward to focus on "the unfreedom of tradition" in the previously uncolonized parts of the archipelago after 1900.

A Discourse on Colonial Labor Relations

Slavery

European society in the days of the Dutch East Indies Trading Company, the VOC, differed little from that of the indigenous slave-owning and slave-trading states scattered throughout the archipelago with which the company traded and treated.[2] After the VOC's demise in 1796, when its possessions reverted to the Dutch state, attempts were made to curb the indigenous trade in slaves in the archipelago. Slavery, however, was not abolished either in colonial precincts or in the archipelago at large, although a series of legal constraints were implemented on the maintenance of slaves by Europeans.

In the nineteenth-century Dutch colony, abolition was a derivative debate.[3] Although considered by a small vocal group within the Dutch colony as a significant moral issue, it was no longer viewed, even by abolitionists, as an issue that seriously impinged on a colonial economy. The leading Dutch abolitionist, Baron R. W. van Hoevëll—who penned the famous antislavery pamphlet *De emancipatie der slaven in Nederlandsch-Indië*

(1848), credited with driving the antislavery debate in the Netherlands—considered slavery a despicable human condition in which the individual "lacks any civil rights, is a creature without nationality or fatherland, . . . has absolutely no will of his own; . . . is and remains . . . not a person but a thing, an object that one buys and that the owner may use as he will."[4]

His more telling argument, however, was far more pragmatic: that the institution of slavery was also anachronistic. He pointed out that as early as 1825, an inquiry had already concluded that "slaves are almost exclusively used in domestic service, which could be undertaken just as well, and no doubt better, by free servants whose number is increasing daily; that they are only rarely employed in agriculture or in factories; that in these cases they could be readily replaced by hirelings who would cost those involved if not less then certainly not much more than slaves, so that the ownership of slaves can be seen as being no more than an extravagant show of wealth."[5] Self-exiled from the Indies in 1850,[6] van Hoevëll continued his antislavery campaign via his influential Liberal journal for colonial reform, *Tijdschrift voor Nederlandsch Indië* (*TNI*), in which he maintained a relentless attack on conservative colonial policy, including the continued tolerance of slavery by European colonial society. In numerous articles, van Hoevëll played on a sense of national shame, embarrassment generated by international comparison, as a powerful incentive to abolish slavery.[7] Elected to a reformed Dutch parliament, he effectively connected his colonially generated politics with the broader metropolitan political Liberal discourse, urging the end of a conservative colonial policy of government monopoly of the economy, the so-called *cultuurstelsel*, a system of compulsory cultivation by Indigenous labor of commercial crops for export.[8]

By midcentury, there was little public evidence of slavery in European public life—it had largely been moved behind closed doors. However, two key phenomena continued to provide the empirical anchors for an antislavery rhetoric after 1848: the (irregular) practice of public slave auctions and public suspicion about the mistreatment of slaves by the Chinese (and Arabs) who, according to van Hoevëll, were "the main owners of slaves these days."[9] By then, the former practice constituted a public embarrassment to a respectable urban public,[10] and the latter was seen to taint the benign behavior of "respectable" European slave owners by association with the practice of non-Europeans within the domain of the colonial environment. Van Hoevëll himself liberally played on this more emotive element in his antislavery polemic, arguing that the colonial state was condoning "Chinese immorality" by its continued toleration of slavery. Although he admitted that it was "almost impossible to penetrate the domestic environment of the Chinese and therefore extremely difficult to ascertain the fate of their slaves in any detail,"[11] he was able to paint a quite lurid image of Chinese behavior. In one of several instances, van Hoevëll described a case "well-known amongst inhabitants of Batavia that in 183x [*sic*] a female slave who was part of deceased estate was bought by an aging, wealthy Chinese for an unheard of large amount of money and that that unfortunate creature had endured extreme hunger for two days before finally giving herself to him. The body of the slave belongs solely to the slave owner and is beholden to his will."[12] How many slaves were actually maintained by Europeans at that time remains unclear, but van Hoevëll's statistics, calculated on the basis of the "slave tax" of *f*2.50 a head that in 1842 raised *f*964,834, indicates there were (at least) over 10,000 registered slaves owned in colonial society, 5,686 of whom were in Java.[13] The tax, initially introduced as an attempt to discourage slave ownership and to promote its gradual disappearance, according to abolitionists now merely created a financial disincentive to the government to abolish slavery.

The Cultuurstelsel

The cultuurstelsel and the arguments of its opponents have been widely discussed,[14] but in reviewing the contemporary nineteenth-century debate as it was conducted in van Hoevëll's Liberal journal, *Tijdschrift van Nederlandsch Indië*, three arguments underpinning the anticultuurstelsel lobby can be defined. These were specifically adapted from—or alluded to—antislavery discourse in their case against "unfree labor." They can be briefly summarized as follows: that forced (unfree) labor was unproductive, that free labor provided the only incentive for moral and intellectual (even physical) development of the native people,[15] and that condoning forced labor reflected on the moral integrity of the Dutch nation.[16] Putting aside the evident self-interest in the Liberal critique of the government monopoly of investment in and export from the colony, the latter two arguments provided the basis for the ongoing recycling of a reformist discourse.

Whatever its authenticity, the argument positing responsibility for native welfare as the moral duty of the Dutch nation assumed a discourse of universal values: the universality of human nature and a human right to liberty as well as the universality of human self-interest as a motive to self-improvement. Representing key elements of a Liberal discourse, these arguments also had a pragmatic significance for a platform promoting free enterprise. As such, the discourse was largely framed in secular, liberal terms rather than religious ones.[17] Colonial critics of the government's monopoly claimed to speak on behalf of the Javanese peasant who, assumed to be no different than the Dutch farmer or Italian peasant, would prefer, they said, to sell his labor freely than to be forced to work under compulsory, unpaid labor contracts: "All that is necessary is that they [Javanese] have personal freedom and that their human labour is released, in the fullest sense, from the bonds of the system of forced delivery and labour that has enslaved it."[18]

This argument became muddied, however, by the force of the (conservative) counterargument, which held that "the natives" had not developed sufficiently to be capable of being free in a modern sense—to respond according to the universal motivations of self-interest ascribed to them by critics. Defenders of the status quo argued that in coercing labor, the cultuurstelsel provided the necessary training for a population trapped in tradition. The labor system was therefore not akin to slavery in any sense but an example of benign colonialism, and for the indigenous people, it provided a necessary stage in their (accelerated) evolutionary development. It was a system of "guided production," which, its defenders argued, was educative and thus an expression of colonial care.[19] In response, opponents of the cultuurstelsel—epitomized by the colonial official E. Douwes Dekker (whose 1860 book, *Max Havelaar: or, The Coffee Auctions of the Nederlandsche Handelsmaatschappij*, popularized the notion of colonialism as a civilizing mission)[20]—argued the scheme was oppressive and exploitative and no better than and indeed a facilitator of the arbitrary exploitation practices of traditional feudal overlords and thus a moral stain on the Dutch nation. Later, Douwes Dekker argued just as vehemently against free labor: paternalistic colonialism needed to be reformed and intensified, not abolished.[21]

Another target of criticism but seemingly less immediately motivated by self-interest was the system of compulsory *herendiensten* (corvée labor), which obligated villagers to perform unpaid labor on public works and other unpaid *gemeenten* (community) or *desa* (village) duties. Like compulsory labor under the cultuurstelsel, herendiensten was also justified by government as "payment in kind" of land taxes, but it continued well after the demise of the former. Lumping both forms of coerced labor together, one contributor to the *TNI* declared: "The herendiensten, as a result of which the Javanese is not master of his time and labour; [and] the compulsory production [of agricultural exports], as a result of which the Javanese is not master over his production—see there, the existence of slavery in Java."[22] Echoing the conclusions of Douwes Dekker's exposé of the cultuurstelsel, the writer added that these practices, which delivered "great profits" to the country, equated the Netherlands with the worst of feudal potentates.

Slavery-like conditions had not declined with the decline and formal abolition of slavery. By the second half of the nineteenth century, unfree labor had, in fact, increased, as had the volume of critical political discourse directed at it. If actual slavery was no longer an issue of economic significance and if it was portrayed as being characteristic of the now discredited VOC era—that is, as belonging to the old days and as an embarrassment to modern society—and associated with the immoral practices of non-Christian, non-European elements, the polemic associated with slavery remained. It was now regularly recycled in the campaign by midcentury, laissez-faire Liberal critics of the cultuurstelsel. But it also entered the vocabulary of a new generation of "progressive Liberals" who directed their invective against the so-called free labor system that had largely replaced it after the formal abolition of the cultuurstelsel in 1870.

Free Labor

At its height, between 1840 and 1860, the cultuurstelsel involved the employment in compulsory labor of up to 72.5 percent of Java's agricultural population, in the production and export of sugar, tobacco, coffee, tea, and indigo.[23] The practices and colonial attitudes this system produced, unsurprisingly, continued to shape the subsequent free labor market operated by the privately owned sugar factories,[24] as well as the new "corporate" plantations in Sumatra in the latter part of the nineteenth century.[25] In response, a new generation of "small *l*" (progressive) liberals had begun to argue not for the withdrawal of the state but for the expansion of the state's role in protecting and advancing the interests of the native citizen. By the late 1860s, as Siep Stuurman shows for the Dutch political arena more generally, laissez-faire liberalism, which had campaigned against both slavery and the cultuurstelsel, was now in decline, and in its place emerged a progressive liberalism that was more attuned to policies of social reform.[26]

The "new politics," as Douwes Dekker had foreshadowed, argued for greater government intervention and placed more emphasis on colonialism's civilizing mission. This change had become evident in the colony toward the end of the century in the writing of journalist and newspaper editor Pieter Brooshooft.[27] In a major report in 1888,[28] written in the midst of the economic depression induced by a combination of falling agricultural prices and devastating plant diseases, Brooshooft defined a new version of a discourse on unfreedom. He argued that the financial servitude imposed by the weight of taxation as well as the continuing demand for unpaid work stole from the Javanese peasant (assumed to be a male worker) both the profits of his labor and the time available for him to labor in his own interests. This was, he argued, merely another manifestation of the former cultuurstelsel it had replaced. These inordinate impositions on the population contrasted, he declared, with the "first [duty] a [modern] government is obliged to undertake, in which any state [should] find the justification for its existence: the maintenance of public order and security."[29] The Javanese, Brooshooft argued, were enslaved by the "unmodern" operations of an anachronistic state.

With the growth in both the number and the circulation of colonial newspapers and company-owned sugar and tobacco plantations, specific employment practices under the wage labor regimes came under increased scrutiny. Operating largely beyond the ken of a metropolitan public, the indentured labor schemes—the so-called coolie-contract system—adopted by plantation managers[30] or the burdensome village contracts arranged by sugar factory owners[31] largely replicated the worst excesses of the early years of the cultuurstelsel. The conditions experienced by plantation workers, relocated far from their homelands and practically isolated on their employers' estates, were considerably worse. In 1902, a local lawyer, J. van den Brand, revealed in a sensational exposé, a pamphlet entitled *De Millioenen van Deli*, how indentured laborers were treated "little better than slaves." An official government investigation confirmed the allegations, and in a report that was subsequently suppressed by the Dutch parliament, it confirmed a large number of cases of *onwettige vrijheidsberooving*—"illegal denial of freedom"—lack of hospital and medical facilities, underpayment and illegal withholding of payments, and numerous other practices that dehumanized the conditions of the "freely contracted" migrant laborer.[32] It found conditions "utterly in conflict with the first principles of morality and civilisation" due to "the vicious relationship . . . that exists between employer and contract worker."[33]

It can be concluded from this brief sketch of colonial labor that in the nineteenth century, a discourse on the unfreedom of the native had become both more detailed and more generalized in scope, and its moral underpinnings were increasingly firmed up by reference to universal principles the iteration of which had become more than merely rhetorical. Its empirical basis had come to delve more intimately into the conditions of daily life, and its conclusions were disseminated more widely and rapidly by modern media. Though this was still a minority view, more frequent exposés of labor conditions provided the kind of sensationalism that generated public indignation, not only in metropolitan Europe but also in the colony itself. Increasingly also, the discourse came to infuse a critique of colonial domestic life. Here, too, the institution of domestic service, the free labor of domestic servants that had now replaced domestic slaves, came under similar critical review.[34] Ever more urgent, however, under a burgeoning Dutch denominational politics was the concern expressed about the sexual exploitation of native women and the conditions under which the next generation of colonials was being raised.[35]

Gendering Slavery

Concubinage and the Colonial State

Throughout the debate on the various colonial coercive labor regimes, the implication had been that what was at issue was the unfreedom of the male worker. The argument was largely ungendered, as its primary drivers had been economic and Liberal.[36] But as the 1902 van den Brand exposé made clear, unfree labor practices had a specific impact on women. Ultimately, he implied, the "smooth operation" of this system of colonial plantation capitalism depended upon practices of prostitution. Though largely conducted by indigenous or Chinese *mandurs* (overseers), it was nevertheless condoned by Dutch and foreign plantation managers, said van den Brand in quoting one manager, on the grounds that "after all, they [native women] are all whores by nature."[37]

By the same reasoning, of course, the survival of the colonial regime had always depended on the role played by women: as slaves, coworkers, childbearers, and concubines.[38] Once again, however, the persuasive force of this critique was what it implied about Dutch culture overseas. By the end of the nineteenth century, the discursive focus of the critique increasingly shifted from the condition of the (male) native worker as being the litmus test of European civilization to a more sophisticated reformist argument that now measured the state of civilization in the colony by the condition of women and on the more intimate issue of the quality of family life. By the turn of the twentieth century, this was extended to include the condition of native women and the native family in indigenous societies under colonial care.[39]

Even more than the colonial labor institutions of slavery, the cultuurstelsel and indentured labor, the very fabric of colonial society had, in fact, been constructed by the "institution of concubinage."[40] Officially, concubinage had been long condoned by the colonial regime, but it too now came under scrutiny. By the end of the century, it came to be seen as damaging to the prestige, quality, and indeed security of colonial society. The results of the "inappropriate" and unequal (sexual) relations were seen to manifest themselves physically and psychologically in the demoralized condition of that part of European society most directly associated with the native, that is, the mixed-race community that typically constituted a European pauper class in every colonial city. Although the issue had been addressed sporadically throughout the 1800s, a series of reports at the turn of the twentieth century now came to define the *concubinaat* (literally, the state of concubinage) as the core cause of the decline in the moral status of the colonial European community and a danger to state security.[41]

"Garrison concubinage" raised particular concerns.[42] It was evidently extensive, and it resulted in an overwhelming number of "natural" or out-of-wedlock births, in contrast to children born in wedlock—in 1889, the figure was 2,238 compared to 215 "legitimate" children.[43] If the problem appeared more visible in the garrison towns, this was probably only because the situation there was more concentrated and easier to statistically verify: it was, however, only part of a widespread phenomenon.[44] Nevertheless, as one influential contributor to the investigation, the evangelical missionary and garrison reformer Johannes van der Steur,[45] argued, the *huishoud-stelsel* (the traditional domestic arrangements of European men) that involved the temporary maintenance of native women as *huishoudsters* (housekeepers), involved a practice only a little better than prostitution. Van der Steur, whose fame came to rest on establishing an orphanage for the children of such partnerships, made no secret of his moral judgment of these mothers. But he was more concerned about their offspring, who constituted "the most dangerous element within the category of *onbeschaafde* [uncivilized] paupers."[46] For van der Steur, the essence of the problem was social, although it ultimately threatened colonial security. He reasoned that the existing colonial structures failed to adequately ensure a differentiation between European and native society, thus endangering the standing of the former and the quality of Europeanness when "the many wandering European children who, although legally categorised as Native, have been more or less raised as Europeans and later go around dressed as such, use their position to undertake all kinds of bad practices."[47]

The problematic space between colonizer and colonized that for most of a century had already been the standard by which European prestige was measured was now invested with further ethical and increasingly also racist considerations whose effect was to more thoroughly separate the two, both physically and metaphorically. Driven in large part by the morally charged denominational rhetoric of the late nineteenth-century Netherlands,[48] the new discourse was transported to the colony via media, newly arrived civil servants, and migrants. It shaped and broadened a public discourse concerning the quality of the colonial European community, central to which, as always, was the native question—the place the native should occupy in a colonial society.[49] Although the focus had changed as, one by one, target issues had been addressed, the colonial debate continued to be couched, as it had been for half a century, in terms of contrasting what was civilized or modern with what was styled as conservative or colonialist and now increasingly considered immoral.

In relation to slavery and the cultuurstelsel, the argument that illiberal practices damaged European prestige had been directed primarily at the colonial regime itself, since almost all Europeans were in government employ. But progressively, the focus of the argument had moved toward the need to reform private behavior. As the European community expanded with an increase in migration, the problematic morality of the colonial European resident now became a matter of concern.[50] This latest turn in the discourse was encapsulated in what its proponents referred to as an "ethical colonial policy."[51] It implied that even the public institutions were now to be imbued with a degree of morality and, in particular, a moral responsibility for the welfare of the members of society under their care. As this debate passed from a critique of the system to an attempt to reform its moral underpinnings, the discourse again oscillated between deploring the unfree circumstances of the native and the condition, or *mentalité*, of the colonial European community—between placing blame on those who created the situation and on the moral defectiveness of its victims.

As with earlier debates concerning the colonial institutions of slavery, cultuurstelsel, and herendiensten, here, too, significant colonial interests attempted to maintain an institution that "modernizers" now considered unacceptable. In relation to the huishoud-stelsel in garrisons, some argued that abolishing it would increase expenses in providing accommodations and widow and orphan pensions; it would make the soldiers' lives even more uncivilized; or it would increase soldiers' recourse to prostitutes, which would lead to a rise in venereal disease and thus medical expenses and loss of service. Experienced generals argued that depriving soldiers of their women would result in general unruliness among the troops; further, if a soldier was responsible for a "real wife," this would sap his fighting spirit, since "having divided loyalties and a more cultivated nature, he would have more reason in the hour of danger, to allow his head to work more than his heart, compared to the less cultured soldier."[52]

Those reflecting the more explicitly moral mood of the Dutch electorate tended to base their criticism on an abstraction—the concubinaat—according to which all native women were castigated as garrison whores. But those who knew the situation viewed these women as "exercising a positive influence on the soldiers they served." Such a woman offered some compensation for the sparseness of garrison life and comfort to the returned fighter, and her *eigenaardige levensopvattingen en karakter* (particular character and attitude to life) and the loyalty she showed to her man made her ideally suited to her role.[53] In the words of Lt. Gen. (ret.) de Rochemot, she was neither *bijzit* (concubine) nor prostitute but a member of

> a class of woman which is unknown in our fatherland. It is constituted by Nyais. A Nyai is the housekeeper of a European and is at the same time his *maintenée* [mistress]. Nyais are numerous and are to be found in all classes of our Indo-European society. Not only do the soldiers in garrisons, but also generals and other officers, and also governors of provinces, residents, [department] heads and other colonial officials normally have, when they are not married, a nyai. Both in the Netherlands and in our colony one can find many important and celebrated people born of a nyai. . . . [I] have regarded the women of the garrisons during the 24 years, always with a sense of admiration for their selfless, sacrificial attachment to their masters. I say masters, because the Nyai is in fact the servant of the man with whom she lives. I have also regarded them during battle, on the battle field against the enemy, during tiring marches, on bivouac, in the ambulance. . . . It speaks to the heart of the European soldier in the East Indies whose unenviable lot is not a little alleviated by the Nyai. The Nyai knows how to bring some comfort to his loneliness. The Nyai scatters flowers on his life's journey.[54]

Among those spearheading public concern and reflecting the "new morality," not surprisingly, were such morally charged organizations as the Vereeniging tot Bevodering der Zedelijkheid in the Nederlandsche Overzeesche Bezittingen (Society for the Promotion of Moral Standards in the Dutch Colonies) and the Nederlandsche Vereeniging tegen Prostitutie (Netherlands Society against Prostitution).[55] These two organizations initiated a private "investigation into the condition of the Netherlands-Indies army seen from a moral perspective," conducted, it was claimed, according to rigorous modern scientific methods, employing extensive surveys and questionnaires and garnering responses from all levels of the armed service.[56] Their report represented the eighteen thousand–strong

European male element of the colonial army, not as demoralized "Indos" but as "mostly fine upstanding Dutch boys at the peak of their lives" and "fight[ing] under the banner of the flag of the fatherland." In contrast, the garrison nyai was not a *gezellige* wife substitute but, in fact, a prostitute; she was not a partner but a woman "akin to what one can find in a brothel";[57] she was not the faithful servant of one man but had need of many.[58] Such women were "taken out of the kampongs and without any education."[59] In a state of affairs produced by these indiscriminate relations "where the term 'respectability' (*kuischheid*) is absent, a sense of morality withers and so the desire for respectability in one's environment steadily decreases . . . and the sense of responsibility becomes weaker."[60] The state of concubinage, of colonial sexual relations, they concluded, was "indubitably one of *national interest*."[61]

In this portrayal, the nyai was no longer presented in a passive role as the victim of a colonial institution, in the way the slave, the villager under the cultuurstelsel, or the indentured laborer, male or female, was presented to underscore the moral decline of European society. Rather, the colonial institution had transformed her into "the dangerous native," attempting to gain illicit advantage from her presence within European society

> with her vague sense of morality sufficient merely as a defence in the battle of life, [she comes from the kampung] to an environment which is without love, and [characterized by] wealth and pleasure seeking, which is organised in a way designed to kill any moral sense . . . so that nothing remains but the bestial element which is so evident in this child of nature. And yet very soon she comes to realize the lowly position that she has come to inhabit: that she will only be tolerated and only finds herself there to satisfy the desires of her *master*; that she, beyond the bed, has no relationship with her master; in short, as far as the permanence of her position is concerned, that her position is lower than that of the lowest servant. This of itself generates in her a desire to improve her position and this she does by seeking her pleasure. The master does not raise the woman up to his level but he sinks down to hers until he often becomes a miserable figure and totally under the influence of his uncivilized Nyai.[62]

Here, the "slave"—the original report places emphasis on the term *heer* (master)—is simultaneously pitied and vilified. She is both the victim of the European man's desires and also the cause of his downfall, both apparently the innocent "child of nature" in her original state and "bestial" and dangerous in her present condition. For his part, the European (male) is initially superior but ultimately emasculated. "Is it not to be deplored," the report asked in conclusion, "that . . . our Colonies are grounded on a foundation of immorality and bestiality? Don't those who hear this blush, when they learn that our authority there is not founded on the prestige of a Christian nation but in part on prostitution (*hoererij*)? Not moral authority but the lack of morality is what safeguards our possession, a possession which the Netherlands is very proud of?"[63] In short, the intimate and immoral relations with the native endangered the moral and physical position of European civilization.

The Unfreedom of Tradition

The reform of colonial domestic arrangements that turned on the separation of the European and native elements of colonial society was the prelude to a much wider campaign: the reform of the native and the institutions of native society. If colonialism inevitably impacted native tradition, unleashing, as in the case of the garrison nyai, potential dangers to the maintenance of European domination, this inevitably required colonialism to address the world beyond the boundaries of European colonial society. Resolving the problem as it was understood at that point implied a much more confident colonial stance, together with a belief in the efficacy of European/Dutch morality and racial superiority. In the early twentieth century, then, an ethical colonial policy saw its role as freeing the native from the slavery of tradition. In the words of one influential contributor to this discourse, the Islam scholar Snouck Hurgronje: "The chains of Muslim law which encircle the followers of Islam and which will prove to be too oppressive in this modern age and society will undo themselves as soon as our cultural life succeeds in one way or another to draw them to us."[64]

Snouck's "progressive" Islam policy was not to condemn Islam but to advocate a policy of associating Muslims, through education—enlightenment—with European civilization. Over the longer term, he argued, this would free the individual Muslim from the anachronistic dictates of Islamic law as well as avert the potential threat to the colonial state of a pan-Islamic movement. Snouck's argument for association, premised as it was on a criticism of tradition and the superiority of modern Western civilization (Christian or otherwise), assumed a perspective in which freedom was equated with modern colonialism and unfreedom with tradition from which it became the duty of colonialism to save its victims. The characterization of tradition as oppressive had a long lineage—indeed, it had been central to the critique of "old colonialism" itself—but it was now used extensively, as here, to legitimate the expansion of (modern) colonial rule. This did not necessarily mean that Indonesians were to be transformed into pseudo-Europeans, since, as was suggested in the discourse on garrison whores, that would trap the native in a dangerous no-man's-land. Cultural hybridity, as noted earlier, was regarded with suspicion. But the Indonesians needed to be modernized.

In many instances—as in the case of Bali—the eradication of (indigenous) slavery and of slave-trading regimes had become the declared motivation for this new era of colonial imperialism.[65] Contemporary accounts of undesirable native regimes often implied that the condition of civilization could be measured by how a society treated its women. But more generally, it seemed that in the twentieth century, slavery (and other forms of oppression) was now a practice undertaken only by uncivilized peoples. Among the many examples that could be cited in this regard is central Sulawesi. There, missionaries, encouraged by the colonial government to bring Christianity to the heathen, advised the prohibition of a range of "abhorrent and inhuman practices," such as head-hunting, witch trials, and slavery.[66] These practices, declared mission leader Albert Kruyt (echoing Snouck Hurgronje), formed part of the culture of an "animist religion" that "hinders social progress because [their beliefs] petrify society into a solid block of conservatism. In this situation we feel that what is necessary in the first instance is to free them from the fetters forged by their religion."[67]

Kruyt highlighted the way slavery impacted family life and population growth. It produced both "slavish" and irresponsible slaves and lazy and arrogant freemen and freewomen. It encouraged illicit sexual relations, and it fostered "unnatural behavior" such as infanticide, committed by female slaves not wishing to see their children become slaves, and abortion, on the part of female slave owners who neither wanted the trouble nor needed the services of children of their own.[68] Abolition of slavery was thus an important step in forming so-called modern families and in encouraging women to more diligently undertake their destined role as the basis for progress. Progress was understood implicitly in terms of improved agricultural production, population growth, reduction in morbidity, and evidence of modernity specifically in terms of improved hygiene and orderly domestic and village arrangements. School attendance and the payment of taxes were further marks of progress.[69] All these were seen as the outcome of the liberating effects of colonization, and for the missionary specifically, they were viewed as freeing the mind from the oppression of the fear induced by animistic beliefs and tradition.[70]

In his study of the (earlier) British imperial antislavery discourse, David Turley suggests that although changes to economic forms of production are important in explaining the rise of the antislavery movement, they cannot be seen as the sole factor. As in the case of the Dutch East Indies, political and ideological arguments and motivations were always present. Turley's discussion of the British example also suggests that the debate in the Indies was part of a broader shift in metropolitan politics that increasingly involved an appeal to a populist politics; thus, the issue of slavery—and, by extension, other forms of unfreedom—formed part of a broader cultural, political, and social transformation in the metropole. But the reformist movement cannot be explained purely from an imperial perspective. In the Dutch case, the discourse about the reform of colonial society—economically and socially—found an important stimulus in a colonially centered debate. At the very least, its "progressive" members saw reform of colonial relations as central to reform of (European) colonial society. This required, from their perspective, a clear separation between all things European and native.

The connection between the earlier antislavery discourse and the later antiprostitution/anticoncubinage discourses in the East Indies lies not so much in the common experience victims of these colonial institutions suffered (although in hindsight, this can be demonstrated) but in their perceived impact upon colonial society and, more broadly, European civilization abroad. The gendering of this discourse reflected, again, not simply the gender of its object but also the broader shift in colonial and metropolitan social discourses away from purely economic, material, and institutional concerns toward a more complex concern about culture and race and individual moral responsibility. Having once reformed European colonial society in the twentieth century, a reformed regime—or at least a more self-righteous and self-confident one—set out to transform the native society over which it claimed guardianship. Here, too, it claimed to reform the economic relations between men and men, as well as the more intimate relations between men and women in the interests of prosperity, "healthy living," and increased population. This broader colonial conceit implied that freedom was the gift of colonization, thus justifying the continuation of the unfreedom that its very expansion was intensifying. This, in turn, reflected a more deep-seated and contradictory process that could be termed modernity.

Notes

1. Susanne Miers, "Slavery: A Question of Definition," in *The Structure of Slavery in Indian Ocean Africa and Asia*, ed. Gwyn Campbell (London: Frank Cass, 2004), 12.

2. P. Boomgaard, "Human Capital, Slavery and Low Rates of Economic and Population Growth, 1600–1910," in Campbell, *The Structure of Slavery*, 83–96; Anthony Reid, ed., *Slavery, Bondage and Dependency in Southeast Asia* (St. Lucia: University of Queensland Press, 1983).

3. Laws regulating slavery in the colony had, however, been implemented prior to British laws abolishing slavery; see R. W. van Hoevëll, *De emancipatie der slaven in nederlandsch-Indië: Een verhandeling* (Groningen, the Netherlands: C. M. van Bolhuis Hotsema, 1848), 5–12.

4. Ibid., 15.

5. Cited in ibid., 31.

6. Van Hoevëll was also at the forefront of the colony's 1848 "liberal rebellion" in Batavia; see P. van 't Veer, "Een revolutiejaar, Indische stijl: Wolter Robert baron van Hoevël, 1812–1879," in his *Geen blad voor de mond: Vijf radicalen uit de negentiende eeuw* (Amsterdam: Arbeiderspers, 1958).

7. Van Hoevëll refers particularly to the embarrassment occasioned by criticism in English-language press accounts in the nearby British colony of Singapore.

8. Siep Stuurman, *Wacht op onze daden: Het liberalisme en de vernieuwing van de Nederlandse staat* (Amsterdam: Bakker, 1992).

9. Van Hoevëll, *De emancipatie der slaven*, 17.

10. Examples of public sales, sometimes of entire families with children, were highlighted in news sections of *Tijdschrift voor Nederlandsch Indië* well into the 1860s. Van Hoevëll notes that even the highest colonial officials—members of the Indies Council (Raad van Indië)—maintained slaves at home.

11. Van Hoevëll, *De emancipatie der slaven*, 17.

12. Ibid., 15.

13. Van Hoevëll notes further that the number of slaves registered in the Moluccas was 2,656; in Timor, 707; in Makassar, 797; in Padang, 369; in Bangka, 37; in Riouw, 5; and in Westcoast Borneo, 2.

14. See Cornelius Fasseur, *The Politics of Colonial Exploitation: Java, the Dutch and the Cultivation System* (Ithaca, N.Y.: Cornell University, 1992); Robert van Niel, *Java under the Cultivation System* (Leiden: KITLV Press, 1992).

15. "Wherever free labour manifests itself one sees general welfare and progress. Where forced labour exists the better off classes progressively decline and one sees misery increase"—"H," "Verhooging van arbeidsloon op Java," *Tijdschrift voor Nederlandsch Indië* (hereafter *TNI*) 15, no. 2 (1853): 124.

16. This summary is based on a review of articles on the cultuurstelsel in the *TNI* between 1850 and 1865.

17. Stuurman, *Wacht op onze daden*, 142–45. Van Hoevëll, a preacher, began his pamphlet on slavery with a perfunctory statement: "The point which forms the basis of our position, our *point de départ*, is the clearly expressed feeling of Christendom, that one person does not have the right over the freedom of another."

18. Herman Warner Muntinghe, "Het stelsel van handel, gedwongen arbeid en verplichte leverantie, vergleken met dat eener vrije kultuur en regelmatige belasting" (The system of trade, forced labor, and compulsory delivery compared to a system of free cultivation and regular taxation), *TNI* 13 (1851): 13. Another regular polemicist was G. H. van Soest; see his "De behoeften van de partikuliere nijverheid op Java," *TNI* 22, no. 1 (1860): 299–306.

19. J. A. Caspersz, "De voordelen die Nederland kan verwachten van de beschaving van den Javaan" (The advantages the Netherlands can expect from the education [*beschaving*?] of the Javanese"), *TNI* 13, no. 1 (1851): 63–66. Caspersz, a colonial controller, claimed the stimulus to increased exertion would result in greater income and eventually help eradicate the "collection of absurdities" that represented Javanese religion, which was "Mohammedan in name only."

20. "The book was republished numerous times throughout the 19th century and, according to one writer, became the bible for a new generation of young and idealistic colonial officials"; see Rob Nieuwenhuis, *De mythe van Lebak* (Amsterdam: G. A. van Oorschot, 1987), 8.

21. Eduard Douwes Dekker, "Over vrije arbeid in Nederlandsch-Indië" (1867), and "Nog eens vrije arbeid," in *Multatuli: Volledige werken*, ed. Multatuli (Amsterdam: G.A. van Oorschot, 1951), 2:180–298, 3:428–60.

22. "W," "De koloniale kwestie op het Internationaal Kongres te Amsterdam in het buitenland beoordeeld" (The colonial question at the International Congress in Amsterdam as discussed abroad), *TNI* 26, no. 2 (1864): 456–57.

23. Fasseur, *Politics of Colonial Exploitation*, 239. This figure varied over time and from region to region; in some places, it was as high as 100 percent of households, with the amount of agricultural land occupied in places being as little as 6 percent; see Merle Calvin Ricklefs, *A History of Modern Indonesia since 1200* (London: Palgrave, 2001), 157.

24. T. J. Lindblad, "Key Themes in the Modern History of Indonesia," in *New Challenges in the Modern Economic History of Indonesia*, ed. T. J. Lindblad (Leiden: Indonesian Studies Program, 1993), 6–7.

25. Jan Breman, *Koelies, Planters en Koloniale Politiek: Het arbeidsregime op de grootlandbouwondernemingen aan Sumatra's Oostkust in het begin van de twintigste eeuw* (Leiden: KITLV Press, 1992).

26. Stuurman, *Wacht op onze daden*.

27. Elsbeth Locher-Scholten, "Mr P. Brooshooft: Een biografische schets in koloniaal-ethisch perspektief," in Locher-Scholten, *Ethiek in Fragmenten: Vijf studiën over koloniaal denken en doen van Nederlanders in de Indonesische archipel* (Utrecht: HES, 1981), 11–54.

28. P. Brooshooft, *Memorie over den toestand in Indië* (Semarang: H. van Alphen, 1888). This 178-page letter of protest, signed by 1,255 colonial residents, railed against the "situation in the Netherlands Indies," claiming that oppressive taxation and unpaid labor demands caused the Javanese farmer to do "everything in his means to ensure he does not die of hunger and any higher aspiration has become forever impossible" (p. 7).

29. Ibid., 85.

30. Ann Laura Stoler, *Capitalism and Confrontation in Sumatra's Plantation Belt, 1870–1979* (New Haven, Conn.: Yale University Press, 1985).

31. Robert E. Elson, "Sugar Factory Workers and the Emergence of 'Free Labour' in Nineteenth-Century Java," *Modern Asian Studies* 20, no. 1 (1986): 139–74. Elsewhere, I show that critics and defenders of sugar factory labor management effectively repeated arguments for and against the cultuurstelsel; see Joost Coté, "'A Teaspoon of Sugar': Assessing the Sugar Content in Colonial Discourse in the Dutch East Indies, 1880–1914," in *Revisiting Sugarlandia: Sugar and Colonialism in Asia and Africa, 1800 to 1940*, ed. Ulbe Bosma, Juan Giusti-Cordero, and G. Roger Knight (New York: Berghahn, 2007), 113–44.

32. According to Rhemrev's report, more than 181,182 indentured laborers were employed on 645 estates. The majority were landless and unemployed Javanese villagers transported to Sumatra on contracts; see Breman, *Koelies, planters en koloniale politiek*, 450–95.

33. Ibid., 532.

34. Elsbeth Locher-Scholten, "So Close and Yet So Far: The Ambivalence of Dutch Colonial Rhetoric on Javanese Servants in Indonesia, 1900–1942," in *Domesticating the Empire: Race, Gender and Family Life in French and Dutch Colonialism*, ed. Julia Clancy-Smith and Frances Gouda (Charlottesville: University of Virginia Press, 1998), 131–53.

35. R. W. van Hoevëll, "De slavenij in Nederlandsch Indië," *TNI* 15, no. 1 (1853): 269. See also Schölten, "So Close and Yet So Far," 131–53.

36. Several famous literary images of the oppressed native female, however, exist in the nineteenth-century discourse. The most famous is that of Adinda, the victim of the cultuurstelsel immortalized in *Max Havelaar* and, earlier, the 1820s figure of the servant Tjampaka and her evil mistress, Kraspoekol, both victims of the culture of slavery in the now forgotten drama by Dirk van Hogendorp; see Paul van 't Veer, *Geen blad voor de mond: Vijf radicalen uit de negentiende eeuw* (Amsterdam: Arbeiderspers, 1958).

37. Breman, *Koelies, planters en koloniale politiek*, 412. A facsimile of the pamphlet is reproduced in Breman's book.

38. Clifford Geertz's well-known argument about "cultural involution" implies that the burden of the cultuurstelsel on native society was carried by women as increased childbearing became an essential means to provide extra contributors to help the Javanese family survive; see Geertz, *Agricultural Involution: The Process of Ecological Change in Indonesia* (Berkeley: University of California Press, 2000).

39. Joost Coté, "Feminizing Modernity: Images of Women in Early 20th Century Colonial and Nationalist Discourse in Indonesia," paper presented at the Women in Southeast Asia Workshop, Monash University, Clayton, July 9, 2007.

40. Jean Taylor shows that under the VOC and nineteenth-century colonial regulations, it was assumed that (male) colonial employees would take Asian wives; thus, concubinage had become an accepted arrangement until questioned toward the end of the colonial era. See Jean Gelman Taylor, *The Social World of Batavia: European and Eurasian in Dutch Asia* (Madison: University of Wisconsin Press, 1983); Nicole Lucas, "Trouwverbod, inlandse huishoudsters en Europese vrouwen: Het concubinaat in de planterswereld aan Sumatra's Oostkust, 1860–1940," in *Vrouwen in de Nederlandse kolonien*, ed. Jeske Reijs et al. (Nijmegen, the Netherlands: SUN, 1986), 78–97; Stoler, *Capitalism and Confrontation*.

41. The issue was regularly raised in education reports; see Joost Coté, "The Sins of the Fathers: Culturally At Risk Children and the Colonial State in Asia," *Paedogogica Historica* 45, no. 1–2 (2009): 129–42.

42. See Hanneke Ming, "Barracks-Concubinage in the Indies, 1887–1920," *Indonesia* 35 (April 1983): 65–93.

43. "Het pauperisme onder de Europeanen in Nederlandsch-Indië," *Algemeen Overzicht* (Batavia: Landsdrukkerij, 1902), 80. Of the 13,062 European

troops in 1900, only 147 were officially married, and almost 3,000 lived with huishoudsters, whereas of the 1,854 Ambonese soldiers, 87 were married, and 764 lived with huishoudsters; see *Het Pauperisme*, 37. The report noted that 4 percent of the Indo-European community was serving in the colonial military in the decade between 1885 and 1895.

44. Official statistics after 1854 did not distinguish between Europeans of "pure" and "mixed" descent in the colony. The rate of concubinage only began to decline significantly after 1915, when it coincided with an increase in both mixed marriages and prostitution; see A. van Marle, "De groep der Europeanen in Nederlands-Indië: Iets over onstaan en groei," *Indonesië* 5, no. 3 (1952): 491–96. Van Marle concludes that even as late as 1940, "possibly just as many Europeans lived in concubinage with non-European women as European men who had entered into a mixed marriage" (p. 499).

45. Der Steur was nicknamed "Pa van der Steur" for his work with orphans, primarily the "motherless" children of European troops, where native mothers—concubines—either had been rejected or had departed.

46. The "civilised paupers" he considered were those of a mixed race gainfully employed in lowly clerical positions.

47. "Het pauperisme," *Algemeen Overzicht*, 34.

48. In Dutch historiography, this had been referred to as the *beschavingsoffensief* (a civilizing project) that focused on rural and working-class families and targeted, among other things, the widespread practice of prostitution. See Martin P. Bossenbroek and Martin Jan H Kompagnie, *Het mysterie van de vedwenen bordelen: Prostitutie in Nederland in de negentiende eeuw* (Amsterdam: Bert Bakker, 1998).

49. Joost Coté, "'A Conglomeration of [. . .] Often Conflicting Ideas': Resolving the 'Native Question' in Java and the Outer Islands in the Dutch East Indies, 1900–1925," *Itinerario* 27, no. 3–4 (2004): 160–88.

50. The European population doubled between 1836 (11,345) and 1860 (22,663)—see *TNI* (1864): 313—but thereafter climbed rapidly, reaching 240,417 by 1930.

51. *Ethiek in fragmenten:* "Een onderzoek naar den toestand van het Nederlandsch-Indisch leger uit een zeedelijk oogpunt beschouwd ter ernstige overweging aangeboden door de Vereeniging tot Bevodering der Zedelijkheid in de Nederlandsche Overzeesche Bezittingen en de Nederandsche Vereeniging Tegen de Prostitutie" (unpublished report, 1898), 5–6.

52. "Het Pauperisme," *Algemeen Overzicht*, 81.

53. Ibid., 38.

54. Locher-Scholten, *Ethiek in fragmenten.* Other positive views advanced included the value of the nyai as an intermediary between the newly arrived male colonial or agricultural functionary and indigenous society; see Elsbeth Locher-Scholten, "The Nyai in Colonial Deli: A Case of Supposed Mediation,"

in *Women and Mediation in Indonesia*, ed. Sita van Bemmelen, Madelon Djajadiningrat-Nieuwenhuis, and Elsbeth Locher-Scholten (Leiden: KITLV Press, 1992), 265–80.

55. Bossenbroek and Kompagnie, *Het mysterie van de vedwenen bordelen*, 139–40.

56. Responses were obtained from nineteen other ranks, two officers and six "persons working for the moral welfare of soldiers."

57. Locher-Scholten, *Ethiek in fragmenten.*

58. Ibid., 14.

59. Ibid., 15.

60. Ibid., 11; Liesbeth Hesselink, "Prostitution: A Necessary Evil, Particularly in the Colonies—Views on Prostitution in the Netherlands Indies," in *Indonesian Women in Focus: Past and Present Notions*, ed. Elsbeth Locher-Scholten and Anke Niehof (Leiden: KITLV Press, 1992), 205–24.

61. Locher-Scholten, *Ethiek in fragmenten*, v–vi.

62. Ibid., 15.

63. Ibid., 22.

64. Snouck Hurgronje (1911) cited in Joost Coté, "Colonialism and Modernity in Indonesia: Christiaan Snouck Hurgronje and Islam in Indonesia," *Journal of Arabic, Islamic and Middle Eastern Studies* 3, no. 2 (1997), 79.

65. Ricklefs, *History of Modern Indonesia*, 175–76.

66. Joost Coté, "Colonising Central Sulawesi: The 'Ethical Policy' and Imperialist Expansion, 1890–1910," *Itinerario* 20, no. 3 (1996): 87–107.

67. Kruyt cited in Joost Coté, "The Colonisation and Schooling of the Pamona of Central Sulawesi, 1895–1925" (master's thesis, Monash University, 1980), 170.

68. Coté, "Colonising Central Sulawesi"; Nicolaus Adriani and Albert C. Kruyt, *De Bare'e Sprekende Toradjas van Midden Celebes* (Batavia: Lansdrukkerij, 1912), 1:159–61, and 2:40–41.

69. Albert C. Kruyt, "Gegevens voor de bevolkingsvraagstuk van een gedeelte van Midden Celebes," *Tijdschrift van het Koninklijk Nederlandsch Aardrijkskundig Genootschap* 20 (1903): 190–205.

70. Albert C. Kruyt, "The Influence of Western Civilisation on the Inhabitants of Poso," in *The Effect of Western Influence on Native Civilisations in the Malay Archipelago*, ed. B. J. O. Schrieke (Batavia: G. Kolf, 1929), 1–9.

25

LURE OF THE IMPURE

Sexuality, Gender, and Agency of "Slave" Girls in Contemporary Madagascar

SANDRA J. T. M. EVERS

This chapter discusses how girls who are living in marginalized conditions use their gender attributes and sexuality to create agency in a very stringent social configuration where others have predetermined their role in society, status, and future possibilities. This study was conducted over a ten-year period (1989 to 1999)[1] among the Betsileo people dwelling in the zone between Ambalavao and Ankaramena. Topographically, the region is a hilly transition between the highlands and the arid semidesert flatlands of southern Madagascar.

By the early 1990s, Madagascar was ensnared in the poverty trap, characterized by low investment and slow growth. About 70 percent of Madagascar's total population lived under the poverty threshold, as compared with 39 percent for sub-Saharan Africa and 32 percent for all developing countries.[2] More recent figures calculated per capita income to be approximately $290 in 2005, with two-thirds of the population living below the poverty line;[3] at least 70 percent of those were living in rural areas.[4]

At the time of this study, the research setting was still relatively unfettered by state regulation. The downward political and macroeconomic spiral of Madagascar left its inhabitants to fend for themselves. Pervasive poverty conditioned every aspect of day-to-day existence. Nobody was immune to its effects, regardless of his or her position in the socioeconomic hierarchy. Poverty brought with it an array of other social ills: localized forms of justice and retribution and radical expressions of inequality. These conditions perhaps even reinforced the belief that people live in a stable and timeless universe, where things never change and where the "Malagasy customs" (*fomba gasy*) predetermine an individual's fate from cradle to tomb.

The Creation of a Society and Status Groups

Prior to the mid-1960s, settlement and acquisition of land were still relatively easy in the arid zone between Ambalavao and Ankaramena.[5] The mere occupation of land gave settlers the opportunity to accede to the status of *tompon-tany*, or "master(s) of the land." The concept of tompon-tany is known throughout Madagascar. The term is translated as "master(s) of the land" and not "owner(s) of the land" because despite the fact that their claims to land are considered legitimate by all villagers, tompon-tany do not have registered title to the land. Words in this article such as *tompon-tany, andevo, andriana, hova, olompotsy, olona madio, olona maloto,* and *fomba gasy* have been in currency at various points in Malagasy history. However, one should be aware that they represent dynamic concepts, which vary based upon local setting and historical context. Even during the relatively short period of this research, these concepts evolved and mutated significantly.

For both the Merina and the Betsileo, living, respectively, in the Northern and Southern Highlands, possession of land and a family tomb are markers of family origin in a particular region.[6] Thus, the initial wave of migrants became tompon-tany simply by building a family tomb on their land, thereby conferring upon it the status of ancestral land.[7] These settlers formed the established group. They claimed either commoner (*olompotsy*) or even noble (*hova* or *andriana*) origins. Based on reports of slave settlement in the Archives d'Outre Mer, however, it appears more likely that this migrant group is of slave descent.

Attempts were made to verify whether the migrants who became tompon-tany were actually of free descent. Most of those interviewed were willing to disclose their place of origin. Follow-up inquiries involved visiting seven villages that were claimed to be the ancestral lands of seven tompon-tany families in the region. A certain number of family members indeed lived in these locations, but it was difficult to conclusively determine whether the villages were in fact their ancestral homelands. Often, the relatives admitted that they also were migrants who had themselves only recently become tompon-tany by establishing a family tomb on their newly acquired land. Unsurprisingly, people with tombs were not reluctant to discuss their family tomb, a significant source of pride and status. In the *tantara* (tale or [hi]story) about their lives, the tomb generally constituted the point of departure. People of slave descent, however, skirted the topic of ancestral lands and tombs, which might reveal either the absence of a tomb or its recent pedigree.[8] After several long trips on foot (ranging from 15 to 50 kilometers) to places that people had identified as their ancestral homeland, I decided that it would be more fruitful to examine perceptions and claims in this area, which seemed to be more relevant than alleged historical reality. In sum, I was increasingly coming to the conclusion that it was not authentication of the tompon-tany's free origin that entrenched their status but its legitimization through the tomb.

The tompon-tany consolidated their position as masters of the land by the creation of a land monopoly. In 1967, they held a meeting in the village of Marovato.[9] At this gathering, all unclaimed land was divided between them. The tompon-tany concluded a pact pursuant to which land could henceforth only be leased, not sold. This amounted to nothing less than a de facto exclusion of later migrants (*mpiavy*) from tompon-tany ranks.[10]

Entrenching Inequality

The settlement and land lease policies of the villages in the region were administered by the tompon-tany village councils. In principle, the tompon-tany did not allow non-Betsileo to live in their villages, and even Betsileo migrants were only admitted after rigorous scrutiny.[11] Every Betsileo migrant who wished to live in Marovato[12] had to first report to the members of the tompon-tany village council.[13] This council united the heads of the five largest tompon-tany families of Marovato. They routinely demanded to know where an applicant's ancestral land and family tomb were located. Their aim was to gain an understanding of the origins of the newcomer. Any migrant who was vague about his or her descent was presumed by the tompon-tany to be of slave origin (*andevo*), since all free-born persons in the highlands have ancestral land and a family tomb in their native region. Tompon-tany referred to Betsileo who could not name their ancestral homeland as people who did *tsy misy tantara* (not have a history) or who had *very tantara* (lost their history). This amounted to an automatic cause of marginalization, as their past afforded them no status or claim to recognition.[14]

Since the 1967 meeting, the tompon-tany have only allowed migrants presumed to be of slave origin to settle in Marovato if they have agreed to live in the western periphery. Migrants of free origin resided in the eastern part of the village.[15] Dwelling in western Marovato automatically entails being deemed by other villagers to be a member of an inferior group. Generally, Betsileo ideology considers the west to be the least favorable ritual location.[16] In Marovato, land in the western quarter was openly seen as impure. No Betsileo of free descent would consider living in the western periphery. Those who dwelled in western Marovato were referred to as *andevo*.[17] People with tombs designated them as *olona maloto* ("impure" or "dirty people"), whereas they called themselves *olona madio* ("pure" or "clean people").

The fact that migrants were unable to prove their free descent by means of a family tomb does not necessarily mean that they were of actual slave descent. Sometimes, their place of origin and family tomb were too far away for the tompon-tany to conduct an in-depth inquiry. However, in such cases, the tompon-tany left the newcomers with two options—departure or settlement in the western part. In other words, the andevo label was conferred upon them.

After numerous futile attempts to verify claims of tompon-tany origin, it appeared that any similar research into the origin of migrants in west Marovato would yield comparably fluid results. The important and central reality was that tompon-tany shaped the destinies of newcomers by ascribing their social identities according to their own criteria. These identities became part of the world with which migrants had to deal and even formed part of their own conceptual scheme.

Social exclusion of the "impure people" was articulated through the fear villagers had of being polluted by the andevo. Not only did they feel superior to them, they also kept a great physical distance from inhabitants of the western periphery. Villagers who came into contact with andevo immediately became impure themselves. This pollution could only be eradicated by a ritual cleansing carried out by the oldest member of a former royal family in Anjoma (located approximately 20 kilometers to the northeast of Marovato). However, there can be no doubt that the principle of keeping a "safe" distance away from andevo was sometimes best honored in the breach, as demonstrated by the seven mixed marriages in Marovato.[18]

Internalization of the andevo label was a significant component of social relations in Marovato. It was most poignantly demonstrated by the andevo bowing to passing tompon-tany nobility and in their self-imposed adherence to rules of avoidance determined by the so-called pure people. According to the tompon-tany, the andevo deviated from the norms of Malagasy customs, which they said only served to confirm their inferior status. In fact, the andevo displayed a number of behavior traits different from those of other villagers. For example, unlike other villagers, none of them ever shook hands. They also seemed to suffer from amnesia when asked about their place of origin. Another distinguishing facet of life in west Marovato was that every household functioned as a different socioeconomic unit, hardly interacting with other villagers. This was a distinct departure from the usual practice in the rest of the village, where both women and men carried out their daily activities on a communal basis.

The Economic Anchoring of Status and Exclusion

Tompon-tany social domination was coupled with economic control over migrants. This subordinate link was created through the dependence of newcomers upon tompon-tany families for land. All migrants entered into a land lease agreement with the tompon-tany upon arrival. This ensured that the tompon-tany monopolized not only superior social status but also the basic means of subsistence.

The inhabitants of Marovato practiced both agriculture and cattle breeding. Although cows were important as status symbols, economic life in the village revolved principally around the cultivation of rice, manioc, maize, and vegetables. The tompon-tany only cultivated one-third of their land in 1992. The rest lay fallow or was leased out. They said that this land could be used in the future to replace the land under cultivation. Each year, just before the rainy season, villagers burned their land, a practice they referred to as *tavy*. They did this to prepare for the new agricultural season, to set aside fallow land for a period of years or as a means of asserting uninterrupted "ownership."

In Madagascar, the Betsileo have the reputation of principally being rice cultivators. This is certainly true with respect to the northern Betsileo. From Ambositra to Ambalavao, the landscape is dominated by rice paddies. However, farther south, the rice paddies give way to hills that have undergone serious erosion, thereby making rice cultivation difficult or impossible. Inhabitants of the region between Ambalavao and Ankaramena constantly complained that the rainy season, historically from November to March, had been commencing later each successive year. They nevertheless continued to cultivate rice at the Zomandao riverbanks, although production was steadily declining.

None of the andevo cultivated rice land. As a tompon-tany family leader explained in July 1992, "The rice fields we need ourselves. And it never is a good idea to give the best away to people you do not even know."[19] Such a statement is not insignificant, as it indicates that the deliberate leasing of poor-quality land is no accident of marketplace economics but an instrument of socioeconomic policy to prevent migrants, with whom tompon-tany share no social bond, from gaining access to good land. This was particularly true for the andevo of western Marovato.[20] Andevo land was, for the most part, located near the northern Ifaha mountain range, at distances of between 1 to 5 kilometers from the village. In 1992, andevo and mixed andevo/free descent households cultivated an average of 0.10 hectare per person. This compared with the average allocation for tompon-tany families of 0.38 per person (measurements taken during 1992 fieldwork).

Tompon-tany family leaders used proximity of social relations as their primary criterion in determining the allocation of land. The family leader managed the ancestral family land (*tanin-drazana*) and the agricultural fields. Ancestral land referred to the plots of land where the parental house and the family tomb were located. This land could not be divided and was jealously protected by the tompon-tany family leader. Farmland commonly was divided more or less equally between him and his brothers.

They either cultivated it with their children or leased it out to other relatives. When sons married, parents bestowed farmland as a gift to the newlyweds. Daughters did not enjoy the same privileges, as they became part of the economic unit of the family they married into. There were exceptions; for instance, parents might occasionally grant a daughter usufruct rights upon marriage to an underresourced groom. But generally, land succession passed through the male line. The first part of the inheritance passed by inter vivos gift, called *lova voalohany* (the first inheritance). This inheritance system fragmented the family land. In July 1992, the village leader in Marovato, Rafidy Andriana, recognized this as problematic: "I have to oversee the fair division of land in my family. Every generation, we have to divide it between more people. I can hardly control it. This is why my father advised me to take as much land as possible, even if we cannot cultivate it. All tompon-tany families did this, since there was lots of land at the time. Now we use this land to practice tavy and to earn money by leasing it out to migrants."[21]

Tenancy agreements concluded with tompon-tany survived from one generation to the next. Children inherited usufruct rights from their parents as part of the inheritance, but they also incurred any accumulated debts. The debts were often more than the children could bear. Migrants arrived with little, and conditions scarcely improved over time. The dream many migrants had of quickly accumulating riches based on manioc crops quickly faded. Upon arrival, migrants were unable to pay for the land immediately. The tompon-tany postponed payment until after the first harvest. Further credits were needed just to seed the land. And here again, the tompon-tany were ready to help. As a result, any potential harvest profits were mortgaged well in advance. The cycle immediately perpetuated itself. As soon as one production season ended, the cultivators had to invest in the next by buying new seeds and fertilizers, which were supplied by the tompon-tany. According to Rafidy Andriana, "All migrants owe us debts, especially those in western Marovato. You see they need us; what would they become without us?"[22] Thus, these leases, despite being oral agreements that were not formally ratified, were key instruments used by the tompon-tany to create a structure of economic dependence.

In 1992, the tompon-tany employed no labor from outside the village. They cultivated their land themselves with the help of the migrants residing in the village. Under the lease agreement, a tompon-tany retained control of the land and held certain rights over the newcomer. He could, for example, demand the newcomer's labor during harvest time. The marginalization of the andevo, however, provided tompon-tany claiming noble descent with permanent workers throughout the year because they were able to demand the labor of andevo at any time. Often, andevo were called upon to perform the more demeaning and dirty tasks, such as cleaning cattle corrals and digging holes for the foundations of tompon-tany houses. As for living conditions in the andevo quarter, west Marovato was materially impoverished. The huts all were of poor quality, and unlike tompon-tany families, the andevo possessed little or no cattle or farming equipment. All of these external signs pointed to the exclusion of the andevo from community life even as they remained a vital part of its socioeconomic dynamics.

The tompon-tany regularly referred to socioeconomic relations and the so-called Malagasy customs as a stable and timeless system. Reality was far less rigid and absolute. Socioeconomic relations were constantly evolving and subject to ongoing negotiations. Even the labels andevo and andriana had recently been introduced by the tompon-tany.[23] However, since such labels evoked notions that were deeply rooted in the historical memory of the Betsileo, the use of them succeeded in legitimizing and perpetuating the inferior status of the andevo.

This observation was confirmed by village leader Rafidy Andriana, who stressed that that was how andevo were supposed to be treated and how the tompon-tany had to consolidate their position in the village. That was what his ancestors expected from him, and it constituted part of fomba gasy. As he stated in an interview on September 22, 1992: "My ancestors see to it that I follow the Malagasy customs. When I am dead myself, I will see to it that my children will also live according to the Malagasy customs."

Marriage Prospects for Andevo Girls

Marriage served as a clear identity marker, and one of the Malagasy customs that Rafidy Andriana referred to was that tompon-tany elders usually arranged the marriages of their children in order to prevent supposedly impure people from entering into their family networks. Fathers of andevo households in western Marovato also arranged marriages for both their daughters and their sons. However, this was not because they wanted to exercise influence upon their children but out of fear that their children might remain unmarried. Because they were labeled andevo and "impure people," they were considered inappropriate marriage partners for free descent families. As a consequence, one could expect them to arrange weddings with other andevo families in western Marovato. But they were reluctant to do so, as they feared that this would confirm their andevo status and background.

Thus, marriage was a troublesome issue for the andevo families in Marovato. In the process of arranging marriages for their children, parents became painfully aware of their ascribed social identity. Being labeled andevo hindered them in achieving life goals that villagers of free descent took for granted. Getting married and having children were the two principal goals named by youngsters, irrespective of status group, when asked to express their desires for the future. In the words of Raozy (August 12, 1992), a girl[24] living in western Marovato:[25] "Other girls know that they will get married some day. I know that I most likely will not be able to, since nobody wants me. Surely not when I wait for my father. But I know who I want to marry. When I tell you, you will not believe me because it is impossible."

Although marriage could be a hazardous enterprise for the andevo girls, by putting their gender attributes and sexuality into play, they created possibilities for themselves that would, in theory, not be available to them under other circumstances. Raozy's story provides insight into these dynamics, as she had set a clear goal for herself. She confessed this to me during the evening preceding my departure for the Netherlands, saying: "I will marry Lahy, Rafidy Andriana's son" (September 23, 1992). Although this prospect appeared virtually impossible under the 1992 Marovato social configuration, Raozy's sister Voahangy had, in fact, defied the odds the previous year, marrying someone of free descent. The following is an excerpt from my field journal (from June 2, 1992, the day of an interview with Voahangy, her husband, and her father-in-law):

> Voahangy (24) married into the *tompon-tany* family of Ragaby. His family compound is located in North Marovato. It consists

of various huts surrounding his brick house. Voahangy and her husband Rakoto (41) dwell in a tiny hut just opposite the house of Ragaby.

The hut accommodates eight inhabitants: Ragaby's nephew Rakoto, his wife Voahangy and their daughter. They each already had one child prior to marriage. These children form part of their household, as do two children of Rakoto's deceased sister. Maro, the father of Rakoto, also lives with them. He is the brother of Ragaby. Rakoto came to Marovato in 1988. Despite his short settlement history, he is perceived as *tompon-tany* due to his family affiliation with Ragaby.

Rakoto was forced to flee his birthplace Ihosy, when he fell prey to cattle thieves. They burned his house to the ground. Rakoto was able to escape, but his wife perished in the fire. Traumatised by the memory of this incident, he left Ihosy with his father, whose wife also had recently died. They hoped that the settlement in Marovato would provide them with a good future.

In 1991, Ragaby ordered his brother to find a wife for Rakoto. Maro contacted several fathers with available daughters in the village, all of whom came from free descent families. Unfortunately, the fathers of the eligible brides immediately refused after a cursory review of Rakoto's financial position. Materially, he had nothing to offer, since he had lost everything in the Ihosy fire. Maro: "It was difficult. I thought I would never find a wife for my son. There was only one solution . . . Western Marovato!" It was late at night when Maro knocked on the door of Ratsimbazafy, who had five daughters of marriageable age. Maro: "I only went after the villagers had withdrawn on the grass mat for the night so they should not notice me." For Ratsimbazafy, Maro's arrival was a dream come true since he had great difficulty in finding husbands for his daughters. He selected Voahangy because she was the eldest and already had a baby. Ratsimbazafy: "Rakoto is a good husband for her. She remains in Marovato and I can call on her when her help is needed" (interview 3 June 1992).

> That same night the marriage arrangements were made. Ratsimbazafy settled for a bridewealth of four chickens, and within the week Rakoto and Voahangy were husband and wife. The marriage, however, was received as an affront by other villagers of free descent. To this day, the mention of this mixed marriage provokes harsh criticism. Ragaby was the principal target of censure after the marriage, which was considered to be a serious violation of *fomba gasy* ("Malagasy customs"). But Ragaby remained stoic: "*Fomba gasy?* It is also *fomba gasy* that you can get cleansed by the oldest member of the former royal family in Anjoma. I go to see him every week, so everybody should be happy" (interview 2 June 1992). This seemed sufficient to silence some villagers, but did not prevent the *tompon-tany* nobility from speaking ill of Ragaby. Not unexpectedly, Rafidy Andriana was harshest in his criticism: "I am sure that my ancestors will one day rectify this violation of *fomba gasy*" (he mentioned this in a meeting on 2 June 1992).

During early 1992 fieldwork, this was the only mixed marriage brought to my attention, although it was clearly not, as will be discussed, the only mixed sexual relationship. Later that year, somebody claimed that Rafidy Andriana had an andevo in his own family: "He obviously did not check her out sufficiently. I know for a fact that the wife, Tsija, of his nephew is the sister of Lalao" (statement recorded on July 5, 1992). Lalao lived in western Marovato with her husband, Ratsimbazafy, and nine children. In first instance, it seemed unlikely that they were actually sisters, since they were never seen together. But some time later, I recorded in my field journal of July 12, 1992:

> Today there is a meeting of the elders from villages within proximity of Marovato. They are discussing the case of Rakazy, the nephew of Rafidy Andriana, and Tsija. Tsija is now openly acknowledged to be the sister of Lalao and therefore seen as an *andevo.*
>
> The elders rule that Rakazy and Tsija do not need to separate, which is normally demanded when mixed couples are discovered. The elders came to this decision because the couple already has

two children. Tsija and the children, however, would not be allowed to enter Rafidy Andriana's family tomb.

After the public condemnation of Tsija as andevo and an impure person, mixed marriages became the talk of the village. Gossip (*resa-be*) and "reality" seemed inseparable. I tried to solve this methodological problem by double-checking claims and stories with many informants. But in the process, it became obvious that it was not so much what was true or untrue that was relevant. The attention had to be on the accusations themselves. Why were they made? And what were their consequences? It was quite obvious that the villagers expected the andevo to behave in accordance with their inferior social status. It appeared just as significant that the disclosure of the supposed slave origin of a marriage partner led to ostracization by the other villagers of free descent. Whether or not an accusation was founded, its consequences were very real.

Gossip, indeed, was an important tool employed by the tompon-tany to force the compliance of free descent people while keeping the andevo in their subordinate position. Gossip about the andevo usually concerned their alleged misdeeds, but insinuations concerning contacts between pure people and impure people also gave rise to discussion within the village. Gossip served a double function. First, it was a mechanism of social control within the established group, strengthening its internal cohesion. Second, "talking bad" about the andevo served to confirm their inferior position as outsiders. Gossip proved highly effective in sharpening the social divisions of Marovato. On one side were the supposedly pure tompon-tany, who claimed social recognition as the established group. On the other side—literally as well as figuratively—were the supposedly impure migrants of western Marovato, whom the tompon-tany portrayed in scurrilous terms.

The heads of tompon-tany families regarded keeping their families pure as one of their most important tasks. Here, pure is to be understood in the sense that no olona maloto should enter into their families. Pure also meant adhering to the dictates of their ancestors as understood by them. The tompon-tany were able to keep olona maloto away by arranging marriages for their children with partners whose genealogical roots could be identified as free.[26] As for the second goal, adhering to ancestors' dictates, the tompon-tany claimed they achieved that by respecting and maintaining the traditions of the ancestors. Thus, by marginalizing the andevo as the others, the tompon-tany tried to maintain a pure cultural identity.

Portraying the andevo as outsiders was necessary for the tompon-tany to maintain their superior position.[27] They described themselves as the "backbone" of the Marovato community, and the responsibility to ensure that other villagers lived according to the Malagasy customs fell upon their shoulders. By presenting themselves as interpreters of the wishes of the ancestors, they elevated their own group to the position of "guardians of justice." They also perpetuated the myth by condemning the andevo's alleged failure to observe the cultural norms of the Betsileo. Tompon-tany of noble descent were particularly vehement in their negative opinions of the andevo, which were expressed in the form of rhetorical monologues recited during feasts and ceremonies.

As mentioned, marriage partners sometimes were only identified as andevo after the marriage was concluded. If this occurred, a number of means were available to solve the problem. The most critical of these was determined by the ancestors, according to the tompon-tany: anyone entering into marriage with an andevo was—and remained—polluted until the dissolution of the marriage. Children born into these marriages were also considered impure. This form of pollution could not be cleansed, as the villagers viewed it as an impurity of the blood (*ra*). For the parent of free descent, this already was sufficient reason to end the marriage, although a more fatal consequence decided the issue. Upon their death, the impure children and andevo wife or husband could not be placed in the tomb of the free descent parent. Therefore, when a man was of free descent, his andevo wife and children could not be buried in his family tomb. Informants told me that this meant that they could not be together as a family in the hereafter. This form of exclusion constituted a highly effective tool used by people claiming free descent to exclude impure people from their families.

Andevo Girls, Sexuality, and Agency

The andevo's position in the village had further deteriorated in 1996, when I returned to Marovato for a second research phase. By then, the tompon-tany had repossessed their leased land from the andevo. This was repeatedly justified by tompon-tany rhetoric about how lazy and useless the andevo were, explaining why it had been decided to evict them altogether. In reality, thirty-one andevo continue to live in Marovato, as they claimed to have no place to go. They no longer held land or worked for the tompon-tany; they survived from the petty theft of field crops and by sending their sons to Ambalavao and Fianarantsoa in search of work.[28] The andevo acknowledged their ascribed status during interviews.

I will return to Tsija, Roazy, and Voahangy to discuss how their living conditions had changed since 1992. Tsija and Rakazy lived together in the same house as in 1992. Tsija had given birth to two more children during my absence. The following section comes from my 1996 field journal:

> Upon my arrival, in the early morning of July 16 1996, Rakazy, Tsija, and their four children are huddled around a nearly extinguished fire.
>
> Rakazy: "Come in. How are you?"
>
> SE: "Thank you. I am fine and how are you?"
>
> Rakazy: "Difficult. You must know about my conflict with Rafidy Andriana. You always know everything. . . . That is very difficult. I promised Rafidy Andriana that I would send Tsija back home. She is not like us. But, I didn't send her back. And now, there are more children. She wants to stay. What can I do? I do not know. Rafidy Andriana does not understand this. It is difficult that Rafidy Andriana is upset with me."
>
> SE: "What can you fear from him?"
>
> Rakazy: "He says that I do not respect him. That is dangerous. You know about *fanafody gasy*.[29] I do not want to speak of this anymore. It is bad."
>
> Tsija: "It is also because my three brothers came to live with us. None has married yet. Ralahy is 19, Fara 20 and Patrick 21. They have no work and my family has no land. So they can work for my husband on his land."

Rakazy: "That reminds me. We really have to go now and help them. The sun is already out for a long time."

The conversation comes to an abrupt end, and they depart for the fields.

Rakazy's brief allusion to fanafody gasy is noteworthy because it was an important tool used by the tompon-tany to enforce conformity. Villagers often employed the term *fanafody gasy* to mean either actual poisoning or sorcery. But the precise term for poisoning is *fanomezana poizina*. Sorcery, *fanafody gasy*, may be defined as the harnessing and transforming of destructive occult energy (*hery*) originating in the ancestors into "medicines" that are used to harm people.

Mechanisms of Control: Poisoning and Sorcery

Villagers generally stated that administration of the poison was a matter for the *ombiasy* (traditional healers), exclusive specialists in the preparation of poisons, protections, and antidotes. They were either unwilling or unable to tell me the ingredients used to make the poison. In Marovato, each tompon-tany had his own ombiasy, who was not accessible to other people in the village. Migrants of free descent commonly still relied on the ombiasy of their region of origin. Andevo did not consult ombiasy. They said this was because the ombiasy refused to provide them with their services. The ombiasy were even more emphatic, stating that they would not even consider allowing an andevo to approach.

That poisoning was far from being just a personal vendetta became increasingly evident after the event. In Marovato and neighboring villages, the family of the victim had the option of bringing the matter of the alleged poisoning before the tompon-tany village council. The council then deliberated and determined which family was responsible and even levied sanctions. In several cases of migrant men who were poisoned after having sexual relations with tompon-tany women, the village council determined that the victims "called it upon themselves" (*fahadisoan'izy ireo izany*). As Marovato village leader Rafidy Andriana explained: "Everybody knows that taking the wife of somebody else is dangerous. And the migrants also should have known better. *Tompon-tany* women belong with *tompon-tany* men" (interview of August 17, 1996).

During my 1996 fieldwork, there was one case that was never put before the tompon-tany village council. Sambo, who openly acknowledged his andevo status in 1996, related the poisoning of his stepsister Mamy as follows (excerpt from fieldwork journal entry of May 3): "The bad things started not long after you left. Mamy died. I know who did it. She was pregnant with a baby from somebody outside western Marovato. You know, they always feel better than us. When his father found out, they arranged for Mamy to die. They poisoned her. It was terrible. Then her sister was always afraid afterwards. You see, she also got pregnant. I think it was the same situation." About the fact that this poisoning was never brought before the tompon-tany village council, Sambo said during the same interview: "They will never punish one of their own. And remember, we are just the *andevo.* Nobody is going to defend us."

None of the cases I witnessed was ever referred to the legal tribunal. Villagers claimed they resorted to local elders to resolve disputes because they had more faith in this system than in the official one. Courts of general jurisdiction were considered far too expensive and were rumored to be rife with corruption. The people held to this belief despite the fact that the villagers had no direct dealings with the tribunal.

Poisoning, however, was not a form of dispute resolution that was random or without consequence, as indicated by the extensive formal discussions that followed any poisoning concerning free descent villagers and the collective sanctions eventually applied after the fact. Furthermore, family seniors and the ombiasy had to approve the poisoning.

The social status of the persons and families involved played a central role in the tompon-tany assessment of a poisoning. In all cases I observed, tompon-tany were accused of being behind the poisoning. When these poisonings took place between tompon-tany families, they were heavily condemned by other tompon-tany and the cases were submitted to the local tompon-tany village councils. Poisonings within tompon-tany families were seen as even more grave offenses. The alleged poisoning of this kind that took place in Marovato was the only one where a sanction followed. Poisonings of migrants by tompon-tany were all blamed on the migrants themselves, and no sanctions for the assumed perpetrators followed. And in the case concerning the andevo victim Mamy, villagers of free descent claimed that the poisoning was her own fault.

Another mechanism of control is fanafody gasy, or "poisoning at a distance." Like actual poisoning, fanafody gasy was used to punish disrespect. The choice to take revenge by poisoning or sorcery was generally made by senior family members in concert with the ombiasy. If they failed to come to a decision, the ombiasy would consult the ancestors of the concerned family on the matter. He did this via a divination system, which is beyond the scope of this chapter to discuss, or he waited to receive a message from the ancestors in a dream.

When sorcery was the method chosen to settle a conflict, the ombiasy would prepare a small bundle of selected herbs. Only ombiasy had the power and right to make these "Malagasy medicines," which were believed to be infused with hery directly transmitted from the ancestors. People said that once fanafody gasy was placed in the house of the presumed victim, the person would fall ill or even die.

Migrants of free descent, in principle, were unable to use sorcery against fellow villagers, primarily because their family ombiasy lived far away. They also stressed that it would be particularly ill advised to perform sorcery against tompon-tany, since the reprisal measures of the tompon-tany would be far more powerful. The fear of tompon-tany sorcery was omnipresent in the villages. The people believed that the tompon-tany, with the assistance of their ombiasy, were able to manipulate ancestral energies and use them for sorcery.

Poisoning and sorcery were last-resort options to settle disputes. But unlike cases of poisoning, sorcery cases were not referred to the tompon-tany village council. To do so would be considered by its members as an intermingling of affairs. Sorcery was the domain of the ancestors, as they provided the malignant forces (the hery),[30] and this could cause the hery of the Malagasy medicine to be misdirected toward them. Hery was to be avoided at all costs.

Although the andevo were named as potential poisoners and sorcerers, I heard of no such cases in the Marovato region. Even if andevo had such intentions, they were not allowed to socialize with other villagers, so how could they plant the Malagasy medicine? Nor did they have access to the ombiasy who were the principal disseminators of poison and Malagasy medicine used in sorcery. Andevo themselves stressed that they had no access to or knowledge of sorcery. They asserted, however, that sorcery could be used against them by the tompon-tany.

Poisoning and sorcery were mainly mechanisms that operated within and between tompon-tany families. It was difficult to determine to what extent the threat of poisoning and sorcery was effective in making villagers adhere to the social mores. There is no doubt that at least the rhetoric of poisoning and sorcery was actively employed as an instrument of power or to avenge wrongs. Both poisoning and sorcery were sometimes "spontaneously" deployed as a means of revenge and seeking "justice," particularly to enforce codes of family honor. They were both part of the social morality and subject to ratification by the internal justice system of the villages. Andevo always felt they risked being the victims. Yet despite this threat, andevo girls continued to try to stake out their own turf in the oppressive social configuration where they had to operate.

Andevo Girls' Exploration of Sexuality and Agency at the Riverbanks

Let us return to Voahangy to illustrate how andevo girls navigated the narrow confines of their predefined roles. In 1996, Voahangy tried to take her destiny into her own hands. My field journals again pick up the story:

> It is August 17, and I am returning to Marovato from Fenoarivo, where I have just visited the parents of Voahangy who have taken up quarters there. Further up the road, approaching me, is a woman with a bundle on her head. As we near each other, I recognise Voahangy. Fresh blood from a wound just above her eye is still trickling down her face. She is maintaining herself upright with great difficulty. At my insistence, she attempts to sit down, and loses her footing, nearly falling as she does so. She removes the bundle from her head. When she bends over I notice a baby tied to her back.
>
> Voahangy: "This time I am not going back."
>
> She takes a patch of cloth from the bundle and roughly dabs at the still unclotted blood.
>
> SE: "What do you mean?"
>
> Voahangy: "It is Rakoto. He treats me badly. He is with other women all the time but he is angry with me. I

do not even know why. And if I ask him, he says that I should not complain and that I am just an *andevo*. I go to my parents when he gets too angry. Sometimes I remember how nice he was in the beginning and go back. But then it starts all over again. It is because people speak about us. It is because I am just *andevo*."

SE: "What do you mean, just *andevo?*"

Voahangy: "It must be clear to you. You know so much about us. You speak to us like you speak to the *olona madio*. But you know that we are different . . . I am not going back. But I feel bad for Pascaline, our daughter. I could not take her."

SE: "But you did take the baby."

Voahangy: "Yes, this is my baby! It happened when I was with my parents. Rakoto took another woman home again. I was sad, so I went to the river at night. I just made a baby with somebody else. Rakoto did not like that when he discovered it. He got angry again. I have to leave now."

SE: "Would you like me to walk with you?"

Voahangy panics at the thought of me accompanying her: "No, I want to go by myself. My parents will be angry with me."

She picks up the bundle, puts it back on her head, and continues on her way.

Using Sexuality to Circumvent Marginality

Andevo girls defined themselves as being inferior to other girls because they had no tombs.[31] They shared this assessment with their brothers and parents but, above all, with other villagers. This awareness was exacerbated by their capacity to "pollute" others. During the day, they would refrain from associating with the so-called pure people insofar as possible. They behaved submissively and did as they were told. At the same time, they suffered physical and mental abuse, as the cases discussed earlier testify.

Under cover of night, andevo girls used other avenues to explore their gender possibilities. This occurred along the banks of the river Zomandao. Girls of free descent were careful not to be seen at riverside during the night, as this would compromise their status. For the andevo girls, however, the riverside represented a place where they could temporarily reverse their submissive roles in relation to other villagers. Andevo girls reported that they had little to lose and that the riverside at least offered the chance to better their bleak prospects. It could potentially bring them access to fertile land, food, and other material wealth. It also was a place of agency where they were no longer considered odious but even became desirable.

Free descent boys and young men (both migrant and tompon-tany) were frequent visitors to the riverside in the evening. Although villagers publicly disapproved of this practice, that did not prevent many from engaging in mixed relations. The consequence of sexual intercourse with andevo was practically seen as becoming impure, which opened the way to a solution. Most male villagers visited the oldest member of the former royal family in Anjoma on a regular basis in order to undergo the purification ritual. It is hypothesized that the harshness of the daily regimes of conformity could be sustained precisely because of the nocturnal loosening of the contact rules between pure and impure people. The consequences naturally had to be rectified to bring actors back into the ambit of the rule-governed space during daytime by way of the purification rituals. In this manner, free descent boys and men could reenter village life again as full members.

Let us now return to some examples. Tsija claimed that she had first seduced Rakazy at the river. And Rakazy also confirmed this during later research. He thought that she was very pretty despite her state of impurity. She became pregnant. Rakazy's interest in her only increased, as it was his first child. The stories of Voahangy and Raozy were very similar. Raozy was most explicit about her strategies. She knew precisely whom she was targeting and how she could win the desired favors. In 1992, she informed me that she had already picked her future groom. Her eye had fallen on Lahy, a son of tompon-tany village leader Rafidy Andriana's third marriage. In 1993, she gave birth to a boy, whom she called Sambatra, "the happy one." During the early stages, she raised the child with her parents, but about a year later, she convinced Lahy that he was the father of the baby. Several months afterward, they moved in together. They were allowed to stay in a little room in the house of Raboba, Lahy's stepbrother. During early 1996, Raozy gave birth to a baby girl named Soa. As soon as I heard that Raozy had given birth, I visited her, on April 2, 1996. What follows is an excerpt from the fieldwork journal notations of that day:

> When I arrive, she is alone.
>
> SE: "Good morning Raozy, I heard about your baby and I come to see her."
>
> Raozy is a beautiful girl. Like her mother she has replaced her natural teeth with "golden" ones. With a happy smile she hands Soa to me. The baby stares at me but does not cry.
>
> Raozy: "I have to tell you many things. I am married to Lahy now. Just like I told you."[32]
>
> SE: "That is right. I am happy for you. But where is Sambatra?"
>
> Raozy: "Oh you do not know. He died. That made me cry. It was just after I married Lahy. Lahy's father did not agree and even now says that we are not really married because my father never arranged the *tandra*. I do not care. I think that I am married to him. Lahy liked Sambatra. That is why he had to die."
>
> SE: "What do you mean?"
>
> Raozy: "Rafidy Andriana does not want people like me. He got really angry with Lahy. He said that Lahy could not have any babies with me. But then Sambatra was already there. After that Sambatra got very sick and died. My husband thinks that his father has something to do with it."

The Legacy of Slavery

Despite the lapse of more than a century since the abolition of slavery, social, economic, and cultural relations in Marovato appear to be grounded in the memory of slavery and the exclusion of slaves from principal cultural components such as tombs, ancestors, and kinship.

The emancipation of slaves in 1896 did nothing to resolve the slaves' economic and sociocultural dilemma, freeing them in name only. As it proposed no substitute system, the net effect was simply to unhinge slaves from their environment, without providing them any useful reference, *other than the past,* to commence their new life.

During the period of slavery and its aftermath of emancipation, the tompon-tany experienced a radical and traumatic rupture, departure, and separation from their place of origin. Thus, the tompon-tany, who ceaselessly reiterated that history and Malagasy customs are their essence, were unable to trace their family histories back further than one generation.

They did, however, preserve a powerful sense of themselves as a people, apparently by internalizing their cultural history and preserving the memory of tombs, kinship, and ancestors. When the conditions became appropriate, that is, with the founding and early development of the village of Marovato, their cultural knowledge was once again externalized, literally born from the ashes of their memory. But the resurrection of this memory also brought with it a malaise, one that made it imperative to create the andevo and relegate them to pariah status. This exclusion, it is suggested, may be due to the slave origins of the tompon-tany themselves.

The prohibition against andevo establishing tombs effectively denied them any possibility of playing an active role in Marovato society. Thus, the creation of the andevo by the tompon-tany was a technique for survival. Its sustainability depended upon the extent to which it evolved and adapted to circumstances. Although portrayed as such by the tompon-tany, its constituent features were in no way a stable and timeless system. Their flexible and fluid contours formed part of a construction of history, culture, and inequality that allowed the tompon-tany to establish a society under harsh conditions.

The andevo were forced to eke out a living on the margins of this society. This entailed a life of conformity, hardship, and humiliation. Within the small confines of their predetermined roles in village life, andevo girls used their sexuality and other gender characteristics to try to improve their prospects. The andevo girls discussed in this chapter, who entered into relationships with free descent men despite all the odds against doing so, indeed endured hardship and even dealt with poisonings and sorcery. But they all boasted about how their beauty, sexuality, and fertility (having babies) lured free descent boys and men onto a path that was disapproved of by their parents. The andevo girls engaged in these sexual relationships on a voluntary basis and with a clear agenda. They usually sought marriage as a result. Thus, the decision to go to the river was born out of the desperate social configuration that governed them, but at least this allowed them to create an environment and a forum for themselves where they could succeed in gaining an ascendancy not otherwise available to them during their daytime existence.

Notes

1. Throughout the initial research phase (1989 to 1992), I used a principally socioeconomic approach, while also relying on the life history method, the interactional perspective, and network analysis. Upon my return to the region in 1996, villagers felt that I was sufficiently "behaving Betsileo" (*mitondra tena Betsileo ianao*) to be allowed to participate in funerals and their accompanying rituals. Financial support for the fieldwork was provided by the Research School CNWS (Leiden University), the Netherlands Organisation for Scientific Research, NWO (section: WOTRO, Science for Global Development), and the Amsterdam School for Social Science Research (ASSR, University of Amsterdam).

2. World Bank, *Madagascar: Poverty Assessment* (Washington, D.C.: World Bank, 2006); cf. International Monetary Fund, *Country Report Madagascar* (Washington, D.C.: IMF, 1997).

3. World Bank, *Madagascar Country Brief*, accessed January 3, 2009, http://web.worldbank.org.

4. B. Sarrasin, "The Mining Industry and the Regulatory Framework in Madagascar: Some Developmental and Environmental Issues," *Journal of Cleaner Production* 14, no. 3–4 (2006): 389.

5. The empirical sections are written in the past tense. Although the hallmarks of the socioeconomic configurations and access policies of the tompontany were still in force during follow-up research in 2007, internal subtleties and changes had occurred, as is also noted in the comparison between 1992 and 1996 discussed in this chapter. For more ethnographic details on these and other case studies see S.J.T.M. Evers, *Constructing History, Culture and Inequality: The Betsileo in the Extreme Southern Highlands of Madagascar* (Leiden: Brill Academic Publishers, 2002); S.J.T.M. Evers, "Expropriated from the Hereafter: The Fate of the Landless in the Extreme Southern Highlands of Madagascar," *Journal of Peasant Studies* 33, no. 3 (2006): 413–44; and S.J.T.M. Evers, "*Lex Loci* meets *Lex Fori*: Merging Customary Law and National Land Legislation in

Madagascar," in *Contest for Land in Madagascar: Environment, Ancestors and Development*, ed. S.J.T.M. Evers, Gwyn Campbell, and Michael Lambek (Leiden: Brill Academic Publishers, 2013), 119–41.

6. M. Bloch, *Placing the Dead: Tombs, Ancestral Villages, and Kinship Organization in Madagascar* (London: Seminar Press, 1971), 106–8. Kinship groups are organized around the tomb. Communal rituals related to the ancestors perpetually strengthen their family bonds.

7. In reality, this land only became "ancestral land" (*tanin-drazana*) by virtue of a *razana* being placed in the tomb. *Razana* means both "ancestor" and "dead person" or "corpse." Bloch, *Placing the Dead*, 106–8. Those calling themselves tompon-tany said that they never replaced an ancestor from elsewhere in order to make their land ancestral but simply waited until somebody in their family died. This does not comply with the customary highland practice of transferring at least one corpse from the old to the new tomb whenever a new tomb is erected. The practice is, however, consistent with the hypothesis that those who currently claim the status of tompon-tany actually are of slave descent and did not have tombs.

8. Most slaves lost their tombs upon enslavement. Slaves were prohibited from having permanent tombs throughout the period of slavery. They were forced to bury their dead in perishable tombs. See Bloch, *Placing the Dead*, 136.

9. To protect the privacy of the villagers, place-names and names of individuals have been changed in this chapter.

10. The 1967 meeting was obviously a crucial turn in the region's history. Although not backed by the state (Madagascar lacks a working centralized land registry system), one could argue this is an inchoate form of a land registry system, albeit orally recorded. Since the tompon-tany had a general consensus on land divisions and their borders, it had local legitimacy. From the angle of a French civil law analysis, there is no doubt that tompon-tany enjoyed the three components attributed to landownership in the civil law: *usus* (the right to use the property), *fructus* (to enjoy its fruits), and *abusus* (the right to alienate/dispose of the property). It should be understood that there is no real land shortage in the Marovato region. The tompon-tany artificially created the shortage in their 1967 meeting.

11. The migrants' claim to be Betsileo was accepted by the tompon-tany at face value, whereas their social origin within the Betsileo group was subject to a further inquiry into whether the ancestral lands and family tombs of these migrants really are in the Southern Highlands.

12. Marovato is a migrant village. Some 36.2 percent of its people have settled since 1970. They are called *mpiavy* ("migrants") because they do not have family tombs in the region. Later in the fieldwork, I discovered six more migrant villages in the Marovato region. The region includes these and other villages located within a 15-kilometer radius of Marovato.

13. The tompon-tany village council functioned next to the formal *fokon-tany* ("village") council. Marovato had one representative in this assembly, and he and four members from two neighboring villages constitute the council. The Marovato representative was appointed by the tompon-tany council. Generally, tompon-tany chose one of their relatives. The fokon-tany delegates represented the national government at the local level. They did not interfere with the tompon-tany settlement policy. In practice, I found fokon-tany councils to be passive entities, meeting only a few times per year.

14. Bloch writes on this issue: "Without an ancestral homeland one was a non-person"; see M. Bloch, "Modes of Production and Slavery in Madagascar: Two Case Studies," in *Asian and African Systems of Slavery*, ed. J. L. Watson (Oxford: Basil Blackwell, 1980), 120.

15. This would appear to be a general phenomenon in the Marovato region, as there are six Betsileo villages other than Marovato with similar east-west configurations in the area. Compare also C. Kottak, *The Past in the Present: History, Ecology and Cultural Variation in Madagascar* (Ann Arbor: University of Michigan Press, 1980), 137–38.

16. Cf. ibid., 137–41.

17. In 1992, Marovato counted 458 inhabitants (292 referred to themselves as tompon-tany and 166 as migrants). Of the total, 57 people were called andevo by other villagers. At this point in the research, the people referred to as andevo denied this status.

18. A distinction needs to be made between unregistered, traditional marriages and registered, church marriages (these are rare). Both free descent and andevo villagers said that, according to Malagasy customs, it is the bridewealth payment that confers public legitimacy upon the marriage.

19. Interview with Rafidy Andriana (tompon-tany village leader), July 7, 1992. All dates mentioned with the quotes and cases refer to the date of the interview. Most interviews were held in Malagasy and later translated into English.

20. In his book on Betsileo villages near Ambalavao, Kottak observes that andevo there also are prohibited from buying land. Usufruct rights are passed from father to son, but the tompon-tany can reclaim the land whenever he feels like it. This is also the case in Marovato. Kottak observes that andevo generally cultivate 0.45 hectare per holding, whereas tompon-tany exploit more than twice that amount—1.2 hectares per holding. The term *holding* lacks precision, as it is unclear how many people live on and cultivate each unit of land. Kottak also states that this land is not sufficient to support the andevo. Kottak, *Past in the Present*, 135, 163.

21. Rafidy Andriana interview.

22. Ibid.

23. *Andriana* (meaning "noble descent") seems to be borrowed from the Merina.

24. From an emic perspective, girls become women when they have proven their fertility by giving birth.

25. Raozy is one of the seven daughters of an andevo family in Marovato. Both parents and their children confirmed that they actually are of slave descent during the 1996 fieldwork.

26. For further discussions concerning slavery and social exclusion through marriage politics, see the original monograph. Evers, *Constructing History*; Evers, "Expropriated from the Hereafter"; and Evers, "*Lex Loci* meets *Lex Fori*."

27. The terminology of *established* and *outsiders* is taken from N. Elias and J. L. Scotson, *The Established and the Outsiders: A Sociological Enquiry into Community Problems* (London: Cass, 1965). The tompon-tany/stranger dichotomy is an established/outsiders configuration common to Madagascar (see Evers, *Constructing History*).

28. For details about the andevo who left the village, see S. J. T. M. Evers, "Solidarity and Antagonism in Migrant Societies in the Southern Highlands," in I. Rakoto, *L'esclavage à Madagascar: Aspects historiques et résurgences contemporaines: Actes du Colloque international sur l'esclavage, Antananarivo (24–28 septembre 1996)* (Antananarivo: Institut de civilisations, Musée d'art et d'archéologie, 1997), 339–47.

29. Here, Rakazy expresses the fear of poisoning and sorcery (see Evers, *Constructing History*).

30. The concept of hery is highly ambiguous for the Malagasy. Hery commonly means strength, and it is neither positive nor negative; it is morally neutral or amoral. For Bloch, it is a good thing only if you can control it. A. Delivré, however, describes hery in more negative terms, as informants in the Marovato area do. Delivré writes: "La signification du hasina dépend donc essentiellement de l'utilisation qu'on en fait: cette puissance n'est bénéfique que lorsque les rapports hiérarchiques entre certains être . . . sont soigneusement sauvegardés. Mais si ces rapports sont inversés et que le hasina est détourné de sa fin propre, il devient accidentellement une force du mal, et on emploie de préférence le terme 'hery' pour le qualifier." See A. Delivré, *Interprétation d'une tradition orale: L'histoire des Rois d'Imerina* (Paris: Klinsieck, 1974), 188. In this regard, A. Southall translates *hasina* as "sacred ritual potency." He considers it to be a central tenet held by all groups in Madagascar. See Southall, "Common Themes in Malagasy Culture," in *Madagascar: Society and History*, ed. C. Kottak, J.-A. Rakotoarisoa, A. Southall, and P. Vérin (Durham: Carolina Academic Press, 1986), 414. Bloch also writes that the notion of hasina is the "kernel of Malagasy thought." It is crucial to note here that the villagers see hery as the flip side of hasina. See Maurice Bloch, "The Disconnection between Power and Rank as a Process: An Outline of the Development of Kingdoms in Central Madagascar," in *Ritual, History and Power: Selected Papers in Anthropology by Maurice Bloch* (London: Athlone Press, 1989), 65.

31. Key informants mentioned during early 2014 that the andevo were still burying their deceased in unrecognizable, makeshift graves in the nearby Ifaha mountains. They are ashamed that they cannot offer their beloved proper tombs, considered to be the portal to the hereafter. They believe that their deceased cannot pass to the hereafter due to the lack of family tombs. Andevo argue that their dead cause them harm in the form of illness and death, since they are frustrated that they cannot go to the hereafter and take revenge upon their descendants.

32. It was later confirmed by Raozy that there had been no bridewealth (*tandra*) transfer to legitimize the relationship, as Rafidy Andriana was strongly opposed to the marriage. For Tsija's marriage, bridewealth was paid to her parents, but that was at a time when her andevo descent had not yet been disclosed. In Voahangy's case, four chickens comprised the whole bridewealth transfer.

26

WAGES OF WOMANHOOD

Managers and Women Workers in the Jute Mill Industry of Bengal, 1890–1940

SUBHO BASU

In the late nineteenth century, Calcutta, dubbed as the second city of the British Empire, witnessed rapid industrialization. Pivotal to this process of industrial expansion and urban growth was the jute industry. Jute mills stretched over an area of 20 miles along the banks of the Hooghly, both to the north and to the south of the city. By 1912, there were sixty-one jute factories in this region employing nearly two hundred thousand workers.[1] A small minority of these workers were women, who faced systematic marginalization and were concentrated in the low-waged jobs in the mills.[2] In 1921, the government of Bengal appointed Dr. D. F. Curjel of the Indian Medical Service to investigate the condition of childbirth among Bengal women working in the jute mill. Curjel's investigation indicated that the mill managers not only were uninterested in knowing the living conditions of their female employees but also believed that the women workers were primarily "prostitutes."[3] Many managers constantly employed rhetoric that castigated the women as sex workers.[4] Even during the strike of 1937, they portrayed women workers as prostitutes.[5] By castigating female workers in this way, male managerial elites obviously sought to indicate that such women were not primarily workers and that their life experiences could not even be understood within the context of work-family balance. With the colonial state considering maternity benefits acts, casting demeaning the role of women workers obviously had an immediate political economic logic. By denying moral legitimacy to female workers, mill managers were trying to avoid the need to take extra measures to improve their living conditions. Yet such stereotyping was also the product of a particular form of managerial perception regarding the female workforce.

By engaging with the life of women workers in the jute mills, this chapter argues that the very use of the term *prostitute* underlay an attempt to commoditize the bodies of women workers in order to further marginalize their position. The availability of a cheap migrant workforce from the famine-devastated regions of colonial India had deeper gendered implications for the formation of the industrial working class in Bengal. More important, the spatial organization of the mill towns also made it difficult for young women workers to balance their productive and reproductive activities. In many ways, the absence of the urban infrastructure for a stable workforce was the reflection of a deliberate policy choice by the managerial workforce in an overcrowded labor market.

The neoliberal incarnations of labor studies celebrate the recent spate of industrial employment of women workers in garment industries in the majority world as a liberation from domestic work.[6] In contrast to this assertion, however, I argue that my investigation of the labor history between 1890 and 1940 in Bengal reveals that the very process of the political economy of labor migration and the nature of urbanization initiated by the employers shaped the survival strategies of women workers. I contend that these women preferred fluid conjugal relationships outside the heteronormative family structure in an overwhelming male work environment. Samita Sen, the pioneering historian of women workers in the jute industry in colonial Bengal, has already emphasized the complexity of the relationship between class and gender in conceptualizing the life experiences of women workers. Through an analysis of the interplay of both production and reproduction and work and family, she highlights how patriarchal norms restricted the life opportunities of women workers in the jute industry.[7] Sen's argument illuminates our understanding of the subject In this chapter, I go a step further and highlight the process of the formation of working classes under the specific impact of colonial capitalism. I also assert that the rhetoric of managerial elites foregrounded the sexual lifestyle of workers to marginalize their positions within the hierarchy of the labor force not simply materially but also ideologically in order to problematize their very identity as workers. The managerial projection of women as sex workers rather than productive workers was a discursive strategy to avoid incurring the economic costs of providing better shelter, crèches, and a supportive work environment for women workers so that they could continue to work in the mill.

From Field to Factory: The Making of an Adult Male Working Class

The uneven geography of industrial development helped to shape the labor market formation of the rising jute industry in Bengal. In the early twentieth century, two-thirds of the industrial undertakings in all of Bengal were located in Calcutta and the metropolitan districts of Howrah, Hooghly, and the Twenty-Four Parganas. In 1911, in the rest of the province, with an area of 70,000 square miles and a population of 38.25 millions, there were only two hundred works that employed thirty-five thousand workers.[8] Urban expansion in Bengal was also limited to this region. According to the 1911 census, apart from Calcutta and the metropolitan districts of Howrah, Hooghly, and Twenty-Four Parganas in Bengal, there were only three other towns containing over thirty thousand persons.[9] Thus, the urban industrial enclave stood like an isolated promontory in the midst of subsistence agriculture.

Despite the prevalence of subsistence agriculture in the primarily monsoon-fed rice economy of Bengal, local workers were reluctant to obtain jobs in the jute industry. In 1888, the magistrate of Howrah remarked that many of the workers who came from neighboring villages were content to do just twenty-one days of work in a month, saying that they could earn sufficient money in that time and did not care to work on the remaining days.[10] In the early phase of the jute industry up until the late 1890s, when local workers were preponderant in the industry, women workers constituted nearly 20 percent of the workforce.[11] As a substantial number of male workers were engaged in agricultural work, rural women who were rendered outcasts in their society for being widows or because of supposed transgressions of patriarchal social norms[12] took up jobs in the jute industry. For example, of the twenty-five workers interviewed by the Indian Factory Labour Commission of 1890, eight were women, six of whom were widows. In this period, many of these women workers were employed in the weaving department and were the highest-paid workers in the industry.[13] Some were from the northern highland of the United Province (UP), and the rest of the workers were local Bengalis (see table 26.1).

Yet the bottleneck of labor supply from local sources, complained managers, stood in the way of rapid industrialization.[14] The apparent shortage of labor was resolved in the late 1890s when adult male migrants from the distant regions of north and central Bihar and United Province (UP) flooded the labor market. The very nature of this migration also led to different patterns of urbanization and the spatial organization of labor settlements that helped to reduce the number of women workers and push them to the margins of the workforce. The sudden influx of migrations of workers from a particular region in Bihar and eastern UP can be explained by the way the colonial reorganization in industry impacted the local ecology and demographic structure, in terms of the land revenue system, policy of the expansion of agriculture, and free trade.

In the early part of the nineteenth century, under pressure from the colonial administration to expand agriculture as a solution to rapid population growth, virtually all arable land in this region was put under cultivation. Pasture started disappearing as population density increased. In the Hazipur subdivision of Muzaffarpur in Bihar, for example, it was reported that the only available grazing was on raised earthen boundaries encircling fields and on the sides of village roads. The cattle in the region increasingly survived on an inferior quality of grass and suffered from various diseases.[15] The disappearance of pastures had an adverse effect on the pastoral communities in Bihar and east UP; by the turn of the century, these communities gave up pastoral pursuits and became cultivators, intensifying the pressure on land.[16]

As the pressure on the land mounted, family holdings were increasingly subdivided. Villages in eastern UP and Bihar became mosaics made up of little pieces of land, each piece belonging to a different holding. In the Lakshnewar *thana* (police station) of Balia, for instance, one property of 34,384 acres held by 32 parent families came to be divided between

TABLE 26.1 THE AREA OF ORIGIN OF THE WITNESSES EXAMINED BY THE 1890 FACTORY COMMISSION, INCLUDING THE AGES OF THE OPERATIVES

Name of mill	*Name of worker*	*Age*	*Adult male*	*Adult female*	*Boy*	*Girl*	*Area of origin, district*	*Area of origin, province*
Union Jute Mill	Rajoni	23		Female			Nuddea	Bengal
Baranagar Jute Mill	Taroni	20		Female			Medinipur	Bengal
	Sookhwaria	25		Female			Chaprah	Bihar
	Sukhni	8.5				Girl	Patna	Bihar
	Noderchand	40	Male				Hughly	Bengal
Budgebudge Jute Mill	Samacharan Samuth	25	Male				Twenty-Four Parganas	Bengal
	Bepin	11			Boy		Twenty-Four Parganas	Bengal
	Degambari	28		Female			Twenty-Four Parganas	Bengal
Union Jute Mill	Shama	10			Boy			
Bengal Cotton Mill	Kedar Dass	32	Male				Calcutta	Bengal
Ghoosrey Old Cotton Mill	Ganpat	24	Male				Gaya	Bihar
Balley Bone and Paper Mill	Jungi Khan	45	Male				Bhagalpur	Bihar
	Durga	40		Female			Bankura	Bengal
	Benimadhab	25	Male				Howrah	Bengal
Empress of India	Hemchunder	24	Male				Twenty-Four Parganas	Bengal
	Fakir Dolie	13			Boy		Twenty-Four Parganas	Bengal
	Bepin	11			Boy		Twenty-Four Parganas	Bengal
	Degambari	28		Female			Twenty-Four Parganas	Bengal
Victoria Cotton Mill	Abdul Barik	23	Male				Twenty-Four Parganas	Bengal
	Jagoo	25		Female			Medinipur	Bengal
	Jaffer	12			Boy		Calcutta	Bengal
Cossipore Gun and Shell Factory	Omerdoodee	42	Male				Calcutta	Bengal
	Kamasi Midoo	14			Boy		Calcutta	Bengal
	Boiragi	25	Male				Cuttack	Orissa
	Suckram	24	Male				Jaunpore	United Province

Source: This table was prepared on the basis of witness accounts in *Indian Factory Commission* (Calcutta: Government of India, 1890), 77–88.

27,781 shareholders in the space of forty years, by the 1880s.[17] Moreover, these small holdings were scattered, and a tenant might hold parcels of land under different landlords.[18] The subdivision and fragmentation of holdings increased the costs of cultivation and reduced returns. Ultimately, as C. M. Fisher has argued, population pressure caused a decline in the marginal productivity of labor.[19]

The steady growth of population and the relentless extension of cultivation adversely affected the natural resources for agriculture. Bihar and east UP were not areas of heavy rainfall.[20] Here, cultivation relied to a great extent upon irrigation. But marshes and creeks, which were sources of water supply, dried up, and tanks were filled up for new cultivable land. The proportion of irrigated areas to total cultivable land was stagnant in this period.[21] The impact on the rural poor of population growth and land scarcity was made far worse by the introduction of the permanent settlement by the colonial regime from the 1790s onward, which enabled *zamindars*, or landlords, to establish a powerful hold on the rural economy at the expense of actual cultivators. Zamindars imposed various forms of exactions on the peasantry that never appeared in the government's calculations, such as forced labor on the zamindar's land, the payment of homage, or appropriation of the produce of orchards.[22] The zamindars also imposed arbitrary levies known as *abwabs*. Despite being declared illegal by the government, these abwabs were numerous.[23]

The exactions and levies, coupled with increased rent demands, caused widespread indebtedness among the tenants. The zamindars, who often combined proceeds they received from moneylending with income from landed estates, acquired land from indebted peasants. More and more, as zamindars acquired large landed estates, land distribution became extremely unequal and the average size of peasant holdings fell.[24] More important, as a Sahabad officer wrote, "a cultivator not in debt is viewed with dislike and suspicion, and debt is their common burden. Fifty percent of the cultivators are in debt for grain lent by their land lords, and forty percent are in debt to *mahajans* (village merchants and bankers) for either grain or money. The latter section consists of men of some substance who can command credit but the former are of the poorer class of cultivators and the grasp of landlord on them is firm and unrelaxing."[25]

During the nineteenth century, the zamindars increasingly became absentee landlords.[26] In most cases, the collection of revenues and the village administration were left to *thikadars* (contractors). Originally tax-collecting officials, the thikadars in the nineteenth century leased land and paid rent to the landlords. They also raised rent and extracted levies from their tenants whenever they could. "There could be no doubt whatsoever," declared the lieutenant governor of Bengal in 1877, "that the combined influence of zamindars (landlords) and ticcadars (land speculators) has ground the *ryots* (farmers) of Behar to a state of extreme depression and misery."[27] Ironically, the judicial system served to enhance the power of the thikadars over the tenants. Zamindars and thikadars had the time and money to use the judicial system to their benefit, whereas the poor tenants could not afford to spend money or invest time in long legal wrangling. The rent disputes ruined the tenants in the region. As a frustrated local official in Sahabad wrote to his superiors: "It is certainly a remarkable country where this sort of thing can go on. Here have the lives of a large number of persons [been] embittered, their worst passions roused and a large part of their savings dissipated, simply and solely because one man wanted to exploit a village. This has gone on for half a century, during all of which there has been administrative headquarters at Arrah about 20 miles away."[28] In the closing decades of the nineteenth century, the commercialization of agriculture led to a further decline in the condition of the peasants. The introduction of railways enabled local cultivators to sell their produce in distant markets. This integration of trade boosted the prices of the food crops in the long run. In Bihar, wider access to the market enabled zamindars and affluent tenants to store produce until prices rose and to make large profits. Meanwhile, spiraling rents for the land forced poor peasants to sell their crops to the zamindars.

In the late nineteenth century, with the deepening of the agrarian crisis, numerous small peasants faced starvation. It was reported that in some districts of Bihar, the size of peasant holdings was so small that peasant families could not even afford two meals a day. Wages of agricultural workers were low and remained stagnant for a long period of time.[29] Hunger was a normal condition of life for the rural poor, and because of the patriarchal structure of the family, women comprised a significant portion of the victims. Following the suicide of a twenty-year-old woman at Etawah in 1872, a local official observed that "her husband was an agricultural labourer, and . . . in addition to his wife he supported an aged mother. His daily earnings when in regular employment during the whole day were twenty five *chittacks* (fifty ounces) of behjur. His wife in weeding times obtained fifteen chittacks or thirty ounces of behjur. He only eats salt once in eight days . . . oil spices or vegetables he never tastes. The three grown up people were always in [a] state of hunger"[30] The implication of the story was that the woman had been driven to suicide by hunger. Indeed, the politics of food distribution within the family often put pressure on women. In patrilocal Indian households, the practice was to provide the food first to male members and elders within the family; children came second, and after completing the distribution of food to everybody else, young housewives were allowed to eat their own meals. Prisoners in the local jails who were also day laborers told officials that starvation had compelled them to steal.[31] Indeed, not surprisingly, famines and scarcities marked the region from the 1860s onward. By the 1890s, the rural population had become vulnerable to diseases, and many succumbed to epidemics of malaria, kalazar, and the plague.[32] Colonial officials sometimes subscribed to the theory that the fair play of the market would eventually put food in the mouths of the hungry.[33] Accordingly, they left the day-to-day relief measures in private hands. The interests of the peasantry of Bihar and eastern UP were sacrificed at the altar of the free market economy.[34]

This situation led to a mass migration from the regions that fundamentally altered the pattern of location for the jute industry in Bengal. In the early stages, mill owners feared that the labor supply from local areas would become inadequate if too many mills were located in closely packed areas. They preferred isolated sites to ensure that their workers would not be approached by rival companies.[35] To guarantee a permanent supply of labor, some mills sent foremen-cum-jobbers, known as *sardars* in local parlance, to the villages to recruit workers.[36]

At this crucial juncture, the flow of migrants from the famine-devastated areas of Bihar and eastern UP resolved the problem of labor supply. The structural bias in the newly emerging colonial rail transportation network, which was oriented toward the Calcutta port, led a large number of workers to migrate to this region. In 1895, Sitanath Roy, the honorary secretary to the National Chamber of Commerce, wrote that places formerly covered with "marshes and jungles" were soon transformed into busy and beautiful towns by the establishment of mills and factories "teeming with a prosperous population."[37] The recent and rapid growth of the mill towns was reflected in the changed linguistic composition of their residents. The compiler of the Twenty-Four Parganas district gazetteer in 1914 commented, "Some of the mill towns are now practically foreign towns planted in the midst of Bengal." In Bhatpara, according to the same source, "four persons speak Hindi to each person speaking Bengali." In the mill town of Titagarh, 75.1 percent of the inhabitants were Hindi speakers, and only 11 percent spoke Bengali (apart from the 8 percent who spoke Telegu and the 4 percent who spoke Oriya).[38] The most densely packed migrant-dominated industrial enclave in the region was the Kankinara-Jagatdal-Bhatpara-Naihati belt, where in twelve jute mills and three other large factories, around eighty-five thousand people were packed into an area of 5.5 square miles.[39] Most of these millworkers were recruited from the Hindi-speaking region of Bihar and eastern UP.

The concentration of migrant workers in densely packed industrial enclaves created an overcrowded labor market, and the preponderance of adult male workers reduced the bargaining power of the relatively smaller number of working women. Initially, the uncertainties of life in a distant land may have discouraged the migration of women and children to the mill municipalities. Mill managers took advantage of this situation to depress wages to the extent that they would only support adult male migrants. In 1929, according to one calculation, a working-class family consisting of a husband and wife and three children required Rs7 per week to subsist in the mill towns, but an average millworker at that time earned only Rs5 per week.[40] As late as 1946, a survey of family budgets showed that expenses exceeded income in 70 percent of the working-class households in the urban areas. This indicates that workers could not maintain their families in the mill towns on urban wages alone. In 1929, Dr. Batra, a Bengal government health official, found that the jute workers' average caloric intake was much lower than that of prisoners in Bengal. According to the survey conducted by Batra in 1929, there was little in the way of fresh vegetables, protein, or milk products in the average worker's diet, and vitamin D was totally absent.[41] All these indicators pointed to the fact that mill managers preferred to pay the wages of single adult male migrants even to workers with families. From 1881 onward, the colonial government enacted legislation to restrict working hours for women.[42] In the early stages when managers were desperate for workers, they recruited women, but the steady supply of male workers eventually made the employment of women workers unnecessary. Thus, following the logic of political economy, mill managers inscribed the birth of the workforce with adult male characteristics, which I will discuss in the next section.

Spatial Organization of Mill Towns and the Marginality of Women in the Workforce

The jute mill towns in Bengal that emerged as a result of the mass migration of adult male workers from north India and pockets of south India were placed under the control of primarily Scottish mill managers. These managers dominated municipal boards, controlled the local police force, and acted as judicial magistrates of the mill towns. They maintained their control over the municipal administration by forging alliances with propertied, high-caste Indians, generally from white-collar professions.[43] Mill managers and propertied Indians often competed with each other in bringing down the cost of investment in the infrastructure of the mill towns.

In these towns, workers lived in extremely unsanitary and overcrowded, privately owned slums. Thomas Johnston, the Scottish Labour member of Parliament (MP) who visited the Kankinara slum in Bhatpara in 1925, has left us with a vivid picture of living conditions in the slums of the area:

> Two thirds of the workers in this industry . . . are housed in vile, filthy, disease-ridden hovels, called *basti* [slums]. These . . . are one storied blocks of mud plaster on wicker and matting with thatched roofs; [there are] no windows or chimneys . . . the smoke oozes through the thatch if it cannot get out through the doorway, which is so low that one has to go down almost on hands and knees to enter. The basti have neither light nor water supply; the floors are earthen; sanitary arrangements there are none; and usually access . . . can only be had along a narrow tunnel of filth where myriads of mosquitoes and flies breed and the stench is such that one fears to strike a match lest the atmosphere, being combustible, should explode.[44]

In 1946, the Labour Enquiry Committee noted that the rooms in the workers' dwellings were usually no more than 8 feet square and were "liable [to] be flooded during the rainy season."[45] The surroundings were filthy. Makeshift latrines were built a few yards away from these tenements and had a fearful stink. The only sources of drinking water were open and dirty tanks.

Epidemics of cholera, malaria, and smallpox remained constant features of life in the mill towns. The high infant mortality rates in working-class slums also helped explain why women preferred not to remain in factory jobs. According to the municipality report of Bhatpara in 1931, 108 out of 822 deaths tallied in the town were of children under one year of age, and 93 were of children between the ages of one and five.[46] Women workers in many cases went back to their own families to give birth to their babies and returned when the latter became old enough to work in the factories.[47] Johnston, the MP from Dundee, was told by an old man in the Kankinara slum that half of the babies there died every year.[48]

Mill managers made only superficial attempts to improve the situation. In the 1920s, they opened baby clinics and crèches in the mills. But a report of the mill doctor mentions that "the conditions of these [workers'] children are often pitiful because those looking after them are either too old or too young to find employment in the mills, or are the sick, and the blind or an occasional out of work. The mother does not return to feed her infant between 5:15 a.m. to 10:45 a.m. or between 1:15 p.m. and the mixtures which the children are given when they cry is enough to ruin all but the strongest digestion and to swell the death rate enormously. Many are doped with opium and die eventually from inanition."[49] These high rates of infant mortality might have also discouraged workers from bringing their wives and children to the mill towns. This too resulted in an increasing marginalization of women in the jute mills (see table 26.2).

TABLE 26.2 SEX COMPOSITION IN BENGAL TOWNS, 1872–1911 (NUMBER OF WOMEN PER THOUSAND MALES)

	1872	*1881*	*1891*	*1901*	*1911*
Average county town	947	971	903	842	816
Average industrial or commercial town	798	767	685	582	537

Source: John Henry Whiteley, *Royal Commission on Labour in India*, vol. 5, pt. 1 (London: H.M. Stationery Office, 1931), 4–18.

Thus, the very nature of labor settlement, the absence of investment in the social infrastructure of the mill towns, and the presence of large numbers of adult male migrants made it difficult for women to work in the mill towns. Indeed, the managerial elites who dominated the mill towns remained committed to the idea of maintaining an adult male migrant working class. Accordingly, the spatial organization of the towns privileged male dominance in the workforce and further marginalized the few women who did work in the factories.

Women Workers in the Jute Mills: Work and Habitation

Women migrated to the mills in situations of distress. According to Samita Sen, "Single women migrated because of 'marital infidelity,' or 'deprivation through desertion, barrenness or widowhood.'"[50] Indeed, in most cases, single women went to mill towns when all their means of support were exhausted in the rural areas. Ranajit Guha has alerted us to the critical deprivation of support for widows in rural Bengal by excavating the story of the death there of Chandra, a young widow who was given poison to induce an abortion in order to avoid public shame for her family, which was headed by her mother.[51] Among the fragments of information available to us regarding single female workers, the factory commission reports also indicate that widows constituted a significant segment of the women workers in the jute mills. Some of these women found a way to develop a new conjugal life in the mill towns by cohabiting with male workers. As early as 1890, Durga, a Bengali widow, told the factory commission that she was staying with her "adopted husband."[52] Such instances indicate the emergence of different forms of familial ties in the mill towns. In many cases, the male partner had two different *samsars* (household establishments), one based in the mill town and another in the village. Manikunatala Sen, a Communist activist in the 1940s, has recalled her experience of such relationships: a women who cohabited with a man to whom she was not formally married put a vermillion mark on her forehead but did not use it on the part in her hair, which was the mark of marriage among Bengali Hindu women.[53] Such relations cut across boundaries of religion, region, or caste, and many of these women earned their living by working in the mills.

In an overwhelmingly male environment, where networks based on family, village, and region constituted a crucial way to enter the labor market, such nonmarital conjugal ties were also a part of survival strategies for single women. The women were aware that these ties did not have the social sanction of either the Hindu patriarchy or colonial law, which did not provide security to women and men, as can be gleaned from the fragmented biographies of women in the mill areas. For example, Narsama Kurmi went to the jute mills on her own from Ganjam District in Orissa. She had married at the age of thirteen but became a widow at an early age. One day, she heard from a man who had just arrived from Calcutta that there was work for women in the jute mills of Bengal. Narsama borrowed train fare from her sister and set out for Calcutta. She arrived at the Howrah station and was put on a streetcar by an acquaintance she met on the train. Her escort told the driver to drop her off at the "Madrassi line," which was primarily where Telegu speakers from the southern Orissa region lived. Narsama only knew Telegu at the time, and the tramway driver instructed her to get off at a slum where, it was said, she found "a place among [her] countrymen." Later on, she developed differences with the sardars, the powerful jobbers and foremen who often controlled such slums and access to workplaces, so Narsama moved from Howrah to Rishra through her regional networks.[54] Regional and ethnic-based networks thus constituted crucial sources of support for women and men in their efforts to survive and obtain access to work, credit, shelter, and food.

Colonial officials often interpreted such networks as reflecting regional and linguistic ties or, in other words, primordial loyalties. Yet for most women, the relationship with male partners cut across these so-called primordial loyalties. According to Mr. Williamson, the Scottish manager of the Kinnison Jute Mill in the 1920s, single male Oriya workers often cohabited with Telegu women[55]—thus, they came from different linguistic groups. Yet in the same mill, a Telegu woman was refused housing in the Madrassi line if she had a Hindustani partner.[56] In the Lothian jute mill, Dr. Curjel found that "upcountry workers" generally selected their partners from among Bengali women.[57] Clearly, given the complex social mosaic of ethnic and religious ties among the workers, social and sexual relations often cut across imagined primordial ties. The relationships that women workers entered into with their male colleagues outside the limits of recognized patriarchal norms in Indian society indicated a particular type of familial formation that emerged under conditions of colonial capitalism and was an integral component of class formation.

Of course, the temporary and fluid familial structure of factory jobs hardly constituted the entirety of the familial experience of women workers in the jute mills. Many families migrated to the mills under extreme economic distress, and as a consequence, husbands and wives sometimes worked together in the factories. For instance, Ramkalyan and Parvati, as described through their narratives to the Royal Commission on Labour in India, provided the other dimension of the story. The two went to the mills after having exhausted all possibilities of earning a livelihood in the country. They were up at 5 AM every day and worked the first shift in the mill until 11 AM. After a recess of half an hour, they continued to labor until 7 PM. At the end of the day, Parvati cooked food while Ramkalyan and the children collected discarded coal from the mill or gathered wood from the fields. Their entire family worked, including their five-year-old girl and two-year-old boy.[58]

Curjel wrote in 1921 that "the weavers were the autocrats of [the] mill and their women folk did not work." She observed that "the rooms of weavers were screened with Purdah" and "were much lacking in light and ventilation." At the end of her description, she wondered, "Was the pseudo-Purdah a symbol of social superiority as published in newspaper?"[59] Weavers, who were generally the best-paid workers, obviously sought to achieve social mobility through the observation of high-caste norms and gender segregation. In an overwhelmingly male, overcrowded labor market, it appeared that women sought to survive through fluid temporary alliances with male colleagues, thereby seeking to develop their own ties in order to survive the labor market situation and particularly their entrapment in the low-waged jobs into which managers and male workers sought to push them.

The World of Work and the Gradual Marginalization of Women Workers

Work in the mills was organized along gendered lines. In the early twentieth century, women increasingly were concentrated in sewing bags and in the winding departments. Some women were also employed in feeding jute softener and carding machines along with men. However, the relatively better-paid jobs, such as roving, spinning, and weaving, were monopolized by the men. Sometimes, women could find employment in the spinning department, but these opportunities became rare in the 1920s and 1930s. In the first two decades of the twentieth century, children were generally used to shift the bobbins. They worked in gangs of ten or twelve, shifting a set of about seventy-two bobbins in one or two minutes.[60]

The very language that managers and colonial official used to describe the work process was completely gendered. For instance, in 1906, the chairman of the Indian Jute Mill Association listed the time it took workers to learn their jobs in the following manner:

Coolie('s) Work	(one) week
Women's work mainly Preparing and hand sewing	(one) week
Shifter('s) Work	(one) week
Spinner('s)work	Graduate from shifters may be a year or more on shifting
Weaver('s)	A year to be first class workmen.[61]

The very language used to describe the work reflected an implicit gender bias. The work of skilled workers, which required nearly a year's worth of training, was described in a gender-neutral term, but the work of women was specified and tied to the particular department of sewing. The huge gap in the training in skilled positions of spinners and weavers, as opposed to the hand-sewing department, was reflected clearly in the differentiation in wages. Women's work was often treated as subsidiary to men's work. Yet in most cases, women earned wages for the family, particularly for children. Indeed, given the fluid sexual relationships between women and men workers, such low wages actually reinforced the instability of the partnership, whereby the fragility of the conjugal ties often left women deserted and fending for themselves. The low wages of women remained the key locution here, as men often refused to pay for their partners' offspring from earlier cohabitations. The work burden women carried was often not less than that of men. Indeed, in her testimony before the Indian Factory Commission of the 1890s, Rajoni, a woman worker, pointed out that she used to wake up at 4 AM and went to the mill at 5:30 AM. She would sleep after 10 PM. Moreover, she had to walk half a mile to her job. There were no regular breaks, so mothers would have to go out to feed their children only when they could manage to take the time.[62] Nearly forty years after this testimony, in 1929, another woman worker, Babunya, narrated a similar experience from her own working life. She informed the commission, "I leave my home at 5 am in the morning to come to work in the mill and go at 9:30 am; I come again to work at 11. I do not get sufficient time [to] do proper cooking. If I am late at work the babus reprimand me. I feed my children after 9:30 when I go home. . . . As I cannot be at home to serve food to my husband he takes it himself, it becomes cold by the time he takes it."[63] The testimony was revealing in many ways. First, it indicated the double burden a woman had to bear as factory worker and wife/mother. Her concern about serving cold food to her husband probably did not simply indicate love but also pointed to the politics involved in a woman's duty to serve her partner a hot meal. The politics of domesticity were further complicated by the fact that women had less job security than men. According to a survey of workers in 1929, in the eleven jute mills employing over 74,963 workers, nearly 72 percent of the women were employed for less than five years whereas around 61 percent of men (10 percent less than the women) worked fewer than five years. Only 2 percent of the women worked for more than thirty years. The survey further indicated that women workers were for the most part daily employees and had much less continuity and security in their employment compared to their male counterparts.[64]

The rapidly dwindling number of women workers, their low wages, their insecure job tenure, and their role as providers for their families put women under enormous pressure. A vast majority of jute mill workers were also indebted to various types of moneylenders. Indeed, without the supply of credit, women workers would not have been able to maintain themselves in the factory jobs. In such circumstances, establishing sexual partnerships remained the most critical choice women workers made in their attempts to develop networks of survival. Encumbered with the double burden of working within the household as well as the factory, they needed to have conjugal partnerships with men. In an overcrowded labor market with a high turnover rate among workers, coupled with the absence of job security, women workers had to change their residences within the mill town areas frequently. In many instances, men also had to change their jobs and places of residence. This obviously contributed to cohabitation with different partners. In the colonial era, though Hindu men were allowed to marry as many times as they wished and Muslim men could remain married to four women simultaneously, women could not marry more than once. It was only among Dalit (former untouchable communities) and "tribals" (indigenous groups) that women enjoyed more freedom in terms of widow remarriage and divorce. Then, the new forms of conjugal relationship that emerged under the impact of colonial capitalism also transformed women workers' lives, which, in turn, led managerial elites to perceive women in the jute mills as sex workers. But the question remains as to why managerial elites constantly highlighted the idea of women workers as prostitutes.

Managerial Elites: Rhetoric and Practice

Why did the managerial elite, who were not generally concerned about the living condition of the working classes, depict women workers as prostitutes? Why did they invest their rhetoric in such depictions? The answer could be located in the newfound interests of both the colonial state and the Indian nationalists in the condition of women workers. The International Labor Organization (ILO) increasingly promoted the welfare of the Indian working classes. The Indian nationalists, though not always champions of the working classes, became more critical of Scottish managerial elites' treatment of workers as the demand for independence gained ground. Trade unions and the growing socialist and Communist movements similarly remained vocal critics of worker exploitation, though they typically were less interested in women workers. Although the triad of colonial state, nationalist elites, and managerial elites tended to ignore the everyday living conditions of working-class women, issues involving women remained politically sensitive and prompted various types of protective legislation. Among these was a maternity benefit act, although jute mill owners, through lobbying, were able to stall the bill between 1922 and 1939. All these factors led managerial elites to adopt the rhetoric that privileged women's sexual activities over and above their role within the production processes. This also enabled them to claim the moral high ground while evading the basic question of the welfare of working-class women in relation to work and life in the mill towns these elites governed.

Notes

I am grateful to my colleague Auritro Majumder for his close reading and comments on this chapter. Like Bengal workers, I am also deeply indebted to Rachel Sandwell for her excellent copyediting and Elizabeth Elbourne for her comments.

1. *Royal Commission on Labor in India* (hereafter cited as *RCLI*), vol. 5, pt. 2 (London: His Majesty's Government Press, 1931), 126–27.

2. For details, see *RCLI*, vol. 11, pt. 2, "Evidence Based on Testimony of Workers," 356–66.

3. D. F. Curjel, "Report of Dr. Dagmar Curjel on the Condition of Employment of Women before and after Childbirth," 1923, Commerce Department Commerce Branch, April 1923, West Bengal State Archives, Calcutta (hereafter cited as Curjel Report).

4. Managers of the Angus Jute Mill, the manager of the Kinnison Jute Mill, and the managers of the Union Jute Mill all asserted that women workers were prostitutes. See Curjel Report.

5. Report of Managers to Directors, Angus Jute Mill, April 27, 1937, Dundee University Archives, Dundee, Scotland.

6. An example of such an attitude can be found in the arguments of Anisul M. Islam and Munir Quddus on the rise of the garment industry in Bangladesh. See Islam and Quddus, "The Export Garment Industry in Bangladesh: A Potential Catalyst for Breakthrough," in *The Economy of Bangladesh: Problems and Prospects*, ed. Abu N. M. Wahid and Charles E. Weiss (Westport, Conn.: Praeger, 1996), 167.

7. Samita Sen, *Women and Labour in Late Colonial India: The Bengal Jute Industry* (Cambridge: Cambridge University Press, 1999).

8. LSS O Malley, *Census of India 1911* (Calcutta: Bengal Secretariat Press, 1912), vol. 5, pt. 1, 8–9.

9. Ibid.

10. Report on Condition of Lower Classes in India, December 1888, para 25, Famine nos. 1–24, National Archives of India, New Delhi (hereafter cited as NAI).

11. E. A. Gait, *Census of India*, 1901, vol. 6, *Calcutta* (Calcutta; Bengal Secretariat Press, 1902), 83.

12. For detailed analysis of this view, see Sen, *Women and Labour in Late Colonial India*, 16.

13. *Indian Factory Commission, 1890* (Calcutta: Government of India, 1890), 77–88.

14. For details, see Ranajit Dasgupta, "Material Conditions and Behavioural Aspects of Calcutta Working Class, 1875–1899," Occasional Paper no. 22, Centre for Studies in Social Sciences, Calcutta, 1981, 12.

15. Muzaffarpur had as many as 1,257 persons per square mile of cultivated area. B. N. Ganguly, *Trends of Agriculture and Population in the Ganges Valley: A Study in the Agricultural Economics* (London: Methuen, 1938), a 124. According to the district gazetteer of Saran, "The cattle are generally of poor quality . . . owing to appropriation of available land for cultivation, pasturage is insufficient." LSS O'Malley (revised by A. Middleton), *Saran District Gazetteers* (Patna 1930), 67.

16. In Sahabad, Ahirs (a pastoral community) constituted nearly 13 percent of the population. They earlier combined cow herding with cultivation for their livelihood, but increasingly, most Ahirs gave up pastoral pursuits. LSS O'Malley (revised by J. F. W. James), *Sahabad District Gazetteer* (Patna: Bihar Secretariat Press, 1924), 46. In Saran also, Ahirs were numerically the largest caste. Many of them gradually migrated to the banks of the Gondak and Gogra Rivers because these areas afford good grazing grounds for their herds. Elsewhere in the districts, they became cultivators. LSS O'Malley (revised by A. Middleton), *Saran District Gazetteer* (Allahabad: United Province Secretariat Press), 44. In Ghazipur, Ahirs constituted 17.64 percent of the population. They all became cultivators at the turn of the twentieth century. H. R Nevill, *Gazipur District Gazetteer* (Allahabad: United Province Secretariat Press, 1909), 84–86.

17. Orders of Government, no. 898/1–710 of 15 June 1889, Nainital. By order W. C. Benet, Secretary to Government, North Western Provinces and Oudh, attached to William Irvine, *Report on the Revisions of Records and Settlement in Ghazipur District, 1880–1888* (Allahabad: United Province Secretariat Press, 1886), 3.

18. O'Malley, *Saran District Gazetteer*, 109.

19. C. M. Fisher, a historian of indigo plantations in Bihar, maintains that "because most of the labour was unpaid family labour, peasants continued to add until the marginal product of labour reached zero." See Fisher, "Indigo Plantations and Agrarian Society in North Bihar in the Nineteenth and Twentieth Centuries," (Ph.D. diss., Cambridge University, 1976), 230.

20. The monsoons generally arrived in June, and the heaviest rainfall occurred in July and August, varying from 11.40 to 13.15 inches. From the middle of September, the monsoon rains gradually disappear. O'Malley, *Sahabad District Gazetteer*, 16.

21. Nevill, *Gazipur District Gazetteer*, 44.

22. A. N. Das, *Agrarian Unrest and Socio-economic Change in Bihar* (New Delhi: Manohar, 1983), 37.

23. O'Malley, *Saran District Gazetteer*, 111.

24. For example, by the 1880s in the Ghazipur district, though 118 persons owned nearly 29 percent of the area and paid to the government nearly 30 percent of the land revenue, there were 50,000 recorded proprietors who owned on average about13.46 acres each; meanwhile, 1,552 *mouzas* (an Indian term used in colonial English, meaning land revenue settlement units in rural areas) with proprietors covered an area of 269,041.78 acres and were owned by less than 10 persons. Irvine, *Report on the Revisions*, 61.

25. C. J. O'Donnel, *The Ruin of an Indian Province: An Indian Famine Explained–A Letter to the Marquis of Harlington, Secretary of State in a Liberal and Reforming Government* (London: C. Kegan Paul, 1880), 6–17.

26. In Ghazipur, out of the seventy-two families, only forty-one were resident. Thirty families were entirely nonresident. Irvine, *Report on the Revisions*, 61.

27. O'Donnel, *Ruin of an Indian Province*, 22.

28. J. A. Hubback, *Final Report on the Survey and Settlement Operations in the District of Sahabad*, 1907–1916 (Calcutta: Bengal Secretariat Press), 55–57.

29. During the 1874 famine, the lieutenant governor of Bengal noted that the wages of agricultural laborers in north Bihar were lower than those in the rest of north India. *Minute by the Honorable Sir Richard Temple, KCSI Lieutenant Governor of Bengal Dated 31st October 1874* (Calcutta, India: Bengal Secretariat Press, 1874), 4 (hereafter cited as Temple Minute). Another report in 1896 also mentions that the wages of the agricultural workers had not increased for the ten years between 1886 and 1896. *Selection of Papers Relating to the Famine of 1896–97 in Bengal*, vol. 1, *October to November*, 1896 (Calcutta: Bengal Secretariat Press, 1897), 3–4.

30. *Census of India*, 1871,1:1; W. C. Plowden, *Report on Census of North Western Province*, 1872 (Allahabad: Government Press, 1878), lxvi.

31. *Census of India*, 1871, 1:lxvi.

32. Ira Klein, "Population Growth and Mortality, Part 1: The Climateric of Death," *Indian Economic and Social History Review* 26, no. 4 (December 1989): 393 (387–404).

33. B. Foley, *Reports on Labour in Bengal* (Calcutta, India: Bengal Secretariat Press, 1906), app. 1.

34. Neville, *Ghazipur District Gazetteer*, 49–50.

35. The early historian of the jute industry D. R. Wallace recalled, "In those days it was considered by the mills a matter of life and death to prevent a rival company settling down in proximity to their labor supply." See Wallace, *The Romance of Jute* (Calcutta: Empire Press, 1909), 46.

36. Foley, *Reports on Labor in Bengal*.

37. Indian Jute Mill Association, *Report of the Committee for 1895* (Calcutta, 1895).

38. LSS O'Malley, *24 Parganas District Gazetteer*, 63–65.
39. *RCLI*, vol. 5, pt. 2, "Oral Evidence of S. C. Bhattacharya," 348–49.
40. Ibid., 132.
41. Ibid., vol. 5, pt. 1, 254.
42. See the detailed discussion of the origin and impact of the Indian Factory Act of 1881 in Subho Basu, "Labour Movement in Bengal: From Community Consciousness to Class Consciousness–A Case Study of Jute Mill Workers" (Master's thesis, Jawaharlal Nehru University, New Delhi, 1988), 149–58.
43. Subho Basu, *Does Class Matter? Colonial Capital and Workers' Resistance in Bengal, 1890–1937* (New Delhi: Oxford University Press), 90–99.
44. *RCLI*, vol. 5, pt. 1, 31.
45. Report on an enquiry into the conditions of labour in the jute mill industry, 1946, Delhi, 31.
46. *Administrative Report on Bhatpara Municipality* (AARBM), 1931, 34.
47. *RCLI*, vol. 5, pt. 1, 52.
48. Ibid.
49. Dr. Jean Orkney, "Report on the Titaghur Health Centre," Manager's Report to the Director, Titaghur No. 2 Jute Mill, 9, Thomas Duff Archives, Dundee University Archives, Dundee, Scotland.
50. Sen, *Women and Labour in Late Colonial India*, 33.
51. Ranajit Guha, "Chandra's Death," in *A Subaltern Studies Reader*, ed. Ranajit Guha (Minneapolis: University of Minnesota Press), 34–62.
52. *Report of Indian Factory Commission 1890*, 88.
53. Manikuntala Sen, *Sediner Katha* (Kolkata, India: Nabapatra Prakashona, 1982), 124.
54. *RCLI*, vol. 11, 360.
55. Commerce Department Commerce Branch, April 1923, B77, Appendix B, West Bengal State Archives.
56. Curjel Report, app. B, interview with John Williamson of Kinnison Factory, West Bengal State Archives.
57. Curjel Report app. B, interview with Mr. Malish of Belighata Jute Mill, West Bengal State Archives.
58. *RCLI*, vol. 22, pt. 2, 356–66.
59. Curjel Report, app. B, Malish interview.
60. D. H. Buchanan, *The Development of Capitalistic Enterprise in India* (New York: A. M. Kelly, 1966), 298.
61. Foley, *Report on Labour in Bengal*, app.
62. *Report of the Indian Factory Commission*, 1890, 77–88.
63. *RCLI*, vol. 11, 335.
64. Ibid., 348–49.

CONTRIBUTORS

ANA LUCIA ARAUJO is Professor in the Department of History at Howard University. Her work explores the history and memory of slavery. She is the author of *Romantisme tropical: L'aventure illustrée d'un peintre français au Brésil* (2008); *Public Memory of Slavery: Victims and Perpetrators in the South Atlantic* (2010), and *Shadows of the Slave Past: Memory, Heritage, and Slavery* (2014). In addition, she edited *Living History: Encountering the Memory of the Heirs of Slavery* (2009), *Paths of the Atlantic Slave Trade: Interactions, Identities, and Images* (2011), and *Politics of Memory: Making Slavery Visible in the Public Space* (2012). She also coedited *Crossing Memories: Slavery and African Diaspora* (2011) with Paul E. Lovejoy and Mariana P. Candido. She is the general editor of the book series Slavery: Past and Present by Cambria Press.

GABEBA BADEROON is the author of *Regarding Muslims: From Slavery to Post-apartheid* (2014) and the poetry collections *The Dream in the Next Body* and *A Hundred Silences*. She is Assistant Professor of Women's Studies and African Studies at Pennsylvania State University, and Extraordinary Professor of English at Stellenbosch University. Further details of her work are at www.gabeba.com.

SUBHO BASU is currently Associate Professor in the Department of History and Classical Studies, McGill University. His work includes *Does Class Matter?* (2004). Other works include a coedited volume with Suranjan Das, *Electoral Politics in South Asia* (2000). With Crispin Bates he edited *Rethinking Indian Political Institutions* (2005). With noted political scientist Ali Riaz, Basu coauthored *Paradise Lost: State Failure in Nepal* (2007). He is currently working on two projects related to the construction of space, race, gender, and nationalism and popular movements and the rise of Bengal Marxists.

GWYN CAMPBELL, Canada Research Chair in Indian Ocean World History at McGill University, is the author and editor of many works, including *Abolition and Its Aftermath in Indian Ocean Africa and Asia* and *An Economic History of Imperial Madagascar.*

MARIANA P. CANDIDO teaches in the history department at the University of Kansas. She is the author of *An African Slaving Port and the Atlantic World: Benguela and Its Hinterland* (2013) and *Fronteras de Esclavización: Esclavitud, Comercio e Identidad en Benguela, 1780–1850* (2011); and coeditor of *Crossing Memories: Slavery and African Diaspora*, with Ana Lucia Araujo and Paul E. Lovejoy (2011). She has also published in *Slavery and Abolition, African Economic History, Journal for Eighteenth-Century Studies, Portuguese Studies Review, Cahiers des Anneaux de la Mémoire*, and *Brésil(s): Sciences Humaines et Sociales.*

JOOST COTÉ is Senior Research Fellow in the School of Philosophical, Historical and International Studies at Monash University, Australia. His research focuses on colonial discourses and colonial modernity in the Dutch East Indies. Recent publications include "Assessing the Sugar Content in Colonial Discourse in the Dutch East Indies 1880-1914" (in Bosma et al., eds., *Sugarlandia Revisited*, 2007, 2010); "Postcolonial Shame: Heritage and the Forgotten Pain of Civilian Women Internees in Java" (in Logan et al., eds., *Places of Pain and Shame*, 2009); and "Creating Central Sulawesi" (*BMGN* 126, 2011).

DAVID BRION DAVIS is Sterling Professor of History Emeritus at Yale University, and is also the Founder and Director Emeritus of Yale's Gilder Lehrman Center for the Study of Slavery, Resistance, and Abolition. Davis is the author and editor of sixteen books and a frequent contributor to the *New York Review of Books*. He has played a principal role in connecting the study of American slavery and antislavery with a broader Western and New World perspective. His most recent books are *Inhuman Bondage: The Rise and Fall of Slavery in the New World* and *The Problem of Slavery in the Age of Emancipation*, the conclusion of a trilogy. He was awarded a 2013 National Humanities Medal by the National Endowment for the Humanities.

ELIZABETH ELBOURNE is Associate Professor of History at McGill University, Montreal. She is the author of *Blood Ground: Colonialism, Missions and Contests over Christianity in Britain and the Eastern Cape, 1799–1852* and has served as the coeditor (with Brian Cowan) of the *Journal of British Studies.*

MARIE-LUISE ERMISCH is a PhD student in the Department of History and Classical Studies at McGill University. Her research focuses on British-based internationally operating nongovernment organizations (NGOs) that worked with children and youth in Britain and overseas in the 1950s and 1960s, organizations such as the British Red Cross Society, Christian Aid, Oxfam, and Save the Children. Prior to her doctoral research, Marie-Luise worked in Uganda with Environmental Women in Action for Development (EWAD), a local NGO, and the Ugandan government. While completing her PhD she also worked for the Montreal-based International Bureau for Children's Rights (IBCR).

SANDRA J. T. M. EVERS is Associate Professor in Anthropology at VU University Amsterdam. Her research and publications deal with migration, slavery, and cultural transmission in Madagascar within the context of globalization, natural resource management, poverty, and sustainable development. Dr. Evers directs a research program on foreign large-scale land acquisitions in Africa and Madagascar.

DR. RICHARD HELLIE was Thomas E. Donnelly Professor in History at the University of Chicago and an eminent scholar of medieval and early Russian history. He was the author of numerous important works, including *The Economy and Material Culture of Russia, 1600–1725* (1999), *Slavery in Russia, 1450–1725* (1982), and *Enserfment and Military Change in Muscovy* (1971). The editors are honored to publish this article, which he completed just before his death.

MATTHEW S. HOPPER is Associate Professor in the History Department at California Polytechnic State University, San Luis Obispo. He completed his PhD in history at UCLA in 2006, and was a postdoctoral fellow at the Gilder Lehrman Center at Yale University in 2009. His writing has recently appeared in *Annales*, *Itinerario*, and the *Journal of African Development*. His book on the history of the African Diaspora in Eastern Arabia will be published by Yale University Press in 2014.

TARA A. INNISS is Lecturer in the Department of History and Philosophy at Cave Hill Campus, The University of the West Indies (UWI) in Barbados. The areas of focus for her teaching and research include history of medicine; history of children and childhood; history of social policy; and heritage and social development. She is a Commonwealth Scholarship alumnus and holds a master's in international social development at the University of New South Wales in Sydney.

MARTIN A. KLEIN is a retired professor of African history from the University of Toronto. His best-known book is *Slavery and Colonial Rule in French West Africa.* He edited *Women and Slavery in Africa* (with Clare Robertson), *Slavery and Colonial Rule in Africa* (with Suzanne Miers), and *Slavery, Bondage and Emancipation in Modern Africa and Asia.* In 2002, he was given the Distinguished Africanist Award of the African Studies Association.

GEORGE MICHAEL LA RUE is a professor of history at Clarion University of Pennsylvania. He conducted field research in Dar Fur province of Sudan on the *hakura* system (a precolonial land tenure system), and the sultanate's social and economic history. He has written on trans-Saharan trade from Bagirmi and Dar Fur. Most recently, he has been using French medical sources to investigate African slavery in nineteenth-century Egypt, and gathering slave narratives and biographical material.

BRIAN LEWIS is Professor of History at McGill University. His books include *The Middlemost and the Milltowns: Bourgeois Culture and Politics in Early Industrial England* (2001), *"So Clean": Lord Leverhulme, Soap and Civilization* (2008), and an edited collection, *British Queer History: New Approaches and Perspectives* (2013).

After postdoctoral fellowships and teaching at Dalhousie, Duke, York, and Toronto Universities, E. ANN MCDOUGALL joined the Department of History and Classics, University of Alberta, in 1986. Her research explores Islam, slavery, and identity in the Saharan societies of Mauritania and southern Morocco. She recently edited a special edition of *The Maghreb Review:* "Who are the *hratin*? The Invisible People of Mauritania and Southern-Morocco" (2013) (SSHRC funded project 2007–11); and *Engaging with a Legacy: Nehemia Levtzion (1935–2003)*, (2012).

FRANCESCA MITCHELL is a graduate of the University of Edinburgh. She completed her MA(Hons) English Literature and History in 2013, having spent an academic year on exchange at McGill University from 2011 to 2012. For two years, she held the position of Features Editor at *The Student*, the UK's oldest student newspaper. She completed a research internship with South African History Online in 2012, and currently lives and works in Oxford, England. She takes a keen interest in human rights, current affairs, and social justice.

CHARMAINE NELSON is Associate Professor of Art History (McGill University). She has made contributions to the fields of the visual culture of slavery, race and representation and black Canadian studies. Nelson's books include *Racism Eh?: A Critical Inter-Disciplinary Anthology of Race and Racism in Canada* (2004), *The Color of Stone: Sculpting the Black Female Subject in Nineteenth-Century America* (2007), *Ebony Roots, Northern Soil: Perspectives on Blackness in Canada* (2010), and *Representing the Black Female Subject in Western Art* (2010).

JOHANNA RANSMEIER is Assistant Professor of Modern Chinese History at the University of Chicago. She was previously on the faculty of the Department of History and Classical Studies at McGill University. She earned her doctorate from Yale University.

MARIE RODET is Lecturer in African History at the School of Oriental and African Studies (University of London). Her principal research interests lie in the field of migration history, gender studies and the history of slavery in West Africa in the nineteenth and twentieth centuries. Her most recent publications include *Les migrantes ignorées du Haut-Sénégal (1900–1946)* (Karthala 2009) and the chapter "'Under the Guise of Guardianship and Marriage': Mobilizing Juvenile and Female Labor in the Aftermath of Slavery in Kayes, French Soudan, 1900–1939" in *Trafficking in Slavery's Wake: Law and the Experience of Women and Children in Africa*, edited by Benjamin N. Lawrance and Richard L. Roberts (2012).

SHIGERU SATO teaches Asian Studies at the University of Newcastle, Australia. He has authored *War, Nationalism and Peasants: Java under the*

Japanese Occupation, 1942–1945 (1994), coedited *The Encyclopedia of Indonesia in the Pacific War* (2010), and is completing a comparative study of social and economic impact of World War II in British Borneo, the Netherlands Indies, and French Indochina.

DR. ULRIKE SCHMIEDER teaches Iberian and Latin American history at the Leibniz University of Hanover. She got her PhD in modern history from the University of Leipzig with a thesis about Spanish history and its entanglements with German, European, and Spanish American history (1820s), and wrote her second book about the image of Latin America in German journals of the eighteenth and nineteenth centuries. Her second doctoral thesis at the University of Cologne compares Mexico, Brazil, and Cuba with respect to gender history (1780–1880). Recently she published a series of articles about slavery and postemancipation in Cuba, Brazil, and the French West Indies and a book comparing the postslavery societies of Martinique and Cuba in the wider context of debates on postemancipation processes in the Caribbeen.

ABDUL SHERIFF was born in Zanzibar. He studied at UCLA and SOAS (PhD 1971). He taught history at the University of Dar es Salaam (1969–91), was Principal Curator of the Zanzibar Museums (1993–2005), and was Executive Director of the Zanzibar Indian Ocean Research Institute (2007–12). He has published *Slaves, Spices & Ivory in Zanzibar* (1987) and *The Dhow Cultures of the Indian Ocean* (2010), has edited a number of books, and has written numerous scholarly articles.

SALAH TRABELSI is Maître de conférences at the Lumière University Lyon 2 (France). He is also Associate Director of the Groupe de Recherches et d'Etudes sur la Méditerranée et le Moyen-Orient (GREMMO). He is a member of the scientific committee of the Centre International de recherches sur les Esclavages (International Center for Research on Slavery) at the École des Hautes Études en Sciences Sociales. His most recent publications include *Résistances et mémoires des esclavages. Espaces arabo-musulmans et transatlantiques*, edited by Olivier Leservoisier and Salah Trabelsi (2014) and *Les Esclavages en Méditerranée. Espaces et dynamiques économiques*, edited by Faibienne Guillen and Salah Trabelsi (2012).

ROSELINE EMEH UYANGA holds a bachelor's degree in biology education and a doctorate degree in educational administration and planning. She is Professor of Educational Administration and Planning at the University of Uyo, Nigeria. She has served as Dean of Faculty (1998–2002) and as Head of Department (1996–2009) at the Federal University of Technology, Yola, Nigeria, from where she transferred her services to University of Uyo in 2010. Professor Uyanga is a registered member of the Commonwealth Council for Educational Administration and Management (CCEAM). Her research interest covers contemporary issues in educational management, gender studies, and education for sustainable development.

RONALDO VAINFAS is Professor of Modern History at the Universidade Federal Fluminense (Rio de Janeiro), which he joined in 1978.He earned a master's degree in history from Brazil (UFF, 1983) and a PhD in social history (University of São Paulo, 1988). He is the author of *Trópico dos Pecados: Moral, sexualidade e Inquisição no Brasil Colonial* (Tropic of sins: Morals, sexuality, and Inquisition in Colonial Brazil), published in 1989 (last edition in 2010), and "Brazilian Moralities: Sexual Relations and Erotic Language in Colonial Brazil" (in *History of Private Life in Brazil*, 1997; last edition, 2012).

GRIET VANKEERBERGHEN is Associate Professor in the Department of History and Classical Studies at McGill University. She specializes in the history of early China, particularly the intellectual, social, and political history of the early imperial period. She has published on texts such as Huainanzi, Shi ji, and Shangshu dazhuan, and is currently engaged in a project on the urban history of Chang'an, the capital of Western Han (202 BCE–8 CE).

JAMES FRANCIS WARREN is Professor of Southeast Asian Modern History at Murdoch University. He has held teaching and research positions at the Australian National University, Yale University, McGill University, National University of Singapore, and Kyoto University. James Warren's more recent publications include *The Sulu Zone, the World Capitalist Economy and the Historical Imagination* (1998) and *Pirates, Prostitutes and Pullers: Explorations in the Ethno- and Social History of Southeast Asia* (2008).

In 2003, he was awarded the Centenary Medal of Australia for service to Australian society and humanities in the study of ethnohistory, and in 2013, The Grant Goodman Prize in Historical Studies.

INDEX